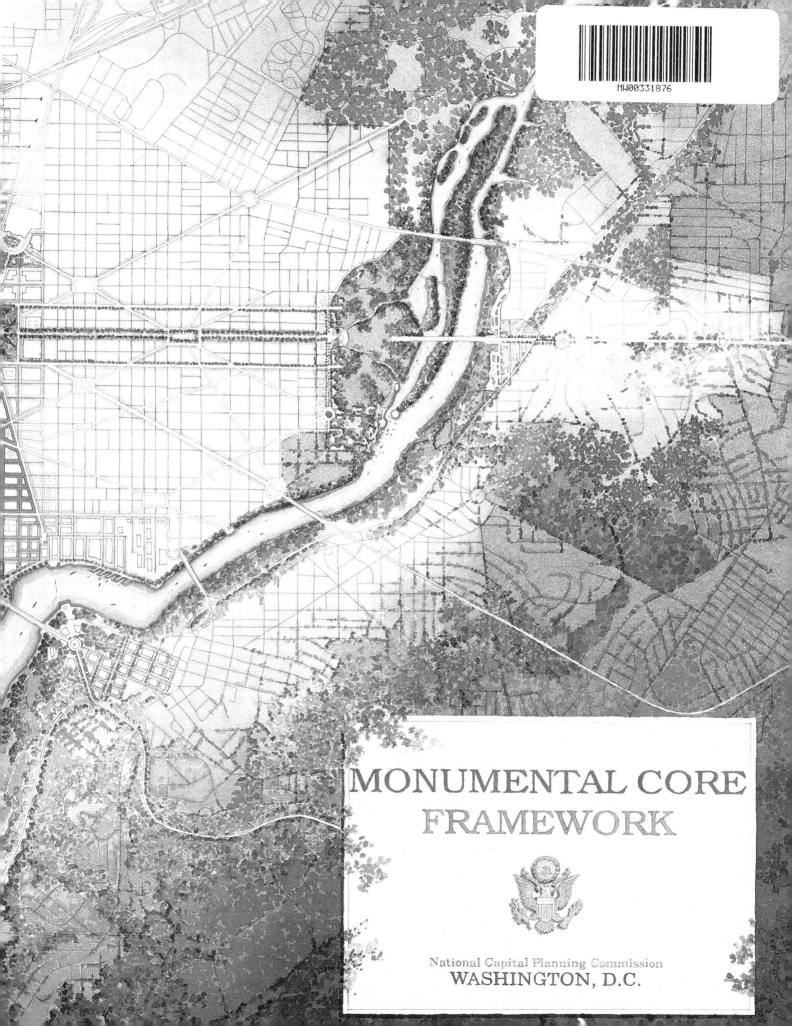

MONUMENTAL CORE
FRAMEWORK

National Capital Planning Commission
WASHINGTON, D.C.

WORTHY OF THE NATION

Washington, DC, from L'Enfant to the National Capital Planning Commission

SECOND EDITION

Frederick Gutheim ✶ Antoinette J. Lee

Foreword by Laura Bush, First Lady of the United States

THE JOHNS HOPKINS UNIVERSITY PRESS Baltimore

This book has been brought to publication
with the generous assistance of the
National Capital Planning Commission.

Originally published by the Smithsonian
Institution in 1977
Johns Hopkins edition published 2006

9 8 7 6 5 4 3 2 1

The Johns Hopkins University Press
2715 North Charles Street
Baltimore, Maryland 21218-4363
www.press.jhu.edu

LIBRARY OF CONGRESS
CATALOGING-IN-PUBLICATION DATA
United States. National Capital Planning
Commission.
Worthy of the nation: Washington, DC,
from L'Enfant to the National Capital Plan-
ning Commission / United States National
Capital Planning Commission; Frederick
Gutheim and Antoinette J. Lee. — 2nd ed.
p. cm.
"United States National Capital Planning
Commission."
Includes bibliographical references and
index.
ISBN 0-8018-8328-8 (hardcover: alk. paper)
1. City planning—Washington (D.C.)—
History. I. Gutheim, Frederick Albert,
1908– II. Lee, Antoinette J. (Antoinette
Josephine) III. Title.
HT168.W3U52 2006
307.1'21609753—dc22   2006001813

A catalog record for this book is available
from the British Library.

PHOTOGRAPHY AND ARCHIVAL
PHOTOGRAPHIC RESEARCH
Peter R. Penczer

Frontispiece: View of the Mall from the
Washington Monument, ca. 1897. DC
Public Library, Washingtoniana Division,
DC Community Archives
Page vi: Logan Park in Anacostia, ca. 1913.
National Archives

CONTENTS

Foreword, *by Laura Bush, First Lady of the United States* • vii

National Capital Planning Commission: A Note from the Chairman • ix

Prologue: The Place of Washington in National Memory • 2

1   The Planned Capital City, 1790–1800 • 8

2   The Port City, 1800–1860 • 36

3   The Civil War, 1860–1865 • 62

4   The Postbellum City, 1865–1900 • 76

5   The McMillan Plan, 1901–1902 • 118

6   Toward Metropolis, 1901–1926 • 144

7   The Year of Decision, 1926 • 166

8   Expansive Planning Visions, 1926–1933 • 192

9   The New Deal in Planning, 1933–1941 • 220

10   World War II and Postwar Years, 1941–1952 • 234

11   Planning the City of Tomorrow, 1952–1960 • 256

12   The Environmentally Conscious City and Region, 1960–1975 • 286

13   Changing Dynamics in the Metropolitan Area, 1976–1990 • 316

14   The Global Capital City, 1991–Present • 346

Epilogue: The National Capital City in the New Century • 374

Acknowledgments • 388

Bibliographic Essay • 390

Index • 418

FOREWORD

WASHINGTON, DC, has been called "the city that dreamers had in mind." Our nation's capital is a city filled with history, yet fresh with promise. I marvel at Washington's natural splendor and the beauty of its design, architecture, monuments, and public spaces. And I delight in the mix of people the city attracts.

Since its beginnings as a few scattered buildings on muddy streets, Washington has drawn visionaries and dreamers of every kind, as well as visitors from every corner of the world. From Pierre L'Enfant, who was commissioned by George Washington to create the capital city's original plan, to those responsible for the new World War II Memorial and the National Museum of the American Indian, Washington has been the beneficiary of grand plans, well executed.

The first edition of *Worthy of the Nation,* published in 1977 by the National Capital Planning Commission and the Smithsonian Institution, chronicles Washington's history from its inception. Illustrated with hundreds of maps and photographs, it explains how an empty swampland became a small town and then the seat of government for our great country.

In the last thirty years much has changed in Washington, inspiring new visionaries and the creation of new realities in the city. I hope that you enjoy the continuing epic of our nation's capital as told in this new edition of *Worthy of the Nation,* a book that offers a wealth of insights and information.

LAURA BUSH
First Lady of the United States

The National Capital Planning Commission is the federal government's planning agency in the District of Columbia and the surrounding region. The commission provides overall planning guidance for federal land and buildings, oversees long-range planning for future development, and monitors capital investment by federal agencies.

MEMBERS

Presidential Appointees
John V. Cogbill, III, Chairman
Herbert F. Ames
Jose L. Galvez III

Mayoral Appointees
Arrington L. Dixon
Patricia Elwood

The Honorable Donald H. Rumsfeld,
Secretary of Defense
The Honorable Dirk Kempthorne,
Secretary of the Interior
The Honorable Lurita Alexis Doan,
Administrator of General Services
The Honorable Susan M. Collins,
Chairman, Senate Committee on
Governmental Affairs
The Honorable Tom Davis,
Chairman, House Committee on
Government Reform
The Honorable Anthony A. Williams,
Mayor of the District of Columbia
The Honorable Linda W. Cropp,
Chairman, Council of the District of
Columbia
Patricia E. Gallagher, AICP,
Executive Director

NATIONAL CAPITAL PLANNING COMMISSION

THE NATIONAL CAPITAL PLANNING COMMISSION is pleased to bring this updated and beautiful new edition of *Worthy of the Nation* to Americans across the country and to readers around the world. In the nearly thirty years since the commission first published *Worthy of the Nation* as a special project to celebrate America's bicentennial, Washington has become a very different place for planners, residents, visitors, and policy makers. The city has shaken off all vestiges of its sleepy, small town past, to emerge as one of the nation's most vibrant and diverse urban centers. Today, downtown Washington offers big-city excitement with a resurging arts and entertainment scene, lively nightlife, and a booming housing market offering trendy lofts and condos to eager new arrivals.

The city is the center of one of the fastest-growing metropolitan areas in the country. In 2002 and 2003 the Washington area, fueled by the thriving technology and biomedical industries, led the nation in job creation and population growth. The region's exploding population now approaches 5 million, making it the seventh largest metropolitan area in the nation. The federal government remains the region's single largest employer, federal procurement spending contributes more than $30 billion to the region's economy each year, and more than 20 million visitors to federal attractions add $4 billion annually to regional economic activity.

Today, in the opening years of the twenty-first century, the role of Washington as the symbolic heart of the nation remains essentially unchanged since America celebrated its bicentennial in 1976. Washington is the seat of government of a great democracy and remains one of the most admired capital cities of the world. The museums, memorials, and great public buildings that define Washington's monumental core express America's connections to its past and aspirations for its future. They help us understand what it means to be an American. As the federal government's central planning agency for Washington and the surrounding region, the National Capital Planning Commission continues to fulfill its mission as a principal steward of the extraordinary historical, cultural, and natural treasures of the nation's capital.

Washington is the beneficiary of two hundred years of visionary planning, and my colleagues on the commission and I, through this book, pay homage to the dreamers and doers who preceded us in shaping Washington's future. Although the genius that inspired Pierre L'Enfant and the giants of the McMillan Commission is undeniable, their visions could not have been achieved without the labors of the planners, designers, builders, and public servants who followed in their footsteps and brought their plans to life. The work of surveyor Andrew Ellicott was critical in advancing L'Enfant's proposals; the US Commission of Fine Arts was established in large part to realize the McMillan Plan. Similarly, today's bold new plans to reclaim Washington's waterfront, create opportunities for memorials and museums in all quadrants of the city, and create an inspiring but livable capital city are being realized by legions of often unsung public servants and dedicated citizens. *Worthy of the Nation* chronicles their efforts and celebrates their achievements.

JOHN V. COGBILL, III
Chairman, National Capital Planning Commission

WORTHY OF THE NATION

PROLOGUE THE PLACE OF WASHINGTON IN NATIONAL MEMORY

Note.) All the Lines coloured red, are
finished and those coloured yellow
are intended to be compleated this Season

Washington, DC, is the nation's finest urban achievement. Its city plan is a world-class creation. The city's monuments, memorials, and public buildings are engraved in the public memory and figure prominently in widely read literary works. The greenswards that make up the Mall, parklands along the Potomac and Anacostia rivers, and green stream valleys throughout the region weave the buildings and neighborhoods into a rich urban tapestry. Residents and visitors to Washington make their way through the city, with its familiar landmarks fixed in their imaginations. Even those who have not had the opportunity to make the trip in person see these images in their minds' eyes.

The plan prepared by Pierre Charles L'Enfant in 1791 established the foundation for the city, charting developments that would take place over the next two centuries. Unparalleled in its scale, scope, and complexity, the original plan brought forth a new capital city from what was sylvan landscape. In spite of crisis, criticism, and shortcomings, the power of L'Enfant's vision inspired successive generations of planners and developers and endured as a foremost example of urban excellence.

For many years after its establishment, even with the construction of the President's House and the Capitol where L'Enfant had sited them, Washington was viewed as a struggling urban center, a curious experiment that might not succeed. Diaries, guidebooks, and novels written during the first half of the nineteenth century point up its shortcomings: the lack of passable streets, the limited housing stock, the extremes of the climate, and the seemingly great distances between major settlements.

The French nobleman Alexis de Tocqueville, author of the classic treatise on the United States and its institutions, *Democracy in America*, studied the new nation for a model of how the French political system might evolve. Although his general views about America were optimistic, he thought that its capital city exemplified youthful ambition exceeding its grasp. "The Americans have traced out the circuit of an immense city on the site which they intend to make their capital," he observed in 1831, although at the time it was "hardly more densely peopled than [the French town of] Pontoise." Insisting that the future would bring "a million inhabitants" to the city, the Americans had "already rooted up trees for ten miles around lest they should interfere with the future citizens of this imaginary metropolis," Tocqueville reported skeptically.

Others voiced positive opinions about the lack of urban coherence. The inveterate traveler Frances "Fanny" Trollope was another European who journeyed throughout the new nation, recording her impressions. In *Domestic Manners of the Americans*, the international best-seller that established her reputation as a social critic, Trollope wrote that Washington reminded her of any number of English "watering places." "It has been laughed at by foreigners, and even by natives," she wrote, "because the original plan of the city was upon an enormous scale, and but a very small part of it has been executed." Trollope for one found this character to be agreeable. The absence of "sights, sounds, or smells of commerce" added much to the city's charm.

Famed Victorian novelist Charles Dickens described Washington in 1842 in *American Notes* in the context of London and Paris. It resembled "the worst parts" of both cities: the "straggling outskirts of Paris, where the houses are smallest, preserving all their oddities, but especially the small shops and dwellings occupied . . . by furniture brokers, keepers of poor eating-houses, and fanciers of birds." He continued the description: "Burn the whole down; build it up again in wood and plaster; widen it a little; throw in part of St. John's Wood; put green blinds outside all the private houses, with a red curtain and a white one in every window; plough up all the roads; plant a great deal of coarse turf in every place where it ought *not* to be." Dickens advised, "Make it scorching hot in the morning, and freezing cold in the afternoon, with an occasional tornado of wind and dust; leave a brick-

field, without the bricks, in all central places where a street may naturally be expected; and that's Washington."

The city's incomplete form reflected the nation's own political instability. Henry Adams, great-grandson of the second president, John Adams, and grandson of the sixth, John Quincy Adams, recollected that in 1860, "as in 1800 and 1850 . . . the same rude colony was camped in the same forest, with the same unfinished Greek Temples for workrooms, and sloughs for roads." Writing from the vantage point of 1905, Adams recalled that on the eve of civil war the city and the national government had an air of "instability and incompleteness." Southern secession was thus "likely to be easy where there was so little to secede from. The Union was a sentiment, but not much more."

Although Washington suffered, the Civil War ultimately gave the city its raison d'être—it transformed the struggling capital into a unifying force that cemented the Union. Sanctified by the carnage of some four years, the city became a sacred space where the formerly warring parties could meet to heal their wounds. Increasingly, Americans began to visit Washington as a civic duty. Although various politicians lobbied for the removal of the federal government to a midwestern location, one observer proclaimed: "The time will soon come, if it has not already arrived, when the most infatuated of Capital movers will look upon the task of tearing down Washington with dismay."

Of the some 9 million Americans who visited the US Centennial International Exhibition, held in Philadelphia in 1876, a very large proportion continued their pilgrimage to Washington. As tourists walked through the "noble marble corridors" of the Capitol, gazed upon the "broad Potomac," or followed the outlines of the great city spreading to the "very edges of its amphitheatre of hills," pride "animated almost every heart." Upon returning home, visitors were "ele-

vated with the experience, with a new and more fervent sentiment of loyalty to our common country, and breathing for the great Republic a prayer that it may last forever."

Famed abolitionist and orator Frederick Douglass summed up prevailing opinions about the city at the turn of the nineteenth century. "Among the great capitals of the world," Douglass wrote, "Washington was preeminently the capital of free institutions." He continued, "Let it stand where it does now stand—where the father of his country planted it, and where it has stood for more than half a century." Washington was "no longer sandwiched between two slave states; no longer a contradiction to human progress; no longer the hotbed of slavery and the slave trade; no longer the home of the duelist, the gambler, and the assassin; no longer the frantic partisan of one section of the country against the other; no longer anchored to a dark and semi-barbarous past." For Douglass, Washington was a "redeemed city," "beautiful to the eye and attractive to the heart." It symbolized the "bond of perpetual union, an angel of peace on earth and good will to men, a common ground upon which Americans of all races and colors, all sections, North and South, may meet and shake hands, not over a chasm of blood, but over a free, united, and progressive republic."

By the end of the nineteenth century, civic improvements, including street pavings, plantings, and reclamation of the Potomac River flats, had transformed Washington into a tourist "mecca." City guidebooks proliferated to satisfy the public's seemingly insatiable demand for information about the capital. This period also saw Washington increasingly regarded as a "historic city" populated by old houses that had withstood waves of redevelopment.

Influenced by the 1893 World's Columbian Exposition in Chicago with its focus on the "City Beautiful," Washington became the test case for rebuilding the central city according to those precepts. Starting in the early twentieth century, massive construction projects anchored the city in national memory. The design of memorials, like the Lincoln Memorial, and museums, like the Natural History Museum, the National Gallery of Art, and the Freer Gallery, along with the Federal Triangle project gave the impression that Washington was throwing off its Victorian gowns and replacing them with Roman robes. Journalist David Brinkley reminisced using classical terms: "Washington in the summer of 1939 gleamed white and green in the sun as if Rome had sent its leftover marble columns, arches, plinths, architraves and friezes to be set down there among the trees."

By the mid-twentieth century, Washington had become that city of timeless beauty of rise and river, street and circle, dome and diagonal, monument and Mall, that fastened itself on the imagination. The nation's foremost architectural critic, Ada Louise Huxtable, wrote in 1967, "At its formal best, Washington has a solemn, full-blown beauty. It is a sybaritic city in correct academic dress. Spring is a romantic overstatement. Summer is a surrealist nightmare as the cool temples shimmer and dissolve in steamy heat. Winter buries the proper palaces in snowdrifts, while the sun hints warmly and regeneratively of spring." Even the times of day were memorable. "There is an hour before twilight, with the glow of the sun still illuminating the horizon, when serene white buildings stand luminous against a clear sky, set stagily amidst the flowers or foliage of a warm spring evening or the bare benches of a crisp winter day. Then the city is touched with its own magic. In the Venetian light the art of politics recedes into the art of architecture. The eye rejoices and the soul expands."

Huxtable added, "The experience is more than the pleasurable recognition of an impressive vista or a successful dialog between structures and spaces. It is an act of love between citizen and stone, and Washington has many lovers, in the tradition of all great cities that have captured the hearts of men." On balance, Huxtable concluded, "Washington succeeds as a city because . . . [of its] singular grace, character and charm."

More recently, the popular historian David McCullough wrote an essay aptly titled "I Love Washington." In it he stated, "What I'm drawn to and moved by is historical Washington, or rather the presence of history almost anywhere one turns. It is hard to imagine anyone with a sense of history not being moved. No city in the country keeps and commemorates history as this one does. Washington insists we remember, with statues and plaques and memorials and words carved in stone, with libraries, archives, museums, and numerous, magnificent old houses."

The city continues to inspire writers, thinkers, and urban critics. Unlike the images of larger urban centers, most notably New York City and Los Angeles, Washington is not defined by dominating heights, sheer magnitude of size, or lavish rewards of commerce and industry. Instead, its form is derived from the highest ideals of nationhood and patriotism. It is a sacred place where national and world events come to place their marks on the city's landscape.

At the outset of the twenty-first century, the city's powers on the human imagination remain undiminished—even with the spread of the city into suburban and exurban jurisdictions. Nevertheless, the processes that established the national capital city and developed it as the center of a major metropolitan region did not always run smoothly. The city's evolution represents a long, often arduous effort by many people, famous and anonymous. How the city developed over two centuries to secure its place on the world stage is the subject of this book. ★

THE PLANNED CAPITAL CITY 1790-1800

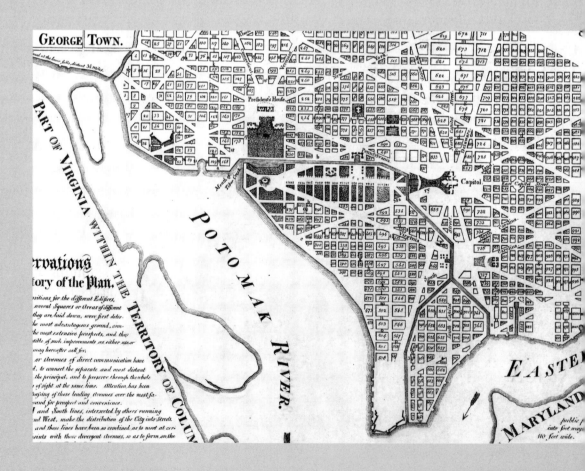

The New National Capital City and Its Potomac Site

That Pierre Charles L'Enfant's plan for the city of Washington survived two centuries is one of its prime enigmas. It was incomplete as it came from his hands, soundly conceived in its fundamentals but hardly more than a sketch, greatly lacking in significant details. Soon after the initial sketches were completed, the city's design was rejected and its creator resigned. Over time, the manuscript itself suffered physical deterioration. Given these challenges, how did it survive as a plan to guide and direct the growth of the nation's capital?

The key to the plan's survival cannot be readily found in L'Enfant's own biography. How could an artist and military engineer with limited architectural training conceive so superlative a city plan that its realization is recognized as one of the world's major planning achievements? The greatness of the Washington plan is more than a tribute to L'Enfant's genius of synthesis and creation or to his ability to produce a city plan in so little time and in the face of political and economic obstruction. The plan reflects L'Enfant's careful integration of the physical form of the Potomac River site with his firsthand understanding of the new nation's aspirations.

THE FEDERAL DISTRICT

Well before Congress passed the Residence Act on July 16, 1790, signed by the president four days later, a substantial legislative history of the proposed federal district had been written. Legislative maneuverings from 1783 to 1789 show a reasonably steady evolution and accumulation of concepts about the federal city. Outstanding among these was the notion of a federal "district," reflected in the Constitution itself. The "district" concept has been traced to the 1783 debates of the Continental Congress on the proposed Delaware River site. The term "district" was repeatedly used after that, and despite the efforts of Jefferson and Madison to popularize the usage of "territory," it is as the *District* of Columbia that the city has maintained its identity.

The Potomac site ultimately chosen by Congress for the national capital was the result of several years of deliberation. In addition to the primary competitor, Philadelphia, Congress leaned strongly toward a site on the Delaware River in the vicinity of Trenton, not far from the government's onetime provisional location in Princeton. In the spring of 1784, however, a congressional committee visited Georgetown and inspected several alternative sites in the vicinity before concluding that the most desirable of these was the land north of Tiber Creek and west of where the White House now stands. Although nothing came of this recommendation—it was unmarked even by legislative history—it established in Congress, and in the minds of the residents of Georgetown, the possibility that the national capital city would be situated there. This further supported George Washington's efforts first in the designation of the Potomac as the seat of government and, second, in the later steps of acquiring the land and building the capital city.

A third element was the realization that the proposed federal district required a substantial area of land. Having started with a minimal concept that embraced only sites required for federal buildings, Congress had gone on, in its authorization on December 23, 1784, of the Delaware River location, to describe an area of two to three miles square. Such an area was in President Washington's mind, apparently, when he began his consideration of the Potomac River site in 1790, and one of the notable factors in the evolution of the national capital city was Washington's decision to increase its size to ten miles square, the maximum allowed by the Constitution.

THE TEN-MILE SQUARE

The constitutional provision to create a national capital city was the starting point for the plan. Article I, section 8, provides that "Congress shall have power to exercise exclusive legislation in all cases whatsoever, over such District (not exceeding ten miles square) as may, by cession of particular States, and the acceptance of Congress, become the seat of the government of the United States." Legislation to further this provision was enacted by Congress on July 12, 1790. This act specified a temporary location for ten years in Philadelphia and the permanent location of the capital on the Potomac at such point between the Eastern Branch and the Conococheague (a small Maryland stream near Hagerstown, in the Cumberland Valley) as the president should designate.

No evidence has been found that George Washington influenced the provisions of this legislation, but much exists to document his long residence on the Potomac and his consequent familiarity with this region—not to mention what was probably of greater significance in the eyes of Congress, the identification of the Potomac region with the president. Moreover, the Potomac River site recommended itself to George Washington, and later to Jefferson, Madison, and others, because among the Atlantic port cities it appeared to offer the best access to the Ohio valley and the West, the key to territorial expansion and national unity. Such access was also the key to the widely disseminated ambitions and expectations of the Patowmack Company canal—indeed, urban growth of the port cities of Georgetown and Alexandria appeared to support the same hope. The actual transaction between Alexander Hamilton and Thomas Jefferson that resulted in agreement on the Potomac site could have applied, however, to a number of different locations. In seeking the reason for the location of the capital city on the Potomac, the most compelling is that the president made the selection.

THE NATURAL SETTING: SIZE, SHAPE, AND EARLY SETTLEMENT

Presidential responsibility for the specific location and boundaries of the city is more explicit. As the new nation shaped its capital city at Washington, several formative influences can be identified. The natural setting and the geography of rivers and streams; the soils, forests, and other resources; the shape of the land, its lowland marshes and heights; and, at finer detail, the springs, the places where streams could be crossed, the commanding views, and other qualities of the landscape—all bore on the decision to locate the city here, to give it specific boundaries and a certain size and shape.

A second set of factors is associated with the earlier settlement of the area: the ten thousand years of occupation by Indian tribes and nearly a century and a half of plantation life with its distinctive slave economy and culture. By 1790 this area was largely a built landscape, not a raw frontier, and what was known of the land was the result of prior use. Most significantly, the land had been divided into plantations and towns held by private owners; both a way of looking upon land as an investment and a business and a philosophy of urbanization had taken clear and firm shape.

There had also developed a strong awareness of the locality's regional position, especially as a place where travel and traffic north and south could cross the broad tidal rivers that indented the coastal plain. The location commanded the chief route to the West with its rapidly developing agriculture and natural resources—and its potential industries. Finally, the city was a creation of its historical period. It incorporated not only the experience of building colonial towns but also the larger European view of urban design, amenity, architecture, and city life. As the barely articulated hopes took form for a democratic capital city to be deliberately created, these were the principal influences at work.

Plantations in the Potomac Valley
The traditional plantation system in the Potomac region paid immediate rewards but held out little benefit for the future. Absent fertilizers, crop rotation, and agricultural improvements, the thin, sandy coastal soil became rapidly exhausted under the intensive single-cropping system. Often fields were abandoned after only three years. Although the typical large plantation may have embraced five hundred to a thousand acres, as few as thirty acres may actually have been cultivated for tobacco. The rest was woodland that

was cleared as needed for fresh tobacco acreage. A variation of this system was the ownership of supplementary farms in the vicinity of the home farm, a practice illustrated by George Washington's land holdings at Mount Vernon.

In the vicinity of the federal city, lands had been settled in the latter half of the seventeenth century. Thus, by the time the national capital was moved here, the traditional tobacco culture was in decline. Plantations were being farmed by second- and third-generation settlers. Many were poor: nearly all were eager to liquidate their real estate holdings. Urbanization provided an answer. A long history of "paper towns" in the Potomac valley, as John Reps referred to them in *Tidewater Towns*, had refined the technique of development. This experience, however, had also produced a quantity of abortive efforts to develop towns, and of those that had achieved any settlement, few had flourished. What caused new hope for future increases in land values—as plantation acres would become town lots—was the interest of the national government in creating a capital city.

Planned Towns in the Potomac Valley
By common practice in the Potomac region, towns were established by an authorization from the colonial legislature designating both the site and the initial governors of the town. A survey then would determine more precisely the boundaries and the lots into which the town was divided and would designate whatever public facilities or amenities might be considered part of the total development. In addition to these sites for public buildings, such tidewater town plans would provide for wharves, warehouses, and other commercial facilities.

Some small port cities were created by the tobacco trade; yet the ease with which cargoes could be collected from plantation wharves (often reached by "rolling roads" along which casks tightly packed with the weed were hauled) and the small number of towns actually required doomed the speculative efforts to failure. Nor were there feasible sites for such towns below

Alexandria on the Potomac. Even the requirement that the exported tobacco be inspected and graded caused only a moderate need for centralization in towns. In contrast with the wide experience in land speculation and such related work as surveying, there was little understanding of the more complex and costly activities of town building: the time needed, the skills demanded, the financing required.

THE DELIBERATELY CREATED CITY

Deliberately created towns, whatever motives lay behind their origin, had much in common with colonial urbanization elsewhere in the British Empire, not only in America but also in Ireland and the West Indies. Additionally, they provided a marked contrast to the organic growth of towns occurring gradually over long periods of time and circumferentially around a center, often a river crossing, a concentration of transportation routes, or some single industry or economic activity like a port or source of power. Whatever the environmental deficiencies, for example, of Boston and New York City, they were reasonably complete towns at each stage of their growth. So, for that matter, was William Penn's more carefully planned "green country town," Philadelphia. By rejecting the established urban creations, Washington's planners had to accept nearly a century of a half-formed city in which the contrast between its aspirations and its urban reality was a continual subject of ridicule and satire.

Yet as a deliberately created city—and in contrast to many other cities of this kind—Washington did succeed. It grew. Its growth followed the earlier expectations and the original plan. And unlike the myriad other deliberately planned cities and capitals (as illustrated in certain capital cities of South America), Washington managed to divest itself of its earlier colonial origins and definitely assert the identity of the new nation and its capital city. More than a century later, in 1930, Washington became the city of five hundred thousand that L'Enfant had envisioned and provided for, the capital of the coast-to-coast

nation of imperial scale he had foreseen. Only then was the significance of the 1791 plan fully recognized and the greatness of its designer appreciated.

Pierre Charles L'Enfant

The selection of Pierre Charles L'Enfant as Washington's planner tells something about city planning at the end of the eighteenth century, that it could be considered the province of "the artist of the army." This aside, it is more reasonable to look upon the expectations of the creators of the capital city as hopes that would be realized in ceremonial arrangements and the symbolism of architecture and garden art rather than in any products of engineering and economics.

That L'Enfant had been the architect of Federal Hall, where Congress met in New York City, a building widely regarded as the most beautiful of its time and place, further recommended him as a planner. Nor should it be overlooked that part of L'Enfant's commission to design the capital city was that he propose designs for its principal buildings. When he undertook the design of the new capital city, he was firmly established in New York City and evoked the admiration and respect of Charles Bulfinch and other leading architects—whatever one thinks of the claim he later made of being "able of commanding whatever business I liked." Finally, L'Enfant was French. That Americans owed their independence to the French intervention led the United States to favor many things French. That France (as against England) hoped to reestablish in the New World the hegemony that had ended in 1759 with the loss of the Caribbean and Quebec meant that it eagerly promoted many things French.

Despite his conspicuous French origins (an impression reinforced by his erratic command of the English language), by the time of his Washington commission in 1791, L'Enfant had been living in the United States for fourteen years. He had served in the army, practiced architecture in New York City, and in other ways assimilated himself into the American scene. That he reflected his artistic background is to be expected, but it is also true that he translated this into language of the New World. Nowhere is this more evident than in his respect for the landscape and its treatment and the buoyant confidence and optimism with which he viewed the expansion of this nation and the growth of its capital city. This is true despite the more obvious contrast between Jefferson, who "accepted" nature in the New World fashion, and L'Enfant, who boldly restructured nature, especially water, in the fashion of André Le Nôtre. In the heavily forested river bottom, sparsely settled with modest plantation dwellings, L'Enfant envisioned a new kind of city suited to the American space and reflecting the conditions of its national growth. It was new by contrast to the contemporaneous densities of Paris (before the boulevards of Georges-Eugène Baron Haussmann and the growth and improvements of the nineteenth century), as new as the Garden District of New Orleans was by contrast to the Vieux Carré.

The mandate that L'Enfant received to design a new capital city was hardly original. Many new capitals had been carefully laid out in the colonies and states. Many other nations in the New World had been provided with new or transformed capital cities, and European nations and principalities were liberally furnished with examples of capital cities created de novo. In these backgrounds, however, there was nearly always the factor of concentrated power. Thus, L'Enfant might be forgiven for expecting from President Washington the autocratic will, just as he had expected and received from him the patronage he considered necessary to create the new city.

L'ENFANT AND WASHINGTON

The selection of L'Enfant is most easily explained by asking, "Who else?" In the selection of architects to design the Capitol and the White House, public competitions were held and numerous applicants submitted designs. In choosing the planner of the capital city, it was difficult even to establish required qualifications. L'Enfant's desire for the commission; his military record; his acquaintance with President Washington, Thomas Jefferson, and other political leaders; and his previous experience as an architect in New York City were all important, but more significant appears to have been his generally acknowledged design abilities in engineering and landscape design as well as in architecture and the decorative arts. In fact, it can be said about L'Enfant's commission to design the city that he sought it; that George Washington appointed him; that the commission was vaguely defined by Washington and Jefferson; that the planner's relationship to the commissioners appointed to be in charge of building the city was poorly described; and that no businesslike contractual agreement defining the work to be done, the schedule, or the fee was ever concluded. Throughout, the initiative remained L'Enfant's.

George Washington's selection of L'Enfant has found many defenders. Less noticed is that he kept the French designer on a short leash. Washington's first concern was to secure the capital on the Potomac against those who were intent upon keeping it in Philadelphia, relocating it in New York City, or moving it elsewhere. President Washington was steadfastly aware of the thin margin of legislative victory that had placed the capital city on the Potomac. As the difficulties of that decision increased, they seemed to strengthen those who wanted the capital located somewhere else.

A CAPITAL CITY WORTHY OF THE NATION

Certainly a great and glorious city plan, "worthy of the nation," as the phrase would run for many decades, would strengthen the Potomac's claim. That L'Enfant could provide this plan better than any other designer was President Washington's initial motivation. But as general and as president, Washington had experienced L'Enfant's temperament, had little confidence in his judgment or tact (particularly in negotiation), and thought him extravagant, overoptimistic, egocentric, and prickly.

L'Enfant's biographers have been intent on using him for their own purposes. Elizabeth Kite presents him as an exemplar of French artistic genius; H. Paul Caemerer aims at strengthening the claims of the designers of the McMillan Commission, and their advocate Charles Moore, that L'Enfant's plan formed the basis of the 1901–1902 plan and of the modern city; Fiske Kimball reinforces L'Enfant's professional and technical stature. More recently, historians like Kenneth R. Bowling seek to understand "Peter" L'Enfant as a gifted designer who was sought out by the nation's early political leaders, many of whom he met during service in the Revolutionary War. Given the complexity of his plan for the federal city and the range of his genius, historians will continue to cull through surviving documents and possible influences and to offer new insights into L'Enfant's biography.

THE EARLY YEARS

Pierre Charles L'Enfant was born in Paris on August 2, 1754, the son of a court painter and a decorative artist. He knew Paris and Versailles, the cities whose formal influence upon the Washington plan is most apparent. He received training in architecture and military engineering and at the age of twenty-three was a lieutenant in the French army when he was recruited as one of a clandestine group of French military engineers and artillery and cavalry officers whose mission was to aid the American Revolutionary War and embarrass the British.

L'Enfant's ambition was rewarded by a creditable military career and advancement to captain, then major. Although he undertook the design and construction of fortifications and other engineering works, he achieved greater distinction from artistic odd jobs: he illustrated Baron Fredrich Wilhelm Von Steuben's drill manual, designed medals and insignia, drew portraits of colonial military leaders, and devised appropriate ceremonies. After the British surrendered at Yorktown, L'Enfant was well remembered by his comrades and took a leading part in organizing the politically powerful veterans' organization, the Society of the Cincinnati; in converting Federal Hall in New York City to frame Washington's first inaugural; and in performing other tasks required by the young republic and its political leaders.

Whatever may have been the influence of L'Enfant's Versailles boyhood or the Paris he knew when he left it at the age of twenty-three, a more proximate experience would have been his visit to Paris from December 1783 to March 1784. At this point he would be facing both the architectural and urban problems of the new nation and the matter of his own professional career as an architect. Such awareness as he may have had might be related to Père Marc-Antoine Laugier's *Essai sur l'architecture* (1753) with its emphasis on urban squares and the straight, wide avenues explicitly derived from the hunting rides of the royal forests. Equally germane are the later designs by Pierre Patte, whose *Monuments* (1765) reproduced the detailed plans of Germain Boffrand and others and expressed a design philosophy based on the development of important squares connected by wide avenues or circles from which avenues radiated. But since so little is known of L'Enfant's activities in 1784, obvious stylistic resemblance between contemporary proposals for Paris at this most important period in its urban development and L'Enfant's plan for

Washington formulated seven years later can only be pointed out. The urban designers of this period were concerned with creating more than urban landscapes: they dealt with the new urban agenda of commerce, waterfronts, and transportation; the new social architecture of hospitals, prisons, and educational institutions; and the design of new towns. L'Enfant was one among such urban designers.

THE PLANNING BEGINS

As L'Enfant addressed the planning of Washington, fully recognizing its importance, the ambitious scope had many consequences. It obliged him to rationalize a development strategy based on multiple centers of growth. More than anything else, this strategy brought him into conflict with the commissioners. The Residence Act of 1790 created a presidential commission to survey the district, purchase land, and supervise construction of public buildings. On January 22, 1791, President Washington appointed three commissioners: David Carroll and Thomas Johnson of Maryland and David Stuart of Virginia. The large-scale investment needed to provide the extensive infrastructure for the multicentered city led L'Enfant to the quixotic recommendation of a large bond issue, a further point of conflict with the commissioners and the pay-as-you-go policy to which they were committed.

Over longer periods of time the decentralized multicentered city encouraged a diffusion of industrial and commercial locations and the growth of distinctly separate communities in each of which were found diverse income and ethnic groups. The walk-to-work city affected rich as well as poor, although from the start there were some individuals like Benjamin Latrobe who were willing to travel on horseback from his residence in Kalorama to his work in the Navy Yard six miles distant. If wealth and ethnicity did not shape Washington as they had shaped the older and larger cities of the East Coast, some distinctly separate character was given to parts of the city that were predominantly oriented to trade, manufacturing, shipping, or certain government functions and installations, like the Navy Yard.

L'Enfant did not present himself as an imperious figure, but he was. He appeared to some as truculent and obstinate. He had difficulty getting people to accept him at his own estimation. With other architects and engineers, his relations were better, but to them as to his political employers, he appeared first and foremost as an artist. As an artist, capable and confident in resolving problems, he boldly assumed that his solutions were the right ones. This self-confidence may have been just what a new and still shaky nation required, but at times that nation did not seem to appreciate it. What L'Enfant was most confident about was the urban program, and since that had not been given to him by Washington or Jefferson, who produced his own sketches for the new city, and not by the commissioners, he made it up. Churches, embassies, universities, monuments, gardens, public buildings, the large public functions, and the small domestic details—all were delivered with a charming French accent and without hesitation. Thus, the biography of its designer was translated into the form of the city.

The Land and the Watercourses

At the time of L'Enfant's appointment, Congress had agreed on a location on the Potomac River at the head of navigation of, as specified in the Constitution, "as much as ten miles square to be organized as a federal district." The land to be occupied by L'Enfant's city comprised the river "flats" (the floodplains both of the Potomac and of the Anacostia northward to the Talbot terrace) and the Wicomico terrace, a step higher, extending from just north of the Mall to the boundaries of the formal city at the Wicomico-Sunderland escarpment as later generally defined by Boundary Street (Florida Avenue). The subject of L'Enfant's design was defined, therefore, by the Potomac and its Eastern Branch, the Anacostia, and the hills that framed the basin city to the north. In its future growth, the city would expand upward into the higher lands surrounding the initial core, in all directions save down the Potomac.

These old river terraces, north of the flats, were further slashed by the stream valleys, most notably Rock Creek. In the larger geographical context, the site embraced the fall line at Little Falls, where the coastal plain meets the Piedmont Plateau, and thereby symbolically linked the tidewater plantations with the Piedmont farming areas. Like London, Washington was located at the extreme end of navigable water, far enough inland to be protected from sea attack but accessible to a flourishing sea trade.

PLAIN, PIEDMONT, AND TIDEWATER

Apart from the small but growing ports of Alexandria and Georgetown, the site selected for the city contained nothing but a few agricultural clearings and plantation houses in its predominantly wooded expanse. The varied geology, from the floodplains to the palisades of the Potomac and the steep ravines of Rock Creek, combined with the highly differentiated climates within a small radius, allowed a wide range of plant species. The environmental detail accurately reflected the fundamental condition of the site: the conjunction of coastal plains and Piedmont. L'Enfant's Washington was framed at Boundary Street by the first evidences of the Piedmont, the Wicomico-Sunderland escarpment. Within this boundary, the old sea beds with their layers of sediment and their susceptibility to erosion were clothed in sweet gum, oak, and hickory forests. Sycamore, willow, and birch filled the stream valleys of the floodplains of the Anacostia and the Potomac. The higher lands of the Piedmont offered a more complex geology with a greater variety of soils and rocky outcrops on its characteristic terraces. Here the forest cover was composed of oak, tulip poplar, sassafras, beech, and basswood.

Given the tidewater character of the area, the outstanding natural resource was the Potomac fishery, particularly the herring, shad, salmon, sturgeon, and other anadromous varieties that seasonally teemed to spawn in the river at the falls. This fishery—together with the oysters, clams, and crabs—had supported the relatively dense population of Indians and their characteristic village life. Until nearly the end of the nineteenth century, it sustained the local community and also provided an important economic activity as well. Associated with the fishery as an element of the local economy in addition to the ecology, and expressing equally the underlying geographical character of the area, was the bird life. The migratory waterfowl were an outstanding element, and turkeys, quail, and other game birds were also abundant.

These characteristics of the Potomac at the head of navigation, where that geological factor known as the fall line presents a distinctive topographical feature, have received much comment. Perhaps no one has better summarized it than Henry Fleet, who in 1631 eulogized: "This place without all question is the most pleasant and healthful place in all this country, and most convenient for habitation, the air temperate in summer and not violent in winter. It aboundeth with all manner of fish. The Indians in one night commonly will catch thirty sturgeons in a place where the river is not above twelve fathom broad. And as for deer, buffaloes, bears, turkeys, the woods do swarm with them and the soil is exceedingly fertile." Other observers noted the abundant water power and excellent mill sites, the ease with which the river as it narrowed could be crossed by ferries and bridges, and additional desirable conditions for settlement and urban growth.

THE DRAINAGE SYSTEM AND HYDRAULICS

The drainage patterns of the area included the primary elements of the Potomac and the Anacostia rivers; the important boundary between Georgetown and the federal city, Rock Creek; and the large tidal inlet, Tiber Creek. This estuary, also called Goose Creek, originated in an extensive watershed, the upper part of which had been named Tiber Creek nearly a hundred years earlier by a settler who had entitled his plantation "Rome." (Tiber Creek is not, as some historians have assumed, a name that derived from the neoclassicism that engulfed the early city.) Major tributaries of Rock Creek—notably Pine Creek, now Piney Branch—reached north and east through the city, and important streams like Reedy Branch and Slash Run were topographical features noted on early maps.

Because they presented initial obstacles to travel (because they created important flood-plains), because they determined forest species and plant communities, and because their steep banks were easily eroded, these watercourses had important effects on later development. They also had significance as a water supply, and parts of the drainage system, such as Rock Creek, supported significant water-powered mills or, like Tiber Creek and lower Rock Creek, were navigable to the river craft of the day. Much of L'Enfant's extensive canal system simply straightened out and rationalized the natural stream locations, improving their use for navigation, while still allowing them to serve their primary purpose of drainage.

As will be seen, however, L'Enfant would not be satisfied simply to solve the city's drainage problem; he wanted to use water in fountains, reflecting pools, and—his most spectacular proposal—a cascade that was to emerge from the base of the Capitol and flow down to join the projected City Canal in a carefully designed reflecting pool that formed an integral element in the functional canal system. In such proposals L'Enfant's debt to European landscape design is most evident, echoing the great Renaissance tradition of cascade design.

Although the aim was aesthetic, the hydraulics were entirely practical. Something had to be done with the waters of Tiber Creek, and the cascade was an ornamental and dramatic means of carrying it to tidewater. The great cascades of the Renaissance involved important iconographic themes. L'Enfant appears to have been content to use water for its dramatic effect. He can hardly have been oblivious, however, to its potential to echo the stairs that would be needed to provide access to the Capitol, and there is no doubt he

envisioned a truly monumental building on this site.

Travelers' Descriptions of Early Washington

The approach to Washington from the north offered travelers a synoptic view of the town and its natural setting from the hills above the Bladensburg road. The view stretched to Georgetown and showed both the Anacostia and the Potomac rivers framing the beginnings of the federal city. Many travelers commented on the panorama from this point, and indeed the progress of the city's growth could be described by the evolution of the Capitol and other principal buildings. In the spring of 1797, French traveler the Duke of La Rochefoucauld-Liancourt set down in his journal characteristic details of the city at the time.

La Rochefoucauld-Liancourt's journal is the most comprehensive account by a contemporary traveler of the creation and development of the city to this date. It embraces the city's legislative authorization, land acquisition, financing, and administration. The author takes the measure of the speculation in land and identifies the effect of this activity in stimulating the initial urbanization around the Capitol, the several competing ports along the Potomac and the Eastern Branch, and other early urban growth centers.

Despite La Rochefoucauld-Liancourt's approval of the location and commercial prospects of the city, his expectation for its future was gloomy, taking into account its overlarge size, its widely separated centers of urban development (he mentioned particularly the distance from the Capitol to the President's House), and the land speculation and influence of mercantile interests. He correctly foresaw a long period of inconvenience and physical discomfort for the city's inhabitants. The adverse impact of the conditions upon the federal establishment and on official visitors to the city seemed to La Rochefoucauld-Liancourt to imperil the entire venture. "One cannot say that [visitors] are pursuing the idea of 'comfort' to extremes when they wish to be preserved from falling into mud holes for lack of paved roads, or from breaking their necks for lack of street lights. This sort of inconvenience will endure here for many years, given the size of the city's plan and the great distance between the two centers of public affairs," he concluded.

Over time, this disbelief that "the Federal City will ever develop to the point where it will become a pleasant place to live for the kind of people who are destined to inhabit it" proved as wrong as the author's larger expectation that the federal union itself would soon dissolve.

THE TIMELESS HYPNOTIC CHARM

That the French visitor should have totally ignored the contribution of his countryman to the city is surprising. Without mentioning L'Enfant by name, his most direct comment is that "the plan has been well conceived and cleverly, even magnificently drawn; as a matter of fact, it is the very magnificence of the conception that gives it its dreamlike quality." In that single insight, he perfectly expresses the timeless hypnotic charm of L'Enfant's drawing, deliberately designed to touch the imagination.

Travelers remarked on the densely wooded character of the land to be occupied by the city. The stage from Baltimore passed through almost uninterrupted forest, and arrival at Washington was announced by the sound of trees being lopped to facilitate the work of surveyors. In limited areas in the center of the projected city, the woods had been more fully and systematically cleared. Here the sites for public buildings were to be found. Isaac Weld Jr. reported in 1796 that "excepting the streets and avenues and a small part of the ground adjourning the public buildings, the whole place is covered with trees." A few locations, wrote Thomas Twining in the same year, "assumed more the appearance of a regular avenue, the trees having been cut down in a straight line." Francis Baily thought that perhaps half of the area projected for the city had been cleared of trees by the fall of 1796 and perceived the site as "broad avenues and a park bounded on each side by thick wood."

THE PORT TOWNS: ALEXANDRIA AND GEORGETOWN

Two towns, Alexandria and Georgetown, were already to be found at the head of Potomac navigation. Both closely resembled the British provincial town. Red brick buildings and green trees pleasantly and closely arranged themselves along the waterfront. Here could be found on a limited scale the amenities of eighteenth-century urban life: homes close to occupations and recreation, inns, and taverns; lively streets and markets crowded with cattle, sheep, hogs, poultry, produce, eager buyers, and curiosity-seekers. Of public buildings and churches there were, as yet, few. Theaters and concert halls were unknown, and, with some exceptions, the mansions of the rich and influential were still built on a small scale and with rudimentary taste. The parks and pleasure grounds of the city plan had not yet appeared, but a short walk brought the hunter into woods or open fields, and the river teemed with fish for the angler.

Like all port cities, Georgetown and Alexandria were cosmopolitan, and whatever transpired or was produced in the world soon found its way here. The waterfronts bristling with masts and the warehouses crammed with merchandise announced the purpose of these towns—to ship and receive goods. These port functions were recorded in hogsheads of tobacco and flour exported and in goods of every description imported from Bristol, Glasgow, and other British ports. The population of Georgetown and Alexandria from the start had been predominantly composed of Scots; their names were stamped on plantations, streets, landmarks, business firms, and establishments of every sort, and their accent marked the place among colonial towns.

Whatever their shortcomings, the towns were distinctly urban creations, complete with town governments, public works, courts, prisons, and other municipal institutions. Here also one found the early water-power industries—the flour and grist mills, foundries and forges, sawmills and lime furnaces—distributed along

Georgetown, ca. 1795. Library of Congress

lower Rock Creek and lesser streams. The Potomac port towns were regularly laid out, with streets at right angles. Although travel was still mainly by horseback, the streets were wide and modern, with no trace of the winding lanes of some older cities. The river was crossed by ferries; the single bridge proposed at Georgetown lay in the future.

It was possible in 1791 to entertain the highest hopes for the "Potomac route to the West" and its stimulus to urban growth at the fall line. Expectations for Washington's growth were sustained by the improvement of river navigation and by canals around the falls. Downriver traffic five years later took the form of narrow barges loaded with tobacco, flour, and other commodities that passed Great Falls on an inclined plane down which the cargoes of hogsheads were lowered and, afloat again, passed Little Falls via a canal on the Maryland side of the river.

L'Enfant's Survey, March 1791

On Wednesday, March 9, 1791, Pierre Charles L'Enfant arrived in Georgetown and immediately started his reconnaissance. Quartering the river bottom and ridges of the site of the future city on horseback, he came quickly to an appreciation of its streams and marshes, its uncertain and fragile river edges, its few really commanding heights of land, the ridges and terraces, as well as the strategic importance of a few feet in elevation. These factors had already determined the drainage, roads, and stream crossings, the existing and prospective settlement, and the siting of many individual plantation houses.

L'Enfant had been directed by President Washington to commence his reconnaissance "at the lower end and work upwards." He continued his work as weather allowed over the next ten days. He carefully noted the approaches to the city from Baltimore and the north and the few but important ferries, fords, bridges, and stream crossings. Starting at the point where the

Potomac and the Anacostia come together, he traveled north toward the height of land where the future Capitol would stand. Turning east he examined the shoreline of the Anacostia as high as the ferry road that led into the future city. Here he turned west and passed Jenkins Hill on the north side, continuing along the Talbot-Wicomico ridge to the crossing of Rock Creek that led into Georgetown.

L'Enfant noted that the days were cold and rainy. The landscape was obscured by a heavy fog, but he managed to see enough of its principal features to form an immediate and important opinion: the high flat land to the east of Jenkins Hill offered far greater opportunity for urban development than the more constricted area north of Tiber Creek on which Jefferson and Washington had been concentrating. He also decided that Jenkins Hill, the highest spot in the land between the Potomac and the Anacostia, was the most desirable location for the Capitol.

Nearly 150 years had passed since the first explorers had passed through the region, and it had long been divided into plantations, large in acreage but typically occupied only by a small dwelling and accommodation for a few slaves. Only the largest plantations could command a Potomac headland for a mansion site. This was an agricultural frontier. Signs of change were witnessed in the growth of the port towns of Alexandria and Georgetown, and there was evidence, however frustrated, of urban aspirations in the platted but still unoccupied riverside towns of Hamburg and Carrollsburg. It was the end of the tobacco boom. The soils of the immediate locality could not support a thriving colonial agriculture. Port towns at the head of Potomac navigation—such as Georgetown and Alexandria—were growing because they had tapped a more distant hinterland of wheat farming deep in the Piedmont and become exporting centers for the Atlantic trade. The future growth of this business depended on the improved access provided by new turnpikes, canals, improvements in river navigation, and the large expansion of grist and flour mills.

PRESIDENT WASHINGTON'S STRATEGY FOR THE PROPRIETORS

L'Enfant's initial reconnaissance had been craftily specified by President Washington to confuse the proprietors, particularly Robert Peter and others who had been bidding up the price of real estate in the initially favored site north of Tiber Creek immediately east of Georgetown. Washington disclosed this strategy to Francis Deakins and Benjamin Stoddert. Noting in his letter of March 2, 1791, to Deakins that L'Enfant was "directed to begin at the lower end and work upward," Washington added that "nothing further is communicated to him." This cat and mouse game backfired. Not many days passed before Washington had greatly enlarged his conception of the amount of land required for the federal city and accepted L'Enfant's estimation of the greater desirability of the land between Jenkins Hill and the Anacostia. Within a week of L'Enfant's first view of the site, Washington was writing Deakins and Stoddert that he intended to view this part of the federal district on his next visit. How this changed attitude came about is not known, but in addition to some meeting, or letter now lost, or other direct message from L'Enfant to Washington, the French planner's enthusiasm may have been communicated to young Daniel Carroll who owned the largest tract of land commencing with Carrollsburg and reaching north, to the east of Goose Creek, to the tract owned by Deakins, with whom Washington was in close touch.

Through the wet, early spring months, L'Enfant pressed his survey. Before March had ended, Washington enlarged his instructions to embrace more fully the task of planning the city. In his letter of March 31, 1791, to Jefferson, Washington confirmed his enlarged oral instructions to L'Enfant and further described his expanded view of the size of the city, now seen as "containing from three to five thousand acres," the whole of which "shall be surveyed and laid off as a city (which Major L'Enfant is now directed to do)." The same letter, written from Mount Vernon, also described for the first time an arrangement with the proprietors that promised to solve the major financial problems posed by the necessity of purchasing sufficient land for the future city.

THE PROPRIETORS ENTER PARTNERSHIP WITH THE GOVERNMENT

The new arrangement provided that the proprietors should convey their lands to the federal government, and after the city plan had been prepared, they would receive back, in exchange, every other one of the platted lots. For a set price of twenty-five pounds per acre, the proprietors would be compensated for federal building reservations, as well as for the unplatted lands required for public use as squares, walks, and similar elements. The land required for streets and alleys would be dedicated by the proprietors without charge. At one stroke, this new arrangement placed the proprietors in partnership with the federal government—and with each other— in urban development.

This partnership departed from the way in which the development of those earlier "paper towns" of the Potomac had been attempted. In these towns, the original owner sold outright to a new party who proposed to undertake the tasks of urbanization. Where did the new arrangement come from? The research of Louis Dow Scisco attributes the concept to George Walker, a small businessman of Georgetown who also owned one tract of land and part of another in the valley of the Anacostia, the prime center of L'Enfant's city. The overwhelmingly Scottish character of Georgetown and Alexandria and of the proprietors themselves, however, suggests that the scheme may well have reflected the real estate and legal arrangements for James Craig's "New Town" in Edinburgh in 1767.

The details of the arrangement were also very congenial. The planters were left in possession of their homes, the sites of which were excluded from the partnership arrangement. Family burying grounds were left undisturbed. And, for the other side, the decisive factor was that the developers of the federal city secured the land substantially without cost, thus allowing their lim-

ited funds to be devoted to the heavy expenses of building.

PLANNING ON A VISIBLY GRAND SCALE

In his important meeting with the proprietors on March 29, 1791, at Suter's Tavern in Georgetown, which Washington described in his diary, the president reviewed the need to enhance the feasibility of the city building project and thus counter the still-present threat that the capital might not be moved from Philadelphia at all; the desirability of planning on a visibly grand scale; the absolute necessity of overcoming the limited financial resources available for building the city; the self-defeating competition for public building sites among the proprietors, particularly as between those of Georgetown and Carrollsburg; and the need for a tract of land so large that it would embrace both Alexandria and Georgetown, the two established urban centers at the head of Potomac navigation, whose commercial success appeared to ensure the future of the national capital city. Above all, Washington urged recognition of the "common cause" to build the city that would stretch from Georgetown to the Anacostia. The meeting was successful, and on the following day the eighteen proprietors signed the agreement to convey their lands by the proposed deeds of trust.

The terms of the agreement certainly were conducive to a liberal view of the city's size. Since land acquisition costs had been drastically reduced, the earlier restraint no longer obstructed Washington's increasingly expansive view of the city's boundary, which now moved steadily northward. First the boundary was seen as the Bladensburg-Georgetown road; then it moved to what is now Massachusetts Avenue; and ultimately it moved to what is now Florida Avenue, along the rugged base of the old river terrace called the Wicomico-Sunderland escarpment. These changes caused perturbation among the proprietors, for L'Enfant's personal view of the city *en grand* was now being affirmed by the expansionist view of his patron, and despite uncertainties about land acquisition, L'Enfant

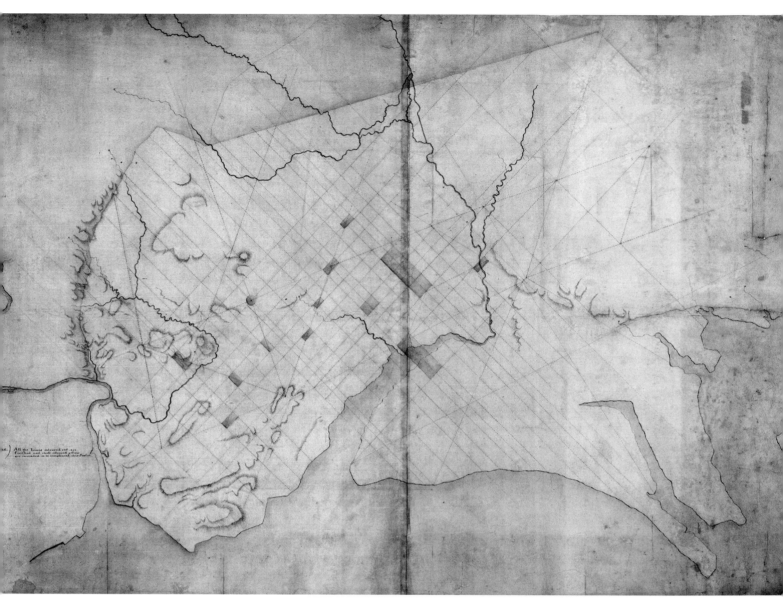

"Map of Dotted Lines" by L'Enfant Showing Survey of Sites for Major Public Buildings, 1791. Library of Congress

proceeded steadily with his planning work. By June 27, 1791, all difficulties with the landowners had been resolved, and deeds of trust were executed with fifteen of the proprietors.

L'Enfant's Memorandum: Urban Design, Landscape Image, and a Development Strategy

By June 22, L'Enfant had prepared an initial plan, which he took to Mount Vernon and discussed with the president at what must have been a decisive encounter. While minor changes were incorporated in this plan before the version dated August 19, which Washington accepted in

Philadelphia and used as the basis for the sale of lots and other decisions, it is remarkable that so complete and detailed a conception could have been created in such a short time and under such uncertainties. From March 9, when L'Enfant arrived in Georgetown and commenced work, to June 22, when his preliminary plan was completed, less than three-and-a-half months had elapsed. To be sure, his efforts were accelerated by frequent reminders from Washington and Jefferson, as well as the commissioners, of the need for dispatch. But by contrast to the concerns expressed about the city's boundaries and the negotiations with the proprietors, almost no attention appears to have been given to the plan itself, nor did Washington mention the meeting of June 22 in his diary. Fortunately, both the plan itself (in the August 19 outline version known as the "Map of Dotted Lines") and a memorandum to accompany it were prepared by L'Enfant and have survived. The memorandum describes how the planner went about his work as well as the plan he created.

After some preliminary qualifications as to the nature of this initial design—the limited time available; the unfinished graphic presentations; the small scale of the plan, which precluded much detail—L'Enfant moved to the positive character of his proposal, "correct only as it respects the situation and distance of objects" but adequately reflecting the topography and illustrating the major features of the proposed city, as well as emphasizing the unity of its several parts. The President's House was sited on a rise just north of the Tiber Creek. From this site major radial avenues stretched outward and crossed grid streets and other radials at points intended by L'Enfant as nodes of urban development. The major radial avenue commenced at Rock Creek and was traced by L'Enfant through the President's House; it then ran southeast, where it met the foot of Jenkins Hill, site for the Capitol, and ended at the Anacostia River. Thus, Pennsylvania Avenue became the city's principal avenue and eventually the nation's great ceremonial and processional route.

L'ENFANT'S STREETS AND AVENUES: "THESE I MADE BROAD"

"Having determined some principal points to which I wished to make the others subordinate," L'Enfant's memoir explained, "I made the distribution regular with every street at right angles, north and south, east and west, and afterwards opened some in different directions, as avenues to and from every principal place, wishing thereby not merely to contract [contrast?] with the general regularity, nor to afford a greater variety of seats with pleasant prospects, which will be obtained from the advantageous ground over which these avenues are chiefly directed, but principally to connect each part of the city, if I may so express it, my making the real distance less from place to place, by giving them reciprocity of sight, and by making them thus seemingly connected, promote a rapid settlement over the whole extent, rendering those even of the most remote parts an addition to the principal, which without the help of these, were any such settlement attempted, it would be languid, and lost in the extent, and become detrimental to the establishment. Some of these avenues were also necessary to effect the junction of several roads to a central point in the city, by making these roads shorter, which is effected [by directing them] to those leading to Bladensburg and the Eastern Branch—both of which are made above a little shorter, exclusive of time advantage of those leading immediately to the wharves at Georgetown. The hilly ground which surrounds that place the growth of which it must impede, by inviting settlements on the city side of Rock Creek, which cannot fail soon to spread along all those avenues which will afford a variety of pleasant rides, and become the means for a rapid intercourse with all parts of the city, to which they will serve as does the main artery in the animal body, which diffuses life throughout the smaller vessels, and inspires vigor, and activity throughout the whole frame.

"These avenues I made broad, so as to admit of their being planted with trees leaving 80 feet for a carriage way, 30 feet on each side for a walk under a double row of trees, and allowing 10 feet between the trees and the houses. The first of these avenues and the most direct one begins at the Eastern Branch and ends over Rock Creek at the wharves at Georgetown, along the side of which it is continued to the bridge over to the Virginia shore, and down to the lower canal to the Potomac, along the sides of which it may be of great advantage to have such a road extended to the upper canal to facilitate dragging the boats up and down."

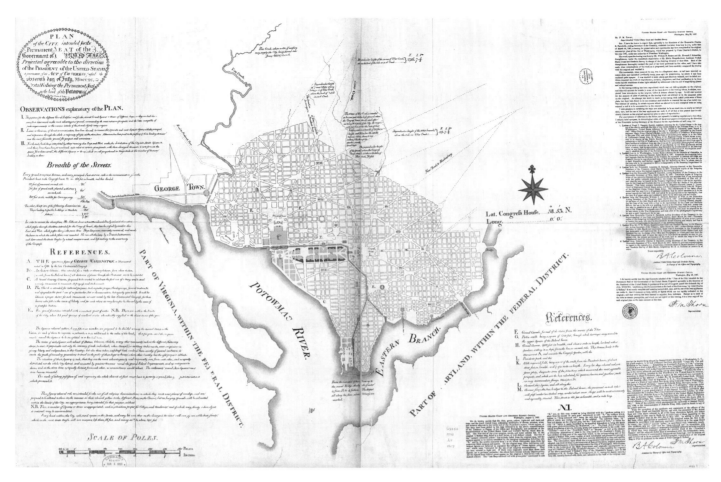

The L'Enfant Plan of 1791 (as shown in a facsimile published in 1887 by the US Coast and Geodetic Survey Office). Library of Congress

L'ENFANT'S UNIFIED VIEW

Throughout his presentation, L'Enfant urged "embracing in one view the whole extent from the Eastern Branch to Georgetown, and from the banks of the Potomac to the mountains [the hills surrounding the city]." Although not understating his concern with the urban design, L'Enfant stressed consistently his aim to generate development of the city throughout its entire large area and the simultaneous development of its several major districts. What L'Enfant offered was not simply the urban design that has survived and attracted admiration over the centuries but also a theory of urban growth and development that was both original and far in advance of its time. This growth strategy brought him into conflict with President Washington and the commissioners and eventually caused his downfall and his dismissal. The man was rejected but never his plan.

By his system of avenues, L'Enfant the planner aimed both to unify the vast extent of the city and its many well-distributed functional centers of development and to provide a means of directing the development effort. This development, he believed, would occur initially along the avenues and later in the more intensive local growth of the various districts around their centers, these to be established by major public buildings. He also considered that by such disposition he could engender competition among the several key points of the multinucleated city. Nor did he evade the designation of what he regarded as the principal artery of initial development, "across the Tiber above tidewater"—or approximately Pennsylvania Avenue. "Where the tidewater comes into Tiber Creek, is the position the most capable of any within the limits of the city, to favor those grand improvements of public magnitude which may serve as a sample for all subsequent undertakings."

In favoring this spot as the principal focus for initial development, L'Enfant was influenced by the alignment of his proposed City Canal. This canal was a means both of draining the low-lying marshland on either side of Tiber Creek and at its head and of supplying a means of transportation for goods into the heart of the city. The canal would "facilitate a conveyance" that would stimulate the growth of markets to supply the city.

THE CAPITOL AND THE PRESIDENT'S HOUSE

Here within the principal focus, too, L'Enfant located the Capitol, for as his memorandum explains, he could discover no other location as advantageous as the one he first identified at the top of Jenkins Hill, "which stands as a pedestal waiting for a superstructure." Balancing this, he proposed a site for the presidential "palace" on the edge of the Wicomico terrace, shrewdly reminding President Washington that it was precisely this location "which very justly attracted your attention when first viewing the ground which is upon the west side and near the mouth of the Tiber." Minor adjustments in the site, he explained, would provide a more extensive view down the Potomac and connect with the Capitol through the system of public walks, gardens, and avenues. Finally, L'Enfant's memorandum described the Mall, "the vast esplanade," in whose center, at the point where the views from the Capitol to the west and from the President's House to the south intersected, he found the appropriate site for an equestrian monument, with suitable landscape embellishments.

Anticipating the objection that the Capitol and the President's House should be closer together (reflecting Jefferson's conception and other earlier and more limited conceptions of the city), L'Enfant argued that the distance between the two buildings was not all that great in his plan and further that "no message to nor from the President is to be made without a sort of decorum which will doubtless point out the propriety of Committee waiting on him in carriage should his palace be even contiguous to Congress." In addition, L'Enfant noted, the interest and delights provided by the gardens and walks of the President's House and the Capitol and the development of the connecting avenue with "play houses, rooms of assembly, academies, and all such sort of places as may be attractive to the learned and afford diversion to the idle" would make the apparent distance seem less.

THE CITY OF ILLUSION

Following the theory expressed in L'Enfant's multinucleated city plan, appropriate sites were designated for the major capital city functions; it was expected that around these sites functional districts would develop. Thus, along the most desirable waters for navigation, the Navy Yard, the marine hospital, the arsenal, and the city's commercial waterfront with its wharves, warehouses, and industries were situated. By contrast to these working elements arranged along the north bank of the Anacostia, that part of the capital oriented to the Potomac was proposed as the monumental, residential, and official quarter. The critical location of the City Hall immediately south of the Capitol was closely linked to the location of the commercial heart of the city along the Eastern Branch and the expectations for the City Canal as a commercial waterway. In the overall conception, the federal and local functions were closely interwoven. There was no sense of economic or social class segregation. If the city as a whole was to function as it was planned, L'Enfant was correct to assert that its various functional elements should be simultaneously developed and able to interact with each other.

The city of illusion was reinforced in its architecture and urban design by provisions for the landscaping. Functional elements of the city, such as the canal, were to become decorative features as well, their turning basins and port features being used as reflecting pools. The grounds of major public buildings were designed as gardens, parks, and promenades. At the Capitol a magnificent cascade forty feet high and a hundred feet wide, a size that would permit it to be seen from the President's House, was proposed by L'Enfant to carry the water of the Tiber from its bed beyond the city to its ultimate destination at the base of Jenkins Hill, where it would augment the waters of the canal and urge them toward the Potomac. In these features of his plan, L'Enfant is most clearly the child of the great Le Nôtre, whose ingenious use of water is a compelling feature of L'Enfant's boyhood home, Versailles.

L'ENFANT'S LANDSCAPE DESIGN

L'Enfant's masterly and brief memorandum concluded with this vividly expressed landscape image: "the whole will acquire new sweetness being laid over the green of a field well level and made brilliant by the shade of a few trees artfully planted." In this comment on the open central composition, L'Enfant reflects the spirit of the age that was creating St. Petersburg and other princely capitals, that age in which the French designers were achieving their renown. It was a period when the divorce of engineering from architecture and landscape design had not yet materialized; so, in the work of L'Enfant, it is impossible to determine where one set of professional interests ends and another begins.

In two distinct ways Washington was conceived as a landscape design. The plan looked forward in its recognition and adaptation of the natural features of the riverfront, the surrounding hills (especially across the Potomac to the west), and the spacious river meadows to be occupied by the city. Yet it expressed continuity with the formal tradition of landscape design. This tradition L'Enfant knew best from the work of Le Nôtre at Versailles and the great chateau gardens of the Loire valley, but it was also part of the larger body of Renaissance garden art of Italy and indeed informed the deliberately planned princely cities of the Rhineland. In the formal landscape tradition, the modern distinction between landscape design, urban design, and architecture had not appeared, however, particularly in the crucial matter of siting the principal buildings. In this, as L'Enfant knew, practical considerations of drainage were as important as the commanding prospect or the prominent situation.

THE FORMAL CITY

To later generations, the Washington plan in its formal characteristics has seemed a paradoxical echo of Old World baroque autocracy in the design of the capital city of a democracy. Such a judgment not only projects Jacksonian democracy two generations ahead but also attributes to the late eighteenth century design alternatives that only a more sophisticated, historically later period possessed. In plain fact, Washington and Jefferson as well as L'Enfant saw only one form of excellence in urban design, that of the age: the formal city. It could be ignored, as it had been in the gridiron cities. It could express a standard of excellence. But there was no alternative. Historical criticism has allowed the present day to see the design of Philadelphia and Savannah, with their regular plans, their park squares, and their waterfronts, as key representatives of a native town planning tradition. They were not so regarded at the time of the planning of Washington, however, and the civic virtues that today they are seen as having were little appreciated at the earlier time.

Meanings of L'Enfant's Plan

The year 1791 was a time of political revolution in the United States as well as in Europe, particularly in France. The last half of the eighteenth century was the Enlightenment, the Age of Reason, the period that called its great men—not kings and rulers but scientists, artists, and philosophers—immortal. Science, especially mathematics, reigned supreme, and all aspects of civilization and the arts responded to its leadership. In architecture, from the mid-eighteenth century forward, neoclassicism had expressed absolute rationality in the work of Étienne-Louis Boullée and Claude-Nicolas Ledoux in France and the Adam brothers, Dance and Soane, in Great Britain. L'Enfant developed his artistic talents under these conditions; his art was inspired by these ideals and purposes. His plan for Washington, despite the derivation of certain elements from Versailles, was less the work of any late baroque style than it was a classically inspired design, fully characteristic of its time. Viewed in these terms, the apparent contradiction between an urban design suited to a tyrannical Renaissance prince and his absolute state and the needs and beliefs of a young democracy vanishes. Instead one sees the revolutionary spirit that inspired L'Enfant to offer his services to the army of the young American republic, that sustained him through difficult military campaigns, and that nourished his veneration of George Washington, commander-in-chief and president, for whom he planned a great city.

NEOCLASSICISM AND THE MATHEMATICS OF THE AGE

By 1791 the characteristics of neoclassicism had been well established and translated not only into literature, painting, and sculpture but also into landscape design and urban forms. Echoes of the earlier Renaissance and subsequent Greek revivals and forms of academicism are to be distinguished from this unique historical period with its sympathies toward reform and revolution, its endeavors to purify and simplify, and its search for absolute values and ideal forms. This was the age L'Enfant knew in France, heartland of neoclassicism. It was to this tradition that L'Enfant reoriented himself on his return to Paris in 1783, and this same neoclassic impulse is reflected in his plan for Washington.

That the United States was an integral if distinct part of this artistic movement cannot be doubted when one examines the aspirations of Thomas Jefferson at Charlottesville, the achievements of Benjamin Latrobe in Baltimore, the paintings of Benjamin West, as well as the work of Jean-Antoine Houdon. Urban design shared the architectural aims enunciated in 1793 by Leon DuFourny in this statement: "L'Architecture doit se regner par la geometrie" (Architecture must be guided by geometry). The new architecture was based on cubes, cones, cylinders, pyramids, and other mathematical models. The design of cities was based no less on geometry. Indeed, urban design was inspired by the search for the ideal city, in which the fundamentally moral

quest of the age would be expressed in elevating experiences: the city would aim at making better citizens. Such a city would be filled with great aesthetic experiences, with monuments commemorating great men and heroic acts, all set in a Virgilian landscape.

The mathematics of the age is fully expressed in the geometry of L'Enfant's plan with its evident roots in the principles of Descartes and its perfect right triangle formed by the Capitol, the President's House, and an equestrian statue of George Washington—that prime expression of the great revolutionary personality and the starting point of the plan. The system of Cartesian coordinates to which L'Enfant's plan is fundamentally oriented establishes what has been called the gridiron element of his plan. A closer examination, however, discloses no affinities with that mechanical checkerboard element that characterized Philadelphia and countless later cities to which it was applied. In L'Enfant's Washington plan there is instead a carefully worked out plaid (as Elbert Peets has called it) of differentially spaced streets, calculated to relate to the earlier selected sites for public buildings, to principal squares and functional places, and to intersections with the system of radial boulevards.

In the view of contemporaries, when the plan of Washington was first exhibited in Paris in 1793, it was correctly received by a culture immersed in the rationalism of neoclassicism and was compared with Pierre Patte's paradigmatic assemblage of proposals for the city's reconstruction rather than with any actual cities or their plans. It was immediately set into the broader canvas of the world's cities, of urban thought, and of the contemporary search for the ideal city—in the case of Washington, a city oriented to a new nation, to a new continent, and to the future.

INSTITUTIONS AND THE ARCHITECTURE OF THE AGE

A political interpretation of L'Enfant's plan must begin with the dominant position assigned to that most representative body, the Congress. For all his veneration of George Washington, L'Enfant did not regard him as a divinely ordained ruler. Nor was L'Enfant's city designed to focus on a ruler and his palace. The planner's eighteenth-century view of the city showed a rich assortment of institutions assigned to key sites throughout the city. These institutions were popular as well as cultural in character: a nondenominational national church (literally a pantheon in which monuments to revolutionary heroes would be placed), colleges, academies, and learned societies. What could be more appropriate to the spirit of the age? Although there is little evidence of the architecture that L'Enfant would have provided had he continued work according to his initial instructions, his collateral activities as an architect firmly establish his affinity with contemporaries.

The origins of this plan are as celebrated as the city's present form. In ancestry the plan of Washington points back to the heroic landscape designs of kings and emperors. The salient lessons of mathematics, triumphal architecture, and green avenues were absorbed by the city's designer, Pierre Charles L'Enfant, and transplanted to the frontiers of democracy. Here, in a land previously dividing its allegiances between London, capital city of the British Empire, and the local colonial capitals, a new focus was demanded. The new national capital would embrace actual as well as symbolic importance in uniting the nation—and its potency, as reflected in its physical form, would predict the ability of this new capital to serve as a unifier of diverse sympathies.

L'Enfant's Plan: Beginnings of Built Washington

L'Enfant's sketch plan of June 22, 1791, was laid before the proprietors by George Washington the next week, and their approval was noted in the president's diary. There is disappointingly little evidence, however, of Washington's own appreciation of the creative dimensions of this work; on the contrary, his expressed concern was the city's boundaries and the procurement of deeds from the landowners. Hence, Washington's participation in such changes as were made by L'Enfant in the plan between its presentation to the proprietors and its subsequent development must remain unknown. It can only be conjectured that L'Enfant made these changes, incorporating Washington's wishes as he understood them. That the plan had secured the measure of approval that would allow it to be translated immediately into building activity is evident. And, as L'Enfant had recommended, the work of clearing and building began with the system of avenues he had planned. It was along these avenues that he anticipated the initial development of the national capital city would take place.

If detailed response of President Washington to L'Enfant's plan was obscure, the commissioners to whom the development of the city was entrusted were equally silent. And if Jefferson's sole substantial comment was a suggestion on draftsmanship, the commissioners in commenting on the plan confined themselves to deciding that the federal city should be called Washington, that the streets of the gridiron should be designated by numbers and letters, that river soundings be specified on the plan, and that the plan itself be entitled "A Map of the City of Washington in the Territory of Columbia."

Attention of all officials from the president to the commissioners was concentrated on the pragmatic issue of the promotion and sale of the city lots, since this provided the entire source of funds for urban development and the construction of public buildings. For this the officials needed quantities of engraved copies of the city plan, at a scale that would show both the lots to be sold and the principal streets and public improvements proposed. Intent upon perfecting his conception, L'Enfant did not produce the engraved plans and chose to withhold his manuscript plan. In February 1792, L'Enfant resigned his position because of his refusal to subordinate himself to the commission. As an indication of this attitude, L'Enfant demolished part of Daniel Carroll's house that stood in the way of his

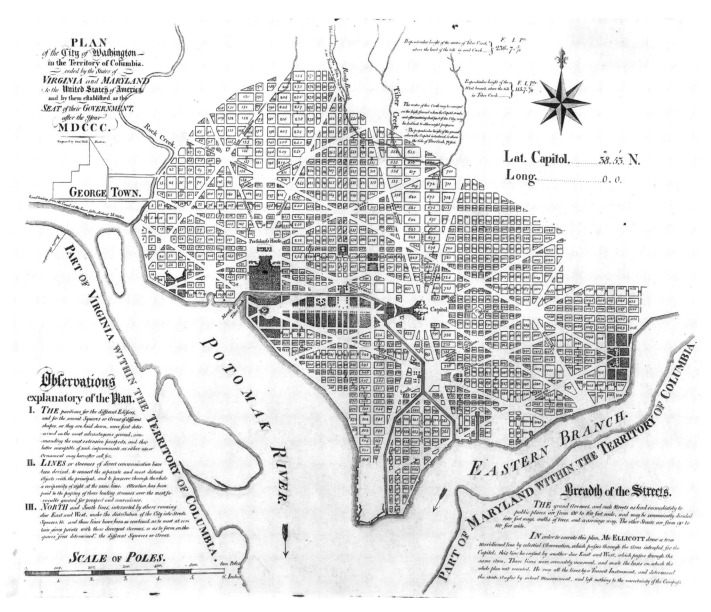

planned New Jersey Avenue. The work of producing the engraved plans was handed over by President Washington to Andrew Ellicott, the city's surveyor, who followed L'Enfant's earlier plans with little change.

THE WORK OF ANDREW ELLICOTT

With his own surveyor's notes and some direct or indirect access to L'Enfant's work as well as his own memory of the designer's plan, Andrew Ellicott in 1792 produced the plan that was transformed into the "official city plan" of streets and lots. The map was engraved by Thackara & Vallance of Philadelphia and published in October 1792. The publisher, Samuel Hill, subsequently produced the Ellicott plan in 1792–1794 (shown here). Ellicott did not alter the major physical features of the plan that L'Enfant had proposed, nor did he resolve its major problems. Sites for major buildings, radial avenues, gridiron streets, open spaces, and environmental features—all are approximately as L'Enfant proposed. Ellicott straightened several radial avenues and eliminated others and, as instructed, provided information on the depths of the navigable waters. Ellicott also numbered the blocks so that the necessary land sales could be efficiently carried on. "Observations explanatory of the Plan,"

Andrew Ellicott's Plan of the City of Washington, 1792. Library of Congress

30

abbreviated from L'Enfant's manuscript plan, appear in the margins of Ellicott's version. In 1793 Ellicott also drew a topographical map that defined the land formations around the L'Enfant city. In this drawing Ellicott followed the suggestion Thomas Jefferson had made earlier to L'Enfant that the map should be oriented to the northwest to make the rectangular boundaries of the planned city congruent with a rectangular sheet of paper.

THE MANUSCRIPT MAP AND THE RECONSTRUCTIONS

Of the many versions of early Washington plans that are in common reference, only the one entitled "Plan of the City intended for the Permanent Seat of the Government of the United States . . . By Pierre Charles L'Enfant" (undated but prepared in 1791)—the manuscript map—can be accepted as showing L'Enfant's intentions. The manuscript map was the most complete version of the Washington plan prepared by the designer himself. L'Enfant also provided "Observations" and "References" for the various features noted on the map. L'Enfant clearly defined the sites intended for the President's House and the Congress House, or Capitol. These two sites were connected by a public walk, the "Grand Avenue."

L'Enfant likely completed this drawing late in 1791. The manuscript map thus does not incorporate subsequent revisions and developments made by the designer. The faded manuscript drawing was copied in 1887 by the US Coast and Geodetic Survey and then varnished over. During the map's handling by the commissioners in Washington's time and by the Army Corps of Engineers and unknown others later on, and then the varnishing and other measures taken in the effort to preserve the manuscript original, certain features appear to have become obscured. These include some of the most significant architectural details of critical areas, such as the Capitol grounds, the Municipal Center, the White House, and the public market. Various efforts at "reconstruction" have been made, most notably by William Partridge and Elbert Peets.

THE WORK OF WILLIAM T. PARTRIDGE

In 1926 William Partridge, chief draftsman of the 1901–1902 McMillan Commission design staff, was retained by the National Capital Park and Planning Commission to interpret and reconstruct L'Enfant's design of the federal city. Among other study drawings, Partridge prepared a drawing showing the comparative plans of L'Enfant and Ellicott. On this comparison map, the major deviation is the straighter course taken by Massachusetts Avenue on the Ellicott plan. Without doubt Washington endorsed L'Enfant's plan and wished only to translate it into a form that met the practical requirements of development. Ellicott himself had neither time nor inclination to prepare any significant planning alternatives. Consequently, what resulted legitimatized the plan—despite the resignation of its creator—and justified L'Enfant's later claim that his work had been used without his being compensated.

THE REINTERPRETATION BY ELBERT PEETS

In 1932 Elbert Peets published an essay titled "The Lost Plazas of Washington" in which he sketched what L'Enfant likely had envisioned for the President's House, a large building with a strongly silhouetted dome. Such a building would have helped to unify a city that stretched over L'Enfant's "magnificent distances." Pennsylvania Avenue, traced southeast toward the Capitol, was to have been lined, Peets thought, with low vernacular buildings.

Peets's reconstruction of L'Enfant's intentions is most persuasive, enlightened as it is by a broader view of urban design, the origins and probable motives of the designer, and contemporary eighteenth-century usages. Yet all the reinterpretations contribute to understandings of the original plan for Washington. Among the important considerations that have emerged from these efforts at reconstruction is the greater integration of urban design and architecture, as in the siting of buildings, the use of arcades and other civic design features, and the embellishment of the plan with such details as fountains

Ellicott's Topographical Map of the Territory of Columbia, 1793. Library of Congress

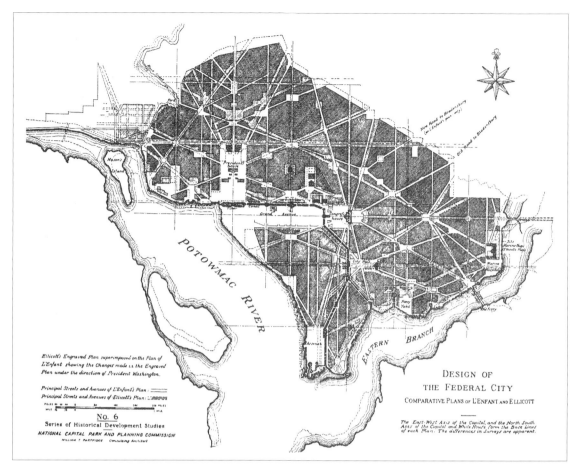

and sculpture. We can understand and sympa-
thize with L'Enfant's reluctance to regard his plan
as complete when we appreciate how gripped he
was by creative fervor. Certainly no estimation or
appreciation of L'Enfant's plan can ever be complete without weighing the reconstructions and
interpretations made of the plan through all the
decades.

THE REAL CITY AND THE ENDURING PLAN

L'Enfant's advice respecting the sale of lots and
the simultaneous development of dispersed centers was not followed. Wholesale speculation in
land and lots escalated until the inevitable collapse of the inflated land values. As early as 1800
and the removal of the government to Washington, this downward trend in land values put its
stamp on the city. The effect of the speculative
boom would be seen for a century in the ragged,
dispersed character of urban development
ridiculed by several generations of visitors and

commentators on the city's form. Thus appeared
the dichotomy between the real and the ideal city:
the former revealing the immediate facts of
poverty and the slow pace of urban development;
the latter, the artistic and unified intent of its
planner. L'Enfant's intent, however, as well as the
comprehensiveness of his design for Washington,
would not become evident for another century.

In the early years the city's few key structures,
the Capitol and the White House, seemed hardly
more than isolated monuments without sufficient urban connection. Indeed, the urban activity contained by the plan responded chiefly to
the operations of the private real estate market
and other dimensions of private enterprise. The
speculative pressures unleashed by the desperate
if misguided effort to finance the building of the
city were nevertheless responsible for the location and building of significant improvements
such as bridges over the Potomac, the Anacostia,
and Rock Creek; roads and turnpikes; churches,

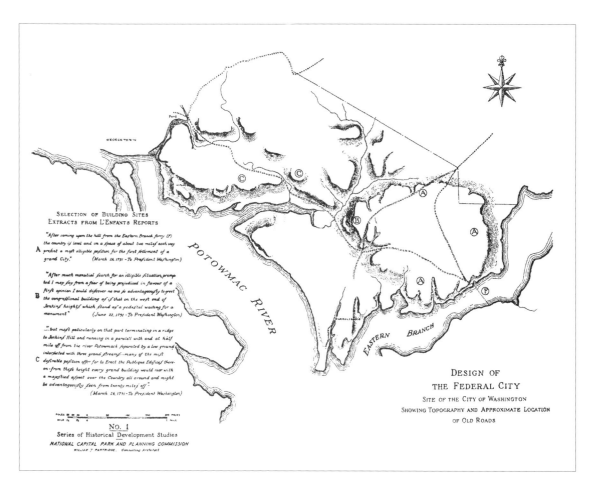

wharves, and public buildings; and civic undertakings that were influenced by the interests of major landholders and speculators and in turn shaped the further development of the city.

This pattern is most clearly illustrated by the development of the area south of the Capitol, an area initially significant because here merged the two broad tidal streams, the Potomac and its Eastern Branch (the Anacostia). In this area were focused the commercial interests of Daniel Carroll of Duddington and the activity of the real estate speculator Thomas Law and his associates in the firm of Morris, Nicholson, and Greenleaf. What was lost in the conflict was not only the topographical significance of the rivers' merging but also the importance of the entire sector designated from the very beginning by L'Enfant as the most explicitly municipal element of his overall plan.

Development of the waterfront facing the deepwater channel of the Potomac, from its junction with the Anacostia upstream for nearly one-and-a-half miles, was naturally handicapped by a shoreline bluff fifteen to twenty-five feet in height. Only at 6th and 11th streets could traffic descend to the level of marine commerce, and it was at these points and between them that development was topographically favored. Here, then, in spite of the greater inherent advantages of the Anacostia shoreline, and contrary to the specific expectations of L'Enfant, was the principal commercial waterfront of the city located and deliberately developed.

As the street system proposed by L'Enfant was laid out with only slight modifications, so were the canals described in his plan also built with but small changes. By the Civil War, the City Canal entered the city directly south of the White House and continued east along the current Constitution Avenue to 6th Street. Here it had been changed from the more graceful alignment proposed by the city's designer. Instead it

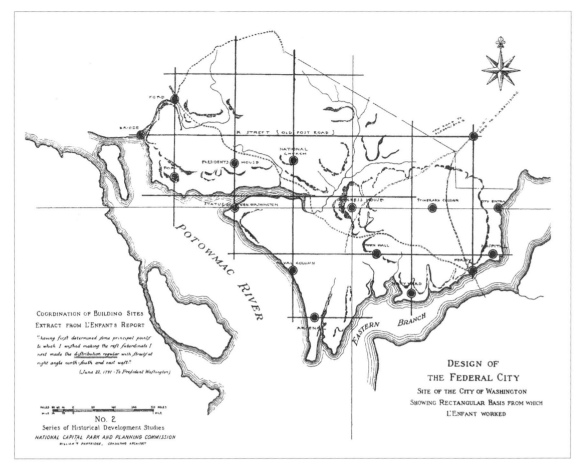

turned directly south to the center of the Mall, where it again turned due east. At the foot of Capitol Hill it again turned south and, closely following L'Enfant's proposed route, divided at Virginia Avenue into the two sections leading to the Anacostia. Above the main Potomac inlet, an extension connected the City Canal to the Chesapeake & Ohio Canal at Rock Creek by extending the design to include a protected waterway along the shoreline.

ANALYSIS OF L'ENFANT'S PLAN
What L'Enfant intended, what he proposed, what survived Andrew Ellicott's translation of his plan, what the 1901–1902 McMillan Plan recognized and continued, and what has endured to the present day are all important and interesting problems. They have been analyzed from time to time by careful and intelligent students among whom Elbert Peets, Fiske Kimball, William Partridge, and John Reps are the leaders. This analy-

sis is being continued by the National Capital Planning Commission, the Commission of Fine Arts, and others, working with sketches and documents. It is therefore only reasonable to expect revisions in what has been thought in the past.

In the end, however, a large measure of judgment and interpretation will be required to answer the questions posed by L'Enfant's plan. How large did L'Enfant intend the Capitol or the President's House to be? Were his squares intended as paved and built-up urban designs or leafy green intervals within the built city? In further detail, were the urban trees proposed by L'Enfant to take the naturalistic forms of the elms and maples found along the streets of Washington and other American cities or the more geometrical shapes of the pruned and trimmed plane trees, limes, and other trees indigenous to European cities? Was the Mall essentially a visual conception as a line of sight, or was it seriously and functionally intended as a pedestrian walk and carriage drive?

THE DESTINY OF L'ENFANT AND HIS PLAN FOR WASHINGTON

Kenneth R. Bowling offers the fullest treatment to date of the story of L'Enfant's resignation and of his subsequent career. It may be emphasized that the planner was a perfectionist who resisted to the end halting the creative process by an imposed deadline, that he refused to recognize the authority of the commissioners or anyone other than the president, that he may have followed his pecuniary as well as his professional interests, and that he steadfastly maintained his position that the city should be developed simultaneously from many centers and along the principal avenues. Although in all of this Pierre Charles L'Enfant stood alone, posterity has sustained his views—and his plan for Washington. ✩

THE PORT CITY 1800-1860

The City of Washington, 1800

The place that greeted the federal government in 1800 restated its sylvan origins but held the promise of a city commensurate with the country's foremost urban centers. The vision of the new capital could not fail to inspire. Its growth depended in large part on governmental commitment to provide public buildings, grounds, public services, and other improvements. This commitment was at best haphazard, timid, and in many respects unmindful of L'Enfant's larger concepts. During the city's first four decades, it struggled to assert its primacy in the region. However, the ultimate outcome of the city's slow but deliberate development was not in doubt.

The port cities of Georgetown and Alexandria, whose early commercial prosperity and rivalry had argued for the present site of Washington, found a new rival in the capital city, with its commercial growth and expectations of future growth. Tripartite rivalry among the cities forced many compromises in the government's willingness to invest in Washington's commercial future. In the long run, however, as in the beginning, the fates of the three cities were seen to be inextricably intertwined, especially in the effects of the physical changes in the river and in attempts to tap the riches of the western hinterland. Nonetheless, Washington, newest of the three cities, never became the commercial giant L'Enfant had intended. Still, by 1840 it was the dominant urban force along the Potomac River.

The city survived crisis, failure, and threat: the many recurring thoughts about removal of the national capital to a more western location, the halfhearted attempts to build a canal and drainage system through the city's center as planned by L'Enfant, the increasingly hazardous environmental conditions in the lowlands caused by an altered river, and the upheavals of the British invasion in 1814. Yet, by the eve of the Civil War, the city would emerge with its own identity, distinct from the nearby urban centers. With classically styled public architecture, pleasure grounds, attractive private dwellings and gardens, and a modern water supply system, Washington by the 1850s began to present an image of the nation's capital powerful enough to subdue future uncertainties.

THE BUCOLIC CITY

In 1800 both buildings at either end of L'Enfant's ceremonial avenue, the President's House and the Capitol, were unfinished. Small public and private buildings were scattered widely throughout the settlement, clustering near these two major federal centers and near the arsenal at Greenleaf Point (today Fort McNair) and the Navy Yard. Open fields, pastureland, and produce gardens spread out over the land in between. Tiber Creek stretched lazily toward the Capitol, but its natural winding form was on the verge of man's improvement. This bucolic city—although it offended the notion of a city as compact, dense, and defined by mortar, masonry, and wood—nonetheless appealed to many of Washington's newcomers. One of these early settlers, Margaret Bayard Smith, was favorably impressed by the romantic beauty of the natural landscape, watered by the Tiber, Potomac, and Anacostia rivers, their banks shaded by trees and wildflowers. "Indeed the whole plain was diversified with groves and clumps of forest trees which gave it the appearance of a fine park." Her friend, Thomas Jefferson, resided at Conrad's Boarding House on Capitol Hill so that he would be able to "enjoy the beautiful and extensive prospect described above." In his appreciation of the countrylike surroundings, Jefferson shared regrets at the tree felling necessary for clearing the land and for fuel.

WATERFRONT AND SHORELINE

Early real estate investments made by entrepreneurs like John Greenleaf produced scattered clusters of row houses in the southeast and the southwest quadrants of the city, close to both the employment centers of the arsenal and Navy Yard and the anticipated thriving wharves. The rush to the waterfront sites verified the strategic location of Carrollsburg along the Eastern Branch, as well as L'Enfant's siting of the arsenal point, and with it the commercial orientation of much of the city east of the Capitol. Prominent men envisioned speculative building activities primarily as commercial investments rather than

as locations for their in-town residences, but all such prospects became clouded as prime riverfront land fell victim to the uncertain shoreline.

Almost as quickly as the area became settled, the shoaling process manifested itself in both the Potomac River and the Eastern Branch, the lifelines to the city's commercial health. As deforestation of Washington City proceeded, and as the Potomac River watershed upriver was cleared of forest cover, the Little River causeway became dammed, its narrow channel suddenly forced into a wider channel at the foot of 27th Street. Sediment carried by freshets became deposited along the riverfronts downriver. A more intensified version of this shoaling process from Bladensburg downriver filled the channel of the Eastern Branch and produced extensive marsh areas along its shores. Communication across the land between the riverside developments and the rest of the city was hampered by the natural terraces, some sharply defined as bluffs measuring as high as thirty feet and only occasionally pierced by dirt roads. The uneven landscape had yet to be flattened by successive cycles of development and renewal. As late as 1830, the lower sections of the Carrollsburg settlement were dotted with "simple wharves and shacks about the shore."

THE INDIGENOUS CITY: ROW HOUSES AND MANSIONS

Looking to the form and architectural style of the row houses of Philadelphia, Georgetown, and Alexandria, the investors in residential developments both in the riverfront areas and in other sections of Washington clearly anticipated a compact city inhabited by a cosmopolitan citizenry. Georgian-styled Wheat Row, a multifamily complex named after one of its early residents, was completed in the southwest quadrant in the mid-1790s, induced by Greenleaf's investments. The row-house vernacular sprang up in the northwest quadrant along Pennsylvania Avenue (the anticipated heavily traveled route between Georgetown and the President's House), although not all developers reflected complete

VIEW OF GEORGETOWN D. C.

confidence in the quick development of a major city.

In addition to row houses, single houses with generous gardens also were commissioned. Within the context of L'Enfant's plan, a villa architecture began to flourish, and a new kind of villa life established the style. Large houses surrounded by flower and vegetable gardens were so prevalent in this dispersed city of the early nineteenth century that, according to the historian Wilhelmus Bogart Bryan, "the cultivated gardens and lawns about the houses in Washington were regarded as one of the distinctive features of the city." In the earliest years of the capital city, the best qualities of the regional life of the Potomac plantation aristocracy were being transplanted to urban conditions and given new form. Thus, an indigenous city from the beginning paralleled the official city and contributed to its character.

In the early turn-of-the-century city there were a significant number of mansions, their owners in most cases having been attracted to the city by its unique role as the seat of government. Some of the most prominent of these mansions were built as town houses by planters from nearby Maryland and Virginia. The Octagon, built for Colonel John Tayloe in 1798–1800 to a design by William Thornton, first designer of the Capitol, was complete with kitchen gardens, smokehouse, and other plantation features, as well as a stable, a carriage house, and dependencies. In shape, the house presented a novel facade, and its interior woodwork testified to the family's tastes acquired in the genteel tidewater tradition—and to the early attractiveness of the city to men of means.

Many newcomers to Washington, especially congressmen, viewed the city as a temporary

home during their short sessions here. Housing was adapted to this transient population in the way of boarding houses, hotels, and taverns. Temporary accommodations for related residential activities revealed a remarkably flexible use of existing structures. The only church on Capitol Hill was fashioned from a tobacco barn that once belonged to Daniel Carroll. Religious services were held in the Capitol, a popular center for socializing and entertaining, for cultural as well as political activities. Despite its scattered and transient pattern, the population of fewer than nine thousand in the entire District made Washington an intimate city. Especially among the affluent and politically prominent, houses were not just shelter; they bespoke the inhabitants' penchant for a social life of formalities and rigorous etiquette.

THE CITY OF GEORGETOWN

Platted in 1751, the city of Georgetown exhibited some of the desired indications and physical results of advanced urbanization. Rising to prominence in the eighteenth century, first as a tobacco port and then as a milling center, Georgetown reached its commercial peak just before removal of the government to Washington. Serious environmental difficulties, however,

barred further development of this port city at the head of oceangoing navigation. Deforestation and cultivation of the land upriver along the Potomac silted up the shoreline between Analostan Island and the Georgetown wharves. As sandbars formed, dredging machines were used, and causeways for diverting the water current were attempted to resolve these hazards to navigation. Nevertheless, in the early decades of the nineteenth century, because of its faltering port capabilities as well as changes in agricultural production in Maryland, Georgetown was well advanced in its gradual transition from a tobacco port to a flour-milling center. In Georgetown itself, years as a profitable port had produced a sizable concentration of warehouses along the Potomac River, with commodious residences extending northward up the steep hill toward M Street.

Around this nucleus of trade, related commerce developed: produce, game, fish markets, and diversified goods attested to the tastes of a more affluent society. Then, with the construction of the Patowmack Canal by the Patowmack Company, George Washington attempted further to improve the town's commercial health. Although the Patowmack Company venture failed, the canal route from Harpers Ferry past the falls of the Potomac and into Georgetown presaged Benjamin Latrobe's 1802 "Plans and Sections of the Proposed Continuation of the Canal at the Little Falls of the Potomac" and ultimately the actual route of the Chesapeake & Ohio Canal. Despite Georgetown's difficulties as a port, the turn of the city's fortunes was such that in 1800 it contained excellent brick houses and prosperous business establishments—advantages that early on led many congressmen and affluent Washingtonians to live in Georgetown and to commute to Washington City.

THE CITY OF ALEXANDRIA

Farther downstream lay Alexandria, formally incorporated in 1748. Notable in the colonial era for its associations with George Washington, it thrived as a collecting point of several tobacco roads. As in Maryland's tidewater and Piedmont agriculture, so also in Northern Virginia tobacco gave way to wheat, and Alexandria became the accessible port for the lower Shenandoah valley. Thus, the city became a wheat export center, reaching far into the western lands through the gaps in the first ranges of the Appalachians. Alexandria's most prosperous decades were the wheat boom years of the late eighteenth and the early nineteenth centuries. A distinctive Federal architecture blossomed during Alexandria's heyday and endured as the city's trademark long after national architectural styles evolved into the romantic revivals.

Building the City: The First Four Decades

In the first four decades of public improvements in Washington, the government concentrated on completing the President's House and the Capitol, building the City Hall, beginning construction of its illustrious buildings to house the executive functions (such as the Treasury, the Post Office, and the Patent Office), and developing the Navy Yard and arsenal along the Anacostia. In the early years of this period, the talents of Thomas Jefferson and Benjamin Latrobe were definitive; the later years were dominated by Robert Mills. The city's physical face was affected by private interests: clients for the genteel homes designed by Latrobe and George Hadfield and spirited business groups that financed and developed markets, mills, and manufactories that supplied city and government needs. In the process of growth, the city survived the 1814 burning of its main buildings by the British, a shattering experience that, in Margaret Bayard Smith's words, "gave civic spirit to the people of Washington" and reinforced the public and the private sectors' commitments to the city's rebuilding. The national capital, only a decade and half old, had acquired permanent enough characteristics to stand on its own, a symbol of patriotism that not even major devastation could destroy.

BENJAMIN LATROBE AND THE CAPITOL BUILDING

Benjamin Latrobe's initial government commission came in 1802, when President Jefferson invited him to Washington to design drydocks for the Navy Yard. Although the drydocks plan was never carried out, Jefferson had found an intellectual kindred spirit in Latrobe, and in the following year Latrobe was commissioned to design and build the south wing of the Capitol. To this commission Latrobe brought considerable architectural and engineering background. Born in Yorkshire, England, Latrobe had studied architecture under Samuel Cockerell and engineering under John Smeaton, both among England's outstanding practitioners of the day. Grieved by the death of his first wife, Latrobe immigrated in 1796 to Norfolk, Virginia, where he was quickly engaged in architectural and navigation projects in the Richmond and Norfolk areas. In the next six years, Latrobe worked on a great variety of architectural and engineering projects in America's large cities.

In 1803 Latrobe was appointed surveyor of public buildings, which included superintending the construction of the south wing of the Capitol Building. From the start, the Capitol was the scene of architectural controversy—not least among its successive architects. William Thornton provided the winning design, but construction of the south wing was supervised by a succession of architects including—besides Latrobe—Stephen Hallett, James Hoban, and, later, George Hadfield. Strong-minded designers like Hallett attempted to redesign Thornton's plan to overcome technical deficiencies, to provide details where Thornton had offered none, and to place their personal stamp on this important public building. Because Thornton also served as one of the three city commissioners and was thus directly responsible for the building of the Capitol, he was in frequent conflict with the architects who superintended construction.

During the construction of the south wing, Latrobe—over strenuous objection by Thornton—was able to alter some interior arrangements. Latrobe's stature as the architect and engineer personally selected by Jefferson enabled Latrobe to overrule Thornton. After the completion of the south wing in 1807, Latrobe then began alterations to the Capitol's north wing, the two sections being joined by an inappropriate but temporary "hyphen." After the Capitol was burned by the British in 1814, Latrobe supervised its rebuilding with zest, incorporating at the time the famous tobacco and corncob column capitals. Charles Bulfinch succeeded Latrobe on the Capitol project and substituted his own design for the dome.

THE PRESIDENT'S HOUSE

In 1800 the President's House was nearly the only public building that was "completed." President Washington selected James Hoban's design after a competition and retained him to superintend construction. In the design for the President's House, Hoban looked to his roots in Dublin, Ireland, most likely to Leinster House, for inspiration. The north side of the building was two stories in height and constructed of smooth Aquia stone; the south side, where the ground sloped downward, had an exposed basement constructed of rusticated blocks of stone.

The cornerstone was laid in 1792, and construction continued until 1800. The stone carvers came from Scotland, where they had gained considerable skill in constructing new buildings in Edinburgh. Rather than the severely plain stone carvings for the buildings of that city, the stone carvings for the President's House included—at Washington's direction—roses, garlands, leaves, griffins, acorns, and ribbons. Because of the gray color of the stone, the whole exterior was painted in whitewash, which gave the building its ultimate name, the "White House."

In 1814 the British invaded the city and set the President's House on fire. Benjamin Latrobe was asked to prepare designs for the rebuilding of the house and provided an updated version with porticos on both the north and south facades. Hoban was hired to oversee the rebuilding of the residence and incorporated porticos into the new design. By 1818 the President's House was repaired and made whole again. For much of the first half of the nineteenth century, the President's House, the largest building in the area, dominated its surroundings.

Architect George Hadfield designed two two-and-a-half-story brick "executive office buildings" on either side of the President's House between 1798 and 1800. The building on the east housed the Treasury Department, the one on the west the War Department. Both buildings were burned in 1814 and were replaced with four buildings, all replicas of the first two buildings. The additional buildings housed the State and Navy departments. Together, these buildings and the President's House formed an executive branch "enclave" that would grow over the next two centuries.

THE WASHINGTON CITY CANAL

In the private sector, the versatile Latrobe was commissioned in 1802 by the Washington Canal Company, incorporated by an act of Congress, to engineer construction of the City Canal. Operating under severe financial constraints, Latrobe was obliged to route the canal in a straight line along the north side of the Mall, then turn it in an abrupt bend in front of the Capitol, and continue it southward toward the arsenal, where it

met the Eastern Branch at Buzzard Point. In the canal's passage through the city's interior, many aesthetic and drainage features planned by L'Enfant were denied for financial considerations. Omitted were the turning basin at 8th Street, the cascade down Capitol Hill, and the settling basin at the foot of the Capitol. Still, the cutting of the canal did affirm the northern boundary of the "Grand Avenue" as defined by L'Enfant. Wood lined the canal, as well as the locks. As a result the canal enclosed water often too shallow and silted for navigation. It also lost its locks and linings during heavy storms, and frequent repairs repeatedly forced grudging congressional appropriations.

The failure of the City Canal to fulfill L'Enfant's or even Latrobe's expectations for a major commercial route indicated in part the federal government's unwillingness or inability to commit sufficient funds for the building structures to endure. To be sure, the roving congressmen were more often preoccupied with their own constituencies back home than with the economic health of their Potomac River abode. Congressional decisions were sometimes swayed by the business sentiments of the competing port cities of Georgetown and Alexandria that still argued against the emergence of a major commercial center in Washington City. The canal project was further hampered by the more remote turnpike

Daguerreotype of the US Capitol by John Plumbe Jr., ca. 1846. Library of Congress

interests that fought any new schemes to siphon off land trade.

THE YOUNG CAPITAL: JOEL BARLOW'S PLACE AT KALORAMA

At the less material end of the spectrum, others in the young city responded to the ideals that the founders had institutionalized in provisions like those for a national nonsectarian church and a university. Enterprise and advancement were combined, for example, in one of the most attractive of Washington's developers, Joel Barlow, settler of Kalorama and close friend of Latrobe. In Barlow's mind the great national university "should be the center of a national educational system. It should include a school of mines, a school of roads and bridges, a conservatory of art, a national library and museum of painting and sculpture, a military school, a mint, a veterinary college, an observatory." The vision was characteristically Napoleonic, but the inception—the need to which it responded—was characteristically American. Barlow, also a friend of Robert Fulton, creator of American internal waterways through the use of steamboats, reflected the national taste for the mechanical arts. Intellectual and educational in intent, Barlow's conception of the city's development incorporated practical measures: "Washington must be the center of a network of national highways and canals linking all the rivers."

At Kalorama, at the edge of town, overlooking the Potomac and Rock Creek, Joel Barlow established himself in a country house remodeled by Benjamin Latrobe and became—in the Jefferson and Madison administrations—a social fixture of the city, his house being "the place to go in the swampy young capital for good company and good talk." The retired diplomat-poet's taste for homegrown vegetables and fruit from his own orchard paralleled Jefferson's, as did the style of his house. The close friendship of Barlow and Latrobe took explicit form when the architect moved to a house at the edge of Kalorama and a connecting gravel path was laid down.

The heights of Kalorama did not discourage Jefferson and others from visiting nor Latrobe from walking to his work at the Capitol. "We reside on the top of the range of beautiful eminences that surround the cities of Washington, Georgetown, and Alexandria on every side. By the aid of a good telescope, my wife sees me ascend Capitol hill, three miles distant, and can trace me on the whole of my return home," Latrobe wrote in 1816. A romantic landscape painting by Charles Codman shows a bit of meadow ornamented with a large urn and the rather sheltered cove at the mouth of Rock Creek; beyond, the Barlow house appears perched on a terrace behind which rises the more dominant Wicomico escarpment. It is possible that this view shows the pond Barlow created by damming Rock Creek so that his friend Fulton might have a suitable place for his steamboat experiments. That conjecture, however, like the event itself, awaits further documentation.

LATROBE'S WASHINGTON: DOMESTIC ARCHITECTURE

In addition to remodeling the house for Barlow, Latrobe designed several of the capital city's outstanding residential and religious structures in a style so representative of the early affluence of the constituent city that the era can rightfully be called "Latrobe's Washington." The capital was indebted to Latrobe for his classical public buildings as well as the City Canal designs. In 1813 Latrobe designed a grand mansion at 17th and B streets—just north of the City Canal's first lock—for John Peter Van Ness. The Van Ness House, sited next to the modest childhood home of Mrs. Van Ness, the former Marcia Burnes, was the largest house Latrobe had ever designed. When completed in 1816, it was a handsome residence, described by Talbot Hamlin as "its author's domestic masterpiece. . . . The house was worth waiting for. Its exterior was deceptively simple, with all the restraint and originality of which Latrobe had become such a master. Thin, guttered eaves, supported on pairs of widely spaced wooden brackets, replaced the usual cornice." The principal rooms occupied the

George Hadfield's City Hall, ca. 1865. Library of Congress

second floor and—new in the United States—separated the activities of the owner's family from those of the servants. Considered to be "more elaborately finished than any private home in the District," the Van Ness House and its carefully laid grounds epitomized the country-estate quality of the city's affluent residential areas. Around Lafayette Square, Latrobe designed a stately residence with spacious grounds for the naval hero Stephen Decatur and St. John's Episcopal Church, which served the president as well as congregants from the residential district sprouting up in the immediate area.

GEORGE HADFIELD: CITY HALL, 1820

The architecture of George Hadfield echoed the clean classical lines that were Latrobe's signature. Although an accomplished designer, Hadfield was a tragic figure. Among the succession of superintending architects on the construction of the Capitol, Hadfield, like Stephen Hallett, had also succumbed to the tirades of William Thornton. British-educated, Hadfield began a brilliant career in London, promising to rival John Nash as court architect. Refused membership in a prestigious architectural club, however, Hadfield immigrated to Washington, where his mentors thought he might find a more immediate outlet for his considerable talents. After a few painful years under the strain of the "rogues then employed in the construction of public buildings," Hadfield enjoyed a relatively successful career as a private architect, designing, for example, a home for Commodore David Porter on 16th Street just at the northern boundary of L'Enfant's city, the location later called Meridian Hill. Hadfield also designed the Custis-Lee mansion in Arlington, the Van Ness mausoleum in

Oak Hill Cemetery, and the home for John Mason on Analostan Island.

Washington's City Hall, constructed in 1820, was Hadfield's greatest commission. Located a few blocks northwest of the Capitol at 4th and D streets on a site earmarked by L'Enfant to accommodate some monumental building, City Hall signaled a major departure from the functions outlined in the original Washington plan. L'Enfant had intended the municipal functions to develop not to the northwest but facing the south leg of the canal, far enough from the federal functions to assert an independence but near enough to the port-industrial area and major arteries to play an integral part in the life of the city. Thus, in its location, City Hall, the seed of what would much later become the sprawling Municipal Center that is now called Judiciary Square, revealed the lack of a comprehensive scheme for siting public buildings. This uncertainty was to endure for the rest of the nineteenth century.

In itself, Hadfield's building bespoke the simplicity and economy desired in buildings constructed with public funds. Its quiet exterior, a central Ionic portico flanked by two Ionic-columned wings, enclosed interiors that were notable for their stark simplicity. The building, much admired in the first half of the nineteenth century, inspired a new appreciation in the early twentieth century as it conformed to Classical Revival tastes. The construction of City Hall, in effect, provided the initial link connecting and making visually comprehensible the long distance between the Capitol and the President's House, although in fact the building is located several blocks north of Pennsylvania Avenue, the planned visual connection.

ROBERT MILLS: PATENT OFFICE, TREASURY, AND POST OFFICE

The burning in 1834 of the Hadfield-designed Treasury Building east of the President's House pointed up the inadequacy of the city's water system. The event also occasioned the design of a new structure on a larger scale as compared to the modest dimensions Hadfield had given the initial structure. Sited on 15th Street directly in front of the President's House as viewed from the Capitol, the new Ionic-styled Treasury Building was designed by Robert Mills, who reigned as the government's architect of public buildings between 1836 and 1851.

A Latrobe protégé, the Charleston-born Mills brought to the capital city considerable experience in both public and private architectural and engineering works. He had worked in Philadelphia, Richmond, and Baltimore, and for ten years had been state engineer and architect of South Carolina. In the Treasury Building, Mills achieved what he considered a "good common building" constructed of masonry vaulting derived from groined arches cemented and coated with the newly perfected "hydraulic cement." Through the Treasury Building and other structures that he designed, Mills established what historian Robert L. Alexander describes as "his version of the Greek Revival as the style most expressive of the new American political system."

Owing to financial constraints, the building as completed in 1840 was much smaller than Mills had intended. In its subsequent enlargement according to designs by Thomas U. Walter, Ammi B. Young, and Alfred B. Mullett between 1855 and the mid-1870s, the completed building presented what later planners termed a "spoliation" of the view inasmuch as it blocked the vista between the Capitol and the President's House.

Seven blocks to the east, on the site that L'Enfant had designated for the national nonsectarian church, Mills superintended construction of the Patent Office, commencing in 1836, after designs by William P. Elliott. Having designed many public buildings and developed in the process a well-grounded philosophy of the design priorities that applied, Mills altered the Patent Office according to his own tastes. The large building, constructed with bold vaulted galleries, presented a powerful Doric facade extending beyond the original building lines along F and G streets. At the building's completion just before

the Civil War, the white granite exterior resembling the Parthenon faced the axis of 8th Street toward the Center Market, across the canal, and through the southwest quadrant to the waterfront, at least partially fulfilling L'Enfant's intentions for a compelling visual experience.

One block from the Patent Office, the Corinthian-style Post Office designed by Mills rose according to no formal plan on a site facing E Street between 7th and 8th streets. Begun in 1839, construction of the original section was completed in the mid-1840s. Thomas U. Walter designed the northern extension, completed by 1855, that faced F Street and the Patent Office. Articulate exponent of economy in public archi-

tecture, Robert Dale Owen praised the Post Office as "a graceful example [of the Italian style], creditable to the architect who designed it." The construction of these buildings indicates what was seen as the grandeur of the government's presence in the city, as expressed in individual structures. Before long, however, the thickening up of the central core with government edifices forced a broader than architectural view of these individual structures. There developed a growing concern with the larger environment surrounding public buildings, the relationship of the buildings to each other, and the structures and functions that clustered around them.

Southeast Corner of the Treasury Building Facing 15th Street as Designed by Robert Mills. Library of Congress

THE NAVY YARD AND THE OMNIBUS TO GEORGETOWN

The federal presence was felt in the southern quadrants too. A major employment center along the Anacostia River was the Navy Yard, whose shipping activities, functional buildings, and wharves attracted many craftsmen and laborers as well as midshipmen attending the navy's training school. The nearby federal arsenal on Greenleaf Point stored weapons manufactured at Harpers Ferry and the Foxhall foundry near Georgetown. A large volume of trade was generated between these government installations and manufactories in the area and between the workers and small businesses serving this neighborhood. In 1830 the opening of an omnibus line between the Navy Yard and Georgetown created a route by which the ties between the waterfront communities and the developing monumental core as well as Georgetown were strengthened. This linkage of communities to each other by an expanding transportation network followed the essential growth pattern predicted by L'Enfant, who had visualized distinct communities, developed around multiple centers of growth, eventually merging as the population increased—and producing a continuous if diversified urban fabric. The ability of these centers to be closely tied to the rest of the city's prosperity rather than to function as competitors depended on the fortunes of the transportation networks.

THE CANAL NETWORK: THE CITY AND THE C & O CANALS

By the 1820s the Potomac River's channels had become so silted and impassable that neither Georgetown nor Alexandria could survive on river navigation alone. The two port cities looked to a large canal scheme. In 1828 construction of the Chesapeake & Ohio Canal commenced. Its route began in Georgetown and ran parallel to the Potomac westward to Harpers Ferry. From Georgetown, the canal was extended eastward, entering the Washington City Canal at 17th and B streets. According to the plan, Alexandria also was to benefit from the new canal by means of the Aqueduct Bridge and Alexandria canal constructed between 1833 and 1843 and located just west of Georgetown to carry the Virginia trade southward; there the canal emptied through an outlet lock into the Potomac. By the mid-1830s, the system was completed from Harpers Ferry to the Washington City connection. The southern route to Alexandria, barely realized in fact, proved commercially unprofitable.

The canal system as a whole never lived up to its expectations. Not only did the three cities

thwart each other's portions of the scheme, but any state investment in the project was compromised by commitments to other urban centers, as, for example, Maryland's interest in Baltimore's thriving port. Nevertheless, even in the act of visualizing the canal as a large commercial artery linking western Maryland counties with the urban depots that clustered along the Potomac, the three cities realized that solutions to their economic problems lay beyond their local boundaries. Regional economic viability clearly depended on strengthening the intercity physical linkages in canals, bridges, and ferries.

The canal network and bustling ports oriented Washington City toward the river. The river basin flatlands were occupied by urban functions; the highlands remained devoted to farms and country or summer residences. The orientation to the city's waterpower resources saw the development of manufacturing centers along Rock Creek, the stream that defined Georgetown's eastern borders, where the rushing waters could be harnessed. The falls of the Chesapeake & Ohio Canal within Georgetown offered that port city an additional cheap power source for milling flour. The prosperity brought by the waterpower on two borders and the change of goods at the canal created a Georgetown filled with a sense of self-sufficiency reflected in the large Italianate residences on the terraces facing the waterfront.

THE COMING OF THE RAILROAD: THE B & O

The coming of the railroad diminished the city's river orientation. Abetting the later removal of the affluent population from the lowlands, the railroad displayed its easy conquest of larger highland areas and its emphasis on intercity links. At the same time that the Chesapeake & Ohio Canal was commenced and hailed as generator of the city's future prosperity, the Baltimore & Ohio Railroad was inaugurated with a direct line to Washington City. As soon as the railroad opened for travel, it was established that rails were destined to become the transportation mode of the future, dominating the area's land-

THE WASHINGTON NAVY-YARD, WITH SHAD FISHERS IN THE FOREGROUND.—[See Page 246.]

scape and settlement patterns for the next century—and orienting the city to a stronger
regional context. Baltimore, in fact, offered
strong competition to the Potomac port cities. In
connecting the city to the rich western lands, the
railroad paralleled the Chesapeake & Ohio Canal
and offered a speedier transit of goods and passengers between urban centers. Another intercity
line radiated from Baltimore, reaching the District line in 1835. This line cut in half the travel
time normally required by the stagecoach.

BRIDGES, ROADS, AND FERRIES

Roads and turnpikes, the earliest transportation
routes through the region, shifted their focus
from Alexandria and Georgetown to Washington
City. The major roads from the Maryland counties into the northern sections of the city were
14th and 7th streets. The southeast quadrant
housing the bustling Navy Yard was serviced by
bridges over the Eastern Branch. The Potomac
River was traversed by ferries and by the 1810
Chain Bridge above Georgetown. Long Bridge,
constructed in 1809 between the Virginia shore
and 14th Street in Washington City, served as a

major turnpike and later a railroad access into
the city. Often damaged by high water and ice,
this bridge was subject to frequent repairs. Its
wide piers hampered the rush of water from
upstream, exacerbating the silting of the river,
preventing large ships from entering Georgetown's harbors, and throwing off excess water
onto the already marshy lowlands south of Pennsylvania Avenue.

THE POTOMAC FISHERIES

The prosperity of the three cities did not depend
solely on the exchange of raw and manufactured
goods at the canals, turnpike, and railroad
depots. The rich fisheries of the Potomac River
strengthened the river orientation and wharf
facilities appended to the three cities. The abundant supply of fish had for thousands of years
attracted aboriginal settlement and only two
centuries earlier had astonished the first white
explorers in the area. In the 1830s, 150 fisheries
lined the Potomac and its tributaries. Those
fisheries along the Eastern Branch produced such
huge fish hauls that farmers from the surrounding rural counties came to the city to sell their

produce and, in the process, took away quantities of fish for use as fertilizer. Deforestation and settlement upriver drastically changed the Potomac as it flowed past the District. Riverine life too was gradually destroyed by the growing residential centers within the District.

SLAVES, SLAVERY, AND FREE BLACKS

Key to the construction of many private and public buildings was the presence of thousands of slaves in Washington City, Georgetown, and Alexandria. In 1800 approximately half of the population was black; the majority of them were slaves. The availability of slave labor for the construction of new buildings was the result of the exhaustion of tobacco farming and its replacement by wheat farming. Unlike tobacco farming, wheat farming was not labor intensive, and slave owners became interested in hiring out their surplus slaves. Slaves were hired out to work as waiters in hotels, servants, artisans, and construction workers. Slaves were also employed in domestic work for their owners or their hired employers.

Numerous slave markets, "pens" (holding cells), and auction blocks developed in Washington, Georgetown, and Alexandria during the first four decades of the nineteenth century. Slave markets were located at Lloyds Tavern and Robey's Tavern near Center Market at 7th Street and Pennsylvania Avenue NW, McCandless's Tavern in Georgetown near Wisconsin Avenue and M Street NW, and Smith's Southern Hotel in Alexandria. The firm of Franklin and Armfield at 1315 Duke Street in Alexandria operated one of the busiest slave pens in the area and through its offices throughout the South supplied slaves to cotton plantations in Mississippi and Louisiana. Other slave pens were located at Decatur House, in sight of the President's House. In outlying areas, slave markets could be found at taverns in

Union Troops in Front of a Slave Dealership in Alexandria, Virginia. Photograph by A. J. Russell, Library of Congress

Rockville, Maryland, and in front of the Fairfax Courthouse in Fairfax, Virginia. These markets and pens held slaves who either were hired out for urban tasks or were sold to owners of plantations in the southern states that were centers of cotton production.

Slaves were required to live on the premises of their owners or the persons who had hired them. The backs of the main houses—including the Van Ness House, the Octagon, Decatur House, and Joel Barlow's Kalorama home—included housing for slaves. Slave housing also was provided behind owners' houses in Alexandria and Georgetown. Thus, backyards became slave domains and "slave spaces." Slaves could acquire both their freedom and property through direct manumission or when provided by wills when their owners died.

In the early nineteenth century, free blacks began to acquire property, mainly near the Navy Yard and on Capitol Hill. No clear pattern separated black and white housing during the early period. As the white population expanded beyond the central core, the black population moved to an outer ring. Blacks also lived in low-lying areas of Tiber Island, in the southwest quadrant between the Mall and the Potomac, and in Foggy Bottom.

The Compromise of 1850 outlawed the slave trade in Washington. This act of Congress resulted from years of lobbying by both white and black activists who urged Congress to abolish slavery and the slave trade in the nation's capital city. Although slaves were still present in the city, auction blocks, markets, and holding pens were removed.

Washington Panorama, 1840

As the mile-and-a-half stretch between the Capitol and the President's House became lined by new Mills-designed public buildings, the residential areas clustered about these two major terminuses also merged. By 1840 a major residential corridor spread northward from Pennsylvania Avenue as far as K Street. Indicators of this residential configuration were the new churches constructed to serve the nearby population. The President's House inspired the clustering of aristocratic residences of the diplomatic corps and important government officials. The Capitol Hill neighborhood generated less stately mansions for a more transient population. The business district formed along Pennsylvania Avenue from the foot of Capitol Hill to 9th Street. Thus, along Pennsylvania Avenue, where L'Enfant had intended a cultural-ceremonial thoroughfare, banks defined the strip, which was filled in with newspaper offices, hotels, eating houses, and small retail establishments.

THE SURGE OF WASHINGTON CITY

By 1840 the District, numbering more than 33,000 in population, became clearly definable. The once autonomous port cities of Alexandria and Georgetown were about to be eclipsed by the surging giant of Washington City. Henceforth, the two older cities would become neighborhoods or suburbs of the large capital city center. In its evolving image, Washington City gathered strength from the new public buildings and installations, the adjoining residential clusters, and the river, canal, turnpike, and rail arteries of trade and communication. In the beginning of the period from 1800 to 1840, the city depended on the prosperity of the older port cities. At the end of this period, attention was focused on Washington City itself. Moreover, public and private decisions about its physical future would affect the region outside the original L'Enfant borders.

RETROCESSION: THE QUESTION OF ALEXANDRIA AND GEORGETOWN

In the two decades before the Civil War, Washington City dominated and directed physical growth in the region. The decline of Alexandria and Georgetown, plus the increasing control that Congress exerted over all the settlements within the District, inspired calls in the two port cities for retrocession to their respective states. In this Alexandria was successful, as the physical barrier of the Potomac River argued for much inconven-

ience in communication with the District as a whole and thus poor prospects for physical improvements. Georgetown never succeeded in separating but remained tied to the city in both physical and social terms. The highlands and opulent residences of Georgetown created an enclave for the fashionable set, many of whom were still rooted in the surrounding plantation life. The new District, although shorn of its Virginia lands, prospered beyond the rural outlines suggested at the time of its early occupancy and indeed doubled its population in the short twenty years between 1840 and 1860.

WHITE MASONRY AND RED BRICK:
THE FEDERAL PRESENCE IN THE
CONSTITUENT CITY

The government's commitment, although not nearly at the scale required had L'Enfant's canal and drainage plan been executed, did bear the

predictive stamp of a strong federal presence. In 1840 Mills's three major public buildings were either completed or well on their way. Their white masonry facades would dwarf the structures of the constituent city and would serve as visual landmarks of national capital grandeur set amid the red brick facades of the residential city. New or expanded federal functions clamored for accommodation in equally dignified surroundings, necessitating construction of new public buildings and extensions of the old. The attention of Congress was now directed to the Mall.

The Mall and the Monumental Core

Until the 1840s, the Mall was used as grazing and agricultural lands. Construction began on the Washington Monument, which was privately financed and designed by Robert Mills, in 1848 and on the Smithsonian in 1849. Several years earlier, the Columbian Institute had built green-

Sketch of the Washington Monument as Designed by Robert Mills, Mid-1800s. Library of Congress

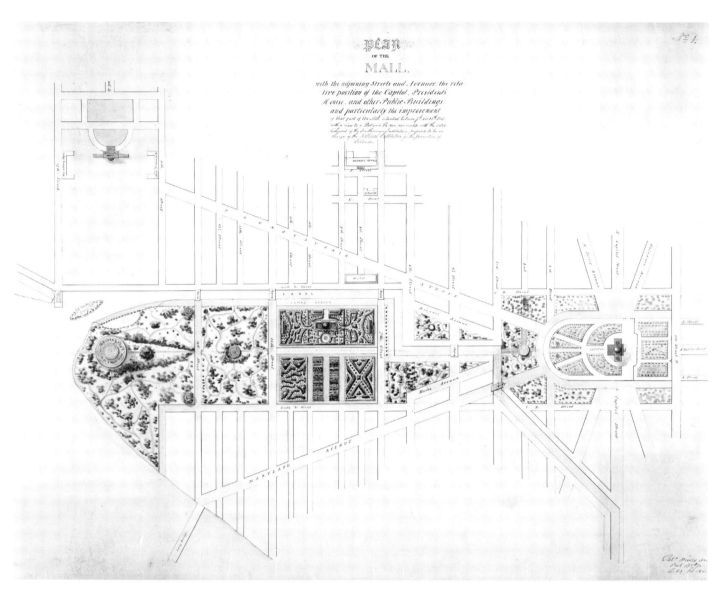

PLAN
OF THE
MALL.

with the adjoining Streets and Avenues; the rela
tive position of the Capitol, Presidents
House, and other Public Buildings;
and particularly the improvement
of that part of the Mall situated between 7 and 12 Str
with a view to a Botanic Garden connected with the estab
lishment of the Smithsonian Institution, proposed to be in
charge of the National Institution for the promotion of
Science.

Nº 1.

Ink Sketch of the National Mall as Planned by Robert Mills, 1841. National Archives

houses at the Mall's east end. The land undulated between hills and swamps. The siting of the obelisk off the President's House and Capitol right angle was the result of fears about uncertain foundations. The monument was built on higher ground, thus presenting a geometric problem later for tidy planners preoccupied with truly symmetrical vistas. Nevertheless, the building of the towering monument, although not completed for nearly four decades, did provide a major interest in retaining the Mall for the ceremonial purposes intended by L'Enfant. In concept and function, however, the Mall gradually changed; instead of becoming L'Enfant's intended site for ambassadorial resi-

dences, the Mall became the setting for cultural institutions.

The cornerstone laying for the Smithsonian Institution in 1849 created a benchmark in the city's history. Small but assertive, the building centered concerns for the larger environment beyond the immediate structure and grounds. The future character of the entire Mall was at stake. The acceptance in 1838 of Englishman James Smithson's bequest of slightly more than half a million dollars set into motion a lengthy period of discussion as to the nature of the institution, its location in the capital city, and an appropriate design for the building. From 1840 to 1841, at the request of General Joel R. Poinsett,

Early Lithograph of the Smithsonian Castle on the Mall. Robert Dale Owens, *Hints on Public Architecture*, 1849

who was associated with the budding institution, Robert Mills prepared a plan for the building and grounds.

Breaking from his Classical Revival trademark, Mills presented a building designed in the Norman style, likely in honor of the British scientist Smithson and "our associations with great literary institutions . . . assimilated with the Saxon style of architecture," as Mills expressed it in a letter to Robert Dale Owen. Mills considered the site of the first Smithsonian Building to be the entire "Public Mall," from the foot of the Capitol to the Potomac River, affording large acreage for horticultural and botanical experiments as well as zoological buildings. Mills planned the Smithsonian Building to be located on a slight rise at the 12th Street axis, which afforded a view of the rolling land, the varied plantings, and a "good variety of rural scenery." The waterways—canal and river— defining the Mall's edges offered the prospect of fountains and other water displays. Reflecting some continuity with L'Enfant's residential

intentions for the area, Mills anticipated the construction of adjacent houses for the "officers of the Institution."

Mills's plans were not executed, but they were not irrelevant to the ultimate fate of the Smithsonian. Further discussion ensued in Congress, which by 1844 defined the institution to embrace a display area for natural history and geological specimens, a library, a laboratory, and a lecture hall, all of which were to appeal to a general audience. Two years later, James Renwick's turreted Norman-style designs for the building were accepted, with the grounds question seemingly a separate matter. In any case, the siting of the building longitudinally along the axis of the Mall, leaving an "open corridor [of] 600 feet," as Daniel Rieff documents, ensured the retention of the long vista from the Washington Monument to the Capitol.

DOWNING'S PLAN FOR THE MALL AND THE "MUSEUM OF LIVING TREES"
In 1850, President Millard Fillmore invited

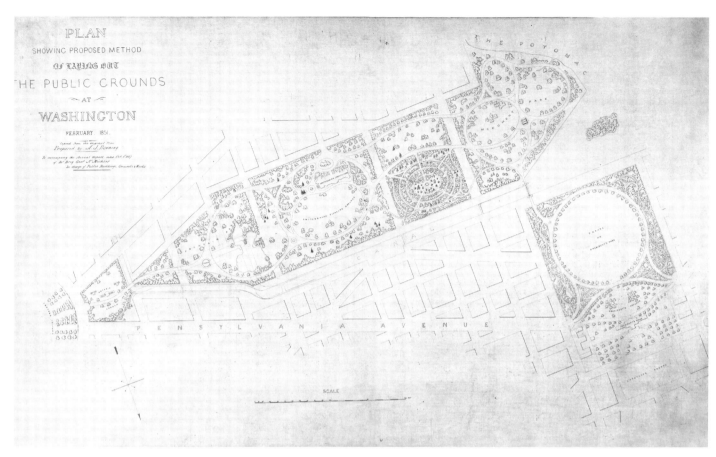

Andrew Jackson Downing's Proposed Plan for Laying Out the Mall, 1851. National Archives

Andrew Jackson Downing, America's pioneer "landscape gardener," to design the grounds on the Mall as well as the parks north and south of the President's House. Downing had already gained nationwide recognition as a landscape designer. His commission on this national project was an outcome of conversations between the Washington banker William W. Corcoran and Joseph Henry, secretary of the Smithsonian, and discussions with city officials about improvement of the grounds around the Smithsonian. A strong botanical focus had been a tradition of the Mall, especially with the founding in 1820 of the Botanic Garden at the foot of Capitol Hill. The Columbian Institute seeded the gardens located here and also incorporated exotic specimens recovered from the Wilkes Expedition (US Exploring Expedition).

Downing's 1851 plan for the Mall and adjoining parks outlined three objectives: (1) "to form a National Park," (2) "to give an example of the natural style of Landscape Gardening which may

have an influence on the general taste of the country," and (3) to create a "public museum of living trees and shrubs." These three objectives were applied to six separate major reservations linked by connecting curvilinear walks and drives. The spaces between were to be filled with trees, pleasure grounds, and lakes, and a decorative wire suspension bridge would connect the Mall with the President's Park south of the White House. The hard geometric lines of each reservation's boundaries were thus offset by the emphasis on undulating ground surfaces and roadways, as if in a built artifact recalling the sylvan glories of the city's first decade. Downing's plan softened the sharp bend of the canal in front of the Capitol into a smooth diagonal along Missouri Avenue, thereby consolidating more ground for public parks. Like L'Enfant, Downing envisioned water displays as critical to the aesthetic fulfillment of the city. Under Downing's plan, Fountain Park, to the east of the Smithsonian Pleasure Grounds, would be supplied from a reservoir in the Capitol with the overflow pumped into a lake that was to be carved out.

The execution of Downing's 1851 plan met financial and political obstacles reminiscent of L'Enfant's time. In fact, the Smithsonian's immediate grounds were the only element to benefit from the overall plan, the other reservations being left to piecemeal improvements. Nonetheless, Downing did succeed in creating a design ideal that influenced the physical realization of Washington's scattered parklets in the post–Civil War era. The continuing influence was then reflected in the frequent revivals of the complete Downing landscape plan by various members of the Army Corps of Engineers—and by wistful mapmakers.

THE CAPITOL EXTENSIONS AND THE NEW DOME

The growth of the nation (and consequently of the number of congressmen) necessitated an enlarged Capitol Building. The architect of the extension to the Mills-designed Treasury Building and Post Office, Philadelphian Thomas U. Walter, was appointed architect of the Capitol extensions. To accommodate new and larger chambers for the House and Senate, extensions were to be added to the original wings, with the original space given over to other uses. But "extension" of the Capitol embraced much more than this work, begun in 1851. The new cast-iron dome, designed to crown the completed building, was an accomplishment in terms of both technology and aesthetics. The dome was only partially constructed at the outbreak of the Civil War, but after a lapse of a few months, work was resumed—so that the new dome might serve as a patriotic symbol of the Union.

The City's Waterways and the Design of a Modern Water Supply

In becoming a more compact city and losing its countrylike appearance, Washington experienced increasingly serious water problems. The water supply that had initially depended on springs was becoming clearly inadequate. When army engineer Montgomery C. Meigs recommended

to Congress the feasibility of a water system originating at Great Falls, Congress appropriated the largest outlay of funds for a single project since monies had been appropriated for its own Capitol. For the new water system Meigs was appointed chief engineer. An important designer who would create several of the city's post–Civil War architectural monuments, Meigs entered the Engineers Corps of the US Army following his graduation from West Point. Possessing a highly inventive mind, Meigs designed engineering structures, integrating mechanical and ornamental fixtures into his large creations.

GREAT FALLS TO CITY PIPES: MEIGS'S COSMOPOLITAN VISION

Ground was broken for the city aqueduct at Great Falls in 1853, although interruptions in the funding retarded completion of the system until nine years later. From a point just above Great Falls, the diverted water was conveyed to the receiving reservoir near Little Falls at Dalecarlia. From this point, at the District line, the settled water was carried to the distributing reservoir just west of Georgetown at Drover's Rest, where it was then piped to the city users. The water had to flow twelve miles over the jagged topography. To convey the conduit over the Cabin John valley, Meigs designed the famous masonry single-arched Cabin John Bridge. To cross Rock Creek, Meigs designed the Pennsylvania Avenue Bridge constructed of cast-iron arches. Meigs's objectives were more than merely to supply water to households and fire hydrants; his cosmopolitan vision saw an increased water supply as feeding into fountains that were necessary health and aesthetic provisions in a congested city.

The immediate effect of Meigs's water system was an abundant water supply necessary to a modern city, even if this supply was not yet consistently clear or healthy. Loose earth rushing downriver from the agricultural lands gave the water a turbid appearance. The design of the system, however, was basically sound. Further improvements were made only in the way of extensions or minor corrections of Meigs's original design; no major changes were undertaken until the twentieth century.

SOCIAL EFFECTS OF THE NEW WATER SUPPLY: SECTORING

In the long run, the water supply system had a profound effect on the city's social configurations, particularly on its residential areas. Since the water came in from the west, it served the western sections of the city first before being piped to the eastern quadrants. This predictability of supply in the city's western quadrants tended to draw the affluent to those areas by reason of the superior services available. The eastern sections, often threatened with water shortages, were left to the less affluent. To be sure, this sectoring of the city along social lines had begun before the construction of Meigs's water system. Blue-collar classes had already clustered close to the Navy Yard, and the affluent had settled early near the President's House and westward into Georgetown. The allocation of public services greatly reinforced this sectoring.

In terms of planning for the water system—as also for the interurban canal and the railroad systems—success depended on more than technological achievements. The functions of the city's vital arteries depended on the cooperation and resources of an area much larger than the local boundaries—in this case the ten-mile square. The Maryland legislature, in response to a federal request, granted to the United States right-of-way for the route of the water mains and support structures through Maryland territory along the Potomac. Later improvements made to the system were necessitated by change occurring miles away, and again solutions had to be found on a regional basis.

FADING PROSPECTS FOR THE CITY'S WATERWAYS

Although in terms of water supply the city benefited from serious commitments on the part of the federal government, Washington's waterfront prosperity was adversely affected by the changed river conditions. The pattern for Washington was the same as the pattern for Georgetown. Repeated silting and poor conditions of the canal boat basin at Rock Creek and the Washington City Canal forced the city to yield the greater part of the coal and lumber business to Alexandria with its deepwater wharves above Hunting Creek. The decline of the Washington City Canal was partly attributable to the sewage that flowed directly from the city to the canal's basins. The canal, a major determinant of the city's commercial core—Center Market and the Pennsylvania Avenue business strip—was by 1860 of little commercial use. It was foul, dangerous, and unhealthy. Water-oriented industries suffered a similar decline. The silting of the Eastern Branch seriously curtailed shipbuilding at the Navy Yard. Manufacturing of armaments at the government arsenal at Greenleaf Point ceased. The important mid-century flour-milling business in the environs of Georgetown declined. Even with the fading of water-oriented industries, the value of manufactures of the District of Columbia actually increased from $2,690,000 in 1850 to $5,500,000 in 1860, evidence of increasing reliance on new rail transportation facilities.

Buildings beyond the Boundary

The location of new government centers away from the river and even outside of the L'Enfant city contributed to the decline of city waterways. In 1851 the US Soldiers' Home, two miles north of the Capitol, was established. In 1852 the Government Hospital for the Insane—now St. Elizabeths Hospital—was located on the former farm of Thomas Blagden along the Anacostia. In 1857 Congress began to support Amos Kendall's Columbia Institution for the Instruction of the Deaf, Dumb and Blind—now Gallaudet College—a mile northeast of the Capitol. The siting of these new institutions in widely separated areas of the District outside the boundary of the city was a significant factor in the city's pattern of suburbanization in the pre–Civil War era.

Mud Machines and Ferryboats

Despite fading prospects for commercial success

East Branch of Potomac R. Washington.

of the city's waterways, the rivers were by no means ignored. Investment both public and private, although generated piecemeal, worked to remold the river edges. As early as 1805, "mud machines" had been employed to remove the sedimentation that adhered to the Potomac riverfront. Throughout this first half of the century, various mechanical devices could be found on or in the river, in the continuing attempt to manipulate the flow of water and to scoop away obstructive marshes. Watercraft plied the Potomac and Eastern Branch; from various vantage points in the region white sails and vertical masts cut across the horizontal waterscape. By 1852 steamboats served all parts of the lower river and the Chesapeake Bay; ferries ran hourly between Washington and Alexandria, daily to Aquia Creek, and weekly to Baltimore and Norfolk. Tolling bells as they saluted Mount Vernon, they added smoke and noise to the environment.

Toward a More Cosmopolitan City, 1850s

The local government contributed to the momentum of urban improvements. The City Council's 1852 prohibition of new cemeteries within the city of Washington, installation in 1853 of gas lamps on major streets and avenues, introduction of modern street signs, inauguration of the city's first system of house numbering in 1854: all these are distinct moves away from a countrylike settlement to a modern city.

THE SOCIAL CITY

Southern habits set the tone of residential life in the antebellum city, a reflection in part of the many presidents who were from the South. Many of Washington's oldest families were descendents of tidewater planters, and most Washingtonians retained strong familial ties to the agricultural societies of Maryland and Virginia. "The gentry," as an English observer termed the citizens belonging to the social set, "are thoroughly Virginian in sentiment." Such sentiment and inclination was played out in the rural pastimes at the several race tracks located outside the perimeter of Boundary Street and was also reflected in the rhythmic life clocked to the sessions of Congress, creating the Washington cycle of social seasons. Opulent French Renaissance and Italianate residences served as set pieces for the urban-oriented winter seasons, and country residences only a short distance away in the unsettled District served as havens of relief from summer heat and the "miasma" of the basin city.

An important indicator of the attractiveness of the city itself for residences was the increased number of legislators who made Washington their home. In 1845 only a little more than 2 percent of the US senators occupied single-family homes in the capital city. By 1860 the percentage of senators living in single-family units had grown to 40. Many built their own houses, sometimes in the unsettled portions of the city beyond Boundary Street, and thus became more sympathetic to physical improvements needed in the region.

The free black population established businesses, such as hotels, barbershops, and restaurants, and began to become property owners. They provided shelter for new black arrivals and havens for slaves on the Underground Railroad. Amid this greater social and economic stability, blacks founded churches and schools, institutions that strengthened the community and inspired them to hope for greater freedom and equality.

The First Suburbs: Uniontown and the Rail Settlements

Working people residing near the Navy Yard and arsenal could spend leisure time in activities oriented to the Eastern Branch, which offered the recreational pleasures of swimming, boating, and fishing. The river-oriented blue-collar community was bolstered in 1854 by the establishment of Uniontown across the Eastern Branch from the Navy Yard. Uniontown is often considered to be the first suburb in Washington. It may have been preceded by settlements along the railroad lines, however, since, according to the historian Wilhelmus Bogart Bryan, "by 1853 so many people were living along the Baltimore and Ohio Railroad, whose business required their daily presence in the city, that the railroad company was requested to have the trains stop at way stations for their accommodation." The growth of suburbs as signified by Uniontown and the rail settlements enlarged the physical dimensions of the city and produced the first inklings of the commuter lifestyle.

The Preservation of Mount Vernon

During the first several decades of the nineteenth century, Mount Vernon was a landmark in travelers' itineraries, even though it remained in the Washington family. In 1832 Frances "Fanny" Trollope, author of *Domestic Manners of the Americans*, recorded her impressions of the property during her river trip to Washington: "It is there that he lies buried: it was easy to distinguish, as we passed, the cypress that waves over his grave." For years the steamboat service between Washington and Mount Vernon was the only way for tourists to get to the late president's house. The popularity of steamboat service to Mount Vernon, among other forms of cultural exploration, tied the city to a larger region and ushered in the city's major source of income made in private enterprise: tourism and its inevitable outgrowth, the guidebook.

When rumors spread about the possible sale of Mount Vernon to developers, Ann Pamela Cunningham appealed to Southern women in 1853 to come to the property's rescue and spoke of its "sacred associations." Edward Everett, a representative and senator from Massachusetts, who later served as the governor of Massachusetts and then as secretary of state, helped champion the cause as a means to save not only the property, but also the Union. In 1858 the state of Virginia chartered the Mount Vernon Ladies' Association and permitted the organization to own the property. Under the leadership of Cunningham, Mount Vernon's future was secured, and the organization's structure served as a template for subsequent private preservation efforts elsewhere.

Cultural Institutions

The growth of cultural institutions gave the leisurely lifestyle of Washington an extra dimension and bestowed a unique image on the city's physical form. The Smithsonian Institution, itself an architectural creature of evolving notions about taste and economy, attracted scientists and other intellectuals who had earlier gathered around the Patent Office and similar agencies. The first permanent argument for the Mall as a cultural corridor, the Smithsonian was joined in 1855 to the east—the site of the current National Air and Space Museum—by an armory intended to exhibit military artifacts. Although the significant decades of such growth still lay ahead, the constituent city of the 1850s enjoyed lectures, concerts, and religious services in the federal buildings, using the space after hours and providing for bustling round-the-clock activities in the city's central core. The city also produced its own cultural landmarks, most notably the assertive Corcoran Gallery (designed in French Renaissance style by James Renwick) facing the Georgian, Hadfield-designed State Department Building.

Conflicts between the interurban centers within the federal district had been hushed by 1860 with the projection of Washington City as the decisive voice. That city's own intracity clusters that formed about major public installations and buildings by the period's end had merged, all still framed largely by the L'Enfant boundaries. And just when the capital city had overcome its interurban rivalries and had at last become physically unified, it was faced with a divided and warring country. ✯

THE CIVIL WAR 1860-1865

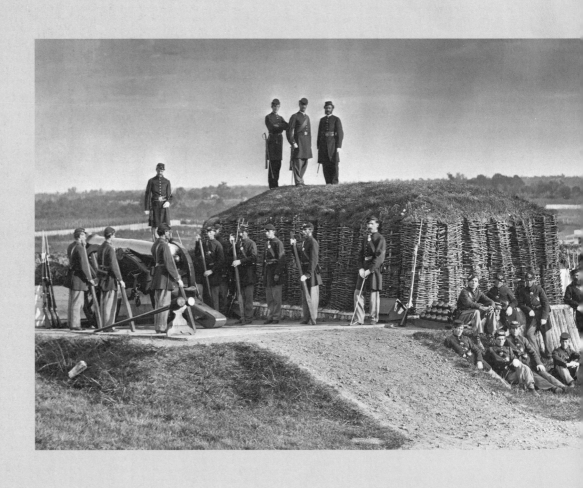

3

Washington in Wartime: The Military City

Any indecisiveness of the federal government concerning the capital city's future was swept aside at least temporarily in the exigencies of war. The city was a salient; projecting into the Northern Virginia front, it was surrounded by Southern sympathizers. Washington needed to be protected, and in the process a vast area was swept into the defensive perimeter. The city became an armed camp; later, a vast hospital. The city's defenses encompassed not only military posts but also new methods of acquiring food, housing, and raw and manufactured materials necessary to the military and civilian functioning. These requisite goods and services were acquired outright by the Military District of Washington, identifying the federal government as the dominant force in the city's daily existence. With its prominent architectural and monumental features, the city also produced patriotic symbols of an ever-united country.

In the military control of the city, it can be said that the government dedicated itself to the city's survival as never before or since. It also can be said that in many respects the military never left the city. Defending the city also represented a dramatic expansion in power of the federal government that made the capital city more central and relevant to the life of the country. Utilizing the city's extant buildings and grounds to suit wartime needs, the government subsequently provided a new physical pattern upon which the future city would rise.

Military preparedness had been an integral part of L'Enfant's plan for the city. The long expanse of the Potomac River downstream was intended to act as a buffer to sea attack. The Eastern Branch, site of the Navy Yard and the arsenal, was the first face of the city to accost any waterborne invasion. Fort Washington, constructed in 1809 on the Maryland side of the Potomac slightly north of Mount Vernon, had served as the only defense on the river before the Civil War. Little else had been planned in the interim, and by all standards the city's defenses were meager. The decline of the Eastern Branch installations had accompanied the growth of similar facilities in other locations, such as the federal arsenal at Harpers Ferry. Although national sectional differences

The Mall Looking toward the Washington Monument, ca. 1863. Library of Congress

had been endemic for years, the designers of Washington never anticipated a civil war and therefore had not planned for defense against attack from surrounding settlements.

John Brown's raid on the Harpers Ferry arsenal raised serious doubts about the capital's ability to defend itself. The transportation routes leading to the heart of the city had earlier functioned as vital links to the city's communications with Virginia and Maryland. These routes now defined its vulnerability. The area's natural topography—a ring of hills surrounding the basin city—offered easy dominance of the central core.

SHELTER AND FOOD FOR THE TROOPS

When Fort Sumter was attacked in April 1861 and hostilities began, fear gripped the capital city.

That Southern sympathizers dominated the ruling elite made the government's commitment to the Potomac River city ambiguous at best. In a few days, however, tens of thousands of troops for defense entered the city at the command of President Lincoln. Over the next few years, the District's population nearly doubled, taxing the city's resources beyond limit.

When war began, the armory on the Mall and the barracks at the arsenal were the only places actually designed for use by troops. In short order, however, the government leased and occupied new sites. Wooden stables and barracks were located on the grounds north of the Capitol and west of 17th Street near the President's House. In a few months, troops occupied other sites, changing drastically the physical appearance of the city. Whole regiments were quartered in the Capitol, the Patent Office, and the Treasury Building; on Georgetown College grounds; in Center Market; in warehouses, churches, and hotels; even inside the White Muslin Palace of Aladdin, which had been built for Lincoln's inaugural ball. Temporary barracks were erected in the open spaces planned by L'Enfant on the Mall and at Observatory Hill.

Beyond N Street, both inside and outside L'Enfant's city boundaries, the open fields were occupied, filling in the original city limits and settling the suburbs north of Boundary Street. Meridian Hill, site of antebellum racetracks, country mansions, and the Columbian College grounds, became a small town of its own, formed around hospitals and barracks. Troops filled country estates, such as William Corcoran's Harewood near the current neighborhood of LeDroit Park. Other estates became hospitals. Montgomery Meigs, engineer of the Washington aqueduct and quartermaster, chose the unfinished but highly visible Corcoran Gallery of Art as his headquarters and set up the army clothing department nearby.

Grounds not devoted to troop accommodations were shifted to new functions, with the concentration of food production in the core of the city and the growth of localized industries

The Grounds of the Washington Monument Served as a Cattle Yard during the Civil War. Library of Congress

replacing earlier reliance on goods shipped in from secessionist settlements. Under the stress of war, Washington acquired industrial characteristics that had been foreign to it before and would be foreign again after the war.

The Washington Monument grounds became pasture for cattle, with a slaughterhouse nearby to provide fresh meat for the soldiers. The vault in the Capitol Building, originally intended for

Cattle on the Washington Monument Grounds in a Photograph by Mathew Brady, ca. 1862. National Archives

Alexandria Wharf, 1865. Photograph by A. J. Russell, Library of Congress

George Washington's tomb, served as the army bakery. Within a year's time, a major center for army equipment and supplies spread over several acres of Foggy Bottom, easily serviced by the river wharves south of G Street. Here corrals and harness and blacksmith shops were located. George Washington Young's mansion on Giesboro Point, located on the Maryland side of the Potomac just south of Uniontown, was leased to the government in 1863. This strategic 624 acres of land in full view of river traffic became the major cavalry remount depot, alleviating the desperate crowding of the corrals near the Naval Observatory. Described as the largest animal depot ever organized by the army, the Giesboro

Point installation accommodated as many as thirty thousand horses at a time.

To transport food and other strategic goods to the city, the military took control of the region's major ports. From the Georgetown flour mills and ships at the wharves, flour was directed to the army bakeries. Alexandria was occupied because of its railroad connections to the South and, like Young's Giesboro Point, because of its commanding situation on the Potomac. Much of the riverfront along the Potomac and the Eastern Branch was thus devoted to military purposes, a usurpation of civilian port facilities that commercial interests would never succeed in fully regaining after the end of hostilities.

The Defenses of Washington along the Ring of Hills, 1865. Library of Congress

THE RING OF HILLS

To build defenses for Washington required a larger view of the city than was to be gained from ground-level maneuvering. In the summer of 1861, the secretary of the Smithsonian, Joseph Henry, sponsored a number of balloon ascensions by Professor Thaddeus Lowe above the city and over many battlegrounds. From such balloon flights, detailed sketches of the region could be made, affording comprehensiveness and current descriptions that were unprecedented. For the first time military strategists could grasp the

Fort Lincoln, 1865.
Library of Congress

entirety of the natural topography: the ring of hills surrounding the basin city and the gaps facilitating roads into the city's core. New military roads began to be built; cut long and straight, by the end of the war those roads measured thirty-two miles in total. These new lines of communication preempted those that in the past had focused on Alexandria and Georgetown. Washington's ascendancy as the primary urban center was augmented and defined.

To secure the ring of highland vantage points surrounding the basin city, a chain of forts was constructed, reinforcing these points throughout that portion of the District located in Virginia and tying once disparate areas into a comprehensive defense design. Built as temporary struc-tures, the earth forts were constructed of timber and some masonry, surrounded by trenches, and flanked by abatis of newly felled timber. Materials to build the abatis were gathered from the woodlands along many parts of the ring. The woods were cleared for several miles in front of the military works to provide for what was described at the time as a "clear field of fire from the forts, batteries, and infantry redoubts." In fact, every movable object in front of the forts was shaved away, including houses and barns.

In the course of the war the military constructed more than sixty forts and more than forty supporting batteries. The location of the forts was determined both by the views offered and by proximity to important arteries. For

example, Fort Reno on the heights of Tenally-town commanded three roads. Fort Foote, on a stretch of land jutting out into the Potomac, was constructed on a bluff a hundred feet above the Maryland shore with a full view of the channel south as far as old Fort Washington. Complementing the new Fort Foote, Battery Rogers was constructed on the Virginia shore inside the corporate limits of Alexandria.

Even with this control over hills and roads, potential weaknesses existed in the line of fortification. A connecting system was therefore devised whereby enclosed field forts were sited at intervals of eight hundred to a thousand yards. Field gun batteries covered the depressions in the ground between the major forts. The entire line

of defense was linked by rifle trenches that also provided a vast network of strategic openings in the line for the passage of troops and artillery.

TELEGRAPHS AND MAPS

The telegraph facilitated communication between these far-distant sites. Reels of insulated wires were unrolled to link the War Department, housed in the Winder Building at 17th and F streets, with critical government centers within the region. A telegraph wire connected to the President's House was taken aboard a balloon flight by Professor Lowe in his reconnaissance of the city. Employees of the Pennsylvania Railroad worked as telegraph operators, headed by Thomas A. Scott, charged with the railways and

Massachusetts Artillery-men at Fort Stevens, 1865. Photograph by William Morris Smith, Library of Congress

New York Avenue Presbyterian Church Where President Lincoln Worshipped during the Civil War in a Photograph by Titian Peale, ca. 1863. Negative N-83-984, Photographic History Collection, National Museum of American History, Smithsonian Institution

Noncommissioned Officers of Company H, Tenth Veteran Reserve Corps, at Washington Circle during the Civil War. Library of Congress

telegraphy. Messages could be relayed with greater ease by telegraph than by messenger. Thus, federal bureaus no longer needed to be physically close to one another. And as much as the telegraph permitted speedier communication between war strategists, it also greatly improved the relaying of news to newspaper reporters—

and to the nation. Furthermore, as an adaptation, flags and the blinking of colored lights permitted long-distance communication. Similarly, a signaling method devised and taught by Colonel Albert J. Myer in Georgetown utilized the techniques of ciphering and coding as well as telescopic observation. His method having

proved successful, Myer prepared a manual on signaling. In 1863 a much-impressed Congress appropriated funds to create the US Signal Corps.

In this same period, the increasingly intense preoccupation of strategists with the natural and built topography fostered mapmaking activities, intended to clarify the outlines of military action in general and to plan coastal blockades and amphibious operations in particular. To keep his scientific staff intact, Alexander Dallas Bache, superintendent of the US Coast and Geodetic Survey Office, cooperated with high-ranking military officers in preparing charts, maps, and data. Such information may have been decisive in precluding the use of the Potomac River as an easy military route into the city. Although in the short run the military evaluations most immediately affected the problems of defense and supply, the new and vivid familiarity with the region as a whole and in detail was to have significance for the future. Many crucial peacetime decisions about the city would later be made by men experienced in the wartime city. Among these men were quartermaster Montgomery C. Meigs and US Sanitary Commission official Frederick Law Olmsted.

PHOTOGRAPHING WASHINGTON

Photography also increased familiarity with the city. The most famous recorder of wartime Washington, Mathew Brady, photographed the important balloon experiments and the mapmaking activities of the topographical engineers. Brady's former partner, Alexander Gardner, was also a major wartime photographer, publishing in 1863 his *Catalogue of the Photographic Incidents of the War.* Both photographers supplied *Harper's New Monthly Magazine* and *Frank Leslie's Illustrated Newspaper* with photographs and daguerreotypes from which woodcut illustrations were made. Through such illustrations, the reading population of the nation was given an unprecedented and immediately compelling view of the wartime city. Illustrations of female civil servants working in the Treasury Department dramatically depicted new personnel policies. Photographs also revealed the war's effect on the physical city, with clean parallel rows of wooden barracks shown in front of the uncompleted Washington Monument. Members of the Army Corps of Engineers made official photographs of the war for governmental records, revealing the new role for the corps.

FREEDMEN AND THE FREEDMEN'S BUREAU

During the war years former slaves, encouraged by the 1862 act of Congress that emancipated the 3,100 slaves in the District, migrated to Washington—a safe haven. Within one year, the population of freedmen increased to approximately ten thousand. Charged in 1862 with easing the plight

Freedmen's Barracks in Alexandria, Virginia, ca. 1865. Library of Congress

of the incoming black population, the Freedmen's Bureau set up several "contraband villages" in the unsettled lands within the fortified region. One such settlement, opened by the Contraband Department of the Military District of Washington in late 1863, was located in the bottom lands of Arlington, on land that had been part of Robert E. Lee's estate. In exchange for housing, the freedmen in this settlement raised hay and vegetables for the army. Photographs record the converted barracks, schools, churches, and shops of these villages.

Washington in Wartime: The Civilian City

The civilian city was able to adapt to the rapid physical changes brought on by the war largely because during the preceding decade it had already undergone extensive change, with basic alterations being wrought by increased private and government investment. For example, the intercity railroad connections of the 1850s initiated the radial configurations of the future city. Interest had already been expressed in intracity street railroads to transport local commuters between residential neighborhoods and employment centers. And the infrastructure for the water supply, crucial to the growth of a city, was under construction.

Further municipal improvements were an outcome of the federal government's preoccupation with military demands. In his annual report of 1863, Secretary of the Interior John P. Usher suggested that the federal government share expenses of paving the city streets. Although his suggestion bore no immediate results, a congressional act that passed in the following year allowed for streets to be lit and paved, and provided sewers without consent from or subsequent taxation of the abutting property owners. A general tax fund was created to finance such improvements, enabling the city government simply to order the work done. Although only little more than half the improvements ordered were actually executed, the law cleared the way for massive improvements in the postwar era.

LAND AND TRANSPORTATION LINES

By the second year of war, Washington was a boom city, inviting investors in real estate and public services. Competition for buildings and land became so intense that during the war assessments for real estate property increased markedly in proportion to market value. The population also became so enlarged and far-flung that many residential areas already were more than a comfortable walk from the downtown. In 1862 Henry Cooke persuaded Congress to grant him a charter to build and operate the city's first street railroad system. In July of that year, the streetcar line between the Capitol and the Willard Hotel at 14th Street and Pennsylvania Avenue opened, serving the major downtown strip along the avenue. In the fall of 1862, the main line from Georgetown to the Navy Yard via the Capitol was opened, with lateral branches along 7th Street and 14th Street added later. The initial handsome profits made by Cooke's line inspired the chartering in 1864 of a new streetcar line, the Metropolitan Railroad Company. This new company constructed its line on the first terrace above the lowland city along F Street, predicting that thoroughfare's eventual emergence as the city's desirable shopping area.

THREAT OF FIRE, DISEASE, AND DISORDER

The congested city filled with roving military men and other newcomers raised questions about daily security. As early as 1860, city officials had asked Congress for a larger police force than the day patrol of fifty officers. In the following year Congress, acknowledging widespread social problems in the swollen city, created the metropolitan police department. At its inception, the force consisted of a superintendent, ten sergeants, and 150 patrolmen.

Fire on the scale of the conflagrations that devastated many American cities almost became a reality in Washington when massive fires broke out at the government stables. Such fires killed hundreds of animals, and those that survived panicked and stampeded through the startled city. Emergencies of this magnitude were beyond

the capabilities of the eight hook, hose, and ladder companies then in existence. In 1864 a consolidated and salaried fire department was created and outfitted with three steam engines, a fire alarm, and a police telegraph.

The congestion of the city also threatened its occupants with disease. Smallpox struck in Washington during the winter of 1862. The metropolitan police, instructed to be on the lookout for conditions contributing to contagion, made inspections for discarded refuse close to crowded quarters and removed obvious nuisances. Not until the following year did the War Department begin to bear responsibility for the waste accumulated by its own overwhelming presence in the city. By the summer of 1863, municipal garbage carts were making regular rounds, at last providing inhabitants with public services befitting a modern city.

THE TRIANGLE

One product of the wartime city that defied police action and protection was the notorious area around "Murder Bay" and "Hookers' Division," formed as a triangle by the canal, Pennsyl-

vania Avenue, and 14th Street. The area's transformation into a crime-ridden neighborhood signaled the twilight of the avenue as Washington's desirable shopping area. Although this triangle had begun its history of decay with increased use of the canal for sewer purposes, it began to live up to its name of Murder Bay as transient military men, as well as the unemployed or underemployed, frequented its various abodes of entertainment. All types of criminals, thieves, and prostitutes collected in dilapidated housing, often using the euphemism "oyster houses," presenting such a concentration of vice that the police were powerless to defend innocent victims. Even so, military officers and government officials frequented this area to patronize its gambling houses, the best of which were located near 14th Street and Pennsylvania Avenue. By war's end, the triangle projected a distinct image, notorious, dangerous, and isolated from the rest of the surrounding city.

In this wartime city, more wholesome forms of recreation and amusement also could be found. The resumption of the Marine Band concerts within a few months after the outbreak of

Murder Bay, a Notorious Slum during the Civil War, Was Located in What Is Now the Federal Triangle. Record Unit 95, Box 67, Smithsonian Institution Archives

Ford's Theatre Just after the Civil War. National Capital Planning Commission Collection

the war projected a reassuring air of normality in the already guarded city. In this secured atmosphere, moreover, three new theaters were established. They were joined by an amusement hall redesigned from the former Odd Fellows Hall on Louisiana Avenue and renamed Canterbury Hall, suggesting the arrival of "high culture" in Washington.

Washington in Transition: The War's End

At the war's end, the reunited Congress viewed a changed city. Although much of the transient military population left, the number of permanent residents in the city jumped 50 percent. Some of the government installations found their wartime locations suitable for the future defense of the city. Services offered and new functions inaugurated by the government during the war could not suddenly be halted. The "temporary settlements" outside the city for which the government had no plans became the nuclei of future permanent neighborhoods. The open spaces within the old city—the Mall and the series of similar parks—had earlier been planned for special functions; these spaces were slowly returned to their prewar state. The rapid munici-

pal improvements that had been implemented to accommodate population influx would continue as the wartime growth proved permanent.

POSTWAR CHANGES IN MARYLAND, VIRGINIA, AND THE DISTRICT

After the Civil War, suburban Maryland and Virginia were oriented to Washington rather than to their respective state capitals. And critical to the future management of the city and its environs was the efficiency in government that had been demonstrated by the Military District of Washington. Here was a model for directness and scope in metropolitan government, a standard of governmental operation difficult to emulate well into the twentieth century.

In the public sector, the government retained the large installation at Giesboro Point (the current Bolling Anacostia Tract). The federal government also retained ownership of many of the wartime fort sites. The ring of forts was dismantled, but the lands with their mossy ruins were not reclaimed as farmland. These lands were available, therefore, for acquisition later on by the National Capital Park and Planning Commission for park development. Today these forts are historic landmarks, artifacts expressing the natural topographical defenses exploited by military strategists. Many of them are operated as parklands by the National Park Service or county parks departments.

Nearly all of the Virginia side of the defended city was returned to civilian uses. Exceptions were the Arlington hills opposite the basin city. The federal government also retained Robert E. Lee's former plantation. Dedicated as the Arlington National Cemetery, the Lee plantation would serve the nation as a new symbol of national unity, a burial place for both Union and Confederate soldiers.

The Freedmen's Bureau continued into the postwar era, converting Campbell Hospital at the head of 6th Street NW into Freedmen's Hospital. A new residential area provided by the bureau was established on the 375-acre farm originally owned by James Barry between St. Elizabeths

Hospital and Uniontown (Anacostia), both of which were established in the 1850s. Barry Farms was established to offer freedmen an opportunity to purchase land and to develop a stable community. The federal government provided further commitment to the black population with the establishment of Howard University, chartered in 1866 and located on a commanding bluff on 7th Street just north of Boundary Street.

The leisurely southern persuasions of the prewar civilian city of Washington survived the Union triumph, although the physical accoutrements of the distinctive lifestyle were never recovered. The large country seats, taken over by the government during the war years, had attracted small settlements and thus opened the way for exploitation of these areas as suburban residential neighborhoods. In much of this nearly cleared metropolitan land, Northerners settled, while Southern sympathizers tended to move west or south to other parts of the country. In the metropolitan area itself, the farming activities originally organized to serve military needs now served the growing urban population.

SUBURBANIZATION

Seen both in far-flung black settlements and in the subdivision of land tracts, suburbanization was made possible by extension of the streetcar system. New postwar routes were established along major commercial and transportation corridors extending from the central city to Georgetown via Connecticut Avenue and P Street and north along 7th and 14th streets. Those routes made large newly subdivided tracts accessible to streetcar commuters. As in the twentieth-century city to come, development patterns would be strongly influenced by the location and extent of transportation facilities. The railroad, indispensable to supplying the wartime city, was given a greater visual presence as well as symbolic linkage to the government's fortunes in the new Baltimore & Ohio train depot and tracks fronting Capitol Hill. Rail traffic would dominate the transportation and communication networks of the peacetime city, further decreasing waterborne traffic. Still, the river was accessible to many of the region's localities that were virtually untouched by the railroad, and so it continued to serve as a carrier of passengers and produce between riverfront settlements for many years to come.

THE VIEW FROM THE SMITHSONIAN TOWER

By the end of 1865, tents and other signs of wartime military activity had largely disappeared from the Mall and other nonmilitary areas of the city. New streetcar tracks imposed their pattern and activity across the city. As viewed from the central tower of the original Smithsonian Institution Building, the uncompleted Washington Monument and tidal swamps beyond to the west seemed to be waiting out the transition. From the same vantage point, a completed Capitol dome was visible. The dome overlooked the awakening city and symbolized the national unity President Lincoln had striven to establish. This new unity would have a permanent effect on the shape and character of the national capital city, affording a clearer vision of new directions for Washington. ★

THE POSTBELLUM CITY 1865–1900

4

The Winds of Peace: Demilitarized City

The salvation of the Union may have been assured, but Washington's future as its capital city was less certain. The earlier failures of the federal government to make the necessary commitment in public improvements, and of the commercial city itself to develop an enduring mercantile trade, relegated the river basin city to severe environmental degradation. In the postbellum era, affluent residents turned away from the river city to higher ground, motivated by both the search for healthier living conditions and the new mobility of the transit system. At the same time, blue-collar workers took over the low-lying areas of this basin city, occupied the older houses, or moved into the new and relatively cheap row houses and alley dwellings. In this pattern, a future polarization of the city was foretold along social and racial lines as well as by locality. Given the abandonment of the basin city by many newly mobile residents, some reaffirmation by the federal government to the city was of primary importance. In the provision of public services—water, sewers, the park system, and street planting—the initial federal concern was environmental quality.

No strong comprehensive policy as yet ruled public improvements. Decisions about parks, public buildings, and sitings of public projects were made on an ad hoc basis, leaving the way open at the century's end for a more systematic approach to the city's physical future.

As the winds of peace blew over Washington, the inhabitants—numbering over one hundred thousand—were faced with the immediate challenge of demilitarizing the city. In the transition, some hospitals constructed for the care of wartime casualties were retained for permanent use. Lumber and other building materials used in temporary structures were recycled for use in public and private buildings. Lands confiscated in and around Washington for military encampments were returned to private use. Samuel C. Busey, whose farm at Belvoir had been surrounded during the war years by troops, observed the return to peacetime conditions: "The soldiers, camps, barracks, parade-grounds, and hospitals disappeared, and labor, help, and hirelings returned in some measure to the accustomed ways and pursuits of former days. But a new era had come, and with it

Arlington National
Cemetery, 1867. Peter R.
Penczer Collection

new methods, new enterprises, and a new impetus to thought and ambition."

Restoring confidence in the newly reunited country was a symbolic task as well as a concern of political substance. Not only did the physical scars of the former military presence need to be removed, but also the city's essential public services—as initiated by Montgomery C. Meigs's aqueduct before the war—needed modernization. Federal and municipal officials faced along B Street a stinking canal that served as an unofficial sewer. The lowlands to the south of the President's House resembled an untamed marsh, its westernmost sections merging into the Tiber Creek as it fed the canal. Wide-piered Long

Bridge, the main route connecting the North and the South, acted as a barrier to the free flow of water downstream, silting up the Potomac River along the shores of Washington and Georgetown. Development of a powerful commercial depot at the capital city's wharves was thus precluded. Inland, public squares that had been set aside as parks in the L'Enfant plan were instead covered by houses.

THE CENTRAL BUSINESS DISTRICT

Center Market had served as the focal point for commercial activity along Pennsylvania Avenue ever since it was established on Market Square in the early years of the nineteenth century. The location was fixed by the intersection of Pennsylvania Avenue and 7th Street, the principal connection between the waterfront and Bladensburg Road, a turnpike and post road leading to Baltimore and points farther north. Here, at the crossing, L'Enfant had proposed a turning basin for canal boats that brought produce into town. Market stalls within Market Square proper contained a large and diversified range of goods. More specialized functions defined the markets that grew up nearby. The area along 8th Street between the market and the Patent Office was devoted to clothing, with secondary lines of other marketing activities along 7th and 9th streets and northeast along Indiana Avenue. A powerful magnet, Center Market attracted the best of the produce and household goods and commanded a competitive position over the localized neighborhood markets, like Western Market at O Street NW, and Eastern Market on Capitol Hill. Out of Center Market evolved the central business district, Washington's retailing core. At the same time, other localized markets assumed a more important position in the expanding residential areas, marking the general trend: the transformation of the capital city from small town to large city. This strong nodal structure of urban growth, hinged on functions like markets, is precisely the pattern predicted by L'Enfant, as his provision for future growth generated from a number of strategic points attests.

PERMANENCY FOR WASHINGTON, CAPITAL CITY

The preponderance of individual enterprise and initiative over that of the federal government for at least a decade following the war led to great uncertainty about Washington's future, especially its future as the nation's capital city. Potential sites for a new "Seat of Empire" included Philadelphia, an old city that had profited handsomely from supplying war materiels. Other invitations came from midwestern states with offers of major cities like St. Louis and Cincinnati as sites for a federal establishment in a loca-

Market Square in a Photograph by Mathew Brady, ca. 1875. Library of Congress

tion closer to the center of the nation that now stretched across the continent.

Advocates for moving the capital city could not, however, overlook the distinctive social and physical city that had blossomed during nearly seven decades. The comings and goings of politicians, foreign dignitaries, and civil servants created a culture unique to Washington. The city was the focal point in a cycle of social seasons. By 1881 *Harper's New Monthly Magazine* was describing the fascinated caravan of "rich or energetic and inquiring inhabitants of other places" who came to live in Washington periodically, so that "Washington may be called the winter end of New York, as Newport is the summer extension of the metropolis." The point is that the highly structured Washington winter season—commencing at New Year's Day with a reception given by the president and his wife and ending at Lent—encouraged these "inhabitants of other places" to invest in opulent residences in Washington.

Just as important to the growth of cultural and scientific institutions in the city (and the nation) was the large number of brilliant individuals who came to Washington during the Civil War, rose quickly through the wartime ranks, and then found in the intellectual and professional opportunities of the government and other public institutions a reason for staying. The Smithsonian Institution, for example, attracted scientific-minded intellectuals, and the various departments of the executive branch of government were staffed by distinguished professionals. Federal bureaus like the Patent Office and the National Observatory also served as magnets to draw the nation's outstanding scientists and social scientists to Washington. Leading architects and artists, attracted to the capital city by major public building projects, also enhanced the intellectual climate. With this concentration of accomplished citizens, Washington through this period was known as the "paradise of a poor man with brains." Indeed the presence, as well as the general tastes, of these highly mobile intellectuals of modest means was evident in the distinctive row houses of restrained proportions nevertheless embellished in a style analogous to the grandeur of the millionaires' mansions in Washington.

PERMANENCY FOR THE L'ENFANT PLAN

This same promise of magnificence was felt in a far more essential way. Critical to Washington's salvation as the capital city, the still unfinished original city plan had a recognized grandeur: a new site could offer only accommodation to an extant set of urban conditions or else the creation of some new and undefined plan. In 1873 a reporter for *Harper's New Monthly Magazine,* writing about the partially executed L'Enfant plan, recounted the relationship of the plan to the symbolism of the major public buildings and to the natural topography. By the third quarter of the century, as the article observed, development over the land's irregular surface had proceeded in such a way that the major public buildings and adjacent development on highland sites, as well as on the hilly terrain of Georgetown and the Eastern Branch Heights, rose from the river bottom settlement to create a city somewhat like Quebec, with upper and lower towns. The writer ascribed the irregularities of the land to the "soil friable under the action of water, and affected by three brooks or creeks," the Tiber, Rock Creek, and the Eastern Branch.

With the advantages of the city reaffirmed, the strategy in retaining the Potomac River site was based on completing, and thus giving permanency to, the L'Enfant plan. A common belief, that L'Enfant's plan was "lost" for much of the nineteenth century only to be "found" and revived for the McMillan Commission in 1901, is an error. In fact, the essential elements of the L'Enfant plan were retained. The sweeping avenues, park areas linked along the Mall, public spaces at the conjunction of the radials and the grid, and locations of the major branches of government as developed between 1792 and the Civil War—these elements dominated public improvements of the postwar city, even if certain major changes in the plan had been made in the decades immediately following its issuance.

L'Enfant's original map, the manuscript plan of 1791, imprinted by the Office of the Commissioner of Public Buildings, was recopied in 1887 under the direction of F. M. Thorn of the US Coast and Geodetic Survey as evidence of the title of the United States to the reclaimed lands along the Potomac River. This evidence was brought to bear in the Potomac flats suit, *Martin F. Morris et al. v. United States.* One can assume from the plan's availability and use in legal proceedings that it was consulted by both federal and municipal officials engaged in public improvements. The Mall, to cite the most obvious focal point of L'Enfant's intentions, was subjected to many grand embellishments throughout the last quarter of the nineteenth century, from the reclaimed finger of land (now East Potomac Park) to the layout and plantings along the Mall proper. The implementation of improvements to the old city was more than cosmetic; a new city steadily emerged. Largely based on L'Enfant's scheme, this city was seen to be worthy of federal commitment to its future as the capital city—and thus worthy also as city of residence for those who had made their fortunes elsewhere but would be attracted to the seat of federal power.

THE CONSTITUENT CITY

The distinction between the public city and the private city was not always clear. One depended on the other. Residents of the constituent city depended on the federal and municipal governments to provide a clean water supply, to lay out and pave streets, to define and develop public parks, to provide sites for public markets, and to maintain the city according to modern sanitation standards. In return, the public city counted on the private residents to support its public works projects, to fill its labor demands, and to build and reside in residential structures befitting the nation's capital city.

Although much public effort was spent on extensive tidying up of federal reservations and buildings in the flatlands, public improvements also carved out new roads into the highlands rising in a crescent of settlements around the basin city. In these newly accessible areas, the government found prime lots of land for federally supported institutions. Among these was Howard University, founded in 1866 on hills to the north of the city center, along 7th Street. New residential areas were also carved out in the highlands, providing after-office-hours escape from the heat and foul air of the lowlands and establishing new patterns of residential activity.

Public Works: The Army Corps of Engineers

In 1867, even before the question of the capital's ultimate future was resolved, the US Army Corps of Engineers shouldered the federal government's responsibilities for the creation and upkeep of public works, buildings, and grounds, responsibilities previously discharged by the Office of the Commissioner of Public Buildings. Nathaniel Michler was the first of a long list of remarkable and versatile engineers who fulfilled these responsibilities as officer in charge of the corps. Born in Easton, Pennsylvania, in 1827, Michler had achieved recognition in the battle of Petersburg, Virginia, and was brevetted brigadier general.

MAJOR PUBLIC WORKS PROBLEMS AND THE WORK OF NATHANIEL MICHLER

Four major and closely related problems facing Michler reflected the immediate public works needs of the postwar city: (1) paving and adorning Pennsylvania Avenue, with special consideration of the President's House; and at the same time (2) inspecting alternative highland sites that might be suitable for a new presidential residence; (3) dredging of the Potomac River, not only to improve navigation and reclaim the lowland marshes, but also to render the Tiber Creek floodplain and the land south of Pennsylvania Avenue floodproof; and (4) defining more clearly the city's public parks starting with the sprawling magnificence of a "national park" along Rock Creek and including many smaller triangular neighborhood greens planned throughout the L'Enfant city.

PENNSYLVANIA AVENUE AND ITS ENVIRONS

At the end of the war, Pennsylvania Avenue remained the city's principal street, although its physical appearance did not in any way connote the grandeur of an urban "ceremonial way." On the north side of this lively street lay hotels and many boarding houses patronized by members of Congress and their staffs during the short legislative sessions. A brick sidewalk facilitated fashionable promenades, even if the avenue itself was largely unpaved. Shops lined the way, most of them occupied above by residential apartments.

A principal feature of Pennsylvania Avenue was the horse omnibus tracks, following the shortest line from Georgetown to the Capitol and on to the Navy Yard. (The other omnibus route led up 7th Street.)

The area south of Pennsylvania Avenue was undesirable. The decaying City Canal presented a barrier, a marshy area, bridged at Maryland Avenue and at 7th, 10th, 12th, and 14th streets. Heavy rains and high tides brought the waters to Pennsylvania Avenue proper, particularly where the old bed of the Tiber Creek crossed it at 2nd Street. Around this center, gambling places, houses of prostitution, theaters, cheap entertainment spots, bars, eating houses, and places of amusement clustered, showing their distinctive faces. In the area, illicit activities formed themselves into "Hookers' Division." To the west, near 14th Street, the area was called "Murder Bay," a freedmen's settlement.

The low-lying topography contributed the popular name to the city's central market: "Marsh Market." At this strategic spot had grown up not only the produce market but also a brisk trade in dry goods, books, stationery, and the banking and business establishments of the antebellum capital city. In the postbellum era, as the city spread beyond pedestrian limits, Center Market was also transformed; no longer serving just the daily needs of city inhabitants, it now provided for more specialized wants. General Michler, in the 1868 *Annual Report of the Chief of Engineers,* took a dimmer view of the market atmosphere, describing the area around the canal as "overrun by market stalls, piles of lumber, and junk shops."

THE PRESIDENT'S HOUSE

The President's House stood to the west of this bustling market area. To the south, the mansion faced sewerlike conditions of the flats and City Canal, the notorious "B Street Main." Smells and malarial mosquitoes became a nuisance and hazard, especially in the hot summer months, forcing even presidents to flee to highland country estates such as Anderson Cottage at the Soldiers'

Home. Moreover, comfort and health conditions aside, the south side of the President's House grounds was clearly an inappropriate conclusion to the parks surrounding the mansion. Set apart in the midst of swirling city life, the Executive Mansion could offer the president little in the way of a haven from the "active cares and business of his high office"—as the *Annual Report of the Chief of Engineers* for 1867 noted—"where he can secure that ease, comfort, and seclusion so necessary to a statesman."

PLANNING, PAVING, AND ADORNING THE AVENUE

Pennsylvania Avenue needed to be paved and adorned—but patterned after what model? In his travels through Europe in 1867 to recover his health, Montgomery C. Meigs sent a letter to Michler describing the paving of streets in the cities of Germany, Denmark, and Prussia. With reference to the brick paving of Pennsylvania Avenue, Meigs observed: "Sidewalks here [in Europe] are never paved with brick." European pavements were created primarily of Belgian blocks or flagstones, laid out at right angles to the line of travel, or with cobblestones and gravel packed closely in a bed of sand. In Berlin, fountains and statues were surrounded by fine mosaic work created out of colored Belgian blocks and marble fragments. Meigs suggested that natural stones available in the Washington area might be readily adaptable to this vivid presentation of street adornment: red and gray sandstone from the Seneca, Maryland, quarries and blue- and white-veined limestone from the Potomac.

DESIGNS FOR WASHINGTON'S STREETS

For an ideal street layout, Meigs studied Unter den Linden in Berlin and sent home his sketch of it showing a wide gravel central walk, four rows of shade trees, and wide sidewalks next to the houses. Berlin's principal hotels and shops faced the parklike street. This arrangement generated much foot traffic during the day while at night the wide walks attracted promenaders, making the street a resort for business and recreation.

Viewing the success of the physical layout of this Berlin street, Meigs hoped it would serve as "authority in introducing improvements as yet novel in Washington."

One year later, in his 1868 report on the improvement of Washington's streets and avenues, Michler presented his own street scheme, patterned after the Champs Elysées. Whereas Meigs had suggested broad paved areas extending out from the houses, Michler placed a row of trees against the houses with a broad paved area separating the residential trees from the street trees. Michler's macadamized central thoroughfare replaced Meigs's graveled promenade. In both designs, however, the width of the paved streets was dramatically narrowed, a necessary prerequisite if all of Washington's streets were to be modernized under the press of time and financial constraints.

Paving and planting Pennsylvania Avenue would go far to reclaim the street from its postwar undeveloped condition. On the other hand, its vulnerability to the periodic freshets of the Potomac River discouraged the federal government from building any major public buildings along or south of the avenue. For example, in the early 1880s during the planning stages of Meigs's Pension Building, the original site in proximity to Pennsylvania Avenue (at the old intersection of Ohio and Louisiana avenues) was rejected in favor of a higher site at Judiciary Square because of concern over the unpredictable behavior of the river. Thus, if Pennsylvania Avenue were to realize development, reclamation of the flats to floodproof the land to the south was essential.

PLANS FOR DREDGING THE POTOMAC

Beyond the benefits that would accrue to Pennsylvania Avenue from river improvements, General Michler viewed the dredging of the river in the process of reclamation as an improvement to navigation and an impetus to expanded commercial trade in Washington and Georgetown. Not having relinquished the expectation that Washington might yet become a major commercial center, Michler suggested the dredging of

two channels—along the city's shores and along those of Virginia—to a depth of twelve feet. The removal of Long Bridge, which functioned more as a dam than a bridge because it "contracted the current and obstructed the flow of the tide," would aid in releasing large volumes of water, scouring the obstructions and securing adequate depths of water for navigation. Breakwaters should be constructed, Michler thought, to deflect water into the new channels, and a cut be opened for the Tiber to allow strong currents of deep water to scour the sewerage, which otherwise was left to spread over the flats and "generate pestilential vapors." So wrote Michler in the 1868 *Annual Report of the Chief of Engineers*. Despite Michler's urgings and those of his immediate successors, little serious attention was paid by the congressional Committee on Public Buildings and Grounds to the improvement of the Potomac until after the massive flood of 1881.

SHALL THE PRESIDENT'S HOUSE BE MOVED?

The proximity of the President's House to the uncompleted Pennsylvania Avenue and the hazards of the Potomac flats encouraged some members of Congress to seek out potential new sites for the mansion, most preferably in the countryside. In ordering Michler to study these sites, the Committee on Public Buildings and Grounds implied some readiness to make a dramatic departure from L'Enfant's site selection, which in the case of the President's House had been made in accordance with President Washington's wishes. Michler, in his *Annual Report of the Chief of Engineers* for 1867, proposed four alternative locations. The first site was at Meridian Hill. "On the first range of hills bounding the limits of the City of Washington," but a mere one-and-a-half miles from the Executive Mansion, it was too near to the city, Michler thought, and would be exposed to the "miasmic influences" rising from the marshes of the Potomac. In addition, the Meridian Hill site offered little as a haven from urban cares. In 1867 "already the street railroad approached, and numerous houses [were] being built on all sides"

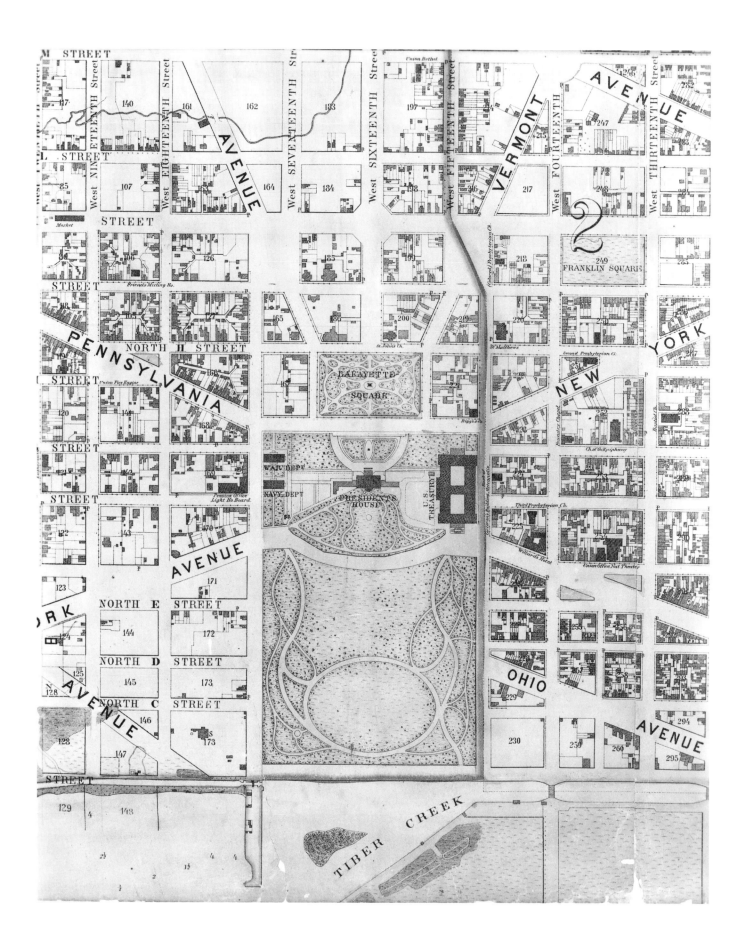

84

of 16th Street, reflecting the accelerating real estate activity in Washington just two years after the close of the Civil War. The remaining three sites, all at least three miles away from the current President's House, were situated in the northeast section of the District on former estate grounds with commanding views of the environs of Washington City. Michler argued strongly for the northeast sites, but no further action was taken on the matter.

PUBLIC PARKS AND THE MALL

In the realization of Washington as a city much like London, Philadelphia, and New York, public parks were now viewed as an urban necessity. Recently established and immediately celebrated park areas totaling thousands of acres graced these other cities. All classes of Washingtonians desired and deserved their own large preserve of greenery for healthy recreation, and the expected expansion of the city in the future envisaged little open space left unless it was procured in the public interest. Only one portion of the Mall fronting the Smithsonian was "tastefully" laid out. The partially developed Lafayette Square to the north of the President's House suffered from grading-induced drainage problems as in the undeveloped marshes to the south. On the east side of the Capitol grounds, croquet games and band music attracted citizens, although the gradual rise of the ground away from the Capitol concealed both these activities and views of the entire Capitol Building from the northeast and southeast sections of the city. The city's other major parks—squares, circles, and triangles—had yet to be cleared and formed.

Rock Creek Park

Nathaniel Michler's suggestions for what he termed a "national park," vividly described by him, were ultimately his most enduring contribution to the physical appearance of the city. The valley of Rock Creek, a "wild and romantic tract," wound as a serpentine canyon through the northwest section of the city and thus acted as a barrier to extensive settlement west of the creek,

except for Georgetown, which was connected to the rest of Washington by the Pennsylvania Avenue Bridge that Montgomery C. Meigs had built to carry water into the city. The lower creek valley, the site of mills and light industry, was divided among several large property owners with land parcels extending up to higher farming land to either side. The combination of rushing waters, deep ravines, and varied greenery—the landscape taste of the times—appealed to Michler, who envisioned winding roads and paths, ornamental lakes and ponds created from the creek's waters. This picturesque tract, in a central position to both Washington and Georgetown, was adaptable to many uses: zoological and botanical gardens, playgrounds, and a processional route. Looking forward to the city's expansion, General Michler suggested in his annual report for 1867 that the Committee on Public Buildings and Grounds "purchase at once a sufficient number of acres bordering on Rock Creek to anticipate the further growth of the city and its increased population," an area of 2,540 acres embracing the forts in the area constructed during the Civil War for the defense of the city.

Hopes for a Unified Mall

Michler recommended that the adjoining open areas or reservations making up the then-irregular Mall should be made to correspond in appearance with the Downing-designed portion that fronted the Smithsonian. Foreshadowing their ultimate agglomeration, the open areas should be "laid out in carriageways, paths for equestrians, and walks for pedestrians, as if the different parts formed a unit." A major hindrance to forming a unified public parkland out of the separate reservations was the Baltimore & Potomac Railroad Station, later called the Pennsylvania Railroad Station, a scene of great activity and noise. As Michler wrote in his annual report for 1868, "The running of the trains is now distinctly heard within the halls of the Senate, and shrill screams of the engine must frequently interfere with debate." Yet in 1868 partial fulfillment of Michler's efforts in the Mall area was at hand: the thirty-five acres of experimental gardens fronting the Department of Agriculture Building were designed to serve as an instructional exhibit with ornamental flowers and shrubbery.

THE SQUARES AND CIRCLES

To the north and east of the public reservations, other public park areas and connecting avenues also faced substantial improvement reflecting the maturation of the surrounding residential developments. Two blocks northwest of Lafayette Square was Farragut Square, adorned by trees and shrubbery, with water pipes laid in anticipation of a fountain. On K Street between 13th and 14th streets lay Franklin Square with its undulating terrain, about to be landscaped in a treatment similar to that of the Downing-planned Smithsonian grounds. Michler described this square in his annual report for 1871 as comparing favorably to Lafayette Square. To the east of the Capitol, at Lincoln Square, miniature lakes were planned. The grounds of the Capitol itself needed to be cleared, however; the northern boundary of these grounds still held a stonecutter's yard, and the southern boundary remained covered with stables and sheds. Other unimproved public squares and reservations restated the Capitol grounds situation: Scott Circle was studded with frame buildings, and Massachusetts Avenue was described in the *Annual Report of the Chief of Engineers* for 1868 as having "remained closed [for many years], houses, gardens, brick kilns, and other obstructions preventing it from being used."

The system of romantic and picturesque public parks envisioned by Nathaniel Michler remained incomplete when he left his Washington position in 1871; it fell to his successors to expand on his work. By the end of the century, the extensions of these projects revealed the makings of a continuous and unified park system, composed of the massive Rock Creek Park and the Mall and its appendages. The two parks were laced by wide avenues, which in turn threaded through the smaller squares, circles, and triangles.

The Territorial Government of Washington, 1871–1874

In the years immediately following the Civil War, a critical issue was the form that municipal government would take and the commitment to it that Congress would guarantee. The future of the city was at stake. In 1871 the problem appeared to be resolved. In that year Congress created a territorial form of government that, although touted throughout the following decades as "self-government" by Washington citizenry, was actually a blend of local and federal participation, the most powerful positions being dependent on presidential appointment. The Organic Act provided for citizens to elect twenty-two members to a house of delegates and a nonvoting delegate to the US House of Representatives. The president appointed the governor, governing council, and heads of administrative departments. The Board of Public Works was created to deal with the city's public improvements and was to be advised by a panel of notable engineers, architects, and landscape designers, including Montgomery C. Meigs and Frederick Law Olmsted Sr.

In the three years of territorial government, three men worked feverishly and brilliantly to improve the face of the city and thus secure Washington's future as the national capital city: Alexander R. Shepherd, as prime mover in the municipal Board of Public Works; Orville E. Babcock, as major in the Corps of Engineers in charge of public buildings and grounds and a member of the advisory panel to the Board of Public Works; and Alfred B. Mullett, as supervising architect of the Treasury Department and architect of the great State, War and Navy Building.

ALEXANDER R. SHEPHERD AND THE BOARD OF PUBLIC WORKS

Of the three men, Shepherd was the best known. Thrust into supporting his family at the age of thirteen, Shepherd began a career in business that very early projected him as an exceptional man. Accumulating a small fortune while working for J. W. Thompson's plumbing and gas fitting company, Shepherd made many business and political friends on his way up. Backed by a powerful group of supporters, Shepherd forced through Congress the territorial form of government that promised federal support for long-deferred public works. Although Henry D. Cooke, brother of financier and railroad baron Jay Cooke, was appointed governor, Shepherd was appointed to the municipal Board of Public Works, a position he made more powerful than Cooke's.

The blending of federal and municipal interests was especially prominent in the public works projects. Federal officials served on the Board of Public Works, presumably to oversee federal interests. Projects undertaken by Shepherd, however—including planting trees, constructing sewers, filling in the Washington City Canal, and laying streets—were distinctly different from the tasks of the Corps of Engineers. The corps's primary concerns encompassed dredging the Potomac River for both navigation and reclamation purposes, improving the water supply, and improving and maintaining not only Pennsylvania Avenue but also associated public parks, reservations, and buildings. For the public buildings, the supervising architect of the Treasury Department or the architect of the Capitol took primary responsibility, except that in the case of the State, War and Navy Building, Alfred Mullett was specially retained by Secretary of State Hamilton Fish. In the three years of rapid public improvements under territorial government, friendships between federal and municipal officials played an important role—to the benefit of the city, if also in some cases to the personal financial benefit of the officials involved.

The Sewer System and the City Canal
Planning and laying gas and sewer pipes and, afterward, grading and paving the streets, marked Shepherd's most dramatic city improvement activity. Attention was paid to the central part of the city, the business sections, and especially Pennsylvania Avenue, 7th Street, and 14th Street. Two major sewers running parallel to the Washington City Canal were laid: one, running from 6th Street to 3rd Street, emptied into the sluggish waters of the City Canal; the other, running from 7th Street to 17th Street, emptied into the Potomac River. Later the City Canal itself was filled, and a sewer pipe was laid along its route to serve as an outlet. Once paved the canal was renamed B Street (now Constitution Avenue) and adorned as other Washington streets, its completion and proximity to the President's South Park and the Washington Monument foretelling its later monumental function.

Already conceived as a ceremonial way, Pennsylvania Avenue demanded special treatment. It was paved with wooden blocks, a material in wide use in other American cities. Lesser streets did not always benefit from an agreed-upon elevation of grading, however, and in some cases improvements plowed through settled areas where houses had been constructed according to the natural contours of the land, now leaving some buildings either perched on the new bluff or half-sunken below the new grade. Hills in unsettled areas were leveled and valleys filled in, providing a flat terrain for development. To crown the completed streets, Shepherd arranged for trees to be planted to provide ornamentation and shade and, as it was popularly inferred, to decrease erosion and provide for ventilation.

SHEPHERD'S LEGACY IN WASHINGTON
The frantic pace and high expenditures, which resulted in a debt of $10 million by the end of 1872, invited congressional investigation and public discredit on Shepherd. His forthright actions in tearing down Northern Liberty market at Mount Vernon Square, for example, and in removing the Baltimore & Ohio Railroad tracks at 2nd Street and Pennsylvania Avenue characterized Shepherd as all the more controversial. Although the territorial form of government was abolished in 1874, after three-and-a-half years of existence, and Shepherd's reputation was too clouded for him to be offered further governmental positions, Shepherd did envision a physical plan that had exceeded in scale anything

undertaken in the city since L'Enfant. Shepherd's legacy to the city was of consequence. In his concentration of efforts on the business section of the city and on residential neighborhoods west of Capitol Hill, the eastern section of the city was ignored, reinforcing the pejorative characterization of that sector as limited to middle- and lower-income dwellings. The area was to bear this negative reputation for years to come.

The central business district improvements caught the eye of congressmen, residents, and visitors, persuading them that the city was indeed worthy of the nation. The 1875 *Harper's New Monthly Magazine* article on Washington enthusiastically alludes to the up-to-date status of the sewer, water, and gas systems servicing the city. In particular the streets, upgraded by Shepherd's efforts, merited special attention, being "covered with the most noiseless and perfect pavements in the world, and embowered in the greenest borders of grass-plots, enclosed with panels of post and chain or graceful paling, and planted with trees. . . . At all points of junction new squares and circles appeared, their verdure relieved with flashing fountains, or bits of statuary, or effects in sodded terraces, all ready for the sculptor." The city, with its new physical appearance and attendant social and cultural "remodeling," shared with the industrial cities to the north a sudden revival of confidence. Washington had "clothed itself anew, thrown away its staff, and achieved a transformation bewildering to its old residents, but very grateful to the patriotic sense which had so long felt the stigma of a neglected and forlorn capital apparently without a destiny." As a final compliment, the newly formed commission system of federally controlled municipal government, adopted in 1874, pledged itself to support and continue the public improvements that had been initiated by Shepherd.

MAJOR ORVILLE E. BABCOCK

Major Orville E. Babcock of the Army Corps of Engineers rose to a key position in public works between 1871 and 1877, his work thus adding to and complementing the municipal improvements. At least as controversial as Shepherd, Babcock began his military career upon graduation from West Point in 1861. His Civil War record, which included building pontoon bridges at Harpers Ferry, taking part in an engagement at Yorktown, and witnessing the surrender at Vicksburg, was marked by brilliance. Attracting the esteem of General Ulysses S. Grant, he became aide-de-camp to the leader of the Union army and made the first contact with General Lee before the treaty at Appomattox. Babcock, continuing to serve as an aide and secretary to Grant, accompanied him to the Executive Mansion when Grant became president in 1869.

In 1871 Orville Babcock had been given responsibility for public buildings, grounds, and works. To this end he pursued a thorough study of the public reservations. Elevating himself above Nathaniel Michler, his predecessor, Babcock complained in the *Annual Report of the Chief of Engineers* for 1871 that "no provision has been made for water in many of the squares and parks." In the next six years, under Babcock's direction, the city's public parks were drained; gas pipes laid for lamps; water pipes laid for irrigation, drainage, and drinking purposes; the walks traversing the parks graveled; and grounds planted and augmented with rustic furniture.

The Drainage System and the Monument Grounds

The apparatus for drainage was constructed on the Washington Monument grounds, which Babcock described as a "primary recipient" of the Potomac's overflow at high tide. Before his 1877 departure, Babcock in the annual report for 1876 referred to the newly drained and adorned monument grounds as follows: "The forming of these lakes, the roadway between them, and the extension of Virginia Avenue, amounting in all to about fifteen acres, has, without doubt, been very beneficial to the general health of the vicinity. Sheets of pure water, green lawns, and roadway now occupy the space formerly a marsh overgrown with vegetable matter." The ground removed in grading the hills surrounding the unfinished monument was transported to the developing park south of the President's House, creating an image of a flat plain stretching into the horizon.

Standing in front of the monument on the newly created public park and looking directly east, Babcock envisioned the mile-and-a-half stretch from the Capitol to the President's House as a unified landscape system. In the 1875 *Annual Report of the Chief of Engineers,* after reporting on the graveling of Armory Square, the plot of green fronting the Pennsylvania Railroad yards, Babcock wrote that "the walls and roads to [Armory Square] harmonize with those in the Smithsonian grounds, the idea being to make the line of the reservation extending from the Capitol to the Executive Mansion one continuous park." Two years later, the public reservations defined by 3rd Street, 4½ Street, Maine Avenue, and Missouri Avenue were drained, graded, and serviced by water and gas pipes. Thus the last gaps in the continuous chain of parks were filled in.

Parks, Squares, and Ellipses
The existing smaller public parks that were scattered throughout the rest of the city as satellites to the Mall also benefited in detail from Babcock's attentions. As an experiment, Babcock attempted to flatten the coarse unscreened gravel forming the public walkways in Lafayette Square with a 3,600-pound roller, only to replace the walkway later on with a finer grade of gravel. Rawlins Square to the west of the President's House was created in 1873 and subjected to the usual process of drainage, grading, laying of pipes, planting, and furnishing. It also received topsoil from the excavations of the new State, War and Navy Building.

To the east of the President's House, Babcock cleared Judiciary Square—which was used as a dumping ground by contractors and punctuated by wooden buildings that had once housed a government hospital and later (until 1874) had been used by the YWCA—as dramatically as his friend Shepherd had removed the Northern Lib-erty Market from Mount Vernon Square in 1872. An ellipse was carved into Farragut Square in anticipation of a statue, honoring the Civil War admiral, for which Babcock designed the pedestal. The trees and plants adorning all of these squares were gathered throughout the nation by George H. Brown, longtime landscape gardener for the Corps of Engineers. In addition, Babcock himself planned and stocked several minizoos made up of birds, deer, and prairie dogs.

THE HARBORS OF WASHINGTON AND GEORGETOWN

Babcock's fellow military engineer, S. T. Abert, was responsible for improving the Washington and Georgetown harbors and integrating them as parts of a permanent, year-round park along Babcock's envisioned "continuous" Mall. In the process of dredging the Potomac, depositing the material onto the flats, and thereby giving sharper definition to land south of the Washington Monument, Abert envisioned deepwater ports necessary to the commercial viability of the city and the extension of the city itself to the waterfront. The freshet of 1873 made it clear to the Board of Survey, created by Congress only one year earlier, that a permanent solution was needed to stabilize the wide expanse of land where the city gradually merged into the river. The general plan as adopted by the Board of Survey was to create a channel sufficiently deep for navigation on the east side of the river between Georgetown and Gravelly Point, the land reclaimed affording approximately "455 acres of land, most advantageously located, for Government purposes," as quoted in the *Annual Report of the Chief of Engineers* for 1875.

Abert also suggested that "much will be saved by making nature an auxiliary" in guiding the natural flow of the river, hindered at the time by Easby's Point (just below Rock Creek's juncture with the Potomac), by Analostan Island, and by the obstruction of Long Bridge. The effort to clear the river was commenced in 1874, when an appropriation was made to continue the dredging operation (initiated in 1869) above Long Bridge, with the material to be deposited on the flats behind the bulkhead of the proposed Washington wharves. Two years later, in 1876, and for several years thereafter, Abert supervised the splitting and removal of several large rocks in the Georgetown harbor by drilling and using nitroglycerine. This initial work, although predicting a radical improvement in the city's waterfront and parks system, remained of minor scope at Babcock's departure from Washington.

ALFRED B. MULLETT, SUPERVISING ARCHITECT

While Shepherd and Babcock worked strenuously to reshape existing lands and by reclamation to furnish new lands upon which the postbellum city would rise, Alfred B. Mullett provided the city with a major public building, an architecturally decisive indication of the federal government's commitment to the city of Washington and, as its rich facades and powerful physical form took shape between 1871 and 1888, a symbol marking the end to any further agitation to remove the capital city. Although Mullett was already working full-time as supervising architect of the Treasury, having succeeded his former Cincinnati associate Isaiah Rogers in 1866, he consented to take on the design for the new State, War and Navy Building at the request of Secretary of the Treasury George S. Boutwell and in consultation with Secretary of State Hamilton Fish. Mullett had already designed Second Empire federal government buildings in New York City, Boston, Chicago, St. Louis, Cincinnati, and Philadelphia, and they were well received by their sponsoring congressional delegations.

In 1870, at the age of thirty-six, Mullett thus found himself the much sought after designer of this public building. Born in Somerset County, England, he had immigrated with his parents to Cincinnati, Ohio, when he was eleven years old. After departing from Rogers's architectural office in Cincinnati in 1860, Mullett traveled through Europe, at the time considered a prerequisite for the architectural profession. In 1863 Mullett was appointed as a clerk in the Office of Construction under the supervising architect while Rogers held that position. In the next two years, Mullett traveled widely throughout the country inspecting federal government buildings and during this time was appointed assistant supervising architect.

In 1874, after serving for nine years as supervising architect, Mullett resigned that position because of poor relations with then Secretary of the Treasury Benjamin H. Bristow. Mullett also had become engulfed in extensive press coverage of the Board of Public Works and his ongoing relationship with Alexander Shepherd. Mullett continued to work on the State, War and Navy Building on a consulting basis, however, until the following year, when delays in the construction schedule prompted the War Department to take control of the project. Secretary of War William Belknap and his ally, Orville Babcock, managed to oust Mullett during a disagreement over funding, bringing in Colonel Thomas Lincoln Casey of the Corps of Engineers and his assistant Richard von Ezdorf to supervise the building's completion over the next twelve years.

The State, War and Navy Building designed by Alfred Mullett was not the first French Renaissance building in the city; it faced the James Renwick–designed Corcoran Gallery of Art, built in the late 1850s, and directly across Pennsylvania Avenue. Unlike the Renwick-designed building, however, Mullett's large and rich facades achieved a heightened sense of dominance and power in the city. The iron structural framework allowed increased floor-to-ceiling heights, giving the entire building a new sense of architectural scale. The tall mansard roof intensified this impression, which was further elaborated by the cast-iron crestings and iron sculpture work in the pediments. Designer Richard von Ezdorf provided the interior furnishings and decor with as rich and artistic a flavor as the exterior, creating "intricate designs," as Lawrence Wodehouse has written, "straight out of the baroque palaces of Austria and Germany." In the State, War and

Navy Building, the executive end of Pennsylvania Avenue acquired a palatial public building that both stimulated and fed the nation's postwar preoccupation with symbols of luxury.

The New Municipal Government: By Commission

The enormous unauthorized municipal debt accumulated by Alexander Shepherd during his term as a member of the Board of Public Works and the financial benefits reaped by his friends in the process caused great concern. By an act passed on June 20, 1874, Congress transferred local authority to three temporary commissioners. The commissioners were responsible for general administration of the city while the territorial government was being phased out and a

permanent system of municipal government was being developed. Based on the work of the temporary Board of Commissioners, a permanent board was established by the Organic Act of June 11, 1878. Among other things, this act provided for the federal government to contribute 50 percent of the municipal revenues needed to operate the city, a funding arrangement necessitated by the rising debts and municipal needs that had been created by Shepherd.

The new municipal government continued, through its various departments, to play an active role in upholding livability in the physical city. Its Board of Health, Office of Engineer Commissioner, Office of Surveyor, and Parking Commission directed teams of municipal employees in maintaining and cleansing the city,

The Eisenhower Executive Office Building When Completed in 1888 Was Known as the State, War and Navy Building. National Archives

reported accomplishments on an annual basis to the commissioners of the District of Columbia, prepared special reports, and promulgated regulations covering such subjects as building codes and sanitation standards for public markets. Under the direction of the commissioners, an officer of the Corps of Engineers, detailed by the president, was charged (as the 1874 *Annual Report of the Commissioners of the District of Columbia* stated) with the "work and repair and improvement of all streets, avenues, alleys, sewers, roads, and bridges of the District of Columbia," as well as performance of "all the duties heretofore devolved upon the Chief Engineer" of the territorial Board of Public Works.

The Board of Public Works was abolished only two days after President Grant named Lieutenant Richard L. Hoxie as a board member. To assure administrative and locational continuity between the defunct territorial government and the new commission form of government, the 1874 act provided that one of the three commissioners should be an army engineer. This position of engineer commissioner as an integral part of Washington's municipal government endured for more than eighty years. Hoxie was immediately appointed to the post of corps officer detailed to the commission. The newly arrayed commissioners occupied the former quarters of the Board of Public Works in the building at 214–216 John Marshall Place.

Thus the corps continued to be instrumental in planning new large-scale public work projects, creating the modern floodproof city, and ensuring the future desirability of the city for residential purposes in terms of clean water, the continuous system of parklands, and public edifices with which a nationwide citizenry could identify.

The Water Supply for Washington, Abundant and Clear

The Washington aqueduct, conceived and built by Montgomery C. Meigs in the 1850s, remained little changed in its essentials through to the early 1880s. The reservoirs fed by force-pump systems allowed the water network to accommodate residential expansion north of Florida Avenue, above the route of direct flow, and to increase the capacity of the network as the city grew. Water served not only the needs of the residential population but also the fire hydrants, drinking fountains, and ornamental fountains as well. Although observers recorded high praise for the city's water, the location, quantity, and quality of the supply were increasingly called into question. Because of the western source of the water and distributing system, water reached the parts of the city west of the Capitol first, often providing much inferior service to the residual areas east of the Capitol. And to be sure, as the city's western residential sections swelled and made increased demands on the existing water system, these western residents, too, complained of an inadequate and muddy water supply.

THE MCMILLAN RESERVOIR

Supplying Capitol Hill and the eastern sections of the city with water had first priority. In 1883 Major G. J. Lydecker began work on a new distributing reservoir on the heights of Washington, the site of Smith Spring, just east of Howard University. A large direct-line tunnel was drilled through solid rock under Rock Creek Park to the new reservoir. It was Lydecker's intention that water distributed from the new reservoir at Howard would flow directly to the eastern sections of the city at a greater elevation than was possible from the old reservoir. Work on the Howard University Reservoir, as well as its receiving and distributing mains, continued until 1888, when all activity at the site stopped for fifteen years. The system was not placed in full service until 1903. Renamed McMillan Reservoir, the new castellated structure utilized a slow sand filtration system for water purification.

The lack of water improvement activity for so many years partially abated in 1890, when the Corps of Engineers laid a large thirty-inch main along East Capitol Street, servicing housing developments as far east as the Anacostia River. Although this new main opened sections of the city to the east of the Capitol to denser populations, the pattern of the most desirable residential areas in the western half of the city had secured itself by the momentum of public commitments and private investment.

THE DAM ABOVE GREAT FALLS

Whereas new extensions to the existing system addressed the eastern section of the city, increasing the overall supply of water depended on raising the height of the water's fall at Great Falls. In 1881 Thomas Lincoln Casey, then a lieutenant colonel and engineer in charge of the Washington aqueduct, had recommended that the dam built from 1863 to 1867 halfway across the Potomac above Great Falls be completed to control the depth of water in the pool above. Casey's recommendation was echoed by Major Lydecker, who three years later urged that the dam be extended across Conn's Island (in the middle of the Potomac just above Great Falls) and the Virginia channel to the Virginia shore. By 1889 the dam was completed, inspiring Lieutenant Colonel George H. Elliott to declare (as quoted in the *Annual Report of the Chief of Engineers* for 1889) that the city was now "abundantly supplied with water," except where corrosion or the small size of city mains impeded its flow. In 1896, however, the demands of the city again outran the supply, forcing the raising of the Great Falls dam to "an elevation of 148 feet above mean tide at the Washington Navy Yard and its extension at that height across Conn's Island and the Virginia channel of the river," as D. D. Gaillard noted in the 1896 *Annual Report of the Chief of Engineers.*

Abundant water was not enough to ensure resident satisfaction with the city's supply. A study of Washington's water supply written by Thomas W. Symons in 1866 led him to declare that other American cities had cleaner water; he also reprinted testimonial letters from prominent physicians as to the urgent need for clean water in Washington. Viewing the extant system in its entirety, Symons observed that the 550 miles of the Potomac River, draining principally from the north and south branches, the Cacapon, the Shenandoah, and the Monocacy, collected pollu-

tants from the cultivated and fertilized lands along its route. Deforestation along the river had increased sediment-laden runoff into the river, especially during storms and heavy snows. In fact, the drainage from the watershed, estimated to number 9 million acres, had so polluted the waters that in the spring of 1888 the Dalecarlia receiving reservoir was thrown out of operation.

The effect of the muddy and impure water on the city's future extended beyond citizen reactions; it was viewed as a significant hindrance to the growth and development of the city. In summer the weather was at its calmest, the water was at its clearest, but the city was at its emptiest. As Lydecker said in the 1886 *Annual Report of the Chief of Engineers:* "It is during the period of the year that the water presents the worst appearance that the city is at its best, Congress is in session, all the Executive Departments are full-handed, and people from all over the country and the world flock to the Capital for the purpose of transacting business and enjoying its social pleasures."

THE DALECARLIA RESERVOIR AND DAM

In 1886 Symons suggested three strategies to cure the water quality ills of Washington: aeration of the water with a hydraulic ram, cleaning and paving the Dalecarlia receiving reservoir, and chemical purification. Four years later, Lieutenant Colonel George H. Elliott saw the problem more in terms of the water's turbid appearance than its fitness for human consumption. The most important improvement needed at the aqueduct was "to furnish the city with better water; or, since the water of the Potomac as brought from Great Falls is, I am convinced, perfectly wholesome at all times, it would be more correct to say with clearer water." With the view that the mingling of the drainage water from surrounding lands at the reservoir was the primary fault, Elliott constructed three diversion dams outside the Dalecarlia Reservoir, one each across Little Falls Branch, Mill Creek, and East Creek, to catch and throw off these waters from the cleaner waters received from Great Falls. By the end of the century, Washington's water supply was judged to be abundant, clear, and wholesome, a public improvement essential to the physical growth of the city.

Reclamation of the River Flats and the Creation of Public Parks

Although the upper Potomac supplied the growing city with water, the portion of river fronting the city proper detracted from the city's waterfront appearance, health, and commercial prospects. The dredging of channels and removal of rocks near the Georgetown harbors initiated by Nathaniel Michler in 1870 and continued by S. T. Abert for several years from 1876 received little serious attention from Congress and even less serious effort toward a permanent solution. Even the major freshet of 1877 that forced the coal merchants of Georgetown to dredge a temporary channel did not bring a change in the policy of temporary patchwork activity despite exhortations of the various army engineers charged with river improvements.

Above and below Long Bridge nearly three hundred acres of bare land extended, created by the sedimentation brought in by the seasonal freshets. These flats, alternately exposed and covered by the daily tides, were especially noxious near the south end of 17th Street, where the sewer main discharged into the Potomac. In 1879 army engineer Abert recommended that the flats be reclaimed by raising the ground one foot above the freshets, using dredged material; he also recommended that the street system be extended to the newly usable land. In Abert's plan, wharves constructed along the extended riverfront would be serviced by water depths of at least sixteen feet.

THE UNTAMED POTOMAC AND THE FLOOD OF 1881

The flood of February 1881 swept aside congressional hesitancy. The melting following a severe winter caused the Potomac to rise more than two feet over Long Bridge, pushing out three spans of the bridge onto the flats below. Although the low-lying portions of the city were accustomed to periodic flooding, as was noted in the 1881 *Annual Report of the Chief of Engineers,* "to an unprecedented extent, the low portion of the city along the Mall and extending across Pennsylvania Avenue was flooded, and a large amount of damage was caused by the flooding of the cellars and first floors." The flood waters swept just three blocks south of the President's House and over as far east as the Botanic Garden at the western edge of the Capitol grounds.

In a spectacular display, the untamed Potomac thus surged in full view of the executive and legislative branches. Added incentive to a radical departure from governmental indecision came in a report on the inferior and unsafe sanitary conditions of the President's House. In November of the flood year, the nationally reputed sanitary and public parks engineer George E. Waring reported that the improvement of the river and reclamation of the flats would be an essential condition to improving the drainage and sanitary requirements of the mansion. Waring regarded the nearly one thousand acres of flats that served as a lodging ground for sewage, the "low and saturated conditions of much of the city lying south of Pennsylvania Avenue," and the drainage from dwellings in the higher parts of Washington to the sewage swamp of the lowlands as part of the related problem of improving the Executive Mansion. Referring to the little-understood disease, malaria, Waring urged that the Corps of Engineers be "guided by our suspicions" and "accept as a common-sense guide of action the rule that all land in or near a town should be kept clean and dry." In filling the flats out to the Michler-proposed line of wharves, Waring envisioned a new public recreational area.

PETER C. HAINS AND THE ELLICOTT MAP

Rising to the task of taming the Potomac, Civil War hero Major Peter Conover Hains studied the river with engineer's and historian's eyes and undertook to direct the river's improvements over the next eight years. In 1883, reviewing the legislative history since 1804 with yearly appropriations of only tens of thousands of dollars for piecemeal improvements, Hains could readily detect the alarmed response of Congress to the 1881 flood, for suddenly the Congress began to appropriate hundreds of thousands of dollars for the reclamation process. More important, Hains looked at the history of the river as revealed in the historical maps, so that he could—as stated in the *Annual Report of the Chief of Engineers* for 1883—"form an idea of the changes that have taken place in the river during a period of less than a century." Referring to Andrew Ellicott's map, Hains pronounced it "the oldest map of the Potomac River in this vicinity" and noted that "the original is now preserved in the office of the Commissioner of Public Buildings and Grounds, but copies of it have been made at various times." The Ellicott map revealed three navigable channels fronting the city. Comparing this map with the 1834 map drawn by Lieutenant Colonel James Kearney of the Corps of Topographical Engineers, Hains detected a rapid shoaling process that had already erased two of the three channels. Summarizing additional studies and Potomac River surveys, Hains stated in the 1883 annual report: "The surveys enumerated here are themselves a history of the river. On the Ellicott map we trace the Washington or City Channel, not deep, it is true, though even above Seventeenth Street a stream of water large enough to be dignified by the name of a channel. . . . In a similar manner the growth of the flats may be traced."

THE WASHINGTON CHANNEL AND THE SLUICING PONDS

Against this legislative and topographical background of the river, Hains outlined the projected improvements as provided in the congressional act of August 1882 that appropriated $400,000. The 1872 plan of the congressional Board of Engineers that had guided Nathaniel Michler recommended that one all-purpose channel be dredged between Georgetown and Giesboro Point with the material simply dumped on the

flats. In 1879 Major William J. Twining, the engineer commissioner of the District of Columbia, modified the 1872 plan by leaving the Washington Channel open as far as Long Bridge and (as Hains stated in the 1883 annual report) constructing "sluicing basins for the purpose of purifying the water in that channel, which would otherwise become stagnant and offensive." Thus, the traditional and natural channel fronting Washington would be preserved and cleansed.

Twining envisioned the purifying sluicing basins as ornamental and projected hundreds of acres of parkland to be created out of the flats. Abert's recommendations of 1881 differed from those of Twining's only in details: the reclaimed land would rise six feet above low water and be enclosed by both a masonry wall resting on piles and riprap along its edges. As with other low-lying parkland throughout the city, this reclaimed land was to be drained by pipes. In 1882 the Board of Engineers recommended to Congress that the permanent improvement be a combination of Twining's and Abert's plans—Twining's sluicing ponds and Abert's filling and embankments.

RECLAMATION OF THE POTOMAC FLATS: THE PROJECT BEGINS, 1882

In the late summer of 1882, Hains began the vast reclamation project according to recommendations of the congressional Board of Engineers, providing in the following year a map of the areas to be reclaimed. Four irregularly shaped flushing lakes were to be joined by meandering walkways, extending from B Street south to the farthest end of the reclaimed area, the ground to be landscaped by clusters of trees. As the dredging process continued, a temporary railroad was built from the outer edge of the fill to the sewer canal so that the dredged material could be deposited on the flats. Four years later, in 1886, Hains modified Twining's four lakes to one large tidal reservoir between Long Bridge and the sewer canal. This reservoir, later named the Tidal Basin, measured "not less than 8 feet deep" and was intended to supply fresh water to the Wash-

Reclamation of the Potomac Flats Using the McNee Dredge, 1891. *Scientific American,* September 19, 1891

ington Channel. A smaller reservoir was constructed near the foot of 17th Street to flush the sewer canal. The Tidal Basin was provided with inlet and outlet gates to flush sewage accumulated along the Washington Channel to the open waters of the Potomac. By the end of the decade, most of the reclaimed area—appended to the Washington Monument grounds—was filled in, awaiting the construction of embankments and landscaping. Dredging activity along the channel and the Tidal Basin continued to the end of the decade and afterward.

Litigation Begins: Morris et al. v. United States
As early as 1882, when Congress was discussing appropriations to be made for the reclamation work, legislators anticipated that individuals and corporations would claim rights to the land. John L. Kidwell and his family owned forty-nine acres of marshland, "Kidwell's Meadows," just south of the Naval Observatory at 23rd Street. Representing more than fifty claimants, including Kidwell's family and the descendents of Chief Justice John Marshall, the case of *Martin F. Morris et al., appellants v. United States* began in the District courts in 1886. The case persisted in the courts for the next dozen years, causing both sides to scrutinize carefully the legislative and topographical history of the District's land holdings and subdivisions. Finally, in 1898 the US Supreme Court made the definitive decision sus-

taining the government's rights to the lands south of Water Street. The Supreme Court also referred to the 1886 congressional appropriation for the reclamation work and its additional provision for compensation to be made for "the private property of individuals situated within the lines of the Government improvement." These compensations, to be settled by the District courts according to estimated values of the land exclusive of improvements, were made possible by the 1896 District appropriation bill, which included over $26.5 million to be paid to the Potomac flats claimants.

THE RECLAIMED LAND AND CREATION OF POTOMAC PARK
As the government's authority over the land neared this confirmation, discussion arose over the use of the land. The push by private real estate interests for subdivision was supported by the example of Boston's Back Bay, which had been similarly reclaimed and transformed into a residential enclave. Commercial interests also argued for such a subdivision of land in Washington because the profits from the sale would reimburse the government for the cost of reclamation.

In the civic atmosphere then current, however, when Rock Creek Park and the Mall, not to mention the many neighborhood parks, were gaining clearer definition as vital elements in the capital city, Charles Glover and other Washington leaders pushed successfully for designation of the reclaimed land as parkland. In 1897, shortly before the final Supreme Court decision, Congress set aside the 621 acres of reclaimed flats and the 118 acres of tidal reservoirs as "Potomac Park . . . to be forever held and used as a park for the recreation and pleasure of the people." (This designation was duly recorded in the *Annual Report of the Chief of Engineers* for 1897.)

The Beginning of the Modern City
Historically, the creation of Potomac Park marked a major departure from the pattern of original public reservations as provided by L'Enfant and elaborated by the Corps of Engineers up to 1874. It was the beginning of the modern city. The filling in of the original boundaries of Washington City inside Boundary Street and the growth of suburban tracts in the District of Columbia, Maryland, and Virginia encouraged the Corps of Engineers to respond to major community interest and seek new areas for landscaped park development. This would maintain the garden city character of the capital and secure the balance between open space and built-up area. Thus, the search for new expanses of parkland outside the L'Enfant city paralleled a significant tidying up of the parkland within the original city.

The creation in 1888 of the National Zoological Park on the western bank of Rock Creek revived Michler's and the community's hopes for the great park along the creek. A congressional bill also inspired by the banker Charles Carroll Glover passed two years later, allowing for the purchase of 2,500 acres. In the following years, more acreage was acquired, greatly satisfying President Theodore Roosevelt and encouraging the philanthropic Glover in the twentieth century to create for public use similar strips of parkland in other sections of the city.

FEDERAL FUNCTIONS IN VIRGINIA
Although Congress had ceded the Virginia section of the original ten-mile square District of

Columbia back to the Commonwealth in 1846, the area had proved of little interest to Richmond. On the other hand, federal occupation of this southern position of the original ten-mile square District of Columbia during the Civil War—and thereafter in the form of military posts and Arlington National Cemetery—served to define the general area within which federal functions were maintained.

From Aqueduct Bridge down the Potomac to Mount Vernon, the traditional tidewater land-

Aqueduct Bridge in Georgetown, ca. 1870. Peter R. Penczer Collection

Procession along
Pennsylvania Avenue
on the Occasion of the
Dedication of the
Washington Monument,
February 21, 1885.
Robert A. Truax Collection

scape still exhibited plantation houses on head-
lands overlooking the river. In 1889 Congress
directed Colonel Hains to survey this historic
area in search of an appropriate "National Road."

Since the new boundary established in 1846
between the District of Columbia and Virginia
was located on the Virginia shoreline of the
Potomac River at the high water mark, any
reclaimed land along the Virginia shoreline
would be under federal jurisdiction. Thus of the
three main routes surveyed by Hains, one was
along the river. That route could be viewed as a
precursor to what became the George Washington Memorial Parkway. Like Lake Shore Drive in
Chicago, this also would be one of the major
parkway projects constructed in America, sym-

bolizing the conquest of space along powerful
natural features. No matter which route was
selected along the Potomac, Hains intended it to
be always in the process of development and
embellishment. Envisioned as having a monumental character, the proposed "National Road"
was a symbolic link between the Mount Vernon
estate, the site so closely associated with George
Washington, and the city that bore his name.

THE MALL: ROMANTIC VISION OR COMPREHENSIVE PLAN?

The romantic vision of the Mall as a continuous
string of informal parks enunciated by Downing
in 1851, and reinforced by Michler and Babcock,
persisted to the end of the century, when the

1901–1902 McMillan Plan proposed a return to the L'Enfant vision of a broad, formal greensward extending from the Capitol to the Washington Monument. By 1900, from the Botanic Garden westward to the monument grounds, the parks developed in response to this romantic vision were considered to be separate public areas that composed the Mall as a whole: the Botanic Garden, a trapezoidal configuration at the foot of the Capitol; Seaton Park, two smaller trapezoids; Armory Square, a rectangular park flanked on the east by the Pennsylvania Railroad yards; the Smithsonian Pleasure Grounds, those carefully landscaped grounds that served as a model for public parks citywide; the Department of Agriculture grounds of landscape quality approaching that of the Smithsonian grounds; and the monument grounds, a rectangular park centered (by 1885) by the completed memorial shaft and merging at its southern end into the area being developed into what was to become the Tidal Basin and Potomac Park.

Frederick Law Olmsted Sr., familiar with the city from his position on the US Sanitary Com-mission during the Civil War, had been appointed to design the Capitol grounds. Existing parks on the Mall represented many bureaus, each employing its own architects, surveyors, and gardeners and each responsible to independent congressional committees. This situation seemed to Olmsted "absurd and wasteful." Olmsted urged his most steadfast congressional supporter, Senator Justin Morrill, that "before anything more is done in regard to any particular ground an effort should be made to simplify and consolidate the present organizations and bring all these grounds into subordination to a comprehensive scheme." Such a scheme would remain elusive for the next quarter century.

THE OLMSTED PLAN FOR THE CAPITOL GROUNDS

Although the Mall's reservations would be subject to changing notions as to their overall design, Olmsted's new grounds and terracing of the Capitol's west front has remained admired and has survived challenges by later arbiters of taste—including his son, whose proposals would

US Capitol Grounds prior to Implementation of the Olmsted Plan, Late 1860s. Library of Congress

be contained in the McMillan Plan. Conceived as an adjunct to the Capitol Building, the grounds as designed by Frederick Law Olmsted Sr. were cleared of the dense forest of decaying trees that had obscured the building from full view. The grounds were refurnished with symmetrically placed and winding walks, with a thin shield of trees ringing the base of the building's new display platform. A grand architectural terrace was completed in 1892, resembling Olmsted's Bethesda terrace in New York's Central Park. The terrace in front of the Capitol served as an unfolding invitation to the building itself and as an improved platform from which to view the expanse of the city. With Olmsted's design for the west front, the Mall could no longer serve as the "backyard" of the Capitol. Until the reclamation process solved what Olmsted termed the "miasma" problem, he proposed a thick belt of trees placed south of the Capitol grounds, as "an efficient means of protection to the Capitol from malarial poison originating on the banks of the Potomac."

PARKS AND HISTORIC LANDMARKS

In planning for the expansion of public parks into new physical areas beyond the borders of the city of Washington, as well as rethinking the forms and functions of park areas within the city, the Corps of Engineers absorbed new types of public properties and sites, then designated simply as public buildings. Current terminology would classify these properties as historic landmarks, and even when they were acquired in the 1890s, they were already seen as objects evoking great patriotic sentiment. In 1893, when Ford's Theatre collapsed, the Corps of Engineers took on their first property. Subsequently, the Petersen House, scene of Lincoln's death, the monument to George Washington at Wakefield, Virginia, and the national military park at Gettysburg, Pennsylvania, were added in response to citizens' landmark preservation efforts. The acquisition of these buildings and sites, responding initially to a preservation motive, inaugurated the federal government's

more explicit commitment to properties of historical value, later institutionalized in the National Park Service.

THEODORE A. BINGHAM AND THE PUBLIC SPACES

By the end of the decade, the corps's responsibility for public buildings and grounds as defined by Congress had expanded well beyond the Mall and the satellite parks, growth centers envisioned by L'Enfant. This expansion demanded a new comprehensive policy and program so that parks and other public properties would become an integrated part of the city's image. Colonel Theodore A. Bingham thought himself equal to the development of new plans and policies. Bingham was born in Andover, Connecticut, on May 14, 1858. Graduating from West Point in 1879, he rose through the military ranks, serving as an engineer officer in various locations. Important for his later Washington work, he was military attaché at the US legation in Berlin from 1890 to 1892 and in Rome the two years following. Transferred to the Corps of Engineers' Public Building and Grounds post in 1897, he remained there until 1903.

Reporting on public grounds in the District of Columbia, Bingham revealed new interests in a dramatic change from the preoccupations with mere maintenance that were characteristic of many of his predecessors. In a sense, Bingham's interests presaged the work of the 1901 McMillan Commission. In Bingham's view (as quoted in the *Annual Report of the Chief of Engineers* for 1901), "Washington [was] not the most beautiful and attractive city in America." He was dissatisfied with the appearance of the city's public and monumental spaces and with the lack of a strong commitment by the federal government to allocate adequate funds for embellishing its green "breathing spaces." Moreover, officials from park agencies in other cities voiced similar disappointment with the capital city's system of parks that should rightly be a "model in what pertains to time development, improvement, and maintenance of parks." Washington's park system was expected to provide both model and inspiration for improved park systems in cities throughout the nation, to elevate the taste of all visitors. On the local level, park improvements were also important amenities for the city's resident population. Echoing the often repeated needs for parks, Bingham stated in the 1897 annual report that parks were crucial in the "promotion of mental growth and cultivating a love for horticulture, arboriculture, and floriculture among our people, who congregate here from all sections of our country." Bingham's style and rhetoric were impressive even if the ideas were already a half century old.

"A Little Touch of the Outside Country"

Colonel Bingham's reports on the shortcomings of the capital's park system reflected the ideals of the national Progressive movement that viewed the physical environment as critical in determining social behavior. By the end of the century, urban life could be depicted by the crowding together of toiling masses, suffering "intellectual degradation and physical degradation" from the demands of city life. In an atmosphere of charity and goodwill, however, enlightened public officials attempted to resolve these social problems by providing "a little touch of the outside country," in much the same spirit that public servants concerned themselves with "the study and conquest of epidemic diseases, the increase and purification of [the] water supply, and the introduction and improvement of drainage systems" as prerequisites to moral improvement. So went the prose of the *Annual Report of the Chief of Engineers* for 1898.

Anticipating a bright future for the resolution of social problems as the new century dawned, Bingham made specific suggestions on Washington's parks, economy dictating that "the parks in and around Washington should form a systematic and well considered whole." The newly created Potomac flats should form, Bingham thought, "the western end of the beautiful system planned by the originators of the city, to extend from the Capitol to the Potomac River," unifying the Mall area. Bingham recommended in the annual report for 1899 that the Botanic Garden

be "thrown open, improved by walks and drives, and made a part of [the Mall]." The much-neglected eastern section of the city, especially the Anacostia flats, deserved development as a balance to the formally designed western sections. Washington's "subtropical climate" demanded more public fountains, Bingham thought, not only as a respite to the summer weather, but also as "a rest to mind and body." And, further justifying increased governmental funding for park development and embellishment, Bingham called attention to the fact that, when compared to expenditures by other cities the size of Washington, the capital city's expenditures for parks were meager indeed.

Recognition of L'Enfant as the First City Surveyor

A January 1898 Senate resolution directed the chief of engineers to assess the "numbers and locations of all lots in the District of Columbia the title to which the records in the Office of the Commissioner of Public Buildings and Grounds show to be in the United States," in order that legal issues over property rights might be resolved. Among the pertinent documents collected was L'Enfant's 1791 manuscript plan. Bingham listed this manuscript plan in 1900 as only one in a long list of documents transferred, under the March 2, 1867, act, from the commissioner of public buildings to the chief of engineers.

In reviewing the papers in the custody of the chief of engineers, especially the early records of the city, Bingham was the initial member of the Corps of Engineers explicitly to credit L'Enfant with the role as "first United States city surveyor" and the first to lay out the city. Any similar recognition by Bingham's predecessors in the corps during the years after the Civil War must be assumed from the actual fulfillment of many L'Enfant plan proposals regarding streets and public parks. Further evidence of interest in the plan was demonstrated in popular publications, such as *Harper's New Monthly Magazine,* which acknowledged the origins and brilliance of the

plan. With renewed interest in L'Enfant's design, especially among those in government circles, began the twentieth century's reverence for the city's first planner and the original intentions of his plan, standards against which all future improvements to the city would be compared.

The Corps of Engineers' responsibilities for public buildings in the post-1874 era were primarily maintenance and improvement of the President's House, with the Government Printing Office and the historic landmarks or shrines as later concerns. As for construction of new public buildings, in the case of the State, War and Navy Building, the corps entered the project after Mullett's plan had been approved and after the War Department had taken charge of the project. Although Colonel Casey as superintendent of construction did little to change the building's design, his assistant Richard von Ezdorf left his mark on the interior details and furnishings.

Public Buildings in the Century's Last Decades

Three additional major public buildings constructed in the post–Civil War era reflected the vision of members of the Corps of Engineers. By special invitation, Montgomery C. Meigs provided designs for the new National Museum (now the Arts and Industries Building), south of the Mall adjoining the original Smithsonian Building, and the Pension Building in the Judiciary Square complex. In both instances, Meigs was chosen for these projects because his diligent public work had won him a good professional reputation among members of building committees. Contrasting with the white classicism of Washington's public buildings constructed before the Civil War, these monumental structures were of red brick. The National Museum's design as adapted by the German-born architect-engineer Adolph Cluss exemplified the polychromatic possibilities of glazed brick, whereas the Pension Building was embellished by Casper Buberl's continuous terra-cotta frieze depicting a procession of Civil War soldiers and sailors. The construction of the Library of Congress in the last three

The Library of Congress, the US Capitol Grounds as Redesigned by Frederick Law Olmsted Sr., and Horatio Greenough's Statue of George Washington, ca. Late 1890s. National Archives

years of the century represented a return to the light-hued classical model for public buildings, although the library's design involved greater elaboration than was characteristic of the pre–Civil War era. The execution of this building involved the talents of private architects J. L. Smithmeyer, Paul J. Pelz, and Edward Pearce Casey, as well as the latter's father, Colonel Thomas L. Casey of the Corps of Engineers.

GROWTH OF THE FEDERAL BUREAUCRACY

With the construction of these major public buildings, the federal government committed itself to the future of Washington as the national capital city. By the end of the century, conditions were ripe for further amplification of the built city by Colonel Bingham and later on by the McMillan Commission. In fact, in Bingham's 1900 report, he stated that, as of June 1900, he was instructed to the "work of making an examination and reporting plans for the treatment of [the newly floodproofed lowlands] section of the District of Columbia situated south of Pennsylvania Avenue and north of B Street, S.W." Improvement of this area had already begun a

few years earlier when the new Romanesque Post Office, designed under the supervision of the supervising architect Willoughby J. Edbrooke, rose out of the deteriorated commercial neighborhood at Pennsylvania Avenue and 12th Street.

The relatively small number of federal government buildings masked the actual growth of the federal bureaucracy in Washington after the Civil War. For example, between 1881 and 1891 the total number of federal employees in Washington rose 50 percent—from 13,124 to 20,834. Department and bureau employees spilled over into many private buildings originally constructed for private commercial functions. Indeed, the federal government's high rent bills served as a powerful impetus for new public building construction in the following century.

COMMERCIAL STRUCTURES AND RETAIL THOROUGHFARES

Private commercial structures, often housing public functions, clustered along the north side of Pennsylvania Avenue and stretched farther northward to G Street, eastward to Judiciary Square, and as far west as 15th Street. The major

Labor Day Parade Showing the Unfinished Post Office Building at 12th Street and Pennsylvania Avenue, ca. 1894. Library of Congress

The Franklin School at 13th and K Streets NW, Home to the World's First Wireless Telephone Call in 1880, in a Photograph by Titian Peale, ca. 1867. Negative N-81-7799, Photographic History Collection, National Museum of American History, Smithsonian Institution

streets devoted to the retail trade—Pennsylvania Avenue, 7th Street, and F Street—were served by the streetcar system, described by an observer in 1875 as "neutralizing the magnificent distances." Pennsylvania Avenue was the first street in the city devoted to commercial purposes, but its low and often flooded location caused its more prosperous merchants and the builders of office blocks to seek higher ground, notably along F Street, the first ridge of highland rising from the lowland basin. Moreover, although the activity surrounding the Center Market at 7th Street and Pennsylvania Avenue had spawned the thriving business thoroughfares to the north along 7th Street, the noise and congestion led many business establishments to leave the avenue. Along the city's major new retail thoroughfares, struc-

tures of decorative cast iron, granite, and brick rose on building lots originally devoted to residential and mixed residential-commercial activities. The regularization of the iron frame permitted enlarged commercial building heights and presented a new awesome image in Washington to match that in other American cities.

EXCELLENCE IN BUILDING DESIGN

The rise of outstanding school buildings marked not only the expanding population but also a concern for an improved physical environment and the high quality of public education in Washington. Most indicative of educational excellence were the school designs that Adolph Cluss provided for the Wallach School in 1864, the Franklin School in 1869, and the Sumner

School in 1872. These buildings—Franklin and Wallach for white students and Sumner for black students—represented both a social and a structural departure from the flimsy frame buildings or rented facilities in church basements that had been utilized for schools in Washington before the Civil War. The construction of the new "citadels of democracy" indicated, as Tanya Edwards Beauchamp points out, an "initial step in the modernization of the city . . . and a promise of better things to come." Cluss, abreast of the latest building materials on hand and conversant with innovative school design in America and Europe, provided the city's children with structures that embodied modern concern for safety, expanded teaching and learning facilities, climate control, healthy conditions, and adequate lighting. The success of these pioneer schools in the city was remarkable.

Starting in 1874, with the commission form of municipal government, the engineer commissioner's department was responsible for public works in the city. The position of inspector of buildings was created in 1878, and this inspector reported to the engineer commissioner. The inspector of buildings supervised the design and construction of new municipal buildings and the repair of existing buildings, including school buildings. The school buildings constructed in the 1880s and 1890s were not intended to rival the celebrated Cluss school buildings but were nevertheless functional and economical and exhibited the latest developments in building materials and techniques. The elementary schools were red brick "boxes," usually two stories in height, with stone, brick, pressed metal, and terra-cotta embellishments. The floor plans were arranged in a "pin-wheel" form that provided for a classroom at every corner.

The growth of the District of Columbia's school system, in terms of both sheer numbers of buildings constructed yearly and new residential populations that they were to serve, was a major barometer for the physical growth of the city. In 1874 the separate school systems for Washington City, Georgetown, and Washington County were merged into a single entity. The schools operated under a single board composed of both white and black members. The black schools continued to function under an independent black superintendent and the white schools under a white superintendent. The segregated public school system was reinforced after the Civil War and endured until the Supreme Court decision in 1954 that banned segregated public schools nationwide. Public school buildings for black and white students were nearly identical at the elementary school level and often were located only a few blocks from one another throughout the city.

In 1882 Washington High School was constructed for white students; in 1891 the M Street High School was constructed for black students. Both were sizable brick buildings. By the end of the century, Western High School was completed in 1898 at the western boundary of Georgetown for white students and was a Classical Revival building sited on a substantial campus. It was in the provision of junior high schools and senior high schools that the "separate but equal" rule broke down. The white schools were larger, had more amenities, and were located on larger plots of land than the facilities provided for black students.

Like schools, churches constructed in the post–Civil War era reflected the cultural needs of the growing population. Second only to federal office buildings, Washington's churches were the chief public buildings, fronting on many of the principal sites L'Enfant had originally provided. The architectural design of church structures was assertive and in many instances hotly competitive. In the residential communities, churches were the largest and most visible buildings and thus contributed most to the community identity. The nineteenth century was not yet the time when Episcopalians, Roman Catholics, Mormons, Presbyterians, and others would erect in Washington symbolic edifices that would associate their national institutional prestige with the national capital city. Yet the churches of the day in the central city did aspire as churches and some as national shrines and religious centers; at

16th Street and Columbia Road, half a dozen faiths scrutinized each other. Mammon had put his stamp on these buildings, dictating their highly visible location and fashionable appearance. In the future, this great interest in a prominent central location notwithstanding, the churches often unresistingly followed their wealthy parishioners to the higher ground of suburban Washington.

During this period, colleges and universities—in addition to Howard University—began to make their mark on the city. Founded in 1789, Georgetown University had a modest presence until the end of the nineteenth century, when Healy Hall was designed by Smithmeyer and Pelz and constructed over a period of decades. Its soaring two hundred-foot central clock spire could be seen throughout the city. Columbian College (now George Washington University) was founded in 1821, and its campus was located on College Hill north of Florida Avenue. After

the Civil War, the college discovered its niche in serving as an evening school for federal government employees and moved its campus to H Street, between 13th and 15th streets, in the heart of the city's financial district. Gallaudet College for deaf students was founded in 1856 on Kendall Green in the northeast quadrant of the city, but its major campus plan by Olmsted and Vaux and buildings were not designed until after the Civil War. Catholic University was founded in 1887 and American University in 1893, but their major construction programs awaited the twentieth century.

Residential Washington and the Growth of Suburbs

The designer of so much of the postbellum cityscape, Adolph Cluss, also participated in the remarkable growth of residential areas of the city. Himself a resident of the architecturally pleasing Judiciary Square neighborhood—cen-

tered on Hadfield's City Hall and Meigs's Pension Building—Cluss developed close friendships with major speculators in his position as a member of Shepherd's Board of Public Works between 1872 and 1874. A result of these friendships was played out in Shepherd's investment activity, not only in the "Row" that bore his name facing Farragut Square, but also in other blocks in the vicinity of rapidly developing Dupont Circle. Shepherd's own house had been designed by Cluss. So also in 1873, "Stewart's Castle," on Dupont Circle at the intersection of Connecticut and Massachusetts avenues, was designed by Cluss. This structure acted like a magnet, attracting similar sumptuous dwellings to be constructed nearby on ground that had been, before the 1870s, an open stretch of commons characterized by swamps and shanties. The process of residential growth was abetted by two developments: Congressmen who now attended sessions of longer duration and therefore

brought their families to Washington were interested in residences of greater permanency than the boarding houses on Capitol Hill or along Pennsylvania Avenue; also, America as an emerging world power attracted a growing diplomatic corps that needed suitable accommodations.

Dupont Circle and Kalorama
The purchase of the building site at the northwest corner of Connecticut Avenue and N Street for the British Embassy further established this clustering around Dupont Circle of luxurious structures commissioned by wealthy and important clients. "In one fell swoop, wealth, political power and diplomacy made this area highly desirable as a residential area." It is interesting to note that although it lay within the walking city, the Dupont Circle area in its heyday was poorly served by public transportation; residents had to be of sufficient means, therefore, to provide their own.

Women on Bicycles, ca. 1890. The Historical Society of Washington, DC

As a neighborhood for those who had earned their wealth elsewhere in the country and had come to settle or even retire in a congenial but politically powerful milieu, Dupont Circle set the pattern for nearby residential development for many years to follow. Henry Adams could have set his novel *Democracy* here rather than on Lafayette Square. And the expansion continued. In the 1880s, a Philadelphia syndicate of speculators moved into the northwest quadrant along Massachusetts and Connecticut avenues onto the old Kalorama estate, considered to be of great natural beauty, chopping out blocks of subdivisions that were fortuitously shaped by the land a particular owner was willing to sell. Erasing the startling contrast between the "unimproved" Kalorama property and the handsome houses that studded Massachusetts Avenue near Rock Creek, the frantic pace of development between 1890 and World War I left the area with an irregular street plan. Some subdivisions followed the Washington grid adopted in 1888 and reinforced in 1893, whereas others were constrained by the contours of the former estate grounds.

For residents of more modest means, the vast majority of whom were ordinary civil servants, Dupont Circle and Kalorama were beyond reach financially. But there were many alternatives. The growing concentration of the city within the original city limits encouraged groups of speculators to settle the Capitol Hill expanse or more probably to look beyond the old city boundary into the highlands of the District of Columbia.

The Row House and the Constituent City
Life in mid-nineteenth-century Washington was marked by a certain comfortable congestion reinforced by the increasing predominance of the row houses. The characteristic type is illustrated by the Petersen House, where Lincoln died. Its origins were solidly planted in the eighteenth-century town houses built in cities along the East Coast. Washington was at the southern end of this region, below which the more distinctively southern house types appeared. From the town-

house type evolved the commercial builder's row house, built in the southern parts of Washington in developments at the scale of a block or even larger areas. Thus, the row house enunciates the true urban vernacular that ultimately produced the constituent city, in contrast to the monumental, official city of Washington. As this city expanded to the north, especially after the coming of the streetcar, whole districts were covered by the characteristic row houses. Brookland, Park View, Petworth, Mount Pleasant, and even Woodley Park were communities whose names were emblazoned on streetcars as destinations. The row-house type also appeared at larger scale on undeveloped lots and blocks at the fringe of the old river-bottom city.

In its typical expression, the row house stood on a full basement. The house was entered from a porch, which as time went on evolved from a stoop or landing with heavy iron railings into a fully developed living porch with room for furniture, swings, grass rugs, lamps, awnings, and other amenities. The earlier red brick was supplanted by lighter hues, and the porch took on Greek Revival overtones. Heating was initially provided by coal-burning stoves, the most popular type being called a latrobe (from its designer), semicircular in form with isinglass doors, and fitted into a fireplace. Illumination came from gas fixtures, in their prime from the Welsbach mantle. The first floor contained a parlor, dining room, pantry, and kitchen opening onto a back porch and yard surrounded by a six-foot board fence. The second and perhaps a third floor were typically given over to bedrooms, although it was not uncommon for larger houses to provide a library or den on the second foot, as a more secluded living or family room. Before the era of the automobile, the residential street was a public environment of continuing interest. The sidewalk offered space for children to play hopscotch, jump rope, tag, statues, and other games, all supervised by the parental eye—from the porch. The row or the block had its distinctive life, its individual characters, its behavior, its morale. Such streets, with their gas lamps, their summertime life in the humid heat of the city, their local standards of removing snow and trash, were found throughout the constituent city of Washington.

Design Vernacular and the Builder's Art

As a design vernacular, the row house was the product of tradition. It was improved by the carpenters and masons, practical builders, and those who graduated from these skills to the entrepreneurial ranks. Progress in design was the result of piecemeal improvements to tradition in building materials, construction techniques, household services, and living habits. Many of the characteristics of the row house were the result of building regulations or codes. When central heating arrived, houses had to have basements for furnaces. The use of air shafts and "notches" provided air and light for interior rooms, especially the little-used "blind dining room." As gas and later electricity were provided, the use of candles and lamps declined. Many design changes were experimental, and some were short-lived fads. The popularity of the front porch was one of the more durable reforms in row-house design. The vestibule, often paved and walled with ceramic tile, and the hallway itself were reinterpreted by successive generations of builders. And in Washington, as in London or nearby Baltimore, it was the large estates encircled by urbanization that provided the principal sites for row housing.

NEIGHBORHOOD LIFE IN WASHINGTON

The population was thus accommodated in a product of the builder's art that expressed the economies and technology of a highly competitive business. That Washington was predominantly a brick city, again like Baltimore and Philadelphia, was ordained by its clay banks gradually being consumed now by brickyards reaching from the Anacostia around to Arlington. The row house possessed the inherent economies of the party wall. Using limited amounts of space with great efficiency, it was eminently suited to the requirements of the

Tenallytown Trolley Car, Early 1890s. The Historical Society of Washington, DC

walking city and later the streetcar city. Many of the most desirable residential streets lay off some principal artery where the trolley car had spawned a commercial strip containing the essential shops and services and frequently churches and schools. Consumer services were seasonally supplemented by the street peddlers, who enlivened the residential streets and heralded the advent of strawberries and watermelons, Potomac shad and saltwater trout, with characteristic cries, and provided such essential services as mending umbrellas, sharpening knives and scissors, or collecting old clothes, bottles, rags, and papers. Along the street at appropriate times came the newsboy to hurl his product onto the porch, the garbage man with his horn, the iceman or baker's cart, the ice-cream vendor or the popcorn and peanut man, and the purveyor of bananas or flavored snowballs made to order of shaved ice.

The distinctive and durable neighborhood with its traditional form of housing was rocked and shaken by the advent of the automobile and the illusion that everyone could live in verdant villas in the suburbs. Enough of these neighborhoods survived, however, to respond to the demand for rejuvenated in-town communities and neighborhood conservation, and the houses were flexible enough in plan to stand being reoriented from the street to the backyard, now become a garden. The row house also inspired the revived vogue for town houses.

Washington in the latter half of the nineteenth century did not develop vast areas of low-income slums. Rather, the poor lived in communities with the rich and middle classes, occupying the characteristic dwellings in alleys that were generated by the large blocks and long lots of the city. These dwellings stood side by side with carriage houses, stables, woodsheds, privies, and commercial structures for services such as horseshoeing. Around the corner from the well-to-do families at Logan Circle or Massachusetts Avenue were the narrow-fronted little clapboard houses of the less prosperous. Black and white, rich and poor, were mingled in almost every block, each housed according to his own circumstances. Only after 1900 did the separation of races and classes take the accentuated form known in most recent times—a reflection of the segregation in employment, in urban life, and, indeed, in the modern city itself.

Capitol Hill: Durability and Restraint
Representing the eastern extension of the row-house speculator's dream, Capitol Hill benefited little from Shepherd's or succeeding public improvements. Grand residences developed by Captain Albert Grant along A Street and East Capitol Street caused a faint flurry of anticipation that this section would become one of the finest residential neighborhoods in the city. In 1871, however, when the British legation considered securing two of Grant's houses, the developer's unwillingness to remove the adjoining partitions sent the legation to look elsewhere, thus relegating Capitol Hill to clients of more modest means. These residents continued to rely on wells, springs, and an unpredictable supply from the city's waterworks. In fact, until the completion of the East Capitol Street water main, the route of the city's water supply originating in the west subjected the eastern half of the city to constant threats of a water shortage—

and this actually occurred in 1889. Thus, although Capitol Hill lured a few residents of wealth, the area increasingly was staked out by people of modest means who could not afford to live in the more lavishly supplied and accommodated (and commensurately priced) western sections. The blocks of tidy brick row houses on Capitol Hill were constructed not only for transients but also for the "stable middle class." Despite the physical isolation from the rest of the city, the Capitol Hill community that developed during the last quarter of the nineteenth century typified the values of a secure permanent population in houses of modest cost, durability, and restraint in detail.

Expansion of the City Northward:
Mount Pleasant
The growing middle-class population of Washington gradually looked northward into the highlands in the District, to higher altitudes where one could escape the heat and congestion of the basin city. In 1865 Maine-born S. P. Brown divided his farmland along 14th Street—with a commanding view of the city—into a subdivision that he called Mount Pleasant. This first subdivision to be created after the Civil War attracted a "large number of gentlemen, mainly clerks in the government employ" bound together by a common New England heritage, who wanted homes in the suburbs of Washington. They were attracted to Mount Pleasant by the convenience of the site to a streetcar line, laid out in 1862 and stretching as far north on 14th Street as Boundary Street (current Florida Avenue). Mount Pleasant also was within range of the walking city. Settlers there built their own detached frame homes around a village green on oddly tilting cross streets west of the major north-south street. Despite the subdivision's proximity to the downtown, the residents were far enough away from the urban orientation to form their own community with strong self-identity. A virtually separate suburban village, Mount Pleasant developed its own social institutions: Bible classes, parties, entertainment, and

the inevitable citizens' association. This identity was physically revealed in Mount Pleasant's irregular business and residential street system and was patriotically celebrated in a history of its first decade written by its citizens' association on the occasion of the nation's centennial.

Columbia Heights

Other suburban subdivisions followed, spreading according to the dictates of transportation lines along 14th Street, 7th Street, and the Baltimore & Ohio Railroad, with the Rock Creek Park gorge an effective western boundary to development until it was bridged for heavy traffic in the early 1890s. Columbia Heights developed in the 1880s along 14th Street, taking advantage of its proximity to Meridian Hill Park and Columbian College, and was serviced by the streetcar line that had been extended north of Florida Avenue. In addition to the advantages of a higher altitude and lower summer temperatures, the physical arrangement initially offered much open space.

LeDroit Park, Brookland, and Petworth

LeDroit Park, developed along 7th Street in the 1870s, offered the amenities of the "suburbs of the city." Here, moreover, the neighborhood identity was reinforced with its own street system and names and its own water and sewer mains. This exclusiveness was physically emphasized until 1890 by a fence built to keep out what LeDroit Park considered undesirable elements of the population. Over in the northeast sector of the city, the development in the late 1880s of the 134 acres of Brookland followed close on the heels of the founding of the Catholic University of America in 1887 and was serviced by the Baltimore & Ohio Railroad. Located on one of the highest points in the city, Brookland developed a characteristic pattern of single-family houses with deep lots, gardens, and trees in what had previously been an isolated and poorly serviced area. By the late 1880s, electric streetcars further engaged the residents to the central city, with additional public improvements to come in response to activity by the powerful citizens' association.

Petworth was laid out in this critical street-planning era in the final decade of the century and was located east of 14th Street in a landscape of short hills. It reflected a strong reaction to privately designed street layouts. Like a piece of fabric cut out of the original city plan, Petworth's pattern embraced the strong diagonals of New Hampshire and Kansas avenues.

Chevy Chase

The blossoming of the residential neighborhoods east of Rock Creek marked the major trend of development until the gorge was bridged—at Klingle Road in 1886 and at Calvert Street in 1891. Designated trustee to the vast land holdings of the late Senator William Sharon along Connecticut Avenue, Senator Francis G. Newlands led the advance into the rural lands west of Rock Creek. Connecticut Avenue extended in perfect alignment beyond Calvert Street to the Maryland border. At the northern terminus of Connecticut Avenue, Newlands created Chevy Chase Village, a graceful haven of tranquility. He correctly envisioned the subsequent development by others along Connecticut Avenue, then graded and conveniently serviced by trolley.

Silver Spring and Takoma Park

The formerly rural Maryland villages of Silver Spring and Takoma Park became more accessible to city residents anxious to find a countrylike respite from their urban weariness. Silver Spring, serviced by the Baltimore & Ohio Railroad after 1873, developed into a middle-class community, increasingly tied by virtue of this popular train service to the fortunes of the District. Takoma Park, a true streetcar suburb, offered large frame houses to a dispersing population and commodious hotels to weekend and summer vacationers. The ads boasted clean spring waters.

Rosslyn and Alexandria

The expanding system of streetcars also radiated out into Virginia, linking the distant towns of Herndon, Vienna, Dunn Loring, and Falls Church to the central city and offering families a farmlike residential setting and the accessibility to a city job. Transportation lines such as the Southern Railroad, which had formerly brought farm produce and dairy products to the city, could be developed to accommodate civil servants as well. Rosslyn, a terminus of several transportation routes that crossed the Potomac at Aqueduct Bridge, was laid out shortly after the Civil War, and its working-class character reflected the concentration of incoming supplies and light industry. Alexandria, once a proud, independent, and prosperous port city, was faced with a similar absorption into the fortunes of the capital city, especially as Peter Hains surveyed a route between Mount Vernon and Aqueduct Bridge.

Anacostia

Across the Anacostia River, Anacostia, often considered to be Washington's first suburb, was founded in 1854 as Uniontown. Established as a white working-class neighborhood close to the Navy Yard, Anacostia found its ties with the central city strengthened in 1875 by a horsecar line and in 1895 by an electric streetcar. In the post–Civil War years, Anacostia witnessed the rise of several residential neighborhoods to augment its market gardening communities. Congress Heights above Bolling Airfield (now Bolling Anacostia Tract) was inhabited by employees of both St. Elizabeths Hospital and the Navy Yard. The neglect of the eastern sections of the city was especially evident along and east of the Anacostia River. Grading operations, essential city services, and street systems such as those provided in the western sections of the city were frequently denied to the eastern sections. Furthermore, Anacostia was dotted by many pockets of poverty, ripe for further enlargement and institutionalization in the twentieth century.

MULTIPLE-FAMILY DWELLINGS AND THE APARTMENT HOUSE

As residents began to move into newly subdivided areas, the homes they left were factors in the phenomenon of the succession of social classes. When the poor moved in on the heels of the rich, the houses, public facilities, parks, streets, and the local environment as a whole were adapted to the scarce means and lifestyle of the new occupants. Many families crowded into previous single-family dwellings or building lots; multiple-family dwellings were improvised or created; and people literally spilled out of the houses onto the streets and back alleys. The Octagon, two blocks from the White House, once the town house of the Tayloe family, was found by Charles McKim at the end of the century to be occupied by seventeen families.

Multiple-family dwellings did not necessarily imply undesirable living conditions. Apartment houses, desired by an increasingly cosmopolitan population with fond thoughts of Parisian flats, made possible the acceptance of similar dwellings in Washington. Cluss and Schulze in 1880 designed at Thomas Circle the Portland Flats, considered to be the first notable apartment house in Washington. Luxury apartment houses in the Dupont Circle area became fashionable places of residence, especially as seasonal homes. Other apartment houses developed along major thoroughfares as a major building type in the city and metropolitan area and served a broad range of residents.

Highway Legislation of the 1890s

As early as 1878, the *Annual Report of the Commissioners of the District of Columbia* had noted the continuing spread of subdivisions beyond Boundary Street (Florida Avenue), woven onto the formerly rural landscape in street plans that did not conform "to those of the city or to each other." Anticipating the need to condemn property within these subdivisions to provide for roads between city and country, the report urged a new topographical survey and an official street plan applied to the District, steps that would ensure the orderly continuation of Washington's plan into the adjoining lands. In the language of the 1878 annual report, "The beauty of the city of Washington arises from the fact that it has not—like most other cities—grown up at haphazard, but in accordance with a well-matured plan framed in advance and uniformly adhered to for the general good without regard to particular interest."

EFFORTS TO REGULATE GROWTH AND THE STREETS THAT GO NOWHERE

By the 1880s, sections of Washington outside the L'Enfant city were experiencing rapid growth and development. L'Enfant had laid out streets only within the area prescribed by President Washington, and thus far no provision had been made for orderly extension beyond that original area. Developers, particularly in the area bounded by 16th Street NW—what is today Florida Avenue NW, North Capitol Street, and Spring Road NW—subdivided their holdings and laid out streets at will, with total disregard for incompatibility of new streets with the planned extension of the L'Enfant streets. By 1887 the District commissioners' annual report was referring to the alarming number of streets that "go nowhere and connect with nothing."

The commissioners and most citizens recognized that there was little they could do about the nonconforming subdivisions that already existed, but they hoped that future development could be regulated. The first step in this direction was taken in August 1888, when Congress passed an act forbidding any plat or subdivision that did not conform with the "general plan of the city." What the commissioners produced was a list of directives that included provisions covering widths of alleys and minimum widths of lot subdivisions. More important, the commissioners ordered that streets and avenues of subdivisions be in exact alignment with and of equal width to those in the city of Washington. New circles and public squares would be laid out and dedicated when the commissioners felt them necessary "to make a subdivision conform to the general plan of the city of Washington." With future subdivisions more or less under control, the commissioners continued to hope that the worst of the deviations in existing subdivisions could eventually be corrected. The Washington Board of Trade, on the other hand, was vigorously opposed to all irregular subdivisions, existing or contemplated, and advocated the ratification of all subdivision streets with the general city plan.

THE HIGHWAY ACT OF 1893

The stricter view of regulation prevailed, and in March 1893 Congress passed an act "providing a permanent system of highways in that portion of the District of Columbia outside the cities of Washington and Georgetown." This act authorized the commissioners of the District of Columbia to prepare a plan for the extension of the L'Enfant streets and required that all subdivisions—including those already extant—conform to this new plan.

A new map of the city was to be made showing the "boundaries and dimensions of and number of square feet in the streets, avenues, and roads" and providing that circles be drawn up at intersections of principal avenues and streets. Anticipating that many legal difficulties would arise between existing subdivisions and condemnations by the commissioners to enforce the lines of this new highway map, the statute provided for a process of hearings and damages to be paid to the landowners.

The engineer commissioner's office was, however, extremely slow in preparing the new plan provided for by the 1893 highway act. In the next four years, under the direction of the engineer commissioner, Charles J. Powell, the map was drawn up and issued in two sections, the first in 1895 and the second in 1897. For the years intervening, a great deal of uncertainty existed as to the exact location of the proposed streets. Real estate transfers in the potentially affected areas came to a virtual standstill: no one wanted to purchase property that might be condemned for a right-of-way.

Not surprisingly, the 1893 highway act was opposed by developers and private property owners alike, and the ensuing legal battles made it obvious that the new legislation was unworkable. By 1898, five years after the legislation had been enacted, only one section of the extension plan had been completed, and not one of the condemnation cases had been decided by the courts. District officials were unhappy with the act's requirement that compensation funds were to come from the District only; the federal government, which they felt also would benefit from the orderly extension of streets, was not required to pay anything.

THE HIGHWAY ACT OF 1898

Protest and opposition to the provisions of the 1893 act reached such a pitch by 1898 that a congressional committee was appointed. This committee recommended that the 1893 act be repealed and new legislation enacted. Congress did just that several months later. Like the 1893 act, the highway act of 1898 authorized preparation of a plan extending the L'Enfant streets, but it differed from the earlier act in that it specifically exempted subdivisions in existence before 1893. The new legislation made no mention of who was to provide funds for compensation when and if the need arose. Despite the failure of the 1893 and 1898 highway legislation to create a uniform District street and highway system, the city and its politicians at the time renewed their interest in Washington's original street plan and attempted to revive its aesthetics and efficiency—even if in the end they were to find that the full enforcement of such provisions was obstructed by public disinterest in the first place as well as the past decisions of private land developers. Nevertheless, what was termed the "Permanent System of Highways Plan" is a major and deliberate extension of the city's plan. As a matter of long and continuous control of growth, the highway plan effort stands respectably above most American cities' suburban sprawl. It provided a coherent network for additional parkways, special sites, and other improvements that were to come under the McMillan and later plans.

THE BUILT ENVIRONMENT: END OF THE CENTURY

At the end of the century, the physical outlines of L'Enfant's plan, still visible after the Civil War, had become strongly defined by public engineering and architectural efforts—and filled in with the artifacts of private investment. The public works of the durable Army Corps of Engineers

and the short-lived Board of Public Works created early stirrings of the City Beautiful movement even before the 1893 World's Columbian Exposition in Chicago. The rising heights of both commercial and residential structures were nipped in 1894 by the District's commissioners, an act that was subsequently reinforced by congressional action.

Residents and visitors of all economic levels met on the common ground of the major business thoroughfares, dispersing at night, however, into their increasingly separate residential enclaves. Strong and socially isolated communities, voteless but represented by citizens' associations, spread the new city beyond the old pedestrian or walking city, temporarily enforcing their separateness, but at the same time heralding their ultimate physical merging in the following century. Topographical hindrances having been conquered by streetcars, railroads, grading operations, and reclamation, the form of the city would no longer be dictated by predominantly natural conditions. The full effect of man's imagination on the city and the creation of what would in the future be termed the "built environment" were now ascendant. ★

Henderson Castle at 16th Street NW on Meridian Hill in a Photograph by Frances Benjamin Johnston, ca. 1890. Library of Congress

THE McMILLAN PLAN 1901-1902

5

Turn of the Century: The Promise of American Cities

The achievements of nineteenth-century science and politics persuaded Americans that they possessed the inventiveness to control and manipulate their physical environment. The Eads Bridge in St. Louis and the Brooklyn Bridge in New York City were early manifestations of this axiom. The 1893 World's Columbian Exposition, which itself celebrated conquest of a vast continent, was another dramatic illustration. The designers who produced the Great White City along the shores of Lake Michigan revealed the ability of a small group of talented people to translate their concepts of architecture and civic design into the reality of plaster.

As the new century opened, resounding memories of the 1893 Chicago spectacle convinced Americans that their seemingly unplanned cities could embark upon a fresh course. In the air was the promise of American cities, sparkling new, but equal to those of the Old World. In accepting the concept that buildings and parklands are interrelated, as the Chicago fair exemplified, designers in Washington at the turn of the century fulfilled the incomplete attempts of their predecessors to build on the work of L'Enfant and plan for areas larger than individual buildings. Modern urban considerations evolved out of this effort. In the city of L'Enfant, a handful of the country's best-known designers were given the task of developing a new design of the city, an early exercise in comprehensive planning and, indeed, for teamwork and institutional aspects a forerunner of the city's later comprehensive planning.

The centennial of the "removal of the government" to Washington only intensified interest in improving the capital city. Most fundamentally, this sense of purpose came out of the post–Civil War decades of growth and piecemeal civic improvement and the increasing conviction that—although Washington had achieved excellence in its residential neighborhoods, its schools, and its parks—it had not orchestrated these gains into a comprehensive urban statement. In 1898 a group of civic-minded Washingtonians formed a committee to meet with President William McKinley and discuss proposals for the centennial celebration.

The World's Columbian Exposition in Chicago in a Photograph by Frances Benjamin Johnston, 1893. Library of Congress

The committee's plans initially included a ceremony in addition to a more permanent memorial, such as an appropriately commemorative edifice or the long-desired and much-discussed bridge to connect the District of Columbia with Arlington National Cemetery. McKinley responded favorably and asked Congress to authorize formation of a committee to oversee planning for the celebration. Congress took action, and a joint committee made up of selected members of the House and Senate, governors of the states and territories, and Washington citizens first met on February 21, 1900.

A BEGINNING: PROPOSALS AND PLANS

During the morning session, a committee of five was appointed to sift through the various proposals made by the citizens' group. Senator James McMillan of Michigan, a wealthy and influential member of the Senate, was the well-qualified chairman. In Detroit, McMillan had been prime mover of Belle Isle Park, which was designed by Frederick Law Olmsted Sr. in 1883 and developed as a public park for city residents. He had served as chairman of the Senate Committee on the District of Columbia since 1890. With the aid of his efficient secretary, Charles Moore, clerk of the

Senate committee and attuned to local sentiments, McMillan initiated numerous improvements in the District. Under his direction, the water supply and filtration system had been improved and a comprehensive sewer system constructed, highways had been extended in a planned fashion beyond the area covered by the L'Enfant plan, twelve streetcar companies had been consolidated into two, and the city's charitable institutions had been reorganized. The city was ready to move into the twentieth century.

McMillan reported back to the joint committee during the afternoon session. His committee recommended that a centennial celebration be held in December and that the event be marked by both the greatly needed enlargement of the Executive Mansion and the construction of a tree-lined boulevard, to be known as Centennial Avenue. This avenue was projected to run through the Mall from the grounds of the Capitol to the Potomac River. The terminus of the avenue at the river might then become the site of the much-discussed bridge to Arlington; moreover, as McMillan rather ambiguously pointed out, "L'Enfant had provided for just such an avenue." Unsure of the feasibility of his committee's recommendations, McMillan also introduced an amendment to create a team of experts to study the proposals and report back to the president. A compromise bill appropriated $6,000 toward the study—to be carried out, however, by the chief of the Army Corps of Engineers, guardian of the city's parks since 1867. Thus began a series of studies and plans proposed between 1900 and 1902 for the Mall and its appendages, as well as for the White House.

The Plans of Franklin W. Smith

The corps's study had in fact been preceded by those studies undertaken by Bostonian Franklin W. Smith in 1890 and 1900. A multitalented but eccentric individual, Smith suggested in his two plans that the land later associated with the Federal Triangle and the Northwest Rectangle be cleared and designated for public buildings and functions. At a time when municipal improvements and the centennial of the city were joined in a reassessment of Washington as the capital, McMillan published Smith's plans as a Senate document for general information and comment. If Smith's diagrams appeared amateurish in their graphic standards, their grand conception for the cleared area nonetheless reflected national interest in the city's image. More than any plans of the decades past, Smith's work was comprehensive regarding architectural methods and effects, popular educational values, the combinations of landscape and other arts, and civic possibilities in parks, street frontages, and schools. By comparison, engineers' plans tended to be street or topographic plats with some incidental planting shown.

The Plans of Colonel Bingham and the Corps of Engineers

In his continuing capacity as the corps's officer responsible for public buildings and grounds, Theodore Bingham prepared two plans in March and April 1900, based on his interpretation of L'Enfant's original treatment of the Mall area. The plans featured a major boulevard from the Capitol to the Washington Monument area. In the first, the avenue terminated in a sculptural grouping just north of the monument; in the second, it terminated at the monument itself. Both suggested that the projected bridge across the Potomac to Arlington National Cemetery be built on the line of New York Avenue, and both retained Downing's park areas and the railroad track and sheds. In the second plan, Bingham showed the triangle created by Pennsylvania Avenue and B Street (now Constitution Avenue) between the White House and the Capitol as providing sites for future public buildings. Colonel Bingham's plans were notable for another reason: he included a treatment of the newly formed Potomac Park created to the south and west of the monument by his associates in the Corps of Engineers during the reclamation of the flats. By including this land in his projections, Bingham significantly enlarged the scope of the study area.

Bingham's plans received adverse publicity in the *Washington Post,* and the *Evening Star* spoke against putting a "mere street" on the Mall. According to the *Post,* Colonel Bingham had shown his plans to President McKinley, members of Congress, governors, and the citizens' committee. Although his plans were technically competent, Bingham was an engineer, not an architect. For a city awakening to feelings of its new prominence as a capital of a world power and having visions of the Great White City on Lake Michigan, an army engineer's plan would not be enough.

The Parsons Plan
In May 1900 Senator McMillan, presumably unhappy with Colonel Bingham's plans, introduced legislation authorizing the president to appoint an architect, a sculptor, and a landscape architect—"each of conspicuous ability"—to prepare plans for the enlargement of the White House, the treatment of the area between Pennsylvania Avenue and B Street NW, and a connection between the Potomac River and the National Zoological Park. The House of Representatives drastically altered the proposal, however, and its final version called for the chief of engineers, Colonel Bingham, to undertake the study with the assistance of only one expert, a landscape architect. Bingham, despite the fact that he had just completed two such plans, employed landscape gardener Samuel Parsons Jr. of New York City, who had worked with Vaux and Olmsted on the plans for Central Park.

Parsons, like Olmsted Sr., viewed a park as a pleasure ground set apart from the sights and sounds of the surrounding city. The desirability of a "people's park" and the efficacious influence of nature on urbanized human beings was a concept, epitomized by Central Park, not appropriate in some eyes for a park running from the nation's Capitol to its principal monument. Parsons's plan, which encompassed the entire kite-shaped area south of Pennsylvania Avenue and north of Maryland Avenue from the Capitol to the Washington Monument, featured a series of connecting oval drives running the length of the Mall and diminishing its size and dropping to lower grades as they approached the monument. Where transverse roads crossed the Mall, they were to be depressed and carried under the linking strips of parkway connecting the oval drives. Charles Moore described the scheme as one of a series of "goose-egg Mall plans."

Parsons submitted his design to Bingham in November and to Congress just before the December 12 centennial celebration. That same day, Colonel Bingham spoke at a White House reception where a model of his proposal for its enlargement was to be displayed. The day's festivities culminated in a banquet sponsored by the Washington Board of Trade, evidence of business interest in the city's future.

The American Institute of Architects' Convention in Washington, 1900

While the joint congressional committee planned its celebration of the city's centennial, the American Institute of Architects (AIA) had been drafting its own commemoration of the event. Glenn Brown, a Washington architect then serving as secretary of the institute, which had moved its headquarters from New York City to Washington, DC, in 1899, had long been interested in the artistic development of Washington. He had recently published an impressive book and portfolio on the history of the US Capitol. Pursuing his historical interest, with a reformer's zeal, he vehemently attacked the federal government for its failure in the past to allow more private architects to design public buildings. Brown saw in the approaching city centennial an ideal time to generate nationwide interest in the improvement of Washington, as well as to emphasize the contribution of professional architects. He arranged to have the AIA convention, opening the day after the centennial celebration, take as its major topic the future development of Washington.

The first session was held on the morning of December 13 at the new Arlington Hotel. Many convention delegates had attended all or some of the centennial programs of the previous day and joined with Glenn Brown in condemning both Bingham's and Parsons's plans, favoring instead a return to the L'Enfant plan for the Mall. H. B. F. McFarland, president of the Board of Commissioners of the District of Columbia and chairman of the joint committee on the centennial celebration, welcomed the delegates, saying: "We hope to receive, while you are here, further instruction as to how to make the city more beautiful than it is." AIA president Robert S. Peabody spoke next: "One does not need a professional education to feel mortified at the sight of certain buildings that have been thrust upon these beautiful highways in comparatively recent times." Peabody vowed the architects' cooperation with the politicians in promoting the "improvement of architecture controlled by the national government."

PROFESSIONAL VIEWS

Papers dealing with the landscape, sculpture, and grouping of public buildings in Washington were scheduled that evening. Brown had worked strenuously to put forward the ideas of some of the best architects in the country. The speakers emphasized the need for a comprehensive study and plan for the capital; of the possible formation of a commission to advise the government on building sites, design, and models for public buildings and sculpture; of the positive attributes of the plan of the "founding fathers"; of the lessons of Chicago in terms of vistas, uniform scale, broad terraces, balustrades, and reflections in water basins; of various treatments for the Mall area; and of restoration of the axial relationships of the Capitol, the White House, and the Washington Monument. They also arrived with plans of their own.

Cass Gilbert, who later served on the Commission of Fine Arts, advocated monumental groups, preferably in the "so-called classic style," with buildings of prominence on axes of streets and a height limitation of three or four stories. He proposed a historical museum as the terminus to the White House axis, projected onto the

reclaimed Potomac Park. Edgar Seeler echoed McMillan's committee and the joint committee in proposing that a Centennial Avenue be constructed through the Mall, not terminating at the monument, but passing north of it. Drawing on the Chicago World's Columbian Exposition and other expositions for inspiration, C. Howard Walker saw the Mall as a national court of honor, with monumental buildings bordering a stretch of park. Paul Pelz, a Washington architect and member of the Washington Board of Trade, said a strong movement was growing within the board, with support from the press, for the purchase of that portion of the District of Columbia bounded by Pennsylvania Avenue, 15th Street, B Street, and 7th Street, an area that contained the notorious Murder Bay, which had deteriorated badly since the Civil War and was considered a civic disgrace. Pelz recommended widening the two B streets (north and south of the Mall) and constructing public buildings along the Mall's perimeter. He proposed a grouping of buildings around the Capitol and located a "Hall of Records" on Pennsylvania Avenue at 8th Street where, after thirty years and many vicissitudes, it would eventually be constructed as the National Archives. Depicting a bird's-eye view of a restructured Mall, George Oakley Totten Jr. regretted that the World's Columbian Exposition had not been held in Washington, because it could have provided a trial run of temporary civic buildings in this study area.

Presenting the point of view founded in landscape architecture, Frederick Law Olmsted Jr. stated that landscape design embraced more than romantic tracts set amid a bustling city. Landscapes, he pointed out, could be formal as well and should be designed in concert with the buildings to which they were related. Prophetically for the outcome of the McMillan Plan, Olmsted suggested that the Champs Elysées be the model for the Mall, a formal park lined with "several parallel rows of trees with several pavement and turf strips."

Glenn Brown himself had a plan for the capital. In an article in the *Architectural Review,* he

advocated a boulevard through the Mall, grander than the Champs Elysées, a common source of comparison in reference to a Mall avenue. Brown also recommended the purchase by the government of the triangle between B Street and Pennsylvania Avenue and urged clarification of the Mall plan before any more vistas were destroyed. The article was illustrated with photographs of formal compositions that Brown had collected at the Paris Exposition of 1900.

To the architects, and particularly the elite represented by the AIA, there could be but one urban design model—Paris. It was in the city of light that the most articulate and influential members had won their professional spurs in the competitions of the École des Beaux-Arts. When they spoke of the "classic," they meant the academicism of the École. Theirs was the white architectural style of the "City Beautiful" and of future Washington, just emerging from the eclectic revival styles and red brick models.

THE CITY OF WASHINGTON, DECEMBER 1900

The architects were generally unhappy with what had been happening in Washington in recent years. The city that presented itself to the Chicago, New York City, and Boston designers was far different from that of today. Its early neoclassicism, reinforced by the public buildings of Mills and his contemporaries, had been effectively obscured by the romanticism that stamped itself upon the landscape, no less than upon the

city's architecture. The Mall was chopped into winding carriage drives and bosky walks. "Overgrown Downing," it was called, in allusion to the romantic landscape plan drawn up in 1851 by Andrew Jackson Downing. The principal new buildings echoed the eclecticism of the past generation; the Romanesque Post Office tower, the Italianate Pension Building, the florid Library of Congress, and the cascading columns that formed the French Second Empire facade of the State, War and Navy Building were elements in the contemporary cityscape. The central city was laced by railroad tracks, and a conspicuously sited depot marked the Mall. The cast-iron shed of "Marsh Market" dominated Pennsylvania Avenue. And back of all this lay the residential city, the characteristic streetscape of tall, narrow row houses with gables, turrets, arched porches, and cast-iron window ornaments.

This individualism in both residential and commercial areas was not greatly different from other American cities, but Washington's role as a national capital suggested a different standard— a "world standard," as Moore suggested—reflecting the dignity, order, and continuity of the national, even an imperial, state. It was to be "all executed by American artists trained in European schools to minister to the satisfaction of American needs." The city to be transformed was also smaller than the Boston or Chicago or New York City from which the designers came; in 1900 Washington numbered 279,000 people, and

View of the Mall from the Washington Monument, ca. 1897. DC Public Library, Washingtoniana Division, DC Community Archives.

most of the developed area was still south of Florida Avenue.

At the close of the AIA convention, a special legislative committee was appointed to bring before Congress a resolution calling for a commission to consider certain improvements in the Capitol. William A. Boring of New York City was designated chairman, and W. S. Eames of St. Louis, J. R. Coolidge Jr. of Boston, George B. Post of New York City, and Glenn Brown of Washington were chosen to serve on the committee.

Meanwhile, Charles Moore, a witness to the grumblings of the AIA, brought these complaints to the attention of Senator McMillan. McMillan had been embarrassed at the outcome of the Parsons plan and now requested through Moore a conference with the AIA legislative committee. As a result of that meeting, McMillan introduced a joint resolution in the Senate on December 17, 1900. It urged "that the President of the United States be authorized to appoint two architects and one landscape architect, eminent in their professions, who shall consider the subject of the location and grouping of public buildings and monuments to be erected in the District of Columbia and the development of the entire park system of the District of Columbia and report to Congress in December of 1901."

Senator McMillan and the Senate Park Commission, 1901

Realizing that opposition in the House would prevent passage of the resolution, McMillan decided to handle the subject in what Moore called a "somewhat different manner." On March 8, 1901, at an executive session of the Senate, Senator McMillan reported from his District Committee a resolution directing that committee to report to the Senate a plan for the improvement of the entire park system of the District of Columbia. The District Committee was to be authorized to employ experts, the necessary expense to be paid from the contingent fund of the Senate. The resolution was adopted and a subcommittee was named consisting of Senators McMillan, Jacob H. Gallinger, and Thomas S. Martin.

At an informal hearing before the subcommittee on March 19, with members of the AIA legislative committee in attendance, McMillan pointed out the difficulty of going beyond improvement of the park system to siting of future public buildings, a topic that would necessitate negotiations with the Senate and the House Committee on the Library and on Public Buildings and Grounds. It was finally agreed, however, that the subcommittee might make "suggestions" as to the siting of buildings. This verbal formula solved the parliamentary dilemma, and it was agreed to appoint an architect and a landscape architect who would then choose their own third member. McMillan summed up the proceedings in the following carefully worded statement: "These gentlemen [the commission to be appointed] could study the question between now and next December and submit privately to this committee a plan which would practically cover the matter of parking [*sic*] of the city and incidentally suggest where the public buildings should be placed." Thus, the Park Improvement Commission of the District of Columbia, commonly known as the Senate Park Commission, or the McMillan Commission, was born out of an elaborate legislative maneuver, avoiding the necessity of the concurrence of the House or conferencing with other committees. As a short-term solution, it contained the seeds of future difficulties.

"THE GENTLEMEN ARE APPOINTED": BURNHAM, OLMSTED, MCKIM, AND MOORE
Daniel Burnham was selected almost immediately by McMillan and Moore to be the architect member of the commission because he had been the "mainspring of the Chicago Fair." Head of the well-known Chicago architectural firm of Burnham and Root, Burnham had been director of works for the 1893 World's Columbian Exposition. He had already designed the Railroad Exchange and Marshall Field's buildings in Chicago and, most important as it turned out, had been chosen as the architect of the new station for the Pennsylvania Railroad in Washing-

ton. Burnham's executive ability and his talent for effecting cooperation among various artists were proven. He was confident and tireless, traveling almost constantly in relation to his work. He thought on a "grand scale" and was greatly productive, with some of his best work, such as his celebrated plan for the city of Chicago, still ahead.

Frederick Law Olmsted Jr., who had made an earlier study of Washington, was selected primarily because of McMillan's experience with the elder Olmsted on the Belle Isle Park. As McMillan reasoned, "I guess the son is as good as the father." Olmsted Jr., "Little Rick," had been his father's apprentice during the older man's last year of active work and in 1898 was himself admitted to the firm, which then underwent another of its frequent name changes, becoming Olmsted Brothers. The youngest of the McMillan Commission members, Olmsted brought to Washington the experience he had gained with his colleague Charles Eliot II in designing the comprehensive Metropolitan Park System in Boston.

Olmsted was already in Washington for the subcommittee hearings. Burnham arrived in Washington on March 21 and that evening met Charles Moore for the first time. Moore offered him chairmanship of the commission. When Burnham inquired about the third member, Moore said the choice was his and Olmsted's but suggested Charles F. McKim. This suggestion Burnham apparently welcomed, for Moore quoted him as saying that McKim was "the man I had in mind. He was the one I most relied on in the Chicago Fair work." Two days later Burnham left for New York City, where he successfully sought McKim's acceptance of the appointment.

Charles McKim had studied at the École des Beaux-Arts in Paris and was the leading exponent of academic classicism in the United States. He headed his own firm of McKim, Mead and White in New York City. Having already designed the Boston Public Library, the Rhode Island State Capitol, and the new buildings and fence in the Yard at Harvard University, after his work on the

McMillan Commission concluded, he would be chosen to remodel the White House and design New York City's Pennsylvania Station.

Charles Moore, who functioned closely with the commission as Senator McMillan's personal surrogate, had an intimate knowledge of how Washington worked. He himself prepared the reports on the District that led to the improvements McMillan initiated through the District Committee. Moore had a reputation on the Hill as a very efficient secretary, and Senator McMillan relied heavily on his judgment and knowledge. Moore had gone to Harvard (as had all of the Senate Park Commission members except Burnham) and had studied with Charles Eliot Norton, who he said had shaped his views concerning art. Moore later wrote biographies of both McKim and Burnham.

Not an artist himself, Moore had profound respect for the elite professionalism these men represented. He shared both their Republican politics and their Brahmin outlook. He enjoyed their sociable dinners at the Century Association in New York City, where projects could be discussed and decisions made. He found his relationship with these men a rewarding experience. Later on, Moore was appointed to the Commission of Fine Arts, where he served for twenty-seven years—twenty-two of them as chairman—and there became a formidable voice in realizing the intentions of the McMillan Commission plan.

THE BASIS OF A NEW DESIGN

Much is known of the working procedures as well as the designs of the McMillan Commission, more by far than is known of L'Enfant's work, even if still not enough to allow a fully detailed comparison of these two major planning efforts. The greatest distinction was that by 1901 planning for the capital city was already set in a context of continuing activity. Plans produced in the years preceding the formation of the McMillan Commission provided an archive of ideas on which commission members could draw. The beautiful natural setting of the city—the river and the hills—and the classic design imposed on it by L'Enfant formed the foundation on which they would build. The inspiration of the World's Columbian Exposition in Chicago made beautifying the capital as important as developing new land and providing for a park system. Above all, the time was ripe for a grand design, and the men with the talent and experience to produce it had been put in a position to do so. The power and personal wealth of Senator McMillan made the venture possible, and the political acumen of Charles Moore would be the guide "through the trying world of officialdom" on what Moore himself called a "quest of good order and beauty made incarnate in the National Capital."

The Optical Survey of the District
The first meeting of the McMillan Commission took place on April 6, 1901. The remainder of April was filled with preliminary studies. The commission made what Burnham called "an optical survey" of the District, going through it in every direction; touring the outskirts; encircling the city on hills; going as far as Great Falls, source of the city's water supply; taking a boat ride to see the city from the river; and visiting Alexandria and Georgetown. But a ground-level view was not enough. Burnham climbed to high points in the city to get a larger view from the heights of Arlington, Meridian Hill, and Anacostia.

Seeking those American precedents and inspiration on which Washington, Jefferson, and L'Enfant had drawn, the McMillan Commission members also toured notable colonial houses. Taking the lightship *Holly* (made available to them by Secretary of the Treasury Lyman J. Gage) down the Potomac to the James and York rivers, they visited the plantations Stratford Hall, Carter's Grove, Upper and Lower Brandon, and Shirley. They also stopped at two colonial capitals, noting the circles and radial streets of Annapolis and the axial relationships of Williamsburg.

"Then," Burnham said, "we examined the documents," the L'Enfant plan and the available maps and surveys. The Senate Press Gallery was commandeered for a drafting room, and J. G. Langdon from Olmsted Brothers was put in charge. Here they studied the fine maps of the outlying areas already prepared by the US Coast and Geodetic Survey Office and drew new and more nearly accurate maps of the older parks and central areas, all "with the aim of making throughout the entire District a well-articulated park system extending as far as Great Falls and Mount Vernon."

Work continued through May with McMillan Commission members commuting between their offices and Washington. Early in June McKim wrote to Burnham that Augustus Saint-Gaudens, the noted sculptor, had been visiting him and taken an interest in the work of the commission. McKim suggested that Saint-Gaudens be made a full member, since "the question of sites refers to sculpture as well as architecture." Burnham, in turn, wrote to Senator McMillan saying they wanted Saint-Gaudens made a member of the commission and then made the appointment simply by placing Saint-Gaudens's name on their letterhead.

The Grand Tour and the City of the Future

On June 11 the McMillan Commission sailed for Europe in search of Old World inspiration. The purpose of the trip, Burnham had explained at their first meeting, was to "see and discuss together parks in relation to public buildings. That is our problem here in Washington and we must have weeks when we are thinking of nothing else." They were also there to track down the European influences reflected in the L'Enfant plan and thus to add substance to the skeleton of L'Enfant's original intentions. But they were also looking further, toward the city of the future, and intended to "make a closer study of the practice of landscape architecture as applied to parks and public buildings . . . what arrangement of park areas best adapts them to the uses of the people, and what are the elements that give pleasure from generation to generation, and even from century to century."

Charles Moore was a member of the party but not Saint-Gaudens, whose health would not allow him to take the strenuous seven-week trip. The itinerary, drawn up by Olmsted, was based on viewing the works of Le Nôtre that L'Enfant had experienced as a young man and had used as inspiration for the original Washington plan. Olmsted brought with him maps of the District of Columbia and a camera. Of this he made good use; many of his photographs were included in the commission's report.

Often inspiration came directly. Moore later wrote that while standing on the steps of the little temple at the Villa Borghese, the commission members decided that the projected "Memorial Bridge should be a low structure on a line from the site of the Lincoln Memorial to the Arlington Mansion—a monumental rather than a traffic bridge, but a significant element in an extensive park scheme." Admiring the vista from the terraces of the chateau of Vaux-le-Vicomte with the *tapis vert* and lines of tall trees, the Americans thought of the Mall in Washington. In England, they measured the green carpet between rows of trees at Hatfield House to find the proper width for the Mall. Olmsted's objections to a central driveway down the Mall were strengthened by seeing a similar scheme in Windsor Great Park.

In London, Burnham found the opportunity to visit Alexander J. Cassatt, president of the Pennsylvania Railroad, and learned that the railroad was willing to abandon its site on the Mall and join with the Baltimore & Ohio Railroad in building a new "Union Station" at their site at New Jersey Avenue and C Street, providing Congress would pay part of the added expense of tunneling under Capitol Hill. Having viewed the tracks on the Mall as a major obstacle to their plans, the commission was now ecstatic. Their plan was already in motion. They telegraphed Senator McMillan and celebrated the good news at dinner.

BACK TO THE DRAWING BOARD
Returning to the United States in August, the commission set up an office in New York City to

Union Station, Early Twentieth Century. Library of Congress

prepare the necessary designs, with a young man from McKim's firm, William T. Partridge, placed in charge of the drawings. A quarter century later, Partridge would serve as consultant to the National Capital Park and Planning Commission.

The McMillan Commission members divided up the work early. Burnham's assignment on the design of Union Station proved very demanding, calling for a second change in location and hence a new design for the site near the Capitol, where the station would serve as a "vestibule" to the city. The Grand Court in front of the depot also needed a design treatment. Burnham's time was consumed in conferences with railroad officials and legislators. As for the McMillan Commission, therefore, Burnham's primary responsibility was to oversee the plan as a whole, just as he had overseen the design and construction of the World's Columbian Exposition. The outlying regional parks and their connections were to be the responsibility of Frederick Law Olmsted Jr. The central composition was to be handled by Charles McKim. Saint-Gaudens was to advise in matters of scale and the location of monuments and statues. Burnham's commitments allowed McKim, who devoted almost all of his time to the work of the commission, to act, as Moore described it, as the "refiner" of Burnham's ideas.

Three-Dimensional Scale Model of Washington Prepared for the McMillan Commission, 1901-1902. National Archives

The commission was painstaking in its planning, especially where details of a major element like the Mall were concerned. They had decided the Mall should have a formal treatment, as earlier suggested by Olmsted at the AIA convention, wiping out Downing's romantic winding paths but preserving the Mall as an appropriate landscape setting for the related public buildings. The commission members envisioned the Mall as similar to Le Nôtre's formal compositions at Versailles and Vaux-le-Vicomte: a wide, open vista with a green carpet down the center, bordered by narrow roadways flanked by rows of elm trees. They had measured similar spaces in Europe, but now to find precisely the right width for the grass-covered panel down the center of the Mall, they had the supervising architect of the Treasury erect flagpoles that could be viewed on the Mall from the Capitol steps and the Washington Monument. Trials were made with the flagpoles 250, 300, and 400 feet apart. They decided on a 300-foot width at the center. (According to Moore, McKim later said in regard to narrowing the Mall, "Rather would I lie down on the floor of this court and die first.")

Great care was exercised also in deciding how many elms should form the rows on either side of the green panel. Burnham said, "Having examined every notable avenue in Europe, we found that not less than four trees constituted an avenue and three produced a bad effect. . . . The American elm was chosen not only because of the architectural character of its columnar trunk and the delicate traceries formed by its wide spreading branches, but also because in the District of Columbia this tree is at its best, notable examples being found in the city parks and in the grounds of the Capitol."

THE SEARCH FOR SUPPORT: CONGRESS, THE PRESS, AND THE PUBLIC

Even before the commission members had gone to Europe, they, along with McMillan and Moore, had understood the need to win allies to their work. For the Senate Committee on the District of Columbia, Moore gathered and published background data and, more important, organized a significant number of hearings, providing the opportunity to record and dissemi-

nate the views of community and civic groups regarding parks. At the commission's inception, Senator McMillan had given a party at which he introduced the members to prominent Washington figures, giving the gentlemen of the commission what Moore called their "social credit." Soon after, McKim sought out Secretary of War Elihu Root for advice. Other cabinet members, as well as influential senators and representatives, were kept well informed about commission activity. Frequent meetings were arranged with the commissioners of the District of Columbia.

Selling the plan was an important aspect of the McMillan Commission's work and would prove immeasurably important in the plan's reception. Moore, a journalist earlier in his career, released just enough to the newspapers to keep the interest of the press and public whetted. McKim's concern about the layman's ability to appreciate plans and drawings led him to ask leading illustrators of the nation's magazines to render the designs and landscaping for public buildings and monuments in relation to the overall scheme. McMillan gave his approval for this project as he had for others, saying, "If the

government will not pay for it, I will." This allowed the freewheeling Senate Park Commission members to move ahead, avoiding penny-pinching and bureaucratic delays. Most of the money was advanced by McMillan through Moore, who paid the bills. Vouchers were then submitted to the Senate, and if they were approved, McMillan was reimbursed. The commission members themselves advanced money, for example, for the scale models of Washington, and at least once Moore sent them money from his own account.

The Commission's Report and the Models of Washington, 1902

The McMillan Commission's report, written by Moore and Olmsted, incorporated photographs of proposed treatments of Washington, analogous compositions in Europe, and examples of parks in Boston and Hartford. Maps were also included, one series comparing current and proposed park areas in Washington to those in Boston, New York City, London, and Paris. The report was a masterful piece of work. It was meant to stir the imagination, and it did. It was

Three-Dimensional Scale Model of Washington Showing Proposed Changes as Prepared for the McMillan Commission, 1901-1902. National Archives

Recommended Design of the Rock Creek Parkway in the McMillan Plan, 1901-1902. *The Improvement of the Park System of the District of Columbia, 1902*

readable and "its essentials were easily grasped even by laymen," a point important in Burnham's view of planning efforts, as Thomas Hines has noted. Burnham wanted the plan to "appeal to the ordinary citizen" and thus wrote the text of the report to "inspire enthusiasm among a broad constituency."

On January 15, 1902, the commission's official report was submitted to the Senate Committee on the District of Columbia. This submission was followed by the opening of an exhibition in the hemicycle of the second Corcoran Gallery of Art, recently built to provide more exhibit space than the original one across from the White House. McKim had worked for three days, staying up almost the entire night before the opening, hanging and rehanging the photographs and illustrations and adjusting the lighting.

The place of honor was held by two models: one of the city as it existed in 1901, the other showing proposed changes. The models, made in Boston by the geographic sculptor George C. Curtis, included an area of about two miles from the Library of Congress to the Lincoln Memorial. Every public building was exactly shown in miniature, every private building outlined. The grades of streets and kinds of trees lining them were exact; five thousand photographs had been taken of buildings, streets, and city blocks to ensure accuracy. A third model, produced in McKim's New York City office, exhibited a proposed treatment of the Washington Monument featuring terraces, a sunken garden, broad marble steps, and a long decorative canal symbolically connecting the monument with the proposed Lincoln Memorial.

Despite snowy weather, the reception was held as planned at the Corcoran Gallery of Art. Theodore Roosevelt and his party arrived first.

President Roosevelt thought the Washington Monument model "too fussy," but when he viewed the entire treatment of the Mall, he began to realize the "greatness of the conception itself." Secretary of State John Hay pronounced himself satisfied, although he noted that the location of executive buildings around Lafayette Square would destroy his house, designed by the great American architect H. H. Richardson as a double house shared with Henry Adams. Secretary of War Elihu Root, already an enthusiastic ally of the plan, was even further enthralled by the exhibit. Members of the Senate Committee on the District of Columbia received the guests, among them senators and congressmen. The exhibition was then opened to the public.

THE PARK SYSTEM AND THE CENTRAL CORE

In the commission's report to the Senate, McMillan called the plan the "most comprehensive ever provided an American city." Actually the plan, as directed by its authorizing resolution, concerned itself with two main problems: the building of a park system and the grouping of public buildings. By connecting existing parkland and carrying the park system to the outlying areas of the District and across the river as far as Mount Vernon and Great Falls, it addressed the regional character of the city. By grouping public buildings in formal compositions, the McMillan Plan created a highly concentrated central core. It gave the city an "official" architecture as well as a plan. Nor did the plan for the monumental city neglect its people.

Frederick Law Olmsted Jr. drew heavily on the Boston Metropolitan Park System in his recommendations for Washington parks. In the published version of the plan, he included photographs of a Boston beach, showing a recreational bridge, bathing house, outdoor gymnasium, and children's sandpiles. In his proposals, Olmsted provided for neighborhood parks where they were lacking, especially in that portion of the District lying outside the L'Enfant city. He suggested additions to Rock Creek Park and outlined individual treatments for important parks.

In transforming parks from the promenading and reposeful variety to those of more intensive recreational use, Olmsted tied parks to the planning process. Park needs thus became an integrated part of a functional program to acquire land. Parks also were now more democratic; they would serve the popular needs in their recreational purpose and form an important element in humanizing the city.

BOULEVARDS, DRIVES, AND PARK CONNECTIONS

Along with the provision of connections between parks, to be related to the area's topography, scenic boulevards were suggested—on the Virginia lands through an as yet undetermined route south to Mount Vernon and on the Washington and Maryland sides along the Potomac Palisades as far north as Great Falls. Another road was planned to follow the Potomac from the Lincoln Memorial to Rock Creek Park, to trace the winding crevice to the zoo, and then to connect the old Civil War sites into a Fort Drive. A second riverside drive emanating from the Lincoln Memorial was planned to lead down the river, paralleling an embanked quay, to a recreational area on the reclaimed land of Potomac Park.

Landscaping in the newly reclaimed Potomac Park, according to the commission's report, was to be modeled after "the landscape of natural river bottoms—great open meadows, fringed by trees along the water side," and would mirror across the Washington Channel an improved commercial waterfront of the southwest quadrant. Olmsted urged the government to reclaim and frame with raised quays the Anacostia mud flats, on the brink of industrial use, to bring recreation space to the eastern residential neighborhoods.

As the planned park connections encircled the city, enveloping the heights of the topography, they also crossed outlying residential areas. Between Rock Creek Park and the Soldier's Home, the much-widened and tree-lined Savannah Street (now Varnum Street) would, according to the plan, set a formal tone to the neighborhood and provide a park facade to an otherwise famil-

Recommended Design of the Potomac Quay in the McMillan Plan, 1901–1902. *The Improvement of the Park System of the District of Columbia*, 1902

The Central Composition of Washington from the McMillan Plan, 1901–1902. The Commission of Fine Arts

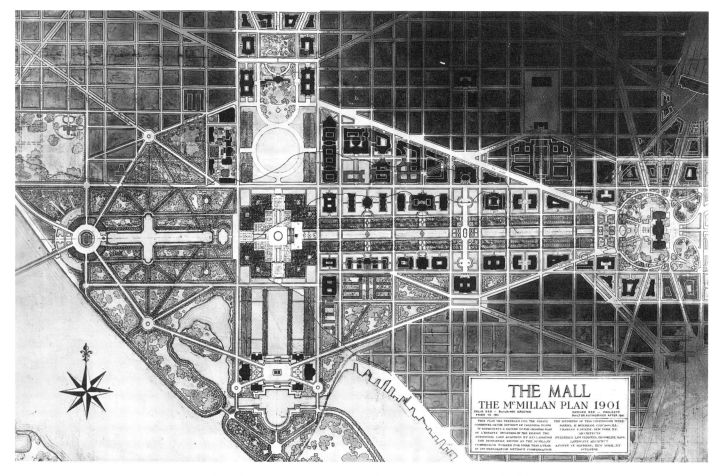

The National Capital Park and Planning Commission's 1929 Interpretation of the McMillan Plan's Mall Design. National Capital Park and Planning Commission

iar street of row houses. On the surrounding heights of the city's topographic bowl, moreover, the plan suggested sites for memorials. Where the radials met the crests of distant encircling hills, it was thought that a "simple white shelter will prove the most effective treatment," whereas closer to the city, such sites for memorials would call for treatment on a "more comprehensive scale."

The Grand Plan for the Mall

The grouping of public buildings and development of the Mall represent the best-known portions of the McMillan Commission's report. Executive functions were to expand into new office buildings surrounding Lafayette Square. Buildings relating to the legislative and judicial functions of government were to be constructed around the Capitol in a relationship already established by the Library of Congress. The Botanic Garden at the foot of Capitol Hill and

the east end of the Mall were to give way to a Union Square with statues of Generals Grant, Sherman, and Sheridan. Fountains, terraces, and statuary would complete the treatment of the proposed square, an American equivalent of the Place de la Concorde in Paris.

The Mall, patterned in part after the Champs Elysées, was proposed to be a green panel bordered by narrow roadways and rows of elms. It was planned to tilt slightly south, forming a new axis with the Washington Monument. According to the plan, it would then follow a vestigial canal, or reflecting pool, recalling the buried waters of Tiber Creek, as well as the decorative canals at Versailles, Fontainebleau, and Hampton Court, and terminating on a site then still a "marshy backwater," later the site for the Lincoln Memorial. The new memorial, recommended in the plan as having a "character essentially distinct from that of any monument either now existing in the District or hereafter to be erected," was

proposed to be set in a *rond-point* or circle in the same way that the "Arc de Triomphe crowns the Place de l'Etoile at Paris." From this proposed circle, avenues were to radiate out into connections with Potomac Park to the south, along the riverside drive to Rock Creek to the north, and across the Potomac to Arlington House on the Virginia hills. This arrangement was similar in form to the avenues radiating out from the Place de l'Etoile into the Bois de Boulogne and several other axial points in Paris.

THE WHITE HOUSE CROSS AXIS
The north-south cross axis extending from the White House to the Potomac River was, according to the plan, to be emphasized by the location of a great sunken garden and a round pool of ornamental water at the base of the monument. The axial line would then terminate at the Potomac, where a future memorial, perhaps a pantheon to honor the Constitution's writers,

was to be located. Critical to this realignment of axial relationships was the design of the Washington Monument grounds. As the commission's report stated, of all the elements in the McMillan Plan, "no portion of the task set before the Commission . . . required more study and extended consideration than has the solution of the problem of devising an appropriate setting for the Monument; and the treatment here proposed is the one which seems best adapted to enhance the value of the Monument itself."

The design for the monument terrace and gardens required a three hundred-foot-wide marble stairway fronting the west and descending forty feet from the monument platform. This feature, surrounded by terraces, paths, trees, and fountains, would have necessitated removal of the high ground that supported the obelisk. The monument's reflection in the round pool was to provide the illusion of the monument's realignment with the north-south axis. Thus, the design

Rendering of the McMillan Commission's Plan for the Mall, 1901-1902. *The Improvement of the Park System of the District of Columbia,* 1902

Rendering of the McMillan Commission's Plan for a Pantheon and Washington Common, 1901-1902. Audiovisual Archives Division, National Archives

would have accomplished the desired geometric aspirations. From an engineering standpoint, however, removal of the hill on which the monument was secured would critically weaken its foundations. In the end, what the commission had hoped would become the "gem of the Mall system" was abandoned. Nonetheless, this emphasis on the problem of the incorrectly aligned monument most clearly illustrates the axial design concern of the architect-planners trained in the French tradition at the École des Beaux-Arts. Few aspects of their work better express the effort that produced their concept of the grand design.

As compared with the majestic respite offered in the monument gardens design, active sports were designated in the area just to the south. A "Washington Common" was planned with a stadium, ballpark, open-air gymnasium, and playgrounds. A realigned Tidal Basin would have facilities for water sports. According to other portions of the plan, in the area south of Pennsylvania Avenue, which it was suggested the government buy, would be municipal buildings, a modern market, and a national "Hall of Records." Public or semipublic buildings such as museums were to front on the Mall.

DEFINING THE WIDTH OF THE MALL

The commission members did not propose demolition of buildings, such as the Treasury, the State, War and Navy Building, or the Library of Congress, blocking original vistas of the L'Enfant plan. They did, however, advocate moving the Smithsonian Institution Castle back from where it projected onto the Mall. Although the commission members did not mention this in their report, knowing the furor it would create, their models and illustrations of the Mall did not show the Smithsonian infringing on it. In addition, Burnham, during his testimony before a hearing of the Senate District Committee on Senator Francis Newlands's resolution to define the width of the Mall, shed some light on the thinking of the McMillan Commission members. "We frankly confess that our scheme would result in moving back the Smithsonian Institution so far as it now projects into the composition; in that scheme involving many millions of dollars if one object already in position can not be made to harmonize with the composition, we frankly confess that in our opinion it ought not to stand in the way of a grand improvement."

THE URBAN AMBIENCE

The static models of the city, largely devoid of human reference, gave credence to the notion that "McMillanism" spelled vacant streets and oppressive architecture. But although Burnham and his associates by no means forged a "new architecture of democracy" in their limited terms of reference, they were oriented to settings and architectural designs that would please both visitors and residents of Washington. The entire discussion of parks referred to appropriate activities to be ascribed to the various park areas—action sports in the Washington Common, the Tidal Basin, and along the Anacostia; riding and hiking in Rock Creek Park; pleasurable walks along the formal parts of the Mall. If the traffic along the Mall between the proposed Union Square and the Lincoln Memorial did not resemble the commercial life along the Champs Elysées between the Place de la Concorde and the Place de l'Etoile, it was because in Washington, the walk was lined only with museums—and flanked by grand office buildings—rather than that mixture of shops, restaurants, and residential functions that give the Parisian street its lively character. Pedestrian traffic might have been generated by retention south of Pennsylvania Avenue of the market functions (moved slightly to the west and under

a new roof in the plan). This pattern was precluded by removal of the Victorian market sheds to make room for the construction of the National Archives Building as part of the Federal Triangle in the 1930s.

Although the piecemeal projects associated with the plan that were ultimately executed did not in themselves create the urban ambience the designers had intended, the aspirations of these men—especially with regard to the District parks outside the river-bottom L'Enfant city—gradually found expression in the planning activities of succeeding generations of designers.

For all of its suggestions of imperial glory, the plan was an amalgam of various foreign and domestic influences. Although the commission members may have stated their indebtedness to Rome, Roman influences were evident primarily in the architectural styles and in the water displays. The Mall itself was derived from French and British sources. Suggestions for river treatment, especially the raised quays, could have been derived from a number of European cities. Nonetheless, the commission members had wanted to understand the motivations of Washington and Jefferson and had also sought examples of urban design and landscaping that the American colonies could provide. In the com-

Rendering of the McMillan Commission's Plan for the Lincoln Memorial, 1901-1902. Library of Congress

mission's recommendations for parks, Olmsted drew on more recent American models and also reflected his long experience and that of his father in Boston, Hartford, and Brookline. The final product of all these influences was a plan that was a uniquely American creation.

Selling the Plan: The Task of Enlightenment

By and large, those who viewed the models, illustrations, and photographs were pleased. The job of selling the plan to the public was, however, still ahead. It was one of the strengths of the 1901–1902 plan that the commission that created it did not neglect it, even after its official function as a commission had ceased. Much of the early opposition to the plan was based on the cost, which bothered the economically minded members of Congress. To money objections, the commission members argued that the plan was intended to guide building projects that were already in the pipeline or were clearly necessary and were to be appropriated in the future. Opponents also attacked the plan because of the genesis of the McMillan Commission; it had been authorized without concurrence of the House, which was not in session during the commission's formation and early work. McMillan regretted having to work without House participation, but he had judged that a comprehensive body of studies or proposals would be a good starting point for the next Congress.

Most of the response from official sources was positive, but Speaker of the House Joseph Cannon of Illinois served as a chief obstacle to the plan, just as he had earlier in forcing compromises in McMillan's original amendments to create a team of experts. Cannon voiced vigorous opposition to the existence of the McMillan Commission and to the various elements of the plan as individual building projects arose. Not inclined to debate the merits of the plan based on its recommendations, Cannon was moved more by issues of prerogative and opposing political philosophies. It was Cannon who made the famous remark that he would "never let a

monument to Abraham Lincoln be erected in that God-damned swamp."

To move Congress, members of the McMillan Commission and supporters of its plan conducted an intensive campaign to make the details of the plan familiar to the public. Burnham in Chicago, McKim in New York City, and Olmsted in Boston "set about," said Moore, "the task of enlightenment." The AIA gave its support, and Glenn Brown made a speaking tour as far west as St. Louis. Charles Moore talked to school children in all parts of the country. Well-illustrated articles appeared in newspapers and magazines, and the report of the commission complete with photographs, maps, and illustrations was published and made available to the public.

The first part of the plan to be tested before Congress was the legislation to clear the railway tracks from the Mall. Burnham also wanted the location of the new Union Station terminal changed to north of Massachusetts Avenue to avoid having to carry that major avenue through a long tunnel under the tracks. The bill, changing the location of the terminal, was passed with McMillan's guidance on May 15, 1902. After McMillan's death in August, progress on the remaining legislation slowed. The toughest fight, involving a large government expenditure to reimburse the Pennsylvania Railroad for part of the extra expense of moving its tracks and terminal, had to be fought without McMillan's influence and over the opposition of House Speaker Joseph Cannon. Although Cannon opposed legislation authorizing any part of the plan, the reimbursement measure finally passed in February 1903.

THE FUROR OVER THE DEPARTMENT OF AGRICULTURE BUILDING

There being no specific endorsement or approval by Congress of the McMillan Plan as a whole, its supporters were summoned to defend its recommendations each and every time they were threatened by opportunistic decisions. One such threat appeared in 1904 in the proposed siting of a new Department of Agriculture Building that would have projected beyond the proposed building line defining the Mall. Secretary of Agriculture James Wilson defied the prescription of the plan and ordered his architects to observe a three hundred-foot setback. This brought the controversy to the desk of President Roosevelt, who was embarrassed to learn that he had earlier given his approval to the building without knowledge of the Mall design issue.

To express the concern of the members of the McMillan Commission and the AIA, Senator Francis G. Newlands sponsored a Senate resolution providing that no building should be erected on the Mall within four hundred feet of its centerline. The hearings on the Newlands bill disclosed a rather thin constituency for the plan, but the arguments advanced by its proponents were persuasive and compelling. The result of the hearings on the Newlands resolution was substantial Senate support for the eight hundred-foot-wide Mall, providing the basis for a presidential directive in support of this provision of the plan. Subsequently, an equally important decision was made to maintain the gradients of the flattened Mall as proposed in the plan. Thus, in piecemeal decisions on closely fought issues, a national commitment to the key provisions of the McMillan Plan built up over the years. Not until more than a quarter century after the plan had been drafted did Congress provide general approval.

For the first decade following the plan's unveiling, the McMillan Commission members maintained a role as unofficial advisory board and arbiter of design. They were often asked to comment on building plans or to serve as jurors for competitions, as they did in the case of the Ulysses S. Grant Memorial at Union Square, the George B. McClellan Memorial at Connecticut Avenue and Columbia Road, and the District Building (as Washington's City Hall is known) in what would become the Federal Triangle. In the case of the Grant Memorial, they were able to choose a design most appropriate for their proposed Union Square site at the head of the Mall and to urge successfully that the memorial be located there.

THE NEED FOR PERMANENT REGULATION . . . AND A MORAL FORCE

After the furor over the Agriculture Building, it was clear that a permanent regulatory body was necessary. President Theodore Roosevelt appointed the members of the McMillan Commission along with Bernard R. Green, superintendent of the Library of Congress, to an unofficial consultative board. This arrangement did not prove satisfactory. In 1907 the placement of the Grant Memorial caused another battle when it was learned that some historic trees would have to be cut to make room for the sculpture in the Botanic Garden. This time, the newspapers attacked both the plan and the McMillan Commission for wanting to "substitute a pantalooned statue for the living sculpture of God." The plan was again upheld, but Burnham was disgusted by having to fight brushfires over and over. He wrote to Moore: "What we need in Washington is a system. . . . When work affecting our plan is afoot it should be someone's business to know about it and to promptly post all of us."

With the formation of the Commission of Fine Arts in 1910, Burnham would have his "system," a watchdog for the national capital. In 1932 Ulysses S. Grant III wrote that "not unnaturally the Commission of Fine Arts becomes the guardian of the plan of 1901; and has not only helped materially in getting various of its projects adopted, but has also deserved the gratitude of the nation for the bad things it has prevented." The Commission of Fine Arts would see that the Lincoln Memorial was located according to the plan and that it was designed by a disciple of McKim's, Henry Bacon. It would lead the fight for locating the Arlington Memorial Bridge by the Lincoln Memorial and enforcing the low and monumental character that the designers of the plan had intended. Saint-Gaudens, McKim, and Burnham would all be dead by 1912, but Moore and Olmsted remained active for another two decades.

Congress did not adopt the McMillan Commission plan in a single action. As the years passed, the plan gained authority in proportion to the diminution in opposition, especially with the electoral defeat of Representative Cannon in 1913. (As a sidelight on history, when Cannon returned to the House two years later and viewed the site of the Lincoln Memorial, he admitted his protests had been a mistake.)

The plan achieved additional official sanction as a body of policy by other routes. One was a series of individual plan-conforming project approvals ranging from the Freer Gallery of Art to the Lincoln Memorial. The second route involved more direct congressional actions. On April 30, 1926, by Public Law 69-159, the National Capital Park and Planning Commission was established and instructed to implement almost all of the McMillan Plan's park proposals, as was implied in the description of parkland to be included in the development of a "comprehensive, systematic, and continuous development of park, parkway, and playground systems of the National Capital and its environs." Then Public Law 1036, an act passed on March 4, 1929, in addition to its basic purpose of enlarging the Capitol grounds, "authorized and directed . . . development of that part of the public grounds in the District of Columbia connecting the Capitol grounds with the Washington Monument and known as the Mall parkway in accordance with the plans of Major L'Enfant and the so-called McMillan Commission, with such modifications thereof as may be recommended by the National Capital Park and Planning Commission and approved by the Commission for the Enlarging of the Capitol Grounds." A third direct action was passage in 1930 of the Capper-Cramton park program, which was based on an assessment of those McMillan Plan features not already rendered irretrievable by time and development.

Seeking legislation for one project at a time made for inadequate progress. This was especially true in the acquisition of parkland. From 1901 to 1925, parkland area in the District increased 24 percent while population increased 70 percent and assessed land values in the District of Columbia increased 240 percent. In the area of public buildings, however, the McMillan Plan did become, as Glenn Brown called it, "a moral force." When Washington prepared for the public buildings program in the 1920s, Moore had the 1901 models set up on the first floor of the new National Museum (now the National Museum of Natural History) where the public could see them and refresh their memories.

The 1901–1902 Plan: Reaction and Response

Just as L'Enfant established the basic design of the federal capital city, the plans of the Senate Park Commission gave Washington its modern dimension. Together they define the capital city known to its inhabitants, the nation, and the world. The L'Enfant plan, translated into Ellicott's survey and then staked out on the ground, became an eternal factor in the physical development of the city. When the McMillan Commission members first looked at the city, they saw both its enhanced natural features in the Potomac basin setting and its physical character as derived from L'Enfant. This framework they had to accept as the basis for their new design.

For all the continuity this represented, the 1901–1902 plan addressed the present and foreseeable future problems of the capital city. The city they designed was for all purposes a new creation: new in its nineteenth-century sense of space and grandeur, its metropolitan regional concept, its appreciation of natural parks and environment, its splendid architecture, and its cosmopolitanism. Perhaps most of all, the capital city was new in a political sense, designed as it was to provide a unified vision for the city as a whole, where earlier efforts had been limited to single buildings or monuments or remained programmatic ideals without significant physical expression.

The plan gathered popular, professional, and political forces to power the great forward leap in urban development, to support the growth of the city, its metropolitan spread, its increasing complexity, and its new cultural institutions and apparatus. In its handling of the railroad, firmly thrust underground as it passed through the monumental core of the city, the plan exhibited a humanistic command of technology. In its development plan for the floodplain of the Anacostia River, the plan offered new quality to urban life and leisure. In its provisions for architectural beauty that extended to bridges and fountains as well as buildings, the plan satisfied a nation's yearning for order and urban significance. In its image, the city was given a symbolic character it would never lose.

THE CITY BEAUTIFUL MOVEMENT

The L'Enfant plan—the plan of the founding fathers, of Washington and Jefferson—was a source of legitimacy for the one offered in January 1902. In reflecting past urban design, reference was made to the L'Enfant plan "restored, developed and supplemented." L'Enfant's Mall was broadened to Victorian scale and lengthened by half to reach the new banks of the reclaimed Potomac flats. L'Enfant's government architecture evolved into the academicism of the École with its Roman overtones. These changes in scale would be accomplished, in time, as the small buildings proposed around Capitol Square, the Mall, and Lafayette Square turned into the huge, if relatively low, structures seen today. L'Enfant's eighteenth-century city of pedestrians, horseback riders, and carriages—promenades, arcades, and urban squares—evolved into the metropolis of railroads, asphalt, elevators, and other products of modern building technology. "Restored, developed and supplemented," indeed, what Burnham, McKim, Olmsted, and Saint-Gaudens offered with such confidence and panache was precisely what the nation wanted at the turn of the century, and for which it soon found a name: "the City Beautiful." Under this banner the new style would be taken to other aspiring cities from coast to coast.

Given its urbanistic expression by the McMillan Commission, the design philosophy of the Chicago World's Columbian Exposition of 1893 was brought to bear on the immediate problems of an emerging urban America. The Great White City of plaster was reconceived in marble, but its dazzling nighttime character; its landscape setting of space, fountains, and greenery; and its sense of order were continued on an even larger scale than in Chicago. As the plan unfolded and materialized, a style of urban design, the "City Beautiful" style, was born. Cleveland, St. Louis, Denver, and San Francisco produced new civic centers whose design had been born in Washington and whose art of mobilizing architecture, landscape design, sculpture, lighting, and other special characteristics became a new technology.

The City Beautiful became a visible expression of the urban reform movement that flowered in the early years of the twentieth century, a movement and a cause. It was voiced most significantly by the planner-publicist Charles Mulford Robinson, who popularized the new unity of parks, plazas, and boulevards and related it to the business progressivism of the age. Robinson's popularizing talents stemmed from the then-new realm of advertising and were first exhibited in his book *Modern Civic Art, or The City Made Beautiful.* It was a comprehensive gathering of urban experiences, but no city more than Washington convincingly illustrated the virtues as well as the authority of the new style. The capital city became an urban model, one that gathered strength from the past and projected it nationwide into the future. Robinson deftly cited the presidential inauguration of 1901, celebrated from roofed stands and pavilions that for the first time had been designed by architects and that were, moreover, "painted white and decorated with vines" to complement the design of Capitol and White House. This joining of the new architecture to the urban design of the city's great processional route was formidable evidence that the City Beautiful was more than another style in the panorama of nineteenth-century architectural eclecticism. It would endure, like the laws of the nation. Or, it could be said, like these monumental structures would the laws of the nation endure.

Whatever its reflection of the national temper or its artistic influence—even the street lighting standards of the national capital city were adopted in other cities—the greatest accomplishment of the McMillan Plan was its ability to perpetuate itself, to expand and develop, and to achieve its goals in the city of Washington. From the moment of the plan's inception to the completion of the Federal Triangle, no public building was erected in the capital city that did not conform to the ideals of the plan and, in most cases, to specific sites and locations. A long generation of artistic dominance extended to the building of the Jefferson Memorial and the National Gallery of Art in the mid-1930s and even into the twenty-first century with the design of the 2004 World War II Memorial on the Mall. Only buildings of acknowledged monumental character were designed in the styles of academic classicism, and those that fell short of that standard became the victims of architectural controversy and shifting standards.

The City Beautiful movement in Washington was not limited, as was the McMillan Plan, by original parks and public building sites but was swept along to include city gateways, parkways, boulevards, monumental bridges, and entire streets. The McMillan Plan, reflecting the vast scope of L'Enfant's creation, became the basis for later comprehensive and specialized planning activity. It spread beyond the monumental core of the official city to the whole of the federal district and far into the countryside beyond. It reestablished the Classical Revival style, pushing aside the eclectic architecture that had characterized the Victorian age. The new city illustrated in the 1901–1902 plan created the image that the public came to associate with the nation's capital in popular magazines, picture postcards, movies, and newsreels. Thus projected across the country and increasingly reinforced by the experiences of tourism, the renewed city served as a unifying force, a national image with which the country could associate its role as a world power. When implemented, this idealized city would look like the capital of a new kind of America—clean, efficient, orderly, and, above all, powerful.

The plan also represented a peak in the development of the architectural profession in the United States. Although few members of the public fully understood the nature of the architectural profession for much of the nineteenth century, the AIA succeeded in bringing public support to bear on architectural matters at the end of that century. Starting in the late 1860s and continuing through the 1890s, the AIA lobbied members of Congress to wrest control over federal government building design commissions from the supervising architect and his staff. In 1893 the professional architects succeeded in getting passed the Tarsney Act, which opened federal government building projects to competition by private architects. Although the Tarsney Act was not implemented until 1897, was applied to only a few dozen building projects, and then was repealed in 1912, the private architects succeeded in making architectural design a matter of public policy by the early twentieth century. Mirroring this development at the municipal level, private architects began to receive commissions to design public school and other municipal buildings in Washington, DC, starting in the late nineteenth century.

Although members of the McMillan Commission did not design many buildings in the capital city, the plan's models and illustrations underscored the Classical Revival tastes of the period. This emphasis on classical forms had a profound influence on both public and private architecture in the city during the first half of the twentieth century. Public libraries, school buildings, banks, and large residences adhered to these classical ideals. Together with federal government edifices, these buildings contributed to what we know as the monumental city.

The McMillan Plan spawned its own adherents. Thirty years later figures like Charles Moore and Frederick Law Olmsted Jr. still held power in Washington and dictated the fulfillment of the 1901–1902 intentions. New generations had been indoctrinated with these ideals. But what was in fact built? The Federal Triangle filled the space between Pennsylvania Avenue and Constitution Avenue west to 15th Street with enormous office buildings never contemplated in the McMillan Plan, which had in fact designated the area for a rebuilt public market and municipal buildings of modest size. In a different fashion, the realization of the 1901–1902 plan did not extend to the building of the Washington Common sports center south of the Washington Monument, the executive group surrounding Lafayette Square, or the Capitol group. On the one hand, advancing demands of federal office space and new building technology outpaced the more modest earlier proposals. On the other, changed city planning priorities and objectives generated projects unknown to the turn-of-the-century planners. ✮

TOWARD METROPOLIS 1901-1926

6

The Plausible Pattern and a Quest for New Planning

By the turn of the century, the capital city's increasing urbanization forced planners to address an area much larger than the original L'Enfant city. This recognition of space needs for the physical future of the city had already been expressed in the nineteenth century's official highway plan and in developments in the surrounding countryside. Although the McMillan Commission looked to L'Enfant's original plan for guidance and inspiration, it also made several recommendations that parkland be acquired outside the original L'Enfant city boundaries, as well as on land reclaimed from the river flats.

As the physical city spread north from Florida Avenue toward the larger boundaries of the ten-mile square and then into the suburban counties, municipal and federal decisions continued to rearrange planning and development priorities in the monumental core. These policy decisions gradually incorporated the whole of the District and provided the basis for extending the radius of planning policy formulation and development activity into the suburbs. Thus, although the metropolitan scale of the capital city had been acknowledged before the Civil War and had gained military recognition during the war, it actually took form in the postwar era. Streetcars and commuter rail lines transformed the former countryside, surrounded and absorbed formerly rural crossroad communities, spawned commuter towns, and eventually generated lineal extensions of the central city. According to contemporary urbanists, the spokes of settlement pinned to the commercial hub represented an idealized city; the rural areas of open space separating the spokes, inaccessible to commuter traffic, offered recreational opportunities and served as reminders to town residents of the landscape's former appearance.

THE AUTOMOBILE AND NEW PLANNING CONCERNS

The automobile drastically altered this plausible pattern of spokes of development and open spaces. As early as 1911, the Army Corps of Engineers suggested that Conduit Road (now MacArthur

Boulevard) be resurfaced for benefit of the
"increasing use of the road by automobiles." By
1925 automotive transportation had been irrevo-
cably adopted by the average Washingtonian.
The automobile projected a host of new planning concerns: What would the impact of the
automobile be on the congested central city and
the sprawling suburbs? What new housing patterns would emerge? Transportation routes were
planned for the motorist. As evidence of this
change, the US Geological Survey in 1924 issued
its first "automobile edition" map of the Washington area, labeling in red the all-year through
and connecting roads. The rush-hour traffic jam
made its first appearance. Parking problems
proved insistent and inspired the construction of
parking garages interspersed among office buildings. In the suburbs, the rural areas of open
space became accessible to the commuter, now
freed from the exigencies of train or streetcar
schedules, restrained only by road improvements. With the scattering of residential settlements, a similar spreading out of employment
followed. What would become a continuing

philosophical battle between the concentrated
government employment and corridor development concept versus proposals for dispersal of
such facilities throughout the region began.

THE ARMY CORPS OF ENGINEERS AND THE PLANNING FUNCTION

In concert with the plans of the McMillan Commission, the Army Corps of Engineers continued
to work on physical improvements in the city,
cooperating with the new federal planning bodies (such as the Commission of Fine Arts) or
being represented there as a member (of the
Public Buildings Commission, established in
1916, and the National Capital Park Commission,
in 1924). Thus the planning function continued
until 1925, when responsibility for public buildings and grounds in the District—save for river
improvements—was transferred to the newly
independent Office of Public Buildings and Public Parks of the National Capital. Important projects of the corps's sunset years in molding the
city were reclamation of the Anacostia flats, provision of parks to fulfill new functions, and

supervision of the construction of several new public buildings. By the 1920s, the corps's Office of Public Buildings and Grounds had become the repository for a wide and diverse range of duties, from the care of statues and monuments to serving as military and social aide to the president. And in the piecemeal procedure of having new structures authorized, an officer of the corps served as executive and disbursing officer for the Commission of Fine Arts (until 1922), the Lincoln Memorial Commission, and many other bodies.

Urban Park Development: Theory and Practice in Washington

In the interplay of theory and practice, Washington was propelled into the front rank of urban park leadership among American cities. In this, it reflected the remarkable assets of its natural setting, the basic city plan designed by L'Enfant, and the opportunity provided by the thousands of acres of newly acquired parkland, especially land reclaimed from the Potomac. Moreover, it reflected the aspiration to build a model city that would exhibit the highest urban aspirations of the period, the Progressive social awareness of parks in creating ideal environments, the talents of Olmsted and other urban designers, and the technological contributions of the Army Corps of Engineers. The park movement also generated its own forward movement as recreational leadership developed, associated with the community role of the public school and a new appreciation of neighborhood life. Although it derived much from comprehensive park development models offered in Chicago and Boston, Washington contributed its share to this planning movement so characteristic of the twentieth century.

ANACOSTIA RIVER IMPROVEMENTS

The fortunes of the twenty-mile-long Anacostia River, tidal but not saline, resembled those of the Potomac before 1881. The wide and extensive flats from its mouth to far north of the District line were caused by widespread deforestation and erosion of cultivated coastal plain lands

Oyster Shucking at the 11th Street Wharves, ca. 1910. Robert A. Truax Collection

upriver. In planning for the river's improvement, the Army Corps of Engineers was chiefly concerned with the "navigable" lower six-and-one-third miles encompassed by the District, although for all practical purposes, the Navy Yard represented the extent of navigable waters. By the beginning of the twentieth century, these flats were covered by a dense growth of grasses. Sewage and other wastes in the river accumulated in this vegetation and were popularly believed to have engendered (in the words of the 1908 *Annual Report of the Chief of Engineers*) the "prevalence of malarial diseases in the portions of the city and District of Columbia which border the Anacostia." In 1898 a congressional act directed that the river be dredged and reclaimed material placed on the flats with the objectives of land reclamation, sanitation, and promotion of navigation and commerce.

Not until 1902, however, did work on the Anacostia River shoreline begin in earnest. It commenced in the portion closest to the Navy Yard, described in the 1903 annual report as "one of the finest gun shops in the world," and the dredged material was deposited on the flats below the Government Hospital for the Insane (popularly known as St. Elizabeths). Hydraulic dredges worked continually until the early 1920s, when the project was largely completed. To provide suitable enclosure for the deposited material, a trench was dug and filled with riprap; then a sea wall was constructed to hold in the dredged material conveyed from the river by discharge pipes.

By 1914 Major Charles W. Kutz (in that year's *Annual Report of the Chief of Engineers*) questioned the objective of the commercial and navigation interests, because "the flats are not now needed for commercial purposes. Until there is a commercial need for this reclaimed area, it is believed that it should be developed as a public park, as was done in the case of Potomac Park, which is made up of land similarly reclaimed." The McMillan Commission had reached the same conclusion in 1901, and the National Capital Park and Planning Commission confirmed the concept as public policy in its 1928 Potomac River Parks Plan.

Thus, what the Commission of Fine Arts in its 1914 annual report called the "Anacostia Water Park," an important element in restoring the "balance in development that has tended toward the northwest," was formally declared in 1919 as Anacostia Park. The proposed park treatment was to embrace an open fifteen-foot channel from the Anacostia Bridge upstream to Massachusetts Avenue and a nine-foot channel continuing north to the District line. The river's edges in the northern portion, according to the 1921 *Annual Report of the Chief of Engineers,* were to be "created by a dam on the line of Massachusetts Avenue, forming a lake of sufficient area to permit pleasure boating . . . and also affording navigation to the District line." Instead, a lateral lake (Kingman Lake) was created along the west shore of the river. Measuring six feet in depth, this lake allowed for the juxtaposition of recreational and commercial activities. The parallel open channel on the east permitted the free movement of silt from upriver, acknowledging that the problem was larger than the District's borders.

By 1921 the improvements sustained the modest $5 million worth of trade then transacted in the area between the Anacostia and Pennsylvania Avenue bridges, relieving what the 1921 annual report termed the "crowded condition in the Washington Channel," whose trade was estimated in that year to be worth $16,206,554. The improved channel also supported activities at the Navy Yard and Buzzard Point. A yacht harbor and allotment gardens, continuing the popular wartime garden activity, characterized noncommercial uses.

The stretch of improved river was given added importance in several ways: by the retention of Bolling Airfield, later called the Bolling Anacostia Tract, after World War I as a permanent aviation facility; by new efforts of the Commission of Fine Arts to devise a park connection between the Anacostia and Rock Creek parks; by completion, in 1907, of the Army War College on Greenleaf Point; and, in 1927, by beginning construction of the massive National Arboretum between Mount Hamilton, Hickey Hill, and Anacostia Park. By 1925 the parks in the northeast quadrant of the city inspired the Commission of Fine Arts to suggest that in cooperation with Maryland a parkway (to be designed by the versatile Horace Peaslee) should be constructed to connect busy Bladensburg Road with the upper end of Anacostia Park.

DEVELOPMENT OF WASHINGTON'S PARKS

The success of the reclaimed Potomac Park, setting an example for the Anacostia Park system, was subject to many more modern notions about social functions of parks beyond the winding walks of the nineteenth century. Although some talk lingered in the early years of the century about the creation of a "rural park" along the Potomac, the influence of Frederick Law Olmsted Jr. and the precedent of the Boston Metropolitan Park System argued for a more varied and distinctively urban scheme for Washington's parks. The move toward more actively used parks stemmed from the belief, expressed in successive annual reports of the Corps of Engineers, that "street play is in a large measure an evil and that the space between curbs is altogether too

narrow and confined for the physical development of child life."

As early as 1890, a congressional statute provided for the temporary construction by the
corps of children's playgrounds on the Washington Monument grounds and the park south of
the White House. In 1903 this authorization, as
quoted in the 1903 *Annual Report of the Chief of
Engineers,* extended to "all other reservations in
the District of Columbia." In the full spirit of
what the annual report called "progressive city
improvements and especially modern park creations," playgrounds were designed to mitigate
undesirable residential conditions. Here "children and young people can take exercise and find
innocent recreation, and [realize] the great value
thereof in developing health of body and mind
in the citizens of the future. . . . A suitable playground draws children by the hundreds . . .
under the care and control of suitable persons."
Through the new combination of open space
and playgrounds, the city gained in the adornment of its landscapes and in the "desirable and
healthful resorts for outpourings of [its] sur-
charged population." Old and new parks were

outfitted with tennis courts, baseball diamonds,
swimming pools, sandboxes, croquet grounds,
and golf courses. Washington was, in fact, in
the process of pioneering urban recreation.
Moreover, with construction in 1917 of a sloping
sandy beach on the shores of the Tidal Basin,
the reclaimed Potomac Park system offered the
most elaborate experiment in recreational park
functions.

THE PARK MOVEMENT AND MODERN
PARK DESIGN

The nineteenth-century public garden had by no
means been eclipsed by the modern enthusiasms
for park recreation. Potomac Park exhibited
another artifact of modern park design developed in New York City and in later parkway
design in the winding "riverside drive" from the
Tidal Basin's inlet to the foot of 26th Street. In
the words of the 1903 *Annual Report of the Chief
of Engineers,* "The soft roadway, or speedway . . .
will be greatly appreciated by all owners and
drivers of fine horses. . . . Nearly every important
city in the country has built and maintains such
a driveway somewhere within its borders, and

whenever one has been built it has contributed
so much to the pleasure and profit of the people
that it is now regarded as an essential."

The aesthetic park system in Washington was
further buttressed by the modest Logan Park in
Anacostia (specifically, in the Uniontown section), constructed in 1913 and outlined by an
elongated brick terrace; by the balustraded stair
that carried 22nd Street NW in Kalorama to
higher levels; and by other grace notes of urban
design.

On a highly formal scale, Meridian Hill Park,
commenced in 1910, was designed by the architect and landscapist Horace Peaslee as an Italian
garden to be built on the "last height along Six-
teenth Street." Patronized by Mrs. John B. Henderson, this monumental park, embellished by a
handsome cascade, was envisioned—apparently
after a conception of Cass Gilbert—by the Commission of Fine Arts (in its annual report for
1921–1925) to serve as a "monumental entrance to
Washington" and "to develop there a great circle
commanding a view of the White House, the
Washington Monument, the Potomac River, and

the Virginia Hills," and thus arguing for a grand
street extending into Maryland and connecting
with Baltimore and Gettysburg.

EARLY PARKLAND ACQUISITION
IN WASHINGTON

As in the case of the proposed Bladensburg-Ana-
costia parkway, the aggrandized 16th Street
entrance to the city, and the suggested Fort Drive
embracing the old Civil War sites, so improvements to Rock Creek Park responded to the same
impulse to provide a screen of parkland between
the suburbs and the monumental core. From
1917—when the Olmsted Brothers were contracted with by the chief of engineers—to 1926,
many additions in parkland were made to Washington's great reserve of natural beauty. The
Olmsted Brothers' plan for Rock Creek Park,
described in the 1921 *Annual Report of the Chief
of Engineers,* recommended that the "moving
principle" was to preserve the natural beauty of
the park while making it available for the use of
the public for riding, driving, and walking. For
this purpose, the area of the park is divided into

"use" areas and "growth" areas, "depending on the location and character of soil and present growth."

In the implementation of this plan, land was graded to allow for new footpaths, roads, and bridges; the old Pierce Mill was used as a teahouse. In the 1922 annual report, the final definition of the park stated that additional lands needed to be protected—even if by easement—to "prevent destruction of the watershed of Rock Creek." By 1923 this requirement had broader metropolitan implications. That year the corps recommended that the remaining unimproved land along Broad Branch from its northernmost point be acquired, because "protection for the park can only be afforded by acquiring control of strips of land at least about 400 feet wide on each side of all tributaries of Rock Creek in the undeveloped sections of the District and Montgomery County."

The urgency of parkland acquisition was prompted by the need not only to protect vulnerable natural and historic resources in the city and to devise a system of connecting and "grand

entrance" parkways but also to correct the potential impact of the complete development of the city according to the highway plan initiated by the 1893 congressional statute. In 1918 the Commission of Fine Arts suggested that the permanent system of highways be revised to allow for the new park schemes. The relentless grid, designed to run over the city regardless of the natural features of the original landscape, did not allow for the development of new park areas. A revised plan "with a view of adapting the suburban highways to the topography" would, in the commission's view, reverse the tendency to "tear down the hills and to fill up the valleys, thereby destroying the charm of large portions of the District. . . . Especially it is desirable to retain the country roads as park entrances and park connections." As it was, the complete connection between Rock Creek and Anacostia, as would have been accomplished by the proposed Fort Drive, could never be fulfilled because of steady development within the grid.

Public Architecture: Constituent Buildings and Orchestrated Urban Form

Construction of public buildings and identifying headquarters buildings for national organizations formed important elements of a strengthened monumental core and set its visual character. The McMillan Commission had favored classical styles patterned after aesthetic ideals taught at the École des Beaux-Arts. This form of eclecticism reached its peak of popularity in the opening decades of the twentieth century. Beaux-Arts architecture found outstanding expression in the United States. Washington contains some of the best examples.

The revered New York City architect William Adams Delano correctly said that Charles F. McKim, Cass Gilbert, Henry Bacon, and John Russell Pope created the modern image of the capital city. The Lincoln Memorial, the Memorial Bridge, the Supreme Court, the National Archives Building, the National Gallery of Art, the modernized White House, and the Jefferson Memorial—these are some of the key buildings contributed by these four leaders of the New York City architectural establishment. There were other architects, like Charles Platt and Ernest Flagg, but Delano's selection was not arbitrary. The taste of this group was nationalized, particularly by Daniel Burnham, his younger associate Edward Bennett, Paul Cret, and the architects of the Federal Triangle (and it can be said that, on the whole, the supervising architect during much of this period, Louis E. Simon, was a force toward this nationalization of an architectural style). But the creative center of this style rested in New York City, probably, as Delano claimed, in the Century Association. This style reflected the presidency of Theodore Roosevelt, the taste inculcated at Yale and Harvard, and the European influence institutionalized in alumni of the École and of the American Academy at Rome, but, most powerfully, it reflected the influence of great wealth, particularly in the banking community.

AMERICAN ARCHITECTURE

The nationalized style has been characterized as imperial, and certainly its flowering coincided with the emergence of the United States as a world power. Too much can be made of that coincidence, however, and architectural history can stand correction from the history of planning by reference to the idealism and reform elements of the City Beautiful movement, as well as to the influence of more romantic elements of American architecture. This influence was best expressed in the tradition of Henry Hobson Richardson, Louis Henry Sullivan, and Frank Lloyd Wright, a tradition that found its stylistic peak in the American version of art nouveau and the Craftsman movement in the first decade of the century. From the first essays toward a modern concept of the city spread before the architectural profession at the American Institute of Architects' meeting of 1900, to the exhaustion of the Classical Revival in the early Depression years, these alternatives were constantly present, and if they never prevailed in the endless quest for a public architecture, they were nonetheless influential.

Washington's select residential streets were filled with Richardsonian Romanesque mansions no less than with copies of the Petit Trianon. The proposed plan of George Oakley Totten Jr. for the capital's monumental core can be regarded as an art nouveau exercise in urban design. Throughout a long generation and down to Eliel and Eero Saarinen's competition design for the aborted Smithsonian Gallery of Art on the Mall and John Carl Warnecke's red brick complex flanking Lafayette Square, this influence was never absent. It was most strongly felt, however, through building designs never realized and in the work of architects never represented in Washington. The selective process of preservation and destruction by which cities grow and renew themselves is, like the writing of history, a reinterpretation of the past, correcting its taste by present standards. The critical examination of Washington's architectural history will set these factors in perspective and thus trace the beginnings of modern architectural design, not in the establishment traditions fostered by the Commission of Fine Arts and its chairman, Charles Moore, but in the broader currents of American art.

In the first quarter of the twentieth century, the Classical Revival in Washington architecture appeared and received the encouragement of the Commission of Fine Arts that produced both its official acceptance and its orchestrated urban form: the architecture not of buildings but of a city. Yet in the early years, and indeed throughout the period, other ideas and dissenting voices were heard, and the steady growth of the constituent building types—office buildings, factory-like structures, museums that were warehouses as well as monuments—was the fertile ground for their expression. If the essence of eclecticism was the association of building types with certain historical styles of building design, these unclaimed building types proved the opportunity for architectural deviation and advance.

The Government Printing Office and the Smithsonian's National Museum of Natural History

In 1904 two architectural events in the city reflected this design duality. Commissioned in 1899, the new railroad-oriented Government Printing Office was commenced, just northeast of the Capitol, after designs of a former supervis-

The Government Printing Office, 1906. Library of Congress

ing architect of the Treasury, James G. Hill. Nearly complete in 1904, Hill's new red brick government building followed the Romanesque tendencies of his earlier Bureau of Engraving and Printing (Auditor's Building) on 14th Street. Also in that year, the new National Museum (later the Smithsonian Institution's National Museum of Natural History) was inaugurated on the Mall. Designed by Hornblower & Marshall, this new classical-style structure emphasized a horizontal mass crowned by a dome. Beneath the masonry skin, however, was a steel skeleton, the functional building of the museum director, George Brown Goode. The key to the design was the module of a museum storage case. The museum was described by the Commission of Fine Arts as the first building to be located and erected according to the McMillan Plan. Noting that the building was aligned to the new Mall axis, hopeful sympathizers with the American translation of Beaux-Arts style expected this new museum to replace the utilitarian red brick National Museum (now the Smithsonian's Arts and Industries Building) on the other side of the Mall.

The Lincoln Memorial, Freer Gallery of Art, and Department of Interior

Other public buildings and monuments on the Mall followed, including the Lincoln Memorial designed by Henry P. Bacon and the Freer Gallery by Charles A. Platt, both structures consistent with McMillan Plan concepts. The Lincoln Memorial grew out of the McMillan Commission plan, although it was not until 1912 that construction began and continued for another decade. Bacon's design called for a temple design with thirty-six Doric columns that represent the thirty-six states in the Union at the outbreak of the Civil War. The accompanying Reflecting Pool—also an element in the McMillan Plan—mirrored the Washington Monument from the top step of the Lincoln Memorial, although the pool's length was shortened to take into account the foundations needed to support the Memorial in the tidal flats. Designed to house the Chinese, Japanese, and American art collections of Charles L. Freer, the Freer Gallery was designed as an Italian Renaissance palace with an interior courtyard. Its roofline followed that established in the McMillan Plan.

Contrary to the neat and coherent clusters devised by the plan, however, the new Interior Department Building (now occupied by the General Services Administration) was located between E and F streets and 18th and 19th streets and represented a technological advance in office building design. Posing a possible threat to the McMillan Commission's plans to unite the White House and the Capitol by stretches of public buildings along the Mall and Pennsylvania Avenue, the Interior Building's massive size and its location to the west of the White House were interpreted by the Commission of Fine Arts as shifting the center of departmental activity to the west, thus adding to the isolation of the Capitol.

As a reaction to the Interior Department's apparent desertion of the McMillan Plan's specifications, the Commission of Fine Arts suggested in 1918 that any further office space for the department should follow the example of the Bureau of Standards, which was then located on sixteen acres far out on Connecticut Avenue where the climate was cooler and "urban pollution and vibrations" were remote. The commission recommended that "in the case of the Inte-

rior Department, as demand for additional clerical room arises, the quarters now assigned to the Geological Survey and the Bureau of Mines be utilized for strictly office purposes and that these two bureaus either jointly or separately secure suburban locations and there construct buildings of separate character on sites adequate in size for anticipated future requirements."

Lafayette Square and the Executive Group
The acute need for increased office space for the executive departments found possible resolution in the new public buildings to be constructed according to the McMillan Commission's configurations: buildings around Lafayette Square facing the White House, referred to as the Executive Group, and buildings in the triangle of land formed by Pennsylvania Avenue, 15th Street, and the Mall, known as the Federal Triangle. In 1913 a Public Buildings Act instructed a Public Buildings Commission to devise standards for new public buildings. This commission's successor bodies, most notably the commission created by the act of 1916, set up a fifteen-member body to "investigate and ascertain what public buildings are needed in the District of Columbia." In the following year, the Treasury Annex Building, facing both the old Treasury Building and Lafayette Square, was constructed according to designs by Cass Gilbert and remained as the sole contribution of the federal government to the proposed Executive Group.

Civic Design: First Quarter of the Century
In the absence of any new comprehensive plan for public buildings, the Commission of Fine Arts as one of its first recommendations had reminded the lawmakers about the McMillan Commission's scheme, suggesting that buildings for the Departments of State, Justice, Commerce, and Labor be located south of Pennsylvania Avenue and east of 15th Street. The possible location of an archives building south of the avenue would aid in restoring greater physical balance in the city and allow executive departments to be more convenient to the Congress.

World War I Tempos on the Mall

With the advent of World War I, rapid expansion of the executive departments and the creation of new bureaus demanded that new office space, if only temporary, be constructed immediately. Long rows of reinforced concrete "tempos" (temporary buildings) lined the Mall and East and West Potomac parks. Temporary dormitories were constructed in front of Union Station. Luckily for the future of the Mall, Colonel W. W. Harts of the corps's Office of Public Buildings and Grounds arranged with the Washington architect Horace Peaslee to design the tempos so that "upon their removal," as the *Annual Report of the Commission of Fine Arts* for 1921–1925 stated, "the roads, walks, and open spaces would be identical with those shown on the [McMillan Commission's] Mall plan. Moreover, the Monu-

ment vista was preserved, and the axis was marked by placing the two smokestacks [of the power plant serving the tempos] in such manner that from the Capitol terrace the Monument is seen between the round brick columns." This was an architectural whimsy. By 1929 the seemingly indestructible character of the concrete tempos plus the proliferation of automobiles over the roads and open spaces caused Charles Moore to complain (in the *Annual Report of the Commission of Fine Arts* for 1926–1929) that the "entire Mall Park has become an open-air garage."

NATIONAL HEADQUARTERS IN THE NATIONAL CAPITAL

The filling in of the outlines in location and architectural style of the McMillan Plan was abetted by the interest of national organizations

World War I Temporary Buildings along Constitution Avenue Near the White House, ca. 1920. Library of Congress

in maintaining headquarters in the national capital. Completion in 1897 of the new Corcoran Gallery of Art on 17th Street south of New York Avenue, after designs by Ernest Flagg, provided the first element in a new monumental grouping to be constructed on what was known as the "White Lot." In 1908 the stately Pan American Union Building, designed by Paul Cret and Albert Kelsey, was located at the northwest corner of 17th and B streets, anchoring the southernmost boundary of the grouping but predicting its extension westward along B Street (now Constitution Avenue) toward the river.

In 1910 the Daughters of the American Revolution (DAR) constructed its national headquarters after designs by Edward Pearce Casey. In 1923 Marsh and Peter designed the DAR's administration building facing D Street, and in the late 1920s John Russell Pope's Constitution Hall for the DAR was added facing 18th Street. Construction between 1914 and 1917 of the building intended to house the American Red Cross, the Memorial Building to the Women of the Civil War, facing 17th Street, constituted another landmark in this lineup of impeccable Beaux-Arts creations. Designed by the New York City firm of Trowbridge and Livingston, the Corinthian-style

white marble memorial not only served as a powerful reminder of women's good works but also provided administrative space. Meticulously detailed with Tiffany stained-glass windows and furniture from Edwin F. Caldwell & Co. of New York City, the building, along with its significant garden and sculpture, was a fitting step in creating a secondary ceremonial way.

To the west of the Pan American Union Building, a less convincing but similar grouping and facade of monumental buildings connected the 17th Street group with the Lincoln Memorial: the National Academy of Sciences Building by Bertram Goodhue completed in 1921, the American Pharmaceutical Association Building by John Russell Pope in 1929, the Public Health Department Building by Jules H. de Sibour in 1933, and the Federal Reserve Building by Paul Cret in 1937.

Indicative of the emphases of the City Beautiful movement on monumental groupings and extensions, homogeneous styles, and the balancing of architectural masses (as intended in the Executive Group to the north of the White House), the proposed grouping of government buildings along 15th Street was envisioned to mirror that of 17th Street and in effect to create a more balanced grouping south of the White

House. It was not until the 1930s and the completion of the Commerce Department Building that this 15th Street facade was achieved, although the two facades certainly were never balanced in scale. Similar in form to the 17th Street grouping, monumental buildings of the Federal Triangle lined Constitution Avenue from the Commerce Department eastward toward the Capitol.

THE COMMISSION OF FINE ARTS: CONTINUITY AND THE CONTINUING PLAN

The membership of the Commission of Fine Arts expressed continuity with the McMillan Commission, with the Beaux-Arts triumphs, and with the combination of varied artistic talents: architect Daniel Burnham, landscape architect Frederick Law Olmsted Jr., architect Thomas Hastings, sculptor Daniel Chester French, painter Francis Davis Millet, and architect Cass Gilbert. And most important for the perpetuation of the "Plan of 1901," as he termed it, was commission member and later chairman Charles Moore. In the early years of the commission, a close relationship was maintained with the Army Corps of Engineers' Office of Public Buildings and Grounds, which occupied offices next to those of the commission on the fourth floor of the Lemon Building at 1729 New York Avenue NW.

Armed with congressional support, the commission reviewed plans for all projects for public buildings and parks in the city. Architectural styles of successive public buildings were molded to conform with the Beaux-Arts sympathies of the commission's members and recommendations of the McMillan Plan. Aesthetic arrangements of public buildings and spaces—especially as applied to the monumental core—motivated much of city planning. In the 1930s, however, practitioners of the modern style, who found support in the growing receptiveness of the architectural profession to design requirements of utilitarian buildings, such as factories and utility buildings, posed serious challenges to this pattern.

Commission of Fine Arts as Planning Entity
Through nearly a quarter century, a self-confident Commission of Fine Arts had supervised an architecturally dominant work of civic design. The heritage of the first quarter of the century was indelible, visible in key buildings and monuments, in whole street scenes and groups of buildings at unprecedented scale. In the Commission of Fine Arts' constant reference to the McMillan Plan, the status of the plan both as a mirror of the L'Enfant plan and as an act of national will was created and perpetuated. Often an effective obstacle to designs contrary to the McMillan proposals, the Commission of Fine Arts justified its stance in the belief that it was "by unanimous consent rather than by specific legislation that this Commission is charged with the maintenance of the plan of 1901, subject to such modifications as possibly may be found necessary owing to changing conditions."

VEHICLES OF CHANGE
To a designer in the City Beautiful tradition, the urban experience was to be realized on foot. The

Headquarters of the Daughters of the American Revolution on 17th Street NW, ca. 1925. The Historical Society of Washington, DC

Row Houses on 13th Street in Brightwood in Northwest Washington, ca. 1920. Library of Congress

scale figure in his drawings was not a Piranesian idler but a businesslike stroller, traversing the malls, riverside promenades, or sidewalks of the city, as purposeful as a traveler or tourist. During this period, the man on horseback, carriage traffic, and the omnibus had waned; the automobile had scarcely arrived. Although planners hardly can be said to have embraced the trolley car—the McMillan Commission report did contain a memorable sentence, undoubtedly written by Frederick Law Olmsted Jr., that referred to the "play of light and shade where the streets break through the columns of trees, and the passage of streetcars and teams give needed life to the Mall"—they did succeed in Washington in getting trolley cars' characteristic wirescape suppressed and put underground.

Washington had fought World War I on foot. City residents used trolley cars, which were never altogether absent from the imagination of the city's planners. Planning studies contained references that could have been aggregated into a comprehensive trolley-car system, but American society was bound elsewhere. By the mid-1920s, automobiles and buses had erupted in a city that was larger, of greater extent, and that needed greater mobility. Vast social changes in urban liv-

ing commenced, extending beyond the separation of homes from workplaces—or the emancipation of suburban wives—to the reverberations caused by continuous waves of dispersal from the city's center. The great transition had begun. Miles of hard-surfaced streets lengthened. Streetcar routes were abandoned; some streets were widened. By 1924 a gasoline tax of two cents per gallon assured highway builders of funds earmarked for highway use.

Varieties of Residential Development: Homes and Houses in City and Suburb

Extensions to the park system into the District and the suburban counties followed the paths blazed by residential development. The spread of development responded to the rapid rise in the District's population, especially between 1910 and 1920, when the city grew by nearly a third. Economy, profit, and technology dictated the perpetuation of the row house. A reinforcement of the rectangular grid as drawn by the highway engineers, the seemingly endless vistas of row houses moving northward through the District were deplored by the Commission of Fine Arts as presenting a "monotonous . . . shape of blocks of houses instead of isolated residences."

The Row House: Building Type and Block Development

The row house stemmed from a long tradition in the city and echoed the predominance of this house type in Baltimore and Philadelphia. The origins of the row-house type in building technology, standardization, and mass production allowed for the separation of housing units by party walls. Economy was achieved in the intensive use of the lot and the lack of a fourth independent freestanding wall. In the row-house mode of living, the front porch or stoop, as well as the backyard, was a platform for neighborhood social life. On Capitol Hill and in the southwest quadrant, the row house had long served the needs of the thousands of middle-class white-collar civil servants. The continuing influx of these employees argued for more of the same block development, following streetcar lines and blanketing the rest of the city—almost regardless of topography.

Located north of Florida Avenue along 14th Street NW, Petworth was a product of various developers, architects, and builders. Its various sections were developed in a piecemeal fashion on land flattened out by steam shovels and

Row Houses in the Trinidad Neighborhood, Northeast Washington. Photograph by Peter R. Penczer

human laborers who cut down hills and forced streets to conform to the highway plan grid. West of Rock Creek Park, Glover Park's street system conformed to fit the topography. East of the Anacostia River, River Terrace appealed to the working classes and was located close to schools, parks, and shopping.

The Petworth Neighborhood, Northwest Washington. Photograph by Peter R. Penczer

designed by architect Arthur Heaton and modeled after English garden cities. Their varied roof and facade treatments gave each adjoining dwelling a unique identity and differentiated the entire complex from surrounding neighborhoods. Unlike earlier suburban subdivisions, Burleith was developed as a whole rather than piecemeal.

Foxhall Village

In the same decade, between 1925 and 1930, Foxhall Village, exemplary of this community design concept, was constructed west of Georgetown University on Reservoir Road. Foxhall's developer, Boss & Phelps, described the "group houses" designed by James S. Cooper in the half-timbered English style as harking back to the old English village: "While adjoining, [they] are absolutely distinctive from so-called 'rowhouses' which are simply a number of houses all identical and adjoining one another. These houses are of an absolutely distinctive character and grouped together in such a way that the total mass makes a pleasing and harmonious composition." As in Burleith, here too were echoes of Baltimore's Roland Park. The Foxhall Village development, promising "city convenience with suburban atmosphere," incorporated the ameni-

Development of Burleith

To the west of Rock Creek Park, new interest was expressed in the development and design of entire architectural complexes or communities rather than single blocks. The development of Burleith between 1922 and 1928 represented an initial departure from the standard row-house design. A creation of the real estate skills of Shannon & Luchs, the five hundred homes were

ties of a verdant background in the form of
Foundry Branch Valley Park (later part of
Glover-Archbold Parkway) with memorable historical associations of the Foxhall Foundry and
antebellum country residences.

Unlike the row-house developments east of
Rock Creek Park, Foxhall Village's network of
streets was adapted to the hilly terrain by roadway layout within straight rights-of-way. To
some extent this "garden city" of row houses as
outlined in the village was made possible by
retention of the natural topography of varying
grades. When the city was dependent on horse-
drawn vehicles, the formal grades needed level-
ing. The automobile was able to conquer wide
changes in the natural grade with less effort.

Wesley Heights and Spring Valley
Development of the land west of Rock Creek
Park continued unabated into the twentieth century despite the best intentions of the Army
Corps of Engineers and the McMillan Commission. Large tracts of rugged land previously inaccessible were—with the automobile—made
available to more intensive occupation. Developer William C. Miller studied prizewinning
suburbs nationwide, including J. C. Nichols's
famed Country Club District in Kansas City. He

Construction of Massachu-
setts Avenue, 1911. Library
of Congress

Street Plan for Spring
Valley and Wesley Heights
in Washington, DC, 1931.
Leaves of Wesley Heights,
August 1931

hired John H. Small III, a landscape architect, to
lay out the affluent suburbs of Wesley Heights
starting in 1925 and Spring Valley in 1929 south
of the extended Massachusetts Avenue. These
subdivisions exhibited aspects of the most sensitive street geometry in the 1893 highway act and
were further defined by retention of the natural
contours of the land marked in careful planting

Advertisement for Spring Valley Homes, 1939. *Leaves of Wesley Heights,* May 1939

of trees and creation of rolling landscapes. Both subdivisions included planned shopping and community centers.

Both Wesley Heights and Spring Valley were controlled developments; all houses were Miller designed and Miller built. Architectural styles included various revivals, including Colonial and Tudor. The houses focused family life on the rear of the house, which led to large private yards. Both subdivisions were largely inaccessible by public transportation, resulting in highly protected living environments for the upper-class and upper-middle-class residents. Deed restrictions that forbade sale of the houses to African Americans and the "Semitic races" further protected the communities from the realities of urban life.

The Miller Company's developments exemplified the cooperative spirit set to work between real estate interests and the National Capital Park and Planning Commission as the latter adapted street plans both to hilly terrain and to the new park frontages. The completion in 1900 of the electric railroad up the Potomac to Glen Echo and the later popularity of the automobile allowed developers to take advantage of the "hilly, long-dormant lands" of the Palisades to create "showplaces of suburban beauty."

Massachusetts Avenue: The Fifth Avenue of Washington

Within the boundaries of the old city, and especially along Massachusetts Avenue, urban living on a grand scale clothed itself in eclectic classical garb. These grand private residences, Washington's equivalent of those on New York City's Fifth Avenue, were gradually converted into embassies with the multiplication of new foreign delegations in Washington. From Dupont Circle and northwest toward Rock Creek Park, these large urban mansions were constructed in the century's first two decades, clear evidence of the political and economic power of their clients. The mansion built for oil baron Senator Richard H. Townsend was constructed between 1899 and 1901 by the firm of Carrere & Hastings. On a powerful corner site, the Townsend residence— now the Cosmos Club—resembles the Petit Trianon at Versailles. Across the street, the Boston firm of Little and Browne created a sumptuous mansion for American diplomat Larz Anderson. The building now serves as headquarters for the Society of the Cincinnati. Described in *Massachusetts Avenue Architecture* as "one of the largest and costliest homes in the city," the structure exhibits the fusing of classical elements into an overall design reminiscent of a grand-style English country house.

Several architects of the École des Beaux-Arts responsible for the monumental public and institutional buildings in the post–McMillan Plan era also contributed to the residential growth of Kalorama and Massachusetts Avenue. The firm of McKim, Mead and White designed the elegant Patterson mansion on Dupont Circle. Jules H. de Sibour was responsible for at least four structures on Massachusetts Avenue, including the luxury apartment building near 18th Street designed for Stanley McCormick, son of the inventor of the reaper, Cyrus McCormick. Other apartment buildings and cultural institutions filled in the interstices, especially along Connecticut Avenue south of Rock Creek Park.

Beside the predominantly New York City architects was the Virginian Waddy B. Wood, designer of more than thirty mansions in the Kalorama and Massachusetts Avenue district and architect of the current Interior Department Building. Without compromising the panache of the Beaux-Arts school, Wood's greater attention to interior design and domestic detail allowed him to reflect in a more intimate fashion the characteristic lifestyle of the native Washingtonian.

CONSTRUCTION OF PUBLIC SCHOOLS

The spread of new housing developments necessitated new schools. The black and white schools that had once been located only a few blocks from one another were becoming spatially segregated as well. The white schools were constructed close to new row-house developments, which were almost exclusively for white residents. The black schools remained close to the black communities of the central city, including Burrville and Deanwood. It was difficult to locate a black school close to or in a predominantly white community; consequently, they tended to be clustered in already existing enclaves. So too did the distinction between the facilities for black and white students become more pronounced. White schools were larger and more numerous and boasted better amenities. During this period, junior high schools developed and served to bridge the intimate elementary schools

The Patterson House, 15 Dupont Circle, Designed by McKim, Mead and White, 1901. Library of Congress

Stoneleigh Court Apartment Building at Connecticut Avenue and L Street NW, ca. 1905. Library of Congress

Embassy Apartments at 16th and Harvard Streets NW, ca. 1925. Library of Congress

Glen Echo Amusement Park in Maryland, ca. 1925. Library of Congress

and the large and multifaceted senior high schools.

In 1909 the position of municipal architect was created under the engineer commissioner, which replaced the position of the building inspector. Under the municipal architect's supervision, a number of outstanding school buildings were constructed in the city. The first municipal architect, Snowden Ashford, served from 1909 until 1921. His buildings reflected his belief that the Collegiate Gothic style was the most appropriate for school buildings. In 1914–1916, he designed the famed and now demolished Dunbar High School Building, which served for decades as the highly competitive academic high

school for black students. Dunbar was located along 1st Street NW, which also was the location of Armstrong Manual Training School and other black schools in a tight enclave. During the same period, Central High School (renamed Cardozo High School in 1950, when it was turned over to black students) was constructed on the commanding ridge at 13th and Clifton streets NW for white students after designs by nationally recognized school architect William B. Ittner of St. Louis. Both Dunbar and Central were model specimens of the Collegiate Gothic style.

Ashford's successor, Albert L. Harris, preferred the Colonial Revival and Renaissance styles, and during his tenure, which lasted until 1934, he designed a great number of increasingly large school buildings throughout the city. Private architects also participated in the design of school buildings, including the well-known firms and designers Marsh & Peter, Leon Dessez, Waddy B. Wood, Appleton P. Clark Jr., and W. Sidney Pittman (a prominent black architect and son-in-law of Booker T. Washington). The schools that they designed were admired for their high architectural standards and for the quality of the education provided within.

FROM THE FAIRFAX COURTHOUSE TO ROCKVILLE

Less affluent residential areas had traditionally spread east of Rock Creek Park, reaching to both sides of the Anacostia River. The deteriorated or inadequate physical condition of housing in these areas inspired Charles Moore to respond to the housing emergency of 1919 by proposing, as reported in the *Annual Report of the Commission of Fine Arts* for 1926–1929, the "establishment of garden suburbs about the city of Washington, either within or without the District of Columbia, as residence places for Government workers of the intermediate and lower grades, both men and women."

Moore's vision of the large metropolitan areas as a resource available to resolve the District's environmental problems was significant because it reflected gradual realization of the city not only as the monumental core but also as the historically defined ten-mile square plus the four adjoining counties in Maryland and Virginia. As early as 1918, the commission suggested "suburban locations" for bureaus of the Interior Department. The following year, the commission stated that cooperation with Maryland and Virginia beyond the District line was necessary, especially if the commission was to influence the creation of Great Falls Park in its picturesque form as well as Mount Vernon Parkway, both recommended earlier by the McMillan Commission. Just six years later, in 1925, the automobile's impact on the metropolitan landscape forced the commission to acknowledge in its annual report for 1924–1925 that the regional city measured forty miles in diameter, extending from the Fairfax Courthouse to Rockville. "The use of the automobile has resulted in the expansion of the city into the surrounding country. The city [of Washington] itself has become the business nucleus." ★

THE YEAR OF DECISION 1926

7

Legitimization of Planning: Metropolitan City, National Capital

The year 1926 was a landmark for planning for the metropolitan city. That year the National Capital Park and Planning Commission was established and the Public Buildings Act passed, authorizing construction of the massive Federal Triangle. In placing major federal commitment behind planning for the monumental core and the city's ever-expanding edges, these congressional acts also responded to City Beautiful ideals. The elements of this abstract conception of the City Beautiful included carefully landscaped, architecturally designed approaches to the city by both land and water; an administrative or "civic center"; business districts whose visibility and access were reinforced by cutting in great diagonal boulevards; residential developments planned around focal points spinning out from the center of the city like a spiderweb; open spaces emphasizing hills, waterfronts, and highlights of the city's topography; and winding parkways connecting open spaces and residential areas with the central city. Washington was fortunate to possess many of these features; other American cities had to create them from scratch.

Promoters of the planning legislation saw these ideals, as translated and enunciated in 1902 by the McMillan Commission, imperiled by the relentless process of haphazard, piecemeal development. The legislation creating the planning commission laid the foundation for an agency that would be affected by evolving expectations of planning and by a rapidly changing city. By contrast, the Federal Triangle stands in style and plan as an artifact of Classical Revival impulses, subject to but not responsive to intrusions of the modern city.

The development of planning in Washington and the rest of the nation represented an outcome of what is called the Progressive era. Although the dates for this period vary from one source to another, generally it covers the last decade of the nineteenth century and the first two decades of the twentieth century. In this period, a newly emerging class of well-educated, professional people sought to overcome the entrenched power of political bosses and to implement rational solutions for society's problems, including the challenges of the cities and the ill effects of industrialization.

One outcome of this period was the emergence of new organizations to address urban issues and advocate reform.

BATTLE CRIES FOR PLANNING

Unlike other American cities, Washington had no body of local constituents that could persuade elected officials of the needs for a planning commission. How was planning legitimatized? National as well as local organizations seized the cause of planning in the nation's capital, congratulating themselves after passage of the 1924 act that created the National Capital Park Commission and then the 1926 act that created the National Capital Park and Planning Commission. A planned capital city would be an inspirational symbol for the nation's cities. To Progressives, it would serve as an expression of municipal reform. To businessmen, a planned city held the promise of an improved urban appearance and a magnet for commercial activity.

The notions of what a planning commission should do were by no means clear. Some thought the city should relate to L'Enfant and the precedents set by Washington and Jefferson. Others, like Charles Moore, thought that the 1901–1902 plan should serve as the controlling design for the city's future. Still others wanted for Washington a metropolitan park system commensurate with the urban systems designed for Boston and Chicago. Observers cognizant of comprehensive planning as already established in many American cities recognized the need for park planning but were also concerned about other considerations, such as traffic, housing, water, and the siting of public buildings. In the push for a planning commission in the capital city, the City Beautiful proponents and business-minded Progressive reformers prevailed over entrenched interests.

The McMillan Plan of 1901–1902 had been the first major achievement in raising the planning consciousness of Washington residents and the nation alike. Drawing on planning experience in other cities, much discussion flowed about the City Beautiful agenda—parks, public building

siting, the monumental core, and extension of physical amenities into the surrounding counties. Although in its time considered a "comprehensive plan," the McMillan Plan was soon overshadowed in scope by Daniel Burnham's Chicago plan of 1909. Burnham, an architectural superstar, was not regarded as part of the embryonic planning establishment. In this effort, he was assisted by Edward Bennett, who later became a noted urban planning consultant in his own right.

Burnham's name and promotional abilities as well as the vastness of the plan (covering a sixty-mile radius around the central city) and the ardent support of the Chicago business interests energized the aspirations of other cities. These aspirations began to be realized when Hartford, Connecticut, established a planning commission in 1907, followed by Milwaukee, Wisconsin, in 1911. But in Washington, with its urban design tradition, it was the need to acquire parks that inspired the initial battle cries for planning. The Chicago plan and newly established planning commissions around the country contributed ammunition as well.

The city's natural landscape and the historical forces that molded the monumental core led to the emphasis on the acquisition of what was left of the city's open space. Parks—as in lower Rock Creek valley—were also a means of urban rehabilitation. By the early twentieth century, the city embodied a strong landscape identity. As John Nolen Sr. said in an interview with Harland Bartholomew, Washington was "a city set in a framework of open space . . . a city proud and aware of its setting and place."

These features were capitalized on by the landscape emphasis that Frederick Law Olmsted Jr. had given the McMillan Plan. Green open space served as the monumental core's basic cloth into which the public buildings were woven. The emphasis on parks was sustained somewhat by the dreamy illustrations of Burnham's Chicago plan as drawn by artist Jules Guerin, although that plan also dealt with many other concerns of physical planning. The Boston Metropolitan

Aerial View of the Neighborhood Around 16th Street and Columbia Road NW, Early 1920s. DC Public Library, Washingtoniana Division, DC Community Archives

Park System offered compelling illustrations of continuous and comprehensive strips of greenery. Emphasis on parks was also an element of lingering interest to romantics in picturesque landscapes and to reformers in the presumed social benefits of playgrounds and recreational facilities.

ZONING ORDINANCE, 1920

The adoption in 1920 of a zoning ordinance for Washington signaled the importance of planning for the nonpark areas of the city. Some controls on Washington's growth earlier had been exercised by regulation of building heights and separation of business activities from residential areas. To draw up the zoning ordinance, Harland Bartholomew, a noted planner from St. Louis, worked closely with District of Columbia commissioners Louis Brownlow and Colonel Charles W. Kutz. Borrowing staff from the Army Corps of Engineers, Bartholomew studied land-use data and made recommendations for the separation of residential, commercial, and industrial

uses, each with specific regulations for "height, use, and area of buildings to be erected." Bartholomew described Washington's zoning as a compromise between the three categories drawn up in the 1916 New York City ordinance and the several subcategories he designed for St. Louis in 1918. Upon completion of the Washington work, Bartholomew recommended the creation of a planning commission to coordinate zoning with future growth of the city—and avoid typical results of the failure to plan land use.

THE AMERICAN PLANNING AND CIVIC ASSOCIATION

Local citizens' efforts were effective in mustering support for planning in their cities and working with planning bodies once they were established. In 1924 John Nolen Sr. of Cambridge, Massachusetts, summarized the work of citizens' groups working for planning in ten American cities, ranging from the metropolis of Chicago to cities of more modest size, such as Johnstown, Pennsylvania. With no local citizen-based group in the national capital, the American Planning and Civic Association (known as the American Civic Association until 1935 and later merged into the National Urban Coalition) performed this function. It was primarily a civic association aimed at numerous and diverse city improvements across the nation. In the 1920s, planning for cities, national parks, and civic centers had been assigned a higher priority than many other municipal activities.

Frederic Delano and Harlean James
President of the American Planning and Civic Association until 1935, Frederic Delano worked for the creation of a planning commission in the nation's capital. He served as chairman of the National Capital Park and Planning Commission after its founding in 1926. Born in Hong Kong in 1863, Delano enjoyed an illustrious career in American railroads in both engineering and executive capacities. A longtime resident of Washington, he was deeply committed to its future. As uncle and father figure to President Franklin Roosevelt, he urged his nephew to make major decisions affecting the city, such as, for example, using presidential influence to support Edward Bennett's proposed Apex Building in the Federal Triangle. With no specific training in planning, Delano was primarily a political and administrative figure and an indubitable business and political leader. Moreover, he had been the leader of the outstanding city planning program in Chicago and was a prime organizer of the *Regional Plan of New York and Its Environs,* which was published in 1928.

Delano "discovered" the future secretary of the American Planning and Civic Association, Harlean James. Delano had brought James to Washington during World War I to be manager of the wartime women's residence halls sited between Union Station and the Capitol. James, born in Mattoon, Illinois, in 1871, graduated from Stanford University in 1898, the class of the future Mrs. Herbert Hoover. Moving to Honolulu in 1901, James worked as a court reporter

and as an executive secretary to various island corporations. Returning to the mainland in 1911, she launched her planning and civic career in Baltimore, where she worked as executive secretary of the Women's Civic League between 1911 and 1916. After her national defense and housing appointments in Washington during the war years, she became executive secretary of the American Planning and Civic Association in 1921 and editor of its yearly publication, the *American Civic and Planning Annual,* and served in these capacities until 1948. Harlean James also achieved professional recognition as author of *Land Planning in the United States for the City, State and Nation,* an important early study in land economics.

The clout exercised by the American Planning and Civic Association could be attributed to the executive talents of James. Grafting association members' expertise onto the congressional process, the association's staff worked with congressmen and their staffs, wrote speeches, drafted legislation, and presented testimony. Acting as an effective lobbying organization by working through the old-boy network of West Point and Harvard graduates and similar connections, the American Planning and Civic Association was able to influence congressional action, appointments, and policies in all government agencies concerned with parks and planning. Through the process of holding meetings, passing timely resolutions, and writing effective letters, the organization's staff exercised remarkable power, particularly in defending parklands from incompatible intrusions.

The Grassroots Committees
Important to the development of planning in the national capital, the American Planning and Civic Association also created "Federal City" committees in various states; seventy-five committees existed by 1924. The popularity of these grassroots committees was explained by a new national awareness of the rapid expansion Washington had experienced during World War I. The city had become a "suddenly enlarged metropo-

lis." These field committees voiced a common cry for the coordination of zoning, park development, and city planning in the nation's capital. They were as weary as other civic and trade organizations of the failure of annual legislation and appropriations to cope with the rapidly disappearing forests and mementos of the National Capital Region's rural past.

Thus, although the voteless city of Washington had no local constituency, it did have national voter concern, as expressed in the appeal of the American Planning and Civic Association and other organizations to "citizens of the entire nation." This sentiment was epitomized by Lieutenant Colonel C. O. Sherrill, officer in charge of public buildings and grounds in the District, in a 1923 address to the Association of City Planners in Baltimore: "If we are ever to have a great national capital, worthy of the greatest nation on earth, we must arouse a deep personal interest among the people of the whole country in the development of the nation's capital. A splendid start has been made in this direction by the American Civic Association."

Besides marshaling support throughout the nation for the planning of the federal city, the American Planning and Civic Association fostered an alliance of the professional societies of architects, landscape architects, city planners, and progressive real estate interests. This alliance was formalized as the Joint Committee on the National Capital for which Harlean James provided the secretarial and executive function. Not only did the nation's citizens look upon the capital city with great affection second only to that for their own hometowns, but they viewed the success of planning the capital city as the inspirational model for other American cities.

In Washington itself, the Committee of 100 served, for all practical purposes, as the local branch of the American Planning and Civic Association and was, in many respects, an extended arm of the Washington Board of Trade. Initially composed of the city's leading businessmen, especially owners of the Washington newspapers, the Committee of 100 served as a power-ful local voice in the push toward a national capital planning commission. Frederic Delano was also a leader in this organization.

HERBERT HOOVER AND AMERICAN INDIVIDUALISM

Organized governmental and business initiative paralleled the rising civic demand for planning in the nation's capital. Ideas expressed by these organizations found fertile ground in the person of Herbert Hoover. An embodiment of the interests of the businessman and government, Hoover followed a notable career as a financially successful mining engineer and a relief administrator during and after World War I. The tools of technology and the politics of a society's renewal prepared him for his key role in planning. As an engineer, Hoover was concerned with efficiency and overcoming waste, both objectives achieved by sound management and standardization. As an administrator of food and recovery programs in war-torn Europe, Hoover had witnessed firsthand the effects on an entire society, especially the children, of war brought on by extremist ideologies.

After nearly four years of European work, Hoover returned to America, grateful for his country's relative detachment from polarizing politics. He found, however, an America unsettled by the war experience of rapid industrialization to provide army materiel and the attendant urban congestion created by settlements close to strategic manufacturing centers. Throughout the 1920s, generally stereotyped as an era of prosperity, large pockets of poverty persisted, ripe for exploitation by what Hoover viewed as un-American economic philosophies. Fearing the "infection of America" by the socialist and communist movements raging in Europe, Hoover wrote *American Individualism*. In this treatise, he attempted to define the American system of capitalism and democracy and its foundation—family life.

THE FIGHT FOR BETTER HOUSING

Appointed by President Warren G. Harding as secretary of commerce, Hoover settled in Washington and commenced to "reconstruct the American economy." Beginning at society's roots, he viewed the supply of more and better housing as critical to America's ability to recuperate from the war. In 1922 he created within the Commerce Department the Division of Building and Housing of the Bureau of Standards, headed by Harvard economist John M. Gries. During Gries's tenure, the division pursued research and published results on housing construction and maintenance as well as zoning and credit. Applying the efficiency procedures of professional engineers, the division sought to standardize building methods and regulations, a concern of the construction industry. Convinced of businessmen's obligation to lead the nation toward better cities, Hoover sought their blessing for government projects and goals. Among several gestures of cooperation, the US Chamber of Commerce also endorsed greater efficiency, lower costs, and the development of resources in the sphere of housing as outlined by Hoover.

The other side of the problem in housing construction was slum clearance. Hoover looked proudly at the decade's major public building projects in Washington, the Federal Triangle and the expansion of the Legislative Group around the Capitol, as significant examples of slum clearance. In promoting housing, Hoover recognized the larger issues of city planning, municipal activities, and land use as affected by zoning, often drawing on Washington for examples of excellence in appearance and management. In his advocacy position as secretary of commerce, Hoover spread the housing theme into the civic sector, creating a volunteer organization called Better Homes in America. Spurred on by Mrs. William Brown Meloney, a talented publicist, the organization served to support the Commerce Department's ideas. Throughout his presidency, Hoover served as president of Better Homes in America.

THE CONFERENCE ON HOME BUILDING, 1931

Hoover's pursuit of the housing cause for more than a decade climaxed in December 1931 with the President's Conference on Home Building and Home Ownership. Organized by Gries and his former Harvard colleague James Ford, the conference brought together thousands of the country's major figures in planning, housing, and business. Symbolic of this coalition, the sessions were held at the Willard and Washington hotels, the US Chamber of Commerce, an office building occupied by the Commerce Department, and the DAR Constitution Hall. Nationwide network radio carried the entire proceedings to the public. The conference commenced with a speech by President Hoover in which he crystallized the deep American sentiment for home ownership and the "sweetness of family life." Underlying this basic philosophy of housing was Hoover's belief that "there can be no fear for a democracy or self-government or for liberty or freedom from home owners no matter how humble they may be." Hoover exhorted conference participants to take advantage of tools offered them by science and technology, to correlate their experiences, to establish standards, and to push for legislative action. Summaries of the conference were published, as well as ten bound volumes outlining the work of thirty-one committees.

Reflecting Washington's experience and aspirations, Charles Eliot, director of planning at the National Capital Park and Planning Commission, recorded the virtues of the planned neighborhood unit. The former president of the Chamber of Commerce, Harry A. Wheeler, chaired the committee on Slums, Large-Scale Housing, and Decentralization and presented illustrations of the alley dwellings in the national capital. These alleys were described as "small, hidden communities in centers of large blocks." John Ihlder, former executive director of both the Massachusetts Housing Association and the Pittsburgh Housing Association and in 1931 a housing consultant to the National Capital Park and Planning Commission, outlined his study of census data, describing housing and family-life patterns deduced from the information. Throughout the published records of the conference, the city of Washington—then at its apogee of middle-class occupancy—was referred to repeatedly, both for examples of desirable housing types and arrangements and for illustrations of the "problem."

BUSINESS SUPPORT FOR THE PLANNING ISSUE

Reliable support for city planning as indicated by Herbert Hoover and Harry Wheeler emerged from strong business traditions exemplified in Chicago as much in the recovery after the 1871 fire as in the successful 1893 World's Columbian Exposition. Business interests in other cities followed suit, bearing the responsibility of influencing the creation of local planning commissions and enactment of zoning laws. And it was, in fact, enlightened and progressive businessmen who promoted the planning issue in the national capital city.

Initially, a sector of business had responded coolly to Harland Bartholomew's 1920 zoning design on the assumption that row housing would be threatened by the imposition of zoning. In some respects, Washington was a bad place for real estate investment, as residency was often only temporary and the future of government operations concentrated in the monumental core was uncertain. Thus a distinctive pattern of tenancy, mortgage lending, real estate, and housing ownership developed, characteristics that when translated into physical form amounted to rental housing and low-cost row-house building. Bartholomew's detailed land-use study in 1920 had revealed only 190 apartment buildings in the city but showed that sufficient land existed for additional housing of this increasingly popular type. The study also showed that whereas of the city's population 71 percent occupied row houses, 14 percent lived in detached houses, and ample additional sites were provided for both categories. In the end, the city's progressive business interests voiced hearty support for the regulation of land use in the city in hopes of stabilizing real estate values and improving the appearance of the city. There was support also for the creation of a planning commission to match zoning with urban growth as recommended by Bartholomew.

THE US CHAMBER OF COMMERCE: NATIONAL PLANNING CAUSES

The businessman's responsibility was further registered in the activities of the US Chamber of Commerce. Founded in 1912 to represent trade and civic associations, the Chamber of Commerce was housed in a number of office buildings close to the financial district along 15th Street. During World War I, the chamber worked closely with the government through its War Services Committee so that war materiel could be supplied efficiently. This government–business community relationship, strained under the trust-busting of the Theodore Roosevelt era, became harmonious in the interest of national defense.

At the chamber's annual meeting in 1919, President Harry A. Wheeler suggested that the chamber construct a headquarters building of its own. Such a building would secure the identity of the Chamber of Commerce, state its permanency, and "commemorate the patriotic part which American business had played in the World War." The building was to mark a climax in business prestige in the capital city. Symbolic of the chamber's sympathies with the planning goals in Washington, the new Chamber of Commerce Building was located on the site of the old Corcoran residence at Connecticut and H streets. As the 1925 *Annual Report of the United States Chamber of Commerce* noted, the site "opposite Lafayette Park places it in a position close to many of the executive departments of government" and "in conformity with the general plan of the Federal Fine Arts Commission for the development of Lafayette Square as an Executive Center."

At the time the chamber's building was being planned for the Lafayette Square site, it was reported that a new State Department Building was also to be sited on the square, just to the west, between Jackson Place and 17th Street,

Lafayette Square, the Hay-Adams House, and the Future Site of the US Chamber of Commerce, 1922. US Chamber of Commerce Library

although this proposal was never implemented. Thus, when its building was occupied in 1924, the chamber had expected that most of the square would be completed according to the outlines of the McMillan Commission report and the plans of the Commission of Fine Arts for the Executive Group that Cass Gilbert had prepared. The chamber building's architectural style was equally harmonious. Designed by Cass Gilbert, architect also of the Treasury Annex on Lafayette Square, the Chamber of Commerce Building displayed a classic Corinthian exterior that enclosed an arcaded court, an important environmental amenity before air conditioning. Having in mind more than just an office building, Gilbert designed several meeting rooms, a library, and a memorial hall on the first floor. In these rooms many significant meetings and conferences promoting improvements in Washington were held.

THE ROLE OF JOHN IHLDER

Reflecting Hoover's and the chamber's common belief that the future of cities' business communities would be "largely determined by their housing accommodations," the chamber estab-

lished a Civic Development Department in late 1920. This department, important in expressing the businessman's interest in housing, was headed by John Ihlder between 1920 and 1928. Best known in Washington history for his later work as director of the National Capital Housing Authority, Ihlder was born in Baltimore in 1876. He began his career as a writer for newspapers and magazines. In 1908 he moved to Grand Rapids, Michigan, where he worked for its Chamber of Commerce. Branching into the housing field in 1910, he worked for a number of social and housing organizations until 1920, when he joined the US Chamber of Commerce.

Under Ihlder, the Civic Development Department echoed Hoover's prescription for a recovered America: maximum use of resources and minimum wastage. The Civic Development Department's Bureau of Housing and City Planning offered member trade associations instructions on zoning and planning, responding to the view that planning was a "modern method of ensuring the use of every natural advantage and preventing waste in city building." Whereas in the past the direction of city growth had been

unregulated, the Civic Development Department stated that, with zoning, businessmen and residents could expect stabilized property values, more building construction and thus prosperity and prevention of "great losses due to the blighting of neighborhoods in unwise developments." A tool of "order and economy," zoning appealed to the scientific and statistical persuasions of Hoover and Ihlder, hence the effort to standardize zoning in the Bureau of Standards.

THE METROPOLITAN WASHINGTON BOARD OF TRADE: LOCAL PLANNING CAUSES

Whereas the Chamber of Commerce espoused national planning causes that reflected heavily the capital city's experiences, the Washington Board of Trade took up the banner of purely local improvements. Founded in 1889, the board was the city's major business and trade association. Its membership was composed of businessmen, artists, civil servants, and architects like Horace Peaslee, Louis Justement, Thomas A. Mullett, and George Oakley Totten Jr. In the absence of a voting constituency to which the Congress and the president might respond, the

board saw itself as representative of "all sectors and interests of the city." The Board of Trade exerted a strong influence on the affairs of Washington, especially in cooperation with such nationally recognized associations as the American Institute of Architects and the American Planning and Civic Association. The board saw the voluntary nature of its work as a strength: "Only through their civic organizations and popular bodies whose standing is entirely unofficial can Washingtonians express their needs and wishes for the general welfare, in such concerted manner as to command the respect and attention of the national legislators who are charged with the duty of maintaining the District government."

The board's motives were not entirely altruistic. In fact, members' prosperity rode on the city's growth and appearance. For several years, the board published *The Book of Washington,* an impressive collection of articles, illustrations, and advertisements reminiscent of nineteenth-century city "booster" publications. Unabashedly, the 1927 issue stated, "Our one aim is to make Washington . . . the most beautiful and the more desirable community in which to live and transact business." Toward this goal, the board established among its committees several that gave special attention to the promotion of public improvements: on Bridges, on Municipal Art, on Parks and Reservations, on Public and Private Buildings, on Sewerage, and on Streets and Avenues.

COMMENDED . . . DISAPPROVED: COMMITTEE REVIEW

The Committees on Municipal Art and on Public and Private Buildings followed ideals of the McMillan Commission and the Commission of Fine Arts. Taking comfort that the Commission of Fine Arts officially oversaw the appearance of public buildings, in an unofficial way the committees sought to set standards for private architecture and artworks. The Committee on Municipal Art issued annual awards for outstanding examples of architecture as judged by two Baltimore architects. Appleton P. Clark Jr., architect and chairman of the committee for much of the 1920s, suggested that in improving Pennsylvania Avenue the "Chicago example" be followed, and thus, through voluntary efforts by building clients, a control of facades was exercised. To stimulate such cooperation—as seen, for example, in the widely admired addition to the Evening Star Building, designed by the firm of Marsh and Peter—tax incentives were proposed although never adopted. As the 1921–1922 *Annual Report of the Washington Board of Trade* stated, "The only feasible method . . . [of] encouraging a certain standard of improvement [is] with subsidies in the shape of remissions of taxes for a period of possibly twenty years."

The board's Committee on Public and Private Buildings attempted to persuade the clients and architects of private buildings by opinions generated by the Architects' Advisory Council. Working through a panel of five "elders of the profession," the committee reviewed all plans filed in the municipal building permit office and rated them by one of four classifications: commended, approved, not approved, disapproved. The committee stated in 1924, "The most frequent suggestion is for simplification of design." Despite the noncompulsory nature of the advisory council's assessments, "with such assistance, freely given, it is inexcusable that any man would put up a building which is a reflection of his own [individual or personal] good taste or a blot upon his city." Architectural design was to be arrived at through a consensus.

EXTENSION INTO VIRGINIA AND MARYLAND

In committees such as those on Bridges, on Streets and Avenues, and on Sewerage, the Washington Board of Trade favored extension of the city into Virginia and Maryland via bridge connections. Virginia was an attractive area in residential and real estate terms, especially when the historic and bucolic charms of Old Virginia were evoked. Keenly aware of the effect of modern transportation on the tourist business, the board in its 1924 annual report recommended the improvement of Chain Bridge to connect with the hard surface road (later Route 50) to Berryville in Clarke County, Virginia, then under construction "to permit tourists to take advantage of a trip to Washington in going to and from this popular tourist section." A similar improvement of the Pennsylvania Avenue Bridge over the Anacostia River was to link the city of Washington to Maryland roads leading to the Chesapeake Bay beaches, Leonardtown, and Annapolis.

The Committee on Streets and Avenues endorsed congressional bills extending 14th Street, New York Avenue, and New Hampshire Avenue to the District line, strengthening the city's impact in Maryland. Yet growth brought its own hazards, as studied by the Board of Trade's Committee on Sewerage. In the board's 1923 annual report, this committee stated that "healthful growth is throttled and imperiled here by a failure to develop the suburban sewerage system of the national capital sufficiently to keep step with the home building." Already the area's rich natural and recreational resources were being defiled: polluted waters entering the Tidal

Row Houses on Princeton Street NW in the Park View Neighborhood, ca. 1920. Library of Congress

Basin's bathing beach caused eye and ear infections. According to the 1921–1922 annual report, raw sewage flowing into the Potomac had "menace[d] the oyster beds of the lower river." In listing the sources of pollution, the Committee on Sewerage had recommended an upper Potomac interceptor to remove sewage between the mouth of Rock Creek and Little Falls, the completion of the interceptor in Rock Creek and the Anacostia to "carry off sewage from Maryland towns," and the construction of purification works at Shepherd's Point on the Potomac to purify the river.

THE COMMITTEE ON PARKS AND RESERVATIONS

Among the Washington Board of Trade's many contributions to planning and parks acquisitions in the city, the achievements of the Committee on Parks and Reservations stand as the most substantial. Like other civic groups and individuals, the committee, chaired by Fred Coldren, decried the loss of open country to the hand of the developer. Citing an address by the former

British ambassador Lord Bryce, a glorious description of Washington as transcending any European counterpart, the committee suggested that his words "should be made a textbook in our public and private schools." In the same annual report for 1924, the committee claimed that as early as 1900 the Washington Board of Trade had adopted a resolution recommending that "Congress pass an act authorizing the appointing of a Commission to devise and report a plan for development of the Capital City." No official response was made toward a general plan, and for the twenty-four years that ensued, the Board of Trade watched the McMillan Commission's recommendations for parks dwindle away under the exigencies of piecemeal congressional appropriations for individual tracts of land and the overwhelming speed of development.

In 1922 the Committee on Parks and Reservations drew up a draft bill to create a National Capital Park Commission, stating that the "forests and valleys are being destroyed far more rapidly than they can possibly be preserved under the present system." Aided by endorsements by the US Chamber of Commerce, the chief of the Army Corps of Engineers, the Committee of 100, and the American Planning and Civic Association, the bill passed "with very slight amendments from the draft as originally framed." Most of the changes in the final bill were in the provisions for membership of the new commission.

Legislation for Comprehensive Planning: The Acts of 1924 and 1926

Although the McMillan Commission's work was not specifically mentioned in the 1924 and 1926 acts, it was constantly referred to in annual reports and in maps prepared by the National Capital Park and Planning Commission. Strongly promoted by the Planning Commission, the McMillan Plan finally received congressional endorsement in 1929. The acts of 1924 and 1926 would thus achieve one of the major objectives—to include basic concepts of the McMillan Plan in all new comprehensive planning for the city and region.

THE NATIONAL CAPITAL PARK COMMISSION

The act creating the National Capital Park Commission was signed into law on June 6, 1924. The membership was composed of the chief of the Army Corps of Engineers, the engineer commissioner of the District of Columbia, the director of the National Park Service (established in 1916), the officer of the corps in charge of public buildings and grounds (who also served as executive and disbursing officer), and the chairmen of the Senate and House committees on the District of Columbia. Outlining the general areas of park and playground acquisition, this act authorized the commission to acquire lands in the District, Virginia, and Maryland, with the advice of the Commission of Fine Arts.

To carry out these acquisitions, the act provided $1.1 million on an annual basis. Both the Boston Metropolitan Park System and the McMillan Plan were invoked in the recommen-

dation that the commission turn its attention to "Rock Creek and the Potomac and Anacostia Rivers . . . and to provide for the comprehensive, systematic, and continuous development of park, parkway, and playground systems of the National Capital."

The Board of Trade and other civic and government groups had won the battle but not the war. To be sure, the Park Commission was created—but Congress still had to appropriate annual funds for parkland acquisition. In Fred Coldren's 1924 annual report of the Committee on Parks and Reservations to the board, he complained that the Bureau of the Budget had assigned only $600,000 to cover the 1924 and 1925 fiscal years. His study of possible park areas revealed the alarming situation that many of these tracts were "now imminently threatened with destruction or . . . irreparable injury," a situation not likely to be reversed by the meager appropriations.

One means for limiting development on the picturesque tracts sought by the Park Commission was to enlist the aid of the Chamber of Commerce and Board of Trade to "informally arrange for individuals to secure critical areas and hold them for later consideration for purchase by the [Park Commission] at the same prices which they paid for the tract." This plan of relying on the beneficence of wealthy citizens to provide a sort of revolving fund seemed feasible in light of the sources of support for the 1924 act. The 1923 gifts by Charles C. Glover and Anne Archbold of the land in the valley of Foundry Branch—later known as the Glover-Archbold Parkway—stood as proof positive of the potential importance of private grants.

Not only were the annual appropriations a severe hindrance to carrying out the expectations of visitors and city residents for the amenities of parklands, but also the commission found itself powerless to influence the city's plan except for structuring growth within the configurations created by the protected parklands. In March 1925, the National Capital Park Commission asked the executive secretary, Lieutenant Colonel

C. O. Sherrill, to hire the park planner James C. Langdon and to create a City Planning Committee to operate under the Park Commission. Drawing on the Park Commission's longtime supporters, this committee was to be composed of a representative of the Committee of 100, "preferably Mr. [Frederic] Delano," and members of the various district engineering and parks offices. Clearly the Park Commission was functioning in a position of weakness. By October

and November 1925, the commission was discussing broadening its functions to include comprehensive planning.

THE NATIONAL CAPITAL PARK AND PLANNING COMMISSION: THE COMPREHENSIVE PLAN

Planning powers were finally granted in April 1926 as an amendment to the 1924 act. Renaming the body the National Capital Park and Planning Commission, the 1926 act outlined a host of new

Glover-Archbold Parkway Site West of Georgetown University. National Capital Planning Commission Collection

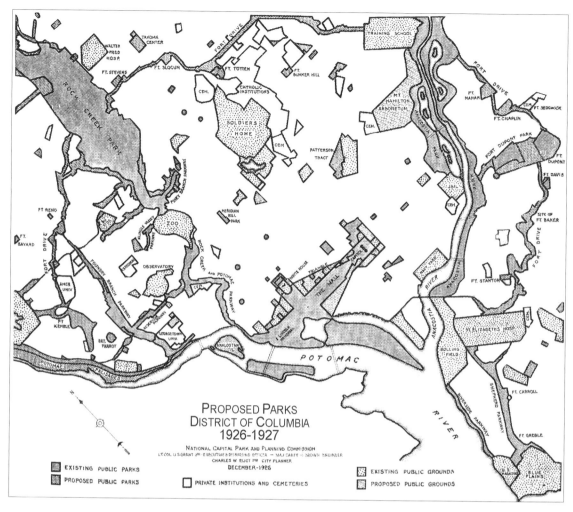

Plan of Proposed Parks in the District of Columbia, 1926-1927. *Annual Report of the National Capital Park and Planning Commission, 1928*

duties in "preparing, developing, and maintaining a comprehensive, consistent and coordinated plan for the National Capital and its environs," embracing transportation, subdivisions, public building sites, sewerage, zoning, commerce, industry, and "other proper elements of city and regional planning." Charged with coordinating the plans of federal and district departments, the National Capital Park and Planning Commission was empowered to exercise influence, although not force compliance, in the planning of the massive building projects inaugurated by the Federal Triangle project, also funded in 1926.

Members of the National Capital Park and Planning Commission responded to the professionalization of planning. In addition to the ex officio members who were members of the Park Commission (except the director of public buildings and public parks of the national capital now

replaced the officer of the Army Corps of Engineers in charge of public buildings and grounds), four "eminent citizens well qualified and experienced in city planning, one of whom shall be a bona fide resident of the District of Columbia, [shall] be appointed for the term of six years by the President of the United States." The National Capital Park and Planning Commission was also authorized to employ a professional staff and consultants. Answering the long-heard pleas of the Commission of Fine Arts and the Washington Board of Trade, the 1895 Highway Commission was abolished and its powers transferred to the National Capital Park and Planning Commission.

The establishment of a planning commission for the capital city can be said to have long postdated the experience of many other cities where planning commissions had been created in the early years of the twentieth century. Yet even before the 1926 act—in fact, since the postbellum era when the Corps of Engineers exercised de facto planning powers—the city had experienced specialized functions of planning such as the platting of extended transportation routes, the regulating of height limitations, and zoning. The city had also been affected by broader conceptions about groupings of public buildings and monuments and by the comprehensive parks system plan enunciated by the McMillan Commission and supported by the Commission of Fine Arts. In this context, then, Washington in 1926 by no means lagged behind planning activities elsewhere.

The 1926 act vested powers in the National Capital Park and Planning Commission to prepare a comprehensive plan, but parkways to and through the city remained the dominant themes in the agency's work program. These landscaped ribbons were basic elements of City Beautiful planning and as such were the foundations of a movement nearing the end of its sway. Although some promoters of planning might have rested content with the motto of the Municipal Art Society of New York—"To make us love our city, we must make our city lovely"—others were looking toward newer goals. For Washington, the 1926 act marked the beginning of newer goals in planning. These were partly expressed in the fact that the business community and government agencies had already voiced concern for housing, traffic, the effects of land use, health issues, and neighborhoods—social issues that would envelop planning in the following decades.

Renewal of large sections of the historic city would produce a strengthened central focus for the metropolitan city. This monumental core would give the larger area its unique character, with which both residents and visitors could identify. Representative of the federal establishment, this core would now demand the attention of lawmakers. New public buildings, on the functional level, would house the expanded bureaus of government and, on the symbolic plane, would embody the nation's cultural achievements. In Washington, the settings and arrangements for these buildings would help determine future planning constraints in the L'Enfant city. At the same time, these powerful images of the federal presence would fuel the mounting forces toward dispersal into the metropolitan city.

The lack of a comprehensive plan for the siting and building of public facilities resulted in a piecemeal decision-making process that appropriated funds for each building project as it was individually deemed necessary. Thus, before the McMillan Commission, which provided the first large-scale plan since L'Enfant's, the city had illustrated many rapidly evolving notions about "good" public architecture. Building sites chosen were often determined by structural feasibility rather than by grand design. Today, this dispersed and variegated pattern speaks of design evolution over historical time. In the early twentieth century, however, these artifacts of a less organized planning process were deplored.

As long as the federal establishment continued to expand, the government was faced with securing new spaces to house its employees. The leisurely pace of public building construction before World War I was hastened dramatically during the war by construction of the seemingly permanent "tempos." After the war, the federal establishment did not shrink back to its prewar numbers but reflected new and enlarged services demanded by postwar conditions. Executive department employees were accommodated in rented spaces secured in private office buildings; thus, the extent of the government's presence in the city was somewhat obscured. In 1925, however, the Department of Commerce alone reported that it was housed in seventeen separate buildings. As the *Annual Report of the Public Buildings Commission* for 1924 had pointed out, the variously housed government departments suffered from a "feeling of separateness, even of isolation, on the part of remoter units, that is harmful." Often these private quarters were deemed to be on the brink of condemnation, posing serious fire risks.

A Scene Near Center Market, the Current Site of the National Archives, ca. 1932. Ross Postcard Collection, DC Community Archives, DC Public Library

The Public Buildings Act of 1926: The Federal Triangle Project

Actively supported by Secretary of Commerce Herbert Hoover, the Public Buildings Act of 1926 provided $50 million for the construction of public buildings in the District of Columbia. Half the amount was to be spent on building south of Pennsylvania and New York avenues and west of Maryland Avenue, the site later known as the Federal Triangle. The other half of the appropriation was to be spent on sites for the Supreme Court and an extension of the Government Printing Office. The triangle area was the large squalid slice of land that had accumulated an infamous reputation in the nineteenth century as a haven for the city's criminal element and included the area known as Murder Bay. Before the Potomac flats reclamation, frequent threats of flooding in the area had discouraged the siting of public buildings in this uncertain lowland.

The Center Market stalls were surrounded by a busy and noisy atmosphere, but the importance of the triangular area was diminished by removal of much of the residential population beyond comfortable walking distance and introduction of light industry. Viewed thus as a blighted area, the triangle was set for marked change. In this direction, completion in 1899 of the Romanesque Post Office on 12th Street pro-

vided a false start but one that nonetheless indicated the government's interest in the area. In 1910 the long strip along 15th Street—facing the White House and grounds—was acquired for executive department buildings intended to mirror the developing monumental lineup of Beaux-Arts creations opposite, along 17th Street. Had Congress appropriated funds for public buildings at that site and the 1910 plans been carried out, the Federal Triangle might never have been realized as a single composition.

Planning for the Project: Initiatives and Responsibility

Responsibility for the Federal Triangle project fell to the Treasury Department, the traditional home of the Office of the Supervising Architect. At the time the office was held by Louis E. Simon, a talented design administrator. Since the project was of unprecedented scale and involved the skills of architect, landscape architect, and planner, coordination called for designers representing the widest national experience. The Federal Triangle project was launched before the newly organized National Capital Park and Planning Commission had a chance to come to grips with the project's urban design. The new commission therefore was unable to influence planning for the Triangle until after the essential form had been agreed upon. As for the Treasury Department, never had it exercised its wide-ranging powers over public buildings to such advantage. Most significantly, for the first time since the McMillan Plan had been formulated a quarter century earlier, there was strong federal commitment to achieving its goals.

The Mellon-Bennett Relationship

Key to the project's success as a work of art was Secretary of the Treasury Andrew W. Mellon. Born in Pittsburgh in 1855, Mellon had had experience almost wholly in financial and industrial corporations and in local public affairs in Pittsburgh until 1921, when he became Treasury secretary in President Harding's cabinet. Mellon gathered the nation's brightest professionals into his daily circles. Later, in 1933, in face of mounting but unsubstantiated accusations of tax irregularities, Mellon resigned from the Treasury to assume the post of ambassador to Great Britain. Although his public image was shadowed, Mellon won the affection of friends and associates by his enthusiasm for sharing his art collection, which later became the nucleus of the National Gallery of Art.

When the Treasury Department was faced with the large-scale Federal Triangle building project, representing an expansion far beyond any earlier dreams for a 15th Street classical facade, Assistant Secretary of the Treasury Charles S. Dewey suggested to Mellon that Edward H. Bennett of Chicago advise him. Dewey had earlier consulted with his friend Bennett on the initial building plans and suggested that Bennett serve as chairman of a new Board of Architectural Consultants. Born in Cheltenham, England, in 1874, Bennett had worked for Daniel Burnham as a planning assistant on the 1905 San Francisco and 1908 Chicago plans. Prepared with an education at the École des Beaux-Arts and several years' experience in the New York City office of George B. Post, Bennett worked with Burnham before launching his independent planning career in 1909. In 1924 he formed an architectural and planning partnership known as Bennett, Parsons, and Frost.

Much of Bennett's midwestern work, especially in Chicago, was derivative of Burnham's far-reaching Chicago regional plan; Bennett also followed Burnham's footsteps in Manila and other cities. Thus, it was a man of considerable and specialized experience that Dewey called upon in September 1926 to advise Mellon on public buildings. Mellon's instructions were broad: he wished Bennett, as the latter recorded in his diaries, to be his "personal architectural advisor." In the six years of the Mellon-Bennett relationship, the architect advised the secretary on the Federal Triangle, the Mall, the site for the intended art gallery, the Legislative Group, the site for the Supreme Court Building, and proposed memorials.

THE CONFERENCE ON THE CAPITAL'S DEVELOPMENT, 1929

With the legislation passed and the designers chosen, President Hoover and other key Federal Triangle supporters realized that the project needed to demonstrate public support if congressional appropriations were to be made on schedule and the entire program accomplished within a few years' time. On April 25–26, 1929, a conference entitled "The Development of the United States Capital" was held at the recently completed US Chamber of Commerce Building. The illustrious program of speakers included Hoover, Mellon, Bennett, Charles Moore, Milton Medary, and Congressman Richard M. Elliott, one of the sponsors of the 1926 bill. Attention focused on the Federal Triangle, its expected effect not just on the face of the physical city but in the minds of patriotic Americans. A star-studded conference such as this drew the nation's attention to important events in planning for the city.

The Board of Architectural Consultants

The Board of Architectural Consultants was composed of the nation's leading architects: Louis Ayers of the New York City firm of York and Sawyer, Arthur Brown Jr. of San Francisco, William Adams Delano of New York City, Milton Medary of Philadelphia, and John Russell Pope of New York City. Bennett himself was at the helm. Although Mellon could not reimburse members of the board for more than expenses, he promised each of the architects the opportunity to design one building in the complex. The efforts of the board were coordinated with the newly established National Capital Park and Planning Commission; with the Commission of Fine Arts; and with Louis E. Simon, supervising architect of the Treasury, whose office was also assigned the design and construction of one of the buildings. The progress of the Federal Triangle project was recorded in the annual reports of the Public Buildings Commission.

Architecture, Design, and Style
In selecting the dominant architectural style, Mellon was much influenced by the McMillan Commission report. As a government official, he felt a responsibility to translate the plan's mandates into reality, agreeing that any "deviation in any important detail might mar great developments to which general approval has been given." One of these important details was the classical style, set by the two major public buildings, the White House and the Capitol, as well as by the buildings occupying other critical sites identified in the L'Enfant plan: the Treasury, the Patent Office, and the District Building. Although the Federal Triangle was to be built of twentieth-century building elements, that is, of steel frame construction with limestone facing, Bennett noted in his diary that "modern 'blunt' architecture [was] not acceptable to Mr. Mellon for Department Buildings in Washington."

President Hoover reminded the Board of Architectural Consultants to address itself to intangible values: "It is our primary duty to do more than erect offices. We must fit that program into the tradition and the symbolism of the Capital." The overall stylistic character of the buildings was to be an "adaptation of the eighteenth century classic," but within this framework, eclecticism would reign: from the Italian Renaissance–style Commerce Department, to the Corinthian-style Archives Building, to the Ionic-order Post Office Building. The mixing of classical orders, rusticated facades, and sculpted pediments with art deco–style metal doors and grilles was typical of the wide variation in the seemingly monolithic Beaux-Arts creations. According to the 1931 *Annual Report of the Public Buildings Commission,* the Federal Triangle represented a distinctive product of the early twentieth century, depicting the revival of classic architecture for the use of modern business demands.

Design Alternatives
By defining the design parameters for Bennett, Mellon expressed his alliance with the prerogatives and precedents that had been offered by the McMillan Commission. Had he been given a free rein, Bennett might have dictated a more uniform Roman style, less eclectic and less Renaissance. He would have argued for a more unified scheme with enriched open spaces and would have given the ensemble greater amenities of fountains, squares, and wide public access. As one who had planned civic centers for other cities and thus had a large view of planning capabilities, Bennett might also have expanded his reach to the entire Pennsylvania Avenue facade, a more comprehensive vision than Congress and others could have accepted. But Bennett's final product probably would not have conflicted greatly with the overall architectural traditions in Washington public buildings.

The modern European design alternatives were certainly visible in the 1920s, but they were little understood by the American public or by the architectural profession, some of whose members translated the Bauhaus ideas into stern factory-like buildings worthy of the clichés of "brutal" or "blunt." Because of his own inclinations, Bennett would not have espoused the more modern or romantic style that characterized the work of Philadelphia architect George Howe or the holistic and highly individualized work of Frank Lloyd Wright.

In 1926 there were few challenges to the Federal Triangle design. Never had there been such unanimity among architectural leaders as to the course that should be followed. Never had there been such a powerful commitment from the president and the principal cabinet-level secretary responsible for this work. These mutually reinforcing influences turned Washington toward its characteristic concentration of government buildings in the central area, particularly in the Triangle and the Mall, and dictated their architectural style, with its roots in Paris and Rome. Whitehall provided the model for the concentration of government departments, as Mellon viewed the capital city. Mellon also suggested to Bennett that the Federal Triangle buildings, "while having each a separate treatment, shall be of harmonious design and grouped around two large interior courts or plazas somewhat after the arrangement of the Louvre in Paris."

THE CIVIC CENTER IDEAL

As a specific undertaking, the Federal Triangle expressed in Washington the civic center ideal. In more general terms, the civic center ideal had been a chief element in plans of American designers for several decades. It may have had earlier origins, but after the triumphs of the 1893 World's Columbian Exposition in Chicago, the City Beautiful movement—of which the civic center was the characteristic expression—had dominated the thinking of designers. It was expected that benefits of the civic center concept would be in the order of civic pride, moral reform, and an integrating device for the nation's diversity of ethnic origins. The aesthetic values communicated by the harmonious groupings would serve to inspire the common man.

The principles of such civic centers had been effectively outlined in 1903 by Charles Mulford Robinson in *Modern Civic Art* and repeated in the reports of the Public Buildings Commission. Land values and individual real estate interests argued for the massing of departmental buildings. In the concentration of public business in one area, efficiency in communication was attained, as well as a heightened sense of the dignity and importance of the individual buildings.

To municipal reformers, as Robinson pointed out, this architecture en masse promised the "cooperation of departments rather than individual sufficiency which separate buildings recommended and which is at the root of so much administrative evil."

In 1922 Werner Hegemann and Elbert Peets published *The American Vitruvius: An Architect's Handbook of Civic Art,* an analysis of the civic center principles. Synthesizing the American experience as illustrated by world fairs and development of college campuses and other institutional groupings, the authors outlined from the perspective of the new art of urban design the elements of civic centers. These elements emphasized the "essential relation between a building and its setting, the necessity of protecting the aspect of the approaches, the desirability of grouping buildings into harmonious ensembles, of securing dominance of some buildings over others."

THE FEDERAL TRIANGLE AND THE CITY BEAUTIFUL

The Federal Triangle expressed more than the civic center ideal; in the Triangle planning, other City Beautiful principles also ruled. The land was defined by the right triangle formed by the city's two major axes, the Mall and Pennsylvania Avenue, with the short leg defined by the White House–Washington Monument axis. It is around this basic geometric form that the rest of the original L'Enfant plan is based. The architectural massing in this area provided a clearer definition to the constitutive triangle and thus to the monumental core of the city. The seventy acres of land were sliced into sites for seven major structures: Ayers designed the long Commerce Department Building between 14th and 15th streets; Brown, the Labor Department Building, the Interstate Commerce Commission Building, and the Departmental Auditorium; Delano, the Post Office with its hemicycle; the supervising architect of the Treasury, the Internal Revenue Service Building; Medary, the Justice Department Building; Pope, the National Archives

Building; and Bennett, the Apex Building, the final structure that later would house the Federal Trade Commission. All the buildings were of the same height and had limestone facades.

Although each was of a unique design, all corresponded to the limitations of classical forms.

The grouping was subordinate to the monumental core's major focal points, the White

House and the Capitol, and great pains were taken to improve the complex's immediate environs. The Federal Triangle enhanced the edges of the Mall and White House parkland, and they in turn served as appropriately formal settings to the Triangle's structures. The complex was designed around two plazas: the Grand Plaza, which drew the Post Office hemicycle laterally toward 14th Street, and the 12th Street Circle, seen as the pivot of the architectural assemblage

and marked by a commemorative column. In Bennett's view, the "vital element binding the entire group is the connection between the two large plazas."

The Competition between Automobiles and Architecture

In designing this large complex, the board was faced with problems larger than those of architectural design. The concerns embraced traffic

The Federal Triangle before Completion of the Apex Building. National Capital Planning Commission Collection

flow and parking. The street system of the Triangle area before 1926 was based on the original layout by L'Enfant: a grid cut by two diagonals, Ohio and Louisiana avenues. To ensure maximum usage of the land for the Federal Triangle complex, the existing street system was abandoned and a new street system drawn up emphasizing the north-south thoroughfares and relying on the peripheral avenues for east-west circulation. The new street design, however, was not solely oriented to traffic; it provided for generous sidewalks and landscaping, as well as broad roadways, to produce a more open character for the new public precincts. The grand facade facing the Mall allowed for the aggrandizement of Constitution Avenue as a "great, new artery." To improve traffic conditions in the area, the National Capital Park and Planning Commission suggested that the north-south thoroughfares pass under the Mall, that a streetcar line form a loop within the Triangle, and that the Triangle be "self-contained as to parking." When land values and building costs were assessed, the Planning Commission viewed parking provided on open ground to be more expensive than parking space within the building network.

The impact of automobiles, especially in the Federal Triangle–Mall area, was a nagging problem from the conception of the Triangle. Because the McMillan Plan predated the automotive age, no provisions were made in the plan for accommodating cars. Later City Beautiful plans for other cities also did not provide for parking either under or above ground. Thus, the plaza spaces shown as formal design elements on many city plans were turned into parking lots. This was the fate of the Federal Triangle's Grand Plaza until construction of the Ronald Reagan Building.

It was not that Bennett and the Board of Architectural Consultants never recognized the problem but that parking was considered only after the architectural and landscape outlines had been agreed upon—and the board's response to the problem was by no means unanimous. Speaking for the Commission of Fine Arts, Charles Moore in an annual report termed the parking situation a "nuisance that could well nigh destroy the beauty of the National Capital." Bennett and Brown recognized that parking was one of the unpleasant realities that had to be incorporated into a static building arrangement.

Seeking a solution, the Board of Architectural Consultants commissioned the advice of traffic experts, National Garages, Inc. For the projected 7,415 automobiles, the firm suggested that provisions be allowed in spaces under the Ellipse (the park area located between the White House and the Washington Monument), under the Triangle, under the Mall, and in two spaces north of Pennsylvania Avenue. In response to the firm's suggestion that 1,300 spaces be designed under the Great Plaza, John Russell Pope objected, urging that the "point of view of the Board should not be lost sight of, namely, its efforts to conserve the beauty of the public park and the beauty of the buildings." Representing the National Capital Park and Planning Commission, and sympathetic with most of Bennett's views, Frederic Delano suggested that a parking lot, enclosed by an eight-foot wall and planted with shrubbery and trees, be allowed at the base of the Washington Monument. Additional parking was proposed by Delano in low garages on the north side of Pennsylvania Avenue and under the Ellipse if four to five ventilating stacks could be constructed. Pope objected to Delano's schemes as too conspicuous and destructive to the 1901–1902 plan and detrimental to the foliage of the monumental core. Less satisfactory suggestions included parking north of Pennsylvania Avenue as far as G or H Street and on sites south of the Mall.

In the last analysis, parking was incorporated into the Federal Triangle building scheme only on a highly restricted basis (as in the Apex Building basement). Contributing factors were difficulty in justifying additional costs during the Depression and openly expressed fear of dangerous ramps and underground driving. Solutions to the traffic problem were also severely limited by poor soil and drainage conditions in the area. Realistic long-term solutions were further thwarted by the assumption that 65 percent of the nearly thirty thousand employees then to be located in the Federal Triangle would use mass transportation or walk to work. Taking solace in this assumption, the board in its disarrayed response to the parking problem allowed for saturation of the area with auto parking in every available large open space within the Triangle, a result that no member of the board foresaw or desired.

The Final Days

Edward Bennett remained with the project until its virtual completion in 1937, but the first six years, from 1926 to 1933, would stand as the most satisfying. In those halcyon days, as he recorded in his diaries, he enjoyed the confidence and support of President Hoover, Secretary of the Treasury Andrew Mellon, Assistant Secretary Charles Dewey, and Frederic Delano of the National Capital Park and Planning Commission, all of whom might accompany him on site visits and to hearings before congressional committees. A realist in terms of what could be accomplished, given the cooperation of these important figures, Bennett worked to incorporate their views into more contemporary terms, especially in the matter of parking facilities. After Mellon's resignation, Bennett was suddenly faced with the prospect of dealing with a new secretary of the Treasury—and a rash of conflicts between himself, members of the Board of Architectural Consultants, and Charles Moore. With his original sources of support—except for Delano—gone, Bennett saw his own Apex Building almost expunged from the project because of fears of some that the Apex would screen the Pope-designed Archives Building and because of the hope of others for possible use of the Apex site as the location for a Thomas Jefferson memorial. By the end of his service, Bennett designed and, through the efforts of President Franklin Roosevelt, saw his Apex Building realized, although in finished form it was stripped of original ornate detail as well as plans for a terraced fountain where the Federal Triangle met 6th Street.

CRISIS AND CRITIQUE: EVALUATIONS AND SECOND THOUGHTS

In the heady days of affluence, the emphasis on inspirational and patriotic symbols appeared justification enough for the large expenditures on the Federal Triangle project. The terminology of the 1926 Public Buildings Act underscored aesthetic concerns: the secretary of the Treasury was to provide "suitable approaches" to the buildings and to beautify and embellish their surroundings "as nearly in harmony with the plan of Pierre Charles L'Enfant as may be practicable." In proposing that the several buildings of the Triangle be designed as a harmonious whole, supporters of the bill desired that the Triangle look as if the elements had been designed and constructed at the same time, present a monumental image, and preclude any chance of further additions of "incongruous new buildings." Charles Moore reflected satisfaction with the Federal Triangle plans as of 1929 in that they conformed to the 1901–1902 McMillan Plan; the Lincoln Memorial and the siting of new Mall buildings would fasten that plan on the city for the ages. Taking the Federal Triangle project together with other public building projects in the city, Congressman Louis C. Cramton, chairman of the House District Committee, saw the nation's capital city "on the threshold of glorious things."

FUNCTIONAL CONCERNS AND SHORTCOMINGS

Functional concerns had been voiced in early discussions by members of the Public Buildings Commission. They were torn, as the commission's annual reports from 1922 on reveal, between a "modern office building" type constructed with an "appropriate but simple finish" and what some viewed as "Greek temples" that were "foolish and unnecessary . . . exceedingly expensive and wasteful of space." Nonetheless, it was recognized that the clustering of buildings for many agencies remedied the legislative confusion of "various departments and bureaus submitting plans for individual needs to Congress" and the past unsatisfactory experience with piecemeal planning. Efficiency was also served in that formerly scattered bureau offices were now in close proximity to one another, to the policy makers of the legislative branch, and to the executors in the White House.

The larger perspectives of city planning showed the environmental shortcomings of the Federal Triangle plan, especially its parking deficiencies and the congestion associated with the daily ebb and flow of government workers. Few benefits of the plan touched the adjoining parts of the city. The north side of Pennsylvania Avenue, for instance, with its wealth of commercial buildings evoking the historic urban past, would remain under the shadow of speculative blight and uncertainty for at least a half century. Shortcomings of the Triangle plan were sufficient to vitiate efforts through successive administrations to complete it (for example, to build the Great Plaza facing the Commerce Department Building) and contributed to the air of disenchantment that surrounded the Pennsylvania Avenue redevelopment efforts.

ECONOMIC REALITIES

After the stock market crash, the Federal Triangle project was interpreted less as an aesthetic symbol than a sign of governmental efficiency. In the expanding role of the government in dealing with the economic crisis, the Public Buildings Commission suggested in its 1930 annual report that "the impression of well-ordered and properly designed Government buildings insures popular respect for the Government." The discordant conditions in the nation would be overcome by heavy injections of planning as symbolized by the Triangle's "example of good taste and intelligent planning." In 1932 Karl K. Hardy, secretary of the Public Buildings Commission, labeled the project as "one of true conservative economy," in contrast to the earlier and limited view of planning that had stressed beautification. The Federal Triangle offered a solution to the problem of unsafe working conditions in private buildings. Moreover, the building program was held out as now "concerned primarily with the

utilitarian problem of housing adequately the Federal activities in order that they might function efficiently and economically."

AESTHETIC AND FUNCTIONAL SUCCESS

The Federal Triangle complex offered remarkable potential attraction to visitor and resident alike. Soon after completion and for decades afterward, each building offered numerous lobby displays and exhibitions depicting the department's primary activities, mirroring the interaction with the public that took place in the cultural institutions flanking the Mall. Lobbies and auditoriums were handsomely adorned, offering a warm welcome to visitors. The Department of Commerce Building even boasted a large aquarium, and in the Department of Justice Building, the FBI museum offered a shooting demonstration straight out of "Gangbusters."

In the federal perspective the Triangle helped define the tourist's Washington and the focus on the monumental core of the city. It gave a clearer definition to the northern boundary of the Mall and in the process cleared the vista for a new ceremonial route along Constitution Avenue. Such a street had already been foreshadowed by the monumental frontage along 17th Street and westward on Constitution Avenue toward the Lincoln Memorial.

To the north along Pennsylvania Avenue, the project could be incorporated into the promise of a proper ceremonial way, it was thought, if private development along the north side of the avenue would conform in height, architectural flavor, and cornice line with the Triangle. Reflecting national interest in the future of the capital city, Alfred Granger, representing the Chicago chapter of the American Institute of Architects, submitted plans for proposed buildings on the north side of the avenue. His plans fused new office buildings with compatible existing elements, cornice lines of the Washington Hotel, the Willard Hotel, and the Evening Star Building. At the far eastern end of Pennsylvania Avenue, the proposed Municipal Center to be constructed around Hadfield's much-admired City Hall

Proposed Municipal Center for the Eastern End of Pennsylvania Avenue, Design by Albert L. Harris, 1929. *Annual Report of the National Capital Park and Planning Commission,* 1929

would initiate public improvements along that side of the street.

The aesthetic and functional success of the proposed development also encouraged future plans for a Northwest Rectangle, west of the White House as far as Rock Creek Park, thereby vindicating the "mistaken" siting of the old Interior Department Building (now the General Services Administration Building); a Southwest Triangle south of the Mall; and the unimplemented plans for similar clusters along East Capitol Street and in the southeast quadrant surrounding the Navy Yard. Of these proposals, the largest realization was the extensive massing of federal departments south of the Mall, where nearly three times the population of the Federal Triangle would ultimately be concentrated.

The replacement of a large section of the decayed mid-nineteenth-century business district by the Federal Triangle complex did not fulfill all expectations. Although it may have satisfied some critics in that the architectural quality of the area had been improved, the office buildings filled with a large mass of workers did not generate business activities, nor life after working hours. Instead, when night fell, the complex illustrated the fate of many downtown areas of cities: empty office caverns through which only the brave would walk by night.

THE EXPANDED FEDERAL PRESENCE

By 1937 the design decisions and most of the construction of the Federal Triangle were virtually complete. In the comprehensive view, the Federal Triangle project and proliferation of similar groupings and large land acquisition programs throughout the city indicated a substantial realization over time of the broad concepts of the McMillan Plan. Although many of the 1901–1902 proposals faded with changing conditions, the federal presence and investment in the city forced a remarkably comprehensive realization of its City Beautiful plan, a result totally unlike the fragmented development of many other American cities. ☆

EXPANSIVE PLANNING VISIONS 1926-1933

8

Planning in the Nation's Capital

The 1920s and early 1930s represented a peak in planning activities for the national capital city. The establishment of the National Capital Park and Planning Commission, the passage of the Shipstead-Luce Act that enlarged the scope of the Commission of Fine Arts, and park funding legislation contributed to this feverish period. Not since the grand days of the McMillan Commission had so many illustrious political figures sought to associate their names with the appearance of the capital city. The personnel of the planning entities, including staff members, commission members, and consultants, were professionals at the forefront of the still-young planning movement. With the city extending into the far reaches of the historic ten-mile square District and into the adjoining counties, planners looked not only backward to the turn-of-the century McMillan Commission recommendations and the even earlier L'Enfant plan but also forward to the emerging regional city with its range of modern concerns.

In devoting daily energies to inspecting, recording, and planning the city, planners stretched their comprehension of the city into the unexplored questions of slums, pollution, urban sprawl, and waste of resources, problems unrecognized in the tourist's view of the static, serene, monumental city. Studies and recommendations revealed both the magnificence of the monumental core and the heretofore obscured constituent city beyond and served as the basis for planning in Washington for at least the next twenty-five years. This vision of the city, present and future, strongly established it as a national city expressive of the federal interest and aware of its identity as the capital.

MEMBERSHIP OF THE PLANNING COMMISSION

In 1929 Representative Louis C. Cramton described the members of the Planning Commission and staff as "men of the widest experience and greatest ability of any planning commission in the country." In general, the six ex officio members came and went according to changes in the agencies and congressional committees. It was in the four presidentially appointed members that the Planning Commission secured its professional status and its continuity. These members often volunteered to carry out special planning or design studies for the commission or became professionally engaged in work related to the commission, as was Frederick Law Olmsted Jr. in his continuing work on various projects in the city.

In the early years the leading figures were commission members Frederic A. Delano and Frederick Law Olmsted Jr. and staff member Charles W. Eliot II. Delano was a longtime activist in planning in Washington. By 1926 Olmsted had established his own reputation distinct from that of his famous father. As a figure of long professional experience nationwide and a former member of the Commission of Fine Arts, who had secure lines of communication with influential people, Olmsted made substantive contributions to the Planning Commission in its early years, taking on much of the work himself. His wisdom mesmerized people like Delano, and they trusted him implicitly.

Charles Eliot was the nephew and namesake of the famed landscape architect who with Sylvester Baxter had in 1893 drawn up the Boston Metropolitan Park System, a model that many Washingtonians admired. He was born in Cambridge, Massachusetts, in 1899. Like Delano and Olmsted, Eliot was a graduate of Harvard University. In 1923 he enrolled in Harvard's Graduate School of Landscape Architecture, which offered professional training in city planning. Before his employment by the National Capital Park and Planning Commission, Eliot had worked for Olmsted on plans for several Massachusetts towns. There he gained a "strong sense of the popular interest in historic shrines, landmarks, and scientific features of the landscape." Eliot's appointment as the commission's "city planner" at the age of twenty-seven startled many activists in Washington, chief among them Harlean James, who on first meeting him viewed Eliot as "that kid." Nonetheless, Eliot's educational background, his sturdy historical orientation, his

familial roots in the New England landscape tradition, and especially the decisive experience under Olmsted allowed him to deal effectively with Washington as a vast metropolitan area, especially in the matter of parks. Eliot saw his job as the function of "allowing for necessary municipal growth, yet preserving as much as . . . I can of the flavor of the past."

THE COMMISSION'S WORK PLAN

At the outset, the commission outlined a work plan. When questioned later about this first work program, Eliot recalled, "Olmsted dictated it; I wrote it down." First, basic data would be collected to guide comprehensive planning. Second, coordinating the more immediate plans of other federal and local agencies would make up the administrative core of the work. Third, a comprehensive plan would be formulated to provide for long-range guidelines in controlling physical growth. The second and third activities were broken down by geographical districts and then by functional subheadings: highways, transportation, water supply, parks, neighborhood centers, and zoning. A timetable was imposed for development of the comprehensive plan to guard against its postponement under pressure of more expedient piecemeal planning decisions.

The City Planning Committee created under the old Park Commission was reborn in the Coordinating Committee empowered to recommend for or against the actions of federal agencies. By 1933 the Coordinating Committee met every two weeks and consisted of thirteen members representing the several government agencies that composed the commission's membership. From the start, the original Coordinating Committee was directed to deal with the major federal agencies and to reconcile their physical plans for the city. Later, other committees were created within the Planning Commission to deal with specific subjects, such as federal and municipal projects, school and recreational plans, and the broad question of water supply for the region.

Work Agenda for Members, Staff, and Consultants

Work was allocated according to the experience of the members, staff, and consultants. Olmsted volunteered to supervise planning for parkways, parks, and neighborhood centers, with the work actually carried out by Eliot, who was designated staff director in 1930. Harland Bartholomew, author of the city's 1920 zoning ordinance, was contracted to work on highways, with many of his ideas translated at the staff level by staff engineer Major Carey Brown. Commission member J. C. Nichols brought his experience with the phenomenal residential growth of Kansas City and its distinguished Country Club District to bear on the molding of new residential sections of the city; here attractiveness would be defined by parks and transportation planning. Nichols was particularly valuable as a practical, money-making type who supported planning as eco-

nomical and was able to communicate this conviction to real estate people.

In the area of housing for low-income families, John Ihlder, valuable for his experience as executive director of the Massachusetts Housing Association and the Pittsburgh Housing Association, was engaged as a consultant. Member of the commission, executive officer until 1933, and chairman of the commission from 1942 to 1949, Colonel and later Major General Ulysses S. Grant III served also as director of the independent Office of Public Buildings and Public Parks of the National Capital. (This office accounted for one of the ex officio memberships on the Planning Commission until the office was absorbed by the National Park Service in 1933.) Grant's contacts with President Hoover prompted Eliot later to credit Executive Officer Grant with "managing the White House" on policies affecting planning in the city. Presidential appointee to

Construction Work on the L Street Bridge over Rock Creek Parkway, 1933. The Historical Society of Washington, DC

the commission Milton B. Medary, the architect, represented the City Beautiful tradition, concerning himself with the aesthetic values of the city in the monumental core and naturally landscaped parkways.

The Automobile

The automobile was at the foundation of Washington as a metropolitan city verging on a regional city. Other functional issues—housing, parks, highways, and siting of public buildings—now hinged on the spatial dimensions afforded by this most private mode of transportation. As congestion increased steadily during the 1920s and 1930s, programs of additional street widening and various structural changes were undertaken. Later on, Washington's circles, considered to be bottlenecks in L'Enfant's generous street system, were refashioned. Tunnels and underpasses were provided to carry streetcars and, later, automobiles underground in the most con-

gested stretches, such as Dupont Circle and Thomas Circle.

In the 1920s, the city grew toward the northwest across Rock Creek as major arterial roads were provided with bridges. In the following years, the Potomac was bridged at Georgetown and above, at Chain Bridge; historic Long Bridge at 14th Street was given greater capacity by building a parallel bridge nearby. The priority earlier given to crossings of the upper Anacostia to carry Baltimore-bound traffic was followed by bridges across the lower Anacostia. Thus, the early river-bottom city burst the natural bounds imposed by its rivers.

Between 1920 and 1930, automobile registrations in the District of Columbia quadrupled. Consequences of this growth and change in travel habits were felt in every sector of city life. Meetings of the Planning Commission now dealt directly with street widenings, new road-planning proposals, bridge construction, parking arrangements, and more fundamentally with regulatory and zoning changes. Regulations were needed both to provide direct accommodation—in the form of parking—and to recognize the pervasive shifts in population location and density that were primarily motivated by adjustments to the automobile. Not the least of these shifts occurred in residential neighborhoods, as pressure for higher densities stimulated the building of apartment houses and as streets were preempted by cars, both parked and moving. The decline of the small-scale neighborhood commercial districts followed as business concentrated in larger-sized units at shopping centers where parking was provided.

J. C. NICHOLS AND THE PROTECTION OF RESIDENTIAL SUBDIVISIONS

As early as 1928, Planning Commission member J. C. Nichols correctly predicted the automobile's effects on the city. He observed that, contrary to public notions about city planning's ornamental results, "the growing acuteness of automobile congestion in all our population centers . . . is forcing upon the public . . . the dire need of better planning to meet the rapidly changing conditions in the size and number of our transportation units." This enlarged physical dimension of the city increased the "tendency of business to move from downtown districts to suburban neighborhood shopping centers, accentuated by the building of outlying apartments and kitchenettes, neighborhood picture shows, filling stations, and chain stores." These massive intrusions into formerly rural lands intended as settings for new residential groupings had "thrust city planning problems—particularly zoning—into the residential areas of nearly all urban communities."

Nichols's primary interest was in the development and protection of residential subdivisions, the focus also of his earlier work in Kansas City. He defined the ideal subdivision in both economic and aesthetic terms. The expense of street maintenance would be lessened, Nichols pointed out, by the "fact that the automobile has annihilated distances and that blocks may be greatly lengthened." As opposed to the common grid cross-street pattern found in many central city areas, the platting of subdivisions in suburban areas was adapted to the topography of the land and was not dictated by some arbitrary street scheme. Highways constructed to handle automobile traffic, although facilitating economy in movement of people and goods, were found detrimental to the value of property facing such highways.

Nichols blamed the street plan ordered by the 1893 highway act for the wasteful "checkerboard plan of streets with short blocks" forced "throughout all these beautiful hills and valleys." To execute the 1893 highway plan, expensive grading operations had ripped out forest trees in the far reaches of the District, "resulting in large sections of our capital city becoming characterless and unattractive." Nichols suggested that the National Capital Park and Planning Commission restudy "these street plans, and their better adaptation to the peculiar contours of the land, and the conservation of the valleys and brooks for park purposes."

HARLAND BARTHOLOMEW'S STUDY OF WASHINGTON STREETS

The highway was the focus for this increased concern about mobility expressed by Nichols and others. The planning act of 1926 placed responsibility for city highway planning in the National Capital Park and Planning Commission. Harland Bartholomew, employed by the commission to conduct highway studies, looked sharply at the ribbons of paving that by 1930 accounted for nearly 30 percent of the city's usable surface. Bartholomew's characterization of the evolution of the city's street system was a precise and skillful summary. Development, as Bartholomew depicted it, began with the narrow streets of Georgetown in the precapital-city era of the eighteenth century. Although these old streets possessed charm, it was difficult to join them via major arteries to the rest of the city. For Bartholomew, the second stage of development was represented by the wide streets and avenues

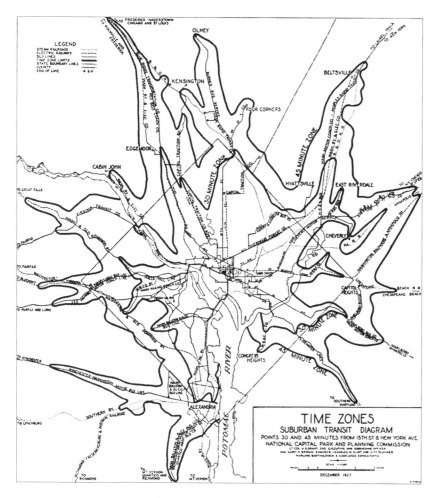

TIME ZONES
SUBURBAN TRANSIT DIAGRAM
POINTS 30 AND 45 MINUTES FROM 15TH ST & NEW YORK AVE.
NATIONAL CAPITAL PARK AND PLANNING COMMISSION
LT. COL. U. S. GRANT 3RD EXECUTIVE AND DISBURSING OFFICER
MAJ. CAREY H. BROWN, ENGINEER · CHARLES W. ELIOT 2ND CITY PLANNER
HARLAND BARTHOLOMEW & ASSOCIATES, CONSULTANTS

DECEMBER 1927.

National Capital Park and Planning Commission's Suburban Transit Diagram, 1927. *Annual Report of the National Capital Park and Planning Commission, 1928*

designed by L'Enfant, "proof of the value of proper planning." Then followed the third stage, which Bartholomew characterized as the "dark days of the capital city, as far as its circulation system is concerned," where streets beyond the boundaries of the old city were independently determined by the landowners and subdividers.

The drawing up of the 1893 highway plan represented the fourth stage, which Bartholomew described as "belated but praiseworthy" in its effort to control land platting. Unfortunately for the natural landscape of the city, the extension of the grid and radials of the L'Enfant flat basin city over a more rugged terrain destroyed many of the city's distinctive features, especially east of Rock Creek Park. In the final stage of developing the street system, the National Capital Park and Planning Commission was entrusted with altering the 1893 highway plan (as amended by the 1898 highway act and subsequent congressional

acts). In March 1932, the commission reported that since 1926 it had made 107 changes in the plan. The commission was to be guided by what Bartholomew boldly diagrammed as three goals: differentiation of street functions, planning for subdivisions according to the natural terrain, and an attempt to "restate the L'Enfant ideal in the terms of a motor age."

In planning for the circulation pattern of the future, Bartholomew designated several streets as major thoroughfares to serve in-town, crosstown, and streetcar traffic. He suggested that these thoroughfares be differentiated from the secondary streets by distinctive street lighting, traffic signals, paving, public service institutions, and tree planting. He recognized that employment centers were sprouting out beyond the monumental core, and he planned for bypasses as well as crosstown and interchange routes. L'Enfant's radials had provided well for through traffic, but the 1893 highway system reflected the more restricted view of daily commuting patterns as movement primarily between the suburbs and the monumental core. Bartholomew's plan sought to overcome this.

Outside the District's boundaries, Bartholomew studied the commuting zone within Prince George's, Montgomery, Arlington, and Fairfax counties. Because of the limited construction of county highways and heavy use of streetcar and railroad lines, the commuting zone resembled spokes about the hub of the L'Enfant federal city. Bartholomew recommended the strengthening of radial highways already largely defined by preautomobile transportation routes. To adapt these radials to the automobile, the routes were to be dramatically widened. To connect these radials and fill in the spokes, Bartholomew drew up a series of bypass routes resembling many belt roads encircling the District. The intersection of the radials with the belt roads was intended to be located at extant county towns to maintain the already developed points of concentration. Thus, the configuration of highways outside the District would resemble a vast built spiderweb.

Housing

New patterns for residential development came into being as a result of changes in the 1893 highway plan. More attention was paid to the natural contours of the land in outlying locations where little or no development had taken place. Within the District, more attention likewise was given to identification of various income groups and their housing needs. Rehabilitation of existing deteriorated housing stock received high priority.

JOHN IHLDER'S HOUSING PROGRAM FOR THE DISTRICT

Housing for the vast middle class was provided in less dramatic proportions throughout the District and suburban counties. In 1930 housing consultant John Ihlder reported to the National Capital Park and Planning Commission on the local and national importance of residential development of the capital city. In his report to the commission, Ihlder argued that "the prestige and appeal of the Capital do not lie wholly in its governmental structure, but do lie largely in its dwellings." The automobile had changed the demands for housing in requiring parking and garage space and in opening to development new areas beyond the streetcar network.

The ideal housing package would include accessibility, detached single-family dwellings, and open spaces. With spaciousness as the primary objective in housing, Ihlder decried the trend of housing toward more intense development. To plan for housing, Ihlder recommended that the Planning Commission gather data on family incomes and sizes and project each income group's housing needs based on economic considerations, rather than continuing to anticipate these needs on "the trial and error method," persisting in the trend toward providing first for the well-to-do. In housing for the lower-income groups, Ihlder predicted the study would reveal that such families were forced to accept unsuitable dwellings. He also predicted that the study would demonstrate that the "lowest income people are not self-supporting."

ALLEY DWELLINGS IN WASHINGTON

Alley dwellings had long been regarded as the most blatant illustration of substandard housing in Washington. In 1930 Ihlder counted more than 250 inhabited alleys, some dating back before the Civil War. These alleys were distributed throughout the old L'Enfant city and in nearby District blocks, especially in the southwest quadrant and in the industrial area of Foggy Bottom. Alley dwellings began as quarters for servants employed in houses fronting on streets. Throughout the nineteenth and twentieth centuries, these hidden communities were the subject of much public discussion. A landmark bill was passed in 1914 providing for the phasing out of all alley dwellings within a period of ten years, with the inhabitants to be relocated. Mrs. Archibald Hopkins, a leading advocate of the 1914 act, organized a corporation to build new low-cost housing for evicted alley-dwellers.

To deal with what Ihlder termed this "difficult problem," new housing was to be sought in other blocks where the black population lived. As the alley population was relocated elsewhere, the next problem to be solved, according to Ihlder, was reuse of the property on which the dwellings were located. The 1914 act had not resolved this issue except to forbid the property's future use for dwellings. Alternative uses suggested by Ihlder included space for parking and loading or, in the tradition of Gramercy Park in New York City, for "tea gardens or outdoor dining rooms appurtenant to hotels, semiprivate gardens or parks appurtenant to apartment houses or private dwellings."

GEORGETOWN: AN EXAMPLE OF THE HISTORIC AND DISTINCTIVE OLD NEIGHBORHOOD

Rehabilitation and relocation were two sides of the housing picture in the old city. Before thoughts of demolition and rebuilding gripped housing officials as they would in the post–World War II era, interest was expressed in the distinctive historical and aesthetic qualities provided by old Washington neighborhoods,

A Georgetown Street in the Late 1930s. Library of Congress

especially Georgetown. This interest was expressed as social workers walked through old Georgetown photographing derelict housing and children's play areas in the narrow streets. Initiated by the wives of junior officers and war workers during World War I, the process of upgrading Georgetown houses had continued afterward.

Both neighborhood residents and outsiders began to see the area as a self-contained community. The 1933 Allied Architects study made by Horace Peaslee had suggested that future plans focus on Georgetown's uniqueness, its separateness from any other part of the city. Georgetown enjoyed a distinctive architecture that by the 1930s coincided with the vogue for colonial and early Federal-style houses.

The old port city was surrounded on all sides by open space and the Potomac River. To enforce this self-contained identity, Peaslee's study recommended that principal traffic arteries and

other barriers be confined to the outskirts of the community. Peaslee suggested that traffic from the north, from the newer developments of Burleith and Foxhall Village, should bypass Georgetown via R Street. Traffic from the south should be funneled on a proposed road on the old Chesapeake & Ohio Canal bed, which would have destroyed this unique historic feature, or else connected with R Street by a road from Key Bridge. Not only would these proposed traffic routes help outsiders bypass Georgetown on their way to the monumental core, but when joined with natural barriers such as parkland and waterways, they would also symbolically bind the self-contained community to the "larger fabric of the whole city."

Although far from complete, by 1931 the process of transforming Georgetown was compared to that of Beacon Hill in Boston, where restoration had revealed the "original charm of the fine old houses, packed tightly together

under the shade of ancient trees and as closely
crammed with the memories of silk and top
hats, capes, and creaking coaches, gay parties and
political intrigue." Georgetown would recapture
this élan by the late 1940s, when the restored
buildings attracted back the rich and powerful.

But in the 1930s, Georgetown was viewed
more as a potential laboratory for experimental
social programs to combat the effects of the
Depression and to create a sense of community
among its inhabitants rather than as an example
of restoration efforts. For example, studies of
Georgetown architecture were instituted in 1933
primarily for the purpose of employment relief.
This was a theme more of the mid-1930s than of
the Planning Commission's earliest years, the
Depression having forced many architects and
draftsmen, as well as carpenters and members of
the building trades, out of work. Restoration of
Georgetown houses was viewed as a lever for
renewing the construction industry locally.

Park Planning

Park planning drew heavily on the Chicago experience. At the behest of Frederick Law Olmsted Jr.,
in 1928 Frederick F. Stephen of the Community
Research Council of the University of Chicago
summed up the Chicago experience begun more
than twenty years earlier. Olmsted Sr. had
planned Chicago's first large parks in the 1870s
primarily as an introduction of nature's amenities into the booming prairie city. Like Washington's nineteenth-century parks of repose and
moral uplift, many of Chicago's boulevards and
large parks were later converted in part to recreational uses at the end of the century.

In a movement to limit the conversion of
these Chicago parks and in recognition of the
often long distances between home and recreational facilities, the South Park Commission
began creating small local recreational parks
throughout the city. By 1928 there were 135 of
these specialized parks, located according to the

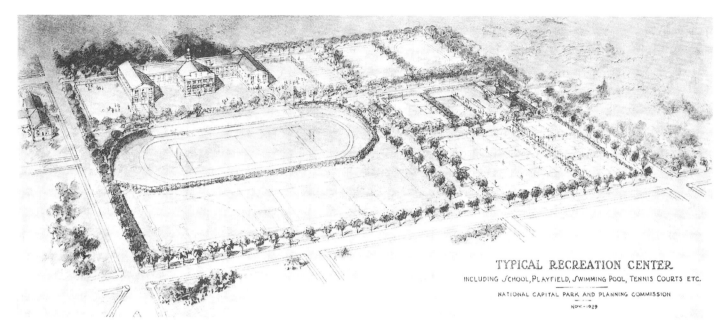

TYPICAL RECREATION CENTER
INCLUDING SCHOOL, PLAYFIELD, SWIMMING POOL, TENNIS COURTS ETC.

NATIONAL CAPITAL PARK AND PLANNING COMMISSION

NOV.-1929

A Recreation Center as Planned by the National Capital Park and Planning Commission, 1929. *Annual Report of the National Capital Park and Planning Commission, 1929*

ethnic, social, and physical barriers already extant in the city. Chicago's immigrant groups tended to live among their own, thereby creating social barriers between one neighborhood and another. These well-defined neighborhoods were often further delineated by physical barriers: railroads, industrial centers, and business thoroughfares. The South Park Commission offered a variety of attractions: playgrounds, gyms, swimming pools, and buildings for indoor sports and craft activities. In addition, some of these parks were situated next to libraries and school buildings.

NEIGHBORHOOD AND RECREATION CENTERS IN WASHINGTON

Local Washington parks had been generously provided in the L'Enfant plan, but the 1893 highway plan had made few such allowances. In its 1927 annual report, the National Capital Park and Planning Commission predicted that the intensification of urbanization across the District—by both the automobile and residential development—would erase the "many vacant lots and unused open spaces in private ownership [that] provided amply for such physical exercise as was needed by the young people." Recreational facilities inaugurated by the Army Corps of Engineers were often in the monumen-

tal core, inconvenient to much of the expanding population.

Taking a leaf from sociologist Philip Archibald Parsons, the report predicted that lack of properly supervised recreational facilities within neighborhoods might be expected to increase the tendencies of children toward delinquency. Therefore, the Planning Commission in 1927 recommended that between ten and twenty small residential parks be provided. Olmsted and Eliot changed the recreational center to a neighborhood center concept by insisting on the simultaneous location of library and school buildings in one place. With such a cluster, children and adults would be brought together and the family unit thus strengthened. Community life would also benefit from the attraction of entire families to a common focus. Olmsted saw the creation of "simple, carefully planned and systematically managed recreation units" as an efficient and economical way to obtain desirable physical planning and social results.

The Planning Commission proposed that the centers be situated so that residents of any neighborhood would not be more than a quarter of a mile from a center. As the physical city had already engulfed much of the land bordering the old L'Enfant city, the commission considered demolition of existing buildings to make way for the centers. The following year the commission drew up a map displaying natural and built boundaries and thus designated the physical and social neighborhoods that were to be served by neighborhood centers. To provide the combination of educational and recreational facilities, the plans of the commission were coordinated with those of the District for new public schools and branch libraries, as well as with the provision of public utilities.

The Depression eclipsed this energetic planning for the constituent city, however, and only three centers were constructed: the Banneker Recreation Center near Howard University, the Eckington Center, and the McKinley Center. Centers were later constructed at the Wilson, Coolidge, Taft, and Spingarn-Phelps schools, some in conjunction with the National Park Service's regional parks system, as at Fort Reno. Still later, the combined educational/recreation center would become the mainstay of the 1960s comprehensive planning.

Washington's approach to neighborhood recreation showed more than flexibility in reinterpreting the city's notable park tradition. Washington planning clearly was in step both with developments in other cities and with the times. The most notable exposition of the neighborhood unit in city planning was just being put forward by Clarence Arthur Perry in his part of the *Regional Plan of New York and Its Environs*. Although Washington had not embraced Perry's philosophy of housing, it articulated more clearly—and in advance of Perry's exposition—the underlying social theory and provided a concrete expression suited to the existing rather than the redeveloped city.

PLANNING FOR NATURAL AND CULTURAL LANDMARKS

With the Planning Commission's interest in incorporating natural and cultural landmarks to enhance its utilitarian planning work, blank maps were sent out to knowledgeable individuals who were requested to locate important sites. Architects listed structures that should be pre-

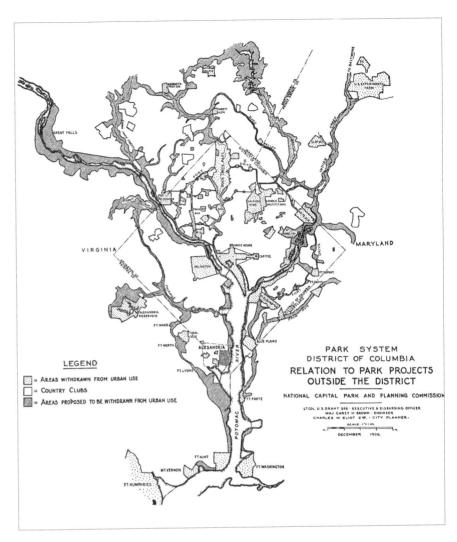

The District of Columbia Park System and Regional Park Projects, 1926. *Annual Report of the National Capital Park and Planning Commission, 1928*

served: Pohick Church, Cabin John Bridge, the locks at Great Falls. Historians pointed out battlefields, ornithologists identified bird sanctuaries, geologists defined important rocky formations, and botanists described stretches of woodlands. When these special interest maps were incorporated with other planning studies, the L'Enfant city, according to a July 1931 newspaper account, marked the center "with its abodes of past and current history setting the motif for the surrounding variations and repetitions of the design." It was reported that the commission anticipated there would extend outward from this nucleus "beautifully landscaped radiating parkways, with frequent connecting links, all of which would serve as approaches or settings for numberless exhibits in a vast outdoor museum."

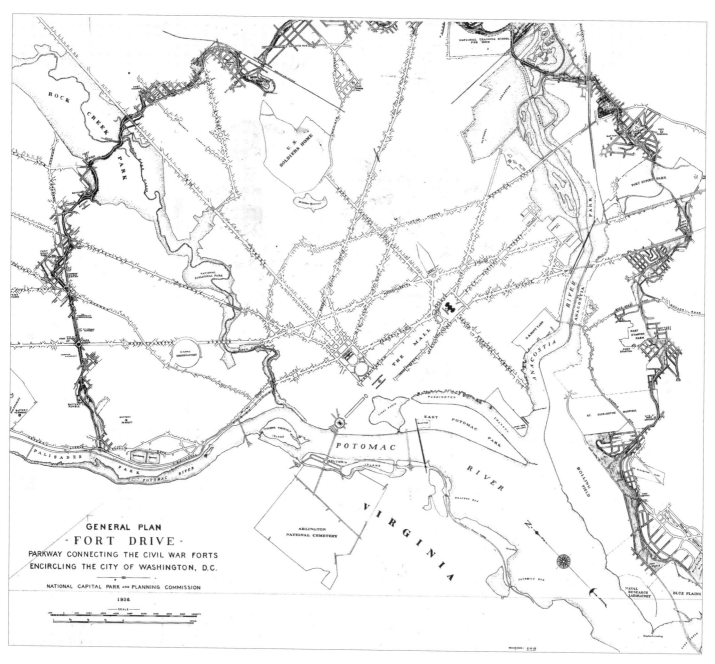

GENERAL PLAN
·FORT DRIVE·
PARKWAY CONNECTING THE CIVIL WAR FORTS
ENCIRCLING THE CITY OF WASHINGTON, D.C.

NATIONAL CAPITAL PARK AND PLANNING COMMISSION

1936.

General Plan for a
Fort Drive Parkway
Connecting the Civil War
Forts Encircling the City
of Washington, 1936.
National Capital Park
and Planning Commission

FUNDING THE PARKLAND SYSTEM PLANS
FOR WASHINGTON

Development of the larger citywide and regional
parks was still severely hampered by low funding
for the intended vast acquisitions. The funding
of $1.2 million over two fiscal years was inade-
quate to preserve land being rapidly eaten away
by development. Nevertheless, the Planning
Commission continued to entertain hopes that
private citizens would donate land or funds for
these acquisitions. After all, national interest in

the capital city's appearance had been important
in creating the commission itself. In the acquisition of parkland as outlined in the 1926 act, especially additions to Rock Creek Park, the commission suggested that in the case of Piney Branch
valley a group of private citizens raise the funds.
The land could be bought and donated immediately to the city or else held until the commission
received sufficient appropriations to purchase
the protected land. In this way, the commission
reasoned (as its minutes for December 1926

reveal), the nation could participate in development of the national capital, as the citizens "are all interested in their Government in some way or other."

In November 1926, Stephen T. Mather, director of the National Park Service and member of the National Capital Park and Planning Commission, offered to use his "connections with wealthy people" to urge them to purchase parklands. In favoring such arrangements, the commission resolved that it could not under the law bind itself to purchase the tracts but that future acquisition by the commission would be considered.

FORT DRIVE: AN UNFULFILLED PASSION

The parkland system outlined by Olmsted and Eliot followed closely the 1901–1902 McMillan Commission plan, although neglect of the park proposals had wiped out chances for realizing the vast park schemes, especially within the District. The attention of the Planning Commission and lawmakers focused on the proposed park strip of Fort Drive and the George Washington Memorial Parkway from Great Falls to Mount Vernon. The projected program was progressive by comparison with the new parkways of the New York City metropolitan area and Connecticut and in design looked even further ahead. The concept of a parkway to link the ring of Civil War forts into a pleasure drive of natural and historical interest—this a proposal of 1901—took on added importance in light of Harland Bartholomew's emphasis on bypass and belt roads to prevent congestion in the monumental core. In the commission's study of historical points of interest, the Civil War forts ranked high.

Throughout the early years of the National Capital Park and Planning Commission, requests for funds to realize Fort Drive as a "single and unified project" never captured the imagination of Congress. By 1926 the land required for the drive lay too close to the built-up city, so that the cost of this land would be much inflated over possible parkland farther out. Additional inertia in realizing the Fort Drive dream may be attrib-

uted to the circular drive's being unique to Washington and not an element of City Beautiful prescriptions. In the next forty years of readjustments to McMillan park proposals, planning issues related to the city's fort system gradually shifted away from circulation to open space and recreational uses extending through residential neighborhoods. The individual sites were fine enough—high, cool, airy, commanding impressive views—but they were also related visually and physically to each other and to the central city.

To implement the proposal after 1926, however, most of the sites still had to be purchased. Although the forts themselves were already partially connected, in many cases by old military roads incorporated in the official street plan, it was suggested that a unifying drive would greatly increase accessibility. In addition to scenic and recreational value, the forts had historic associations reinforced in some cases by surviving earthworks, rifle pits, and other structures; as late as 1920, the forts were still fruitful locales for surface archaeology, yielding military buttons, buckles, and other wartime trophies. Above all, it was the topographical value of the forts that was most esteemed: they ringed the city, defined its rim of surrounding hills, and (before trees had grown again over the cleared lines of fire) offered such superb views of the city itself, the broad and gleaming Potomac, and the surrounding metropolitan landscape. Yet, however reinterpreted, even as a circumferential highway, the Fort Drive failed to win sufficient support to be realized.

GRAND APPROACHES: MOUNT VERNON PARKWAY

Construction of a Mount Vernon Parkway also had been one of the recommendations of the 1901–1902 McMillan Commission. This entrance to the capital in the form of a parkway connecting George Washington's home and the city was intended as a combination of utilitarian highway between north and south and an aesthetic creation. In 1926 the Bureau of Public Roads had

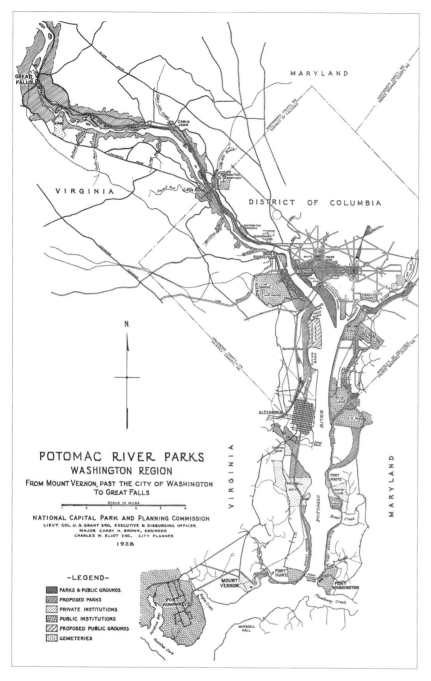

POTOMAC RIVER PARKS
WASHINGTON REGION
FROM MOUNT VERNON, PAST THE CITY OF WASHINGTON
TO GREAT FALLS
SCALE IN MILES
NATIONAL CAPITAL PARK AND PLANNING COMMISSION
LIEUT. COL. U.S. GRANT 3RD, EXECUTIVE & DISBURSING OFFICER
MAJOR CAREY H. BROWN, ENGINEER
CHARLES W. ELIOT 2ND, CITY PLANNER
1928

-LEGEND-
PARKS & PUBLIC GROUNDS.
PROPOSED PARKS
PRIVATE INSTITUTIONS
PUBLIC INSTITUTIONS
PROPOSED PUBLIC GROUNDS
CEMETERIES

Proposed Plan for Potomac River Parks from Mount Vernon to Great Falls, 1928. *Annual Report of the National Capital Park and Planning Commission, 1929*

already surveyed the area and planned the landscape treatment. It was hoped that financial backing for the nearly fourteen miles of proposed road would come in part from private contributions for a memorial to commemorate the upcoming bicentennial in 1932 of George Washington's birth. During congressional hearings in 1924, the celebration was viewed as a "world event," of enough importance to justify public expenditures.

In 1926 the chief of the Bureau of Public Roads, Thomas H. MacDonald, voiced the disappointment many Americans probably felt upon leaving the capital city for Mount Vernon. MacDonald viewed it as a "disgrace to allow the large numbers of people who annually come here from all over the world to visit this national shrine to be dumped into the mud at the entrance gate [to Mount Vernon] in the way that they now are." In regard to the Washington end of the parkway, in 1928 Milton Medary, an architect and a member of the Planning Commission, criticized the appearance of the southern approach to the city: "Those of you who came from the south passed four or five miles of railroad yards and rubbish heaps." Mount Vernon Parkway, to be constructed close to the river, would pass important historical sites and the historic city of Alexandria, an emotional experience that some congressmen argued would transform visitors into better Americans. Plantings for the entire stretch were to follow the same general plan used in Arlington National Cemetery near the parkway's Washington end and in Potomac Park across the river.

Extension of the landscaped parkway concept to other major land approaches was suggested in 1928 by Medary, who admired the scenic views in the approach to the city "over the Virginia hills where you find at the brow of those hills, suddenly and dramatically at your feet, the whole city of Washington across the Potomac." Thus, he also spoke highly of the approach to Washington from Baltimore by way of the Anacostia valley, or from the north down 16th Street or through Rock Creek Parkway, or from the west by Great Falls. Unfortunately, development of the proposed Mount Vernon Parkway—as well as other city parkway approaches—had to await future definitive congressional action.

THE POTOMAC PALISADES PARKWAYS PROPOSAL

As early as 1926, Eliot had studied potential parkland in the rugged topography west of Rock Creek Park and recommended a drive along the

Construction along the George Washington Memorial Parkway near Mount Vernon, 1931. National Capital Planning Commission Collection

Collingwood Turnout on the George Washington Memorial Parkway. National Archives

length of the Potomac Palisades. East of Rock Creek Park, he reviewed the new bridge proposed between South Capitol Street and the rural shore of Anacostia, predicting that the "route into Maryland through the now blighted area of the southwest would have an important influence toward rehabilitation and effectively utilizing an area very near the heart of the city." Looking over the river to Anacostia and its sweeping views of Washington, Eliot suggested a parkway along the ridge between Oxon Run and the Eastern Branch. One year later, Eliot spoke of the desirability of creating a riverside drive from Potomac Avenue in Georgetown out to the District line. To duplicate the proposed Mount Vernon Parkway on the Virginia shore and to serve as a southern extension through Prince George's County of the proposed Potomac Palisades Parkway, Eliot suggested that a similar parkway on the Maryland side "should some-day extend to Fort Washington so as to form a circuit drive 29 miles in length down the Virginia shore to Mount Vernon, across the river by ferry to Fort Washington, and back to Washington on the Maryland side."

THE FOREST BETWEEN WASHINGTON AND BALTIMORE

The City Beautiful preoccupation with landscaped entrances extended to the main route between Washington and its regional urban neighbor, Baltimore. Such an entrance from the north to the capital city had long been an interest of various members of the Commission of Fine Arts and other residents and politicians. In 1931 the Planning Commission, with the cooperation of the American Planning and Civic Association, the National Council for Protection of Roadside Beauty, and the American Nature Association, surveyed the appearance of major entrances to the city. Along US Highway 1 connecting Washington and Baltimore, surveyors counted 1,099 signboards.

Implementation of proposals for the entrance lagged over the years because, as the Planning Commission noted in its minutes for June 1933,

Maryland officials had "never been warm toward the idea of the Government buying land in the State." In that same year, however, the US Department of Agriculture's Forest Service received an emergency fund of $20 million to purchase forest lands. The Planning Commission suggested establishing a forest "adjoining the fall line" between Baltimore and Washington. Acquisition of forest lands in this important location was accomplished through use of these emergency funds.

This strategic landscape connecting the Piedmont Plateau and the coastal plain would serve as a "sample plot at the door of the National Capital" to teach congressmen and the public about the Department of Agriculture's Forest Service activities. It was envisioned that such a forest would serve the recreational needs of a vast region and secure future sites for expanding Washington's water supply. The Planning Commission cited the beautiful municipal forests adjoining old German cities that "gave a marvelous setting for such cities compared with the usual unkempt surroundings of American cities. There is a large field for the development of the city forest idea in America, and the establishment of such a forest here at the gateway to Washington would dramatize the whole idea."

Public Buildings: Location, Design, and Concentration

Passed in 1930, the Shipstead-Luce Act provided for the Commission of Fine Arts to review building permits for new construction next to or abutting existing or proposed public buildings and parks to ensure that there would not be a negative effect on these public properties. The area defined for such review covered the whole of Rock Creek Park in the District; the Potomac Parkway; and the monumental core of the Mall, White House, and Capitol. The scope of review embraced the new buildings' "height and appearance, color and texture of the materials of exterior construction." The act affected all residences constructed in view of Rock Creek Park. With later expansion of federal government facilities,

the geographic boundaries of the Shipstead-Luce Act's jurisdiction were partially expanded but were not adjusted to account for the location of all new government facilities developed during the following decades.

ECHOES OF THE MCMILLAN PLAN: THE WASHINGTON MONUMENT GROUNDS, MEMORIAL BRIDGE, AND THE JEFFERSON MEMORIAL

It is a paradox that although the McMillan Commission's recommendations for the location of public buildings and features such as bridges and parklands generally succeeded, its most painstaking and elaborate proposal—for the Washington Monument grounds—in the end failed. This design proposal was intended to reconcile the relocated Washington Monument with the geometry of L'Enfant by a series of terraced parks and ornamental bodies of water. In 1928 legislation was proposed for the completion of the Washington Monument grounds. Engineers recommended that the plans be abandoned, however, because any changes to the grounds could endanger the stability of the monument. It is likely, however, that changing architectural taste and altered convictions concerning design precision were contributing factors as well.

Memorial Bridge was recommended in the 1901–1902 plan as a symbolic connection between

Construction of Memorial Bridge, ca. 1930. National Capital Planning Commission Collection

the Lincoln Memorial and the Custis-Lee mansion. The bridge also was viewed as a monumental approach to the city and Arlington Cemetery, a fitting prelude to visiting the Tomb of the Unknown Soldier. Inspired by Roman aqueducts, the firm of McKim, Mead and White designed the bridge with nine low arches. The design was organized by three traffic circles—around the Lincoln Memorial, around the Virginia shoreline, and around the entrance to the cemetery. The bridge's sculptural groups reinforced the symbolic role of the bridge as reconciliation of the two sides—the North and South—that fought the Civil War. Constructed from 1926 to 1932, the bridge was viewed as an integral part of the city's park system rather than as a mere traffic bridge.

Echoes of the 1901–1902 plan were also apparent in the approved location and design of the Jefferson Memorial. The McMillan Commission had initially proposed the site for a national pantheon of monumental character with a sight line to realign the Washington Monument on its true axis. The idea for the pantheon assumed massive

regrading and landscaping of the Washington Monument grounds as a prelude to the highly formal Washington Common setting for the pantheon.

Representing the Thomas Jefferson Memorial Commission in later years, the Jefferson scholar Fiske Kimball favored the Tidal Basin site because of its proximity to the Lincoln Memorial and the Washington Monument, thereby giving the memorial to the third president an equivalent national character. The Planning Commission was skeptical about the site because of its relative isolation and suggested a location in Lincoln Park to stimulate improvements east of the Capitol.

The Commission of Fine Arts supported the Jefferson Memorial Commission on the memorial's location as well as the selection of the project's architect, John Russell Pope. Pope's pantheon design was developed over the years during the 1920s and 1930s. After his death in 1937, the successor firm of Eggers and Higgins prepared a downsized building plan in 1938, which was ultimately constructed between 1939 and 1943 along the sight line from the White House toward the Potomac River. Kimball justified the design as embodied in Jefferson's rotunda at the University of Virginia. When the Jefferson Memorial was completed, it was viewed as having a sorely outdated design. Only later did it grow in the public's affections. The Commission of Fine Arts described the Jefferson Memorial as "the last of the great Beaux Arts monuments in Washington."

THE HORIZONTAL CITY

The conviction, expressed in the 1928 *Annual Report of the National Capital Park and Planning Commission,* that "the dominance of the Capitol, both real and apparent, over the federal City should not be destroyed" supported the perpetuation of the horizontal city. Zoning provided for specified height limitations that varied according to the locations of buildings. In 1929 the Planning Commission acknowledged nationwide trends toward increased heights of buildings but rejected such an increase in Washington not only for aesthetic and symbolic reasons but also because of congestion problems anticipated as a result of more intensive use of land. The increasing trend toward dispersal of new low-rise public and private buildings throughout the District and the region was strengthened by building height limits, which tended to produce lower-density development. In addition, as the annual report pointed out, "Before the telephone, the trolley, the autobus, and the automobile, when communication and transportation were slow and laborious, there may have been an economic advantage in bringing all kinds of business into a small area. This is no longer the case."

THE CENTRAL URBAN CORE AND ALTERNATIVES TO CONCENTRATION

The location of public buildings in Washington involved a fundamental decision on the shape and functions of the central urban core. In the initial difficulties of moving and parking automobiles in the central area and the conspicuous failure of the Federal Triangle to deal with such elements of congestion, the problems of concentrated federal buildings were clearly posed. The alternatives to concentration were either modest decentralization to the edges of the downtown federal core or more drastic dispersal to the urban fringe.

To those who saw the center of Washington as the Capitol, most notably the Planning Commission, it was an attractive possibility that federal establishments could be encouraged to locate east and north of that point. To those who saw the center of the city as the White House, such as the Commission of Fine Arts, development had to be west and north. Between the two key points lay the Federal Triangle and the congestion it had produced. For these reasons the struggle between opposing viewpoints on the location of federal buildings focused on the areas west of the White House and east of the Capitol.

THE EAST CAPITOL STREET CORRIDOR

As a result of continuing concern for balance and sight lines, the Planning Commission envisioned a lineal development of public and semipublic buildings along East Capitol Street, terminating in a sports center facing the Anacostia River. Also called the "Avenue of the States" because of plans for new structures to house exhibits and information centers for each sovereign state or groups of states, the East Capitol Street corridor was to relieve traffic congestion west of the Capitol, a problem heightened by construction of the Federal Triangle. The plan also physically strengthened the corridor that L'Enfant had designed to be the major commercial strip of the city. By the late 1920s, when the Planning Commission was first considering areas appropriate for possible public building sites, the Capitol Hill neighborhood, with row upon row of Victorian houses, appeared deteriorated.

Just as development of the Federal Triangle had eliminated another blighted urban area, so the planning for East Capitol Street aimed to replace the worst of the deteriorated residential areas with modern office buildings, to start similar upgrading of the immediately adjacent neigh-

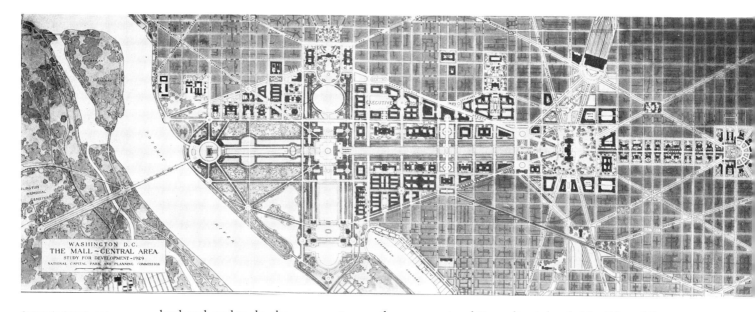

WASHINGTON D.C.
THE MALL ~ CENTRAL AREA
STUDY FOR DEVELOPMENT ~ 1929
NATIONAL CAPITAL PARK AND PLANNING COMMISSION

Suggested Eastward Prolongation of the Mall and Development of East Capitol Street as the Avenue of the States, with a Stadium at Anacostia Park, 1929. *Annual Report of the National Capital Park and Planning Commission,* 1930

borhood, and to develop new centers on the Anacostia. Over the next three decades, several design proposals were cast for East Capitol Street, since many of the new buildings proposed for location along this street required new studies and design proposals of the overall route. These design proposals became more graphically detailed in 1941 with the Downer-Clarke plan for the Federal Works Agency. In contrast to the tightly knit consistency of the Federal Triangle, however, the East Capitol Street "mall" always exhibited highly individual buildings surrounded by ample green spaces. Neither the mall's hoped for civic features nor the planned interaction with adjacent residential areas ever took hold. Many, indeed, felt that the decades-long threat of land acquisition for development of new public facilities encouraged further deterioration of neighborhoods such as Capitol Hill.

THE NORTHWEST RECTANGLE

Chief among the departments in need of new accommodations were the War and Navy departments. The intended large massing of buildings for these agencies would have a significant impact on the monumental core. The Commission of Fine Arts favored the new buildings' sites to be along the ridge paralleling Pennsylvania Avenue west of the White House. Alternatively, the Treasury Department's Board of Architec-

tural Consultants headed by Edward Bennett suggested the Independence Avenue areas just southwest of the Capitol, facing across the Mall to the planned Municipal Center at Judiciary Square.

As another possibility, the Northwest Rectangle—defined by the Mall on the south, E Street on the north, between 17th Street and the Naval Hospital grounds facing 23rd Street—offered little-developed but distinctive sites overlooking Potomac Park and the new Lincoln Memorial. Seeking relocation from its massive concrete tempos along the reflecting pool, the Navy Department was interested in the historic site of old Observatory Hill (above the equally historic "Key of Keys") with its appropriate marine environment along the Potomac.

The 1901–1902 McMillan Commission report and Commission of Fine Arts had stressed the importance of the White House as the focal point for future public buildings. In 1931 the Planning Commission altered its earlier emphasis on East Capitol Street by agreeing with the Navy Department and recommending the Northwest Rectangle for the site of the War and Navy departments. This break with the past reflected the commission's claim that it was "looking many years into the future" in planning for buildings of a permanent character that might well house different departments in gener-

ations ahead, an idea later embraced by public buildings officials.

Duplicating the planning for the Federal Triangle, the Planning Commission, in its annual report for 1931, recommended that "all the permanent buildings existing and proposed in the northwest building area should be regarded as part of a single related group insofar as the varied character of the existing buildings to be retained will permit." These extant buildings included the semipublic buildings facing the Mall and the Interior Department Building (now the General Services Administration Building).

The Planning Commission was concerned about the height, style, and appearance of the new buildings in the Northwest Rectangle. Once the Planning Commission had the power under the Shipstead-Luce Act to influence planning in the Rectangle, it requested that the new group be "self-contained as to parking . . . and that parking be prohibited outside of buildings." To coordinate plans for the Northwest Rectangle, the Planning Commission organized a northwest building committee to agree on "basic principles governing the design of the area, including such items as building lines, heights, materials, and location of axes." These plans addressed, among other concerns, buildings close to the Mall that should harmonize with the Lincoln Memorial.

In rejecting the Commission of Fine Arts' suggestion of Pennsylvania Avenue west of the White House as a public building site, the Planning Commission in its 1931 annual report stated that the Commission of Fine Arts, traditionally assigned the task of protecting the McMillan Plan, was digressing "from and to some extent violating the principles of the L'Enfant and McMillan plans." Additional investment in the northwest sector, beyond that proposed for the Northwest Rectangle, would reinforce the tendency toward unbalanced development of the city toward the northwest. "From the larger standpoint of regional and city planning any such stimulus would be hurtful rather than helpful to the development of a balanced, efficient, and well-coordinated national capital." The Planning Commission had already considered sites along East Capitol Street between the Capitol and the Anacostia River.

Although accusing the Commission of Fine Arts of deviating from the McMillan Plan, the Planning Commission nearly followed suit in questioning the need for the Executive Group around the White House. The Planning Commission noted that the Agriculture Department on the Mall appeared to function satisfactorily. Fearing that a White House Executive Group would again increase the northwest emphasis of the city, the Planning Commission wobbled on its commitment to concentrated clusters in stating in the same breath that the "commission sees a real menace to the future of the city if all Government activities are packed very closely together. It would be a great mistake to emphasize the trend to the northwest, ignoring the splendid possibilities to the east and northeast."

Regional Parks and Planning

Visions of regional parkways required a dramatic increase in funding. In 1930 a bill sponsored by the House and Senate District Committee chairmen, Louis C. Cramton and Arthur Capper, was passed authorizing $16 million in the District alone to be used for parkland acquisition. The Capper-Cramton Act, a legislative gesture of support for the Planning Commission, provided an opportunity for the commission to show concrete results of its work program. The act also served as model for similar grant programs later instituted in other parts of the country.

Representative Louis Cramton summarized his belief that investing in parks was more important than funding buildings and monuments when he said, "artificial beauties such as monuments, boulevards, and pretentious buildings, if they are not built this year, they can be built next year or twenty years from now." Cramton was more interested in the natural beauties of Washington, beauties that "if not now [in 1929] preserved . . . cannot be restored later." An ideal ex officio member of the National Capital Park and Planning Commission, Cramton displayed an unusual interest in the city, owning a large library of Washington-related books, walking the streets and roads of the city, and faithfully attending Planning Commission meetings. He possessed a formidable knowledge of the city and its unique physical attributes, much beyond the scope of many residents. As chairman of the House Committee on the District of Columbia, Cramton was able to overcome the shortsighted opposition of power and energy development interests and to secure passage of the Capper-Cramton Act. The act was jointly sponsored by Senator Arthur Capper, chairman of the Senate Committee on the District of Columbia.

THE GEORGE WASHINGTON MEMORIAL PARKWAY

The Capper-Cramton Act provided land acquisition funds for the regional George Washington Memorial Parkway along both sides of the Potomac, on the Virginia side from Mount Vernon north to Great Falls and then south again on the Maryland side to Fort Washington. For the land in Virginia and Maryland needed for the parkway, both states were required to commit one-half the cost, either directly or through eight-year no-interest federal loans. The route of the George Washington Memorial Parkway ran through many reservations already owned by the government; nevertheless, massive coordinating efforts with the several federal agencies with interests along the route were required. In addition, the state agencies needed to be consulted about acquiring rights-of-way and making direct purchases of land. Some of the land, however, was to remain in private hands with restrictions placed on development.

Commercial development along the route was discouraged, except in those areas of Alexandria traversed by the parkway. Passage of the Capper-Cramton Act had been accomplished despite impending development of a power plant at Great Falls and the option taken by the Sun Oil Company on land above Key Bridge for a pier and oil tank farm. In the late 1920s, the Potomac Electric Power Company was in the process of negotiating with the local US district engineer, Major Brehon B. Somervell, to develop a power plant at Great Falls. All members of the Planning Commission, save Major General Edgar Jadwin of the Army Corps of Engineers, vigorously urged retention of Great Falls for a park, defending what had been proposed in the McMillan Commission report. Although the power company had presented a "combination park and power scheme" in its annual report for 1929, the Planning Commission argued that incidental creation of a park on the margins of the public utility development "would be a totally different kind of park from the natural valley."

Reminding its constituency of the unique scenic and historic qualities of the gorge, the Planning Commission concluded that it was "inadvisable to decide now upon the destruction for all time of the scenic and recreational and inspirational assets of such large prospective importance as those included in the Valley of the Potomac at the doors of the National Capital." The impending Sun Oil Company tank farm brought up the question of future use of the Rosslyn waterfront, then in decline. Although many Virginians favored creation of the landscaped parkway and aggrandized bridgeheads as portals to the city in the automobile age, local Rosslyn businessmen protested against the park development.

On the other side, several national organizations supported commission proposals for the parkway. In addition to providing general support, the American Engineering Council offered to preserve the locks and other works of the Patowmack Company at Great Falls as part of a "Washington engineer memorial parkway." The American Society of Landscape Architects proposed that a portion of the river park be dedicated to Frederick Law Olmsted Sr. The Theodore Roosevelt Memorial Association purchased Analostan Island with the intention of retaining it in its sylvan state as a tribute to Roosevelt's interest in conservation. The George Washington Memorial Parkway's future was further secured by the organization of a George Washington Memorial Parkway fund for collecting monies to match federal grants provided by the Capper-Cramton Act.

The primary legacy of Capper-Cramton legislative efforts on the city of Washington's behalf was the creation of the George Washington Memorial Parkway. The Capper-Cramton Act also provided $1.5 million in funds for an extension of Rock Creek Park into Maryland and an extension of the Anacostia Park system farther up the valley of the Anacostia River. In this act, Washington finally possessed the makings of a truly regional park system and at the same time had an important opportunity for demonstrating cooperation among the National Capital Park and Planning Commission and the Virginia and Maryland planning agencies.

Since the National Capital Park and Planning Commission's approval authority did not extend beyond the District line, the future of commission plans for the regional city lay in its ability to influence through planning policy recommendations and by coordinating with planning agencies in Virginia and Maryland. The Planning Commission believed that its plans were appropriate guidelines for the surrounding counties because, as it stated in its 1931 annual report, the "region must be responsive to the influences of the dominant center."

CAPPER-CRAMTON ACT BENEFITS TO MARYLAND

Like the National Capital Park and Planning Commission, the Maryland-National Capital Park and Planning Commission, established in 1927, was strengthened by passage of the Capper-Cramton Act, which provided for implementation of park plans. The tax base even in Montgomery County was very low, inadequate to purchase the massive park systems envisioned by the two planning commissions. Thus, financial aid provided by the Capper-Cramton Act was crucial. Chief among the benefits of the act was the extension of Rock Creek Park and its major stream valleys into Maryland "to preserve the flow of water in Rock Creek."

In 1929 Irving R. Root, city planner, and Roland W. Rogers, a landscape architect consultant at the Maryland commission, drew up a plan for Rock Creek Park in Maryland in close consultation with the National Capital Park and Planning Commission. The thin ribbons of green commenced just southwest of the northern corner of the ten-mile square and followed the crooked route of Rock Creek northward, with some of the creek's tributaries encompassed as parklike appendages. Root's plan for Rock Creek provided a protected stream valley richly furnished with recreational facilities, as well as dramatic overlooks, and a lake created in the broader stretches of the creek closest to the District line.

The Capper-Cramton Act plans for other regional parks in Maryland were implemented. Anacostia Park was extended northward, branching to the west in Sligo Creek Park. Other branches were extended to protect the minor stream valleys. To the east, Anacostia Park fed into what later became the massive Greenbelt Park and the Baltimore-Washington Parkway. The valleys of the Potomac River in Maryland were absorbed into Montgomery County's park system, including the valley of Cabin John Creek, which was an appendage of the George Washington Memorial Parkway. These thin slivers of protected parkland radiating from the District's parks followed the irregular routes determined by nature and provided a faint hint of the wedges of greenery that would be translated into the wedges and corridors plan of the 1960s.

The coordination of parks and highways between the District and the Maryland counties persuaded planning officials of the feasibility of regional planning. No official coordinating body existed. The success of cooperative public improvements depended instead on the willingness of the District and Maryland planning agencies to pay attention to each other's plans.

PLANNING FUNCTIONS IN MARYLAND

Some early planning powers in Maryland had been exercised by the Washington Suburban Sanitary Commission. Created in 1916, this commission controlled and operated the water and sewer system, approved plats of subdivisions, established street grades, and surveyed and platted future subdivisions. By the 1920s, the Washington Suburban Sanitary Commission was also considering preparing a highway and park plan. When rumblings of a suburban planning commission were heard, several members of the Sanitary Commission argued that their commission ought to be given the larger planning powers.

The local leadership in Montgomery County was well exercised by E. Brooke Lee, speaker of the Annapolis House of Delegates. Lee secured House support for the planning act through the "courtesy system" by which bills of a local nature could be passed if they had support of the local delegation. The movement for planning in Montgomery and Prince George's counties had been largely stimulated by the establishment in 1926 of the National Capital Park and Planning Commission, which in its organizing act was instructed to cooperate with local planning agencies. None of these existed at the time, but they soon appeared.

A hereditary power and large landowner in Montgomery County, Lee saw support for planning as stemming from educated people living on the edge of the national capital and from those who ran the national government downtown and wanted to improve county conditions. Lee worked to cement these interests at community meetings and at dinners at the old City Club on G Street, across from the Epiphany Church. Key members and staff of the Planning Commission attended these functions, explaining the work of the national commission to the suburbanites.

THE MARYLAND-NATIONAL CAPITAL PARK AND PLANNING COMMISSION

The Maryland legislature passed legislation in 1927 providing for a district containing the two counties contiguous to the District of Columbia. The Maryland-National Capital Park and Planning Commission was provided authority to plan, acquire land in the public interest, levy taxes to pay for park acquisitions, and draw up zoning ordinances. Important especially in the post–World War II dispersal of federal agencies, the Maryland-National Capital Park and Planning Commission was given an advisory role in the location of public buildings. The area initially covered by the Maryland commission consisted of 141 square miles in the southern portions of Prince George's and Montgomery counties closest to the District of Columbia and embraced twenty-seven incorporated towns and villages. With six appointed members, the commission included three from each county, appointed by the governor and approved by the respective boards of county commissioners. The chairman of the Washington Suburban Sanitary Commission was an ex officio member, providing continuity with the past and the possibility of overall plan coordination with sewer and water plans.

Although the Maryland-National Capital Park and Planning Commission was set up as a joint effort of two counties, in reality the past and present needs of the two counties were very different. Montgomery County was the more affluent of the two with a topography of rolling hills and rich soils. Its location was conducive to high-value real estate developments. Montgomery County residents proved willing to be taxed to support a county park system. Prince George's County was characterized, especially along the highway between Washington and Baltimore, by old tobacco farms and new industrial development, functions unattractive to high-cost housing. As a less affluent county, it did not enact any park legislation or a tax for such amenities for many years.

The relationship between the National Capital Park and Planning Commission and the Maryland-National Capital Park and Planning Commission was one that saw suburban planners identifying with the aspirations set forth by the federal commission. This relationship between the suburbs and the city was characterized by the similarity in the name selected by the Maryland commission. Also symbolic of this identification with the regional goals set by the federal Planning Commission, the 1927 law directed the Maryland commission to maintain offices in the District of Columbia as well as in the two counties.

The Work of Irving R. Root
Attracted to the national capital, Harvard-educated Irving R. Root joined the Maryland-National Capital Park and Planning Commission as the commission's first planner and engineer. Root, a city planner of high caliber in the landscape architect tradition, was from Flint, Michigan. At the commission he was instructed to prepare a comprehensive plan for the two counties. Root maintained a close relationship with the National Capital Park and Planning Commission, and as Charles Eliot described the situation in 1928, "their engineer [Root] is in our office every week and is thoroughly conversant with [our] plans."

Later on, amendments to the 1927 act added more detailed transportation planning responsibilities to the Maryland commission. In drawing up a highway plan, Root retraced the major thoroughfares of radial and connecting highways

outlined by Harland Bartholomew. Many of these highways were not built in the 1930s, but their location on the Maryland commission's plans ensured their retention for future consideration. Progress was made in the construction of a highway connecting Bethesda and Silver Spring (East-West Highway). Plans were under way also for linking Silver Spring and 16th Street, paving the Rockville–Potomac–Great Falls Road, and improving River Road to connect with Massachusetts Avenue (later with Wisconsin Avenue as well). Highways planned and constructed provided visible signs of public improvements that assured residents of the counties that the Maryland commission was producing vital public works and thus justified its planning powers.

PLANNING IN THE OLD DOMINION
The state of Virginia created the Virginia Park and Planning Commission, but its lack of authority throughout the 1930s hampered any effective regional participation. In 1930 the Virginia legislature set up a planning commission "with authority to make plans for a district including Alexandria, Arlington County, and all or parts of Fairfax County." The acceptance of the act hinged on the agreement by two of the three jurisdictions named, but as of 1932 no acceptance by any of them was actually at hand. In the absence of a concerted Virginia voice, therefore, the National Capital Park and Planning Commission dealt with the jurisdictions separately, noting the zoning ordinances adopted by Arlington County and the city of Alexandria and the comprehensive city plan under consideration by the Alexandria City Council.

REGIONAL COOPERATION ON WATER SUPPLY AND SEWAGE PROBLEMS
Regional cooperation was also evidenced in 1929 with the creation of the Washington Region Water Supply Committee formed by representatives from the Maryland-National Capital Park and Planning Commission, other Maryland agencies, Virginia agencies, District representatives, and the National Capital Park and Plan-

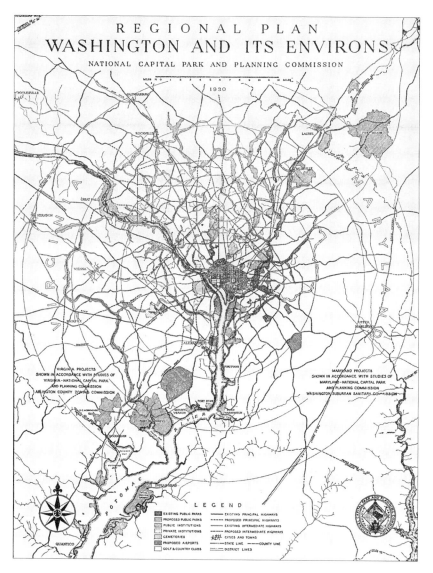

REGIONAL PLAN
WASHINGTON AND ITS ENVIRONS
NATIONAL CAPITAL PARK AND PLANNING COMMISSION
1930

Regional Plan for Washington and Its Environs, 1930. *Annual Report of the National Capital Park and Planning Commission, 1930*

ning Commission. The committee was requested to advise the National Capital Park and Planning Commission on the adequacy of the present water supply and to make recommendations on future sources of water. The 1929 sources of water—from Great Falls, from the Northwest Branch of the Anacostia River, and from Holmes Run in Virginia—were reported by the committee to be "lagging considerably behind the urban development of new areas." The committee report commented that "like highways, parks, and other elements of planning, water service plays a part in determining the direction of urban growth."

The increased demand for water by cities and towns north of Washington, such as Cumber-

land, Martinsburg, and Hagerstown, diverted water from the Potomac above Great Falls and affected the supply available to the District. The committee considered several joint or independent arrangements for the District, Maryland, and Virginia, simultaneously studying possible water sources to be found in the Patuxent River and Seneca Creek in Maryland and the Occoquan Creek and River in Virginia. Although no decisions were made about permanent regional cooperation or new construction, in general the Maryland and District representatives on the Water Supply Committee favored separate action by different authorities, whereas the Virginia representatives were in favor of continuing to depend on cooperating with the federal government and the District. (Arlington County and even the town of Falls Church received aqueduct water.) Articulation of the inclinations of the tripartite region and the areas intended to be developed was viewed by the committee as "important" in anticipating "an ultimate plan of development [of the water supply], which will include all the work done in the immediate future."

A similar representative regional committee was established in 1929 to report on drainage and sewerage problems. No sewage treatment plant existed in the region except for small facilities to serve Gaithersburg and Washington Grove. Thus, whether by direct discharge or by interceptor sewers, all sewage was discharged into the Potomac River or other streams. District Commissioner J. B. Gordon reported that the District was contemplating construction of a treatment plant at Blue Plains and had already acquired the property. When built, the Blue Plains Treatment Plant could service both the District and Maryland, but in 1929 the Maryland authorities were inclined to favor separate treatment plants on all streams then serving as discharge points for sewage.

Even if the sewer system—complete with trunk lines, interceptors, and treatment plants—was accomplished, the committee anticipated persisting problems of pollution. "The condition of the river is a matter of great economic interest to the shellfish industry as well as to the people of the Washington region," the committee reported. Pollution of the Potomac stemmed largely from overloaded sanitary sewers flowing into storm drains at high water, especially along Rock Creek. Planning for sewage influenced other elements in planning since, as the committee noted, construction of treatment plants in the region "would affect the proposals for parks along the Potomac River and smaller streams."

Planning for parks was also affected by the open valley treatment adopted in Maryland and Virginia whereby strips of land along streams were secured to absorb and channel high waters during flood conditions. In the treatment of these floodplains as park areas, the states thus obtained both recreational and drainage advantages. The committee concluded its work, recommending that the representative regional committee continue meeting to discuss regional sewage and drainage needs.

REGIONAL AND PROJECT PLANNING

The farseeing, wide-ranging studies produced by such representative committees and by the regional planning commissions represented a significant body of data on which the future of the region could be projected. Those who had worked earnestly for fulfillment of the McMillan Commission's recommendations could find concrete satisfaction in the massive George Washington Memorial Parkway, the preservation of Great Falls in its natural state, and the overriding emphasis on concentrated groupings of public buildings in the monumental core. Planning for the constituent city and for the region as a whole was also in full gear, with interest expressed in Washington community life—and in cooperation on resources, cutting across jurisdictional lines. This work was carried out in an atmosphere of high professionalism enhanced by substantial staff work and the support of key political figures.

Yet the circumstances of decision making by the National Capital Park and Planning Commission were still far from ideal. In its 1928 annual report, the commission admitted: "The most striking shortcomings of the situation at Washington as it begins to be studied closely are not in the quantity but in the quality of the planning that has been done in the past and is being done today." The tendency to make decisions of consequence based on brief studies was characteristic of "our hurried time." To be sure, the commission had produced many studies. The exigencies of project and specialized planning to deal with immediate problems, however, had forced the effort away from comprehensive and master planning and away from pursuing and updating basic studies. As for the cooperative committees representing agencies from the District, Maryland, and Virginia, this relationship was informal, not fixed by law, and not institutionalized in any single authority.

The Great Depression and its problems superseded the buoyant early years of the National Capital Park and Planning Commission and the land acquisition programs of the Capper-Cramton Act. Social issues such as unemployment had already brought Georgetown to the Planning Commission's agenda. Public works programs, rather than comprehensive planning, influenced planning for public improvements.

Symbolic of this transition in the planning picture, Frederick Law Olmsted Jr. retired from the commission in 1932, refusing reappointment. Upon his departure, the commission cited Olmsted for his "devoted and unselfish service to the cause of farsighted planning in Washington over more than 30 years, and [expressed the] hope that he will join the meetings of the Commission in the future as member 'emeritus' " Henry V. Hubbard, a Harvard professor and president of the American Society of Landscape Architects, replaced Olmsted. In the following year, 1933, Charles Eliot was appointed director of the newly created National Planning Resources Board and left the commission. Planning direction at the commission staff level was then taken over by John Nolen Jr., who had joined the commission staff two years earlier. ✯

THE NEW DEAL IN PLANNING 1933-1941

The Shift from Comprehensive Planning to Short-Term Goals

The New Deal transformed Washington and accelerated the city's growth. Suburbanization became the overwhelming form of growth, most particularly in the Virginia counties after completion of Key Bridge in 1923 and Memorial Bridge in 1932. New federal programs spurred this suburban development. Thus, to a noticeable extent, began the dispersal from the central city of not only residential functions but also commercial and governmental ones.

Despite concern with unemployment and recovery and a progressive orientation to social problems, the New Deal in Washington, as in many metropolitan areas, was less innovative in urban planning than in other areas. Fundamental urban problems were largely ignored; unable to function in the vacuum, city planning became almost totally ineffective. Many federal programs, particularly the Federal Housing Administration mortgage insurance program and expanded federal-aid highway programs, directly subsidized suburbanization without comparably strengthening the planning arrangements that would have guided it into more compact forms.

Ironically, the federal government was dramatically expanding its involvement in many aspects of American life, whereas in the national capital city, planning was underfunded and became ineffectual. The effects of weak planning were everywhere to be seen in sprawling subdivisions and eventually in the placement of major federal government facilities according to the wishes of department heads. Another generation would pass before planning for the capital city became revitalized.

NEW DEAL INITIATIVES

The New Deal initiated public programs aimed at stimulating employment by providing funds for public works projects, many of them long overdue. There was a distinct tendency to build what had already been planned and was ready to go. Many administrators of these new agencies looked to the Washington area as a case study of what could be accomplished nationwide—as, for example, in the model city of Greenbelt, in Prince George's County, Maryland.

Greenbelt represented the first time that the federal government became involved in building total communities. Under leadership of Rexford Tugwell, the Resettlement Administration oversaw the construction of the original section of Greenbelt dating from 1935 to 1937, which consisted of 885 houses designed by Reginald S. Wadsworth and Douglas D. Ellington. Influenced by sociologist Clarence Arthur Perry's views on the neighborhood unit, the homes were arranged in clusters within superblocks and included row houses, apartments, and prefabricated detached houses. As a self-sufficient community, Greenbelt also embraced a school, community center, and shopping center. Modeled after Clarence Stein's plan for Radburn, New Jersey, the roads and sidewalks were arranged so that residents could walk through the community without crossing streets. The community was incorporated in 1937

and placed under the Farm Security Administration. Greenbelt received international and national attention for its progressive plan. Many political leaders, including President and Mrs. Franklin D. Roosevelt, visited the community during its early years. In 1954 the residents formed a cooperative and purchased most of the houses and vacant land from the federal government.

Nationally, federal government funds were channeled through agencies like the Works Progress Administration, the Public Roads Administration, and the Public Works Administration. New areas of public activity appeared in housing and other fields. As these new agencies rose to prominence, the National Capital Park and Planning Commission continued to provide local coordination and advice but found increasing resistance to such planning guidance among federal agencies, intent upon short-term program goals. The drop in funding to the National Capital Park and Planning Commission, through

The Model City of Greenbelt in Prince George's County, Maryland, 1938. Library of Congress

both direct appropriation and the Capper-Cramton Act, cut the Planning Commission's ability to update or even to sustain its comprehensive planning. Planning decisions were largely made independently by federal agencies. The funding challenge, and hence the commission's diminished influence on planning decisions, led to increased demands by architectural and planning professionals—even from members of the Planning Commission itself—that the commission's structure be reorganized. The comprehensive plan, project planning, and coordinating efforts that were among the accomplishments of the Planning Commission's early years were no longer adequate for a city rapidly spilling into Virginia and Maryland in seemingly haphazard

directions. By 1941 the overwhelming requirements of the defense establishment dominated urban needs.

THE MALL DEVELOPMENT PLAN

In September 1933, Harold Ickes, secretary of the Department of Interior and administrator of the Public Works Administration, announced an allotment of $600,000 for the Mall Development Plan. It was estimated that the project would provide jobs for 350 men. This plan included the Mall proper and Union Square, the plot of land joining the Capitol grounds to the Mall, and provided for "roadway construction, general grading, landscaping, tree planting, and water supply system." In 1929 Congress had authorized the

Monumental Core prior to Completion of the Mall Development Plan, 1932. National Archives

Mall Development Plan, but it had never been funded.

The 1929 act instructed that modernization of the Mall be in accordance with the L'Enfant plan and the McMillan Plan, "with such modifications thereof as may be recommended by the National Capital Park and Planning Commission and approved by the Commission for the Enlarging of the Capitol Grounds."

As early as 1927, Frederick Law Olmsted Jr., Frederic A. Delano, and the other commissioners—along with Charles Eliot—prepared guidelines for the Mall development according to their interpretations of what L'Enfant would have done and what the McMillan Commission had recommended. Eliot interpreted L'Enfant's intentions for the Mall as an open vista between the Capitol and the Washington Monument. Eliot, in his 1927 memorandum, combined this aesthetic with the McMillan Commission's recommendation that the central vista be "enframed by rows of elms."

Olmsted built on Eliot's proposal by stating that to accomplish this geometric stretch of greenery three major elements had to be coordinated: first, new public buildings had to be designed to ensure the longitudinal boundaries and open vista; second, the "obstructive trees along the axis" had to be removed; and third, the entire Mall's length had to be graded and planted with formal rows of elms. Olmsted's 1927 memorandum recognized that many public officials and residents "jealously cherished" the Smithsonian grounds and Department of Agriculture grounds as artifacts of earlier romantic landscaping. Nevertheless, Olmsted justified his plan by the promise of "a very great permanent advantage" in the future clearance. The Commission of Fine Arts approved Olmsted's and Eliot's plans, which served as the basis for later work on the Mall Development Plan.

Olmsted was also influential in the overall design of Union Square. He conferred with W. L. Parsons of the Chicago firm of Bennett, Parsons, and Frost, the firm responsible for the new Botanic Garden at the foot of the Capitol as well as landscaping the extension of the Capitol grounds north of Constitution Avenue and toward Union Station. In planning Union Square, Olmsted had to design a connection between an essentially Beaux-Arts creation and the romantic Capitol grounds designed by his father years earlier.

PLANS FOR PUBLIC BUILDING SITES

The Mall development inspired new plans and studies for the adjacent urban environment. Accordingly, the Municipal Center, located at what is now called Judiciary Square, was reviewed, as were traffic arrangements through the Federal Triangle. It was proposed that the south side of Constitution Avenue should mirror the style and grandeur of the Federal Triangle buildings. Still, the ability of the federal government alone to effect extensive rehabilitation of the central area was limited, especially in the area north of Pennsylvania Avenue. As Henry V. Hubbard, successor to Olmsted on the Planning Commission (but with a different philosophy of design), stated, "It is evident that the Government has neither the funds, intention nor desire to spend public money for actual construction of buildings on the north side of Pennsylvania Avenue. . . . The actual construction must be a matter of private initiative." Hubbard suggested that local architects make tentative sketches for that side of Pennsylvania Avenue "as suggestion and an inspiration" to architects actually commissioned to design the separate private buildings.

John Nolen Jr., Planning Commission director, anticipated that the Mall Development Plan would spur interest in several long-term projects such as the Northwest Rectangle and the Southwest Triangle as sites for future public buildings. This represented a significant shift in emphasis away from the East Capitol Street plan for the location of federal buildings. The Northwest Rectangle was defined by E Street NW, 17th Street, Constitution Avenue, and 23rd Street. Boundaries of the Southwest Triangle were B Street SW (now Independence Avenue), Mary-

land Avenue, and 15th Street. Both sites had been studied as potential locations for public buildings and were deemed compatible with McMillan Commission plans inasmuch as this planning, according to Nolen, "recognized the Mall and the cross axis of the White House as the basis for the central composition of the city." Nolen also envisioned that the Mall Development Plan would inspire the "moving of [the] old Smithsonian Building" and construction of

the 12th Street and 14th Street underpasses to facilitate traffic in the monumental core.

A major investment in the Northwest Rectangle was construction of the massive new headquarters for the US Department of the Interior. Covering five acres on a two-block site, the new building was connected to the earlier Interior Building by a tunnel under Rawlins Park. Although spartan in its exterior design, the interior was decorated with murals, sculptures, other

The National Mall, 1937. National Capital Planning Commission Collection

artwork, and ornamentation. Interior Secretary Harold Ickes was so involved in the building's construction that he personally selected the architect, Waddy B. Wood, and oversaw its construction. The building possessed many innovations for a federal government building: a central vacuum cleaning system, air-conditioning, and interior parking garage.

THE MODERN MOVEMENT IN AMERICAN ARCHITECTURE

In the 1930s, a body of planning and architectural professionals conversant in the modern design alternative confronted the persistence of Beaux-Arts sympathies in Washington public architecture. The important 1932 exhibition, titled Modern Architecture: International Exhibition, at the Museum of Modern Art in New York City, as well as its accompanying catalog by Henry-Russell Hitchcock and Philip Johnson, crystallized the challenge of the modern movement in America. The battle between New York City establishment architects versus New York

City modernists was replayed in Washington, and the Jefferson Memorial project was the first of successive design conflicts in the capital. The millions of visitors saw little in the Washington skyline to indicate the rising tide of modernism, unless by accident or by astute observation they discovered William Dewey Foster's streamlined Central Heating Plant in Georgetown. Foster's beige triumph was the first federal building of this era to knock aside the Classical Revival forms.

The more obviously classical National Gallery of Art, constructed between 1936 and 1941, and in particular the Jefferson Memorial inspired a vocal outpouring of letters, speeches, and testimonials by the modernists against the Pope design. For the memorial project, the modernists did not provide a design alternative (they advocated a competition), but the strength they exhibited forced Pope, his successor firm, and the Memorial Commission to compromise by relocating, reducing, and simplifying the original scheme.

Reduced Influence of the Planning Commission

The undercutting of effectiveness of the National Capital Park and Planning Commission in influencing planning decisions was symptomatic of the Planning Commission's increasingly weakened financial and political standing. Demands of the Depression spending reduced funding to the Planning Commission through the District's appropriations. From the high of $1 million exclusive of Capper-Cramton funds in both 1929 and 1930, there was a sharp decrease; by 1932 Congress appropriated only $47,185 to the Planning Commission through the District of Columbia budget.

New programs set up by the New Deal—for example, employment programs—further reduced the Planning Commission's role as a shaper of policy; at the worst its role among the new agencies was that of an observer. The National Industrial Recovery Act funded highway improvement schemes intended to create employment opportunities, the plans for which followed largely, but not entirely, the Planning Commission's earlier major thoroughfare system.

The Public Works Administration's Housing Division provided for demonstration housing projects in the District of Columbia, issuing its own policies covering location, construction method, and financing arrangements.

HOUSING AND THE NEW MOBILITY

Private housing developments mushroomed in the suburbs, often oblivious to any regional plan. Observing that new homes and apartment buildings were being located in both Maryland and Virginia without consultation with the planning agencies, the Planning Commission deplored private decisions made without study of water and sewage facilities and other necessities of residential living.

The popularity of the automobile with Washingtonians, a taste indulged not only by L'Enfant's wide streets and boulevards but also by generous modern highways, facilitated mobility in the vast metropolitan area. A traffic study performed in 1934 by planner Charles Herrick for the Planning Commission revealed that the "proportion of people in Washington who use private automobiles or taxicabs is over twice the average

Looking East on K Street toward 16th Street NW. The Historical Society of Washington, DC

reported from six other cities," a larger proportion even than in Los Angeles. Herrick discussed the possibility of imposing economic disadvantages on the automobile driver and encouraging greater use of public transportation. In 1934 Herrick predicted that without incentives to change riding habits, there would be no end in sight to the "prohibitively expensive projects that may be necessary if the proportion of automobile drivers continues to increase." Chief among these "expensive projects" were parking facilities and improved highways to handle rush-hour traffic. The Planning Commission considered recommending staggered office hours but did not possess the necessary resources to draw up a new traffic plan to update the Bartholomew guidelines from the commission's early years. The result was the continued increase of parked cars on every street and green space in the central city.

Later in the 1930s, the Federal Aid Highway Act of 1938 launched continuous road planning in the District of Columbia. This planning commenced with the 1939 Highway Planning Survey. For the first time, the District was treated "as a state" in the distribution of federal road funds. The first highway plan for the city (replacing the earlier periodic road programs) was drafted in 1941. It was a more specialized and strongminded highway planning effort than had been the street extensions offered in the 1893 highway plan or the more rounded and comprehensive thoroughfare plan of 1930 developed by the young Planning Commission. The 1941 planning efforts were succeeded by new ventures that would confirm the city's planning for the motor age.

NATIONAL AIRPORT AT GRAVELLY POINT

In contrast to dispersal activities unrelated to any comprehensive plan, National Airport was carefully sited in 1940 at Gravelly Point—between the 14th Street Bridge and Alexandria—after a number of sites in the metropolitan area had been studied. Washington had seen aviation history in the making since the days of the Wright brothers

and Samuel Langley's unhappy termination of his flight in the waters of the Potomac. Washington's small flying fields like that at College Park, Maryland, had many vivid associations with aviation's infancy. Dirigibles had flown from Alexandria / Hybla Valley Airport in Virginia, and the earliest commercial passenger services operated from Washington-Hoover Airport. This airport—originally improvised from a merger of two privately owned airports, Hoover Airport near what became the Pentagon site and what was called Washington Airport—eventually became impossibly constricted. Spurred by wartime exigencies, President Franklin D. Roosevelt decided in 1938 to build a new federal airport to serve the capital city's expanding air traffic.

The most likely alternative location for this facility, other than Gravelly Point, was Camp Springs, Maryland, where Andrews Air Force Base would one day be built. Camp Springs in the early days, however, posed major access problems that could not be resolved fully until completion of the Capital Beltway. Gravelly Point, on the other hand, was wonderfully accessible to the central city via the Mount Vernon Parkway and US Highway 1, the main highway south. By continuing the extensive fill of the Potomac river-bottom meadows, moreover, the need for large-scale acquisition of developed areas was avoided. Nor was the air traffic of the early years much of an environmental nuisance, save in the Old Town of Alexandria (where it was regarded as third in order of importance as a nuisance, after the soot from the Potomac Yards and the odors of a riverfront fertilizer factory). As finally built, the airport terminal itself became a work of architectural distinction. Nominally designed by Howard Lovewell Cheney of Chicago, but more largely the work of then government architect Charles M. Goodman, the design was ultimately inspired, as was that of so many public buildings, by a sketch headed "Stolen from the desk of Franklin D. Roosevelt."

Thus National Airport, a work of lasting urban significance, materialized and became the

capital city gateway for millions of travelers in the burgeoning era of air traffic. The image of the capital city from the air approach and via the riverside parkway, an image seen by day but even more spectacularly by night, strongly recaptured the formalism of the monumental city. The airport's location also recaptured that sense of a national city on the Potomac, largely lost in the days of rail and highway travel. Finally, National Airport's notably convenient location to central city destinations embedded it in the fabric of the city despite the deafening noise, vibrations, and atmospheric pollution that came with expanded aviation services and the advent of jet planes.

THE GRAB-BAG METHOD OF DEVELOPMENT
The low funding and lack of a comprehensive plan that could be implemented led to the loca-
tion of new public buildings almost at random. In 1941 Harold Ickes described the process of locating new public facilities as the "grab-bag method of putting a road or a building on any bit of vacant land that can be discovered." The influence of both Frederic Delano and Frederick Law Olmsted Jr., the latter a continuing Planning Commission consultant, was still formidable in the planning field, although both leaders were elderly by then. New figures at the National Capital Park and Planning Commission seemed unable to inspire either the confidence or the attention of federal officials responsible for agency plans. Such a situation could only invite criticism.

The diminished effectiveness of the Planning Commission was reflected in Frederic Delano's letter of resignation in April 1942 to his nephew,

National Airport, Constructed on Land Created by Dredging the Potomac River, 1941. Copyright *Washington Post,* Reprinted with Permission of the DC Public Library

President Franklin Roosevelt, addressing him as "his Excellency, the President of the United States." Describing the original National Capital Park and Planning Commission as the "best that could have been worked out fifteen or more years ago," Delano reminded Roosevelt that the commission's only administrative duty was the purchase of parks and playgrounds. "Otherwise it was solely a planning and coordinating committee." Many of the ex officio members gave little if any time to the work of the commission and rarely attended meetings. The commission had no compulsory relationship with important agencies such as the Bureau of the Budget. Delano concluded that "now is an appropriate time to reconsider the set up [of the commission] on a sounder basis."

This concern with the effectiveness of the commission was reflected by the ever-vigilant Committee of 100 and the faithful American Planning and Civic Association in their suggested new philosophy for Washington planning: "No longer should we regard planning as a method of setting up restrictions to prevent officials and citizens from free action; but rather as a means of positive determination of the pattern of the future, under which sound plans are devised and practical projects outlined on an economic schedule." The two organizations recommended a mandated, integrated set of relationships among agencies most responsible for the appearance and functioning of the city. Most important, they recommended that sufficient funds be appropriated to the Planning Commission to draw up regional plans and keep them current.

The Multicentered Regional City

The effectiveness of the National Capital Park and Planning Commission was significantly reduced by the shifting of the War Department installation from a long-intended building site in the Northwest Rectangle to the Arlington site next to Arlington National Cemetery. Many tugs on the city's neat central core and surrounding area had already dispersed public buildings far-

ther into the District and beyond. As these public installations became large office buildings filled with armies of employees, the buildings themselves became subcenters in what was rapidly becoming the multicentered regional city. New buildings in dispersed locations necessitated provisions not only for access and parking but also for other facilities such as water, power, sewage disposal, and housing for employees—and housing entailed more complex relationships with schools, stores, and recreation accommodations.

BUILDING THE PENTAGON

In the 1930s and early 1940s, historic lands associated with the Washington, Custis, and Lee families became a battleground between the National Capital Park and Planning Commission and the War Department. As part of the dénouement, early in 1940 the War Department conceived of a vast structure to contain its consolidated activities, accommodated from World War I days largely in the concrete, so-called temporary buildings along the Mall. The Planning Commission had expected that the War Department's needs in replacing these tempos could be met by the officially designated Federal Office Building No. 2, to be located in the Northwest Rectangle. As the pace of national defense activity quickened and the scale of war involvement became evident, however, the War Department put aside earlier building plans and began to search for a site on the Virginia side of the Potomac River.

The Arlington Site: Background and Battleground

First to be considered by the War Department was the Arlington Experimental Farm, a tract of two hundred acres located west of the railroad. Part of the former Custis estate, the tract had long been used by the Department of Agriculture and was scheduled to be turned over to Arlington National Cemetery. Possible use of this site by the War Department met with objections: both the Planning Commission and the Commission of Fine Arts felt that such use would conflict with the siting of the Lincoln Memorial directly across the Potomac. The two commissions won this skirmish but not their original struggle to locate the War Department Building in the Northwest Rectangle as planned.

The entire river lowland area of Arlington between the 14th Street Bridge and Arlington National Cemetery was under intensive development pressure at the time. The recently constructed bridges and highways and the freeing up of the old Washington Municipal Airport land increased this pressure. This lowland area was to accommodate several major projects, including a proposed facility for the Navy. The chief of the Army Corps of Engineers surveyed the area and identified the major subcenters: Fort Myer, Arlington National Cemetery, Arlington Experimental Farm, the projected federal airport at Gravelly Point, and the projected War Department site, which underscored the heavy military presence in the entire area. Because of its location in Virginia, however, the area lay outside the jurisdiction of the National Capital Park and Planning Commission, although certainly not beyond its regional sphere of interest. From October 1933 on, when John Nolen Jr. had reported to the Planning Commission that the Department of Agriculture was about to abandon its Arlington Experimental Farm and move to new facilities at Beltsville, Maryland, the general site had been very much within the Planning Commission's range of vision.

Once the commission made the decision to abandon the old Washington Municipal Airport, the land and its future use became a topic of much speculation. The Planning Commission saw the best reuse of the old airport land as accommodating expansion of Arlington National Cemetery beyond what would be provided by the acquisition of the Arlington Experimental Farm. Planning details for this expansion and land reuse had been put forward. The Planning Commission was alerted that these plans were in jeopardy, however, when John Nolen Jr. reported in July 1939 that a detachment of troops from Fort Washington had occupied the Arlington land "with a view to developing permanent quarters at this site." This was the beginning of the critical phase of the long engagement.

War Department Moves in Virginia

In the following months, the Planning Commission lost its bid to use the Arlington Experimental Farm for park activities, especially as the Bureau of the Budget wrote bills transferring the entire lowland site to the War Department. A compromise plan was reached—by the War Department, the Bureau of the Budget, and the president of the United States on the one hand and the National Capital Park and Planning Commission on the other—providing for the land to be divided between the Departments of Interior and War. The needs of Interior's nursery, greenhouses, and camp site were to be met first, with the rest of the land to be allocated to the War Department. The War Department agreed with the Planning Commission's overall plan, provided that the commission would cooperate in getting the proposed compromise plan through Congress. In fact, the resulting bill as processed by Congress eliminated all mention of the Department of Interior and the Planning Commission, except that a right-of-way was given to Interior for an approach to Memorial Bridge.

Design of the Pentagon

Once the War Department owned its large and commanding piece of Virginia land, as established by congressional act, the Planning Commission and others waited anxiously to see what the department planned to build. For several months, there were announcements that only temporary buildings would be constructed on the site. With sounds of war becoming louder, Congress then appropriated $35 million for construction of the War Department Building, the five-sided structure later called the Pentagon, to occupy sixty-eight acres of land immediately north of US Highway 1 on a portion of the old airport land and a portion of the Arlington Experimental Farm. The structure was to house approximately thirty thousand office workers at

Stretch of Highway South of the Pentagon, 1946. National Capital Planning Commission Collection

its peak occupancy. What was in the works was a virtually self-contained city served by railroad and bus lines, shops, churches, health and recreation facilities, and restaurants. Most visibly, vast parking lots and an extensive network of highway interchanges surrounded the building. A commuter launch would connect it to the Naval Air Station at the juncture of the Anacostia and the Potomac rivers.

Objections and Outrage

When the full ramifications of this behemoth of a building emerged, the Commission of Fine Arts issued an anguished press release on the first day of August 1941. Referring to the illustrious history of the Commission of Fine Arts, the press release reminded readers that the McMillan Commission had requested that the land destined for the Pentagon be kept open and free of permanent buildings, a sacred haven of repose for Arlington National Cemetery, certainly in the

category of a "great park," and an appropriate foreground to the capital city. The Commission of Fine Arts evoked arguments in favor of dispersal to spin out federal buildings into a vast regional city in the post–World War II era. As for the needs of the War Department, "we are sure that there are other and better solutions to this particular problem which, incidentally, might result in decentralizing the offices of the Army to prevent that remote possibility of wiping out the whole establishment incident to the dropping of two or three bombs."

Harold Ickes's warning "against further encroachment upon the parks and playgrounds of the National Capital" was as powerful as the outrage of the Commission of Fine Arts. As secretary of the interior, Ickes deplored not just the independent action of the War Department but even more the irreparable damage to the orderly development of the city. He accused the War Department of single-handedly creating "upsetting influences involving shifting population, traffic congestion, and a general disturbance of the whole city pattern." Ickes objected that "at the rate we are going, the parks in Washington will soon be nothing but glorified boulevards."

THE APPROACH OF WAR: DEFENSE CONSTRUCTION AND OUR NATIONAL CAPITAL
Several months before Pearl Harbor, Washington had already begun to draw up its battle lines. Tempos and especially transitory defense housing began to rise again—a repeat performance of World War I. This time, however, defense construction reached far into the suburbs: tempos in Suitland, Maryland, and defense housing in Falls Church and on the farmlands of St. Elizabeths Hospital. Barracks were everywhere. Perhaps spurred by the warnings of the Commission of Fine Arts that only a few bombs were needed to immobilize the government, the Bureau of the Budget made studies regarding relocation of federal employees outside the National Capital Region. Access by roads and bridges from the city and suburbs to the War Department's Pentagon city and widely dispersed tempos had to be constructed, superimposing wide ribbons of highway on the once bucolic landscape.

The head of the Public Roads Administration, provider of this new mobility, planned to move testing facilities from the National Airport area to far away and undeveloped Langley, Virginia, to avoid future agency moves that would be necessitated by encroachment of development on these facilities. The War Department Building itself attracted smaller auxiliary buildings. The National Capital Park and Planning Commission and the Washington chapter of the American Institute of Architects discussed air raid protection in the area, suggesting studies be performed to determine the "location of wooded areas in the region suitable for evacuation in relation to access and transportation, such as the Catoctin Mountains of Maryland and Chopawamsic recreation area in Virginia."

A few days before the nation went to war, T. S. Settle, secretary of the Planning Commission, delivered a patriotic radio message entitled "Our National Capital." Settle recalled the many instances of tourists who, on looking over the monumental core, became better citizens with a heightened sense of patriotism. During the war emergency, Settle saw among the nation's problems the need for protection both from the enemy outside and from those who would disrupt and destroy from within. He cited a list of insensitive public officials who for the sake of expediency would destroy the carefully planned city of public buildings and parkland. He stated that destruction of open spaces in the city would cripple the efficiency of employees. Settle blamed the tension in the city on the unwillingness of governmental agencies and Congress to look ahead and to work with the National Capital Park and Planning Commission in planning for the future. In coupling war emergency with the protection of Washington as the patriotic national shrine, Settle defined the Planning Commission's work as an important element in the nation's morale and thus a contribution to winning the war. ✪

WORLD WAR II AND POSTWAR YEARS 1941-1952

10

World War II Growth and Development

Washington had always grown with war, economic crises, and national emergencies. The years of World War II and of postwar readjustment were no exception. An analysis of Washington's population showed that 67 percent of the city's increase had occurred in five of its thirteen decades of history. The analysis also showed that the wartime increase in the 1940s was a suburban metropolitan phenomenon. The District's population had grown from 663,091 in 1940 to 802,178 in 1950—a peak—and the metropolitan area population increased from 967,985 in 1940 to 1,464,089 in 1950. Growth in the Virginia counties came from construction of bridges and even more from location of the Pentagon and other federal establishments on the south bank of the Potomac.

After World War II, unprecedented prosperity and population growth continued almost unabated for two decades. Americans' pent-up demand for goods, combined with federal government programs to help veterans return to civilian life, caused the suburban housing boom, with the attendant problems of sprawl, traffic congestion, and the decline of the central city. Although the District was governed in a different fashion than other American cities, it too experienced these problems. The work of the National Capital Park and Planning Commission illustrates the variety of problems addressed, the difficulty of finding solutions to metropolitan-wide issues in a fragmented local government structure, and the confusion and uncertainty attendant in trying to adapt a nineteenth-century urban fabric to the automobile-dominated mobility of the postwar era.

POPULATION AND HOUSING

The settlement pattern that earlier had followed main transportation corridors, especially those defined by the streetcar system, grew more diffuse as the automobile became the primary mode of commuting and as the city decentralized its employment and retail trade. Lower population densities were also reflected in the pattern of sprawl, a new and specific condition of urban settlement, defined at the time as development at densities too low to enable the economical provision of full municipal services. Along with the building of wartime temporary office buildings came wartime temporary housing, much of it in the form of prefabs or mobile homes. The temporary type of construction was dictated equally by shortages of copper, iron, lumber, and other critical building materials; by scarcity of skilled building labor; and by fear that the local economy would collapse with a postwar glut of housing. Even conventional housing of the wartime and postwar periods reflected the qualitative decline.

Under all these expectations lay two assumptions that were to prove spectacularly wrong: that the nation would enter a postwar recession on the model of the years following World War I and that national population growth would decline. To these mistaken premises, Washington's experience was to add a third. The expectation that the end of the war would see a return to prewar conditions was blasted by the postwar obligations of the national government to its international responsibilities, to the Cold War, and to a new agenda of domestic programs, especially those that affected cities.

Downtown Washington Bustles with Activity at 11th and F Streets NW, ca. 1940s. Copyright *Washington Post*, Reprinted with Permission of the DC Public Library

WARTIME WASHINGTON

World War II brought massive changes to the city. Temporary structures covered open spaces in the monumental core and in many outlying areas. Although some of the outlying buildings were later removed, the land seldom returned to its former open condition. This development of land and transportation connections predicted permanent development and extensions to the city's edges. The automobile allowed for larger and more remote pieces of fringe areas to be enveloped into the wartime city. Whereas the city during the Civil War and World War I had spilled into the open lands that lay within the District's boundaries and were heavily defined by routes of public transportation, the city of the 1940s spread far into the surrounding counties.

The growth in numbers of federal government civilian employees, which reached a wartime peak in 1943 of 284,665 employees, accelerated this development. In 1918 the federal government had employed a maximum of just over 120,835 civilian employees.

World War II caused permanent changes to the city. In contrast to the post–World War I city, the wartime population endured especially in terms of government employees. Beginning in 1918, the number of employees had steadily decreased until the Depression years. Conversely, after World War II, the federal government maintained a largely consistent number of employees, hovering at about 225,000 until 1951, when the Korean War again catalyzed an expansion in federal employment. World War II Wash-

Temporary Federal Office Buildings on the Mall as Viewed from the Top of the Washington Monument, 1943. Library of Congress

ington grew in response to the dictates of the
War Department and the Bureau of the Budget.
The most planners could hope for was either a
return of the city to its prewar order or an
opportunity to draw up a new comprehensive
plan for the postwar era.

Wartime Residences and Office Centers
The sudden need for wartime office and housing
space involved more than buildings alone. Residences needed to be supplied in convenient, or at
least expedient, locations for workers. This need
in turn entailed planning for water, sewerage,
schools, shopping, parking, and recreation. Facilities in the central core were already taxed to

their personnel limit (40,000 at the Naval
Weapons Plant on the Anacostia River;
30,000–40,000 at West Potomac Park in tempos;
25,000 at the old Navy Municipal Buildings on
Constitution Avenue).

New office centers, generally of contemporary
style, began to be constructed in the District and
suburban counties on the once-open spaces that
had been part of the regional park system. For
such developments, the Planning Commission
recommended that "additional temporary Federal office buildings should be constructed in
outlying locations so distributed that concentration shall normally not exceed 2,500 employees
in any one location, with a possible maximum of

Interior of Union Station, 1942. Copyright *Washington Post,* Reprinted with Permission of the DC Public Library

Fort Dupont Houses Located East of the Anacostia River, 1944. Library of Congress

5,000 employees." Even with the development of these low-density office centers, the commission saw limits to packing defense needs into the Washington area and therefore proposed decentralization of some government offices to other cities.

McLean Gardens

Among housing sites on former open space was the project undertaken on the McLean estate on upper Wisconsin Avenue NW, a garden apartment complex designed by Kenneth Franzheim. Construction of this large concentration of apartment buildings pointed up the tendency to build first and plan later. In the early stages, con-

Aberdeen Hall, Men's Dormitory for War Workers, at McLean Gardens in Washington, DC, 1943. DC Public Library, Washingtoniana Division, DC Community Archives

Planned to include a complex of apartments plus a shopping strip, McLean Gardens was sited before the boundaries of the northern extension of the Glover-Archbold Parkway were defined. In addition to congestion, McLean Gardens also generated transportation problems. In 1942 the Defense Homes Corporation, which constructed the development, was unwilling to design a streetcar loop at the intersection of Wisconsin and Idaho avenues, as recommended by the National Capital Park and Planning Commission. This modest incident symbolized a nationwide failure to integrate planning for mass transportation facilities with comprehensive planning, a shortcoming later illustrated many times over in urban renewal and large-scale suburban development.

siderable opposition to the complex was expressed because the neighborhood contained single-family dwellings with high property values rather than housing projects. A highly concentrated population in blunted Georgian-style boxes on a shaven landscape was inimical to the neighborhood of individual lawns and trees, well-defined architectural details, and generous proportions. Moreover, residents of the housing project would add to the already congested streetcar lines and major thoroughfares.

Washington's housing picture was further clouded by differences in facilities for war workers, white and black workers, and the displacement of a "small village" of black families in Arlington from the site of the Pentagon. Washington differed little from other cities responding to nationwide demographic changes. For the most part, the Planning Commission and the National Capital Housing Authority supported the development of housing for black families

A Suburban Subdivision with Newly Constructed Single-Family Homes in Arlington, Virginia, 1942. Library of Congress

east of the Anacostia River, closer to the Navy Yard, Union Station, and other employment centers.

POSTWAR PLANNING ON THE HORIZON

As World War II drew to a close, the National Capital Park and Planning Commission discussed the shape of postwar planning, especially for housing, in view of the increasing rather than decreasing population projections. Alfred Bettman, a national planning authority and specialist in municipal corporation law, who would later serve as consultant to the Planning Commission on redevelopment legislation, first attracted the attention of the commission when

he reported that as a planning body it had "been criticized by architects and others from time to time with having done most of its planning for the central area and done nothing about the redevelopment of the older parts of the city." Chairman Ulysses S. Grant III invited Bettman to submit more recommendations. Much of the zeal in providing housing for war workers had obscured the continuing problem of housing for the poor, so that the problem surfaced anew in the postwar era.

Mobility

Postwar planning was concerned with mobility and its effects on the traditional structure of the

Americans Swarm F Street after Learning of the Japanese Surrender, August 14, 1945. DC Public Library, Washingtoniana Division, DC Community Archives

city. This matter was taken up by the Washington Board of Trade. In October 1946, the Board of Trade created a City Planning Committee, with four subcommittees devoted to the comprehensive plan, coordination, research, and public relations. Fischer Black, chairman of the City Planning Committee, suggested that some regional authority be created to scrutinize planning within the several jurisdictions. As the official city chamber of commerce, the Board of Trade was also acutely aware that the increasing dispersal of population and employment centers would radically affect business operations.

Fueled by the programs of the Federal Housing Administration, federal-aid highways, and nationally assisted public works, postwar suburban development surged forward and was welcomed heartily by real estate interests, home builders, and such professional organizations as the Urban Land Institute. Few gave an appropriate measure of critical evaluation or, indeed, recognized suburban development for the momentous change it was.

DEVELOPMENT IN MARYLAND

Development beyond the District line had largely erased the state of Maryland boundary in popular usage, but its jurisdictional significance had been reemphasized by the separate plans for highways that had been drawn up in Maryland, Virginia, and the District of Columbia. A notable illustration of the need for coordination was the Northwest Freeway proposed by the Maryland-National Capital Park and Planning Commission. This route was proposed to collect traffic from Gaithersburg along a line parallel to US Route 240 (the historic road to Pittsburgh and the West since the days of General Braddock's ill-fated expedition) and to unload it at MacArthur Boulevard just outside the District line or possibly at Cabin John.

The remainder of this route into Washington lay conveniently beyond the jurisdiction of the Maryland commission. The route from MacArthur Boulevard or Cabin John to downtown destinations—through the natural obstacle of the Potomac Palisades, the built obstacle of the Washington Aqueduct from Great Falls, and existing narrow streets and roads—was difficult and costly. In this particular case, the Planning Commission's Regional Highway Committee and the Coordinating Committee in the 1950s showed their strength by elaborating the alternative route possibilities in both Maryland and the District before exploding the simplistic Northwest Freeway scheme. This experience showed the dangers inherent in the piecemeal approach to highway planning.

THE COMPREHENSIVE TRANSPORTATION PLAN

Postwar transportation planning culminated in the vast programs of urban expressways, bypasses, grade separations, and circumferentials that homogenized American cities, structured future growth, and everywhere changed lifestyles into an approximation of Los Angeles or northern New Jersey. In Washington, what had begun as a regional expressway system born of wartime transportation needs and experience was distorted into a system whose largest costs were incurred in metropolitan areas. Thus, it was no accident that Washington's Capital Beltway was the first major circumferential route to be planned, completed, and evaluated in any American city.

In facing the postwar period, the District of Columbia Department of Highways had taken the initiative with several successively bolder plans, culminating in the 1946 Greiner-DeLeuw report, which also spoke for the District commissioners and the Public Roads Administration. The plan was spectacular and sweeping. It interpreted the doctrine of continuous flow in a system of below-level highways and subways. In contrast to this plan, the Planning Commission wanted more gradual, incremental improvements. The March 1947 report of the Planning Commission pointed to the unsubstantiated cost-benefit aspects of the Greiner-DeLeuw report and criticized the expensive highway tunneling proposals in particular.

In short, the Planning Commission argued that first there were a number of remedial measures that were needed and should be undertaken for the existing highway system before embarking upon costly, sweeping, and generally unproved programs of new construction. The Planning Commission restated its 1945 recommendation to the District commissioners that they adopt a thoroughfare plan (a system of through streets) as the first step before starting any program of below-level or other grade-separated highways.

These recommendations, effective and moderating, further expressed the conviction that highway planning was no longer a spasmodic affair of individual project proposals to be dealt with piecemeal but rather had become a continuous process requiring specialized attention. The Planning Commission thus acted to form a continuing committee on the Comprehensive Transportation Plan. This action recognized the exceptional significance and influence of transportation planning and its steadfast presence on the planning agenda.

Proposed Inner Loop Freeway System, 1955. National Capital Planning Commission Collection

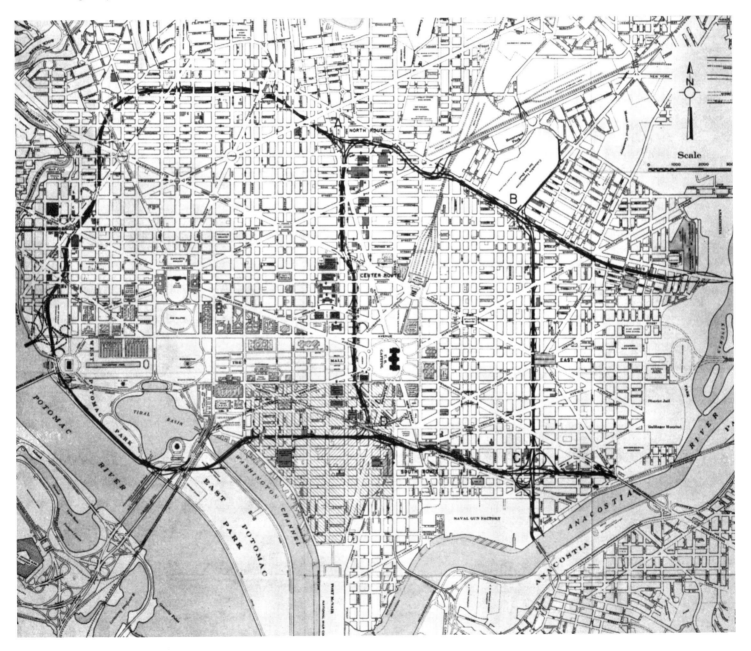

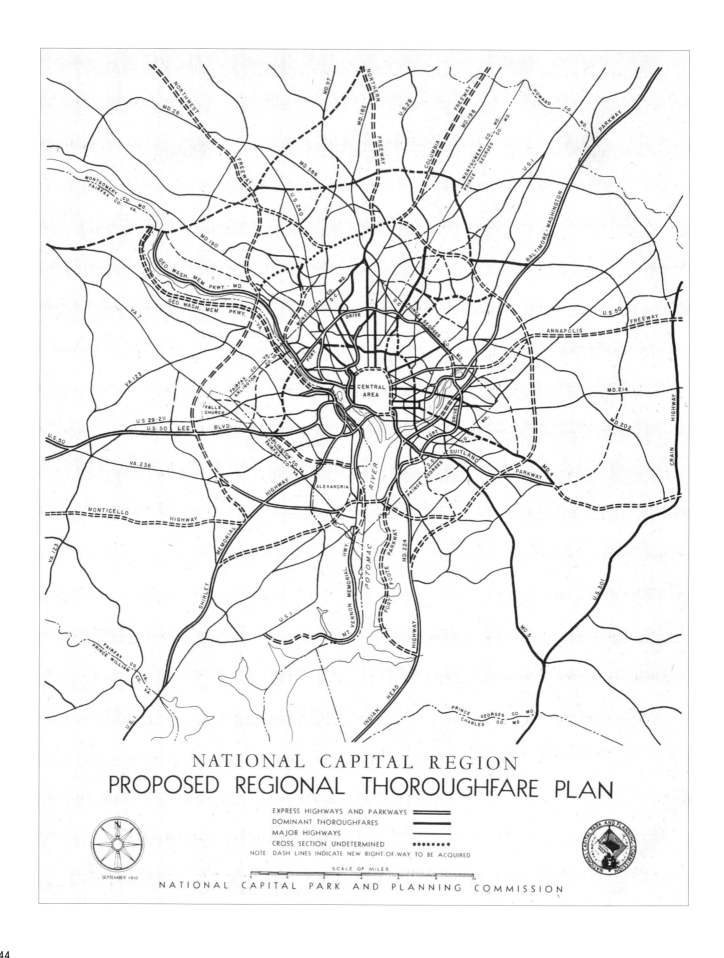

NATIONAL CAPITAL REGION
PROPOSED REGIONAL THOROUGHFARE PLAN

EXPRESS HIGHWAYS AND PARKWAYS
DOMINANT THOROUGHFARES
MAJOR HIGHWAYS
CROSS SECTION UNDETERMINED
NOTE: DASH LINES INDICATE NEW RIGHT-OF-WAY TO BE ACQUIRED

SCALE OF MILES

SEPTEMBER 1950

NATIONAL CAPITAL PARK AND PLANNING COMMISSION

The 1950 Comprehensive Plan

Rebuilding obsolete areas of the city became the primary focus of the 1950 Comprehensive Plan, since a comprehensive basis was required for funding of renewal projects under new national programs and policies. Other requirements also contributed to the plan's form: parks and community facilities, population and land studies, transportation, and housing were included. Employed by the Planning Commission to direct preparation of such a plan, Harland Bartholomew looked back to the McMillan Commission plan and through it to the L'Enfant plan, especially its parks, and to plans from the early years of the National Capital Park and Planning Commission that he had influenced so much, primarily in the area of recreation and neighborhood identity.

Almost a quarter of a century had passed since those early days. The postwar city offered new challenges and opportunities. Chief among these were questions of the increasing dispersal effects created by the automobile, ideas about security from atomic attack, congestion, and the environment. In response to these concerns, the 1950 plan recognized the need for a healthy and expanded employment center and therefore proposed the East Mall, the Northwest Rectangle, and the Southwest Rectangle as suitable settings for government office building development. It also proposed the transportation facilities that would be required if those areas were developed.

RINGS AND RADIALS: PLANNING FOR THE BELTWAY AND RAPID TRANSIT

The 1950 plan modified Bartholomew's circumferential road scheme proposed in the Planning Commission's early years and applied the same circumferential idea to the center of the city where inner rings and crosstown routes were drawn. The inner loop of three circumferential or ring routes would be located one mile from the White House to carry traffic around parts of the central congested area. The second loop was planned for three to five miles from the White House, tracing the route of the McMillan Com-

mission–inspired Fort Drive, which would have connected the two riverside drive systems. The third loop was to be a new beltway completely around the city between six and ten miles from zero center. Strengthened radial roads would provide access between circumferential roads and allow access between dispersed employment centers.

As illustrated in the plan, however, none of these thoroughfare proposals approached the scale of later freeway programs, either in extent as a system or in size as individual roads. Bartholomew rejected plans proposing development of mass transportation facilities beyond the extant bus and streetcar system, pointing to the large proportion of Washingtonians traditionally tied to their automobiles, the low population density that could not efficiently support a rapid transit system, and the assumption by transit planners that the commuting pattern could be concentrated along a few radial lines. In short, Bartholomew viewed rapid transit as incompatible with the horizontal, dispersed, low-density capital city. As the plan stated, "Neither the existing nor the probable future population pattern contains sufficiently high population densities over a large enough area to warrant the extremely high cost involved in the development of a rapid transit system." In 1961 the Planning Commission disavowed this view in the Year 2000 Policies Plan.

THE CONSTITUENT CITY AND THE FEDERAL PRESENCE

Central to all of these 1950 proposals was the constituent city, the city of homes and residents, and the services they demanded. The plan pictured in vivid graphic form the problem areas of the District, characterized by slums, overcrowding, alleys, and disease. The Washington mosaic of the three categories of "obsolete, blighted, and satisfactory" areas was compared to those of other cities.

Beyond recommendations that the plan made for the constituent city, it defined the important employment role of the federal government in

Proposed Regional Thoroughfare Plan for the National Capital Region. National Capital Park and Planning Commission, *Comprehensive Plan for the National Capital and Its Environs*, 1950

Greenway Shopping Strip
at Minnesota Avenue and
Ridge Road SE, 1942.
National Archives

molding the metropolitan city. "The Federal establishment itself, as the major economic base of the community, can make or break the future of the city by its policy—or lack of policy—on geographic arrangement of its operations." In conclusion, the plan suggested that to effect regional planning on the scale outlined in its transportation recommendations, a formal association of planning agencies in the area be created.

THE GUIDE FOR FUTURE PLANNING

The 1950 plan broke considerable new ground, and it gained strength from the city plans that had preceded it. But such a stance did not guarantee its ability to generate action and compliance. In the general summary of the plan, the commission acknowledged the provenance and clouded expectations of the 1950 recommendations. "The plan here published evolved out of a series of earlier plans, on which the Commission has been working since its start. . . . Its broad goals will not change. . . . To the extent that it is known and approved by the community at large, it will also be an effective guide for the whole metropolitan area." The reception of the 1950 plan was weakened, however, by its issuance at a time when the composition of the commission was significantly altered by a change in chairmanship. Moreover, a bill to restructure the National Capital Park and Planning Commission was pending.

In 1950, the new commission chairman, William C. Wurster, presented the all-important comprehensive plan, the expected foundation for all future planning, to the public. Wurster had

succeeded Major General Ulysses S. Grant III, whose career had been associated with the Planning Commission from the beginning. Grant was a symbol of the continuity of commission policies, which were strongly oriented to conventional planning approaches traditionally supported by groups such as the American Planning and Civic Association. In marked contrast, Wurster's appointment reflected President Truman's concern for urban minorities. Wurster's professional qualifications were impressive, beginning with his chairmanship of the Massachusetts Institute of Technology's departments of architecture and planning; he was also married to one of the great leaders in public housing, Catherine K. Bauer. Certainly his appointment broke decisively with the past, and had Wurster not decided to return to the University of California–Berkeley after serving a year on the commission as chairman, his leadership would probably have left a more permanent mark.

Upon Wurster's resignation, Harland Bartholomew, a longtime Truman associate originally from St. Louis, was appointed commission chairman and began immediately to show that association with the commission and the city since 1920 did not prevent him from reaching independent judgments. Bartholomew's most immediate past service to the commission was in directing the development of the 1950 Comprehensive Plan, and this, too, he was willing to jettison in tune with the times.

Metropolitan City at Mid-Century

The metropolitan city of the mid-twentieth century was actually defined by factors other than public decree. As a capital city Washington evolved from the federal presence, but this evolution was expressed variously at different historical periods. During most of the nineteenth century, the federal establishment was of direct importance; it was concentrated, but it was relatively small. By contrast, after World War II, between 1946 and 1950, the federal establishment had increased to what seemed to be a plateau of about 225,000 civilian employees and was relatively decentralized throughout the city and the region. The federal government also represented a diminishing share of the total employment in the area because a large private sector had developed separate from, if not independent of, the federal establishment.

DISPERSAL OF FEDERAL FACILITIES

Sporadic location of federal establishments beyond the District boundaries entered a new phase under pressures of World War II. Led by the siting of the Pentagon, the Naval Medical Center, the Beltsville Agricultural Research Center, the Naval Ordnance Laboratory at White Oak, Maryland, and other major centers of employment, a spate of so-called temporary buildings on temporary sites followed. Many, such as the facility in Suitland, Maryland, were destined to become permanent.

Under wartime conditions, these locations were roughly determined by existing transportation and in-place utilities, by availability of housing, or by feasibility of supplying these necessary services at a time when all such efforts were rigorously limited and controlled. The suburban pattern thus fostered was a campuslike federal installation located on a major transportation artery, surrounded by new communities of single-family homes. This was followed by the filling in of open land by additional residential development, commercial centers, schools, and other local government services.

Contrary to the expectations of many planners, there was at the time neither a decline in population growth nor an abatement in building and development. The intense pace of wartime and postwar development relentlessly drove Washington toward metropolitan government and its dilemmas. In Washington, unlike other American cities, annexation of surrounding suburbs to the central city was impossible given the legal barriers of the Constitution and the Residence Act of 1790. Creation of metropolitan agencies proceeded in the Maryland counties, but Virginia lagged, and no regionwide cooperation emerged.

The Intercontinental Ballistic Missiles Threat
At this confused juncture in the immediate postwar years, Washington was obliged to face its vulnerability to attack by intercontinental ballistic missiles armed with atomic warheads and seriously to consider urban dispersal as a means of defense. Top-secret studies, such as "Project Lincoln's" analysis of Manhattan, demonstrated a general urban vulnerability. This fact of life had been illustrated clearly by the saturation bombing of urban areas during World War II; the lessons of Dresden, Hiroshima, and Nagasaki could not be forgotten. British experience with shadow capitals in wartime and the forced decentralization, also during the war, of many nonessential agencies from Washington to other parts of this country presented themselves as tested solutions.

Federal contract allocation could motivate firms that were willing to move to dispersed locations, and fast amortization rewarded such moves with significant tax reductions. Although the problem of civil defense was immediate and nationwide, and many strategic centers equaled

Perpetual Savings Building at 11th and E Streets NW, 1950. Arteaga Photos, DC Public Library, Washingtoniana Division, DC Community Archives

Aerial View of Suitland Parkway from the Projected New Federal City at Suitland, Maryland, 1949. Copyright *Washington Post,* Reprinted with Permission of the DC Public Library

Washington in both importance and vulnerability, the nation's capital presented greater opportunities to execute new civil defense plans as a demonstration for the rest of the country and as a way to spread the benefits of public works projects.

On December 16, 1950, a national emergency was declared because of this recognized threat of atomic attack. Legislation was proposed for the relocation of sensitive government agencies. According to bills introduced in the House and Senate, cross sections of the government's vital

systems were to be dispersed in eight facilities with a total of forty thousand employees. These facilities were to be constructed in a radius outside of but accessible to the city and were to be built of special materials resistant to blast and atomic fallout. One such facility was built for the Atomic Energy Commission in Germantown, Maryland. To complement this planned dispersal of sensitive agencies into the greater Washington metropolitan area, the Bureau of the Budget proposed removal of about 25,000 employees to decentralized locations totally outside of Washington in other parts of the nation. The 1950 proposals, in short, attempted to provide for a systematic dispersal policy within the context of purposeful planning.

Reaction and Response in the Suburban Counties

The Pentagon experience in Arlington had dramatically demonstrated what happens when a major installation is suddenly constructed in the suburban landscape without planning or preparation. In response to the legislative proposals for dispersal, residents in the counties next to Washington could envision what the results might be in their suburban areas. During the 1950 congressional hearings on this dispersal legislation, county residents testified on the probable effects of such construction and fielded suggestions for more comprehensive planning. Dismissing the potential economic benefits and added jobs in rural Loudoun County, the "Washington milkshed," for example, Mrs. Robert S. Pickins, chairwoman of the Loudoun County Planning Board, testified: "When the government moves in, school burdens increase; water problems and sewage problems increase; and the change in the economy is very disturbing."

Professionals committed to regional planning recommended that the government study the effects on housing patterns, on roadways and highways, on urban and rural communities, and on the public utilities necessary to support additional growth. The simplistic suggestion that large office structures should be separated by open spaces, which would soon be filled in by housing, was not sound planning. The regional planner Clarence S. Stein insisted in a strong statement to the congressional Committee on Public Works that no dispersal of federal installations "should be attempted without providing both housing and full community facilities, including markets and schools, for the major part of the personnel."

Even jurisdictions not immediately affected by the proposed legislation were apt to be involved indirectly. Arlington County, site of the contro-

versial Pentagon, did not anticipate any further federal installations within its boundaries. Hearing testimony suggested that even so "Arlington will be directly affected by the proposed dispersal" in the burdens thrown on transportation routes and facilities, water supply, and sanitation. Facilities in the District and Virginia would necessarily be affected, it was predicted, because "all routes across the Potomac into the District of Columbia pass through the county."

Dispersal and Civil Defense

Planning for the eight dispersed facilities was further complicated, as the legislative hearings revealed, by questions of whether an atom bomb attack would occur during working hours when office buildings were crowded with people or at night when these buildings were virtually empty. There was no way to know whether atom bomb attacks would focus at the center of the target area or in the vicinity, and therefore safety could not be presumed for the proposed twenty-mile radius.

Other questions were raised. Would eight facilities that were spread out in the counties but linked by highways be truly convenient to each other and to the District in the event of emergency? Would larger bombs necessitate an even larger radius from point zero? Could government really function with mechanical communication systems, or would face-to-face conferences still be necessary? Leaving aside the uncertain defense justifications for dispersal, some government officials regarded the proposed eight facilities as investments in relieving congestion in the central city. Planners of this decentralizing persuasion were quick to pick up the theme. Quite apart from the issue of atomic war, they pointed out, the problem of overconcentration of government buildings in the downtown was still unresolved.

Although no legislation would emerge from the 1950 hearings, the government's dispersal policy was furthered by executive action, culminating in Executive Order 11035, dated July 9, 1962, which established a continuous review of locations for public buildings. Fear of atomic attack on the city continued to pervade building location policies for most of the 1950s, but acceleration of weapons technology shifted the focus from passive civil defense to the doctrine of countervailing weapons.

Strategic dispersal was seen in the location of the Atomic Energy Commission in Germantown, Maryland; the Central Intelligence Agency in Langley, Virginia; the National Bureau of Standards in Gaithersburg, Maryland; and the National Security Agency in Fort Meade, Maryland. Other smaller movements took place, and highly secret installations, such as the standby "underground Pentagon" near Camp David, in Blue Ridge Summit, Pennsylvania, and an "underground Congress" at the Greenbrier in White Sulphur Springs, West Virginia, were created in this period. The dispersal movement declined as more powerful weapons appeared. At the same time, the inconvenience of outlying locations was voiced more often. This awareness coincided also with increasing interest in central city revitalization.

SPLENDID ISOLATION REVISITED

The federal office buildings sitting in splendid isolation in the suburbs forced planners to reconsider recentralization. The supposed proximity of home to work was more an idealization than a reality; in fact, employees at dispersed installations often commuted many miles from equally dispersed residential areas elsewhere in the region. Although located close to urbanized centers, the dispersed installations simply could not offer the convenience of the central city. Despite the many connecting highways, in practice there was little face-to-face communication with the president, the Congress, other agencies, or indeed other facilities of the same agency. Since little or no public transportation existed between the installations and the city or other suburban areas, most employees were forced to use their automobiles.

The dispersed installations were inconvenient for out-of-towners; agencies were forced to hold meetings and conferences in the central city. There was the constant need to attend upon Congress. Finally, as weapons technology advanced and eventually nullified the early 1950s policy of dispersal, civil defense needs reached beyond the limited scope of building location. In an atmosphere of détente, moreover, there seemed to be no need to sacrifice the efficient day-to-day functioning of centralized government to plans for civil defense. In spite of the long historical experience of medieval walled cities, military considerations usually proved a poor basis for city building and urban design.

SERVICES AND TRADE IN THE NATIONAL COMMUNITY

Service employment had always formed part of the Washington economy. This took the form of a large building industry, printing plants, transportation and communications, and other distinctive activities. Large numbers of men and women also engaged in retail trade, in hotels and restaurants, and in a wide variety of health, legal, and other services. With the postwar era there came, in addition, a host of new activities reflecting Washington's attraction as a national center. Business and professional associations brought their important national conventions, lobbying, and communications activities to Washington. Headquarters or branch offices of many firms with contractual arrangements with the federal departments located here, as did a booming television industry and an enormous establishment devoted to higher education and academic research. Here also was the apparatus related to federal administrative decisions and appeals, licensing and regulation, lawyers, expert witnesses, and influence peddlers.

TALL BUILDINGS IN THE URBAN RIM

By 1950 tall buildings, often considered evidence of a commercial society, began to rise along the rim of the metropolitan city. The horizontal city within the boundaries of the District of Columbia was one of the features that distinguished Washington from most other cities. Thus, pres-

sures to build upward had pushed high-rise construction to the very rim of the metropolis, on land in the Maryland and Virginia counties not subject to the capital city's height controls. Tall buildings were not just those built by private interests; the federal government also created these artifacts inimical to the city's traditions.

Between 1947 and 1948, Commissioner of Public Buildings W. E. Reynolds brought new building plans for the National Institutes of Health in Bethesda to the Planning Commission for consideration. The National Institutes of Health research hospital as proposed would rise thirteen stories on the site's highest ground, with subordinate buildings grouped around the main building in a relationship reminiscent of the City

Beautiful civic center formula. An epitome of the management-oriented civil servant whose philosophies influenced the spartan public buildings of the early postwar years, Reynolds justified the building's height from the "standpoint of economy and efficiency of operation." In January 1948, the Planning Commission approved the building plans with the thought that they were far enough away not to impinge on the monumental core.

EARLY PRESERVATION PLANNING AND THE NEW GEORGETOWN

Disturbed by the alteration of the old fabric of the city through proposed redevelopment and highway construction, the Commission of Fine

The Georgetown Waterfront, with the Whitehurst Freeway Paralleling the Potomac River, Early 1950s. National Capital Planning Commission Collection

Arts chairman David Finley expressed the desire to preserve the features of the L'Enfant plan that had influenced so much of the city's development. As the minutes of the National Capital Park and Planning Commission for the June 1952 show, Finley suggested that his commission supply the Planning Commission with a plan outlining the essential elements of the L'Enfant Plan: "the streets, plazas, parks and structures that should be considered inviolate to any but the most necessary and generally approved changes."

The Planning Commission also received suggestions in 1946 from Colonel Byron Bird of the District Engineer's Office that the declining waterfront be surveyed for new uses, a proposal that reflected his examination of the changing functions of the entire Washington riverfront. Construction in 1949 of the elevated Whitehurst Freeway siphoned traffic off Georgetown's congested narrow cross streets.

The realization of a new Georgetown, a maturing of Georgetown as a distinctive community, had produced a strong concerted voice among residents and supporters against allowing the area north of M Street to be altered at will. Responding to these interests, Congress in 1950 declared all of Georgetown a historic district and placed the design of all future construction under the judgment of the Commission of Fine Arts. As the city's first official historic district, residential Georgetown served as an index of comparison with other historic neighborhoods. It also typified a lifestyle that would attract high-income residents to the District.

Development in Suburban Virginia

Rapid physical changes forced regional planning agencies to respond quickly. In January 1942, the Arlington County Board reported that changes were made in the zoning map at almost every meeting. Major commercial areas were created at Clarendon, at Rosslyn, and along Columbia Pike, with smaller centers established to serve more local needs.

A new zoning plan proposed in 1942 by the National Capital Park and Planning Commission called for apartment buildings visible from Washington to be restricted to sixty feet with a few allowances made for buildings of ninety feet. Special treatment was to be accorded the "Vista of Washington Line" that followed the ridge on which the Civil War forts had been located. John Nolen Jr. stated his opposition to the ninety-foot limit as blighting the low-rise buildings surrounding them. No action was taken on the proposal of the commission.

The Arlington County Board suggested, however, that such apartments, "scattered here and there, would tend to break up the monotony of the skyline." In 1945 the Commission of Fine Arts warned the National Capital Park and Planning Commission that private developers owning land in Northern Virginia contiguous to Arlington National Cemetery proposed to construct apartment buildings that would be visible from the Mall. Such a discordant view from the ceremonial core would be a "threat to the integrity of the central composition of the Capital." Eventually, through the efforts of the Planning Commission, enough land, such as the Nevius tract addition to the Arlington National Cemetery, was acquired along the length of the river to push back future high-rise development. In this way, a minimal landscaped foreground was provided to offset the mushrooming Virginia high-rises visible from many sections of the Mall.

Aesthetic problems posed by high-rise apartments and office buildings close to the Virginia waterfront must have caused Planning Commission members to regret that the Virginia lands within the original ten-mile square had been ceded back to the Commonwealth a century earlier. Faced with uncontrolled development, the commission began to consider the entire skyline of the national capital and its possibilities for coherent design. Pressures for loosely controlled development on what was once the backdrop to the Potomac intensified in the postwar era as the demand for permanent housing steadily increased. Entire portions of Planning Commission meetings were devoted to reviewing development plans in Virginia and protesting their impact on the view from the District. In the search for leverage to mitigate these effects, the Planning Commission recognized as one offsetting item the fact that the development was also subject to financing regulations of the Federal Housing Administration.

ARLINGTON TOWERS

In 1949 the Planning Commission was faced with the proposed thirteen-story Arlington Towers project designed by architect Donald H. Drayer. The Arlington County Board had approved a "relaxation" in the zoning regulations to allow for the unusual height and density of the proposed building. The Planning Commission vigorously opposed the generation of more traffic in the area of Key Bridge, the creation of an "unsightly background for the Mall" in the special spot zoning, and the light color of the buildings that would compete with that of the Washington Monument, the Capitol, and other monumental structures. Eventually constructed in spite of commission opposition, Arlington Towers correctly predicted the height of future construction, such as the high-rise office cluster in Rosslyn. Even today Arlington Towers remains a major element in the Virginia landscape.

GEORGE WASHINGTON MEMORIAL PARKWAY

Other new developments sprang up along the extant access roads to Washington. For example, the memorial character of the George Washington Memorial Parkway, originally conceived of and approved by the Planning Commission as a picturesque parkway, was threatened by the flood of new demands made on the land. Harland Bartholomew saw these problems as symptomatic of large areas of disagreement among federal, state, and city planning officials. Threats to the special character of the parkway included National Airport; commercial zone changes along Washington Street in Alexandria; Belle Haven, just south of Alexandria, on the brink of apartment construction, most notably in the form of the massive Hunting Creek apartment development; and the Woodland Manor subdivi-

sion, where the sponsors proposed a recreation and commercial area fronting on the parkway. In all cases, until the relationship between the National Capital Park and Planning Commission and suburban planning agencies could be formalized, preservation of the scenic qualities of these extensions of the national capital depended on the piecemeal resolution of each individual case.

SPRINGFIELD

Extending the sight lines into Virginia, the Planning Commission had little influence beyond suggesting how proposed developments should be coordinated with federal, District, and metropolitan area needs. In the summer of 1947, John Nolen Jr., then executive director of the Planning Commission, reported on a major development about to occur in Springfield, then "nothing . . . but a cross road" at Shirley Highway and Franconia Road. Six thousand acres along Shirley Highway had been assembled by developers to provide a residential community for more than 45,000 residents.

In the process of development, large tracts of agricultural land had been rezoned to residential, business, and industrial uses. Although this virtual city lay beyond the limits of Planning Commission purview, the commission suggested that new residents of Springfield could not funnel themselves entirely into Washington. "The development should not be planned solely as a tributary of Washington, but should be more of a self-contained community. . . . Consideration ought to be given to the development of employment centers in the vicinity."

Planning for Growth in the Maryland Counties

Growth was being generated in Maryland in such volume that M. Bond Smith, general counsel to the Maryland-National Capital Park and Planning Commission, characterized the situation as uniquely tied to the national capital city. In 1948 Prince George's County, Maryland, was the fastest-growing section in the Washington

metropolitan area, forcing the boundaries covered by the Maryland commission to be extended ever outward. Urban sprawl threatened the comprehensive stream valley park program that the Capper-Cramton Act had authorized but never entirely funded. The director of the Maryland commission, Fred Tuemmler, stated that Prince George's County parks were being acutely affected by "both federal and private development of employment centers and the expansion of Maryland University." These much-threatened stream valley parks were more than decorative; they conserved natural resources, assisted flood control efforts, framed the metropolitan city, and added to the value of adjacent residential developments.

THE HOME RULE CHARTER, 1948

With the end of World War II, the pent-up demand for land pushed home construction and its related needs for schools, shopping facilities, and recreation into the forefront for the suburban counties. The population of both Montgomery and Prince George's counties had nearly doubled in the ten years between 1940 and 1950. (Montgomery County's population increased from 89,490 in 1940 to 194,182 in 1950; that of Prince George's County increased from 83,912 in

1940 to 164,401 in 1950.) Pressures for developing land to its maximum density—and thus for developers to reap huge profits from the radical increase in value of the land—led to rumblings against the planning powers of the independent Maryland-National Capital Park and Planning Commission. In what was billed as a fight for home rule, forces in favor of the counties' controlling development of their own land succeeded in passing a home rule charter in 1948. The charter failed, however, to extract the planning powers from the Maryland commission. Antagonism over who would benefit from development dominated the activities of the counties' political and planning bodies for at least two decades. It was not until environmental and no-growth policies came to the fore in the late 1960s that these unchecked tendencies toward development for profit's sake were questioned.

PARKS AND HIGHWAYS

The Maryland-National Capital Park and Planning Commission's most effective tools in directing growth were its park acquisition and highway plans, both areas in which the commission achieved considerable distinction. Purchased jointly by the National Capital Park and Planning Commission and the Maryland-National

Capital Park and Planning Commission, stream valley parkland acquired before World War II with Capper-Cramton funding, as well as land acquired with the same funding in the postwar era, funneled residential development in between the wedges of open space. That development was usually close to major highways radiating out from the District.

Following the lead taken in the National Capital Park and Planning Commission's 1950 Comprehensive Plan, the Maryland commission unveiled its highway plan two years later. The proposed spiderweb of radials and circumferential dual highways provided a basis for public discussions. The proposed new radials included the relocated route that became Interstate 270 to Frederick and the Annapolis Freeway (US Route 50), both under construction in 1952. The proposed circumferential roads were named the Intercounty Belt Freeway and the Outer Belt Freeway. Both bypassed the District and linked suburban population centers. The Intercounty Belt Freeway anticipated the route later followed by the Maryland portion of the Capital Beltway. The Outer Belt Freeway, proposed to be located even farther from the population center established by the District boundaries, was never constructed.

THE REGIONAL VIEW: REDEVELOPMENT, MOBILITY, AND FUTURE GROWTH

The ability of the Maryland commission to retain its planning powers throughout the postwar era of expansion did not necessarily reflect great effectiveness in structuring the urbanizing counties. The full effects of uncontrolled and uncoordinated growth had yet to shock development-minded officials into an appreciation of the waste in resources and large public costs incurred. Yet the Maryland commission did not need to be reconstituted; it needed to express a regional point of view rather than the more parochial bicounty point of view that reflected the different traditions and outlooks of Prince George's and Montgomery counties. The ability

to develop this larger view of the interrelationships with each other and with the District of Columbia would portend the ability of all the national capital's jurisdictions to set common goals and to put aside immediate gains in favor of long-term regional benefits.

Although the growth of the postwar capital city often appeared directionless, several themes emerged in the decade following World War II that were important in recharting the metropolitan city's future. Of these themes the most important were redevelopment by both public and private efforts, mobility, and the need for future growth to be guided by comprehensive and specialized planning, based on the strengths of previous plans and continuity between the historic and modern city.

Public redevelopment was an urban reflection of the heady postwar era of world leadership and unprecedented national wealth. Private redevelopment was finding new and profitable uses for older, settled areas in the region; new development was changing towns into employment subcenters, farm property into housing subdivisions with appropriately historical names, and rows of town houses into commercial strips.

On a less disruptive level, old areas of the city were undergoing renewal by self-regeneration, by discovery of the values of historic buildings and neighborhoods, and by growth of a strong community consciousness, as exemplified in Georgetown. Tying together concepts of residence and work, new platforms of mobility were planned, making the city accessible and siphoning traffic from sensitive areas but at the same time creating new environmental hazards. Although the 1950 Comprehensive Plan was rooted in policies dating from the National Capital Park and Planning Commission's early years and reflected the dispersal trends of its time, it did reestablish the need for such comprehensive planning and for project and functional studies. The postwar city, suffering from the effects of planning by many independent agencies, had already inaugurated the tools to restructure its future. ⋆

PLANNING THE CITY OF TOMORROW 1952-1960

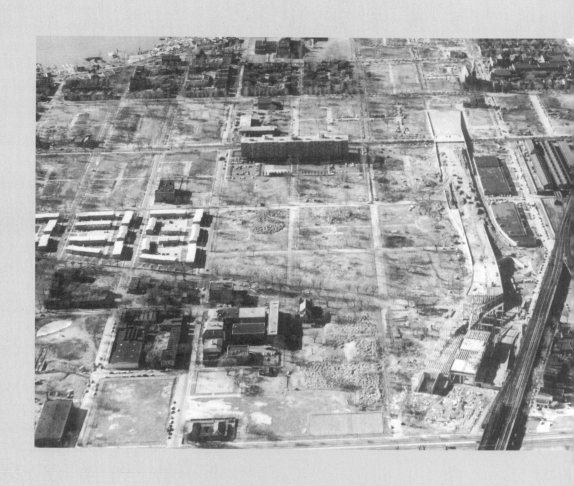

New Planning Visions and Authorities

Urban visions that emphasized city rebuilding reflected the supreme confidence of the post–World War II period. Sentimentality for the old did not constrain this outlook. Postwar housing and urban renewal legislation, the creation of the interstate highway system, the construction of dams and other water control systems, and the triumph of modernism in architecture all exemplified the rush toward the modern city. Washington was not immune to this national planning fever. The movement of the middle classes out of the central city convinced planners that it needed to be rebuilt to compete with the new suburbs. The urban fringes were developed on seemingly "clean slates." The Washington metropolitan area offered a grand opportunity to display the art of modern city planning.

Suburban growth catalyzed this broad canvas of metropolitan Washington, populating an increasing number of counties in Maryland, Virginia, and even West Virginia. In common with many of the nation's metropolitan areas that were fueled by government housing finance and transportation policies, Washington displayed glaring proof of the region's sprawl. Entire weekend sections of the *Washington Star* and the *Washington Post* reported suburban homebuilders' activities. The characteristic low densities and sprawling nature of development led to a huge demand for transportation, water and sewer lines, and other services provided by local governments. These demands were difficult to satisfy because all came at a predictably higher cost per family. Reality soon outstripped the initial illusions of suburban economy.

THE SUBURBAN BOOM: NO FREE LUNCH

There was no such thing as a free lunch. The mystique of a parklike environment, the appeal of "newness" in housing and schools, the apparently more manageable scale of small local communities, and the feeling of escape from the problems of the central city added to the postwar suburban boom. Besides, that was where the houses were.

The automobile, a fascinating "adult toy," made possible this escape to the suburbs. By greatly enhancing the mobility of entire families, the car gave access to new forms of leisure, as well as greater opportunities in employment, education, and social and cultural experiences. The central core in most cities was filled with obsolescent industry, an increasingly abandoned commercial downtown, and housing that was rejected by all but the most needy. People abandoned this scene with little regret. In Washington, however, the downtown was filled with federal agencies, offering the most significant concentration of employment and sustaining a viable metropolitan center.

As a metropolitan center, Washington served a nation of citizens increasingly identified with their national government and obliged to visit the capital for both business and pleasure. Such comings and goings did not benefit the retail shopping center. Instead, older settlements within the metropolitan area were subject to renewal in the form of new office complexes and employment subcenters, as also occurred along K and L streets and north toward Dupont Circle. The temporary wartime boom extended by national growth, increasing industrial and social complexity, and unavoidable worldwide responsibilities gave the city's center a solid foundation.

THE NEED TO ACT

Demands for new growth in the capital in 1950 produced the movement toward regional planning embodied in the 1952 legislation reorganizing the National Capital Park and Planning Commission as the National Capital Planning Commission and creating the National Capital Regional Planning Council. The need to act also was implicit in the various transportation and metropolitan studies and other examinations of projected needs in the capital. Finally, in 1957, the voluntary Washington Metropolitan Regional Conference of Governments evolved into the Metropolitan Washington Council of Governments, the area's first voluntary but formal organization on a regional scale.

The major development overall in this period was the move to facilitate regional planning, the scope of which had been recognized in the McMillan Commission's proposals and in the work of the National Capital Park and Planning Commission's early years. Regional powers were implicit in the Capper-Cramton Act, which had assisted the National Capital Park and Planning Commission in planning for and acquiring regional parklands. The Planning Commission had also helped to create suburban Maryland and Virginia planning commissions.

The activities of the National Capital Park and Planning Commission in the region had diminished in the Depression and wartime years, however. The dispersal of new development had flooded the countryside with so little warning that regional plans assumed new urgency. It became imperative to formulate planning policies for acquiring additional open space, for building a mass transportation system, and for restructuring and developing a central employment and commercial center to offer conveniences superior to those available in dispersed office clusters and suburban shopping centers.

EFFORTS TO REORGANIZE THE COMMISSION

Some of the same groups that had actively supported the creation of the National Capital Park Commission in 1924 and the National Capital Park and Planning Commission in 1926 urged the creation of a new planning commission, but like the American Planning and Civic Association, these groups had lost their political clout. The Capper-Cramton program was completed, and the built-up District precluded major new park acquisitions. At the same time, the Planning Commission entered a transition; its park planning and acquisition function was phased out, and its city planning function gained importance.

The most influential congressional figures, particularly Representative Howard W. Smith of Virginia, the formidably powerful chairman of the House Rules Committee, believed that the region was not sufficiently united in its views to permit successful action by the Congress and that it was better to let local opinion mature. Smith's district had been redrawn in response to growth in the Virginia suburbs. Because Northern Virginia was rapidly urbanizing and becoming less "southern," the redrawing of the congressional district made Arlington and Fairfax a separate congressional district represented by Joel Broyhill. Representative Smith retained a constituency, outside Broyhill's district, with conservative views to match his own and was therefore able to maintain his political power in Congress and in the committees of which he was a member. In the end, however, Smith and other members of the House District Committee were persuaded by Virginia planning bodies to act, and Congress passed the National Capital Planning Act in 1952.

THE NATIONAL CAPITAL PLANNING ACT OF 1952

The National Capital Planning Act of 1952 gave more authority to the National Capital Planning Commission. The word "Park" was significantly absent from its institutional title. The National Capital Planning Commission became a national government agency that received its annual funding directly by congressional appropriation rather than through the District government budget. Commission membership was also changed. Given the importance of highway planning, the director of the Bureau of Public Roads was added as an ex officio member. The director of the Forest Service was dropped. The presidential appointments were expanded to five members, two of whom were to be residents of the District of Columbia or the metropolitan area.

Recognizing that the National Capital Planning Commission's planning powers focused both on the national capital region and on the settled city within the ten-mile-square District, the 1952 act specified that the commission plan for the "appropriate and orderly development and redevelopment of the National Capital and the conservation of the important natural and historical features thereof." Like its predecessor commission, the new commission was empowered to establish coordinating committees to "correlate the efforts among the various agencies." The National Capital Planning Commission was instructed to prepare and adopt a comprehensive plan, and as a critical area, a thoroughfare plan was suggested. When matters of new federal development or construction were proposed, the agencies involved were directed to consult with the National Capital Planning Commission as to the effect on the comprehensive plan: "After such consultation and suitable consideration of the view of the Commission, the agency may proceed to take action in accordance with its legal . . . authority." This provision of mandatory review was based on the earlier experiences of the National Capital Park and Planning Commission and the Commission of Fine Arts.

Redevelopment

Of all the post–World War II redevelopment projects in Washington, the southwest quadrant was the most dramatic. It involved the clearing of four hundred acres and the forced removal of 23,500 people, of whom 76 percent were black residents. The redevelopment process exacted a huge human toll, mainly on the large number of people displaced because no replacement housing was provided. Many blocks of potentially historic buildings were leveled. The effects of the southwest redevelopment reverberated for years afterward in citizens' attitudes toward planning, local governance, and neighborhood conservation. The roots of the southwest redevelopment project went as far back as the McMillan Plan's efforts to refashion the monumental core and were tied to rebuilding efforts in other American cities during the first half of the twentieth century.

Redevelopment synonymous with demolition and building anew had already given the city its dramatic Federal Triangle, an early example in Washington of the phoenix rising out of the ashes. Redevelopment offered what Washington architect Louis Justement called "an opportunity to exercise a degree of control never before attained." Yet the definition of redevelopment differed among those who sought control of the land to be cleared of slums.

NATIONAL AND LOCAL JUSTIFICATIONS FOR REDEVELOPMENT

To hard-pressed mayors and city councils, the redevelopment issue was frequently seen in fiscal terms and a search for an improved tax base. In areas where taxing authority was restricted largely to the real property tax, redevelopment took the form of high apartment buildings and high office buildings that reflected high property values and high densities. Washington's traditional character as a horizontal city and restrictions placed on development by the 1910 Height of Buildings Act prevented the worst excesses of the trend toward high-density development, and Washington's role as the national capital allowed it to escape some of the pressures that other cities faced. Nonetheless, to some extent Washington redevelopment in the early years responded not only to urban economic and ideological considerations but also to fashions in urban planning that were seen in other cities.

Washington's urban history and its long-established planning arrangements were an important strength in understanding and dealing with urban problems; early on the city was represented in most of the federal aid programs that benefited other cities. One of the most important federal aid programs was urban redevelopment or urban renewal, as it was redefined by the Eisenhower administration. The earlier idealism of the public housing movement became associated with the more comprehensive goals of urban reconstruction, the building of more viable and attractive central business districts and core cities, and the more unified and effective guidance of suburban and metropolitan development. Insofar as the urban problem at mid-century was seen as urban decay induced by the steady drift of the middle class to the suburbs, urban renewal sought to offer home-owning families an inner-city alternative.

Postwar housing and redevelopment legislation was also a creature of its time; the reigning ideas were those of Frank Lloyd Wright as expressed in *Disappearing City* and of Eliel Saarinen in *The City, Its Growth, Its Decay, Its Future.* Other prophets of decentralization had translated into architectural terms both the suburban future and the potentialities of reconstructing central cities like Detroit, Chicago, and Washington.

Redevelopment theory contained the hope that a "turnaround" trend could be stimulated, bringing people back from the suburbs to the city. The assumption was that through redevelopment, or urban renewal, vital new communities could be created within the central city to give homeowners a realistic alternative to suburban living, a positive urban choice. Redevelopment was seen as a way to reverse the outward-bound movement to the suburbs by revitalizing the central city. Thus, along with regional planning efforts, redevelopment plans moved ahead.

Rebuilding the old city had been authorized by the District of Columbia Redevelopment Act of 1945, as amended and institutionalized in the Redevelopment Land Agency, but was not funded until the passage of the National Housing Act of 1949. The National Capital Park and Planning Commission had been authorized to designate the land and to prepare the plans. The Redevelopment Land Agency possessed the novel authority to assemble land and to prepare it for the developers. The Redevelopment Land Agency also had unique access to federal loans and subsidies for redevelopment.

GOODWILLIE PLAN FOR THE SOUTHWEST QUADRANT

The southwest quadrant plan began in the midst of housing scarcity during World War II. Arthur Goodwillie, director of the Conservation Service of the Home Owner's Loan Corporation, first broached the topic. In line with the government's emphasis on conservation of critical resources, Goodwillie suggested that extant housing in old neighborhoods also be viewed as resources. In

1942 he presented a report, *The Rehabilitation of Southwest Washington as a War Housing Measure,* to the Planning Commission. In the report, Goodwillie delineated the nine-block area closest to Capitol Hill and produced assessments showing that rehabilitation of the old buildings would be cheaper than razing them and building anew. Not only would the government incur considerable savings by this plan, but also the residents could walk to work in many government office buildings, Union Station, and the commercial waterfront. The report also showed that additional densities could be achieved by constructing apartment houses in some of the interiors of city blocks where notorious alley dwellings had once stood. Although the Planning Commission approved of the Goodwillie rehabilitation plan in principle, it was never executed.

The 1942 Goodwillie plan was less an outline for neighborhood conservation than it was an economical design for housing in the face of severe material shortages. His survey of conditions in the quadrant reminded the city's planners that conspicuous "slums" existed within eyeshot of the Capitol. Significantly, and contrary to later conceptions of the Southwest's social situation, this 1942 plan recognized that the population of the quadrant was almost evenly divided between white and black residents, with the overwhelming majority of white residents desiring to continue living there.

Goodwillie described the area's verdant atmosphere, with wide and well-shaded streets and large interior blocks available for green commons and playgrounds. As an area physically and psychologically isolated from the rest of the city, first by the City Canal and later by the railroad, the Southwest had developed a homogeneous physical environment: small brick or wooden row houses, decorated with picturesque ironwork and gingerbread, and surrounded by front and back yards often richly planted with the characteristic landscape materials of the urban poor, ailanthus and pink Rose of Sharon.

Planning for the new city had traditionally been based on new construction in open land.

Yet the old city had a well-recognized example of revival in Georgetown where, during World War I, the wives of war workers who simply needed convenient housing had pioneered what came to be termed "unslumming." The Goodwillie plan for the Southwest offered similar advantages. Neighborhood conservation, however, as a means for meeting postwar housing needs was not in the forefront of federal planning philosophy in the late 1940s and early 1950s.

JOHN IHLDER AND THE NATIONAL CAPITAL HOUSING AUTHORITY

John Ihlder, proponent of housing for the poor, drafted a bill for federal funding of housing to be built on sites cleared by the urban renewal program. He spoke from substantial knowledge of the housing needs of the poor, having worked to establish the Alley Dwelling Authority in 1934, directed its early work, and then directed the successor organization, the National Capital Housing Authority in 1943 as it pursued its mission to build new public housing throughout the metropolitan area.

During World War II, the diversion of monies from his housing program to wartime needs had crippled the National Capital Housing Authority, and Ihlder hoped discussions of redevelopment in the District would find an outlet in his housing agency. Both business interests, most notably the National Association of Home Builders, and real estate boards fought off efforts like those of Ihlder out of concern that public housing would compete with private building interests. Battle lines over the impending Redevelopment Act were further complicated as some supporters of public housing did not admire the Housing Authority's past performance and sought to disassociate themselves from Ihlder. As a result—as housing policy became absorbed into redevelopment planning—Ihlder's frequent warnings about the fate of low-income residents fell on deaf ears.

For a country emerging as the undisputed leader of the free world, vestiges of nineteenth-century slums that marred its major cities were an embarrassment. In April 1943, Alfred Bettman offered a broad interpretation of postwar redevelopment: "It should include the replanning and rebuilding of the built up and subdivided areas of cities and metropolitan regions." The settled areas of cities were no longer to be regarded as static entities around which planners could insert parks, housing, and public buildings. Instead, these settled areas were available to the planners' alterations so as to fit into new urban ideologies.

THE REDEVELOPMENT ACT OF 1945 AND THE REDEVELOPMENT LAND AGENCY

The passage in 1946 of what was known as the District of Columbia Redevelopment Act of 1945—largely based on Alfred Bettman's draft bill—paved the way for redevelopment. The National Capital Park and Planning Commission was authorized to designate redevelopment areas and boundaries and to prepare and adopt plans in accordance with the existing comprehensive plan. In a bicameral action, the District commissioners were authorized to approve plans adopted by the Planning Commission.

The five-member Redevelopment Land Agency was created and empowered with the unique public authority to acquire property designated for redevelopment. The land would then be prepared for transfer to public and private developers. To attract private developers, on whose participation the program depended, the cost of the land could be reduced by as much as two-thirds of the original price. If no private developers were willing to take on a particular project, then the National Capital Housing Authority could step in and receive public funds for developing the property. A $20 million revolving trust fund was authorized, but no appropriations were ever made by the District commissioners.

In the language of the 1945 act, the limits of redevelopment were defined as "replanning, clearance, redesign, and rebuilding of projects." These projects had to be located in slums or blighted areas or "be redeveloped for this hous-

ing purpose," although some of the cleared land could be transferred to commercial and public purposes. Despite these definitions, various public bodies had in mind different priorities and different results from development. These divergent views set redevelopment in Washington on an uncertain course as the various interests argued their positions.

Although passage of the 1945 act created a battleground for housing versus business interests, little actually happened in the way of redevelopment for the next three years. The Redevelopment Land Agency existed, but only by the beneficence of a public-spirited member, department store executive Mark Lansburgh, who financed the agency's administrative costs. The Planning Commission was appropriated $75,000 to prepare plans and to select sites. Until the commission actually issued a new comprehensive plan, however, no redevelopment sites could be designated. The commission therefore expanded its staff by engaging Harland Bartholomew, a link with the commission's golden years of the early 1930s, to supervise development of such a plan.

THE NATIONAL HOUSING ACT OF 1949

When the National Housing Act of 1949 was passed, the Redevelopment Land Agency under Title I was entitled to receive funds for slum clearance and redevelopment from the Housing and Home Finance Administration (later folded into the Department of Housing and Urban Development). John Ihlder's National Capital Housing Authority was also able, under Title III, to receive funds to construct low-rent public housing as an "essential part of the redevelopment program." To harmonize the agencies and procedures involved, the Planning Commission set up a coordinating committee on housing and redevelopment, made up of representatives of the Planning Commission, the Redevelopment Land Agency, the National Capital Housing Authority, and the District commissioners.

The Redevelopment Land Agency actually began its statutory functions in 1951, when

John R. Searles Jr. became the first director.
Princeton-educated Searles injected a high
degree of administrative ability into the agency,
as well as a commitment to the health of the District's business community. Guiding the agency
for ten years through what was for all practical
purposes a new national experiment in rebuilding cities, Searles steered a middle course between
the short-term vision of developers and the
long-range vision of planners.

The radical redevelopment authorized by the
1949 Housing Act led some planners to believe
that removing decayed housing and creating new
communities in new physical surroundings
would transform the inner city into an alternative attractive enough to retain or lure back the
middle class. However, even before the results of
redevelopment were fully realized, the course of
redevelopment thinking altered. The Housing
Act of 1954 provided for redevelopment planning
to include retention and rehabilitation, rather
than removal, of existing structures. This conservation approach was strengthened over the years

and expanded to include retention of existing
community facilities and general community
character.

THE BARRY FARMS AND MARSHALL HEIGHTS PROJECTS

Several years before actual passage of the 1949
legislation, attention had been focused on Barry
Farms and Marshall Heights as sites poised for
redevelopment. Barry Farms was a community
with deep roots in the nineteenth century: after
the Civil War the Freedmen's Bureau had earmarked the land for housing for former slaves. It
was located on the east side of the Anacostia
River, north of St. Elizabeths Hospital and at the
foot of the hill on which Fort Stanton stands,
one of the highest points in the District. Defined
by the higher elevations to the east and the Anacostia River to the west, the isolation of Barry
Farms was reinforced by several nearby public
reservations. Barry Farms's street system, which
developed independently of any District plan,
followed either the ridges or the valleys of the

site. Housing was basic, primarily of wooden construction, and scattered (70 percent of the land was vacant). The neighborhood was mature enough, however, to contain well-developed streets, neighborhood services, churches, and two civic associations.

Barry Farms first came to the attention of the National Capital Park and Planning Commission in 1942, when a new temporary school building was proposed to occupy land already devoted to the neighborhood playground. The Planning Commission pointed out that the playground was a "war necessity" and that it was actually essential because the Navy Department occupied the neighborhood's Fairlawn Recreation Center. This temporary school facility was approved, however, with the recommendation that adjacent lands be acquired to compensate for the loss of the playground.

As part of the Planning Commission's "desire to study, analyze, and understand blighted areas and their causes and effects," the commission, in cooperation with the National Capital Housing Authority, made a major study of Barry Farms in 1944. When land values and costs of public services provided by the District were compared, the study found that the area did not pay its way. In fact, the District was subsidizing Barry Farms by at least $600 per family. "Rural blight" was largely a function of the layout of the area, which was difficult to police and to provide with other essential services.

Convinced that, as things were, the most the neighborhood could expect in the future was piecemeal, sporadic, and unprofitable development, the study suggested that Barry Farms "offers one of the best opportunities in the District of Columbia for the development de novo of a complete and integrated neighborhood unit." The area's advantages could be realized only when it was developed as a whole, the report suggested, especially if development were aimed at establishing a self-contained neighborhood providing for a wide range of economic groups. Thus, the commission defined its initial concept of redevelopment and urban renewal in

keeping with broader national and professional concepts.

Marshall Heights was also considered a redevelopment area, similar to yet different from Barry Farms. Also located east of the Anacostia, the triangular piece of land was defined by Benning Road, Central Avenue, and the District line. Its physical appearance clearly revealed the narrow rectangular street grid drawn up in 1886 and imposed on steep slopes. The area was dotted by frame buildings. Many public improvements, such as grading and paving, provided by the District before 1945 had been made using temporary materials, "anticipating the necessity of complete redevelopment of the area at an early date." Unlike Barry Farms, however, Marshall Heights had no long community past. As late as 1927 it contained only two houses. In 1945 Marshall Heights was characterized as a "shanty town."

The commission's study of the area found that, like Barry Farms, the tax base of Marshall Heights did not cover its costs in public services. This kind of evaluation, however, had not been fully applied to all other areas of the city. The commission saw the Heights as ripe for redevelopment as a self-contained neighborhood of low enough density to result in only limited dislocation for the current population. In the mid-1940s, the cost of acquiring both Barry Farms and Marshall Heights was not prohibitive.

Decisions needed to be made quickly on designating Barry Farms and Marshall Heights as redevelopment areas and presenting plans to Congress for funding. In 1945 citizens of Marshall Heights requested that the District install sewer and water lines according to the old street plan, a proposal that the Planning Commission rejected as obstructing future redevelopment by strengthening the obsolete street pattern. Also, the postwar housing shortage had spurred speculative activities in Marshall Heights; developers were pressing for introduction of the related public services that were anticipated to follow the old grid.

Wishing to avoid further complications to its redevelopment plans, the Planning Commission,

by withholding its approval, placed a freeze on
further improvements in Marshall Heights, an
action that sparked fierce opposition from both
residents and developers. The freeze lasted from
1946 to 1950 while the Planning Commission
drew up plans for the area, attempting during
these intervening years to answer charges that
such specialized plans could not be drawn without a more comprehensive plan developed for
the entire city. Another charge was that few of
the then-current residents of Marshall Heights
could afford to live in the new housing that redevelopment would provide.

Opposition to including Barry Farms in the
Planning Commission's redevelopment plans
surfaced and gained strength in 1947. Ulysses J.
Banks of the Barry Farms Citizens Association
stated that the community had grown during the
war and was providing new homes of high standards. He argued that many building permits
were pending and that these should not be held
up while the Planning Commission, the District
commissioners, and Congress made up their
minds about redevelopment policy in the District of Columbia.

In 1948 the Planning Commission presented
its plans for Marshall Heights to Congress for

funding, but the residents of Marshall Heights
blocked appropriations for both their neighborhood and Barry Farms. The final blow to the two
projects was dealt in the passage of Title I of the
1949 National Housing Act that provided federal
funding to the Redevelopment Land Agency
except for those projects that had been presented
to and rejected by Congress. The District commissioners had already cited the "great hardships
on legitimate private activities" in Marshall
Heights and its instructions from the House
Appropriations Committee that the project be
abandoned and that the District government
"furnish utilities and other municipal improvements on the basis of the 1886 narrow gridiron
street plan." In 1950 the Planning Commission
formally dropped plans for the projects and recommended that the Redevelopment Land
Agency turn its attention to the "inlying areas."

STABILIZATION VERSUS RADICAL REDEVELOPMENT

Postwar Washington viewed federally funded
redevelopment as an opportunity to reverse the
powerful lure of suburbia and to revitalize the
city. Nonetheless, when Washington embarked
on redevelopment of the Southwest, the commu-

nity found itself divided. On the one hand, the Planning Commission as framer of redevelopment plans believed that stabilization was the area's primary need; on the other hand, federal housing and redevelopment officials, the Federal City Council (a private organization representing the progressive downtown business community), and the Redevelopment Land Agency, which was responsible for implementing the redevelopment plan, believed that more drastic urban surgery was required.

The stabilizers came across as conservatives. They argued that Southwest Washington was occupied by blue-collar workers who walked to their jobs on the waterfront—in warehouses and produce markets—or at Union Station. The Planning Commission made the case for improving the housing conditions of these fami-

lies but leaving them and their jobs where they were. By contrast, the federal housing and redevelopment officials and the Federal City Council pushed for more radical large-scale clearance; relocation of the existing population; and design of a large, new, and different community that would give an urban alternative to suburban living in terms of school and community life as well as housing. Because the federal officials had the money, their views largely prevailed.

THE ELBERT PEETS RENEWAL PLAN FOR THE SOUTHWEST

The southwest quadrant of Washington was one of three possible redevelopment areas in the inner city designated by the National Capital Park and Planning Commission after the demise of Barry Farms and Marshall Heights as poten-

Map of Principal Problem Areas in the District of Columbia, 1950. National Capital Park and Planning Commission, *Comprehensive Plan for the National Capital and Its Environs*, 1950

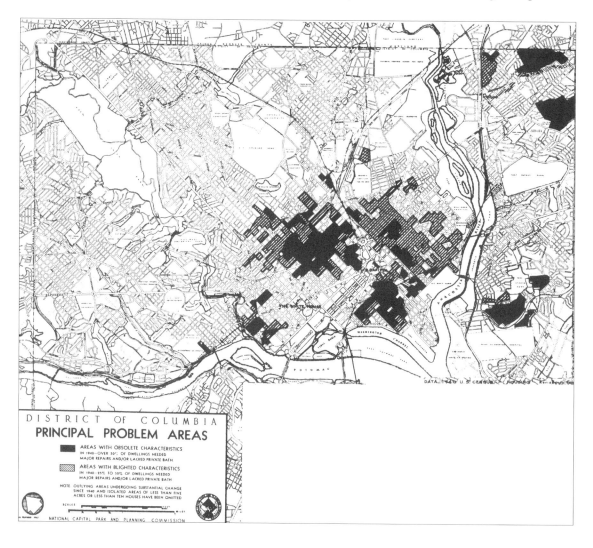

tial projects. According to the 1950 Comprehensive Plan, much of the small southwest quadrant and large areas in the northwest and southeast quadrants possessed high concentrations of "obsolete dwellings," overcrowding, and other potential threats to public health. When these separate conditions were overlapped, however, the Southwest emerged as the principal first target for renewal.

In 1951 the Planning Commission commissioned the landscape architect and urban designer Elbert Peets to prepare a renewal plan for the Southwest. An eminent historian-interpreter of the L'Enfant plan, Peets drew up a "neighborhood plan" that retained the Southwest as predominantly low income, rehabilitated many existing structures, and carefully wove in new low-rise buildings. Peets was strongly attracted to the Southwest as a distinctive, historic area with characteristic old street trees and row houses. Peets's plan closed many streets to

through traffic and reoriented the remodeled houses to gardens in the interior of blocks previously filled with alley dwellings, stables, and shacks for coal and wood. The houses would be saved, reequipped, and given new settings with a fresh neighborhood character.

In the spirit of the wartime Goodwillie plan, the Peets plan did not propose drastic alterations to the appearance of the neighborhood. Rather, the aim was a gradual process of rehabilitation that would entail minimal relocation problems. In view of the active privately financed rehabilitation efforts that had already transformed Georgetown, and the initiation of similar efforts on Capitol Hill, the Redevelopment Land Agency acknowledged in its annual report for 1952 that "the [Southwest] area, though blighted to a considerable degree, does contain many individual structures susceptible to the Georgetown kind of rehabilitation." The report hailed the Peets plan for its faithfulness to L'Enfant. But in the eyes of

Commercial District on the 700 Block of 4th Street SW before Urban Renewal, 1949. Curtis Collection, DC Community Archives, DC Public Library the Redevelopment Land Agency, the Peets plan, in its focus on leaving the area much the way it was, belonged to the rehabilitation brand of redevelopment. For this, the agency could not justify spending public funds.

THE JUSTEMENT-SMITH PLAN FOR THE SOUTHWEST

In 1952 the Redevelopment Land Agency invited Louis Justement and Chloethiel Woodard Smith, the architect-planner whose strongly expressed views about reshaping the city had received wide circulation in her writings and in exhibitions, to explore the more radical alternative of large-scale redevelopment. This approach was in line with Justement's well-known redevelopment philosophies. Reminiscent of Daniel Burnham's legendary advice to "make no little plans," the Justement-Smith plan aimed at a "whole process of rebuilding the city in a purposeful and accelerated fashion." In its introduction, the written plan acknowledged the novelty and challenge of such an opportunity, as well as the absence of prior experience to serve as any guide. When redevelopment was approached under such unrestricted circumstances, it was expected that it would "release and stimulate progress" beyond the borders of the redevelopment area.

Other sections of the city would theoretically follow in a chain reaction, proffering their own plans for redevelopment and construction. Ideally the plan would be detailed enough to provide a basis for attracting developers yet allow "scope for the maximum of individual initiative and imagination on the part of subordinate levels of planners and architects." The creation of "new and greater realty values" and the health of the business community, especially the building industry, were primary motivations in the plan's recommendations. The new residential areas planned in the redeveloped section of Washington were to be attractive enough to bring back the suburbanites who had fled the city. As the planners pointed out, the process of dispersal coupled with the inability of the historic ten-mile-square District to annex suburban territory

(and thus maintain a large affluent tax base) made the specter of the bankrupt city very real.

The broad and original concepts outlined by the Justement-Smith plan included a new entrance or "front door" esplanade to the Southwest, along 10th Street, passing over the railroad tracks and the planned expressway. The entrance was planned to link the formerly isolated quadrant with the cultural facilities along the Mall, most notably the original Smithsonian Building. "The view down Tenth Street to the channel, uninterrupted by buildings, over-passing the highway, bordered by parks on the east and a wide planted park set back along the west, would provide an inviting entrance leading to main east-west access avenues to residential areas and to the attractive waterfront drive leading to Fort McNair." The functional success of this new artery depended on its connection with Maine Avenue, which paralleled the Washington Channel. Engineering problems created by topographic conditions were never fully resolved, and so the connection was not totally realized.

The new residential city was to be formed around groups of buildings, high-rise apartments and town houses like those in Georgetown with front and back yards. According to the plan, "each group of buildings must be carefully studied later to take the greatest advantage of the various sites, orientations to sun, prevailing winds and views, provision of maximum privacy for each family unit, best use of open space, etc." The arrangement of building groups would necessitate closing off many of L'Enfant's streets. Low-income housing was to be maintained in the existing public housing area, in correct proportion to what the plan's authors saw as a well-balanced central urban area.

A strip of high-rise apartments would be developed along the extant waterfront, traditionally the center of the southwest quadrant's commercial and recreational life. The plan also called for the small "corner grocery" type of store and public or semipublic buildings located along the main residential avenue to provide "welcome breaks in the design and scale of residential buildings." In the juxtaposition of private enterprise and public benefits, the plan held the promise of a "richly varied and human urban area."

Some of these values were echoed in the town-house areas of Capital Park where Smith translated ideas into architectural terms through design treatment of parking and public open spaces. There was no wide application of these values, however, because they proved too elusive to survive the bureaucratic conflicts and neighborhood packaging to which future decisions concerning the new Southwest were subjected. Thus, underinvestment in the public sector produced an almost wholly residential character instead of the more diversified and lively urban atmosphere originally intended. Not even the corner grocery survived.

Intended to cut across this newly molded quadrant was an expressway designed to connect the 14th Street Bridge with South Capitol Street. In relation to the proposed 1950 Comprehensive Plan's Inner Loop, the freeway would serve as the first stage of this central thoroughfare. The freeway would not only carry through traffic above the "central congested part of the city," but it would also give residents in the Southwest access to the rest of the city. Rather than cutting through the quadrant as tentatively outlined in the 1950 Comprehensive Plan, the freeway suggested by the Justement-Smith plan should bound and define the residential area to be developed. When the artery was later built, it became that boundary (and barrier) and separated the new federal buildings complex south of Independence Avenue from the residential area.

In the tradition of the McMillan Plan, the Justement-Smith sketch of proposed development provided no restrictive design but rather a stimulative range of possibilities. It was a concept plan. On a more practical level, the sketch was intended to help the Redevelopment Land Agency attract developers and market the redeveloped land. Unlike the "conservative" Peets plan that offered no new dramatic images, the Justement-Smith plan helped to convince financial interests that the Southwest's reputation as a low-rent neighborhood would be completely altered as a result of the redevelopment.

THE SOUTHWEST REDEVELOPMENT WORK OF THE PLANNING COMMISSION AND THE REDEVELOPMENT LAND AGENCY

The Planning Commission–sponsored Peets plan and the Redevelopment Land Agency's Justement-Smith plan had in common their reliance on the southwest quadrant's past lifestyle. Otherwise, their divergent philosophies were marked, which prompted the Planning Commission to name Harland Bartholomew to study and assess the two plans and to make recommendations to both the Planning Commission and the Redevelopment Land Agency. Bartholomew agreed with Peets's emphasis on retaining the quadrant as a low-income residential area because of the convenience to employment centers for those who could least afford to own automobiles and because relocation problems would be minimized. Peets's brand of rehabilitation was by the same token more difficult to define as a redevelopment project and was thus questionable in terms of justifying federal financing. Whereas the Justement-Smith plan responded positively to those who believed there was a need for dramatic action and expression of idealism through extensive redevelopment, Bartholomew questioned the success of attempts to transform the area completely. He also pointed out the acute relocation problems and the loss of industrially zoned land, as well as the expensive rearrangement of the traditional business thoroughfares along 4th and 7th streets.

THE PLANNING COMMISSION'S COMPROMISE REPORT

To reconcile the two plans, the Planning Commission issued a compromise report in November 1952. In this report, written with the assistance of Peets, and drawing on recommendations of the earlier report by Harland Bartholomew, the Planning Commission restated its responsibility under the Redevelopment Act of 1945 to prepare

and to adopt the "general framework or guide of development," which the Redevelopment Land Agency was then supposed to execute. The 1952 compromise report approved large areas for clearance but recommended replacement by low-rise buildings that would follow in form and location the old row-house configurations. This compromise report by design avoided the "extremes of idealism—such as the complete wiping out of this area and of its replacement by a forest of multi-story apartments, and, on the other hand . . . the extreme of expediency, such as replacement or face-lifting of the existing development."

The reduced emphasis on rehabilitation was supported by the highly influential American Public Health Association's Housing Appraisal

Technique that assessed more than half of the living units in the southwest quadrant to be "substandard" and ripe for replacement. Although the Planning Commission was reconciled to demolition of overwhelming numbers of structures, the report reiterated that the area was steeped in "historic and sentimental interest" in both its street plan and architecture. To preserve these values, the Planning Commission sustained its conviction that the quadrant should remain a moderate- to lower-income area. The commission also reaffirmed its long-held concern to design neighborhoods, not individual structures. The compromise report agreed to the desirability of the 10th Street Mall or esplanade but expressed reservations about the interchange between the terminus of the new mall and Maine

Avenue. Based on this report, a final redevelopment plan was prepared.

THE ROLE OF THE REDEVELOPMENT LAND AGENCY

Final adoption of the redevelopment plan for the Southwest was only the beginning of a long, obstructive legal and administrative process for which there were no precedents or useful guides. Moreover, time added complexity as altered redevelopment philosophies and policies stressed a more conservation-oriented approach as opposed to radical reconstruction. With the invitation, issued in 1953, to developers to submit plans for the Southwest, the Redevelopment Land Agency began its legislated responsibilities of assembling land, demolishing buildings, preparing sites, and then disposing of the land. Almost immediately, lawsuits flooded the District courts, challenging the agency's powers of condemnation. In a protracted process, leaving many plots of land vacant over several years, the litigation route led to the Supreme Court. In the landmark October 1954 decision in *Berman v. Parker,* the High Court upheld the right of the Redevelopment Land Agency to condemn, in the public interest, land occupied by "miserable and disreputable housing."

MAJOR PROJECT AREAS IN THE SOUTHWEST

Even before the legal battles were resolved, the Southwest was divided into three major areas, two of which were small demonstration areas to be developed first and in full view of the Capitol. James Scheuer and Roger Stevens were the principal developers responsible for the large Capitol Park complex, one of the major developments of high-rise apartment buildings and row-house groupings in one of these areas. The other small area, located just south of this area, was to be developed as a light industrial enclave. The largest area extended from the waterfront to the western boundaries.

As the smaller projects demonstrated the success of the redevelopment process, the future of the largest area was assured. Covering the entire

Zeckendorf Proposals for Southwest Washington Redevelopment, 1955.
A Redevelopment Plan for Southwest Washington, D.C., 1957

quadrant from the waterfront to the boundaries of the two smaller projects, the large area was the platform for the creative planning to come. The flamboyant New York City real estate developer William Zeckendorf, representing the firm of Webb and Knapp and recruiting the design and technical guidance of architects I. M. Pei and Harry Weese, took charge of the vast project. The detailed plan was developed between 1954 and 1959 and was based on the general plan approved in 1952. The detailed plan was largely a response to the spirit of the Justement-Smith plan. Zeckendorf envisaged the new Southwest as a showcase of unusual architectural beauty. Zeckendorf's Southwest was to be entered via a 10th Street Mall and was to be inhabited by four thousand families of varying incomes. There was to be a modern town center, as well as enlarged waterfront restaurants, marine activities, and a cultural complex.

Zeckendorf's 10th Street Mall took inspiration from the vision of the Justement-Smith plan. The mall or esplanade in the Zeckendorf plan

was described as a "wide and impressive span, flanked by stately government buildings." Contrary to its earlier proposed function as an entrance linked directly with the waterfront along Maine Avenue, this mall would end "in a circular overlook providing motorists or pedestrians a grand view of the waterfront and residential Southwest Washington."

Parallel to the Mall and just south of it, the cultural complex or plaza, as proposed by President Dwight D. Eisenhower's DC Auditorium Commission, was to be developed on nineteen-and-a-half acres. This cultural complex was supposed to be a unified cultural and entertainment center, similar in concept to what was later developed as the Kennedy Center for the Performing Arts in Foggy Bottom. Zeckendorf's concept of the plaza was even more elaborate than the Kennedy Center, however. Zeckendorf saw the plaza as perfectly situated for a central tourist center, a complex of restaurants and other visitor-oriented establishments that would allow

tourists "to savor the best of America's cultural flavor and entertainment talent. . . . In short, the plaza is envisioned as a cultural center for Washington, the nation, and perhaps even the world."

The waterfront in Zeckendorf's design would assume more dramatic proportions than those of "cramped" market stalls. Zeckendorf planned that the waterfront marinas, markets, and restaurants would extend the length of the channel north of Fort McNair (the Army War College's site) and become strategic vistas that could be seen from various vantage points in the quadrant.

The residential community of Capitol Park was to be housed in eight-story buildings with elevators or in town houses. Just as the new mall would provide a new vista, so the high-rise apartments would be visually designed and distributed "to achieve a balanced diversity of visual appeal and to maintain an openness to light and air," especially facing the Washington Channel. The town houses would be organized around

residential squares beneath which extensive parking space was planned. These square open spaces were to serve as the common front yards for the abutting houses (much in the tradition of London's private parks) and were touted as providing "a suburban spaciousness for in-town locations." In addition, each house had its own small backyard, and many apartments their own balconies. The town center as proposed would incorporate both shopping center and community facilities—churches, parks, libraries, and community houses—and unify the separate residential clusters.

The final format for residential clusters was determined less by Zeckendorf's plan than by individual developers who flocked to the Southwest after Zeckendorf's overextended real estate empire collapsed. They completed what he had begun. For example, the Reynolds Aluminum Service Corporation developed the River Park complex to illustrate the use of aluminum in urban renewal projects. Some of the developers

held design competitions; for example, Charles H. Tompkins sponsored a competition for the design of Carrollsburg Square, which the Washington firm of Keyes, Lethbridge & Condon won. Although the prizewinning design was praised for its "humane character," the panel of judges feared that consistent use of high-rise buildings and town houses organized around parklike plazas "could lead to an overdone Southwest style for residential developments." This consistency in residential accommodations was broken somewhat by a few remaining historic buildings: Wheat Row, the Barney Neighborhood House, the Washington Lewis House, and the Law House, as well as several old churches.

The true test of the "success" of the Southwest urban renewal project could be based on whether or not it fulfilled its objectives. The middle-class families who were to have occupied the housing did not return. Instead, single federal government office workers or congressional committee staff members filled the apartments

and houses, and the swimming pools and tennis courts echoed to the voices of a largely transient population. Tourist attractions, hotels, waterfront restaurants, and other limited commercial uses emerged as the characteristic business activities in the area. Relations between the residents occupying new developments and the occupants of existing public housing remained troubled despite the conciliatory efforts of a dozen new churches and community institutions.

FEDERAL OFFICE BUILDINGS ON INDEPENDENCE AVENUE

The problem of the design and land use north of the expressway was solved in 1954, when the General Services Administration received approval to construct new government office buildings along Independence Avenue. The government had already built several facilities in the area, most notably the large Agriculture Department Buildings; the Bureau of Engraving and Printing; the Department of Health, Education, and Welfare; and the Railroad Retirement Build-

ing. A government warehouse located within the bend of the railroad tracks was later transformed into the General Services Administration Regional Office Building.

The Southwest Urban Renewal Plan designated six sites along the south side of Independence Avenue and north of the railroad for public buildings. Facilities were developed on these sites for the new Department of Health, Education, and Welfare Building and the Food and Drug Administration between 2nd and 3rd streets; Federal Office Building No. 6 between 4th and 6th streets; the Federal Aviation Administration Building housing this major agency and offices of the Department of Transportation; and the Forrestal Building at the entrance to the 10th Street Mall and what is now called L'Enfant Plaza. Later, on the south side of the railroad, a site was acquired for the Department of Housing and Urban Development (HUD) Building designed by Marcel Breuer, a set piece for the new architectural policies of the Kennedy administration.

The flat triangle of land directly east of the HUD Building was filled in by the large office building designed by Edward Durrell Stone and leased to the Department of Transportation. The US Postal Service Headquarters Building and the privately developed hotel–office building complex flanked the 10th Street Mall accompanied by underground amenities: a shopping mall, a parking garage, and a small theater.

As with the rest of the city south of Independence Avenue, the principal shortcoming was the absence of any reasonable arrangement for mass transportation and, considering the ninety thousand jobs scheduled for the area, anything resembling a transit terminal. Although the Southwest as a whole was never conceived of as part of the monumental core in earlier comprehensive plans, except for a small area referred to as the Southwest Triangle in the 1930s, the new buildings along the southern border of Independence Avenue provided a stronger public setting for the new Smithsonian museum buildings that would subsequently line the south side of the Mall: the circular Hirshhorn Museum and Sculpture Garden, the two-block-long National Air and Space Museum, and the National Museum of the American Indian.

REHABILITATION AND REDEVELOPMENT PROJECTS ELSEWHERE IN WASHINGTON

The coupling of redevelopment with slum clearance was exemplified most clearly in the new Southwest. When demolition activities were at their peak, however, consideration was given again to an alternative method of redevelopment: rehabilitation. As early as 1948, the Planning Commission had studied what was popularly called the "Baltimore plan." The logic of the Baltimore plan followed from the premise that obsolete, run-down housing was primarily the result of unenforced or ineffective building codes. The solution for such housing was to enforce the code and hold property owners responsible for maintaining their own buildings. Another mechanism for supporting rehabilitation efforts was the 1954 Housing Act, which

allowed federal funds to be applied to rehabilitation projects in urban renewal districts.

It was too late to apply this growing acceptance of rehabilitation in the Southwest because most of the old row houses had already been demolished. The code enforcement method was included, however, in the 1955 study commissioned by the District commissioners and entitled *No Slums in Ten Years*. Written by James W. Rouse and Nathaniel S. Keith, the study was primarily concerned with Washington's role as a national demonstration city. The report listed twenty different steps that planning and governmental bodies should take to rid Washington of slums. These steps included code enforcement, study committees, special "fight blight funds," and new administrative procedures.

Applauding the dynamic concepts that fostered the new Southwest, the report also praised private rehabilitation efforts in Georgetown, Capitol Hill, and Foggy Bottom. The report captured the spirit of the optimistic postwar decade (when problems appeared to be solvable by applying vigorous governmental programs) and outlined further redevelopment areas. Surprisingly, it suggested resurrecting the politically unfeasible Barry Farms and Marshall Heights proposals. To avoid criticism for omissions, the report also suggested areas in all quadrants of the city except the already progressing Southwest. The report left the reader with this final optimistic thought: "Washington can become the country's first major slumless city—an appropriate and exhilarating role for the Nation's Capital."

SUPPORTIVE ZONING STUDIES

The 1955–1956 study conducted by consultant Harold M. Lewis for the Washington Zoning Revision Office supported redevelopment efforts. Lewis's report, *Rezoning Study of the District of Columbia*, was designed to make the zoning recommendations of the 1950 Comprehensive Plan more specific, to coordinate zoning with the plan, and to resolve conflicts between the Zoning Commission and the Planning Commission.

years of the Planning Commission. Lewis studied 137 neighborhoods that he defined by major traffic arteries, parks, and institutional lands, as well as by population densities sufficient to support one public school.

Data collected for each neighborhood included information on playgrounds, parks, and business needs, with the community center focused on the employment and business centers. This involved a redefinition of the neighborhood center concept of the 1920s and 1930s when recreation and education facilities were the key indicators of neighborhood identity. Lewis identified forty "problem neighborhoods"— most of them bordering the monumental core, south and east of the Capitol and north of Massachusetts Avenue—judged to be deficient in several of the criteria for an ideal neighborhood. To improve these problem neighborhoods, Lewis recommended their designation as redevelopment areas and thus gave further support to the

Zoning Commission Hearing on the Harold M. Lewis Study, May 1957. Copyright *Washington Post,* Reprinted with Permission of the DC Public Library

The Lewis report's basic thrust, as well as its major success, was to update the zoning regulations. The report also updated the neighborhood concept as it had been developed in the early

Foggy Bottom Area before Redevelopment, Early 1960s. National Capital Planning Commission Collection

recommendation in the 1950 Comprehensive Plan that Shaw and portions of the northwest and northeast quadrants be redeveloped.

FOGGY BOTTOM

In spite of its brewery, gas works, and coal yards, Foggy Bottom was a popular area because of its proximity to George Washington University and nearby medical facilities. It was also close to government offices in the Northwest Rectangle, the federal office building precinct bounded by E Street NW on the north, by Constitution Avenue NW on the south, by 17th Street on the east, and by 23rd Street on the west. Row houses located in Foggy Bottom were of modest working-class dimensions, since the dwellings had developed close to the industrial establishments along the Potomac.

Rehabilitation of these houses proceeded under private initiative, so that the neighborhood went about "unslumming itself" in the Georgetown tradition. Moreover, studies had been carried out in Foggy Bottom along the route of that area's portion of the Inner Loop. Like a set piece of the two methods of redevelopment, slum removal and rehabilitation, the vast Columbia Plaza complex highlighted Foggy Bottom's new status. Columbia Plaza, the area's only urban renewal project, was a "packaged living" complex of high-rise and low-rise apartments, an office building, and a shopping mall. This development, meant to attract middle- to high-income dwellers, was a symbol of redevelopment for the affluent "24-hour" population—a place, that is, where people lived, worked, and played.

THE EVOLVING RESIDENTIAL CITY

Government-sponsored plans for urban renewal and spontaneous "unplanned" unslumming of historic neighborhoods were only two factors influencing the character of Washington's residential areas during this period. After World

The Columbia Plaza Complex in Redeveloped Foggy Bottom, 1970s. National Capital Planning Commission Collection

War II, middle-class families began to leave the city, not only to buy single-family homes in the suburbs, but also to flee neighborhoods that had become open to purchase and occupancy by black residents. The integration of Washington's public schools in 1954 accelerated this "white flight" out of the city, and a new resegregation of schools and residential areas occurred. The real estate practice of "block-busting" was halted in Takoma Park in far northwest Washington through the efforts of Neighbors, Inc. The turnover of neighborhoods from white to black continued to transform the city well into the early 1970s, however.

The new residential patterns in the Southwest urban renewal area provided opportunities for those who aspired to live in stable integrated neighborhoods. Apparently, it was easier to achieve integrated living in new residential areas than to integrate established residential areas. Integrated living also occurred for limited time spans in newly revitalized areas of Capitol Hill and Foggy Bottom, but the forces of gentrification caused these areas to become economically segregated as property values accelerated and lower-income residents were forced to relocate.

The public school construction program in the District of Columbia, which had become largely built out by World War II, became a symbol of integration and then resegregation. Before the Supreme Court's *Brown v. Board of Education* decision of 1954 that outlawed segregated public schools, changing residential patterns caused Central High School to be turned over to black students in 1950 and renamed Cardozo High School. Fully integrated schools were opened in 1954 but represented only a transitional state to resegregated schools by the end of the decade. White students left public schools as their families moved to the suburbs or sent them to private academies. Critical commercial investment and political power followed the white middle class into the suburbs.

Transportation

The preparation of a mass transportation plan, an integral part of planning activities in Washington at mid-century, was called for in a provision of the 1952 reorganization act. Congress implemented this provision by designating funds in the National Capital Planning Commission's 1955 and 1957 budgets for the Planning Commission and the National Capital Regional Planning Council to conduct the Mass Transportation Survey jointly.

THE MASS TRANSPORTATION SURVEY

The Mass Transportation Survey became the first such study of the national capital city to be based on an integrated approach in which land-use implications of transportation were fully examined. It was also the first such study by a planning agency rather than an ad hoc committee or a highway group. Although overall policy direction was exercised by the Planning Commission, daily work was supervised by a Joint Steering Committee established by the National Capital Planning Commission and the National Capital Regional Planning Council with representatives from both Maryland and Virginia agencies.

Starting in 1955, the two-year-long study was set up to survey both highway needs and mass transit needs so that a unified mass transportation plan resulted. Kenneth M. Hoover, project director of the Mass Transportation Survey, forecast that if the emphasis on the automobile and highways continued, by 1980 the region theoretically would need radial and circumferential expressways with capacities ranging from four to twenty-six lanes. The capacities of thoroughfares would need to be increased and widened not only in the outlying areas but also through the central city as well.

With this startling picture of financial and environmental disaster, the study recommended a balanced transportation system made up of a new rapid transit system, the improvement and extension of existing highways, and a system of parking facilities at mass transit station sites. Supported by the area's planning bodies and local governments, as well as the federal government, the National Capital Planning Commission and the Regional Planning Council presented the recommendations of the survey to Congress.

The survey's basic data had come from a 1948 origins and destinations survey. In the fast-changing Washington metropolitan region, a dozen years was too long an interval between original data collection and the ultimate action by Congress. In 1960 Congress passed the National Capital Transportation Act, which created the National Capital Transportation Agency to initiate planning for the recommended subway and highway program. Because of the lapse of time between the original survey and the enabling legislation, however, congressional action was almost too late.

The transportation problem first drew the attention of planners to modern suburbia and the need for metropolitan integration. Of the many perceptions that emerged from the Mass Transportation Survey, attention focused most on the journey to work from the suburbs to downtown, the heavy reliance on private cars, and the related problem of rush-hour movement. The survey specifically pointed to the growing suburban structure that was generating major centers of congestion around highway interchanges, suburban shopping centers, large educational complexes, and even office building concentrations. Such congestion had hitherto been experienced only in the downtown heart of the city.

The Mass Transportation Survey—after making the maximum allowance for the automobile, including an extensive street-widening program and construction of an outer circumferential beyond the Capital Beltway—projected that by 1980 major problems of traffic congestion would still plague the metropolitan area. The dispersed location of employment centers that lay predominantly in a northwest-southeast alignment from Bethesda to Bolling Air Force Base created a suburban pattern of trips "between districts other than sector zero." A similar outlying pattern, less intensively developed, was described in the Virginia counties from National Airport west-northwest to Tysons Corner, with a possible extension on the Maryland side of the Potomac.

In the Mass Transportation Survey, planners had detected a new pattern of metropolitan mobility, but more significant than this geographical configuration was the concept of a city in motion that the survey described. The dramatic revelation of the new data was the increased number of trips that would be made by the average person each day. The earlier lifestyle that could be fulfilled by weekly marketing, walking to work, and engaging in neighborhood-based leisure pursuits was being replaced by one that demanded extensive transportation resources. Even in a family in which everyone had a car, something like perpetual motion was demanded to take advantage of the employment opportunities, the regionwide recreational resources, or the programs of a dozen universities. These offerings were only a sampling of resources in a region strewn prodigally throughout, wherein each group looked to the entire metropolitan population for its constituency. The cost of and the time required for travel still had to be reckoned with; the social and cultural implications were unknown.

THE NATIONAL CAPITAL TRANSPORTATION ACT

The 1960 National Capital Transportation Act directed the National Capital Transportation Agency, a federal corporation, to plan in detail for the construction of a mass transportation system to service the entire region and to set such plans within the more comprehensive provisions for the region as a whole and the unified treatment of highways as well. It further provided for the negotiation of an interstate compact between the states of Maryland and Virginia and the federal government (including the District of Columbia's municipal government) to create an effective body to take over what the National Capital Transportation Agency had commenced, although the interstate compact as ultimately created did not include federal representation. Nonetheless, the compact provided for the first metropolitan areawide operating agency.

THE REGIONAL METRO SYSTEM

The fundamental advance in the Washington Mass Transportation Survey and plans for the eventual Metro rail system was the newfound appreciation of the interrelationship of transit and land use. In the survey, projections of travel demand had been based on a carefully regulated changing use of the land, and this suggested the appropriate way to pay for the system. When it came to the enabling legislation, it was accepted that revenues from fares would not pay for the system. Therefore new proposed powers were advanced that would provide additional revenues out of the rents from parking structures, shopping centers, and other forms of development to be built by the mass transportation agency at station plazas throughout the system.

Planners also recognized, on the basis of the survey, that rush-hour service alone would not produce an economical operation, and so incentives to use the service for trips other than to work and at times other than peak commuting hours were suggested. Finally, selective higher densities (not necessarily in the form of buildings taller than currently permitted or in conflict with the basic concept of a horizontal city) were projected to overcome the handicap imposed upon the transit system by Washington's characteristic low densities. Aggressive promotion of the system, especially in these innovative uses, was expected to change the city's populace and their travel and social habits gradually, to reorient people to downtown activities and institutions, and to build new patterns of leisure-time behavior. This reorientation had succeeded in Stockholm and other cities, and it seemed a reasonable objective for Washington.

To express this strategy, the survey further assumed that the system should be built in stages, with a nucleus to serve the downtown area and its principal federal establishments between the Capitol and the Pentagon. The area delineated, roughly comparable to that of the 1948 highway plan, was defined north and south by K Street and Independence Avenue, east and west by 4th and 20th streets.

In subsequent stages, the system was to be extended to the District line and to commuter destinations beyond in the suburban counties. As the system expanded, so would the administrative structure that was creating and would be operating the system. The downtown's system was to be built first. This area, Pierre L'Enfant's city, was characterized by the federal presence and federal employment concentration. The practical impossibility of anything other than a subway in this downtown area was evident. For all these reasons, it was logical that the transit system in the downtown area should be built as a federal operation. The National Capital Transportation Agency, a federal corporation, was specified in the implementing legislation for Metro and established in 1960.

These were the planning and implementing guidelines. What actually happened was a different story. The suburban counties and the states helped bring about premature creation of the regional transportation agency compact—the Washington Metropolitan Area Transit Authority—and caused effective control of the system's planning to be transferred from the federal government to the states. There were several results: strong commuter interests subsequently caused priority to be given to current demands for commuter services rather than to unification of the city; Metro gave up its role as provider of station plazas with parking and off-peak uses and the critically needed rental revenues that had been projected. As for the downtown area, proposals to connect the subway directly to the Kennedy Center and other off-peak destinations that might have balanced the transit load were eliminated. In short, the system was based on current and projected demand rather than on a long-range plan for establishing new transportation patterns.

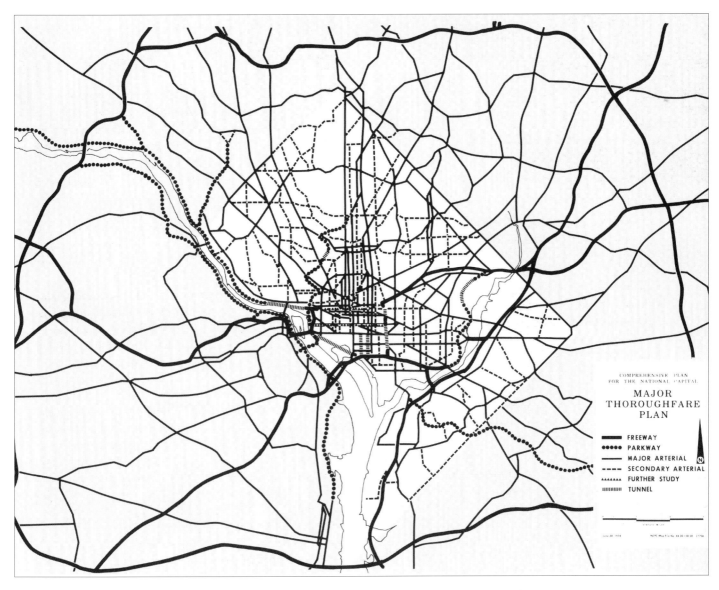

The following text appears within the map image:

COMPREHENSIVE PLAN
FOR THE NATIONAL CAPITAL

MAJOR
THOROUGHFARE
PLAN

FREEWAY
PARKWAY
MAJOR ARTERIAL
SECONDARY ARTERIAL
FURTHER STUDY
TUNNEL

THE CAPITAL BELTWAY

In terms of the proliferation of transportation origins and destinations outside the L'Enfant city, the significance of the Capital Beltway was profound. Encircling the District, at a distance of a dozen miles from the center, the Beltway was planned starting in the 1950s as the Circumferential Highway and completed in 1964 as the I-495 Capital Beltway. When built, the Beltway measured sixty-four miles in length, twenty-two in Virginia and forty-two in Maryland, and bridged the radial routes provided by highways and by the impending Metro. Over the years, the Beltway has been widened from four and six lanes to eight lanes, except for the Woodrow Wilson Bridge. The Beltway's original thirty-eight interchanges have increased to forty.

The impact of the Beltway was described in two notable studies, the *Maryland Capital Beltway Impact Study* and *The Socio-Economic Impact of the Capital Beltway on Northern Virginia*. Published in 1968, these early analyses could not fully appreciate the impact of the new highway, but they easily established its revolutionary importance as it changed travel behavior and the configuration of land use throughout the region. The Beltway actually redefined the position, within the metropolitan complex, of the older District of Columbia, not to mention the city of L'Enfant or nineteenth-century Washington.

The Capital Beltway around Washington. National Capital Planning Commission, *Comprehensive Plan for the National Capital*, 1974

Dedication of the Capital Beltway at the New Hampshire Avenue Interchange, August 18, 1964. Copyright *Washington Post,* Reprinted with Permission of the DC Public Library

Capital Beltway / I-270 Interchange, 1964. Copyright *Washington Post,* Reprinted with Permission of the DC Public Library

Much of the long-term effect of the Beltway was caused by its construction at a time and in a location of extremely rapid urban growth, causing the emerging city to form itself around the new expressways and their major design opportunities at interchanges with the principal radial routes.

THE JOINT COMMITTEE ON WASHINGTON METROPOLITAN PROBLEMS

Metropolitan development planning had long been limited by categorical federal grant-in-aid programs and federal planning for the central city that included many of the metropolitan service networks. To look more closely at how federal interests and responsibilities beyond the ten-mile-square city described in the Constitution were being affected by metropolitan growth, Congress in 1957 established the Joint Committee on Washington Metropolitan Problems. The committee, popularly called the Bible Committee, after its chairman, Senator Alan Bible of Nevada, held hearings, submitted reports, and drafted legislation over the next three years.

The joint committee urged Congress to enact, in the form of a joint resolution, an important policy declaration of federal interest in the proper development of the metropolitan area. The committee published and widely distributed its research and more general recommendations, and it supported enactment of legislation creating a Potomac Interceptor Sewer. By far the most important activity of the Joint Committee was related to mass transportation. In the course of hearings on mass transportation, representatives of the National Capital Planning Commission and the Regional Planning Council presented the findings of the Mass Transportation Survey. Along with the National Capital Planning Commission and others, the joint committee supported a mass transportation program.

Metropolitan Washington: City, Suburb, and Region

The national capital city was similar to other older American cities in its expansion at the edges and its rebuilding of older portions. The rebuilding process was recognizable at the public level and visible in the inner city through redevelopment activities. In the private sector, older portions in various jurisdictions underwent change, most notably the giant office subcenter of Rosslyn. Although constructed by private enterprise, these office buildings, like so many of those in the District, provided offices for federal employees when demands for space spilled beyond the capacity of existing public buildings. Witnessing creation of these office clusters, which were highly visible and made new demands on essential services, the capital city needed to redefine its image: did it represent the ceremonial capital city, or would it become, like other American cities, bespangled by glass office towers and beribboned by connecting highways?

THE IMPLICATIONS OF ROSSLYN

The future role of Rosslyn—a settlement with firm commercial and industrial roots—as a high-density commercial and office building center had been predicted by construction of the Key Bridge in 1923. After World War II, Rosslyn was no longer a terminus of land and water routes but an important portal to the city from the Virginia side of the George Washington Memorial Parkway. A complex of over a dozen high-rise office buildings, luxury apartment

George Washington Memorial Parkway Looking North from Rosslyn, Virginia. Photograph by Peter R. Penczer

Rosslyn, Virginia, 1964. Copyright *Washington Post,* Reprinted with Permission of the DC Public Library

Shirley Highway Looking Northeast toward Shirlington in Virginia, 1953. National Archives

buildings, hotels, and other commercial enterprises, Rosslyn was developed in the late 1950s to incorporate a multitiered segregation of movement. The ground-level streets were devoted almost entirely to automobiles, and upper-level footbridges and elevated sidewalks were provided for pedestrians. Pedestrian concourses, bus interchanges, and automobile parking were located below grade, and later the Metro subway station was built below that.

The crowding in of high-value construction at Rosslyn exhibited, as the *Christian Science Monitor* noted, the "partnership between business and local government that also reaped benefits for the Arlington taxpayer," because the investment added to the county's tax base. Despite the cluster's financial success, helped by large amounts of federally leased space and new rivalry with the skylines of other Virginia cities, its proximity brought what some considered to be "something of a Manhattan look to the Washington area." Others likened it to a "Houston on the Potomac."

THE RANCH HOUSE AND THE CURTAIN WALL

Suburbanization, new transportation technology, the 1952 act that redefined the federal role in the city and the metropolitan area, and a more powerful thrust for planning were all generated by the confirmed growth of the postwar capital city. The simpler days of the New Deal or the even earlier period still fresh in the recollection of some Washingtonians would never return. The ranch house and the curtain wall formed the architectural language of the period. The outstanding determinant of urban design, however, was the sprawling character dictated by the expressways, which were more important now than canals, railroads, or paved roads had been in their own time.

Regional shopping centers, industrial parks, office building complexes, and apartment house developments were some of the important building types to appear in the new suburbs, heralding the future character of the metropolitan fringes. Moreover, new federal establishments modeled on the Bureau of Standards were moving to outlying locations, as other agencies relocated less visibly as tenants in the new office building centers.

Local governments responded to the movement with big consolidated educational centers, including new community colleges. Montgomery County attempted to prime the pump of expressway industrial redevelopment by erecting public buildings along highly visible rights-of-way. Such redevelopment was geographically defined in corridors, and the corridor and the cluster soon became important elements in metropolitan-scale planning. The most important of these corridors were located toward Baltimore. The Baltimore corridor contained not only the ancient post road, now called US Route 1, and two principal railroad lines but also the Baltimore-Washington Parkway and a greatly improved US Route 29. Much of the change had begun earlier, but in the eight-year period from 1952 to 1960, the Washington area, certainly in terms of its metropolitan structure, turned decisively toward its regional future.

By the 1950s, everyone could see what William E. Finley, executive director of the Planning Commission from 1958 to 1962, and the new breed of city planners saw: the contrast between the declining central city and the booming suburban belt. What was more acutely felt by the planners, however, was the lack of coordination between the two planning efforts, city and suburb, and as far as the Maryland side of the Potomac was concerned, a positive decline in the close working relationships that had characterized central city and Maryland suburban planning in the quarter century before World War II.

The basic lack of coordination between planning efforts in the District, Virginia, and Maryland was most visibly stated in the accelerated construction of tall apartment buildings along the Arlington ridge and the dense office building clusters at Rosslyn. Only a short distance away, similar developments were soon to rise in Alexandria, Arlington, Fairfax County, Silver Spring, and Bethesda.

THE WASHINGTON IMAGE AND URBAN BALANCE

During the 1950s, the dichotomy sharpened between the public federal buildings of the monumental core and the privately owned structures of the suburban communities; between the buildings mainly of the first half of the twentieth century and those of the quarter century immediately following World War II; between the carefully planned, architecturally articulated central city and the jumbled anarchy of laissez-faire. Perhaps of greatest consequence for Washington was the dichotomy between the deliberate concept of an exceptional city, a national capital city, and a city that could have been built anywhere in the continental expanse of the United States.

What was at stake was the image of Washington, the entire metropolitan city regarded as a whole: its urban planning tradition of nearly two centuries, its careful regard for the natural setting and the continuity of its built environment, its specially designed entrances and carefully

View along East-West Highway, Maryland, 1953. National Archives

contrived vistas, and its concept of parks and open spaces. Only exceptional measures of regionwide planning could express this image and its underlying philosophy of urban design.

From a practical point of view, sound decisions on the future of the central city were impossible without some assumptions and controls that would guide the future of the suburban subcenters. These understandings of the metropolitan city had to calculate the balance between office space and other types of space in the central city as against that balance in outlying sites. The question had become important to the federal establishment, nearly one-third of which was located outside the District of Columbia by mid-century. Another assumption had to be made, moreover, on the balance between the federal establishment and private enterprise. Calculations of transportation and other urban services would rest on such assumptions. In the end, these understandings would determine the critical elements of the future city and its growth. ✭

THE ENVIRONMENTALLY CONSCIOUS
CITY AND REGION 1960–1975

12

Rethinking the Urban Agenda

The effects of post–World War II planning and development were evident throughout the nation. Highway construction, urban renewal, and suburban development took their toll on neighborhoods and rural settings. The Washington area's enthusiastic embrace of development and progress left its mark on the city and the region. Four hundred acres in the southwest quadrant of the city had been wiped clean, left as a vast mud flat after demolition, before being slowly rebuilt. A major leg of the Inner Loop highway provided easy access between the city and the suburbs, but it also created major barriers between once connected areas of the city. Many observers remarked on the high cost of progress.

No urban critic was more effective than Jane Jacobs. Her book *The Death and Life of Great American Cities,* which condemned wholesale 1950s urban development, became an immediate sensation. "This book is an attack . . . on the principles and aims that have shaped modern, orthodox city planning and rebuilding," she wrote, citing middle-income housing projects as "marvels of dullness and regimentation" that sealed their residents away from the vitality of city life. New highways eviscerated cities and neighborhoods. The urban renewal projects that found their way into many central cities, like Washington's southwest quadrant, resulted from planners' urgings to convert older areas into superblocks and park promenades. These tax-supported, public works programs caused "cruelly shaken-up" cities.

Jacobs's manifesto found a sympathetic audience in many urban residents at a key time in American history. The early 1960s marked the threshold between admiration for physical symbols of growth and the resurgence of environmental concerns, with important implications for the national capital city. Humanists had long decried the negative costs of laissez-faire growth. Their concerns gained increasing support among planners and became institutionalized in that era's new growth policies. The architecture critic for the *San Francisco Chronicle*, Allan Temko, enunciated this awareness of the effects of uncontrolled growth in the nation's capital in 1962. In a long article

Converting the Streetcar Entrances at Dupont Circle into a Fallout Shelter, 1964. © (1964), *The Washington Post* (Dick Darcey), Reprinted with Permission

sterility and the lack of human interaction, and depicted suburban mothers imprisoned in their station wagons. Finley argued for a reemergence of the central city as the focus of urban life, with major traffic routes moving into and out of the center of the city rather than bypassing it. Finley also suggested that instead of continuing to allow for unplanned sprawl, planning should bring about "ordered, attractive growth."

This period was marked by growing dissent in the face of conventional planning wisdom. The impact of redevelopment and highway programs was evident not only in the physical changes wrought upon the city and region but also in the plans for new development projects. During the 1960s, all levels of government responded with the passage of environmental and preservation legislation that provided for public participation. The public would no longer accept the cold, untested analyses of planners and business leaders. Residents and a new generation of local planning leaders took matters into their own hands and forced changes to draconian housing and transportation plans. In the course of this evolution in urban affairs, planning for the city and region became much more environmentally conscious and set the tone for the remainder of the century.

in the *Washington Post*, Temko saw the city as "out of control" despite the "majestic harmonies of the Federal design." He viewed the characteristic spread of settlement over once-rural landscapes, in Washington as in all American metropolitan centers, as dramatically altering urban civilization itself.

Disillusionment with suburban sprawl and the automobile had already seeped into the consciousness of planners. National Capital Planning Commission director William E. Finley surprised the Washington Building Congress early in 1958, when he advocated abandoning the dispersal theme of the 1950 Comprehensive Plan and pointed to the "crack in the picture-window vision of suburbia." He spoke darkly of suburban

The 1961 Policies Plan for the Year 2000

The directions of controlled growth were outlined in 1961 in the dramatic publication *A Policies Plan for the Year 2000*. Written by the staff of the National Capital Planning Commission and the National Capital Regional Planning Council, the Year 2000 Policies Plan presented various alternative approaches to controlled growth: (1) restrict growth in the region; (2) create new independent cities at least seventy miles from Washington, each growing to a population of three hundred thousand to five hundred thousand people in the next forty years; (3) accommodate most new growth in a planned sprawl extending in all directions as low-density development; (4) disperse new cities throughout the region away from the urbanized center and apart from each other; (5) locate a ring of cities approximately thirty miles from the urbanized center; (6) establish peripheral communities along the edges of the urbanized center; and (7) structure growth in corridors along major transportation radials that emanate from the central city.

WEDGES AND CORRIDORS: THE RADIAL CORRIDOR POLICY PLAN

The radial corridor option, referred to as "wedges and corridors," was selected as the most advantageous for the city of Washington in the year 2000. Drawn along the proposed rapid transit routes and a parallel highway system, the radial corridor policy plan expressed the concept earlier stated by Finley: the central city should be the primary focus or hub of the metropolitan region. The corridors were to be created by linking major development centers; each corridor or spoke would be separated by wedges of open countryside. In design this would produce something similar to the idealized nineteenth-century radial transit city, a snowflake pattern where open space was readily accessible to the urban and suburban population. The wedges and corridors plan was magnified beyond the scale of the earlier configuration but absorbed its values.

Diagrams of the radial corridor plan showed more specifically how the radials would embrace clusters of public buildings and services, private office buildings, shopping centers, various housing and apartment types, industrial complexes, schools, and community centers, all of them linked by the kind of urban "greenways" popularized in Philadelphia's redevelopment planning. Contrasting with these urban centers, the wedges of open space would reflect the private agricultural enclaves that still prevailed in the region, from the tobacco lands around Mitchellville in Prince George's County to the dairy and livestock grassland in the Piedmont. These wedges of open space would also reflect the largely undeveloped tracts of federal land, including the Agricultural Research Center in Beltsville, Maryland, and the emerging Dulles

Year 2000 Policies Plan staff including NCPC's William E. Finley (second from left), 1961. Copyright Washington Post, Reprinted with Permission of the DC Public Library

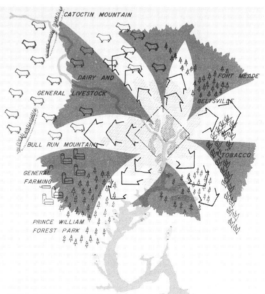

Open Wedges and Developed Corridors. National Capital Planning Commission, A Plan for the Year 2000, 1961

International Airport in Chantilly, Virginia. To secure these green wedges, the Year 2000 Policies Plan urged the designation of the lands as rural in perpetuity by outright acquisition, tax concessions, and zoning, as well as by concentration of future development in the densely populated corridors.

The Year 2000 Policies Plan reflected the ideas of the planner Hans Blumenfeld of Philadelphia, originator of the wedges and corridors theory.

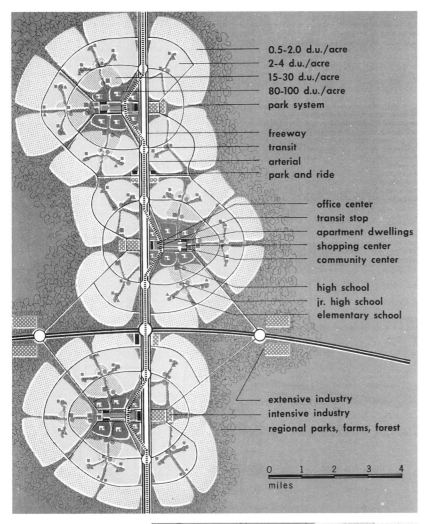

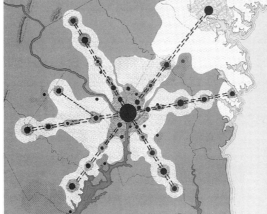

0.5-2.0 d.u./acre
2-4 d.u./acre
15-30 d.u./acre
80-100 d.u./acre
park system

freeway
transit
arterial
park and ride

office center
transit stop
apartment dwellings
shopping center
community center

high school
jr. high school
elementary school

extensive industry
intensive industry
regional parks, farms, forest

0   1   2   3   4
miles

Urbanized Corridors.
National Capital Planning
Commission, *A Plan for
the Year 2000*, 1961

The Radial Corridor Plan.
National Capital Planning
Commission, *A Plan for
the Year 2000*, 1961

The plan insisted on the simultaneous recognition and accommodation of the forces of concentration and dispersal. The scheme also closely resembled the contemporaneous development of the so-called finger plan in Copenhagen. At the time, this pattern was in the mainstream of urban planning, and the popularity of the corridors concept endured for decades.

METRO CENTER

In overall design, the Year 2000 Policies Plan acknowledged the importance of the central city in giving the wedges and corridors metropolis its identity by designating the central area of the District as "Metro Center." This center was defined as the historic L'Enfant city, the area for which Pierre L'Enfant had prepared his original city plan. Metro Center was bounded on the north by Florida Avenue and on the south, east, and west by the Potomac and Anacostia rivers.

Its role as the primary location of federal employment underscored the importance of central Washington. The Year 2000 Policies Plan applauded the monumental public office buildings as consistent with their purpose. The plan recommended, however, that to provide for sheer growth, new buildings should "make more efficient use of ground area; they could be developed at densities as much as twice those of 1960 without exceeding today's height limitations." The plan proposed locations within the central business area for new public and private office buildings to be constructed densely in small clusters or cells of buildings organized around plaza designs and located along mass transit lines. Starting with the Mall as Washington's unique and "most remarkable physical feature," the plan called for development of the historic major diagonal avenues and the vicinities of L'Enfant parks as "Special Streets and Places." These special places were defined by their historic origins, by the existing mature trees, and by the broad dimensions of the places themselves.

In designing the diagonals, planners put forward new ideas. Why not design these thoroughfares as more than vehicular routes? Why not capture the colorful street environment exemplified by the Paris boulevards with their wide sidewalks, landscaping, varied shopping opportunities, and distinctive apartment buildings? The plan suggested that the central business district—another special place—should ideally

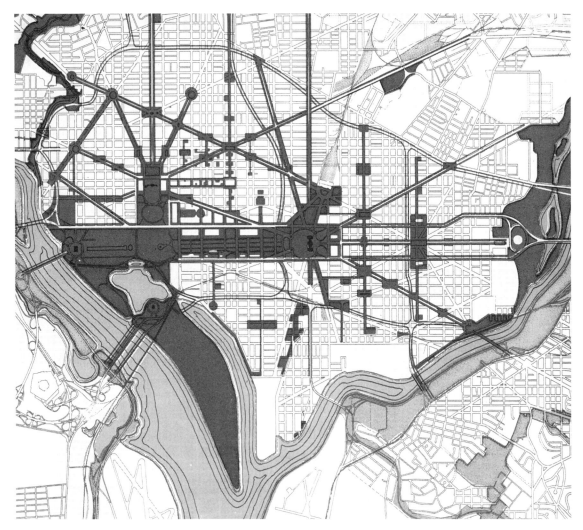

Special Streets and Places in the L'Enfant City. National Capital Planning Commission, *A Plan for the Year 2000*, 1961

incorporate a greater mixture of uses than offices and stores. To provide greater accessibility to this regenerated downtown, the Year 2000 Policies Plan retained the ultimately destructive Inner Loop highway proposed in the Planning Commission's 1950 Comprehensive Plan and viewed extensions into the suburbs along the corridors as compatible with the emerging rapid transit system.

ACCOMPLISHMENTS AND INFLUENCES OF THE YEAR 2000 PLAN

President John F. Kennedy endorsed the Year 2000 Policies Plan and directed federal agencies to refer to the plan when locating new federal facilities. The document stimulated the many planning jurisdictions of the area. A fruitful debate began to define common interests. Large

portions of the wedges and corridors plan were embraced in Maryland and, with modifications due mainly to topography, in Virginia as well. The bold and simple diagram planted itself in the popular imagination and, widely supported by civic groups, survived many challenges by the Council of Governments for as long as fifteen years.

In downtown Washington, redevelopment and the location of federal buildings received support from the plan but were less consistently responsive to it. Nonetheless, the plan influenced the design of the Metro rail system and special project planning for Pennsylvania Avenue and other development centers. Most of all, the Year 2000 Policies Plan also affected the future planning of the National Capital Planning Commission.

The impact of the Year 2000 Policies Plan was most pronounced in the metropolitan region where rural land still existed. For the first time, a structure was suggested that combined the much-desired qualities of order, open space, and mobility. The plan's wedges and corridors scheme fit well with the topography and traditions of growth in suburban Maryland. Nevertheless, pressure existed among developers (who held land in the potential wedges) to disregard the plan and to establish additional corridors or to permit the ad hoc filling in of the wedges.

Reconciling these issues depended on the work not only of suburban agencies but also of regional agencies. For the Maryland-National Capital Park and Planning Commission, suburban growth was reflected in the continuing enlargement of its jurisdiction. This commission issued a new comprehensive plan in 1962 and in principle adopted the wedges and corridors scheme two years later. The various levels of decision making in county planning, from county councils to ad hoc planning by the Washington Suburban Sanitary Commission, dealt the scheme many blows, leading to the Council of Governments' prediction of a "spread city" with development covering the Maryland counties.

On the whole, the wedges and corridors concept survived in Maryland. In Montgomery County, open space provisions, an agricultural zone, a five-acre minimum subdivision requirement, an adequate public facilities ordinance, and the strong provisions of capital budget planning strengthened and reinforced the concept. Intensification of environmental concerns, including air and water pollution, helped mold county policy. Environmental interests led to new zoning categories and subdivision philosophies that included open space. The concept of providing for parks expanded from the early stream valley ribbons to large regional parks, greenbelts around new development, neighborhood parks, and park-school combinations.

On the other hand, Virginia's topography dictated the stream valley park system and so the state's growth was less compatible with the wedges and corridors scheme. The stream valleys of Virginia penetrated the area in concentric circles around the central area, and dense corridors had already developed along Virginia's Route 7 from Alexandria to Leesburg and along Glebe Road from Alexandria into Arlington. In Northern Virginia, the planning activities of Fairfax County became extremely important because of its large size and its proximity to the District. Fairfax County had belonged to the Northern Virginia Planning District Commission since 1948. The Virginia commission was established to adopt a regional plan and aid planning agencies in the various constituent jurisdictions.

The Virginia District Commission prepared a plan in 1965 that espoused a wedges and corridors growth pattern extending through existing concentric development into the still-rural areas of Loudoun and Prince William counties. The plan was adopted in principle by all the major jurisdictions except the more densely settled Fairfax County. The planning functions of the Northern Virginia Planning District Commission were obscured by the question of whether it or the Council of Governments was responsible for regional planning in Northern Virginia and also by the refusal of some jurisdictions to endorse its programs. Despite a late start and various administrative uncertainties, planning philosophies in Northern Virginia steadily evolved, closely mirroring a similar evolution in Maryland: infatuation with growth gave way to environmental concerns, control of growth, prudent land use, and development of more flexible planning tools.

THE METROPOLITAN REGIONAL CONFERENCE OF GOVERNMENTS

Another outcome of interest in regional matters was the Washington Metropolitan Regional Conference of Governments. The conference was founded in the mid-1950s to promote voluntary cooperative action among the metropolitan counties and special-purpose regional organizations. Renamed the Metropolitan Washington Council of Governments, or COG, in 1957, it sought to formulate policies and to coordinate views on a wide range of intergovernmental social and economic issues. When the regional planning responsibilities of the National Capital Regional Planning Council were transferred to the Council of Governments and the National Capital Planning Commission in 1966, the regional planning process crystallized primarily around the development of governmental coordination procedures.

Without actually retracting the wedges and corridors scheme, the Council of Governments raised new planning questions in its pursuit of a Metropolitan Growth Policy Program. The need to establish land-use controls, to allocate scarce resources, and to accept equal responsibility for the burdens of growth throughout the region forced planners to develop new tools. In its 1975 report, the Council of Governments recommended the constant monitoring of employment and migration, which together were regarded as the "key drivers of growth in the region."

To realize the vast wedges and corridors design, regional planning organizations clearly had to include all planning elements: zoning, regulation of new subdivisions of land, transportation networks, public works, and the allocation of funds. The regional growth configurations of the Year 2000 Policies Plan also required more immediate action to regulate development of heavily populated corridors, including the new town centers, highways, the completion of the mass transportation system, and the preservation of three hundred thousand acres of open space required to separate the corridors. Policies worked out jointly between the National Capital Planning Commission and the National Capital Regional Planning Council additionally involved economic analyses; development plans; and studies of legal, administrative, and fiscal arrangements. In this way, new forms of development planning were superseding the older and simpler regulations of land use that had constituted planning for the past half century.

The Council of Governments concerned itself with designing areawide standards for health and social services, public safety, human welfare, salary schedules, waste disposal, and purchasing procedures. In 1974, over a decade after the Year 2000 Policies Plan was issued, the Council of Governments predicted, in the words of its reexamination, that unless the multifarious planning decisions affecting development in the region were enforced through strategic location and timing of water and sewer lines, by the year 2000 the wedges would be filled in and the region would become a "spread city." The Council of Governments reported that the Year 2000 Policies Plan could be realized only by careful and vigilant growth management.

The council also criticized the original 1961 plan for being too concerned with urban form and not cognizant enough of other factors that influence growth, such as taxation, business cycles, financing, and the strata of governmental decisions. According to the council, the plan was not explicitly social minded. Despite this critical reexamination of the Year 2000 Policies Plan, however, the Council of Governments offered no planning alternatives. It continued to study the policies plan to seek better ways to structure growth.

ACTION PLAN FOR DOWNTOWN

Rather than wait for official planning bodies to further detail the Year 2000 Policies Plan, Downtown Progress, an organization supported by Washington area businesses, decided to produce its own "Action Plan for Downtown." Downtown Progress was prompted by what ailed the downtown. Not only was retail activity leaving the downtown, but also the downtown was expanding to the northwest, from the White House westward to Rock Creek Park. In 1963 *Architectural Forum* reported that although $228 million of new construction occurred west of 15th Street, only $32 million was invested east of 15th Street. Corporations and trade associations facilitated the shift of the downtown along K Street, Connecticut Avenue, and Farragut Square, where land was cheaper and easier to assemble.

Downtown Progress prepared a "plan for the

revitalization of Downtown Washington and
assist[ed] in putting that plan into action," refer-
encing the Year 2000 Policies Plan. The Downtown Progress Action Plan recommended that
the many temporary buildings from World Wars
I and II be removed and that downtown employment be increased. It called for a new visitors
center on Massachusetts Avenue near Union Station, a new central library, a new convention hall
and exhibit space, a new law school, and new
churches. It looked to the new Metro system to
address the problems of traffic and the lack of
parking space. The action plan also called for
new apartments to be constructed in Mount Vernon Square East and South.

Although no direct results can be ascribed to
the action plan, it consolidated many recommendations and observations of the early 1960s
and described the downtown at the time: a place
with waning businesses, declining property values, and a poor appearance. The action plan also
made the case for designating the downtown an
urban renewal area so that public powers could
bring about land acquisition and clearance.

UPSCALE PACKAGED LIVING AT THE WATERGATE COMPLEX

Envisioned as a new type of living environment
that would attract affluent residents to the central city, the Watergate complex was located on
the site of former gas works along the Potomac
River. When the gas works and other industrial
uses left Foggy Bottom, William E. Finley of the
National Capital Planning Commission encouraged this large development and saw it bringing
new life to the city. The Watergate complex consisted of five buildings: three cooperative apartment buildings, one hotel, and one office building. The group of buildings was designed to be a
"community within a city," a self-contained
entity where residents could live, work, shop, and
relax in a single place. The Società Generale
Immobiliare of Rome, an Italian investment
company, funded the development, and Italian
architect Luigi Moretti designed the complex.

Because the Watergate complex was sited close
to the Potomac River and was visible from the
Lincoln Memorial, the Commission of Fine Arts
expressed concern about its size and height.

Design reviews caused the building to be constructed of neutral-colored precast concrete panels rather than stark white. The buildings' curvilinear shapes were inspired by an early design for the nearby Kennedy Center but were retained even when the performing arts center dispensed with curvilinear lines in favor of a rectangular box.

The Watergate complex offered a radical concept in city living, complete with unparalleled river views and access to the developing Kennedy Center. Its ground floor shopping center offered a full range of services, from a grocery store to a florist shop and a dry cleaners. Finley regarded the Watergate complex as a major investment in the city because it attracted affluent residents into an area once viewed as undesirable. He also thought that the complex provided a greater "sense of urbanity" than that offered in the new southwest quadrant.

THE KENNEDY CENTER

The Kennedy Center represented another major investment in the city. The center grew out of a long-held dream of many Washington area residents for a facility that would house world-class musical and performing arts productions. The city's desire for this level of cultural offerings far outstripped what could be accommodated in the Daughters of the American Revolution's Constitution Hall or Lisner Auditorium on the campus of George Washington University. After the work of President Eisenhower's DC Auditorium Commission from 1955 to 1958, Commission of Fine Arts chairman David Finley arranged for the review of several possible sites for this facility and recommended the one on the Potomac River to the US Congress.

In 1959 the National Cultural Center Board selected architect Edward Durrell Stone to design the building. Stone's initial designs called for a curvilinear structure. Although the design proved too expensive to build in 1962, Stone presented a revision that would house three major auditoriums. The final design was an enlarged version of Stone's US embassy in New Delhi, with a low-slung box surrounded by a single row of thin columns supporting an overhanging roof.

After the assassination of President Kennedy in 1963, Congress voted to name the center in his honor. The Kennedy Center was built according to the revised design and opened in 1971. Through its offerings, the success of the Kennedy Center contributed to Washington's development as a world-class city.

New Planning Directions

In 1962 local interests assumed leadership of the National Capital Planning Commission, and their views transformed District planning. The newly appointed chairperson, Elizabeth Rowe, began to steer the agency away from the official planning practices of the previous decade. A life-long District resident who had grown up in what came to be known as Adams Morgan and lived in Cleveland Park, Rowe represented those who had intimate knowledge of the city gained through long associations with local traditions. Rowe first became concerned with city planning during her term of service on the DC Auditorium Commission. During this commission's study of an architectural model of the site in Foggy Bottom later occupied by the Kennedy Center, she noticed the "spaghetti" of bridges and approaches planned to span the city and affect many settled areas.

When appointed to the National Capital Planning Commission in 1962, Rowe found that her idyllic view of the city as a collection of neighborhoods, defined by tree-lined streets and handsome buildings, put her at odds even with the relatively environmentally sensitive planning policies in the Year 2000 Policies Plan. These goals called for well-designed highways; higher densities in inner-city areas such as the Southwest and along the intended radials of the Year

New Highways in Foggy Bottom, 1965. © (1965), *The Washington Post* (Charles Del Vecchio), Reprinted with Permission

2000 Policies Plan; intensive redevelopment of the Georgetown waterfront; rehabilitation and redevelopment in Adams Morgan; and construction of monumental complexes of packaged living like Columbia Plaza and the Watergate, which combined office buildings with apartment houses, shops, hotels, and recreation facilities.

Rowe's outlook embraced social concerns, a sense of continuity with the past, and a growing opposition to highways ripping through neighborhoods or any similarly drastic altering of the District's strongly defined neighborhoods and edges. Her views were reinforced by studies that demonstrated that an estimated 11,000 people would be affected by construction of the east leg of the Inner Loop. Rowe shrank from the ad hoc planning of the city by means of highways, then the best-financed government program and a process that the engineer commissioner and highway officials implemented without intervention from citizens or the National Capital Planning Commission. The 1950s highway plan remained on the books, but its various components were defeated in court cases and through new US Department of Transportation policies starting in the 1960s and continuing through the early 1970s.

Government-sponsored urban renewal projects and privately financed office construction caused visible urban disruption. Rowe described modern high-rise buildings as belonging to the "vertical ice-tray school of architecture." In an effort to provide counterbalance, Rowe established historic preservation as an active concern of the Planning Commission's work and, in other planning efforts, sought to encourage grassroots participation.

THE YEAR 2000 POLICIES PLAN
IN THE DISTRICT
In October 1962, William E. Finley left his position with the National Capital Planning Commission to work for developer James W. Rouse on the Cross Keys development in Baltimore and later the new town of Columbia in Howard County, Maryland. Further detailing of the Year

2000 Policies Plan as it affected the District fell to Charles H. Conrad, who became executive director of the Planning Commission in 1965. A member of the commission staff since 1951, Conrad had served as deputy director under Finley in the critical years when the Year 2000 Policies Plan and the subsequent elaboration were developed. The series of plans and reports produced over the following decade reflected a growing environmental consciousness. Many of the major precepts in these plans and reports formed the foundation for planning activities for the remainder of the century.

The first of these reports was published in 1965, when the National Capital Planning Commission issued *1965/1985: Proposed Physical Development Policies for Washington, D.C.*, also called the "Brown Book." Whereas the Year 2000 Policies Plan was a statement of proposed policies applicable to the entire region, the Brown Book was a more detailed statement of proposed policies that focused on the District of Columbia. The 1965 plan treated the District as a collection of distinct special places, from the grand and historical Mall, Georgetown, and the Federal Triangle, to neighborhoods such as Cleveland Park, Brookland, and Brightwood. Special streets included Pennsylvania Avenue, boundary streets such as Florida Avenue, and functional connecting streets. The city's edges gave it a special ecological character, notably along the two urban rivers.

Another kind of environmental determinism was evoked in the conception of the metropolitan area as a unique landscape. This idea was put forward in Ian McHarg's study prepared for the National Capital Planning Commission in 1967 and titled *Toward a Comprehensive Landscape Plan for Washington, D.C.* The ongoing process of human interaction with natural resources characterized the city as a growing and adapting organism. In tracing geological formations, planners pushed the region's past back to the Pleistocene. Terraces were produced in this early age, cut by "steeply dissected valleys," and "two confluent rivers . . . surrounded by a backdrop of

MALL AND PARKS

VISTAS FROM EXTERIOR

VISTAS

L'ENFANT'S CITY

Landscape Identity Study Showing L'Enfant's Washington. National Capital Planning Commission, *Toward a Comprehensive Landscape Plan for Washington, D.C.,* 1967

low hills" offered the natural boundaries of the precapital city. The varied soils offered a wide variety of plant ecology used in both formal and bucolic built landscapes. McHarg ascribed the genius of the L'Enfant plan to the designer's careful "reading [of] the subtleties of land form" and recommended that the city rediscover and reinterpret the waterways, wooded hills, and ridges of the natural setting within the L'Enfant city, thereby offering a "most dramatic contrast between calculated artifice and nature."

The landscape study translated into planning policies in the National Capital Planning Commission's *Proposed Comprehensive Plan for the National Capital,* the "Green Book," published in 1967. As part of a general approach emphasizing social problems, physical planning, and design, this proposed plan sought to detail the broad policy emphasis of the 1965 Brown Book and to orchestrate social objectives in terms of urban

environments. Addressing social problems of low-income Washington residents, the plan reaffirmed the determination to attract and to retain middle-income families in the District.

The Green Book stated that qualities of the city's landscape could be experienced by residents of the city. Ideally, the topographic setting—once seen by the perceptive observer—would strengthen identity and the sense of belonging and thus spark interest in the city's future. The visual experience was available to residents and visitors from many vantage points: in panoramas from hilltop parks and from the upper floors of office buildings and in close-ups from sidewalks and front porches. The topography could be experienced by "strollers and by occupants of vehicles traveling up to a mile a minute." More emphasis on identifying special streets and places and the strengthening distinct communities could sharpen this communication of natural and built values. The plan stated that "most areas have positive characteristics and distinctive features that can be retained and exploited through design."

The Green Book proposed no radical surgery. Washington's distinct communities should be preserved to "give direction to the processes of conservation and regrowth now at work within the residential sections of the city." In recognition of these existing distinct communities, the plan incorporated a map outlining the boundaries and names of each neighborhood. (In testimony to strong community identity, the correct location of neighborhood boundary lines was promptly contested at every neighborhood meeting where the map was discussed.)

The Green Book stated transportation guidelines and more decisively reversed the highway and automobile infatuation that had so influenced (and been accommodated by) planning for over forty years. "Construction of a highway system capable of carrying all peak-hour traffic without congestion would preempt too much land, destroy too many homes, produce too great a change in the overall character of the city, and would cost too much both in

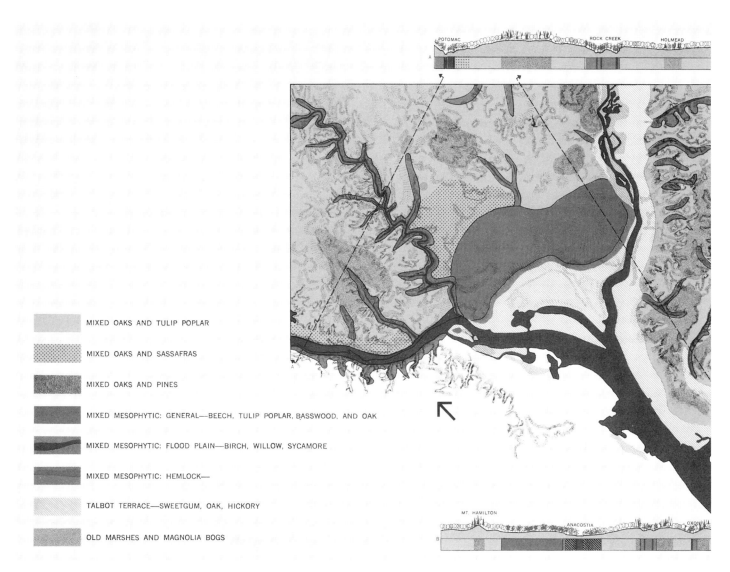

MIXED OAKS AND TULIP POPLAR

MIXED OAKS AND SASSAFRAS

MIXED OAKS AND PINES

MIXED MESOPHYTIC: GENERAL—BEECH, TULIP POPLAR, BASSWOOD, AND OAK

MIXED MESOPHYTIC: FLOOD PLAIN—BIRCH, WILLOW, SYCAMORE

MIXED MESOPHYTIC: HEMLOCK—

TALBOT TERRACE—SWEETGUM, OAK, HICKORY

OLD MARSHES AND MAGNOLIA BOGS

terms of initial investment and in the reduction of the city tax base." The plan anticipated that the Metro rapid transit system would carry a large share of the commuter load traveling to and from downtown Washington. Construction of the 103-mile-long Metro system began in 1969.

Following intense public discussion of the Green Book, the Planning Commission refined and revised the 1967 proposals. These revised proposals were incorporated into four major chapters of the comprehensive plan, or the "Red Book." They addressed Washington as capital city, residential city, and central city of the large metropolitan region. The basic intent of the comprehensive plan was to improve the city's quality of life and not to plan for significant

increases in population or development densities in the District.

In its land use objectives, the Planning Commission continued to advocate the open and horizontal green city by preserving, in the words of the Red Book, "features unique to the District's individual communities." High-density development was proposed to be concentrated in the central area, as well as in what were called uptown centers, with predominantly moderate density of residential and mixed uses in adjacent areas. These moderate densities as planned also served as transition areas between high-density and low-density areas. The plan pointed out, however, that beyond simple land-use geometry, "the character of residential development—

Landscape Identity Study Showing Washington's Ecological Associations. National Capital Planning Commission, *Toward a Comprehensive Landscape Plan for Washington, D.C.,* 1967

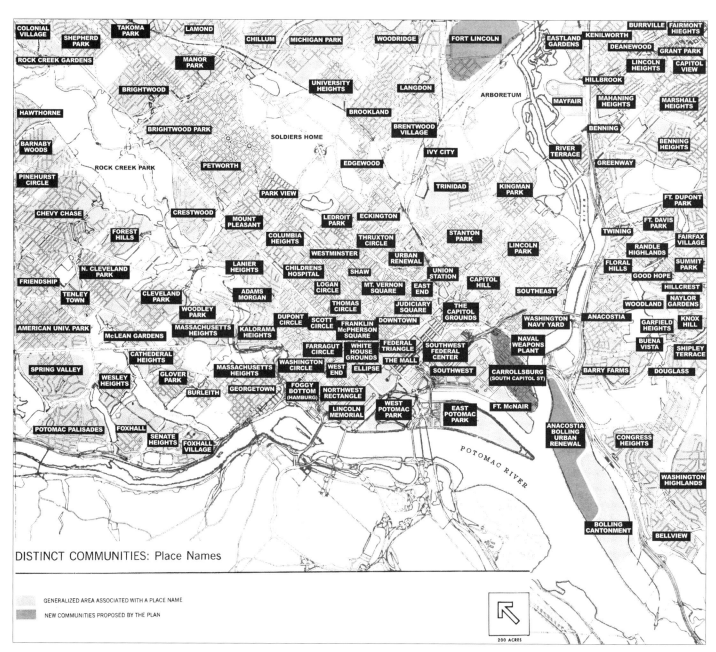

DISTINCT COMMUNITIES: Place Names

GENERALIZED AREA ASSOCIATED WITH A PLACE NAME

NEW COMMUNITIES PROPOSED BY THE PLAN

200 ACRES

Washington's Distinct Communities. National Capital Planning Commission, *Proposed Comprehensive Plan for the National Capital,* 1967

height, density and type—should be related to the relative accessibility, geographic setting, historical context, and existing patterns of each area, and, most importantly, to the needs of the people residing in the city."

RIVERS, BRIDGES, AND HIGHWAYS: FRAME AND FULFILLMENT

As at the city's beginning, the rivers frame the image of Washington today. Those great uniters of the metropolis, the Potomac and the Anacostia, were once the urban focal points of the capital city. When new land routes preempted the rivers as the chief arteries, the rivers became the city's "backyard," where industrial activities and high density threatened its open character. Deforestation and cultivation of lands dictated other changes to the rivers. These practices allowed earth to wash into the rivers with every rainfall and also caused agricultural wastes to flow past the city, drastically affecting the environment and depositing loads of silt when the river currents slowed. Reclamation of the river flats and a new appreciation of river edges focused attention on gateway aspects of bridges and land, as well as the water routes into the city, and inspired acquisition over the next half century of the scenic riverside gateway, the George Washington Memorial Parkway.

Although these entrances to the capital city created a stabilized aesthetic riverfront as far as the District's boundaries, the prolific growth of bridges and highways during the post–World War II era brought new hazards. Along the rivers, strategic areas such as Georgetown and what is called the Bolling Anacostia Tract were poised for new and more intensive development. To plan for this vital environmental and recreational resource, the National Capital Planning Commission in 1972 published the comprehensive study *Urban River*, a detailing of Comprehensive Plan policies. This study argued for restoration of the river's historic character and suggested new design treatments. The Planning Commission provided further detail in the 1976 study *Shoreline Acquisition and Development Policies and Programs.*

Perhaps the most critical if unique area of the urban river was Georgetown, with the obsolescent but still operative Whitehurst Freeway that had stimulated extensive high-rise construction along K Street and in Foggy Bottom. The Three Sisters Bridge and Freeway was abandoned in 1972 and left a publicly owned waterfront without a future. Spurred by a presidential directive to prepare a plan for the Georgetown waterfront, the National Capital Planning Commission and the District of Columbia Department of Transportation sponsored the Georgetown Waterfront Area Study. In January 1975, the consultant's final report recommended replacing the elevated freeway with a cut-and-cover depressed thoroughfare and extending the traditional scale and urban design of Georgetown north of M Street down to the waterfront.

New Design Initiatives

The Kennedy administration's efforts to improve the quality of public architecture further exhibited an increased preoccupation with historical and aesthetic values. Suggestions made by Secretary of Labor Arthur Goldberg produced the Ad Hoc Committee on Federal Office Space to study federal space requirements. As part of its review of this general topic, the committee issued a report entitled *Guiding Principles for Federal Architecture.* These principles were intended for nationwide application, but because of the concentration of federal buildings in Washington, the report had particular importance for the capital city.

The first principle was that public architecture should reflect the "dignity, enterprise, vigor, and stability of the American National Government," with attention paid to regional traditions in architecture and the fine arts. Second, any attempt at promoting an "official style" must be avoided. Third, the site for the building and its relationship to its surroundings should be the first design consideration. Karel Yasko, assistant commissioner for design and construction at the General Services Administration, took up these principles and redirected the design of subsequent public buildings in many American cities. Public buildings in Washington, including Marcel Breuer's double Y-shaped structure for the Department of Housing and Urban Development and Hellmuth, Obata + Kassabaum's National Air and Space Museum, set new civic standards for architectural design.

Department of Housing and Urban Development Building on 7th and D Streets SW, 1968. Copyright *Washington Post*, Reprinted with Permission of the DC Public Library

METRO DESIGN

By the late 1950s, plans for a new rapid transit system for Washington were an accepted reality. In the 1960s, plans for its physical form were worked out in an environment of high design aspirations. Early plans for four rail lines in 1959 gave way to an ambitious 89-mile rail system and, in 1965, a "bob-tailed" system that served primarily the District and Arlington County. When the Washington Metropolitan Area Transportation Authority was established in early 1967, the plan called for a 98-mile regional system that offered service for every major jurisdiction. With this approved plan, the federal core received the service it needed to operate efficiently and for employees to get to work downtown. In addition, the mid-city received service from what would become the Green Line.

The design emerged as a compromise between the engineering demands of the project as represented by the Chicago-based firm of DeLeuw, Cather & Company; the review bodies, including the Commission of Fine Arts; and Harry Weese, who is credited as the architect of the Metro system. The equal stature of the architect with the engineering firm was an unusual arrangement but accounted for the quality of the built system. The various designers involved with the project traveled to existing subway systems in the United States and other countries and tried to avoid what they saw as problems, including ugly columns, graffiti-damaged walls, and deadening boxy stations.

The review bodies, especially the Commission of Fine Arts, absorbed the aspirations of the Kennedy administration's desires to improve the

Metro under Construction, 1974. Copyright *Washington Post,* Reprinted with Permission of the DC Public Library

quality of federal government architecture and insisted on a high quality of design throughout the system as well as "monumentality." Weese developed a plan for the use of vaults in the underground stations, which resembled the coffered ceilings of the Capitol dome and Daniel Burnham's Union Station. The vaults were indented with a waffle pattern of rectangular coffers that increased the drama of the underground stations. Although the Commission of Fine Arts wished that all the stations could be virtually identical, the below-ground stations differed from the above-ground stations, and the "hub" stations like Metro Center differed from the single-stop locations. The same design for the platforms, benches, lighting, and signage in all stations created continuity. The Metro stations reflected Weese's view of subway stations as an "outdoor environment." As the Metro system began service in 1976, both residents and critics admired the comfortable and safe system. It was rapid transit that reflected federal Washington at its best.

LAFAYETTE SQUARE

The Kennedy years in Washington signaled new design directions for federal government projects and continuity with older urban structures. This duality of change and continuity was best exemplified by Lafayette Square, the forecourt of the White House. Surviving nineteenth-century residential buildings, particularly on Jackson Place, as well as Latrobe's Decatur House and St. John's Episcopal Church, framed the square. Several presidents had proposed to locate new executive branch buildings around the square.

The White House and Lafayette Square, 1936. National Capital Planning Commission Collection

In fact, a succession of architectural designs had been proposed for this site. The McMillan Plan included an Executive Group around the White House, a monumental precinct that provided office space. Cass Gilbert's general plan of 1920 for the Executive Group provided details for a continuous colonnade that framed the square. Based on this concept plan, he designed the Treasury Annex and the US Chamber of Commerce Building to conform to this plan. Construction of the Federal Triangle relieved pressure to locate offices at Lafayette Square, and no further buildings were constructed according to the Gilbert scheme.

By the post–World War II era, the constituency for this classical redevelopment of the square had evaporated. The Eisenhower administration supported Henry R. Shepley's five-story Georgian version of a modern office building; this design also failed to arouse enthusiasm. Shepley's scheme envisioned demolishing the Blair House, the old Corcoran Gallery of Art (then used for the Court of Claims), Decatur House, and the old State, War and Navy Building.

At issue was the character of the White House. It could be seen as a public building, a palace, or,

as most Americans traditionally thought of it, a private residence. The development of the buildings around Lafayette Square determined which of these interpretations prevailed. The issue of Lafayette Square's design reemerged during the restoration of the White House during Harry S. Truman's presidency; as time passed, there was growing pressure for resolution. President and Mrs. Kennedy stepped into the situation, relying on advice from their friend William Walton, then chairman of the Commission of Fine Arts, together with architectural assistance from the San Francisco designer John Carl Warnecke. The final solution for Lafayette Square became a celebrated project of its era.

The design for the redevelopment of Lafayette Square retained every historically recognized building around the square and beyond, including the old Corcoran Gallery of Art (subsequently restored to become the Smithsonian's Renwick Gallery). At the edge of the square formed by Lafayette Park, old town houses were preserved, and new compatible, replica town houses filled in the gaps between surviving buildings. The much taller New Executive Office Building and the Court of Claims Building were

placed behind the rows of town houses and were designed in red brick to harmonize with the town houses. Brick walkways tied together the whole ensemble and reinforced the residential nature of the White House. When Walton apologized to President Kennedy for taking up so much of his time to review plans for the Lafayette Square, the president said, "That's all right. After all, this may be the only monument we'll leave."

The Lafayette Square project was indeed a worthy monument. The integration of old buildings and new construction represented a "watershed in thinking about new development in older areas" and was a model for many American cities. Its presidential approval and its large, strategic location made a statement more influential than written directives. The Lafayette Square solution demonstrated that new and old buildings could peacefully coexist; it served as an example to other cities and communities throughout the nation facing similar challenges.

Growth Centers

The 1960s witnessed large-scale developments in the rapidly growing outlying areas. Almost in

spite of planners' efforts, the activities of private speculators in the 1960s offered formidable challenges. A "packaged-living" model developed for Columbia Plaza and the Watergate complex in Foggy Bottom was appealing. The model influenced commercial developments in Rosslyn in the late 1950s and Crystal City in the 1960s, both driven by the need to house government employees displaced when the temporary buildings of the two World Wars in and around the Mall were demolished.

The packaged-living phenomenon was most explicit in Crystal City, a development spawned by National Airport and new expressways. Located along the highly visible Virginia shore, Crystal City had the physical elements of a city—apartments, offices, hotels, shopping, recreation—all unrelieved by any civic, social, or humanistic grace. Washington's largest builders, Cafritz and Tompkins, developed the complex on a flat tract of largely reclaimed land just south of the Pentagon, which conformed to plans of the Arlington County Planning Commission that located high-density development along the Jefferson Davis Highway corridor. Unified by a vast network of underground malls—described as

Key Bridge and the Rosslyn Skyline, 1967. Copyright *Washington Post,* Reprinted with Permission of the DC Public Library

Crystal City, Virginia. Photograph by Peter R. Penczer

"territecture"—Crystal City offered a self-contained lifestyle of convenience and safety.

Phil Stanford of the *Washington Post* asserted that these new neighborhoods, called "omni-buildings," avoided the "sterility of one-use districts like downtown Washington, or much of the suburbs." It could be said that the design of developments like Crystal City defined a new sterility. The high densities of people on the fifty acres of land led some urbanists to fear apathy and disaffection among residents. Architects viewing the project questioned whether the complex truly functioned as a whole or whether it was a disjointed collection of buildings. Unredeemed by even topographic irregularities, as, for example, at Rosslyn, the regulated monotony of Crystal City seemed a crushing blow to the spirit.

The glass office towers that populated Rosslyn and Crystal City obliterated any hope that new outlying office buildings would be patterned

Dulles International
Airport Terminal, 1966.
Copyright *Washington
Post,* Reprinted with
Permission of the DC
Public Library

after architectural traditions of the capital city.
Outside the jurisdiction of the District of
Columbia, the precast concrete facade took over.
Even within the District, squat towers defined
the commercialization of the central city along
Connecticut Avenue and K, L, and M streets in
the Northwest. Limited only in height, these
structures were part of the office-building boom
occurring in cities across the nation. In Washington the buildings were mostly the work of speculative investors and reflected the clustering of
national associations and organizations in the
capital.

Similar office groupings formed around the
region's major thoroughfares, especially next to
the Capital Beltway, as in Westgate at Tysons
Corner. These far-flung office centers offered an
urban lifestyle removed from the central city, so
that people could commute between home and
work entirely within the suburban context. This
change was especially striking in Fairfax County
where the Beltway created, for the first time in
history, a north-south route cutting across the
traditional corridors leading to the south and
west from Alexandria and Washington. Built on
a larger scale than the earlier regional shopping
centers, these suburban subcenters conspicuously altered the traditional landscapes. They
had not been anticipated, however, and their
locations were more often fortuitous than
planned. The result was seen over and over again
in environmental impacts and the stress on limited essential public services.

DULLES INTERNATIONAL AIRPORT

Since the end of World War II, city planners had
anticipated the construction of a new airport.
Passage of the Washington Airport Act of 1950
addressed this need. From a number of recommended locations, President Eisenhower selected
a ten thousand acre site located twenty-six miles
west of the District of Columbia. The site strad-

dled Fairfax and Loudoun counties. Unlike many urban airports, a greenbelt surrounded this airport. Eero Saarinen was selected as the architect for the new airport, which remains one of the architectural landmarks of the postwar period. Construction on the airport began in 1958, and it opened in 1962. The airport was unique for its soaring suspended roof, which Saarinen described as "a huge, continuous hammock suspended between concrete trees"; the 193-foot glass-enclosed central control tower; and the mobile lounges used to transport passengers between the terminal and their flights.

The airport was named for John Foster Dulles, the secretary of state from 1953 to 1959. The importance of Dulles Airport stemmed from its ability to provide an alternative location for arrivals and departures. It was not originally conceived as an economic generator because of the limited access road. Over time, however, Dulles Airport became the center of a massive development corridor of office buildings, housing, and shopping facilities that took advantage of closeness to the airport. Dulles was more than an airport; it was the catalyst for jobs, a massive employment center, and even a "community."

THE NEW TOWNS OF RESTON AND COLUMBIA

The new towns of Reston in Fairfax County, Virginia, and Columbia, in Howard County, Maryland, represented bold privately sponsored alternatives to conventional suburban sprawl. Both towns succeeded because of the careful development of land based on economic feasibility studies, and both depended on the support of the suburban jurisdictions in which they were located. Their locations were interpreted as fulfilling the urban corridors configuration of the Year 2000 Policies Plan. The success of the new towns inspired planners throughout the nation and the world who had vivid examples of a new kind of suburban development that occurred without government sponsorship or funding. These communities were the American answer to the many European planned new towns developed to provide for new housing in

countries where land was scarce. The Reston and Columbia experiences gave their home counties and states, as well as the nation, experience with innovative planning, zoning, and development models.

Reston was the product of Robert E. Simon, who in 1961 took his proceeds from the sale of Carnegie Hall in New York City and purchased seven thousand acres in western Fairfax County for his new town, which derives its name from Simon's three initials. Not only did Simon see an advantage to its proximity to the new Dulles Airport, but he also was smitten by the rolling hills, meadows, and streams in the area. He had visited new towns in Great Britain and other European countries, most notably Tapiola in Finland, and he admired Italian coastal villages. His new town provided for communities organized around lakes, clustered housing, a mix of housing types and sizes, open spaces of commonly held land, and employment for residents. The community was open to all purchasers, making it a racially integrated community from the beginning. Fairfax County facilitated the project through the creation of a special zoning category, "residential planned community."

The architects for Reston, who included Chloethiel Woodard Smith and Charles Goodman, designed the earliest town houses in the modern style as they had in the southwest quadrant urban renewal area and elsewhere. At first these houses sold slowly, which led to the construction of more conventional housing. A major investment came in 1966, when Secretary of the Interior Stuart Udall announced that the US Geological Survey would be relocated to Reston, a promise that became an actuality in 1973. Eventually, Simon relinquished control of Reston to Gulf Reston, which later sold it to the Mobil Corporation and its subsidiary, the Reston Land Corporation. As Reston developed and Dulles Airport expanded, the town became home to satellite, communications, and high-technology companies and a major employment center.

In Howard County, James W. Rouse also drew on new town theory and building in the creation

of Columbia. He had visited new towns in England, Sweden, and the Netherlands, as well as Radburn and Greenbelt in the United States. In 1963 he began purchasing land just off the Route 29 corridor that contained 165 farms and 14,000 acres of land. Columbia also embodied the 1960s idealism of "making America a better place." Rouse, who had hired William E. Finley of the National Capital Planning Commission to plan the Cross Keys development in Baltimore, then assigned him to plan the new town.

The new town of Columbia was organized around the village system. Each village contained five neighborhoods and its own small commercial center modeled after the village center at Rouse's Cross Keys community in Baltimore. The nine villages were placed around a town center that included an enclosed shopping center. In designing the town center, Rouse and his staff looked to Tivoli Gardens in Copenhagen, Denmark, and designed the Columbia Inn, the Columbia Cinema, restaurants, and the dinner theater accordingly. Office buildings that provided employment were integrated into the village structure.

Rouse watched what was happening in Reston and admired the mix of residential apartments and town houses at the Lake Ann Center. He rejected the urban character of the architecture and the use of exposed concrete, however, and opted for more conventional housing design. Like Reston, Columbia was envisioned as a racially integrated community, then a rarity in the Washington metropolitan area. As Rouse promoted Columbia, he cited the alternative. Had Columbia not been built, the same land would have become the site for a multitude of fragmented and piecemeal developments. Columbia offered a quality of life superior to that poised for that large acreage.

Lake Anne, Reston, Virginia, 1977. Copyright *Washington Post*, Reprinted with Permission of the DC Public Library

Wilde Lake Village Green in Columbia, Maryland, 1968. Copyright *Washington Post*, Reprinted with Permission of the DC Public Library

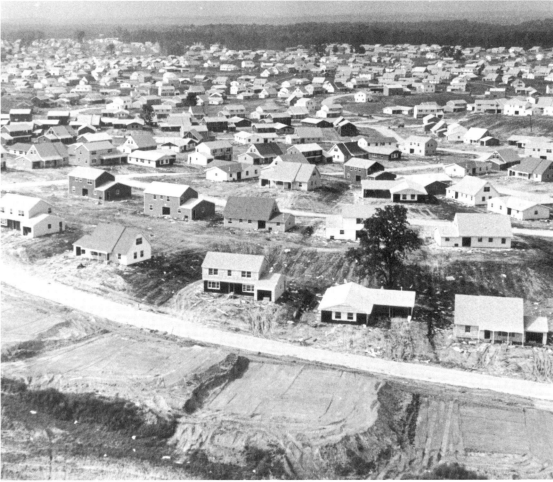

Bowie Subdivision, Prince George's County, Maryland, 1963. Copyright *Washington Post*, Reprinted with Permission of the DC Public Library

In 1969 the economic consulting firm of Hammer, Greene, Siler Associates wrote about Reston and Columbia in the report *The Economy of Metropolitan Washington.* "The two best examples of total new town developments in the nation are Reston and Columbia. . . . The proximity of these two developments to Washington has been a major factor in their success to date. These attempts to concentrate population in planned environments in the suburbs are a major departure from the development pattern of the past."

Redevelopment Projects of the 1960s

Urban redevelopment continued to play an active role in reshaping the city, but in a more subdued and socially oriented mode as compared to the extravagantly overoptimistic redevelopment in the early 1950s. Not only did the earlier redevelopment model focus on upper-income accommodation, but also that model provided no replacement housing for low-income dwellers. The idealistic claim that Washington could become a slumless city within a decade gave way to a realistic and evolving process that addressed the needs of those who had the fewest resources and recognized their concerns and aspirations.

The new spirit of rehabilitation and small-scale renewal, both aimed at providing new communities for low- and moderate-income residents, characterized redevelopment activities after the mid-1960s. As contrasted with urban renewal of the 1950s, rehabilitation and citizen participation became paramount. Urban renewal areas designated in the northwest quadrant included Northwest 1 (just west of North Capitol Street), 14th Street, Shaw (just north of the downtown area), and the downtown. Urban renewal areas in the northeast quadrant included H Street and Northeast 1 (just east of North Capitol Street). Organized by Walter Fauntroy and the Model Inner City Community Development Organization, Shaw emerged as part of Washington's Model Cities Program and was named after the new junior high school in the area.

The National Capital Planning Commission, in consultation with the Redevelopment Land Agency, designated an urban renewal area west of Union Station and North Capitol Street. In terms of successful meshing of new and rehabilitated structures, Northwest 1 could claim the 227-unit Sursum Corda development and Sibley Plaza (sponsored by the National Association of Home Builders), as well as the rehabilitation of substantial blocks of row houses within the area.

One urban renewal proposal that attempted to integrate the objectives of neighborhood conservation and rehabilitation was described in *A Program for Bates Street,* proposed in 1969. Working closely with the neighborhood residents of a two-block area that was part of the Shaw School Urban Renewal Area, the proposal addressed the problem of Washington's thousands of row houses, structurally sound but obsolescent. The proposal suggested opening up the interiors of blocks, building playgrounds, and redesigning streets for better living, all as a background to renovating individual houses to admit sunlight and air to previously dark interiors and to create more convenient layouts. The opportunity to demolish some existing houses and to incorporate some new construction in the form of public housing was also examined. This possibility was a promising exercise in smaller-scaled redevelopment, with less clearance and moderated impact on social structures. Moreover, this possibility was realistically conceived in terms of Washington's characteristic street plan and housing types. The program was to be carefully phased to avoid relocation and was aimed at accommodating the same population in the old neighborhood.

Given the fact that nearly all new housing starts were located in the surrounding suburbs and that the District needed to conserve and to reuse the existing housing stock, alternatives such as those explored in the Bates Street proposal seemed to foreshadow a promising future in terms of urban continuity. Although not directly expressive of a historic preservation effort, the Bates Street proposal supported a technique through which this future objective could be realized in areas that, unlike Georgetown or Foggy Bottom, lacked the resources to "unslum" or gentrify themselves on a house-by-house basis and to pay all the costs involved.

In 1961 Adams Morgan was adopted (by the Planning Commission but not by the District commissioners) as a redevelopment area after much private initiative had already promised a revitalized neighborhood. Plans for the area were dropped four years later, however, when residents opted for a self-renewal approach and a program of code enforcement. This was understandable: when Adams Morgan residents looked toward the new Southwest, they saw money-making developers, demolition of important landmarks, planning of suburban-type plazas, high-density development, and extensive relocation of residents.

The Bolling Anacostia Tract was designated an urban renewal area in 1967, when the air traffic functions of the air force base were relocated. Although the Planning Commission developed various conceptual plans for building a new neighborhood on the site, Congress later deleted the tract from the commission's jurisdiction and directed the Department of Defense to construct military housing and other facilities according to its own designs.

The new town of Fort Lincoln on the former site of the National Training School for Boys in Northeast Washington was another notable urban renewal project. The large site had inspired proposals for a community college or Government Printing Office operation. President Lyndon B. Johnson played a role in securing the site for the new town. Adopted by the National Capital Planning Commission and approved by the District of Columbia Council in 1972, the Fort Lincoln plan incorporated the many revisions in redevelopment thinking since 1949, as well as the historical evolution of planning in the city contained in the Planning Commission's comprehensive and specialized planning reports. The plan for Fort Lincoln emphasized the strengths of the natural topography, the views, and the environmental amenities offered by the natural woodlands as well as the historical sites and events that should be recognized by developers.

As a planned community, Fort Lincoln had as its primary objective the "creation of an attractive and racially, socially, economically, and functionally inclusive community of approximately 16,000 persons." It was developed as a self-contained community, a neighborhood that sought to attract outsiders to its town center, parks, and trails. The community was linked to the rest of the city by a transit shuttle to the nearest Metro station. Provisions for community malls, playgrounds, and schools provided additional elements in creating an attractive area.

The formation of groups like the Model Inner City Community Development Organization in Shaw marked the emergence of community-based organizations over the following decades. Emerging from antipoverty and civil rights advocacy, these organizations addressed the needs of the communities in which they were located. The Neighborhood Housing Services organization in the Anacostia neighborhood administered a high-risk revolving fund and made loans to home owners in the area. In order to serve the needs of other low-income areas, community development corporations, also known as CDCs, became incubators for new approaches to community development. The organizations undertook what initially were considered to be risky rehabilitation and new construction projects that provided rental housing and facilities for needed retail operations. CDCs also played important roles in establishing health centers and enticing businesses to locate in their neighborhoods to provide jobs. As their reputations and track records solidified, their financial bases expanded to include support from banks, foundations, federal and local government funding sources, religious institutions, and private corporations.

In the post–Great Society era, CDCs benefited from the passage of the Community Reinvestment Act of 1978 that required banks to cease red-lining practices and demonstrate that they

served their local communities. In addition, the Tax Reform Act of 1986 established the low-income housing tax credit program and made low-income housing projects attractive to investors. When used in conjunction with the historic preservation tax credit, the low-income housing tax credit generated new rental housing in historic buildings. By 1999, the CDCs demonstrated that successful revitalization initiatives operated "on a smaller scale than the large federal programs of the past."

URBAN RENEWAL AND THE 1968 RIOTS

The assassination of Dr. Martin Luther King Jr. on April 4, 1968, precipitated widespread civil disturbances in major cities across the nation. In Washington portions of the city were burned and looted, thirteen people died, and property damage was widespread. The crisis lasted five days, from April 4 though April 8. Nearly 13,600 federal troops and national guards were called up to protect the city. Destruction was concentrated in three major sections. On 7th Street between Mount Vernon Place and Florida Avenue, 263 buildings were damaged. Near 14th

Street and Park Road, 275 businesses were damaged. On H Street in Northeast Washington, between 2nd and 15th streets, 90 buildings were damaged. The resulting loss of homes and jobs was matched by the destruction of property, the larger disruption of community services, and the damage to the city's morale. As in the earlier civil disturbances in Watts in Los Angeles, it was immediately clear in Washington that the task of reconstruction would not be easy and that reconstruction plans would not find any ready consensus.

Within hours after the crisis began, the National Capital Planning Commission launched a detailed survey to determine the extent of damage. The commission also began to formulate an outline plan for reconstruction. By April 9, the commission could report that estimated property damage totaled $13,330,556. The report of the survey published by the Planning Commission localized the areas damaged and categorized the buildings affected according to the degree of damage (from 0 to 10 percent, from 11 to 50 percent, and more than 50 percent). The survey also sorted the damage between 909 commercial establishments and 283 dwellings. A subsequent analysis by the commission raised the initial estimates to 1,352 affected businesses involving damage to 645 buildings.

Total property damage was calculated at $57.6 million, which included the value of looted and burned inventories of goods as well as real property damage. Nearly half of the damage was in the 7th Street corridor, the historic route that long ago had connected the Potomac port to the Baltimore turnpike. The Planning Commission's report, *Civil Disturbances in Washington, D.C., April 4–8, 1968, A Preliminary Damage Report,* was an immediate response to Mayor Walter Washington's call for "positive action programs and a full mobilization of local and federal resources to assist in rebuilding the damaged sections of the District."

In addition to preparing planning data such as real property maps, assessment and insurance records, aerial photos, and field inspections, planners met with many community groups. The aim was to search for a reconstruction strategy. By August 28, 1968, the cooperating agencies of the District of Columbia and the National Capital Planning Commission published a second report, *Alternative Approaches to Rebuilding,* which specifically addressed the three major concentrations of damage. This report took into consideration a wide spectrum of views expressed in the community. A parallel survey was also issued by the Metropolitan Washington Board of Trade.

During the disturbances, public agencies had shown the value of metropolitan organization of police, fire, and other emergency services. Immediate needs for housing those left homeless and caring for those left unemployed were met with a similarly impressive degree of regional emergency organization. At the same time, preparations for longer-range reconstruction were initiated. In many respects, the entire response resembled that experienced by cities after an earthquake, flood, or other widespread disruption.

The political issues embedded in reconstruction plans had roots in the wide variety of expectations held by different elements in the community. These were only partially recognized in the City Council's report of May 10, 1968, entitled "Rebuilding and Recovery of Washington, D.C., from the Civil Disturbances of April, 1968." What the City Council made clear was the evidence revealed in public hearings that "the lack of housing, employment and other opportunities for ghetto residents were . . . the basic factors contributing to the disturbances." Yet public opinion alone clearly could not resolve the differences between short-term aid and long-term redevelopment, between using the reconstruction opportunity to advance fundamental reforms and simply rebuilding the areas as they had been. Overall, there was a pervasive if less clearly expressed view that the opportunity for fundamental changes in land use, transportation, recreational open space, and other physical characteristics of the damaged areas should not be thrown away.

Of the many experiences from the ensuing decade after the 1968 disturbances that can be examined, redevelopment of the 7th Street corridor is the most representative as well as the most illuminating. Following closely the initiatives and plans of the National Capital Planning Commission, as well as the articulation of community development objectives, the Redevelopment Land Agency worked in close coordination with departments of the District government. By 1976 3 new housing developments with a total of 400 units were completed, and construction had started on 245 more new units, with an additional 50 rehabilitated units. The 7th Street environment was greatly improved by miniparks and new street lighting.

Home Rule

Dissent against the planning and transportation programs of the 1950s and early 1960s found expression in a variety of forums. One of these was pressure for home rule. By 1957 the city had become a black majority city. For the most part, the black community had not been sufficiently involved in the planning process that brought about large redevelopment projects, and their disenfranchisement became the foundation for political action.

In 1964 District residents were granted the right to vote for president. In 1967 President Lyndon B. Johnson reorganized the District's governing structure and replaced the commissioner system with a presidentially appointed mayor and city council. Also in 1967 the mayor and the chairman and vice chairman of the City Council replaced the three District commissioners on the DC Zoning Commission, which also included the architect of the Capitol and the director of the National Park Service. The following year, 1968, marked the first popularly elected school board. In anticipation of support for home rule, local recreation facilities were transferred from the National Park Service to the DC Department of Recreation.

The Home Rule Act of 1973 restored an elected city government—the mayor and city council—and established Advisory Neighborhood Commissions that institutionalized a formal system for citizen participation. One important aspect of the Home Rule Act was the provision for the National Capital Planning Commission and the mayor to "jointly establish procedures for appropriate meaningful continuing consultation throughout the planning process for the National Capital." Local interests were to be given an opportunity to be heard within the context of federal priorities for the nation's capital.

One of the first areas where there must be "appropriate meaningful continuing consultation" was in the planning effort to flesh out the *Comprehensive Plan for the National Capital,* formerly the sole responsibility of the Planning Commission. Elements of the comprehensive plan pertaining to local concerns such as detailed land use plans for specific nonfederal areas of the city were to be prepared by the District of Columbia government, adopted by the City Council, and reviewed by the Planning Commission as to federal interest and inclusion in the comprehensive plan. The success of the process depended on clear channels of communication, an understanding of both federal and local needs and priorities, and a willingness to work toward resolution of any differences.

The District government's Municipal Planning Office, renamed the Office of Planning, began to develop local planning goals and a local land use plan as part of its work to identify appropriate District elements of the comprehensive plan. The National Capital Planning Commission identified and gave priority to the federal elements of the comprehensive plan: together, these efforts represented a basic commitment to continue comprehensive planning for the nation's capital. While providing a framework for future policy decisions regarding physical development and social and economic vitality, the comprehensive planning process allowed for changes and additions to that framework according to new priorities and needs.

By the mid-1970s, planning approaches had turned 180 degrees from where they had stood at the mid-twentieth century. No longer did a relatively small group of design professionals develop and implement plans for the national capital city or, for that matter, any city. Planning had become a grassroots occupation, in which citizens' voices were a potent force. Planners had to respond to private initiatives and develop mechanisms for public consultation and participation. The likes of Pierre L'Enfant or Daniel Burnham would not have recognized or even tolerated these planning approaches. Yet the new participatory planning process offered a new tool to help protect the legacies of L'Enfant, Burnham, and their fellow urban visionaries. ★

CHANGING DYNAMICS IN THE METROPOLITAN AREA 1976-1990

13

The Best and Worst of Times

The 1970s and early 1980s represented a low point in urban living in the United States. Not only had many residents moved out, but also once vital commercial enterprises, most notably downtown stores, cultural offerings, recreation activities, and movie theaters, had vanished. Many cities' downtowns were pockmarked with empty lots located in between isolated modern office buildings, leaving an eerie urban landscape. Few people ventured into downtowns in the evening hours. The District was no exception to this sorry state of urban life. It had several advantages that no other city possessed, however. It was still the location of the federal government, and this reality helped stabilize the city until new investment and revitalization could turn the tide. More than most cities, the national capital city experimented with new tools and projects to revive the central city and became a model for the revitalization of urban America as a whole.

The census numbers tell the story. In 1970 the District's population stood at 756,510. Ten years later, in 1980, the population had declined by 118,177 people to 638,333, a 16 percent decrease. The departure of residents for the suburbs was the primary culprit in the population decline in the city. So, too, was the conversion of sections of the city—such as Foggy Bottom—from residential to commercial and institutional uses. These dynamics played out during a period of slow economic growth in the 1970s and early 1980s, when the nation experienced a significant recession. By 1982 fortunes changed, and the nation, as well as the Washington metropolitan region, experienced a period of growth and prosperity. This buoyant period ended in 1990, when the nation experienced another economic downturn.

Contributing to the District's population decline was the sluggish overall growth in the Washington metropolitan area during the 1970s. These gloomy times caused planners in 1980 to predict that the area's population would grow to only 4.2 million people by the year 2000. The planners of 1980 turned out to be too pessimistic; they underestimated the region's population in 2000 by one million people.

Metro Construction Impacts Downtown Businesses, 1971. Copyright *Washington Post,* Reprinted with Permission of the DC Public Library

The District's population decline should be viewed in the context of what was happening in cities and older suburbs across the nation. All were experiencing significant outmigration. In addition, the size of households declined, as families with children moved out to new residential communities. In the Washington metropolitan area, depopulation was a phenomenon that occurred in several older communities, not just the District. For example, across the Potomac River, the older suburb of Arlington, Virginia, also experienced a significant population decline—a 12 percent decrease—in the same decade.

Still, however universal the problem, the outmigration of residents from the District had a devastating impact on the city's image and repu-

tation. Once the city represented a safe haven; now large parts of it were gripped by abandonment, poverty, and crime. Parking lots, demolition sites, and underused commercial buildings scarred the downtown area north of Pennsylvania Avenue. Streets and sidewalks along downtown commercial streets were torn up, as construction of the new Metro subway system proceeded. Metro's unsightly construction debris lasted for years, causing a huge impact on the ability of affected stores, restaurants, and other small businesses to survive.

Newer suburban jurisdictions drew investment and prosperity out of the center of the metropolitan area and dispersed it around the outer reaches of the suburbs. The population of rapidly developing Fairfax, Montgomery, and Prince George's counties blossomed and spilled into Loudoun, Prince William, Frederick, Calvert, and Anne Arundel counties. Never before had the fortunes of the central city and the rising suburbs stood in such stark contrast.

The aftereffects of the 1968 riots and abandonment caused the physical landscape of the central city to increasingly resemble bombed-out European cities after World War II. Help was on the way, however. Measures were being taken to invest in the central city's long-term viability, but it would take years for the plans to yield visible results. One major investment was the Metro system that placed passenger stops throughout the downtown and connected it with District neighborhoods and the Maryland and Virginia suburbs. Metro's first segment opened in 1976 and ran two miles from Rhode Island Avenue to Farragut North. As additional segments opened, the promise of revitalization was translated into reality. Once opened and operating, Metro became a magnet for growth and offered an unprecedented connectivity throughout the region.

Another factor in shaping the physical landscape was the implementation of historic preservation laws and the change in federal government tax policy that favored preservation of historic buildings over demolition. Preservation

laws resulted in the greater protection of historic buildings. Preservation regulations encouraged developers to rehabilitate historic buildings. They also resulted in compromises that used historic facades as features in new building projects.

With the radical redevelopment of the southwest quadrant a vivid memory, residents sought to protect their neighborhoods through active involvement in traditional citizens associations, new planning organizations, and the Advisory Neighborhood Commissions. They became adept at using historical designations to protect historic districts and landmarks.

New museums, monuments, and memorials brought residents and visitors to the downtown and the Mall. By the end of the 1980s, the city began to reclaim its role as a cultural and entertainment center. At the same time, the suburbs were striving to create a sense of place and coherence in their burgeoning landscapes.

THE BICENTENNIAL

On July 3, 1976, the city witnessed one of the largest gatherings of people ever convened along the Mall. The crowd of five hundred thousand

people lined up peacefully along both sides of Constitution Avenue to cheer a parade that celebrated the nation's bicentennial. The event was important on several levels. It not only provided a retrospective on the two hundred years of the nation's development, but it also was an act of healing. As *Washington Post* reporter Haynes Johnson wrote, the parade provided a tonic "after the rancor and bitter divisions of the recent past." The parade stood in contrast to the events of the previous years that had shattered the faith and goodwill of the American people toward their government.

The year 1976 ushered in a sense of relief and optimism for the future. That year witnessed the end of the Watergate era that had culminated with the unprecedented resignation of President Richard M. Nixon. In 1975 South Vietnam fell to North Vietnam and brought to a close the Vietnam War, a protracted struggle that had sapped the energies of the country for over a decade. Both of these events, in addition to the civil rights movement, had mobilized America's youth and challenged established authorities. Out of these divisive years came the commitment to examine history in new ways and to approach the future with greater public participation.

The bicentennial celebration was a time of introspection as well as rededication. For at least a decade before, the entire nation had worked on the celebration, a series of festivities that did not focus on a single event or exposition. The bicentennial instead became a broadly decentralized undertaking to which communities, organizations, and government agencies all contributed. Projects addressed not only national concerns and themes but also those of state and local history. Some organizations issued books and pamphlets. Others sponsored special exhibits and conferences. Still others undertook building restoration projects.

As part of the decentralized celebration, the National Capital Planning Commission sponsored a new history of planning in the District and metropolitan area, *Worthy of the Nation: The History of Planning for the National Capital.* The book, the accompanying exhibit, "Federal City: Plans and Realities," and the exhibit catalog were produced in cooperation with the Smithsonian Institution and the Commission of Fine Arts. Located in the Great Hall of the Smithsonian "Castle," the exhibit traced the development of the national capital city from the city's founding through the official planning activities of Pierre L'Enfant, the McMillan Commission, and the National Capital Planning Commission. The exhibit also marked the turning point where the future of the constituent, home-rule city could be glimpsed. Although planned as a temporary show, the Federal City show was so popular that the exhibit was displayed for at least five years. Even with this well-attended exhibit, however, the National Capital Planning Commission's future role, as well as its mandate to protect the "federal interest," was still barely defined.

DEFINING THE FEDERAL INTEREST

When the District's home rule became a reality, the National Capital Planning Commission was no longer the primary planning agency for the District of Columbia. It was responsible only for the federal portion, charged with protecting the "federal interest" from local encroachment. Rather than enjoying the status as the dominant planning agency, it was challenged to coordinate its activities with the District government and other planning entities.

The term "federal interest" was first introduced in 1966, when President Lyndon B. Johnson abolished the National Capital Regional Planning Council. The president stated that the National Capital Planning Commission would retain responsibility for the federal interest in regional planning. When the US House of Representatives voted for the 1973 District of Columbia Self Government and Government Reorganization Act, it voiced concern about protecting the federal interest in the District of Columbia. The term remained largely undefined to many politicians, area residents, and almost everyone else for at least another decade, however.

During this new era, the Planning Commission pursued three major mandates. The first was to prepare and to adopt the federal elements of the comprehensive plan for the national capital and its environs. The second was to develop the annual Federal Capital Improvement Program that included federal land acquisition and construction proposals for the region. The third was to review and to comment on state, regional, and local government plans and programs and to approve federal and district development proposals in certain areas.

Uncertainty about the definition of federal interest led to a study by the General Accounting Office (GAO), which resulted in the report *Mission and Functions of the National Capital Planning Commission,* issued in June 1983. The GAO report found that few inside or outside of the Planning Commission could give a definitive statement about what constituted the federal interest. The Planning Commission's efforts that formerly had centered on District planning were now directed to comprehensive planning for the federal establishment and reviewing federal development projects. It was generally agreed that the Planning Commission would define the term as it prepared the federal elements of the comprehensive plan, conducted its review of federal agency projects, and made recommendations on planning to other planning authorities.

COMPREHENSIVE PLAN DEVELOPMENT

First issued in 1983, the federal elements of the comprehensive plan included a thorough discussion of federal goals related to the future capital, federal facilities, federal employment, diplomatic and international functions, preservation and historic features, open space and natural features, environment, energy resources, transportation, tourists and visitors, and intergovernmental cooperation and public participation. It addressed the District and the metropolitan area in majestic terms. The Planning Commission sought nothing short of "a capital worthy of a great nation" and sought to ensure that the needs of the federal government workforce would be addressed.

During the same period that the report was being prepared, the District government hired more staff to develop the District elements of the comprehensive plan and to handle local planning activities. The home rule legislation provided for the direct election of a mayor. Walter Washington, who was appointed mayor in 1967, was elected to the post in 1975. In 1979 he was succeeded by Marion S. Barry, who served until 1991. Upon his election, Mayor Barry became intimately involved in the planning process, because it was so closely linked to lifting the city's sagging fortunes.

Led by assistant city administrator for planning and development James O. Gibson, the District-led planning effort included an analysis of the local economy and challenges for the next two decades. The decline in population was recognized as a result not just of white flight but also of the departure of middle-class black families to the suburbs. In the 1983 planning report, the Barry administration outlined a number of priorities, issuing the comprehensive plan that same year. In these documents, the District plan-

ners expressed the hope of stabilizing the city's population at 633,000 people by 2000 by providing new housing opportunities and by improving the city's core. The planners, along with residents and visitors, observed the significant underuse of the downtown: "Even allowing for buildings that will remain, over one half of the total land area of downtown could be rebuilt by the year 2000." They voiced the need for a "living" downtown with an important residential component and envisioned that the next twenty years would witness the rebuilding of downtown that would attract people in the evenings and on the weekends.

The District elements of the comprehensive plan included land use, economic development, housing, environmental protection, transportation, public facilities, urban design, preservation and historic features, and human services. The plan acknowledged the large percentage of regional growth that occurred in the suburbs as compared with that in the District. It also noted the decline in the percentage of District-based federal government jobs as compared with the total employment in the area—from 40 percent

Vacant Lots in the Central City along Massachusetts Avenue NW. Photograph by Peter R. Penczer in 1950 to 23 percent in 1980. The 1983 comprehensive plan outlined significant challenges for the District and recommended approaches to address them. In 1984 the City Council adopted the District of Columbia comprehensive plan. Over the following years, the Barry administration committed itself to attracting new jobs, housing opportunities, and retail activity to the city.

INTERNATIONAL CENTER

The National Capital Planning Commission's work on preparing the federal elements of the comprehensive plan helped define its unique role in the city and region. The first element to be adopted by the Planning Commission focused on foreign missions and international organizations, which included the expanding World Bank and International Monetary Fund. Foreign missions were encouraged to remain in the District to enhance their ability to communicate with the State Department and other agencies.

An International Center sited on forty-seven acres at Van Ness had been originally conceived in the early 1960s to respond to the numerous requests from foreign governments to identify suitable sites in the District for their chanceries. Restrictive zoning and protracted negotiations with the District government often limited their choices. The International Center provided an enclave of chancery sites on federal government property, formerly the site of the National Bureau of Standards, in a secure and tranquil environment. Two parks and landscaping helped to blend the center into the surrounding community.

Homes for sixteen foreign missions—including embassies for Jordan, Kuwait, Qatar, Ghana, and Israel, among others—were established on nineteen separate lots. The International Center provided low-cost federal land for long-term lease to foreign governments. Countries wishing to locate their chanceries within the compound were encouraged to design their buildings in the indigenous architectural styles of their country. The State Department, the National Capital

Planning Commission, and the Commission of Fine Arts had final design approval. The Van Ness Center also became home to the campus of Intelsat, composed of member countries that owned and operated satellites, and a federal office building to provide services to the center's occupants.

Upgrading Downtown

The revival of the downtown hinged on bringing new uses to the former retail core, as it was generally assumed that the retail establishments that departed for the suburbs would not return. Rather than trying to reinstate traditional retail in the downtown, planners instead worked to transform the commercial core into an office enclave with smaller retail outlets. The logic for this approach lay in the nearly complete buildout of Downtown West, from 16th Street on the east to Rock Creek on the west and Dupont Circle on the north. Little additional expansion could occur in that area, and it was only a matter of time before office development would need to seek new ground to the east of 16th Street. The federal and the District governments cooperated in laying the groundwork for the eventual redevelopment of Downtown East.

Planners studied the qualities of Downtown West and concluded that another kind of development was necessary for the emerging Downtown East. The single-use character of Downtown West led to empty canyons of speculative office buildings in the evenings and during the weekends. Urban critics were disdainful of the uninspired architecture of row upon row of squat glass boxes. New development to the east would need to include a mixture of uses, such as housing, and to employ a different architectural language. Where historic buildings were swept away on the west, they would need to be preserved as development occurred in the east.

PENNSYLVANIA AVENUE DEVELOPMENT CORPORATION

The coordinated redevelopment of Pennsylvania Avenue between the Capitol and the White

House represented a major investment in upgrading the District's old commercial core. It also served as a spark that ignited new development projects in Downtown East. Plans for the rejuvenation of the blocks lining Pennsylvania Avenue dated back to 1962, when the Ad Hoc Committee on Federal Office Space recommended to President John F. Kennedy that the government "should formally undertake the redevelopment of Pennsylvania Avenue." President Kennedy appointed an Advisory Council on Pennsylvania Avenue headed by architect Nathaniel Owings. After Kennedy's death, with the support of President Johnson, the council continued its work and presented its plan to the president in 1964.

The council called for a new image for the avenue, one where the north side of the avenue would evolve into a Northern Triangle office district of government and private office buildings. Similar to the Federal Triangle south of Pennsylvania Avenue, the new buildings on the north side would conform to a new building setback fifty feet behind the existing line. Two large squares would be sited along the avenue. The first, National Square, would be located at 8th Street. The second, Grand Plaza, would be located behind the District Building between 14th and 15th streets. This grand-scale planning envisioned the demolition of three venerable historic buildings along the route—the Washington Hotel at 15th Street and Pennsylvania Avenue, the Willard Hotel at 14th Street and Pennsylvania Avenue, and the Old Post Office, except for its tower. Coincidentally, these recommendations were issued in the same year that the Joint Committee on Landmarks was established.

Although none of these early Pennsylvania Avenue plans were formally adopted, two major projects were built that conformed to the guidelines. C. F. Murphy and Associates designed the new building for the Federal Bureau of Investigation (FBI), which was constructed between 1967 and 1972. Set back seventy-five feet from the avenue, it was originally intended to house retail functions along the street front. Unfortunately, FBI concerns about security precluded this amenity. Another building—the Presidential

The Intersection of Pennsylvania Avenue and 11th Street NW before Revitalization. Copyright *Washington Post*, Reprinted with Permission of the DC Public Library

Building—at the northeast corner of 12th Street and Pennsylvania Avenue was constructed and housed offices of the District of Columbia government.

Despite these presidentially backed planning efforts and building projects, a growing tide of sentiment for the preservation of the city's landmarks challenged the assumptions of the 1964 plan. In 1965 Secretary of the Interior Stewart Udall designated the Pennsylvania Avenue National Historic Site under the authority of the 1935 Historic Sites Act. The boundaries of the National Historic Site included all of the Federal Triangle, the Treasury Department Building, all of Pennsylvania Avenue between 3rd and 15th streets, and a zigzag northern boundary along F and E streets to the north. The boundary included the important 8th Street vista between the National Archives and the old Patent Office Building. The designation was based on the historical importance of Pennsylvania Avenue—as the route of inaugural processions and as the site of important events and landmark buildings.

In 1969 the Pennsylvania Avenue Plan of the President's Temporary Commission on Pennsylvania Avenue responded to criticisms of the 1964 plan by downsizing National Square. The demolitions of the Old Post Office and other major landmarks were still among the recommendations. Two years later, in 1971, citizen activists coalesced around the threatened Old Post Office and formed the preservation organization Don't Tear It Down. Although it focused major efforts on protecting the Old Post Office, the organization also addressed the fate of the Willard Hotel, which had closed after the 1968 riots and was slated for demolition soon afterward along with other older buildings in the area.

In 1972 the US Congress established the Pennsylvania Avenue Development Corporation (PADC), which was directed to develop Pennsylvania Avenue in keeping with its historical and ceremonial role. The new authority for the revamping of Pennsylvania Avenue called for a cooperative venture between the federal government and private enterprise, where the federal presence would merge with other commercial, community, and residential uses.

After an initial survey of the area, PADC planners gave a dismal description of what they found. They described the area as a "drab and depressing place" and "one of the shabbiest and least interesting of the world's main thoroughfares." They did not observe the bustling commercial center or the stately public place that Pennsylvania Avenue should have been as a Main Street in the nation's capital and as L'Enfant had envisioned it more than 150 years earlier.

Two years later, PADC issued the Pennsylvania Avenue Development Plan, which expressed a desire for both residential uses on the avenue and a stronger preservation sensibility. Despite the historical designation of the Pennsylvania Avenue National Historic Site, the planners did not see a coherent historic district. The task was to create a comprehensive urban design by reclaiming and enhancing the monumental and grand urban vision of L'Enfant and "the vitality of the area when it was Washington's 'main street.'" To accomplish this, the planners aimed to develop new designs within the parameters of the height, scale, and quality determined by the older designs of the Washington and Willard hotels, the Evening Star Building, and the cluster of older commercial structures close to 7th Street. Small groups of historic buildings within the area would be demolished and their facades reused.

The first step in generating activity along the avenue was the improvement of the roadway configuration and the provision of new sidewalks and street furniture. By the first inauguration of President Ronald Reagan, these improvements were evident between 13th and 15th streets. By 1984 all of the sidewalks were completed, and seven hundred willow oak trees had been planted. By 1988 a new lighting system was provided. Another early step involved acquiring and offering for development the Willard Hotel and much of the block to the west of it.

The PADC staff oversaw the creation of major public spaces along the avenue. These parks were important design features in the upgraded thor-

New Design of Pennsylvania Avenue from the White House to the US Capitol. *Report of the President's Council on Pennsylvania Avenue,* 1964

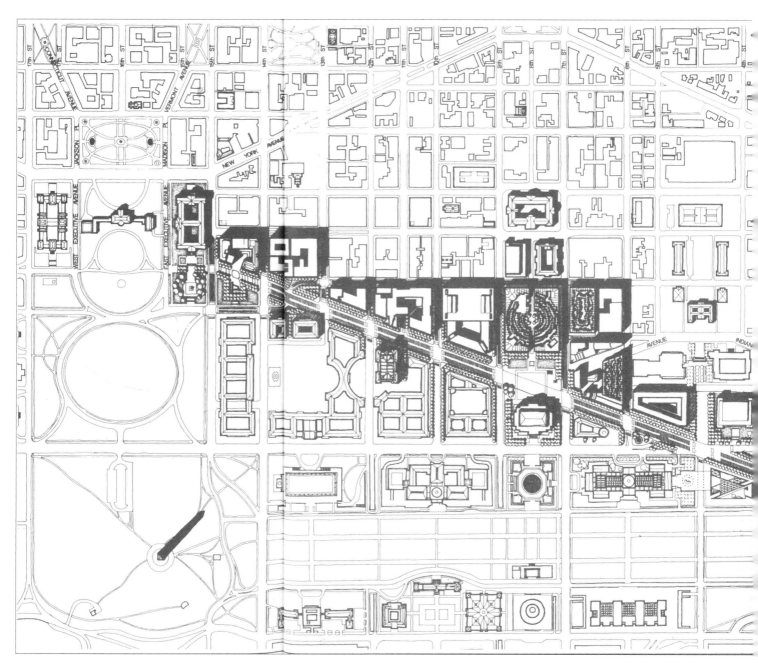

Pennsylvania Avenue.
Pennsylvania Avenue
Development Corporation,
*The Plan for Pennsylvania
Avenue,* 1974

oughfare and complemented the improved physical infrastructure. They included Western Plaza, designed by Robert Venturi and dedicated in 1980 as Freedom Plaza. Stripped down from an earlier design, which contained two ninety-foot-high pylons and scale models of the Capitol and the White House, Western Plaza bore the outlines of the L'Enfant plan on a flat marble surface. Another notable park was Pershing Park between 14th and 15th streets, designed by J. Paul Friedberg and dedicated in 1981. It was designed

to honor General John Joseph Pershing, the commander of the US forces during World War I, and to provide a quiet retreat. Pershing Park was an oasis sheltered from traffic noise by a fountain and pool, which is frozen for ice skating in the winter, and food service. The American Battle Monuments Commission designed and built the memorial.

To transform the avenue's building stock, Congress gave PADC a multimillion-dollar budget, the right of eminent domain over 110

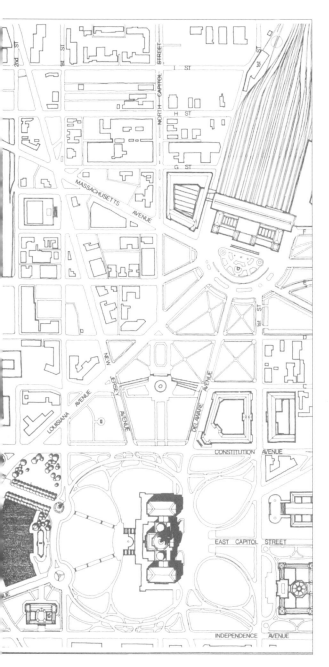

1001 Pennsylvania Avenue that incorporated several historic building facades and opened in 1986. In 1988 the Canadian Embassy designed by Canadian architect Arthur Erickson was completed. This was the first major building constructed at the eastern end of the avenue.

From PADC's beginning, the provision of housing was an essential ingredient in returning life to Pennsylvania Avenue. The ideal location for housing was east of the FBI Building, between 6th and 9th streets, close to the envisioned arts and entertainment activities. The original plan envisioned an "Italian hill town" at Market Square, a name that recalled the short street that cut through the site, the small triangular park (Market Square Park), and the old Center Market, which had once occupied the site. Additional apartment houses were planned for 6th and 7th streets and placed above floors devoted to office and retail uses. Specialty retail was targeted for 7th Street, a traditional arts-oriented artery, as well as for F Street, between 8th and 9th streets. Revisions to the plan retained the existing street configuration, reduced the housing to 1,200 units, and distributed it among eight blocks between 6th and 9th streets.

Located on blocks flanking 8th Street, Market Square emerged as a major mixed-use project that incorporated residential, office, and commercial uses. PADC determined the building's footprint around Market Square Park, a smaller park than initially conceived. As designed by Hartman-Cox, the two buildings are mirror images and reinforce the importance of the 8th Street axis. The buildings were designed to be compatible with the existing historic context and formed the backdrop for the new US Navy Memorial. Two terraced waterfall fountains framed a circular plaza that was designed by Conklin & Rossant and dedicated in 1987. This plaza, encircled with restaurants and cafés, demonstrated the power of memorials in urban settings to help create vibrant urban spaces. Market Square also delineated the southern boundary of what came to be known as the "Penn Quarter."

acres, and the ability to work with private developers to implement building projects. In 1984 the National Place mixed-use project, which included a Marriott Hotel, a renovated National Theater, and a Rouse-operated shopping mall, was completed, as were the office buildings at 1201 and 1301 Pennsylvania Avenue. By 1986 the restored and extended Willard Hotel and office-retail complex designed by Hardy Holzman Pfeiffer of New York City was completed. Hartman-Cox designed the large office building at

The US Navy Memorial at Pennsylvania Avenue and 8th Street NW. Photograph by Peter R. Penczer

View of a Revitalized Pennsylvania Avenue. Photograph by Peter R. Penczer

As the construction projects took shape and were completed during the 1980s, Pennsylvania Avenue was dramatically transformed. In 1994 the Urban Land Institute presented a special award to the Pennsylvania Avenue Plan and to PADC for having revamped "a downtrodden and unsightly segment of the nation's capital. It overcame the area's negative image and attracted private capital for renovation and new construction. The PADC has helped build the kind of Main Street that taxpayers can be proud of." By 1996, when the major projects were completed, Congress dissolved PADC. Afterward, the General Services Administration, the National Capital Planning Commission, and the National Park Service jointly administered the remaining projects of the Pennsylvania Avenue Plan. The National Park Service assumed responsibility for managing the parks, plazas, and other features of the congressionally created Pennsylvania Avenue National Historical Park. The General Services Administration was given responsibility for recommending any plan amendments to Congress that were deemed necessary and appropriate for further redevelopment and for developing the remaining, unsold parcels in accordance with the PADC Plan.

A LIVING DOWNTOWN

In 1981 the District government issued *A Living Downtown for Washington, DC;* this report outlined the various investments that would soon bring—or were already bringing—new life into the downtown. The investments included the new convention center, development projects approved at Metro Center and Gallery Place, the developing Pennsylvania Avenue corridor, and the arts center at the old Lansburgh department store building. A hotel/residential incentive district was established to spur hotel development near the convention center and to spin off new restaurants, shops, and offices. The living downtown concept also called for a higher quality of office building design than could be found in the average speculative office buildings in Downtown West. It envisioned residential development north and east of Mount Vernon Square and the establishment of arts, culture, and entertainment facilities.

The centerpiece of the living downtown concept was the new convention center that was planned as early as the 1970s to house large conventions and trade shows. This type of facility was available in many other cities and served as a tool for economic development and job creation. The District aimed to compete for those conventions beyond what could be accommodated in the city's largest hotels. The largely faceless building was completed in 1983 after designs by Welton Becket. Although the construction of the building resulted in the destruction of historic buildings and the closure of historic L'Enfant streets, it also attracted new hotels and visitor facilities to the area. In the end, its life span was only twenty years; it was superseded by a larger convention center north of Mount Vernon Square that opened in 2003.

REAL ESTATE BOOM OF THE 1980S

In 1986 an observer wrote, "Real estate development is proceeding here at a pace unmatched in any other city in the United States. During the first half of 1986, the metropolitan area absorbed 6 million square feet of new office space. That's

25 percent faster than in 1985." It was estimated that the Washington area added the equivalent of more than twenty-six city blocks of offices that year or the equivalent of the District's K Street office district in a single year.

New developments along Pennsylvania Avenue were symbolic of a larger real estate boom in the area in the 1980s. The national economy recovered from the effects of high interest rates and the severe recession of 1981–1982 with nine years of sustained growth. The office construction boom was fed through the provisions of the 1981 Economic Recovery Tax Act that provided for accelerated depreciation for new office construction. Many tax-sheltered investments in the form of syndications were created. These plentiful sources of capital investment caused a large number of speculative office buildings to be constructed throughout the nation, a phenomenon that led to overbuilding and ultimately the collapse of the office market in the late 1980s. During the office construction boom, a sizable number of new office buildings were constructed in the District's

downtown and in the spreading suburbs of the adjacent jurisdictions.

As development filled in underutilized sites in Downtown West and began to take root in Downtown East, the ubiquitous 1950s and 1960s International Style glass box was swept aside. Completed in 1976, the National Permanent Building at the northeast corner of 18th Street and Pennsylvania Avenue demonstrated that it was possible to design a modern office building and still provide depth and interest. Inspired by the Pompidou Center in Paris, it was designed by Hartman-Cox and constructed of a poured concrete frame with exposed tubes of utility ducts.

Interest in historical forms and details adapted to modern uses also fueled the turn away from postwar modernism. Postmodernism found a comfortable home in the District, which was filled with classically inspired buildings from various architectural periods. For much of the 1980s, postmodern office buildings were constructed throughout the District's central core and enlivened the urban scene.

Two major types of commercial buildings emerged during this period. The first consisted of new office construction using historic buildings as frontispieces, facades, or bases. The second consisted of entirely new office buildings that were designed with echoes of historic styles and features, including the base, shaft, and capital formula for building articulation. Both types represented a dramatic departure from commercial office construction of the preceding decades and were built in both the eastern and western sections of the commercial core.

The use of historic buildings as part of new construction included the Sumner Square project, which restored the historic Sumner School, reconstructed the adjacent Magruder School, and constructed new office spaces in the surrounding area. The historic Army Navy Club was expanded at the top to encompass additional stories, and its interior was completely rebuilt. The Bond Building received a similar addition to its crown. The building at 1100 New York Avenue incorporated the preserved Greyhound bus depot and new construction above and behind it. The corner Demonet Building along Connecticut Avenue was restored, and a new building was constructed to the rear. The Metropolitan Square project across 15th Street from the Treasury Department incorporated three buildings—the Metropolitan Bank, the Keith-Albee Theater, and the interior of the Old Ebbitt Grill. The much-altered Rhodes Tavern, the city's oldest tavern and first city hall, was a casualty of the project. The Warner Theater project provided for a renovated theater, the addition of three floors at the top, and a new building to the side.

The Red Lion Row development at 2000 Pennsylvania Avenue gave facade projects a bad name when leftover portions of the historic buildings were slapped up against a particularly incompatible, bland glass box. Other facade projects, however, were more successful. Examples include Georgetown Park, an upscale shopping center at the southwest corner of Wisconsin Avenue and M Street, and the Penn Theater project on Capitol Hill, which incorporated the facade of a historic theater into a new building. The brick row-house facade project at 1818 N Street NW and the Tudor facade project at 1915 I Street NW were notable examples of this unique approach to melding preservation and new construction.

Notable postmodern-style office buildings included the 1986 Presidential Plaza, designed by Keyes Condon Florance in an art deco–streamline moderne style; the 1987 Republic Place, designed by Keyes Condon Florance with colorful brick bond; the 1984 complex for *U.S. News & World Report,* designed by Skidmore, Owings and Merrill; and the three luxury hotels at the intersection of 24th and M streets. Skidmore, Owings and Merrill designed the 1983 Inter-American Development Bank at 13th and New York Avenue, a massive curving building in the Washington postmodern style.

An anomaly was the Tech World Building project south of Mount Vernon Square, which unfortunately closed 8th Street; it provided hotel, office, and retail space in twin glass blocks and a three-story bridge over 8th Street and overwhelmed the 1903 Beaux-Arts gem of the Carnegie Library Building. Although the developer insisted that the street closure and bridge were necessary to ensure the success of the facility that would display and sell technology goods, the project never fulfilled its aesthetic or economic goals.

NEW MUSEUMS, MONUMENTS, AND MEMORIALS ON THE MALL

In anticipation of the bicentennial, the National Park Service completed a ten-year planning process with the firm of Skidmore, Owings and Merrill for the Mall. The Mall master plan revisited and set aside many of the McMillan Plan proposals. The plan resulted in the removal of Adams and Madison drives, converting them to walkways, and the establishment of Constitution Gardens, which replaced many temporary buildings.

New museums and memorials followed the redesign of the Mall. One prime example of this

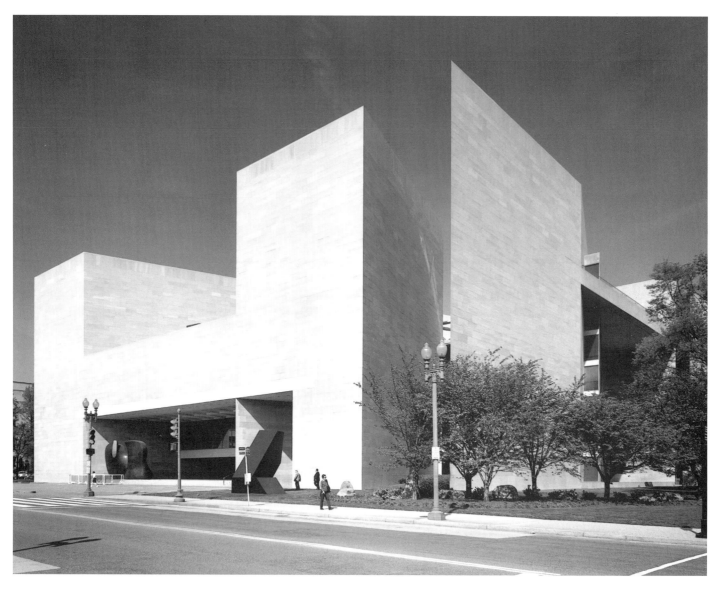

East Building of the National Gallery of Art. Photograph by Peter R. Penczer

period was the East Building of the National Gallery of Art. Completed in 1978 after designs by I. M. Pei, it was an immediate architectural landmark, acclaimed as one of the world's most notable buildings. In a city draped in classical language, the East Building was unapologetically modern, fashioned of interlocking trapezoid and diamond shapes around an immense atrium. Its diamond-shaped glass skylight illuminating an underground visitor center served as the model for Pei's famous addition to the Louvre in Paris.

The design of the Vietnam Veterans Memorial was one of the most publicized design projects of its time. Initiated by the Vietnam Veterans Memorial Fund (VVMF), the memorial was

intended to commemorate a traumatic conflict that remained fresh in the memories of veterans, their families, and the nation. In 1981 the VVMF held a competition that resulted in the selection of the design of Maya Lin, a Yale University architecture student. Although not as graphically sophisticated as many of the other submissions, Lin's design represented the triumph of a noble idea. The two polished black granite walls that intersected in a wide V shape carried in chronological order the names of all 57,000 who died or were missing in action. The walls were set into the earth, with their tops level with the ground.

Because the memorial design was unlike the traditional and classical memorials that blan-

Vietnam Veterans Memorial. Photograph by Paul Jutton, National Capital Planning Commission

keted the city, reaction to it was divided. Some found the design to be powerful, dignified, and exemplary of the trend toward a landscape approach to memorialization. Others referred to it as a "black hole" and a cavelike "black gash of shame and sorrow" and found personal fault with the designer, who was of Asian ancestry. However, the major review bodies supported the design, and the project moved forward. In 1982 ground was broken, and the memorial was dedicated later that year. To respond to the needs of those who desired traditional symbols, a flagstaff and a statue of servicemen were added to the memorial site. A statue paying tribute to the women who served was added as a stand-alone memorial in 1993. A plaque commemorating veterans who died after the war due to war-related causes, but who were not eligible for inscription on the memorial wall, was added in 2004. Today, the Vietnam Veterans Memorial is one of the most emotionally charged memorials in the city. Every Veterans Day, Vietnam veterans travel from throughout the country to pay their respects to their former comrades at the beloved "Wall." The memorial design represents a major episode in the chain of controversies that accompanied memorial design and construction in the capital city.

The critical success of the Vietnam Veterans Memorial and the "modern impulse to exhaustively memorialize people and events" sparked plans to establish other monuments and memorials. The large number of proposed projects led to the passage of the Commemorative Works Act of 1986 that sought to rationalize the process for the many proposed memorials and museums that could crowd the Mall. The Commemorative Works Act set guidelines for new commemorative works, including the requirements that the work receive congressional authorization and that there be a minimum interval of twenty-five years after a person's death or the event before a work could be authorized. The act also established the National Capital Memorial Commission (renamed the National Capital Memorial Advisory Commission in 2003) to advise on future commemorative works to stop the proliferation of military memorials. It limited them to wars or branches of the armed services. The law also established two areas: Area I, essentially the Mall, the White House area, and the Federal Triangle; and Area II, the rest of the city. Area I was reserved for commemorative works of "preeminent and lasting significance" and Area II for works of "lasting historical significance."

The legislation provided a process for establishing a memorial on federal land in the national capital. That process begins with a sponsor's request to the National Capital Memorial Commission to review the concept with the understanding that the memorial will be erected at no cost to the federal government. The memorial sponsor then seeks a member of Congress willing to introduce a bill authorizing the memorial that conforms to the provisions of the Commemorative Works Act. Once Congress passes the bill, it goes to the president for signature. The memorial sponsor organizes the entity that will establish the memorial and plans for the fundraising efforts. The selected design is presented to the National Park Service or the General Services Administration, and if it is approved, it is submitted to the National Capital Planning Commission, the Commission of Fine Arts, and the state historic preservation officer for concurrence. When the memorial is completed, it is dedicated and transferred to the National Park Service or the General Services Administration for management.

Other Development Projects

The construction boom that spread over the downtown and the Mall covered many other parts of the District as well. The placement of Metro stops throughout the downtown core provided the impetus for new development and new life for the central city. So, too, did Metro stops elsewhere in the District of Columbia. In the late twentieth century, Metro stops served a role similar to that of Pierre L'Enfant's late eighteenth-century nodes of development. L'Enfant also had placed public buildings and parks at strategic locations to encourage growth, which he hoped would eventually merge and fill in the living city.

The Southeast Federal Center, also called the Washington Navy Yard Annex, was one of the dense developments planned around a Metro stop. The plan called for federal office and commercial uses and adaptive use of historic structures, all commercial spaces to be next to the Metro stop, and a planned waterfront zone. Although intended as an employment center for thousands of federal employees, plans for this area lagged until the late 1990s, when new development finally began to occur nearby.

The construction of the Frank D. Reeves Center by the District as a municipal office building was envisioned as a major investment in the area scarred most by the 1968 riots. In 1986 the Reeves Center was opened at 2000 14th Street NW, on

The Frank D. Reeves
Center at the Corner of U
Street and 14th Street NW.
Photograph by Peter R.
Penczer

the corner of 14th and U streets, at the heart of the historic African American commercial center. Paul Devrouax, who had experienced the vitality of the area as a boy, designed the eight-story office building. The Reeves Center was named for the first black Democratic Party committeeman and housed more than a thousand District government workers. Soon after the completion of the Reeves Center, the opening of the Metro stop at 13th and U streets reinforced the investment and led to the transformation of U Street and the entire Shaw neighborhood.

GEORGETOWN WATERFRONT

Georgetown's waterfront had fallen into disrepair after the departure of industrial businesses that left an abandoned cement plant, debris, and parking lots behind. The construction of the Whitehurst Freeway in 1949 further contributed to the "backwater" character of the waterfront. The proposed Three Sisters Bridge and Freeway project would have replaced the Whitehurst Freeway with a new massive freeway. In 1964 the waterfront was considered for an urban renewal designation, but given the city's experience with the southwest quadrant, this approach was rejected. In 1967 the waterfront was designated a National Historic Landmark. Starting in the early 1970s, the area became filled with rehabilitated and new commercial and residential buildings, including Canal Square, the Foundry, and the Papermill project.

As the development of Georgetown accelerated during the 1970s and 1980s, developers sought to exploit its appeal to the affluent and to young people from throughout the region. As new and converted buildings filled in M and K streets, the fate of the Georgetown waterfront

Key Bridge and the Whitehurst Freeway in Georgetown. Photograph by Peter R. Penczer

after abandonment of the Three Sisters Bridge and Freeway project was at stake. The Commission of Fine Arts wanted the waterfront to be devoted to park uses, to become a worthy component of a green necklace along the Potomac River shoreline, and so the commission urged the secretary of the interior to acquire the last remaining privately held tract at an estimated cost of $25 million. However, no federal or District funds were available for the purchase of this property, considered in 1980 to be "one of the

most valuable pieces of property in the country."

Instead, the various review bodies hammered out an agreement for development of the Washington Harbour complex, a matter-of-right, mixed-use project that included a publicly accessible boardwalk along the riverfront. The architect Arthur Cotton Moore designed two curving buildings surrounding an elliptical plan and fountain. Considered the best solution at the time, the project, completed in 1987, provided a "sense of place" in the former industrial wasteland and attracted visitors to an area of the waterfront that had long been ignored. In the same year, the District agreed to transfer the ten acres that had been acquired for the freeway to the National Park Service for a park, although this did not occur until 1999.

Historic Preservation in the District of Columbia

The loss of older commercial and residential buildings in the District and, in particular, the threatened demolition of major landmarks along Pennsylvania Avenue led to the evolution of local historic preservation protections. So, too, did passage of the National Historic Preservation Act in 1966. In 1964 the Joint Committee on Landmarks had been established as a cooperative effort of the National Capital Planning Commission, the Commission of Fine Arts, and the District of Columbia government. Its first job was to conduct studies of historic buildings in the District and to compile an inventory of potential landmarks.

Spurred by the passage of the 1966 National Historic Preservation Act, Mayor Walter Washington designated the deputy mayor as the state historic preservation officer and the Joint Committee on Landmarks as the professional state review board to meet the act's requirements. Still, other than nominating historic properties to the newly expanded National Register of Historic Places, there were no effective local protections. Several agencies and organizations cooperated in passing DC Regulation 73-25 in 1975, which called for a delay in demolition and a period of negotiation to determine the fate of threatened buildings. This was an interim measure until 1978 and the passage of the Historic District and Historic Landmark Protection Act.

Also known as DC Law 2-144, the 1978 ordinance strengthened the legal protection for historic properties by establishing the DC Inventory of Historic Sites, which built upon the 1964 inventory. As implemented, the Historic Preservation Review Board, which replaced the Joint Committee on Landmarks, made decisions about local designations of landmarks and historic districts. The board served as the state review board in nominating properties for listing in the National Register. The board also made decisions on requests for demolitions, alterations, additions, subdivisions, and new construction on landmarks and contributing buildings within historic districts. DC Law 2-144 also provided for the mayor's agent to determine if "special merit" existed to warrant demolition of historic resources, which has proven to be a strict standard but, at the same time, provided needed flexibility for important modern projects.

Because Georgetown was designated as a historic district in 1950 before the establishment of the local historic preservation program and was placed under the administration of the Commission of Fine Arts, the commission retained its regulatory role for this community. The staffing of the Historic Preservation Review Board was transferred from the National Capital Planning Commission to the District government in 1983.

To counter threats of incompatible development and inspired by legal protection from DC Law 2-144 and the new tools that the National

Washington Harbour on the Georgetown Waterfront. Photograph by Peter R. Penczer

Union Station Following its Restoration. Photograph by Peter R. Penczer

Historic Preservation Act offered, neighborhood activists organized and nominated historic landmarks and districts for local designation. Citizens living in older neighborhoods sought and received local historical designation for neighborhoods, including Capitol Hill, a large residential historic district in the city that consisted of approximately 5,000 buildings. Other districts included Dupont Circle, Strivers' Section, Logan Circle, Massachusetts Avenue between Dupont Circle and Rock Creek Park, Uniontown in Anacostia, 16th Street, Kalorama Triangle, Mount Pleasant, LeDroit Park, Foggy Bottom, and Sheridan-Kalorama. In addition to historic districts, numerous individual buildings and landscapes were designated as historic landmarks. In 1977 the demolition of Dunbar High School, the city's famed academic black high school, galvanized the African American community to support preservation.

The historical studies and surveys conducted to justify these designations absorbed many of the new historical perspectives of the preservationists. These designations were driven by a desire to expand the scope of what was considered "historic" and to address communities that needed protection and economic revitalization. Preservationists not only were inspired by high-style architecture and the achievements of the founding fathers, but they also were interested in vernacular building types, twentieth-century architectural styles, and the impact of ethnic and cultural groups, especially African Americans, on the growth and development of the city.

THE HISTORIC PRESERVATION TAX INCENTIVES

With widespread historical designations occurring, the rehabilitation of historic buildings for commercial purposes escalated after passage of the Economic Recovery Tax Act of 1981, which provided a 25 percent historic preservation tax credit. This tax credit changed the attitude of developers and, indeed, that of city officials toward preserving older commercial buildings. Even though the credit was reduced to 20 percent in 1986, it remained a powerful force in transforming formerly underused commercial buildings.

The rehabilitation of Union Station was a key example of the use of the federal tax credits. The Union Station Redevelopment Act of 1981 sought to remove the failed National Visitors Center and to replace the building with a functional railroad station and commercial facilities sufficient to support the complex. The resulting project housed mixed uses, including revitalized station facilities, making it a transportation hub for trains (Amtrak, Metro, and regional commuter rail), automobile parking, and buses. Union Station was restored to its original and glorious Daniel Burnham design, and the mixed-use approach was a decided success.

Federal historic preservation tax credits were attractive to many developers, even though rehabilitation standards had to be met before credits could be claimed. Some developers opted not to preserve historic buildings according to the secretary of the interior's standards for rehabilitation, which set out what treatments were acceptable, and sought to preserve only the facades of historic buildings because the financial return was greater. To some degree, this approach followed the precedents used for the upgrading of Pennsylvania Avenue. Facade projects became particularly desirable when the historic buildings were low rise and the zoning called for much higher and denser development.

New Immigration Shapes the City and Region

Upheavals, conflict, and strife around the world during the 1970s and 1980s reverberated in the city and surrounding area by the influx of refugees. The end of the Vietnam War, the Central American civil wars, and the Soviet invasion of Afghanistan were particularly important in the changing population demographics of the area. So, too, was the evolution of immigration legislation that lifted earlier limitations on certain groups.

Before 1965 immigration laws gave preference to Western Europeans. In 1965 the Immigration and Naturalization Act abolished national origin quotas and instead gave preference to immigrants with skills that were needed in the United States, including medical and scientific skills. The 1965 law also sought to reunite families. These changes allowed for a large increase in the number of Asians and Hispanics entering the United States. Within a few years, the effects became visible. Changes to the nation's immigration laws were reflected in the demographics of the region.

After the fall of Saigon in April 1975 and the passage of the Indochina Migration and Refugee Assistance Act of 1975, hundreds of thousands of Vietnamese refugees came to the United States. Although many Vietnamese immigrants settled in California, Texas, and Louisiana, they also came to Washington, DC, which gave them a chance to be politically active on behalf of their homeland. In Arlington, Virginia, they carved out an economic niche for their community. Metro construction had left many commercial buildings abandoned, particularly in Clarendon. Vietnamese families purchased or rented the deteriorated buildings and established stores and

Friendship Arch across H Street in Chinatown, between 6th and 7th Streets NW. Photograph by Paul Jutton, National Capital Planning Commission

other enterprises that served the refugee community. The concentration of Vietnamese shops and restaurants for much of the period of Metro construction led to its informal designation as "Little Saigon." By 1982, when the Clarendon Metro stop opened, rising real estate values caused the community to move to the shopping center known as Eden Center in Falls Church. Later waves of Southeast Asians settled in Mount Pleasant and Adams Morgan.

During the 1980s, thousands of Latinos settled in Mount Pleasant and Adams Morgan, which remained the barrio for the Latino community. They included people from El Salvador and Guatemala, who were escaping economic hardship and political turmoil in their home countries. A vibrant strip of stores and restaurants developed in the area to serve this community. Over time, many Latinos also moved to the suburbs and established bakeries, restaurants, and shops. The first wave of Latin Americans was followed by others from Peru, Bolivia, Nicaragua, and Mexico.

Caribbean immigrants settled along 16th Street and Georgia Avenue and in Silver Spring, Takoma Park, and Langley Park. Many set up small markets, barbershops, and restaurants. Harsh conditions in Somalia, Ethiopia, Nigeria, Ghana, and Eritrea brought new African immigrants to the District. Thousands of Koreans settled in the area and became visible proprietors of convenience stores, gas stations, grocery stores, shoe repair shops, dry cleaners, and tailor shops. A large Korean community formed in Annandale, Virginia, and was visible through the many Korean restaurants, churches, and stores.

Suburban Growth and Self-Sufficiency

The essential phenomenon of suburban growth in the period between 1970 and 1980 was the dramatic influx of population, not only from the District but also from other parts of the country and the world. Between 1970 and 1980, Fairfax County, Virginia, grew from 454,275 to 596,901, a 31 percent increase. A decade later, in 1990, its population of 818,584 exceeded that of the District of Columbia, which stood at 606,900. This population growth necessitated development of subdivisions for housing, office parks for businesses, and shopping centers for stores.

Although the suburban counties continued to accommodate development plans on older commercial crossroads or formerly rural lands, the Council of Governments issued the *Metropolitan Growth Policy Statement* in 1977. The policy statement acknowledged that the radial corridors configuration of NCPC's 1961 Year 2000 Policies Plan was no longer attainable in some parts of the metropolitan area because development had already occurred along the prospective wedges of open space or low-density development. It noted the impact of growth on the region's air, water, land, and energy resources and issued the policy goal promoting growth in specified high-density growth centers that included the metropolitan center, transit centers, outer suburban centers, and rural centers. In the process, growth would be concentrated in dispersed development centers as opposed to uncontrolled growth. The policy direction of growth centers presaged the emergence of major suburban office centers that characterized growth in the metropolitan region for the remainder of the twentieth century.

SUBURBAN COMMUNITIES AS INDEPENDENT ENTITIES

During the late 1970s and through much of the 1980s, the rapidly urbanizing counties that surrounded the District of Columbia voiced a desire to separate themselves from the image of the central city. Most counties viewed themselves not as satellites of the capital city but as mature urban entities with separate economies and independent means. Indeed, they had satellite communities of their own. This growing desire for separation was based on a wish not only to disassociate themselves from urban ills of the central city but also to underscore their superior economic base within their own boundaries.

By the 1970s, Fairfax County saw itself as a leader in defining an independent regional economy. In the early 1980s, Charles Gulledge, chairman of the Fairfax County Economic Development Authority, stated, "We do not want to be the bedroom community of Washington. Our objective was to control the quality of growth, to attract corporate headquarters and high technology companies . . . and also to attract the supporting infrastructure—small businesses, shopping centers, and the like."

The major example of this strategy occurred in the 1980s, when Mobil Corporation moved its corporate headquarters to Fairfax County. During the economic expansion that followed the recession of 1981–1982, the county gained high-tech companies that undertook operations research, electronic research, computer programming and data processing, biological research, and telecommunications services. These industries—represented by firms such as MCI, Flow General, Microdyne, Telenet, and the regional headquarters of AT&T—established the Washington area as one of the most important high-technology centers in the country, behind Boston, San Francisco, and Los Angeles.

The impact of federal government procurement was profound in the establishment of sectors of new industries. The military presence in Northern Virginia led to the evolution of the area for high-tech, security, and eventually Internet businesses. The presence of the National Institutes of Health, the Food and Drug Administration, and the Department of Agriculture in the Maryland suburbs spawned the biomedical industry there.

Companies developed as federal contractors clustered around the new town of Reston and the old community of Herndon. New toll roads that paralleled the Dulles Access Road also attracted a linear cluster of some of the nation's most important education think tanks. These developments contributed to the success of western Fairfax County in the 1990s as it became one of the hubs of the Internet revolution.

Aside from economic developments, Fairfax County developed its own cultural and recreational offerings, the George Mason University's Center for the Arts and the Patriot Center.

The Historic Town of Herndon, Virginia. Photograph by Peter R. Penczer

Although a federal government investment, Wolf Trap National Park for the Performing Arts, a unit of the National Park System, served county residents. Residents no longer had to travel into the District to enjoy world-class musical performances and sporting events. George Mason University, along with branches of other colleges and universities within the county's boundaries, offered a range of educational and cultural offerings.

Not all jurisdictions viewed themselves in such an independent manner. Montgomery County, Maryland, saw itself as inextricably tied to the District, because the latter was the economic and cultural center of the region. The health of the District influenced the health of the county. Montgomery County was the exception, however; other counties voiced independent leanings, although federal government spending remained a major component in their economies.

PIERCING THE SUBURBAN SKYLINE

The rise of suburban urban centers became a problem for planning officials, especially when those centers became visually intrusive on the views from the city's monumental core. In 1978 the Department of the Interior sued Arlington

County over the proposed rezoning for what became the USA Today towers of the Gannett publishing company at Rosslyn Circle, the western terminus of the Key Bridge from Georgetown. The proposed towers rose above the tree line and destroyed the heavily wooded character of the Arlington shore of the Potomac River. The planned development caused visual intrusions on the Iwo Jima Memorial, Arlington National Cemetery, and the east-west axis of the Mall across the Potomac River. At the time, the tallest building in Rosslyn was only fifteen stories high. The development proposal called for a group of buildings ranging from twenty-two to twenty-nine stories in height, almost twice that of most buildings in Rosslyn. The National Capital Planning Commission, the Department of the Interior, and others viewed the rezoning request as a serious threat to the horizontal nature of the city. Although the suit was not successful and did not stop the projects from being constructed, agreement was reached with Arlington County officials that they would protect the vista from the Mall from further encroachment by high-rise buildings to the south of the subject buildings. As the high rises were completed, one critic referred to Rosslyn as "Houston-on-the-Potomac."

In the 1970s and 1980s, the Planning Commission repeatedly complained about creeping building heights along the Jefferson Davis Highway near National Airport. Using its mandate to review area plans for their impact on the federal interest, the National Capital Planning Commission sought to gain a stronger hand to address this problem. Issued in 1980, the parks, open space, and natural features element of the comprehensive plan outlined the federal interest in the Topographic Bowl, the escarpment of hills surrounding the L'Enfant City that swept over the Florida Avenue escarpment, Anacostia Hills, Arlington Hills, and the Potomac Palisades and gorge.

Review of the area within the Topographic Bowl was not enough to address visual intrusions farther out, however. During the extension of the Metro into the suburban jurisdictions, Arlington County made plans for development that would occur around Metro stops along the Ballston Metro corridor. Arlington County was especially insistent on high-density development to attract new residents and office buildings, to increase tax revenues, and to pay for its financial contributions to the Metro system. Arlington County provided plans for the Ballston Metro stop that called for buildings as high as twenty-four stories and approved the Olmstead Building project at the Clarendon Metro stop. Although planners always understood that Metro stops would become the focus for mixed-use development, not everyone was prepared for the massive scale of this development in various jurisdictions.

To measure the magnitude of the threatened intrusion, the National Capital Planning Commission developed the tool known as the "Mall vista cone." From the US Capitol terrace, the Mall vista was described as a conelike view extending into Arlington County—"first as a tree-covered area, close in the background and then as a mixture of trees and buildings in the horizon." The tool called for a Mall vista cone of an eight-degree angle for Arlington County, where close-in areas should be kept low in scale and areas farther out could have gradually higher buildings.

By 1981 the Planning Commission issued the federal environment element of the comprehensive plan that covered a wide swath of land from Fort Meade to Prince William Forest. In 1982 the Planning Commission adopted the open space and natural features element of the comprehensive plan, which called for retention of major features of the Potomac and Anacostia rivers and maintenance of the natural and undeveloped portions of the shoreline. Manassas National Battlefield Park was augmented in 1982 and 1988 with two boundary expansions to protect the battlefield land from high-density mixed-use development favored by Prince William County.

REGIONAL SHOPPING CENTERS

During much of the first half of the twentieth century, retail activities had been concentrated in the central city with branches in the emerging suburbs. As the suburbs developed substantial populations, their shopping centers gained in scale and purchasing power. They began to attract shoppers from larger geographic areas, including central city residents who could no longer count on the lagging offerings of the historic retail corridors where convenient parking was a major consideration.

Tysons Corner in Fairfax County was the region's preeminent example of a power retail center. This role was enhanced by its location along the Capitol Beltway at the conjunction with several other major thoroughfares. It opened to the public in 1968 as one of the first fully enclosed, climate-controlled shopping centers in the region. In its initial form, Tysons Corner opened on one level and included 3 anchor stores, 2 movie theaters, and 100 specialty stores.

In 1988 it was expanded to include 5 department stores and more than 250 stores and restaurants spread over 2 levels. As it evolved, Tysons Corner became a superregional mall and drew customers from a multistate area.

The construction and expansion of Tysons Corner had a profound effect on the surrounding area. Where the immediate area had once been covered with farms, rural stores, and used car lots, the Tysons Corner of the last quarter of the twentieth century became a destination unto itself—the quintessential "edge city." The locale became prime real estate and attracted hotels, office buildings, and apartment complexes, as well as the companion mall Tysons Galleria, a hub of upscale shopping, smaller satellite malls, and "big box" retail stores.

PRESERVATION AND CONSERVATION IN THE SUBURBS

No matter how growth-driven the suburban counties were, all recognized the impact of

The Rosslyn, Virginia Skyline as Viewed from the Memorial Bridge. Photograph by Peter R. Penczer growth on a wide range of community values, including the need for "place" and identity. In 1980 Montgomery County, Maryland, prepared a plan for the preservation of agricultural and rural open spaces. The plan called for both the preservation of farmland and the continuation of farming as an economically viable industry. Agricultural reserves were designated, and a range of tools were used, including the state's agricultural land preservation program, rural clustering, transfer of development rights, and the creation of a County Development Rights Bank.

The plan was farsighted in viewing farmland and rural open space preservation as serving an important public purpose. The importance of agricultural and open space protection lay not just in the survival of the agricultural economy; these spaces also contributed to the protection of air and water resources and natural habitats. They served as the green lung of the county and a sanctuary from an often hectic urban life. Over time, the county's tools worked. In 1990 91,000 acres of farmland were protected.

Montgomery County also operated a Moderately Priced Dwelling Unit Program that gave density bonuses and design flexibility to developers to provide home ownership and rental opportunities to families with moderate incomes. The efforts to view growth within a larger context of an array of community needs set the county apart from many of its neighboring jurisdictions. Both Frederick and Prince George's counties in Maryland, for example, studied the status of farms and rural open space, but neither developed a program comparable to the Montgomery County program to make land preservation a viable option.

In the early 1970s, the city of Alexandria could have gone the way of Arlington County. Alexandria planners and politicians planned for high-rise construction along its historic waterfront. In 1973 the federal government sued the city of Alexandria over the ownership of the shoreline between the Pepco generating plant, north of Old Town, and the southern tip of Old Town.

The suit was based on the federal government's claim to most of the land along the waterfront, because the Potomac River shoreline in Virginia that existed in 1791 had been designated as the District's western border. By the 1970s, because of land reclamation, that original shoreline was well within Alexandria's waterfront boundary.

In 1979 the city of Alexandria and the National Park Service agreed to joint planning and public participation on land uses and management of the waterfront as a means of settling the suit. The 1981 Joint Land Use Plan for the Alexandria Waterfront provided for the protection of open space, low-scale development along the waterfront, landscaping, and public access to the waterfront amenities. The joint federal and local effort prevented the skyline-piercing projects that overtook the development of Rosslyn close to the Potomac River shoreline as well as Crystal City farther inland.

This is not to say that Alexandria did not care about historic preservation; it had created the Old and Historic Alexandria District in 1946. The historic district was established to better regulate buildings along Washington Street, the route of the George Washington Memorial Parkway as it passed through the city. By the 1970s, the Old and Historic Alexandria District encompassed four thousand buildings, many dating from the eighteenth century.

By the 1970s and 1980s, all of the suburban jurisdictions had established local preservation programs that involved the identification of historic buildings, designation, and oversight of alterations and additions. The 1980s amendments to the National Historic Preservation Act provided impetus for local government programs through the recognition of Certified Local Governments and the provision of funding for the activities of certified local government preservation programs.

The federal historic preservation tax incentives that had spurred the reuse of so many historic buildings in the District of Columbia proved attractive to suburban property owners as well. The federal tax credits were complemented by state and local incentives, which encouraged property owners to rehabilitate and reuse historic buildings. Although local government programs provided for local designation that entailed local regulation, they also nominated historic properties to the National Register of Historic Places. National Register status provided eligibility for federal grants and tax incentives and consideration in federally funded and sponsored activities. By this time, historic preservation was such an accepted activity of local government that most included a historic preservation element in their comprehensive plans.

THE NEW URBAN ENVIRONMENT

As development spread over formerly rural areas in the metropolitan region, observers questioned the resulting quality of life. Before World War II, area residents had been tied together by railroads and thoroughfares that ran through the capital city. They identified with the District and its role as the national capital city. By the 1970s, however, the majority of area residents lived outside of the District. Indeed, many never needed to see or travel through it. Suburban lives were conducted along the Capital Beltway, close to major interchanges and mixing bowls, and in "condo canyons" that lined these superhighways.

How the federal government did its work was a major factor in the growing disassociation of suburban communities from the central city. In the 1980s, the number of federal employees in the Washington, DC, area actually declined, albeit slightly. In 1980 the total number of employees stood at 360,120. Ten years later, in 1990, the total was 353,175, even though the federal government's budget had increased from one year to the next. What was occurring was the increased outsourcing of federal functions to private firms, sometimes referred to as "Beltway Bandits." Thus, the federal government's work was becoming invisible, and the workers employed by these firms did not have particular loyalties to a federal agency and did not work in a building owned or leased by the federal government. Even if the funding for private-sector jobs came from the federal government, an increasing number of Washington, DC, area residents viewed themselves as private-sector employees. This context prompted the statements by jurisdictions like Fairfax County that they were independent of the central city.

What kind of urban environment did outsourcing practices create? Employees of private firms (funded with federal government contracts) lived in new housing in the suburbs, traveled on the Capital Beltway or major interstate highways to an office park for their jobs, sent their children to suburban schools, and shopped at increasingly large malls. Their geographic identities shifted from the District to suburban locations, such as Reston, Fairfax City, Alexandria, and Rockville.

The planning challenge for the remainder of the century and the next was to increase regional cooperation and to raise the urban planning standards beyond what was common practice in other metropolitan areas across the country. But the suburban jurisdictions rarely paused to acknowledge the roots of their affluent lives. In times of recession, local governments sought ways to lift their economies. In boom times, they were too busy dealing with seemingly runaway growth. Increasingly, the national capital city resembled a small and precious jewel set in an ever-enlarging metropolitan ring. ✯

THE GLOBAL CAPITAL CITY 1991-PRESENT

14

A Golden Era?

For much of the nation, the late 1990s was a period of unprecedented affluence. The decade started with a recession that gave way to recovery and then an almost giddy period of roaring growth and seemingly overnight fortunes. The challenge for urban areas was to manage the growth that spilled into the central cities and older suburbs and fueled enormous sprawl in the exurbs. For the Washington area, the rising tide of development lifted the central city and transformed it into a desirable place for living, working, shopping, and playing. Development around Metro stops blossomed. At the metropolitan edges, planners sought to protect formerly rural areas from spreading subdivisions and shopping strips and used public and private tools for land protection.

In the Washington area in the early 1990s, the real estate boom of the 1980s had become a bust. The severe economic downturn made construction cranes in the District's downtown almost an endangered species. New office buildings sat vacant and silent. Despite these troubled times for the city and the region, however, planners still viewed with pride their accomplishments in upgrading the central city and in extending the development infrastructure beyond its borders.

The national economy turned upward in 1993 and remained strong for the remainder of the decade before encountering another recession at the decade's end. Unlike the rest of the country, however, the Washington, DC, area was cushioned from the economic downturn. The local economy flourished and remained strong; federal government budgets and federal outsourcing kept it humming. For example, between 1990 and 2000, federal procurement rose from $12.9 billion to $28.2 billion. A beneficiary of many of these contracts, the Washington area's economy emerged as the strongest in the United States. This built-in protection against recession attracted new people, and that in turn required the District and surrounding counties to build accommodations to house them. Such continued growth challenged each of the jurisdictions and the region as a whole to accommodate the increased demand on the planning infrastructure.

The early part of this period also was marked by the dissolution of the Soviet Union and the end of the Cold War. Out of the collapse of the Soviet period came new realities. The United States remained the only world superpower. Nations held together by oppression now dissolved into conflict. Against this changed international scene, Washington, DC, clearly emerged as a global capital. Its major landmarks became unifying symbols for people in the throes of civil war and international confrontations.

Aided by the Internet revolution during the second half of the 1990s, vast fortunes were created, and the appetite for luxury living expanded correspondingly. In the District's reemerging Downtown East, new buildings filled empty spaces. In the downtown, plans were made for high-end housing of a kind that the District had not seen since the early twentieth century. In the suburban counties, residents transformed modest brick colonial and ranch houses into multi-storied residences or moved to houses with more space than their parents could ever imagine.

Extending the Legacy

The "third act" in the planning drama that had begun with Pierre L'Enfant and progressed through the McMillan Commission began in the early 1990s when the National Capital Planning Commission developed *Extending the Legacy* (commonly known as the Legacy Plan). The plan was a visionary framework for America's capital for the twenty-first century, conceived in response to the threat of overbuilding on the Mall and the surrounding ceremonial area and the need to preserve open space, and released in 1997. In many ways, the Legacy Plan enjoyed the same mandate as the McMillan Plan—to make recommendations regarding the location of new monuments and public buildings. During the 1980s and early 1990s, the flurry of new monuments and memorials already constructed or planned to be constructed prompted the National Capital Planning Commission to prepare a new plan for Washington's monumental core to suggest what the Mall and surrounding area might look like fifty to a hundred years in the future.

LEAD-UP TO THE LEGACY PLAN: NEW MEMORIALS, MONUMENTS, AND MUSEUMS
Based on the 1986 Commemorative Works Act, the efforts of the National Park Service and the National Capital Memorial Commission to encourage the location of monuments and memorials away from the Mall found success in the National Law Enforcement Officers Memorial. Located at the Judiciary Square Metro stop, it was built of elliptically shaped memorial walls that formed a "pathway of remembrance," where the names of fallen law enforcement officers were inscribed. Completed in 1989, the memorial can accommodate up to five thousand people, who gather annually on May 15 to commemorate the officers' memorial day.

Other memorials located away from the Mall followed. The Women in Military Service Memorial opened in 1997 at the foot of Arlington National Cemetery and integrated an educational center within an existing hemicycle. Devrouax & Purnell designed the African American Civil War Memorial at the top of the Shaw Metro stop, which was completed in 1999. The National Japanese American Memorial was dedicated in 2000 to honor the Japanese Americans who served in the US military during World War II and those who were interned during the war. The memorial was sited on a triangular park to

The National Law Enforcement Officers Memorial at Judiciary Square. Photograph by Paul Jutton, National Capital Planning Commission

348

the north of the US Capitol. Members of the National Capital Memorial Commission and the project's sponsors negotiated the location.

Other memorials sited on the Mall in Area I included the Korean War Veterans Memorial, authorized in 1986 to honor the members of the armed forces who served in the Korean War. In 1989 its location was approved in Ash Woods in West Potomac Park—on the other side of the Reflecting Pool from its companion memorial to Cold War military conflict, the Vietnam Veterans Memorial. As a result of the rigorous review by the Commission of Fine Arts, the National Park Service, and the National Capital Planning Commission, the original proposal that resulted from a design competition for the memorial was deemed out of scale and was reduced in size, but it followed the same conceptual approach. Cooper-Lecky Architects made significant revi-

sions to the Korean War Veterans Memorial design, which resulted in a platoon-size military unit of nineteen stainless steel statues moving through peace and war zones indicated by juniper bushes and granite stripes. A mural wall consists of forty-one etched panels that depict army, navy, marine corps, air force, and coast guard personnel and their equipment. A granite curb lists the twenty-two countries of the United Nations that sent troops or provided medical support in defense of South Korea. The memorial was dedicated in 1995.

The US Holocaust Memorial Museum, completed in 1993, stands just to the south of the Mall along 14th Street. Although it was originally proposed as a memorial on the southeast corner of the Washington Monument grounds, the National Park Service convinced the memorial's proponents that they needed a museum to tell

National World War II Memorial. Photograph by Peter R. Penczer

this complex story. With General Services Administration cooperation, the Holocaust Memorial Council developed a museum to memorialize the 6 million European Jews and others who were annihilated during the 1930s and 1940s. Architect James Ingo Freed studied the concentration camps in Europe and designed the museum to echo their industrial, warehouse character. *Architecture* magazine described the final design of the museum's interior as "warped, fractured, twisted, dislocated, and ominous" to signify the moral and ethical collapse of German civilization under the Nazis. Its polished exterior fit well with the surrounding federal buildings.

The design of the World War II Memorial incited the most rancorous artistic debate of the 1990s, with many opponents asserting that it disrupted the axial view down the Mall. The memorial was established to honor the 16 million American men and women who served in the armed forces during World War II and the more than four hundred thousand who died. Advocates studied several prospective locations in the Mall area, including a site in Constitution Gardens to the north of the Reflecting Pool; however, the chairman of the Commission of Fine Arts, J. Carter Brown, ultimately convinced other decision makers that this memorial, representing the most significant event of the twentieth century, needed to be located on the east-west axis of the Mall, along with other major memorials to Lincoln, Washington, and Grant. All the review commissions endorsed the Rainbow Pool site on the eastern edge of the Reflecting Pool.

Designed by Friedrich St. Florian, the World War II Memorial was located on a 7.4-acre site and incorporated the Rainbow Pool. Fifty-six pillars, symbolizing the war's unification of states and territories of the country, encircle the main plaza, and two arches represent each theater of the war. A stairway two hundred feet wide descends six feet from 17th Street. A waterfall-

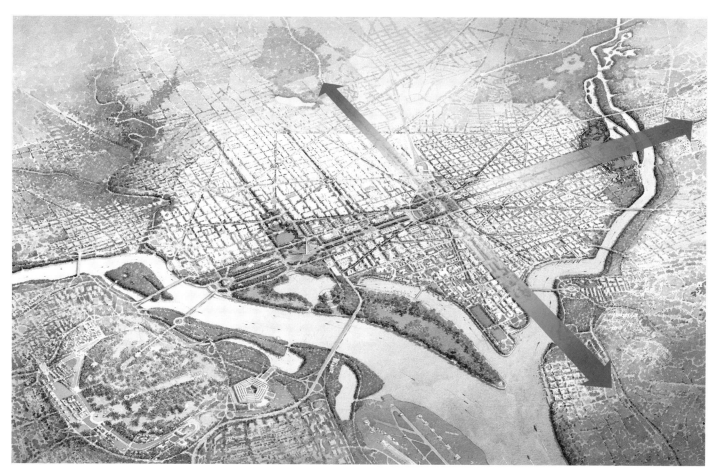

flanked Freedom Wall, a field of sculptured gold stars, symbolizes the human toll of the war, and bronze bas-reliefs depict the war years at home and overseas.

A CROWDED MALL

The development of the World War II Memorial demonstrated the increasing pressure on the open space of the National Mall. Since the early twentieth century, on average, one new memorial had been constructed in the nation's capital each year. In addition, Congress had authorized a dozen more memorials for which sites had not yet been selected. If past trends continued, land for the equivalent of ten new Air and Space Museums would need to be found by 2050. At this rate, the great sweep of civic open space was at risk of being overwhelmed. This concern was the principal impetus for the Legacy Plan.

Extending the Legacy: Planning America's Capital for the 21st Century recommended that new memorials, museums, and public buildings be placed where they could play a role in revitalizing the area in which they were located and, at the same time, protect the Mall and its historic landscape from future building. The defining urban design concept of the Legacy Plan was expressed in an axial diagram placing the US Capitol at the center with bold lines radiating north, south, east, and west. Today, most of the federal government's memorials, museums, and great public buildings are located west of the Capitol, making the Washington Monument the focal point of this official precinct. By using the Capitol as the center, the Legacy Plan expanded the traditional core north, south, and east, creating new opportunities for development and investment in these other, often-neglected parts of Washington.

The plan's themes included the need to build on the L'Enfant and McMillan Commission plans and to unite the city and the monumental

NCPC's *Extending the Legacy* Recenters Washington on the US Capitol. National Capital Planning Commission, *Extending the Legacy: Planning America's Capital for the 21st Century*, 1997

South Capitol Street Facing North toward the US Capitol. Photograph by Peter R. Penczer

A Cement Plant at the Foot of South Capitol Street on the Anacostia River. Photograph by Peter R. Penczer

core with the US Capitol at the center. It also called for the use of new memorials and museums to stimulate economic development, the integration of the Potomac and Anacostia riverfronts with the expanded canvas that protected the Mall and adjacent historic landscape, and an improved transportation system to make the

expanded monumental core accessible. Legacy's proposal for the Circulator—an inexpensive, easy-to-use transportation system that would transport Washington's residents, workers, and visitors to key attractions and businesses around the city—made its debut in Washington in the summer of 2005.

CREATING A "WHOLE CITY"

Taking into consideration the time needed to see plans to their fruition, the National Capital Planning Commission predicted that the Legacy Plan would take from twenty to eighty years to be completed. It was a guide for future development, a "vision plan." The Legacy Plan presented Washington, DC, as one city rather than as a collection of discrete enclaves. It proposed new civic, cultural, and recreational attractions for all quadrants, not just the northwest quadrant or the central core. It also depicted the District and its suburbs as a single entity that deserved a regional growth plan so that all jurisdictions could thrive. Recognizing that there were many places of value throughout the District and surrounding areas, the plan looked at distinctive neighborhoods, topographical high points, natural areas, historic forts, and linkages between notable places.

This focus on distributing the benefits of new developments throughout the District was evident in the draft National Capital Planning Commission study on *Foreign Missions in the District of Columbia: Future Location Analysis.* Issued in mid-2003, this report described the International Center at Van Ness as fully developed and pointed out that all of the existing foreign missions were located in the northwest quadrant. Additional diplomatic districts would need to be established, which the study identified. These potential "opportunity areas" included 16th Street in Columbia Heights, the Anacostia waterfront, and the US Soldiers' and Airmen's Home in the northwest quadrant. These recommended areas, particularly the Anacostia waterfront, reinforced the Legacy Plan.

MEMORIALS AND MUSEUMS MASTER PLAN OF 2001

Almost immediately following adoption of the Legacy Plan, the National Capital Planning Commission established a task force to examine location policies for memorials and museums and invited the other responsible parties—the Commission of Fine Arts and the National Capital Memorial Commission—to participate in approving the location and design of memorials on federal land in the nation's capital. The Joint Memorials Task Force established "the Reserve"

NCPC's *Extending the Legacy's* Proposal for a Revitalized South Capitol Street. National Capital Planning Commission, *Extending the Legacy: Planning America's Capital for the 21st Century,* 1997

NCPC's *Extending the Legacy's* Vision for a New Civic Place in front of the Kennedy Center. National Capital Planning Commission, *Extending the Legacy: Planning America's Capital for the 21st Century,* 1997

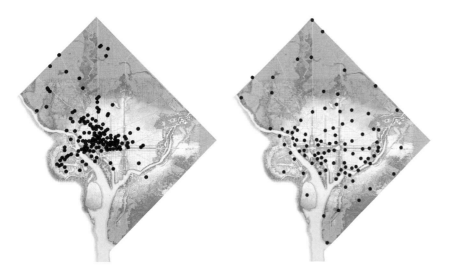

Existing Sites of Museums and Memorials and Proposed Sites for Future Commemorative Works. National Capital Planning Commission, *Memorials and Museums Master Plan*, 2001

—the central cross axis of the Mall—and agreed to approve no new memorial or museum sites in this area. The policy stated, "The Reserve is a unique national space, an embodiment of our democratic ideals and achievements, and must be preserved as an indispensable, nationally significant cultural resource. This setting has matured as the nation has matured. The cross axis, framed by monuments and museums, constitutes the historic urban design framework of the capital established by the L'Enfant and McMillan plans—open spaces, long axes, and dramatic vistas. It must be rigorously protected. No new memorial sites will be approved in this area."

In the same policy, the task force designated the area immediately next to the Reserve—Area I—for a very limited number of memorials of preeminent national significance. It was the rest of the city—Area II—where future memorial locations were encouraged.

Assisted by a group of prominent architects, designers, and planners, the task force developed an urban design framework for the placement of future memorials and museums. No fewer than a hundred new sites for cultural and commemorative facilities were identified. The master plan encouraged future memorial sponsors to think

Concept Redesign of the Anacostia Metro Station as a Potential Memorial Site. National Capital Planning Commission, *Memorials and Museums Master Plan*, 2001

of commemorative works not simply as objects but as "place makers." Memorials and monuments in the form of civic plazas, gardens, water features, and rehabilitated historic buildings could support urban revitalization efforts, define the city's identity, and create new urban destinations for both visitors and residents.

In November 2003, the US Congress passed amendments to the Commemorative Works Act that gave the *Memorials and Museums Master Plan* the force of law. The amendments established a somewhat expanded Reserve at the cross axis of the Mall on which no new commemorative works can be located. In the meantime, sponsors of prospective new memorials, such as one for America's disabled veterans, proceeded with plans according to the master plan's recommendations and were free of controversy over site locations.

ACCLAIM FOR PLANNING ACHIEVEMENTS

The collective planning efforts in the national capital city gained a high level of recognition and acclaim. In 2003 the American Society of Landscape Architects awarded the National Capital Planning Commission its prestigious Landscape Architecture Medal of Excellence for "sustained and significant contributions to landscape architecture policy, research, education, project planning, and design over the past 10 years." This national award recognized the Legacy Plan, the *Memorials and Museums Master Plan*, the South Capitol Street Urban Design Study, and the *National Capital Urban Design and Security Plan* and anticipated the successful outcome of the reconstruction of Pennsylvania Avenue in front of the White House.

With this award, the Planning Commission firmly established its role in protecting the federal interest in the District, a role that was poorly defined in the mid-1970s but had become better defined since that time. As a federal agency, the commission also worked with the District's aspirations for economic development in all sections of the city. In the process, it made an enduring mark in the planning history of the national capital city.

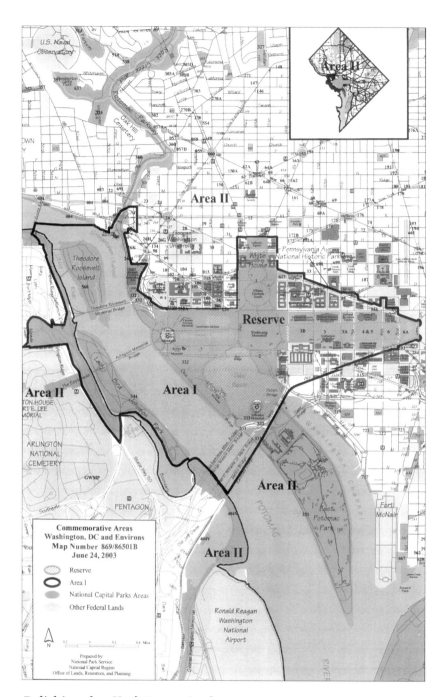

Map of the Reserve as Approved by Congress in 2003. National Park Service

Polishing the City's Image in the Global Community

Where dozens of new building projects in the District's downtown had occupied the area's skyline in the 1980s, by 1992 the American Planning Association's journal, *Planning*, published a special issue on the Washington, DC, area: "It's a new era, and in Washington, as in many other U.S. cities, the boom has come to a crashing halt. The only construction crews on the city's streets today are those putting the finishing touches on projects started years ago. Only one small new office project has begun in the last two years, according to city officials." Still, as the recession waned, the national economy picked up steam. Major projects again rose in the central core and strengthened the city's role as a living city and an attractive place to do business.

REZONING, 1990

To reinforce the living city concept, the DC Zoning Commission in 1990 established new comprehensive regulations in the downtown that demanded housing and encouraged arts and lively retail outlets to build on the concept of a living downtown. The controversial and expansive rezoning covered eighty-eight downtown blocks, from Pennsylvania Avenue on the south to M Street on the north and from 15th Street on the west to 3rd Street on the east. The zoning affirmed the creation in 1989 of a "destination" retail, service, arts, and entertainment area between 9th and 15th streets and encouraged these functions through the availability of density bonuses. It created an arts district overlapping the southern portion of the retail district to create two arts corridors: the E Street theater spine and the 7th Street arts walk. The zoning enhanced Chinatown as the downtown's sole ethnic and cultural area by reinforcing the area's mixed commercial and housing uses and by encouraging retention of businesses and community facilities.

The 1990 rezoning also buttressed the downtown historic district, which had an irregular boundary that included 7th Street and sections of F, G, and H streets. Established in 1982, the downtown historic district included 164 historic buildings. The downzoning of the district removed the economic incentive to destroy the low-rise buildings and allowed for a program to transfer underutilized development rights to other downtown properties. Lastly, the rezoning mandated a limited amount of market rate housing and encouraged developers to make significant contributions to affordable housing

off-site. The Zoning Commission envisioned that two-thirds of the new housing would be located north of Massachusetts Avenue between 3rd and 11th streets.

This dramatic rezoning of the District's old downtown was accomplished as part of the downtown element of the District's comprehensive plan that represented the work of many residents, property owners, and civic organizations. The rezoning also drew on the success of the residential housing projects that had been created through the Pennsylvania Avenue Development Corporation on and near Pennsylvania Avenue and the investments already made in the downtown theaters and arts facilities.

MATURATION OF HOME RULE

Sharon Pratt Kelly succeeded Marion Barry as mayor in 1992. Mayor Kelly brought a fresh face and new ideas to city government, but the city operated with significant budgetary deficits. Kelly lost to Barry in 1995. Only a few weeks after Mayor Barry reassumed office, the US Congress declared the District of Columbia insolvent because it was spending at a rate that exceeded its income by nearly 20 percent. Congress established a Financial Control Board and a mayor-appointed chief financial officer to take over city operations. Essentially, governance of the District fell to the Control Board and the chief financial officer rather than to the mayor. In 1999 the former chief financial officer, Anthony A. Williams, became mayor. Two years later, in 2001, the Control Board ceased operations and turned the city back to the local governance after the city achieved a balanced budget for three consecutive years.

The 1984 citywide comprehensive plan for the District was intended to be effective for twenty years, but within ten years it was already outdated. The plan was amended with the incorporation of ward plans—three in 1989 and five in 1994. In addition, the District undertook a number of "small area plans," including the Union Station / North Capitol Street Plan and the Buzzard Point / South Capitol Street Area Plan. Even as these plans were being developed, the Control Board slashed the District's planning staff from eighty-seven to thirteen people. The scarcity of planners gave the city a reputation for unconstrained development. With the inauguration of Mayor Williams, District planning was revitalized.

DISTRICT PLANNING REINSTITUTED

Having worked at the Boston Redevelopment Authority, Mayor Williams took particular interest in planning. He hired a new director for the Office of Planning, Andrew Altman, and dozens of new staff members. The new planning infrastructure in the District aimed for making Washington commensurate with the great capital cities of London and Paris by shaping and directing the city's considerable financial and business energies into areas of opportunity. The mayor also wanted to use planning to unify the eastern and western portions of the city, segmented since the mid-nineteenth century, and to bring about a unified community. Reinvigoration of the Office of Planning also brought the historic preservation office under its purview for closer cooperation between planning and preservation.

Several projects were targeted for major opportunity areas. The Anacostia Waterfront Initiative Framework Plan outlined a revitalization plan that provided for a 1,200-acre waterfront park system, cultural destinations, and strengthened neighborhoods. The goal of that effort was to provide a significant civic space along the waterfront and pedestrian access to the river and to encourage mixed-use development and the location of high-technology industries. Planners took note of waterfront developments in Providence, Cleveland, and Oakland and thought that Washington should be able to duplicate their success. Included in the Anacostia waterfront framework were plans for the near southeast waterfront; parklands connecting Capitol Hill with the Anacostia River waterfront; the Poplar Point waterfront plan, which provided a cultural park, housing, and impressive views; and schematic designs for the redevelopment of the campus of St. Elizabeths Hospital.

In the downtown, the Office of Planning undertook to manage the redevelopment of the old convention center site to include mixed uses of housing, retail, cultural facilities, and a new central public library to replace the ill-maintained Martin Luther King Jr. Memorial Library, the only building in the District designed by Mies van der Rohe. The District also worked with developers to bring about new housing projects for the downtown neighborhoods north of Massachusetts Avenue and to solicit development proposals for the historic Franklin School at the corner of 13th and K streets.

THE CENTRAL CITY AS DESTINATION

Two venerable downtown department stores—Garfinckel's and Woodward & Lothrop—closed in the 1990s; only Hecht's survived. These stores were casualties of the overleveraged 1980s and the dependence of department stores on ample parking and a strong residential market; their closings signaled the end of a viable downtown retail core and the gradual evolution of the area into a "destination." Now focused on events and nearby employees, the downtown was a place of sports arenas, convention centers, hotels, restaurants, museums, and other cultural facilities. It also was increasingly a magnet for "cultural tourism" opportunities. Nationally, other urban downtowns transitioned in a similar fashion; major new museums and sports arenas increasingly replaced former retail entities.

The success of the Pennsylvania Avenue development projects, which provided condominiums, rental apartment houses, and cultural facilities at the eastern end of Pennsylvania Avenue, generated the kind of downtown twenty-four-hour living long imagined by city planners and politicians. Nevertheless, residential living required grocery stores and other amenities that had long been absent from the city's center. These services were slow to return to the central city.

A major residential investment was the Lansburgh, an apartment house located one block north of Pennsylvania Avenue. The project incorporated the facades of a pair of historic buildings and the abandoned Lansburgh & Brothers department store. The project resulted in 369 apartments above street-level retail and space for the new Shakespeare Theater. In the completed complex, the architect, Graham Gund of Cambridge, Massachusetts, captured the essence of Washington's signature brick building stock using the material in flat and patterned surfaces.

The Jefferson at Penn Quarter was developed on the last major Pennsylvania Avenue Development Corporation site. Located at 616 E Street, the project was managed by the General Services Administration, which set the bar for housing units at 345 and encouraged a performing arts space as part of the project. The resulting project undertaken by JPI resulted in 420 housing units, a theater, and ground-level retail space. The project also incorporated the building used by Clara Barton during the Civil War and restored the building's facade.

The Ronald Reagan Building and International Trade Center at Pennsylvania Avenue and 13th Street NW. Photograph by Maxwell Mackenzie, Courtesy of the Ronald Reagan Building and International Trade Center

FILLING IN OLD DOWNTOWN

When the Pennsylvania Avenue Development Corporation was dissolved in 1996, the National Capital Planning Commission became the "keeper" of the Pennsylvania Avenue Development Plan. The General Services Administration played a major role in several post-1996 projects, including facilitating the Hotel Monaco project and the Spy Museum on F Street across from the old Patent Office Building. The General Services Administration also was responsible for the Clara Barton Office project on 7th Street. During the Civil War, Barton had worked from this office to locate soldiers missing in action. When the third-floor office was discovered in 1997, it was filled with boxes of papers and memorabilia. The General Services Administration will now interpret the building, which was once slated for demolition, as a historic site.

Downtown housing projects included the Mather Studios Loft Condominiums located in a 1917 former office building on G Street across from the Martin Luther King Jr. Memorial Library. Market Square North was developed by a partnership of Kingdon Gould III and Boston Properties. In addition, new shops were incorporated into the rehabilitated Woodward & Lothrop department store building.

Dedicated in 1998, the Ronald Reagan Building and International Trade Center represented a major effort to "complete" the Federal Triangle. The plot of land embraced what was intended to be the Grand Plaza in the original Triangle plan of the late 1920s but ultimately became a massive parking lot. When the General Services Administration prepared the master plan for the Federal Triangle to put a building in the Grand Plaza, it favored federal occupancy in the building. When plans changed to support an international center in the building, the Pennsylvania Avenue Development Corporation administered the competition for the development of the site, and the General Services Administration supervised its construction. A consortium of firms, including Pei Cobb Freed & Partners, with James Ingo Freed as the lead architect, won the competition.

The building included not only offices for government and trade organizations but also a conference center, special events spaces, exhibit facilities, and a food court. Next to the Pentagon, it was the second largest government building in the National Capital Region and the largest government building in Washington, DC.

Key to the development of the District's downtown was the location of the MCI Center (now known as the Verizon Center) at 7th and F streets, NW. The center was planned to provide homes for professional and college teams, restaurants, concerts, and other events. It replaced the US Airways Arena (formerly the Capital Centre) located in suburban Prince George's County with a state-of-the-art facility in downtown Washington near Metro. During the design phase, the Verizon Center was criticized for its scale—it towered over the nearby old Patent Office Building—and it also required the closing of 6th Street, an original L'Enfant street. Designed by Ellerbe Becket and Devrouax &

Purnell, the Verizon Center fulfilled its promise as an economic generator. It attracted restaurants, sports-related retail outlets, and other commercial enterprises to the surrounding area.

By the 1990s Washington's old convention center had become obsolete, too small to house the larger conventions that sought space. Although an alternative site on the Union Station rail yards was proposed, the new convention center was developed north of Mount Vernon Square. It spread over six city blocks at a location formerly planned as a campus for the University of the District of Columbia. The completed new convention center resulted from an extensive planning process and efforts to mitigate the effects of a large building—nearly three times the size of the old convention center—surrounded by low-rise residential and commercial development.

Constructed of glass, limestone, granite, and brick, the new convention center's facade was designed to assimilate the character of the nearby streets and articulated to resemble three

The Carnegie Library Building with the Convention Center in the Background. Photograph by Peter R. Penczer

buildings, rather than a single big one. Approximately 25 percent of the facility was built underground to reduce its above-ground height. Although it was the sixth largest convention center in the country and the largest building in the District, its impact on its surroundings was mitigated through benefits to the surrounding area in new historic designations, grant programs that promoted preservation, and the renovation of the old Carnegie Library into the short-lived City Museum of Washington, DC. Designed by Atlanta-based Thompson, Ventulett, Stainback & Associates and the local architectural firms Devrouax & Purnell and Mariani Associates, the new convention center is projected to pump $1 billion into the local economy each year, to create 17,000 jobs, and to encourage the construction of sixteen new hotels.

TOURISM AND HERITAGE TRAILS

Apart from the "business" of government, tourism is the major industry in the Washington area. Twenty million tourists visit the capital city annually. For years, cultural organizations tried to direct tourists beyond the Mall and monumental core to patronize museums and cultural organizations elsewhere in the city. Toward that end, they initiated "Off the Mall" weekends dur-

ing which visitors and residents were encouraged to visit a collection of museums, such as the Phillips Gallery, the Textile Museum, and the Christian Heurich House (former home of the Historical Society of Washington, DC, now known as the Brewmaster's Castle) in and around Dupont Circle. The success of these efforts depended on the ability of organizations to plan events that would encourage visitors to venture beyond the traditional tourism spots.

The revival of urban neighborhoods and the designation of historic districts catalyzed tourism efforts throughout the city. This initiative coincided with the phenomenon of "cultural tourism," also referred to as "eco-tourism" or "heritage tourism." Internationally, tourists were increasingly drawn to historic and cultural places, generating economic benefits to host countries.

A concerted effort to bring the economic benefits of tourism was represented by the DC Heritage Tourism Coalition, founded in 1996 and later renamed Cultural Tourism DC. Formed to promote "the vibrant life of the Nation's Capital and the city beyond the monuments," the organization promoted tours, trails, and programs. Historic trails and interpretive plaques placed throughout distinctive areas of the city, such as Franklin Square, enhanced tourism development. So did the opening of Metro's long-awaited Green Line.

THE CITY OF LUXURY

The fortunes that developed from the Internet and biomedical enterprises found expression in the development of luxury projects. As in other cities, loft housing became a popular residential choice. In Washington, however, there were few industrial buildings available for conversion to housing because of the historical lack of manufacturing enterprises. Thus, developers constructed new loft residences to meet this demand.

Other examples of new luxury housing included the Ritz Carlton development at 2200 M Street NW, a mixed-use hotel, condominium, and commercial project in an entirely new building, and its sister complex in the former George-town incinerator complete with a "brickyard meeting room." Luxury residences filled in the Penn Quarter as older buildings and their facades were integrated into the construction. In the neighborhoods beyond, formerly modest houses were expanded into "McMansions" and other expressions of "mansionization." Suburban enclaves, such as Great Falls in Virginia and Potomac and Mitchellville in Maryland, became home to the region's business leaders.

Some suburban jurisdictions, such as Arling-ton, Fairfax, and Montgomery counties, became so engulfed with high-end market-rate residen-tial development that programs to integrate affordable housing into housing options became priorities. In the District, the revival of urban neighborhoods gave housing activists additional evidence of the displacement of longtime resi-dents by the influx of affluent new residents. Increasingly, the District became home to both very expensive residential living options and housing for the poor, with a squeeze on middle-class housing.

POSTMODERNISM AND NEOMODERNISM

The buildings in the postmodern style that filled in the District's downtown during the 1980s con-tinued to flourish into the 1990s. Although the postmodern style began to wane nationwide, buildings in this style found a comfort zone in the classical city.

Notable buildings in the postmodernism genre included the Thurgood Marshall Federal Judiciary Building that completed the triumvi-rate of the Postal Service Museum and Union Station and was dedicated in 1992. Edward Larrabee Barnes / John M. Y. Lee & Partners designed the building to blend classicism and modernism. On the exterior of the Federal Judi-ciary Building, the classical facades of its sister buildings were evoked. One of postmodernism's progenitors, Michael Graves, gave the city a major landmark in the International Finance Corporation's headquarters on Pennsylvania Avenue at 21st Street. In the suburbs, the neotra-

An Example of Suburban In-fill Housing in Arling-ton, Virginia. Photograph by Peter R. Penczer

ditional Reston Town Center, designed by RTKL Associates, was opened in 1989. It provided a popular ice rink and community gathering spot amid a hotel and office and retail structures.

As the decade evolved, however, there was a renewed interest in the modern period of the 1950s and early 1960s, which had been so lam-basted by the critics as offering little more than oversized glass boxes. Many original buildings of the period had already been demolished. Surviv-ing modern residential communities, such as Hollin Hills in Alexandria, gained new apprecia-tion. As if to acknowledge the creativity of the modern period, architects and clients sought to secure a place for neomodern buildings in the city and area. In 1997 the new World Bank head-quarters to the west of the White House were opened. Designed by Kohn Pederson Fox and Associates, the new headquarters featured two new buildings grouped around a thirteen-story atrium. Along Massachusetts Avenue in Embassy Row, the new Finnish Embassy was designed as a steel and glass box and reflected the long-stand-ing Finnish modern tradition. Completed in 1993, it was designed by Finnish architects Mikko Heikkinen and Markku Komonen. Both build-ings reaffirmed the importance of modernism in the otherwise classical city.

An interest in neomodernism also found expression in several federal government buildings, including Helmuth, Obata + Kassabaum's new Secret Service headquarters. In the nonprofit sector, Henry Cobb designed the new headquarters for the American Association for the Advancement of Science, which was constructed as two triangular towers. The design for the new Metro system canopies was selected through a competition. Lourie & Chenoweth / Houghton produced the winning design with a curved steel-and-glass canopy, inspired by the coffered concrete ceilings that were part of the original design for the Metro stations. Designed to cover the escalators at forty-six Metrorail stations, the canopies reinforced the best qualities of the modern movement.

Historic Districts

After decades of resistance to historic preservation on the part of real estate developers, District government officials, and many federal agency administrators, the protected enclaves of historic buildings provided the District with strong marketing symbols. Its multitude of historic districts and landmark buildings became a major draw for new residents and businesses.

The American Association for the Advancement of Science Building at 12th and H Streets NW. Photograph by Peter R. Penczer

Canopy at the Virginia Square Metro Station in Arlington, Virginia. Photograph by Peter R. Penczer

During the 1990s, additional historic districts and landmarks were designated. By the early twenty-first century, there were nearly 600 landmarks and 39 historic districts that encompassed more than 23,000 buildings. Approximately 15 percent of the city's building stock was either individually designated or within the boundaries of designated historic districts. Nine historic districts from the White House to the Capitol and from Constitution Avenue to Mount Vernon Square protected the downtown. A ring of historic districts spread from Georgetown on the west, through Foggy Bottom, Dupont Circle, Shaw, Greater U Street, and Greater 14th Street, to Capitol Hill on the east. Other historic districts protected areas within the original L'Enfant city and beyond the L'Enfant boundary of Florida Avenue. In fact, Washington, DC, enjoyed the status of having more landmarks, historic districts, and protected buildings than any other city in the country.

Several executive orders and the tools of the National Historic Preservation Act—most notably Section 106, which called for federal or federally sponsored projects to take into account impacts on historic properties—were helpful in gaining greater support for historic preservation. For example, the construction of the MCI (now Verizon) Center resulted in the opening of the formerly closed "streets for the people" in front of the Martin Luther King Jr. Memorial Library. The new convention center project resulted in a grant program aimed at protecting historic properties that were impacted by the new building. While the large development projects were implemented, the District's state historic preservation officer played a key role in reviewing the projects and leveraging historic preservation benefits to mitigate adverse effects.

Although many preservationists decried facade projects, they continued to embellish the emerging historic District. Facade preservation projects, like the Red Cross Building at 20th and E streets NW, were notable and were valuable additions to the historic city. In the Red Cross project, the front and side walls were retained

and moved forward on the lot to accommodate a large addition at the rear. Although facade projects continued to be constructed, there was a trend toward preserving and reusing whole buildings. Examples of this include the preservation of the old Woodward & Lothrop department store and the former Webster School at 10th and H streets. The General Services Administration initiated the project on the former PADC site that became the Spy Museum.

The former Tariff Commission Building at 800 F Street was preserved as a result of a long-term lease of the property under Section 111 of the National Historic Preservation Act, wherein a private developer agreed to comply with the secretary of the interior's standards for rehabilitation. This was the first time that the General Services Administration had leased an entire historic building to a developer.

Facade Project at 9th and F Streets NW. Photograph by Peter R. Penczer

The Kimpton Hotel and Restaurant Group was selected to lease the building for sixty years and to rehabilitate the building as a hotel. Rents paid to the General Services Administration would be directed to other preservation projects in Penn Quarter. Reincarnated as the Hotel Monaco, the building houses 184 hotel rooms, a restaurant, and meeting spaces and has become a notable addition to the city's growing collection of luxury-class hotels. Nevertheless, the renovations and modifications can be reversed when control reverts to the federal government.

Protecting the City from Terrorism

The bombing of the Alfred P. Murrah Federal Building in Oklahoma City in 1995 and the terrorist attacks on the World Trade Center and the Pentagon on September 11, 2001, forced security planning to the fore. Soon after the 1995 bombing, the Secret Service ordered the closing of Pennsylvania Avenue in front of the White House to vehicular traffic, blocking a key east-west traffic artery in the downtown.

In March 2001, the National Capital Planning Commission established an interagency task force of federal and District agencies to examine the impact of federal security measures on Washington's monumental core. Patricia Gallagher, the Planning Commission's newly appointed executive director, led staff support of the project. The task force undertook intensive consultations with security and terrorism

Temporary Security Barriers Surround the Washington Monument, 2004. Photograph by Peter R. Penczer

The conversion of this building, one of the city's treasured federal government landmarks, into the Hotel Monaco was a preservation triumph. Originally designed by Robert Mills and augmented by Thomas U. Walter, the General Post Office Building was later occupied by the Tariff Commission. The rehabilitation plan grew out of a competition sponsored by the General Services Administration for an adaptive use proposal after the agency determined that the building was no longer suitable for a federal facility.

Hardened Street Furniture and Landscape Treatments as Proposed by NCPC. National Capital Planning Commission, *The National Capital Urban Design and Security Plan,* 2002

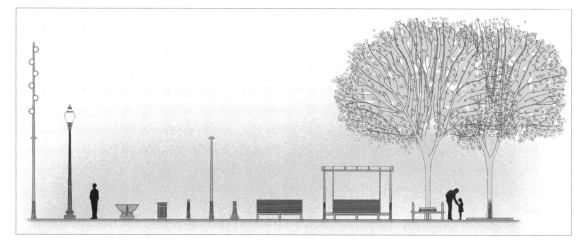

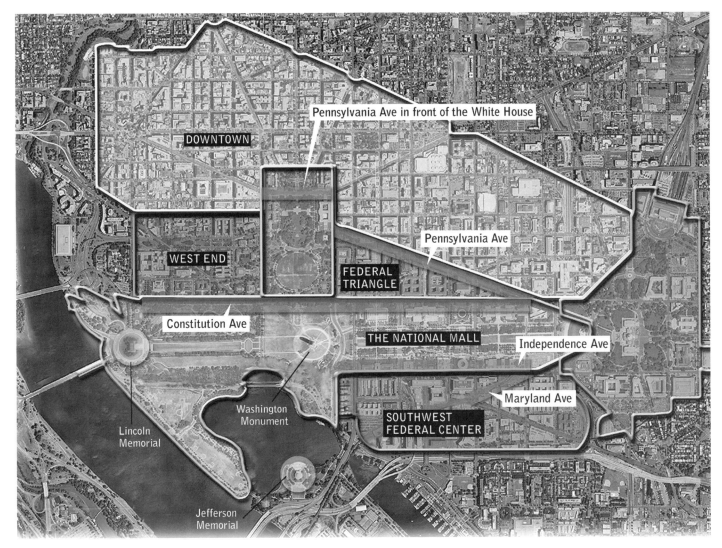

The labels on the image read:

DOWNTOWN

Pennsylvania Ave in front of the White House

WEST END

Pennsylvania Ave

FEDERAL TRIANGLE

Constitution Ave

THE NATIONAL MALL

Independence Ave

Maryland Ave

Washington Monument

SOUTHWEST FEDERAL CENTER

Lincoln Memorial

Jefferson Memorial

Security Design Solutions for Distinctive Precincts within the Monumental Core as Proposed by NCPC. National Capital Planning Commission, *The National Capital Urban Design and Security Plan*, 2002

experts, local and federal government agency officials, planning and design professionals, and the local civic and business community leaders. In November, just two months after the September 11, 2001, attacks, the task force released its report, *Designing for Security in the Nation's Capital*. The report recommended that Pennsylvania Avenue in front of the White House be closed to normal city traffic but open to a circulator urban transit system and traffic improvements in the downtown to relieve congestion. The report also called for the redesign of Pennsylvania Avenue in front of the White House as a landscaped civic space and consideration of a tunnel to facilitate east-west traffic.

In the immediate aftermath of the September 11 attacks, the General Services Administration

and other property managers placed additional barriers and planters in front of major public buildings and monuments in the monumental core. In addition, E Street south of the White House was temporarily closed, and several streets in the US Capitol complex were closed. In general, the responses to terrorism were made on a piecemeal basis to provide for the security of individual buildings and small enclaves.

In Designing for Security, the interagency task force concluded that a more thoughtful approach was needed, one that could yield broader urban design benefits as well. The task force recommended that the National Capital Planning Commission prepare a comprehensive security design plan that would identify permanent security and streetscape improvements. In

October 2002, following an extensive public comment period, the Planning Commission released the *National Capital Urban Design and Security Plan.* The plan sought to provide perimeter security against the threat of bomb-laden vehicles, to propose a citywide program that offers both security and urban beautification, and to expand the palette of attractive street furnishings and landscape treatments that can serve as curbside security. In preparing its plan, the commission called upon the services of some of the country's top design and planning firms, including the Olin Partnership, Peter Walker and Partners, Michael Van Valkenburgh Associates, EDAW, Chan Krieger and Associates, and Wolff Clements & Associates.

The *National Capital Urban Design and Security Plan* offers a variety of design solutions such as hardened street furniture, low plinth walls, planters, bollards, and green curbside hedges with embedded security measures. These elements can be applied in a variety of ways to meet the security and design needs of particular downtown areas. The plan is built on an urban design framework that identifies key areas and streets within the monumental core and recommends solutions that respond to the unique conditions and special character of each precinct. Although the plan proposes several design approaches, all share a compatible aesthetic vocabulary that helps knit together the fabric of downtown Washington. The plan represents a

well-received effort to find less intrusive security solutions that do not shout "fortified street."

Many of the security design measures suggested in the plan were implemented. Along Pennsylvania Avenue in front of the White House, the Federal Highway Administration constructed a public plaza that welcomes pedestrians and is appropriate for the historic setting of the presidential mansion. The redesign included eighty-eight new mature Princeton American elm trees, a natural-looking paving material, new benches, guard booths, and bollards. The project was completed in time for the 2005 presidential inauguration.

The Smithsonian Institution designed permanent security measures for its facilities on the National Mall, including benches, light poles, and urns that complement the historic character of the Mall precinct. At the grounds of the Washington Monument, the National Park Service regraded the site to accommodate curvilinear seating walls and paths that serve as vehicle barriers. The plan included repaving the monument's plaza in granite and planting new shade and flowering trees.

Exploding Suburbs

By the early 1990s, an increasing number of growth centers called the Washington metropolitan area home. To a large extent, these centers formed around the hugely successful 103-mile Metro system, completed in 2001 at a total cost of $12 billion. The General Services Administration

committed to consolidate headquarters of major agencies or to locate parts of other agencies near Metro stops and reinforce development. Other centers, located at the crossroads of major thoroughfares, became destinations unto themselves.

Although it lacked access to Metro, the biggest edge city was Tysons Corner, which offered as much office space as major cities such as Miami, and included two major regional shopping malls. Other edge cities included Crystal City, Landover/Lanham, White Flint Mall, Dulles, Merrifield, and Rosslyn/Ballston. Other growth centers clustered around older suburban downtowns, such as Bethesda in Maryland, and Alexandria and Ballston in Virginia, in addition to the 1960s new towns of Reston and Columbia.

Although some critics described edge cities as employment centers without social and community linkages and without physical coherence, others viewed them as evolving entities that could develop into true communities. Growth centers that formed around existing towns—like Annapolis, Leesburg, and Fredericksburg—were more likely to offer a sense of place than were areas like Tysons Corner that grew up around a rural crossroads. Critics agreed that growth centers needed to be more pedestrian friendly.

Virginia's suburban jurisdictions developed ways in which to channel and to manage growth. The city of Alexandria provided incentives for mixed-use and high-density development near Metro stops. Arlington County boasted that it had planned for the arrival of Metro by providing for high-density development along the Jefferson Davis Highway, Rosslyn, and Ballston corridors; it promoted revitalization of older neighborhood retail centers. As a result, by 2003 Arlington County described itself as among the most densely populated jurisdictions in the country, denser than Seattle, Cleveland, or Pittsburgh.

Fairfax County addressed traffic woes by encouraging people to work close to where they

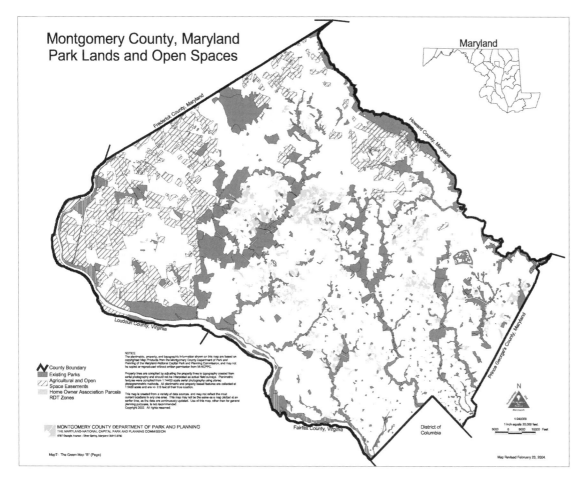

lived and by connecting the southern and western parts of the county with the Fairfax County Parkway. By 2000 Fairfax County took pride in its multifaceted economy that allowed approximately half of its residents to work in the county. The county also spoke of its ability to generate significant retail sales from an "assemblage of retail communities"—Tysons Corner, the Dulles corridor, Fairfax Center, and Springfield. Now that the county had only a dwindling supply of vacant land, however, it relinquished its role as the premier center for regional growth to developing counties, like neighboring Loudoun County.

Challenged to preserve agricultural interests while still fostering economic development opportunities, Loudoun County gained its reputation as one of the three fastest-growing counties in the United States. Known as the "global crossroads of the information technology industry with a vibrant rural economy," it was one of

the nation's leading centers of technology companies, such as America Online; 60 percent of all Internet traffic flowed through it. The eastern part of the county was organized around four major communities—Ashburn, Dulles, Potomac, and Sterling. Historic towns, villages, hamlets, and agricultural land composed the western part. With little supportive state land use or planning legislation, the county's attempts to preserve its rural heritage depended on case-specific uses of conservation, cluster design, and land protection.

Prince William County focused its development near the available infrastructure of Interstates 66 and 95, which the county designated as primary growth areas. It sought to control sprawl through support of the Virginia Railway Express commuter train and development incentives for builders to provide affordable housing. Tension between development and protection was demonstrated in the successful efforts to protect

A Typical Neighborhood in Kentlands, Maryland, Illustrating Neotraditional Development. Photograph by Peter R. Penczer

land associated with the Manassas National Battlefield Park and to prevent Disney from establishing an amusement park in the county.

The Maryland counties benefited from several state planning initiatives in the 1990s that promoted managed growth and "smart growth," including the 1992 Maryland Planning Act and the 1997 Smart Growth and Neighborhood Conservation Initiative. The most populous jurisdiction in Maryland, Montgomery County rightfully boasted of its success in largely achieving the wedges and corridors concept as a means of providing for orderly growth. This policy, originally adopted in 1964, was maintained as an "enduring vision" through the end of the century. The corridor cities of Rockville, Gaithersburg, and Germantown allowed for the clustering of households and jobs. The corridor cities conserved energy, reduced vehicle trips, and minimized the impacts of development. Green wedges of protected lands provided a "green lung" for the county. Older communities such as Silver Spring, Bethesda, Friendship Heights, and Wheaton were revitalized in keeping with their

historic character, even though that character sometimes dated from the middle of the twentieth century.

Planned around centers, corridors, and growth areas overlayed on three major "tiers"—developed, developing, and rural—Prince George's County located twenty-six designated "centers" at existing or planned Metro stations using existing infrastructure. One of these centers does not yet exist, the long-planned National Harbor project near the foot of the Woodrow Wilson Bridge, which would result in commercial waterfront development of more than five hundred acres. Like other Maryland counties, Prince George's County sponsors a Rural Legacy Program and a Community Legacy Program. Prince George's is the first suburban county in the nation to change from a white-dominated to a black-dominated county—African Americans composed 50.7 percent of the population in 1990 and 62.7 percent in 2000—while enjoying a rising income level. In spite of its economic strength, however, Prince George's County continues to be frustrated by the lack of retail amenities comparable to those found in the other suburban counties.

Frederick County was still largely undeveloped when it officially joined the Washington metropolitan area in 1980. In 2000 more than 80 percent of its land was still in agricultural use or located in conservation zones. The county saw its future development occurring according to the "community concept" whereby urbanized areas developed at higher densities and rural areas developed at lower densities. The community concept would avoid the scattering of subdivisions throughout the county and encourage residential development at community centers. Despite this effort to manage growth, the county projected that its population would increase by nearly 20 percent during the first decade of the twenty-first century, fueled largely by the employment growth in Montgomery County.

Wedged between the Washington, DC, and Baltimore metropolitan areas, Howard County emerged as the most forward-thinking proponent of "responsible regionalism." Officially part of the Baltimore Metropolitan Statistical Area, Howard County saw itself as a cooperative party to both the Baltimore Metropolitan Council and the Washington Metropolitan Council of Governments. Its major urban center, Columbia, had evolved from a fast-growing new town to a mature urban center, leaving the western section of the county to be preserved as a rural enclave.

SMART GROWTH

One of the major development trends of the 1990s was "smart growth," a movement that began with a small coterie of designers and spread throughout the nation, as it sought to address sprawl and its aftereffects. Defined by the US Environmental Protection Agency, smart growth is "about being good stewards of our communities and of our rural lands, parks, and forests. It is about ensuring that the best of the past is preserved, while creating new communities that are attractive, vital, and enduring." It changed the development debate from traditional growth/no growth to "how and where should new development be accommodated."

Smart growth advocates questioned abandoning the existing urban infrastructure and rebuilding it farther out. They sought to address increasing commute times and longer distances to basic services of stores and schools. They questioned the practice of abandoning older communities while developing open land and prime agricultural lands on the suburban fringe. Smart growth planning was town centered, accommodated transit and pedestrian activity, provided for mixed uses, and preserved open space.

The Kentlands development in Gaithersburg, Maryland, offered an alternative to the traditional car-oriented, suburban subdivision. It was designed in the late 1980s as a 1,600-unit community laid out over a 352-acre site that had once been a farm. The development incorporated the original residence, farm buildings, and mature vegetation and spread out in tightly bound clus-

Town Houses under Construction in Centreville, Virginia. Photograph by Peter R. Penczer

ters of traditional housing. Designed by Andres Duany and Elizabeth Plater-Zyberk, Kentlands became a highly recognizable "neotraditional" or "new urbanist" community. The firm was best known for the master plan for Seaside, Florida, which was modeled after nineteenth-century small towns, and for several dozen similar communities. By 1991 Kentlands had more than 350 houses and apartment houses. The firm revived a number of architectural and urban design elements that had fallen out of favor, such as front porches, sidewalks, on-street parking, and back alleys as service corridors.

The costs of sprawl in terms of demands on public infrastructure and the environment became part of the national urban debate. The national media carried stories about the promise and plague of "uncontrolled sprawl" on transportation systems, environmentally sensitive areas, the water supply, and the cultural landscape. Smart growth initiatives, such as those sponsored by the state of Maryland, indicated a willingness to offer localities greater planning tools to shape their environments. "Green" devel-

Inside the Cesar Pelli-designed Terminal at Ronald Reagan Washington National Airport. Photograph by Peter R. Penczer

opments also depended on a complex array of building codes that varied across jurisdictions. In Virginia, land use control depended to a greater extent on private tools, such as easements, voluntary compliance with cluster development, and outright purchase of land by a public or non-profit entity.

PRIVATIZED GOVERNMENT IN THE SUBURBS

The size and location of the federal government workforce was a major component in planning for the city and the region. In general, planners sought to maintain the balance of 60 percent of the federal workforce in the District and 40 percent in the suburban counties. By 1996, however, the District's share had dropped to 52 percent, despite an executive order to address this decline.

Of increasing importance was the growing size of the "invisible" government that consisted of the employees of private firms that lived off government contracts. In 2002 Stephen S. Fuller of George Mason University wrote about the effects of increased government procurement in the National Capital Planning Commission report, *The Impact of Federal Procurement on the National Capital Region*. The report addressed the changing role of the federal presence in the region, where federal procurement spending had doubled between 1993 and 2001 and had caused a large expansion in contractor jobs. This expansion represented an ongoing effort to shift the federal budget from direct payrolls to procurement spending.

The outsourcing of federal work had a profound impact on development in the city and the region. No longer did federal buildings house these workers. The outsourcing firms could be located anywhere in the metropolitan region—in older communities, in the emerging growth centers, or in an edgeless city. By the 1980s, Northern Virginia was the center for high-technology companies, whereas Maryland was the center for the biosciences.

DEVELOPMENT OF THREE AIRPORTS

The expansion of Ronald Reagan Washington National Airport, including Cesar Pelli's new passenger terminal, was completed in 1997. It was designed with a footprint in the shape of a capital E. A concourse connects the new terminal with the existing one, which underwent restoration. The new terminal is a vaulted structure built of steel sections and plates. The artistic program—called the architectural enhancement program—was unprecedented in a modern Washington building. Thirty contemporary artists provided mosaics, murals, paintings, art glass, and floor medallions. The completed terminal reflects an alliance of art and architecture and a "time capsule of the state of contemporary American art in the mid-1990s, just as public art produced for Rockefeller Center captured the state of painting and sculpture in the 1930s." The new passenger terminal houses a large number of shops and restaurants, giving the terminal a shopping mall character.

An economic generator for all of Northern Virginia, Dulles International Airport has a huge impact on the state's overall economy. Its continued expansion through the last decade of the twentieth century preserved the signature design of the airport terminal while doubling it in length and allowed for the construction of ancillary terminals elsewhere on the site. The first major expansion occurred in 1985, when a midfield concourse was constructed. In 1997, under the direction of the architectural firm of Skidmore, Owings & Merrill, the existing terminal was renovated and two 320-foot wings identical to the original terminal were added to the east and the west of the original terminal as envisioned in the original Eero Saarinen plan.

The Baltimore/Washington International Airport (BWI) is accessible by Amtrak and MARC trains and light rail service from Baltimore. Although not in the same architectural class as Dulles or National airports, it serves the northern reaches of the Washington, DC, metropolitan area. The fastest-growing airport in the nation in the 1990s, BWI brought with it new opportunities for business development.

THE MULTICULTURAL METROPOLITAN REGION

The immigration of foreign nationals that had begun in earnest in the 1970s and 1980s to transform the demographics of the metropolitan region reached even greater proportions in the 1990s. By 2003 Arlington County described its demographics as 40 percent Hispanic, African American, and Asian American. One in three Arlington residents spoke a language other than English at home; one in four had been born outside the United States. Fairfax, Montgomery, and Prince George's counties evidenced similar demographics.

Some of these groups came to work in the high-tech industry that clustered around the Dulles corridor in Northern Virginia and the biotechnology corridor along Interstate 270 in Maryland. Others formed communities in sprawling suburbs in distant counties. Area schools addressed enrollments of students from around the world. With the immigrants came new religions, institutions, commercial centers, and schools. In far reaches of suburbia, mosques, religious schools, and shopping strips were constructed to meet the needs of these groups.

During the 1990s, when Prince George's County became a black majority county, it also became home to a growing Hispanic community—from 4.1 percent in 1990 to 7.1 percent in 2000—and an increasingly large Asian population. In 2000 the white population in county stood at 27 percent.

FRACTURED OR COMMON DESTINIES?

At the onset of the twenty-first century, the Washington, DC, area faced a paradoxical situation. Increasingly viewed as the global capital city, at the local level it was a fractured mosaic of numerous local jurisdictions with their own planning agendas. Some counties and independent towns viewed their proximity to the national capital city as a business opportunity and sought to siphon business from the District or from the neighboring jurisdictions. Others saw themselves as dependent on the largess of the federal government—whether in federal government employees or outsourced workers—and thus part of the larger enterprise in national government.

In some respects, post–September 11 terrorism planning brought the metropolitan region into a more cooperative compact than had been the case earlier. With terrorism a threat, the destinies of each jurisdiction depended on close cooperation with the larger group. Experience with protecting the federal government from major disruption served to remind surrounding jurisdictions of their essential reason for being part of the national capital region; their futures were closely intertwined with national and international destiny. ★

EPILOGUE THE NATIONAL CAPITAL CITY IN THE NEW CENTURY

The New Century City

Momentous events in the planning of the capital city have marked the turn of each century. In 1800 the federal government moved from Philadelphia to its new location on the Potomac River. In 1900 the McMillan Commission revitalized the L'Enfant Plan, devising new designs for parks and groupings of public buildings and producing a document that endures as a benchmark in the city's planning heritage. In 2000 the National Capital Planning Commission's Legacy Plan gained greater definition through a number of detailed studies.

A major turning point for the new century occurred on September 11, 2001. Terrorist attacks on the Pentagon and the World Trade Center, together with the downing of United Airlines Flight 93 in Shanksville, Pennsylvania, forced planners in the National Capital Region to ponder the unthinkable. How could truck bombs be prevented from smashing into the Washington Monument? Could bioterrorist attacks in the Metro system be prevented? What about a truck carrying a dirty bomb into the monumental core? Speculation about potential terrorist targets and security risks coalesced to form a gloomy cloud of possibilities that hovered over planning deliberations.

Planning for twenty-first-century terrorism recalled reactions to previous threats. The bombing of the Murrah Federal Building in Oklahoma City in 1995 sparked serious antiterrorism planning and closed Pennsylvania Avenue in front of the White House. During the 1950s, government officials planned for the evacuation of the city in the event of an atomic bomb attack and encouraged the federal government to disperse government facilities outside of the monumental core. During the Civil War, the city survived four years near the frontline. In 1814 the British invaded the city and burned its major buildings. Some observers believe that the current focus on terrorism also will be viewed in its proper context.

Planning was not entirely directed at fighting terrorism. As far as normal planning activities were concerned, the sustained boom in the real estate market continued to transform the central city and the spreading suburbs. In the midst of a national and international economic recession and historically low interest rates, real estate remained a thriving industry. Federal procurement dollars kept the Washington metropolitan area out of the recession. In the process, the central city grew and became the living city so yearned for in the 1970s and 1980s. Growth and development continued to expand in the surrounding suburbs, pushing the sprawling metropolitan area into southern Pennsylvania and West Virginia.

This period in Washington's history is fraught with both great tension and great promise. Tension derives from the potentially grave danger to the city menaced by terrorism. The promise springs from the revitalization of the city and older suburban communities. There even is hope for greater rationality in regional planning. Given the benefit of hindsight, each planning era adds to the quality and the strength of the city and region. Whatever the outcome of current tensions, the city has survived great challenges in the past and, without doubt, will prevail again.

Central City and the District

The emergence of the monumental core as the unifying focal point of remembrance had begun in earnest in 1963, when Dr. Martin Luther King Jr. made his "I Have A Dream" speech on the steps of the Lincoln Memorial. The power of King's words, broadcast throughout the country via television and radio, carved that image in national memory. Use of the Mall has become de rigueur for groups to focus national attention on issues of concern, such as antiwar sentiments, civil rights, AIDS, and abortion, among others. The aftermath of some Mall events took physical form. In 2003, by an act of the US Congress, the National Park Service placed an inscription on the steps of the Lincoln Memorial noting the location where Dr. King had stood to deliver his seminal address. (A national memorial to Dr. King was authorized in 1996, to be built on the Mall. As of early 2006, however, the private funds needed to begin construction had not been raised.) Congress also approved in 2003 the National Museum of African American History, for a location on or near the Mall.

Memorialization and commemoration also were manifested in museums. Museums dedicated to the Holocaust, the role of American Indians, and achievements in air and space have added to the patriotic imagery of the Mall. By the beginning of the twenty-first century, the Mall had become a sacred place, a place of pilgrimage, an "open air cathedral," and a place for school groups' "civic rite of passage." Because of its historical and cultural features, the Mall also has become a place to celebrate the American experience.

Many viewed the Mall as a completed cultural landscape and thought that any additions to it would violate the completed artistic canvas. The National Capital Planning Commission's Interagency Task Force, which produced the *Memorials and Museums Master Plan* in 2001, provided many other options for the location of new memorials and museums. The task force introduced the concept of a "Reserve" where no new memorial or museum can be added, declaring the Mall a completed work of civic art. Congress agreed and authorized the Reserve in November 2003.

Not only was the Mall a completed artistic and cultural landscape, but the city was also a national treasure and an icon. Unlike most American cities, Washington is defined by its low profile, which is essential to give proper prominence to the Washington Monument and the Capitol dome. Horizontality also reinforces the importance of the city as the national capital, not just a commercial city with signature skyscrapers.

The central city continues to welcome new museums and cultural facilities and to rehabilitate existing ones. The underground US Capitol Visitor Center, located on the building's east side, is designed to provide additional office space and enhance visitor amenities and security. Although originally expected to be completed in December 2005, changes to the scope of the project delayed the center's opening and escalated the project's cost. It became known as Washington's version of the "Big Dig," the large highway project in

Boston known for its massive cost overruns and delays. When completed, the US Capitol Visitor Center will encompass an area roughly three-quarters the size of the Capitol. On the eastern edge of Pennsylvania Avenue, the Newseum is building its new facility, thereby completing the avenue's redevelopment plan. The building, previously located in Rosslyn, was designed by the Polshek Partnership. It provides museum space as well as condominium and retail spaces, with a transparent facade and central atrium.

Protecting the city from terrorist attacks necessitated the placement of barriers and planters throughout the monumental core. Although some people questioned their effectiveness in the face of an actual attack, these bar-

The August 28, 1963, March on Washington for Jobs and Freedom Led by Dr. Martin Luther King Jr. Copyright *Washington Post,* Reprinted with Permission of the DC Public Library

the Washington Monument, the need for security barriers, combined with the need for walks accessible to those with disabilities, gave the National Park Service the opportunity to enhance the grounds. The redesigned landscape offers full security for the landmark while preserving the beauty of the monument's setting. Nearly seventy-five years of debate had ensued since the McMillan Plan's formal French design of terraces and fountains was set aside.

By 2005 the city's downtown was bursting at the seams with many new buildings that filled once empty lots and blocks of abandoned buildings. High demand for office space caused a six-story addition to be built on top of the Hecht's (now Macy's) department store at Metro Center, as originally planned. The DC Zoning Commission's controversial decision to replace matter-of-right zoning for office space with the Downtown Development District that encouraged mixed-use housing, arts, and lively retail incentives for higher density resulted in numerous apartments and condominiums constructed in the downtown's east end. Many of the occupants were empty nesters and young professionals, who were attracted by the restaurants, museums, theaters, and nightclubs that have flourished within the office buildings.

New development could be funneled along North Capitol Street, South Capitol Street, and the waterfronts in the Southeast and Southwest. Some developers are looking to NoMa, north of Massachusetts Avenue between Union Station and Mount Vernon Square. Development along the Anacostia River waterfront has been spurred by the construction of new buildings along M Street, serving the Washington Navy Yard. The relocation of Navy activities from leased space in Crystal City to the Navy Yard as part of the Base Realignment and Closure Act seems to have served as the catalyst for the M Street buildings.

The unprecedented development by the General Services Administration of a mixed-use project at the Southeast Federal Center next to the Navy Yard, as well as the location for the new headquarters for the Department of Transporta-

riers provided at least the psychological impression of protection. The indefinite closure of Pennsylvania Avenue called for a redesign so that it could function as more than a closed street. In 2003 the National Capital Planning Commission selected Michael Van Valkenburgh's redesign of Pennsylvania Avenue. His design creates a ceremonial way with rows of Princeton American elm trees in a way that will not preclude reopening the thoroughfare to traffic in the future. At

tion there, represents a major investment in the transformation of the Anacostia waterfront. In January 2004, the General Services Administration announced the selection of Forest City Enterprises, Inc., to redevelop forty-two acres of the Southeast Federal Center. The company will construct not only office buildings but also apartments, condominiums, shops, and a waterfront park. The new center will contain enough space to house six thousand residents and accommodate six thousand workers. This project was the first of its kind for the General Services Administration: it allowed private developers to build on federal land and generate tax revenue for the District. The Department of Transportation will be placed on the remaining eleven acres, along with forty thousand square feet of retail space. The mixed-used development of the federally owned site is viewed as a means of revitalizing the Anacostia waterfront as called for in the Anacostia Waterfront Initiative Framework Plan and in *Extending the Legacy*.

Development along the Anacostia River waterfront is also getting a boost from plans for mixed-use development along the South Capitol Street corridor as envisioned in the National Capital Planning Commission's 1997 Legacy Plan. This previously neglected stretch of thoroughfare that serves as a key entry to the capital city is undergoing major revitalization, with plans underway for a new river crossing, parkland, a brand-new baseball stadium, and retail, residential, and office space. In the spring of 2005, the National Capital Planning Commission proposed a variety of development scenarios for the area that would also include a site for a major museum or memorial and a cultural facility.

In much the same way that the military contracted with private firms to develop the high-tech corridors near Dulles International Airport, and that the National Institutes of Health, the Food and Drug Administration, and the Department of Agriculture helped to develop the biotechnology belt in Montgomery County, the District of Columbia is working to attract both federal agencies and related private firms to the

city. In NoMa, north of Massachusetts Avenue, the new headquarters of the Bureau of Alcohol, Tobacco, Firearms and Explosives that the General Services Administration built is near completion. The new XM Satellite Radio Station is also located in this area.

The scarcity of buildable space in the downtown has made the redevelopment of the ten-acre old convention center site especially critical. The development team, headed by the Houston-

Concept Design for the New Department of Transportation Headquarters at the Southeast Federal Center. Computer Rendering by JBG Companies

Rendering of the South Capitol Street Corridor as Envisioned by the National Capital Planning Commission, 2005. National Capital Planning Commission

based Hines Interests, was selected to develop this project, which will include apartments, condominiums, shops, public spaces, and parking. The site also could contain a new central library, hotel, music museum, and offices. District officials think this project builds a "dynamic new identity for downtown's East End" and forms a critical element in revitalizing the downtown core.

Mayor Anthony Williams began to make sizable grants to new and existing cultural organizations as investments in the economic development of the downtown, yet another indication of the "destination" role for the city. The clustering of both public and private museums and performing arts centers sought to tilt the District back toward a city with an active nightlife, to complement its role as a job center.

Despite the upgrading of the central city, some portions of the District continue to contain some of the most impoverished living conditions to be found anywhere in the nation. In the 1980s, these areas were not originally envisioned as part of the living city and were invisible in city promotional pieces. Large sections of

Northeast and Southeast Washington, particularly on the east side of the Anacostia River, have not yet shared in the city's resurgence. The multitude of three-story, low-income apartment houses built in the 1950s and 1960s east of the river are being torn down and replaced with single-family houses that are selling quickly to middle-income families. New developments along the Anacostia River will doubtless contribute to the rising fortunes of these areas.

Updating the District's comprehensive plan—Growing an Inclusive City—was prompted by the outdated 1984 predecessor plan. In preparation for undertaking the new plan, the District Office of Planning issued a vision plan to present overarching themes to community groups. The vision plan acknowledged that the city was divided by income, education, and employment. Although new people were moving to the city to take advantage of its historic neighborhoods, jobs, and growing schools, it was imperative to ensure the preservation of mixed-income neighborhoods, strong community centers, and physical connections from east to west to reinforce the "whole city" goal. Job opportunities needed to be

created beyond the downtown. The District viewed a major area of opportunity along the Anacostia waterfront, which could be transformed into a twenty-mile river walk with new parks, museums, memorials, and cultural sites. New neighborhoods, such as Poplar Point, could be created by developing abandoned areas. In this way, the District's planning goals complemented those of the National Capital Planning Commission's Legacy Plan.

In 2004 the National Capital Planning Commission released the *Comprehensive Plan for the National Capital: Federal Elements*. This plan had not been updated since the mid-1980s. The federal elements include the federal workplace, foreign missions and international organizations, transportation, parks and open spaces, the federal environment, preservation and historic features, and visitors. The new plan absorbs the many planning documents of the 1990s and early twenty-first century to address emerging planning issues and challenges facing the region. Among these are the impact of federal government procurement on the National Capital Region, the large holdings of open space by the federal government in the region, and the

Long a Site for Industrial Activity, the Anacostia River Waterfront Is Primed for Vibrant New Uses. Photograph by Peter R. Penczer

important role of the 20 million visitors who
come to the city each year and the need to
accommodate them. Reflecting on the experience
of the past decade, the plan's principles included
promotion of smart growth and sustainable
development through the discouragement of
suburban sprawl, encouragement of more compact forms of development and mixed uses
within federal facilities, and concentration of
federal development near existing high-capacity
transportation facilities. Building on planning
legacies, the comprehensive plan called for the
preservation of historic properties and important L'Enfant and McMillan Plan design features.

The Region

In 2003 the vacancy rate in suburban offices was
higher than in the District, but the gradual economic recovery and increased spending on
defense and homeland security filled many
empty office buildings in subsequent years.
Older office enclaves, such as Crystal City, were
forced to adjust to a changed market that valued
open, pedestrian-friendly places such as Pentagon Row, part of Pentagon City. New develop-

ment favored street life, busy sidewalks, and
street-level stores and restaurants. The decision
by the General Services Administration to move
the US Patent and Trademark Office to new
offices in Alexandria and the migration of related
patent law firms to the new location has challenged Crystal City's developer to refurbish the
area. The Charles E. Smith Company, the original developer of Crystal City, regards this enclave
as the core of its real estate empire. The transformation of Crystal City will use Ballston or
Bethesda as models, where pedestrian-oriented
shops generate activity and vitality in the streets.

The major question for the future of the suburban areas is how to handle the projected
increase of 1.3 million in population between
2000 and 2020. Will the suburban fabric continue to push new growth centers and the edgeless city farther into the countryside? Will the
region by 2050 fulfill the specter of the "spread
city" predicted in the 1960s? What will be the
impact on the central city?

In the March 23, 1997, issue of the *Washington
Post* writers Glenn Frankel and Stephen C. Fehr
deplored the rapid loss of open space in the

region: "Vast tracts of farm land and forests are being swallowed up, plowed under, smoothed out, and paved over." Ironically, the national crusade against the Disney theme park planned for Prince William County in 1993–1994 turned out to be a choice not between Disney and preserved open space but between Disney and another Centreville-type development. The latter won out.

Even smart growth—the high-density development along transit and other transportation routes using existing infrastructure—has its downside. Where smart growth called for protected open space and greater investment in already developed areas that possessed adequate infrastructure, reactions against it resulted in zoning for one house on anywhere from three to twenty acres. These large-lot residences were described as "lifestyle zoning" or "Gucci sprawl." It is estimated that more than half of the land surrounding the nation's capital was protected from the typical suburban subdivisions. Developers simply skipped over these protected areas for new home sites in West Virginia and even Pennsylvania.

Some planners saw a logic to the configuration of the region. John Parsons of the National Park Service describes a "green belt" or ring of open space. Most of the land is private open space set aside through easement, low-density zoning, or purchase of development rights. The belt runs from the rural east end of Prince George's County northwest to Beltsville and north to Fort Meade south of Baltimore. It embraces the Patuxent Wildlife Refuge on the east, the agricultural preserve in Howard and Montgomery counties, and farmlands in western Loudoun County to the north and west. At its southern border, it includes Prince William Forest Park and the Quantico Marine Base. This ten-mile-wide "protective strip" functions much in the same way that the greenbelt that surrounds the Greater London area offers proximity to open space and low-density development in England's capital city.

Some question the "permanence" of the open spaces that make up the greenbelt, especially in those areas of Loudoun County where the tools to keep agricultural land in farm use (or at least in low-density development) are of questionable utility. Even in Montgomery County, where an astonishing 93,252 acres (one-third of its land area) are protected in the "agricultural reserve," some observers think that this protection is for the short term. Somewhere in the not-too-distant future, the protected lands may be converted to large-lot development.

The economist Stephen S. Fuller detects an even larger region that functions as the National Capital Region. The labor force that grew up around federal government outsourcing produced a regional "laborshed" extending from Baltimore to Richmond and along Interstate 81 in the Shenandoah Valley. Jobs also are more dispersed throughout the area rather than concentrated in "employment centers." Anecdotal stories feature workers who commute nearly an hour to get to a train station that gets them to their downtown jobs in another hour. Commuting two hours in each direction between home and work may become commonplace.

The historian Carl Abbott describes another configuration in *Political Terrain: Washington, D.C., from Tidewater Town to Global Metropolis.* The Chesapeake crescent arches from Norfolk to Baltimore, with Washington as its organizing core. This configuration is based in part on the Bureau of the Census definition of the Washington-Baltimore area as a Consolidated Metropolitan Statistical Area and the strong presence of the federal government in the area from the Aberdeen Proving Grounds north of Baltimore to the Navy complexes in Norfolk–Newport News.

Few planners accept that regional growth occurs randomly. Instead, they try to discern local patterns in the region's growth. If the logic can be determined, they reason, then growth can be managed and transformed into something that works for present and future residents. Planners also understand that Washington's situation cannot easily be compared with that of other metropolitan areas because of its unique underlying economy.

The Capital City's Special Character

The national capital city is a city of ideas and information. As a knowledge- and technology-intensive economy, the city is unlike other metropolitan areas, even in the postindustrial period. Never an industrial center, Washington focuses instead on ensuring a high quality of life to attract well-educated and affluent residents. It also is a center for research and development, populated by think tanks, lobbying organizations, associations, and policy makers. Because it is the nation's capital, it is very much an international city of embassies, immigrants, and world-class cultural facilities. For some observers, the Washington metropolitan area is one of those places that attracts the "creative class" of people who thrive on urban lifestyles and opportunities for innovation. This image is a far cry from the buttoned-down bureaucrats depicted in countless Hollywood sagas.

The Washington, DC, area possesses many attributes that make it home to the best-educated population in the nation. One of these is the stability of federal and contract jobs. The presence of well-educated, creative people forms the basis for economic growth in the city and region. They create new businesses that are tied to government functions, patronize cultural offerings and high-end restaurants, and live in upscale communities.

The attractions of the city and the region and the opportunities in both the public and private sectors serve as a magnet for people not only from other parts of the country but also from around the world. A huge influx of immigrants has transformed the demographics and image of the greater metropolitan area. During the 1990s, 48 percent of the population increase in the area could be ascribed to immigration. In older suburbs, such as Wheaton in Maryland and Arlington County, people from Ethiopia, the Ivory Coast, El Salvador, Colombia, Bolivia, and Pakistan may work together in a single drugstore. An owner of a gasoline service station employs people from Iran, Tunisia, Vietnam, Taiwan, Ethiopia, Ghana, and the Philippines. These groups have revitalized fading inner-Beltway neighborhoods and supported hundreds of small businesses, churches, and immigrant support organizations in new ethnic enclaves.

The location of various immigrant groups has been dictated by who was already there. Israeli immigrants lived in the Maryland suburbs close to the established Jewish community. Arabic immigrants clustered around the Falls Church mosque in Northern Virginia, and Filipinos settled close to Fort Washington, near military bases where many found employment. Koreans formed enclaves in Annandale and Fairfax City. Africans and Caribbeans clustered in Prince George's County, where the majority of residents were African Americans. It is only a question of time before the power of these communities' numbers translates into greater political clout.

Many Roles, Many Players

The planning authorities that developed during the twentieth century in Washington, DC, were created incrementally to address issues as they arose. For example, the Commission of Fine Arts was established in 1910 and continues to operate under its original mandate. The National Capital Planning Commission focuses on the monumental core, the District's downtown, and federal facilities in a relatively confined suburban area. The revitalized District of Columbia Office of Planning handles development by managing growth in "hot" areas and encouraging development in "cold" areas. The Advisory Neighborhood Commissions and traditional citizens associations provide additional review and consultation on District matters.

Surrounding the national capital city is a growing array of town, city, village, and county governments with which to contend. However, the Washington Metropolitan Council of Governments does not include all of these jurisdictions within its regional family. No viable regional planning body exists to direct and to manage growth. The interests of regional entities and states and the values of urban versus rural residents do not always coincide.

Because the city is the nation's capital, various key individuals have exerted personal influence in unique ways to the city's advantage. President George Washington was the first of a long line of illustrious patrons, whose involvement in and commitment to the city's future made it take root. President Abraham Lincoln ordered the construction of the US Capitol dome to continue even during the Civil War. After the Civil War, figures like Alexander Robey Shepherd and organizations like the Army Corps of Engineers supervised many municipal improvements to the city to stave off plans to move the capital to

another location. After the McMillan Plan was completed, Commission of Fine Arts secretary Charles Moore used his position to enforce implementation of the plan's major components.

During the 1960s, President John F. Kennedy, Jacqueline Kennedy, and Lady Bird Johnson supported plans to upgrade Pennsylvania Avenue, to preserve the residential character of Lafayette Square, and to beautify the monumental core. Senator Daniel Patrick Moynihan championed improved architectural design for federal government buildings, a revitalized Pennsylvania Avenue, and residential uses in the city's down-

Montgomery County Farmland Preservation. Photograph by Peter R. Penczer

town. More recently, First Lady Laura Bush took an active role in advocating a redesign of Pennsylvania Avenue in front of the White House and in promoting historic preservation in the city and elsewhere. Eleanor Holmes Norton represents the District as a nonvoting delegate to the US Congress and provides the political leadership for development and revitalization projects.

Few cities have enjoyed such a high level of interest and patronage.

As a result of past and current planning and development, the national capital city possesses one of the nation's most illustrious design legacies firmly rooted in the past two centuries. People throughout the world know its government buildings, monuments, and memorials. These icons offer a universal vocabulary for people who are "coming to America" to seek new lives. In the current climate, the national capital's icons serve powerfully the cause of freedom and democracy. At the same time, planning necessary to sustain the city and its region has never been more challenging.

The L'Enfant Plan, the McMillan Plan, and subsequent plans built upon them remain a powerful legacy for the District of Columbia and the suburban jurisdictions that immediately surround it and are linked to it through the Metro and park systems. In the outlying areas, planning challenges resemble those of many suburban and developing areas elsewhere in the country. The unique quality of the national capital region remains the underlying economic stability that the federal government offers through employment and contracting activities. This financial underpinning continues to drive the outward expansion of the area.

Whatever the future holds for the national capital city, the brilliance of more than two centuries of planning legacies continues to inspire. However insightful successive planning benchmarks were, no single plan has been more influential than the one that L'Enfant created. Although his design dates from the end of the eighteenth century and exerts its greatest influence on the District and the adjacent jurisdictions, subsequent planners have sustained his original vision through centuries of new technologies, radically new transportation systems, national and international conflicts, and cultural transformations. L'Enfant foresaw the nation's rise to international prominence. In light of his faith in the nation's destiny, he designed the blueprint for a capital city worthy of a great nation. ★

ACKNOWLEDGMENTS

This edition of *Worthy of the Nation: Washington, DC, from L'Enfant to the National Capital Planning Commission* is the second edition of a book that I first worked on three decades ago as a graduate student at George Washington University. The first edtion, titled *Worthy of the Nation: The History of Planning for the Nation's Capital* appeared in 1977. Frederick Gutheim, a well-known Washington planner and urban historian who also was my dissertation director, wrote it for the National Capital Planning Commission, and I am honored to have worked on this updated edition, which includes new chapters on the history of planning in Washington since 1977. In addition, drawing on recent scholarship, I made minor revisions to Mr. Gutheim's work on the late-eighteenth to mid-twentieth centuries (chapters 1 through 9), and in the postwar period (chapters 10 through 12), I reorganized Mr. Gutheim's material to present it in a chronological rather than thematic context.

I wish to acknowledge Elizabeth Moss, whose skills as a researcher and editor made it possible for me to complete the project on schedule. Elizabeth located many outstanding sources for the period from the mid-1960s to the present, reviewed and commented on all facets of the manuscript, and paid special attention to the bibliographic essay. Photo researcher and photographer Peter R. Penczer provided many new images that enhance the text and increase its appeal to the public. I also am indebted to the National Capital Planning Commission and its chairman, John V. Cogbill III, for undertaking this project and to staff members Paul Jutton, Denise Liebowitz, Lisa MacSpadden, and Stephen Staudigl. They provided many helpful critiques, thorough fact checking, enhanced graphics, and organizational insight. I extend special thanks to Denise Liebowitz, who facilitated the gathering of information and who coordinated the many comments and contributions of the reviewers. I also thank the commission members who reviewed and commented on the revised and expanded text. They include Chairman John V. Cogbill III, mayoral appointee Arrington L. Dixon, John Parsons of the National Park Service, Jerry Shiplett of the Department of Defense, and Michael McGill of the General Services Administration. I am particularly grateful to

Mr. McGill for his dedication to this project and for the invaluable insight he provided into the history of planning for the nation's capital.

In developing the themes of the past three decades, the National Capital Planning Commission convened a group of experts for a work session in June 2003. The participants included Patricia Gallagher, executive director of the National Capital Planning Commission; Tersh Boasberg, Historic Preservation Review Board; Arrington L. Dixon, NCPC commissioner; Stephen S. Fuller, George Mason University; John Parsons, National Park Service; Joseph Passonneau, consultant; Gail McCormick, City Museum of Washington, DC; Stephen Sher, Holland & Knight; Richard Tustian, former Montgomery County planning director; and Margaret Van der Hye, former NCPC commissioner. These participants identified many important topics for the book's new chapters and provided additional comments during the manuscript review process.

During my research for the period from 1976 to 2003, the following individuals were especially helpful: Judy Daniel and Gwen Marcus Wright of the Montgomery County Department of Parks and Planning; Janet Davis, Frederick County Department of Planning and Zoning; Rick Davis, Urban Land Institute; and Brian Holtman of W. C. & A. N. Miller Companies. Thanks are due to the staff of the Washingtonian Room, Martin Luther King Jr. Memorial Library; the Library of Congress; and the Kiplinger Library at the Historical Society of Washington, DC.

Finally, I wish to thank my former supervisor, John Robbins, then manager of the National Center for Cultural Resources at the National Park Service, and my husband, Joe Wallis, for supporting my work on this project.

ANTOINETTE J. LEE

BIBLIOGRAPHIC ESSAY

Prologue: The Place of Washington in National Memory

The quote from Alexis de Tocqueville is found in *Democracy in America*, vol. 2 (1835; reprint, New York: Vintage Books, 1945), 56. Frances Trollope's observations on Washington can be found in *Domestic Manners of the Americans* (1832; reprint, London: Folio Society, 1974), 163. Charles Dickens's quotation is found in *American Notes* (1842; reprint, New York: Forum International Publishing Corporation, 1985), 115.

Henry Adams's observations are recorded in *The Education of Henry Adams* (1918; reprint, Boston: Houghton Mifflin Company, 1961), 99. The new role of Washington after the Civil War was captured by S. D. Wyeth, *The Federal City; or, Ins and Abouts of Washington* (Washington, DC: Gibson Brothers, 1868), 5. Washington as a place of pilgrimage is described in Ainsworth R. Spofford, *The Founding of Washington City* (Baltimore: Maryland Historical Society, 1881), 62. Frederick Douglass's speech is found in *Life and Times of Frederick Douglass: His Early Life As A Slave, His Escape from Bondage, and His Complete History: An Autobiography* (1893; reprint, New York: Gramercy Books, 1993), 412.

David Brinkley's observations about Washington during World War II are found in *Washington Goes to War* (New York: Ballantine Books, reissue edition 1989), 4. For Ada Louise Huxtable's transcendent description of Washington, see the architecture section of *Washington: The New York Times Guide to the Nation's Capital*, edited by Alvin Shuster (Washington, DC: R. B. Luce, 1967). David McCullough's proclamation, "I Love Washington," was originally published in *American Heritage* (April–May 1986) and was reprinted in *Katharine Graham's Washington* (New York: Vintage Books, 2003), 370.

1. The Planned Capital City, 1790–1800

THE NEW NATIONAL CAPITAL CITY AND ITS POTOMAC SITE

For the origins of the "district" concept, see Louis Dow Scisco, "A Site for the Federal City: The Original Proprietors and Their Negotiations with Washington," 1956, Historical Society of Washington, DC, Manuscript Collection. This paper was later shortened and published in *Records of the Columbia Historical Society*, 1957–1959 (Washington, DC, 1961). On selection of the Potomac site, see Constance McLaughlin Green, *Washington: Village and Capital, 1800–1878* (Princeton, NJ: Princeton University Press, 1962). Green's treatment of the decisions to create, locate, and plan the national capital city is fully documented and tightens up the more discursive treatment earlier offered by W. B. Bryan, A *History of the National Capital*, vol. 1 (New York: McMillan, 1914). Although there is no designation of a name in the Constitution's reference to the "seat of the government," it was anticipated as early as 1791 that the capital city would be named for George Washington; see Elizabeth S. Kite, *L'Enfant and Washington* (Baltimore: Johns Hopkins Press, 1929). The commissioners began using the name "Washington" in January 1794, according to Bryan. George Washington always referred to Washington as the "federal city."

The natural topography—and its abundance—that presented itself to L'Enfant is described in W. L. McAtee, *A*

Sketch of the Natural History of the District of Columbia,
Bulletin of the Biological Society of Washington 1 (1918).
Early settlement of the area is sketched by Bryan; see also
Robert L. Humphrey and Mary Elizabeth Chambers,
*Ancient Washington: American Indian Cultures of the
Potomac Valley* (Washington, DC: George Washington
University, 1976). "Paper towns"—towns established in law
but in fact never developed—are described by John W.
Reps, *Tidewater Towns: City Planning in Colonial Virginia
and Maryland* (Williamsburg, VA: Colonial Williamsburg
Foundation, 1972), and by Fairfax Harrison, *Landmarks of
Old Prince William* (Berryville, VA: Chesapeake Book Co.,
1964). On the reference to Philadelphia as a "green country
town," Samuel Hazard, *Annals of Philadelphia, 1609–1682*
(Philadelphia, 1850), cites William Penn's fifteenth instruction to his commissioners charged (in 1683) with laying
out the city of Philadelphia "that it may be a green country
town which will never be burnt and always be wholesome." This is quoted by Anthony N. E. Garvan, "Propri-
etary Philadelphia as Artifact," in *The Historian and the
City,* edited by Oscar Handlin and John Burchard (Cambridge, MA: MIT Press, 1963); see also Edmund N. Bacon,
Design of Cities (New York: Viking Press, 1967).

Kenneth R. Bowling, *Creating the Federal City,
1774–1800: Potomac Fever* (Washington, DC: American
Institute of Architects Press, 1988), accompanied the 1988
exhibit at the Octagon Museum that explored the political intrigue and turmoil that accompanied the establishment of a national capital city.

PIERRE CHARLES L'ENFANT

The biographies of L'Enfant are thorough and encyclope-
dic. They include H. Paul Caemmerer, *The Life of Pierre
Charles L'Enfant, Planner of the City Beautiful, the City
of Washington* (Washington, DC, 1950), and Elizabeth S.
Kite, *L'Enfant and Washington, 1791–1792* (Baltimore:
Johns Hopkins Press, 1929). Although brief, Fiske Kimball, "L'Enfant," in *Dictionary of American Biography*,
edited by Dumas Malone, vol. VI, renewed copyright
(1933; reprint, New York: Charles Scribner's Sons, 1961),
165–169, offers one of the best appreciations of L'Enfant's
architectural design and his role as a traditionalist
rather than an innovator. For the reference to Père Marc-
Antoine Laugier's *Essai sur l'architecture,* see Helen
Rosenau, *Social Purpose in Architecture: Paris and
London Compared, 1760–1800* (London: Studio Vista,
1970).

A newly crafted L'Enfant biography is presented in
Kenneth R. Bowling, *Peter Charles L'Enfant: Vision,
Honor, and Male Friendship* (Washington, DC: Friends of
the George Washington University Libraries, 2002). In
this publication, L'Enfant's considerable works both
before and after the plan for the capital city are developed. They provide a broader context for understanding

his selection by Washington as well as his dismissal.

The floating appraisal, "worthy of the nation," apparently goes back to the beginnings of Washington and is
sufficiently general to have been employed in other con-
texts—at least as early as 1824 when, in discussion of the
founding of the National Gallery of Great Britain, the
chancellor of the Exchequer expressed hope for the
"establishment of a splendid Gallery . . . worthy of the
nation"; see Homan Potterton, *A Guide to the National
Gallery* (London: The Gallery, 1976). Lieutenant Montgomery C. Meigs, the army engineer who built the Washington aqueduct, voiced the phrase in 1852 or 1853 in support of this project. "Let our Aqueduct be worthy of the
nation," Meigs wrote in his report to Congress. Meigs is
cited in Albert F. Cowdrey, "Design for a City: The U.S.
Army Engineers in the Building of the Nation's Capital"
(MS, Historical Division, Office of the Chief of Engineers, Washington, DC, 1974). No direct documentation
of Meigs's report is given, but references are supplied to
(a) Russell Frank Weigley, Quartermaster General of the
Army, 61; (b) Warren T. Hannum, "Water Supply of the
District of Columbia," Professional Memoirs: Corps of
Engineers, US Army 4 (1912); (c) Edwin A. Achmitt and
Philip O. McQueen, "Washington Aqueduct," *Military
Engineer* 41 (1949); and "The Washington Aqueduct,
1852–1952" (MS, Washington District, Corps of Engineers,
1953). The apparent date of the Meigs report is 1852 or
1853. Of the many references to the phrase "worthy of the
nation" as applied to Washington, this appears to be the
earliest in point of chronology. Although it refers not to
the city but to the aqueduct, the presentation strongly
suggests that Meigs was not originating the phrase but
echoing its currency in the larger urban context.

It was President Grant, however, who gave the phrase
its strong, explicit relationship to the national capital city
by sustaining the point in his many messages to Congress; see H. Paul Caemmerer, *A Manual on the Origin
and Development of Washington* (Washington, DC, 1939).
Grant's commitment to making the national capital city
"worthy of the nation" and his role as a steadfast friend
of the capital city is further substantiated in the biography by his grandson, Ulysses S. Grant III, *Ulysses S.
Grant: Warrior and Statesman* (New York: Morrow, 1969).
Although more detailed documentation of the use of the
phrase "worthy of the nation" in reference to Washington's role as a capital city would be of interest, it is clear
that the ideal was enunciated very early, that it inspired
the city's builders in their most vigorous efforts, and that
it still brightly illuminates the efforts of contemporary
urban designers.

In 1790 Thomas Jefferson drew a small grid, encom-
passing 1,500 acres at the juncture of the Potomac and the
Anacostia rivers (the site of Carrollsburg), to develop his
thoughts on the plan for the new capital city. Although

Philadelphia—the autochthonous American city—provided the immediate inspiration for the right-angled streets shown in this drawing, Jefferson hoped to avoid the monotony of its streetscape by varying the distances between buildings and streets. Fully versed in the functional requirements of an urban center, Jefferson allocated to commerce the fourteen blocks facing the deep waters of the Anacostia and to government purposes the four blocks facing the Potomac. The rest of the city was to develop on the inland blocks. The sketch shown here is reproduced from "Proceedings to be had Under the Residence Act," November 29, 1790, Thomas Jefferson Papers, Library of Congress Manuscript Division.

Following L'Enfant's survey between Rock Creek and Tiber Creek, Thomas Jefferson refocused his planning thoughts on a site facing the confluence of Tiber Creek and the Potomac River where Hamburg and the "Key of Keys," the rocky projection guarding the upper channel of the Potomac, were located. For this site Jefferson drew an elongated grid—with the commercial waterfront much contracted from his November 1790 sketch—to encompass four city blocks along the Potomac. Most important for the spatial relationships and the "genesis of L'Enfant's great mall" was the location of the President's House and the Capitol and their connection along a strip of land by the Tiber—"public walks," as Jefferson labeled it. Although in area this plan appears to be constricted in comparison with the area later covered by L'Enfant's plan, Jefferson actually was envisioning a city commensurate with Philadelphia. The planned city size is shown here by the widely separated "dotted squares" denoting blocks "to be laid off" and sold in lots at some time "in future." This drawing of the elongated grid is reproduced from a manuscript (no title, no date, although likely March 1791), Thomas Jefferson Papers, Library of Congress Manuscript Division.

THE LAND AND THE WATERCOURSES

Henry Fleet's "Brief Journal" is reproduced in Edward D. Neill, *Founders of Maryland* (Albany: J. Munsell, 1876); the passage quoted here is given in Fairfax Harrison, *Landmarks of Old Prince William* (Berryville, VA: Chesapeake Book Co., 1964). The drainage patterns of the Potomac area—the creeks, branches, and tributaries of the river as well as the springs, wells, and other sources of water—have been reconstructed by Garnett P. Williams, a geomorphologist and sedimentarian on the staff of the US Geological Survey; see his *Washington, D.C.'s Vanishing Springs and Waterways* (Washington, DC: US Geological Survey Circular 752.CP107-125, 1977). See also the work on this subject by Paul M. Johnston, "Geology and Groundwater Resources of Washington, DC, and Vicinity," Water Supply Paper No. 1776 (Washington, DC: US Geological Survey, 1964); and "Groundwater in the Wash-

ington, DC, Area and a Brief History of the Public Water Supply," *Journal of the Washington Academy of Sciences* 32 (1962). Copies of the Johnston articles are shelved in the Historical Society of Washington, DC.

TRAVELERS' DESCRIPTIONS OF EARLY WASHINGTON

Quotations from the La Rochefoucauld–Liancourt journals are from the 1974 translation by Professor and Mrs. David J. Brandenburg, *The Voyage in the United States of America, 1795, 1796, 1797*, excerpts of which (containing descriptions of the federal city) are published in the *Records of the Columbia Historical Society, 1973–1974* (Washington, DC, 1975). We are indebted to the Brandenburgs for the opportunity to read their manuscript. For the Weld, Twining, and Baily excerpts, see W. B. Bryan, *A History of the National Capital*, vol. 1 (New York: McMillan, 1914). The preexisting towns of Alexandria (founded 1749) and Georgetown (1731) were assimilated into the District of Columbia by 1791, and by this date both were thriving ports widely described and commented on by travelers. As negotiations commenced with proprietors of the land where the federal city was to rise, these proprietors were generally Georgetown residents.

L'ENFANT'S SURVEY, MARCH 1791

The details of L'Enfant's operations are provided in his letters and reports to Presidents Washington and Jefferson and to the commissioners and in the local press; see Elizabeth S. Kite, *L'Enfant and Washington* (Baltimore: Johns Hopkins Press, 1929); *Records of the Columbia Historical Society* 2 (Washington, DC, 1899). For Washington's instructions to L'Enfant mentioned in the president's letter to Deakins on March 2, 1791, see Kite, and there also see Washington's March 31, 1791, letter to Jefferson. The research of Louis Dow Scisco, as noted earlier, is published in the *Records of the Columbia Historical Society, 1957–1959* (Washington, DC, 1961). James Craig's "New Town" is described in A. J. Youngson, *The Making of Classical Edinburgh* (Edinburgh: Edinburgh University Press, 1966). For George Washington's diary entries on his negotiations with the proprietors in Georgetown, see John Clement Fitzpatrick, ed., *The Diaries of George Washington, 1748–1799*, vol. 4 (Boston: Houghton Mifflin, 1925).

L'ENFANT'S MEMORANDUM: URBAN DESIGN, LANDSCAPE IMAGE, AND A DEVELOPMENT STRATEGY

On L'Enfant's sketch plan of June 22, 1791, and his accompanying memorandum, see Elizabeth S. Kite, *L'Enfant and Washington* (Baltimore: Johns Hopkins Press, 1929).

MEANINGS OF L'ENFANT'S PLAN

A fresh and insightful interpretation of L'Enfant's plan and the system by which the major diagonal streets were named are provided in Pamela Scott, "'This Vast Empire': The Iconography of the Mall, 1791–1848," in *The Mall in Washington, 1791–1991*, edited by Richard Longstreth (Washington, DC: National Gallery of Art, 1991). J. P. Dougherty, "Baroque and Picturesque Motifs in L'Enfant's Design for the Federal Capital," *American Quarterly* 26 (March 1974), presents a still useful analysis of the meaning of the major elements of L'Enfant's plan.

On the swelling of neoclassical art by which L'Enfant was motivated, see Hugh Honour, *Neo-Classicism* (Harmondsworth: Penguin, 1968), who quotes DuFourny; see also Peter Collins, *Changing Ideals in Modern Architecture* (London: Faber and Faber, 1967). On the mathematics of the age and the scientific and cultural milieu that created its architecture and city planning, see Brooke Hindle, *The Pursuit of Science in Revolutionary America, 1735–1789* (Chapel Hill: University of North Carolina Press, 1958); Helen Rosenau, *The Ideal City in Its Architectural Evolution* (London: Routledge and Paul, 1959) and *Social Purpose in Architecture: Paris and London Compared, 1760–1800* (London: Studio Vista, 1970); and Helen M. Fox, *André Le Nôtre: Garden Architect to Kings* (New York: Crown Publishers, 1962).

L'ENFANT'S PLAN: BEGINNINGS OF BUILT WASHINGTON

The commissioners wrote instructions to L'Enfant about naming the city Washington and numbering and lettering the streets: east–west streets to be numbered from the Capitol, north–south streets to be designated by letters of the alphabet. For this communication from the commissioners to L'Enfant dated September 9, 1791, see Edward S. Delaplaine, *The Life of Thomas Johnson* (New York: F. H. Hitchcock, 1927). Lee Otis Colbert, "The Earliest Maps of Washington, D.C.," *Military Engineer* 41 (1949), outlines the details of the L'Enfant manuscript map of 1791, the Ellicott map of 1792, the James R. Dermott map of 1797–1798 defining the public lands, and Nicholas King's plats of 1803 produced by the city's first surveyor. On the speculative boom and its effect on the character of the early city, see Allen C. Clark, *Greenleaf and Law in the Federal City* (Washington, DC: Press of W. F. Roberts, 1901). Also see Talbot F. Hamlin, *Benjamin Henry Latrobe* (New York: Oxford University Press, 1955), for favorable reference to Thomas Law and his real estate activities—as well as for a rare glimpse of Thomas Jefferson's shortcomings as an architectural designer. For Elbert Peets's essay "The Lost Plazas of Washington," see Paul D. Spreiregen, ed., *On the Art of Designing Cities: Selected Essays of Elbert Peets* (Cambridge, MA: MIT Press, 1968).

2. The Port City, 1800-1860

THE CITY OF WASHINGTON, 1800

Filling in the physical city of Washington with a cultural and intellectual life is discussed in James Sterling Young, *The Washington Community, 1800–1828* (New York: Columbia University Press, 1966); the first chapters provide a remarkably keen insight into the effects of the city's plan on the social community as well as on the political community centered around the Capitol. Young also explores the isolation of the legislators from the rest of the city; the creation of Washington "at a distance" from the rest of the nation he sees as evasive and an effort to escape the scrutiny of the nation. Young is far from clear, however, that this consequential effect was a deliberate objective of the city's plan.

In the absence of a detailed history of the port activities that verified the original river orientation of the city, one must draw upon a number of specialized histories. For descriptions of the natural landscape of early Washington, as well as the vast environmental changes that later registered the presence of the federal establishment, see Margaret Bayard Smith, *The First Forty Years of Washington Society* (New York: C. Scribner's, 1906). The expectation that the southwest quadrant along the Washington Channel would become the most prosperous area of the embryonic city is discussed in Herman R. Friis and Ralph A. Ehrenberg, "Nicholas King and His Wharfing Plans of the City of Washington, 1797," *Records of the Columbia Historical Society*, 1966–1968 (Washington, DC, 1969); see also Allen C. Clark, *Greenleaf and Law in the Federal City* (Washington, DC: W. F. Roberts, 1901).

On Carrollsburg, see in the Martin Luther King Jr. Memorial Library, Washington, DC, in the vertical files s.v. Waterfront, the article by William M. Birth. For Bryan's reference to "cultivated gardens," see his *History of the National Capital*, vol. 2 (New York: n.p., 1916). The port, milling, and canal activity that generated considerable prosperity in antebellum Georgetown is described in Constance W. Werner, *Georgetown Historic Waterfront* (Washington, DC: US Commission of Fine Arts, 1968). The lively river traffic that plied the waters of the Potomac and the Eastern Branch and linked together tidewater settlements is noted in John Sessford, "The Sessford Annals," *Records of the Columbia Historical Society* 11 (Washington, DC, 1908), whereas the "Letter From the Governor and Council of Maryland Transmitting a Report of the Commissioners Appointed to Survey the River Potomac" (Washington, DC, 1823) testifies to the hazards and uncertainties of river navigation caused by the "vicissitudes of the seasons." Richard Mannix, "Albert Gallatin in Washington," *Records of the Columbia Historical Society*, 1971–1972 (Washington, DC, 1973), records the rhythm of life in the young city—the social seasons, the muddy roads, and the embryonic neighborhoods situated on high ground.

The idea of a Potomac canal was popular even before the Revolution. The state of Virginia chartered an unsuccessful canal company as early as 1772. Another company (variously known as the Patowmack Company, the Patowmack Navigation Company, the Potomac Canal Company, or simply the Potomac Company) was chartered by Virginia in 1784 and by Maryland in 1785, with George Washington as its president (1785–1789). This company intended to improve the Potomac's river bed by removing obstructions wherever practical and to build a series of short canals around the falls and the unimprovable sections of the river. This system, known as sluice navigation, was the standard method used in England during the late eighteenth century. The Patowmack Company began levying tolls on the improved sections in 1799, and by 1802 five canal links, ranging from fifty yards to two miles in length, were complete. This system was navigable only during floods and freshets. The canal limped along until 1821, when a joint committee of the Virginia and Maryland legislatures investigated the Patowmack Company and found that the company had not fulfilled the proviso in its charter that it provide "navigation for boats carrying fifty barrels of flour even in the driest seasons." The company was disbanded in 1822.

Additional plans to improve the most unsatisfactory sections of the so-called Patowmack Canal between Little Falls and Georgetown were drawn up even while the Patowmack Company was still in existence. Benjamin Latrobe's Plans and Sections, prepared in 1802, was such a proposal. Latrobe's canal was never built, but the route he laid out was almost identical to the one along which the Chesapeake & Ohio Canal was constructed nearly twenty-five years later.

BUILDING THE CITY: THE FIRST FOUR DECADES
For Margaret Bayard Smith's remarks, see *The First Forty Years of Washington Society* (New York: C. Scribner's, 1906). For Joel Barlow's vision of the city of communication, see John Dos Passos, *The Ground We Stand On* (New York: Harcourt, Brace and Company, 1941). See also Mary Mitchell, "Kalorama: Country Estate to Washington Mayfair," *Records of the Columbia Historical Society,* 1971–1972 (Washington, DC, 1973), 1–72. Latrobe's remarks are quoted in Talbot F. Hamlin, *Benjamin Henry Latrobe* (New York: Oxford University Press, 1955); see there also Hamlin's description of the Van Ness residence designed by Latrobe. Mitchell reproduces the view painted by Charles Codman. The original painting is on display in the Jefferson Room, Department of State, Washington, DC. On particular residences, see George McCue, *The Octagon* (Washington, DC, 1976).

The design, construction, evolution, and frequent rebuildings of the President's House are lavishly covered in William Seale, *The White House: The History of an American Idea* (Washington, DC: American Institute of Architects Press, in cooperation with the White House

Historical Association, 1992). For a discussion of the development of the executive branch precinct, see Antoinette J. Lee, "The White House in the Monumental City," *White House History* 11 (Summer 2002), 4–13.

On Hadfield's confrontation with the "rogues" responsible for the construction of public buildings, see G. L. M. Goodfellow, "George Hadfield," *Architectural Review* [London] 138 (July 1965). For Robert Mills's statement about "good common buildings, which was a desideratum in architecture" and his allusion to the hydraulic cement used in the Treasury Building arches, see Helen Mar Pierce Gallagher, *Robert Mills: Architect of the Washington Monument 1781–1855* (New York: Columbia University Press, 1935), where there is considerable discussion of Mills's philosophy on the design and construction of public buildings. An updated summary of Mills is available in Robert L. Alexander, "Robert Mills," in *McMillan Encyclopedia of Architects*, edited by Adolf Placzek, vol. 3 (New York: The Free Press, 1982), 200–208. The National Capital Planning Commission's study, *Downtown Urban Renewal Area Landmarks, Washington, D.C.* (Washington, DC, 1970), describes Mills's arch construction, used by him also in the Patent Office as "an innovation in engineering at the time." For Robert Dale Owen's remarks on the Post Office, see his *Hints on Public Architecture* (New York, 1849). An authoritative work on the Chesapeake & Ohio Canal is Walter S. Sanderlin, *The Great National Project: A History of the Chesapeake & Ohio Canal* (Baltimore: Johns Hopkins Press, 1946); see also his article "The Maryland Canal Project: An Episode in the History of Maryland's Internal Improvements," *Maryland Historical Magazine* 45 (1950).

The history of slaves, slavery, and free blacks has been studied by a number of scholars, including Letitia W. Brown, "Residence Patterns of Negroes in the District of Columbia, 1800–1860," *Records of the Columbia Historical Society,* 1969–1970 (Washington, DC, 1971), 66–79; James Oliver Horton, "The Genesis of Washington's African American Community," in *Urban Odyssey: A Multicultural History of the Nation's Capital,* edited by Francine Curro Cary (Washington, DC: Smithsonian Institution Press, 1996), 20–41; John Michael Vlach, "Evidence of Slave Housing in Washington," *Washington History* (Fall–Winter 1993–1994), 64–74, 102–103; Mary Beth Corrigan, "The Ties That Bind: The Pursuit of Community and Freedom among Slaves and Free Blacks in the District of Columbia, 1800–1860," in *Southern City, National Ambition: The Growth of Early Washington, DC, 1800–1860,* edited by Howard Gillette Jr. (Washington, DC: George Washington University Center for Washington Area Studies in conjunction with the American Architectural Foundation, 1995), 69–90; Walter C. Celphane, "The Local Aspect of Slavery in the District of Columbia," *Records of the Columbia Historical Society* 3

(1900), 224–256; and Frederick Bancroft, *Slave-trading in the Old South*, (Baltimore: J. H. Furst Company, 1931).

WASHINGTON PANORAMA, 1840

On the retrocession movements initiated by Georgetown and Alexandria, see W. B. Bryan, *A History of the National Capital*, vol. 2 (New York: McMillan, 1916). Constance M. Green, *Washington: Village and Capital, 1800–1876* (Princeton, NJ: Princeton University Press, 1962), succeeds in visualizing the physical and social city of the 1840s and cites travelers' accounts that substantiate this panoramic view. See also the first edition of the guidebook by George Watterston, *A Picture of Washington* (Washington, DC, 1840), the first good guide to the city and an unambiguous source on the physical city in the year 1840.

THE MALL AND THE MONUMENTAL CORE

Robert Mills's letter to Robert Dale Owen on the "Proposed Smithsonian Institute" is quoted in Helen Mar Pierce Gallagher, *Robert Mills: Architect of the Washington Monument* (New York: Columbia University, 1935). Daniel D. Reiff, *Washington Architecture, 1791–1861: Problems in Development* (Washington, DC: US Commission of Fine Arts, 1971), offers thorough documentation of the city's major residential and public buildings, illustrated in excellent photographs.

Downing's plan for the Mall comprised both a written and a graphic portion. For the excerpts from the written portion, quoted here, see Wilcomb E. Washburn, "Vision of Life for the Mall," *Journal of the American Institute of Architects* 47 (March 1967). The physical evolution of the Capitol Building and the grounds surrounding it are discussed in two articles in the *Records of the Columbia Historical Society, 1969–1970* (Washington, DC, 1971): "The Capitol," by Philip Van Doren Stern, and "The Capitol in Peril? The West Front Controversy from Walter to Stewart," by Charles C. McLaughlin.

The US Botanic Garden located at the foot of Capitol Hill is the descendent of the Columbian Institute's early efforts. President Washington suggested as early as 1796 that a national botanic garden be established, but the idea was not acted upon until the early 1800s. The role of the short-lived (ca. 1820–1825) Washington Botanic Society in setting up the botanic garden is uncertain, but by 1818 the first president of the Columbian Institute was urging that the institute—a group of Washingtonians who met to discuss the natural world—assemble a collection of native plants that "might be useful in medicine and dye-making."

In 1820 Congress passed legislation that made it possible to lease public land to private parties willing to develop public gardens or parks. One of the first, and possibly the only, grants made under the provisions of

this act was that of five soggy acres at the eastern end of the Mall to the Columbian Institute for a botanic garden. The institute's founders had hoped that this group would become the Washington counterpart to Philadelphia's American Philosophical Society, but by 1826 the Columbian Institute was dying, and with it the botanic garden. A few Washingtonians continued to visit the garden over the next two decades, but on the whole the surviving specimens were ignored and neglected.

Interest in the idea of a botanic garden was renewed in 1842, when the US Exploring Expedition (Wilkes Expedition) returned from South America and the islands of the South Pacific with rare plant specimens. The Wilkes specimens were originally set up in and around the Patent Office (today the Smithsonian Institution's National Portrait Gallery and American Art Museum), but in 1850 the specimens were moved to greenhouses on or near the site of the Columbian Institute botanic garden. The US Botanic Garden is now under the jurisdiction of the Architect of the Capitol.

THE CITY'S WATERWAYS AND THE DESIGN OF A MODERN WATER SUPPLY

The route of Washington's water supply and technical aspects of its original design are covered in Albert E. Cowdrey, "Design for a City: The U.S. Army Engineers in the Building of the Nation's Capital" (MS, Historical Division, Office of the Chief of Engineers, Washington, DC, 1974), and Philip O. McQueen, "The Washington Aqueduct, 1852–1952" (MS, Washington District, Corps of Engineers, 1953). Further insight into Meigs as a designer is provided in Harold K. Skramstad, "The Engineer as Architect in Washington: The Contributions of Montgomery Meigs," *Records of the Columbia Historical Society, 1969–1970* (Washington, DC, 1971). W. B. Bryan describes construction of the water supply routes and support structures in *A History of the National Capital*, vol. 2 (New York: McMillan, 1916); see there also descriptions of the spread of public institutions beyond the District boundaries. The status of the capital city's waterways and shipping trade just before the Civil War can be gauged from the *Annual Report of the Secretary of the Treasury* for the years 1850–1860. The *Annual Report of the Secretary of War* for 1883 presents a ten-year survey of improvements to the Potomac River. See also at the Historical Society of Washington, DC, the file of newspaper clippings on riverfront improvements.

TOWARD A MORE COSMOPOLITAN CITY, 1850S

For the commentary on Washington "gentry," see W. B. Bryan, *A History of the National Capital*, vol. 2 (New York: McMillan, 1916); see there further details on the armory. The importance of tourism to nationwide interest in the capital city cannot be overestimated nor can the impression the city makes on tourists be ignored. For the quote from Frances Trollope about Mount Vernon, see *Domestic Manners of the Americans* (1832; reprint, London: Folio Society, 1974), 162. Roughly coinciding in its beginnings with the inauguration of rail travel (in 1835, when the Baltimore & Ohio Railroad reached Washington) and flooding at the time of the Civil War, tourism is best documented in the publication of literally hundreds of guidebooks. Most influential among the early guidebooks are those done by George Watterston: *A Picture of Washington* (1840), *A New Guide to Washington* (1842), and *New Guide to Washington* (1847–1848). For a more complete list of Washington directories and guidebooks, see Constance McLaughlin Green, *Washington: Village and Capital, 1800–1876* (Princeton, NJ: Princeton University Press, 1962).

3. The Civil War, 1860-1865

WASHINGTON IN WARTIME: THE MILITARY CITY

On this period of Washington history, the Historical Society of Washington, DC, calls attention to two little-known volumes in its collection. The condition of Washington during the war is discussed in Colonel George A. Armes, *Ups and Downs of an Army Officer* (Washington, DC: By the author, 1900). A strategic view of Washington's defenses is reflected in A. N. Waterman, "Washington in the Time of the First Bull Run," *Military Essays and Recollections of the Commandery of Illinois, Military Order of the Loyal Legion* 2 (1894). On the efforts of the capital city to provide modern municipal services to meet emergency wartime needs, see the *Journal of the 61st Council of the City of Washington* (Washington, DC, 1863–1864) and the *Journal of the 62nd Council of the City of Washington* (Washington, DC, 1864–1865), also at the Historical Society of Washington, DC. For contemporary descriptions of the abatis and city fortifications, see in the Martin Luther King Jr. Memorial Library, Washington, DC, Washingtoniana Division, the vertical files s.v. Civil War.

Albert James Myer was born in Newburgh, New York, in 1829. He entered the army as an assistant surgeon in 1854 and was posted to Texas. While there he became interested in the development of a system of visual signals as an alternative to the telegraph. A military board was created in 1858 to consider Myer's suggestions, and two years later Congress passed an act providing for one signal officer, but no signal corps, in the army. Myer was appointed to this post of signal officer, which carried the rank of major, and was ordered to New Mexico to serve in the campaign against the Navajo.

Shortly after the outbreak of the Civil War, he was ordered to Washington to organize and command what, in 1863, was to become the US Army Signal Corps. Myer established a signal school near what is today the junction of Massachusetts and Wisconsin avenues NW to train signal corpsmen in his "wig/wag" system and code. This system, which Myer had perfected in New Mexico, utilized a single flag in a series of prescribed positions. The size and color of the flag varied according to the distance the signal had to be sent (the greater the distance, the larger the flag) and the color of the background behind the signaler (a white flag if the signaler were silhouetted against a dark background, and a red flag if in an open area or against a light background). At night signals were sent by means of two lanterns, one placed at the feet of the signaler as a point of reference while the other was moved according to the same pattern as a flag. Myer published his code in 1864 in *A Manual of Signals: For the Use of Signal Officers in the Field*. When the Signal Corps was reorganized by Congress in 1866, Myer was made chief signal officer with the permanent rank of colonel. He continued as chief signal officer until his death in 1880.

WASHINGTON IN WARTIME: THE CIVILIAN CITY

George Rothwell Brown, *A Not Too Serious History* (Baltimore, 1930), delineates in anecdotal style the social city and the public accommodations generated by the massive influx of soldiers. Graphic documentation for the nearly self-sufficient fortress city is provided in Stanley P. Kimmel, *Mr. Lincoln's Washington* (New York: Coward-McCann, 1957), and in the issues of *Harper's Weekly* that span the war years. For social history of the period, see Mary Mitchell, *Divided Town* (Barre, MA, 1968), which presents a picture of divided loyalties in Georgetown. This theme is pursued at the imaginative level in Alan Tate's novel *The Fathers* (New York: G. P. Putnam's Sons, 1938).

The spelling for the modern Tenleytown section of Northwest Washington has varied over the decades. The area is named for the original Tenally family, but officials—census takers and tax assessors—varied in the spelling of the name. The most popular spelling before the nineteenth century, and probably even before the Civil War, was "Tenallytown"; certainly this is the spelling preferred by longtime residents of the area. A third spelling, "Tennallytown," also occasionally appears. See further Judy Beck Helm, *Tenleytown, DC: Country Village into City Neighborhood* (Washington, DC: Tennally Press, 1981).

WASHINGTON IN TRANSITION: THE WAR'S END

The symbolic value of the city in the Union cause is clearly perceived by Margaret Leech in *Reveille in Washington* (New York: Harper & Brothers, 1941), a remarkable history of the effects of the Civil War on the city. In this work, moreover, events are closely tied to the scale of the neighborhoods and widely dispersed public enclaves that the city then presented. For an authentic and anecdotal visualization of how Washington looked to the viewer in 1866, see the pictorial map and guidebook T. Loftin [Snell], *Stranger's Guide to Washington, D.C.: The City as Mr. Lincoln Knew It, 1865* (Washington, DC: By the author, 1967).

A summary of the role of the Freedmen's Bureau is presented in Lois E. Horton, "The Days of Jubilee: Black Migration during the Civil War and Reconstruction," in *Urban Odyssey: A Multicultural History of the Nation's Capital,* edited by Francine Curro Cary (Washington, DC: Smithsonian Institution Press, 1996), 65–78.

4. The Postbellum City, 1865-1900

THE WINDS OF PEACE: DEMILITARIZED CITY

Samuel C. Busey, *Pictures of the City of Washington in the Past* (Washington, DC, 1898), and *Personal Reminiscences* (Washington, DC, 1895), offer a personalized view of the postwar city in transition as it was expanding beyond the District boundaries into the metropolitan region. On Washington's social seasons, see "A Nation in a Nutshell," *Harper's New Monthly Magazine* (March 1881). For the description of Washington as the "paradise of a poor man with brains," see Henry H. Glassie, "Victorian Homes in Washington," *Records of the Columbia Historical Society, 1963–1965* (Washington, DC, 1967). The 1875 *Harper's* article referred to in the text is "New Washington," *Harper's New Monthly Magazine* (February 1875).

PUBLIC WORKS: THE ARMY CORPS OF ENGINEERS

The essential documentation of federal contributions to the city's development is provided by the annual reports of the Corps of Engineers. In these reports, each of the supervisory personnel relates his efforts to tame and to make navigable the waters of the Potomac and the Anacostia; to provide the city with a clean, clear, modern water supply; to reclaim the malarial flats and also floodproof the city; and to protect the increasingly scarce cultural and historical resources of a city experiencing rapid change. Happily, many of the key figures in the Corps of Engineers during this era possessed a keen interest in the historical roots underlying these environmental issues. A preliminary analysis of the corps's role in the Victorian city is offered in Colonel Alan J. McCutchen, "A Historical Summary of the Work of the Corps of Engineers in Washington, D.C. and Vicinity, 1852–1952" (MS, Washington District, Corps of Engineers, 1952), which is organized around specific structures and natural phenomena, and Albert E. Cowdrey, "Design for a City: The U.S. Army Engineers in the Building of the Nation's Capital" (MS, Historical Division, Office of the Chief of Engineers, Washington, DC, 1974), which traces the career of the corps through the sequence of time. On the water supply responsibilities of the corps, see Philip O.

McQueen, "The Washington Aqueduct, 1852–1952" (MS, Washington District, Corps of Engineers, 1953). The Meigs letter to Michler, dated July 27, 1867, describing European streets is printed in full as Appendix T-2 to the 1867 *Annual Report of the Chief of Engineers.*

THE TERRITORIAL GOVERNMENT OF WASHINGTON, 1871-1874

On this period of Washington history, and especially the brief but influential career of Alexander R. Shepherd, see William M. Maury, *Alexander "Boss" Shepherd and the Board of Public Works* (Washington, DC: George Washington University, 1975), and also the earlier version published in the *Records of the Columbia Historical Society, 1971–1972* (Washington, DC, 1973). See also Maury's "The Territorial Period in Washington, 1871–1874" (PhD diss., George Washington University, Washington, DC, 1975), especially for information on public improvements in the northwest quadrant of the city. In addition, some of the notable designers in this period are discussed in Harold K. Skramstad, "The Engineer as Architect in Washington: The Contribution of Montgomery Meigs," *Records of the Columbia Historical Society, 1969–1970* (Washington, DC, 1971). On the overall condition of sewers, public utilities, and street pavement in the city at the end of the third quarter century, see "New Washington," *Harper's New Monthly Magazine* (February 1875).

On Orville Babcock, see, in addition to the *Dictionary of American Biography,* the *Annual Report of the Chief of Engineers* for the years 1871–1877, when he was in charge of public buildings and grounds. See also Donald J. Lehman, *Executive Office Building,* General Services Administration Historical Study no. 3 (Washington, DC, 1970). On Alfred B. Mullett's government career, see the *Annual Report of the Supervising Architect of the Treasury* for the years 1863–1874. Lawrence Wodehouse's comment on the State, War and Navy Building is in his article "Alfred B. Mullett and His French Style Government Buildings," *Journal of the Society of Architectural Historians* 31 (March 1972). A history of the Supervising Architect's Office, with a chapter on Mullett, is provided in Antoinette J. Lee, *Architects to the Nation: The Rise and Decline of the Supervising Architect's Office* (New York: Oxford University Press, 2000). A fresh look at Alexander R. Shepherd and the transition to the commission form of municipal government is provided in Alan Lessoff, *The Nation and Its City: Politics, Corruption, and Progress in Washington, D.C., 1861–1902* (Baltimore: Johns Hopkins University Press, 1994).

THE NEW MUNICIPAL GOVERNMENT: BY COMMISSION

On the role of the District government in the city's physical evolution, see the annual reports of the commissioners of the District of Columbia.

THE WATER SUPPLY FOR WASHINGTON, ABUNDANT AND CLEAR

The development of the city's water system is not reliably discussed at length in any of the general secondary sources for this period of Washington history. A great deal of information is contained, however, in readily available printed primary sources such as the annual reports of the chief of the Army Corps of Engineers. The annual reports of the water registrar (pre-1887) and the water superintendent (post-1887) contained in the annual reports of the engineer commissioner of the District of Columbia also provide a wealth of information. In addition, the District of Columbia government has maps of the water distribution system for the period after 1871.

A discussion of the condition of the city's sewer system is contained in a report issued by a presidential committee in the mid-1880s. A series of official reports to Congress prepared by the city government before construction of the filter plant (ca. 1905) discusses the condition of the water itself as well as the supply system. During the 1930s, a report to establish the capital cost basis of the water system was prepared under the direction of the engineer commissioner and submitted to Congress. Informally referred to as the "Shingler Report," this document contains historical information on costs, dates, and justification for additions and improvements to the city water system. Like the Shingler Report, House Document No. 480, prepared jointly by the Office of the Engineer Commissioner and the Corps of Engineers during the 1940s, contains historical information on development and expansion of the system for Washington.

RECLAMATION OF THE RIVER FLATS AND THE CREATION OF PUBLIC PARKS

For a contemporary view, see "Improvement of the Potomac Flats," *Scientific American* 65 (September 1891). For Waring's findings, see "A Report of Mr. George E. Waring, Jr., on the Improvement of the Sanitary Condition of the Executive Mansion," as printed in the *Annual Report of the Chief of Engineers* for 1882. For Frederick Law Olmsted's statement of his position on a "comprehensive scheme" for the Mall, see his letter to Mr. V. Hammond Hall, March 28, 1874, Olmsted Papers, Library of Congress Manuscript Division. For discussions of the Olmsted plan for the Capitol grounds, see Charles C. McLaughlin, "The Capitol in Peril? The West Front Controversy from Walter to Stewart," *Records of the Columbia Historical Society,* 1969–1970 (Washington, DC, 1971); Albert Fein, *Frederick Law Olmsted and the American Environmental Tradition* (New York: G. Braziller, 1972); and Laura Wood Roper, *FLO: A Biography of Frederick Law Olmsted* (Baltimore: John Hopkins University Press, 1973). On Theodore A. Bingham, see the entry in *Who's Who in America, 1930–1931* (Chicago: Marquis, Who's

Who, Inc., 1932), and the *Annual Report of the Chief of Engineers* for the years 1897 to 1903, when Bingham was in the Office of Public Buildings and Grounds. See also John W. Reps, *Monumental Washington* (Princeton, NJ: Princeton University Press, 1967).

PUBLIC BUILDINGS IN THE CENTURY'S LAST DECADES

The history of the Renaissance-style Library of Congress Building is traced in four articles in *The Quarterly Journal of the Library of Congress* (October 1972): Helen-Anne Hilker, "Monument to Civilization: Diary of a Building"; John Y. Cole, "The Main Building of the Library of Congress: A Chronology, 1871–1965"; "Album"; and "Smithmeyer & Pelx: Embattled Architects of the Library of Congress." See further John Y. Cole, "A National Monument for a National Library: Ainsworth Rand Spofford and the New Library of Congress, 1871–1897," *Records of the Columbia Historical Society,* 1971–1972 (Washington, DC, 1973). Federal public buildings and structures testified to the government's commitment to Washington as the capital city and directly influenced the configurations of growth in the region. For an important study of evolving philosophies of public design, see Joanna Schneider Zangrando, "Monumental Bridge Design in Washington, D.C., as a Reflection of American Culture, 1886–1932" (PhD diss., George Washington University, 1974). The General Services Administration has sponsored several excellent histories of key federal buildings of this era under the learned authorship of Donald J. Lehman: *Pension Building,* General Services Administration Historical Study No. 1 (Washington, DC, 1964), and *Executive Office Building,* Study No. 3 (1970). See also Gail Karesh Kassan, "The Old Post Office Building in Washington, D.C.: Its Past, Present and Future," *Records of the Columbia Historical Society,* 1971–1972 (Washington, DC, 1973).

For the observation on the streetcar system, see "New Washington," *Harper's New Monthly Magazine* (February 1875). For further observations on Washington's residential architecture and the eccentricities of the L'Enfant cross streets, see the following sequence of articles in *Harper's New Monthly Magazine*: "State and Society in Washington" (March 1878), "A Nation in a Nutshell" (March 1881), and "A Glimpse of Some Washington Homes" (March 1885). For the quotations from Tanya Edwards Beauchamp, see the article "Adolph Cluss: An Architect in Washington during Civil War and Reconstruction," *Records of the Columbia Historical Society,* 1971–1972 (Washington, DC, 1973). A comprehensive history of the development of public school buildings is provided in Antoinette J. Lee, "Public School Buildings of the District of Columbia, 1804–1930," Sumner School Museum and Archives, Public Schools of the District of Columbia, September 1989.

RESIDENTIAL WASHINGTON AND THE GROWTH OF SUBURBS

On the Dupont Circle area, see further in the Martin Luther King Jr. Memorial Library, Washington, DC, Washingtoniana Division, the vertical files s.v. Residential Sections–Dupont Circle. See these same files s.v. Mount Pleasant. In general, these files provide an excellent source for primary materials on residential areas in Washington.

An edited compendium of Washington, DC, neighborhoods is presented in Kathryn Schneider Smith, ed., *Washington at Home: An Illustrated History of Neighborhoods in the Nation's Capital* (Northridge, CA: Windsor Publications, Inc., 1988). James M. Goode, *Best Addresses: A Century of Washington's Distinguished Apartment Houses* (1988; reprint, Washington, DC: Smithsonian Institution Press, 2003), provides a comprehensive history of the apartment building types in the city and surrounding metropolitan area, including a number that have been demolished.

HIGHWAY LEGISLATION, 1890S

On the streets of Washington, see further in the Martin Luther King Jr. Memorial Library, Washington, DC, Washingtoniana Division, the vertical files s.v. Streets. The highway plans prepared by the engineer commissioner of the District of Columbia in response to the 1893 Highway Act (27 Stat. 532), and issued in 1895 and 1897, can be found in bound form at the Cartographic Division of the National Archives, Record Group 351, "Records of the District Surveyor's Office."

5. The McMillan Plan, 1901-1902

TURN OF THE CENTURY: THE PROMISE OF AMERICAN CITIES

John W. Reps describes in detail the pre–McMillan Commission plans for the Mall area, most notably those offered by Franklin W. Smith, Theodore Bingham, and Samuel Parsons Jr., in *Monumental Washington: The Planning and Development of the Capital Center* (Princeton, NJ: Princeton University Press, 1967).

THE AMERICAN INSTITUTE OF ARCHITECTS' CONVENTION IN WASHINGTON, 1900

Discussion of Washington architecture and planning by members of the American Institute of Architects is published in the *Proceedings of the 34th Annual Convention of the American Institute of Architects* (Washington, DC, 1900). This volume of *Proceedings* includes discussion by Cass Gilbert, Edgar Seeler, C. Howard Walker, Paul Pelz, George Oakley Totten, H. K. Bush-Brown, Joseph C. Hornblower, and Frederick Law Olmsted Jr., as well as the opening remarks of McFarland and Peabody, as quoted here in the text. Glenn Brown, *Memories,*

1860–1930 (Washington, DC: Press of W. F. Roberts Company, 1931), provides a highly personalized view of the "revival" of the L'Enfant plan, the role of the American Institute of Architects in its "crusade" to improve civic art, the work of the McMillan Commission, and the array of political and design figures who secured the Beaux-Arts traditions in Washington up to World War II.

Documents related to the McMillan Plan include Glenn Brown, comp., *Papers Relating to the Improvement of the City of Washington* (Washington, DC, 1901); Charles Moore, ed. and comp., *Park Improvement Papers* (Washington, DC, 1903); and William V. Cox, comp., *Celebration of the One-Hundredth Anniversary of the Establishment of the Seat of Government in the District of Columbia* (Washington, DC, 1901). For additional background on Cass Gilbert, see his *Reminiscences and Addresses* (New York: private printing [The Scribner Press], 1935). Glenn Brown's plan for the capital is described by him in "A Suggestion for Grouping Government Buildings: Landscape, Monuments, and Statuary," *Architectural Review* [Boston] 7 (August 1900), reprinted in the *Proceedings of the 34th Annual Convention of the American Institute of Architects* (Washington, DC, 1900). For Charles Moore's view of Washington as a world standard, see Moore's unpublished memoirs, National Archives, Washington, DC, Record Group 42, Section 66, "Records of the Commission of Fine Arts."

SENATOR MCMILLAN AND THE SENATE PARK COMMISSION, 1901

Senator McMillan's carefully worded statement on the formation of the Senate Park Commission is contained in the official report: US Congress, Senate Committee on the District of Columbia, *The Improvement of the Park System of the District of Columbia,* 57th Cong., 1st sess., 1902, S. Rept. 166. This report incorporates a complete description of the proposed plan, excerpts of which are quoted here in the text. The original report continues to make good reading on the city of Washington as it would become and the aesthetic prescriptions to which it would respond. On the roles played by individuals on the McMillan Commission and for anecdotal materials, the following biographies have been consulted and quoted: Thomas S. Hines, *Burnham of Chicago: Architect and Planner* (New York: Oxford University Press, 1974); Charles Moore, *Daniel H. Burnham: Architect, Planner of Cities,* 2 vols. (1921; reprint, New York: DaCapo Press, 1968), and *The Life and Times of Charles Follen McKim* (Boston: Houghton Mifflin Company, 1929); Lewis Hind, *Augustus Saint-Gaudens* (New York: International Studio, John Lane Company, 1908); Louise Tharp, *Saint-Gaudens and the Gilded Era* (Boston: Little, Brown, 1969); *The Reminiscences of Augustus Saint-Gaudens,* edited by Homer Saint-Gaudens, 2 vols. (New York: Century Co., 1913).

THE GRAND TOUR AND THE CITY OF THE FUTURE

The route of the European tour that provided Old World inspiration and clarification of architectural and design sources for commission members is recorded by Charles Moore in the first volume of his biography of Daniel H. Burnham (1921; reprint, New York: DaCapo Press, 1968), as well as in his biography of McKim (Boston: Houghton Mifflin, 1929). John W. Reps, *Monumental Washington: The Planning and Development of the Capital Center* (Princeton, NJ: Princeton University Press, 1967), covers the negotiations between Alexander Cassatt and Burnham, as well as the work of William T. Partridge in the New York City office of the commission.

THE COMMISSION'S REPORT AND THE MODELS OF WASHINGTON, 1902

The official report is titled *The Improvement of the Park System of the District of Columbia* (57th Cong., 1st sess., 1902, S. Rept. 166). The pair of scale models (one inch = 80 feet) of Washington designed and constructed by George Carroll Curtis in 1901–1902 for the McMillan Senate Park Commission enjoyed an exceptionally long and useful life. These models, now the property of the Commission of Fine Arts, were selected for inclusion in the bicentennial exhibition, Federal City: Plans and Realities, sponsored jointly by the National Capital Planning Commission, the Commission of Fine Arts, and the Smithsonian Institution and exhibited in the Smithsonian's Great Hall beginning February 22, 1976. By the early 1970s, Curtis's models had found their way to storage in a hangar at National Airport and were by this time in vast disarray. Two restorers worked for an entire year to reassemble the models, like giant jigsaw puzzles, detail by detail, building by building, tree by tiny tree. A two-thirds section of each of the two original models was restored for display. The exhibition labels for the models read as follows: Washington, Existing Conditions, 1900, and Washington, Proposed Changes, 1902.

The comprehensive parks design that was translated by Frederick Law Olmsted Jr. onto the Washington landscape was derived from the Boston Metropolitan Park Commission by Charles Eliot and Sylvester Baxter. Details were affectionately recorded by the former's father, Harvard president Charles W. Eliot, in Charles Eliot, *Landscape Architect* (1902; reprint, Amherst: University of Massachusetts Press, Library of American Landscape History, 1999).

THE GRAND PLAN FOR THE MALL

Key sources for the design standards to which the commission members subscribed include Glenn Brown, *1860–1930, Memories* (Washington, DC: Press of W. F. Roberts Company, 1931), and Charles Moore's unpublished memoirs, National Archives, Washington, DC,

Record Group 42, Section 66, "Records of the Commission of Fine Arts." Moore's memoirs are an especially rich source on the personal qualities of commission members; see Moore's memoirs also for insight into the political maneuverings of the commission.

SELLING THE PLAN: THE TASK OF ENLIGHTENMENT

For the critical reference to the "pantalooned statue," see the *Washington Post*, October 8, 1907. For Grant's statement and additional background on preservation of the L'Enfant plan, see Ulysses S. Grant III, "The L'Enfant Plan and Its Evolution," *Records of the Columbia Historical Society, 1932* (Washington, DC, 1932). Public Law 1036 on Mall development and the role of the National Capital Park and Planning Commission is documented in *Statutes at Large* 45 ch. 708, 619 (1929).

THE 1901-1902 PLAN: REACTION AND RESPONSE

The historical record traces comment and criticism of the McMillan Plan. Initial enthusiasm for the plan was tempered by the reality of specific building projects, the first group of which were under way by 1908 and could be seen by the *Evening Star* as costly beyond the nation's means. The Mall element of the plan, so said the *Star*, was likely to be as "bare and hot as the Desert of Sahara," the straight-lined formality of the design was "grim," and the new commission that advocated the plan was seen as "self-appointed." The newly conceived Mall and its formal plantings, in the eyes of those still faithful to the curving concealments and surprises of Downing, were seen as the work of "tree-butchers and nature-butchers."

The initial constituency of the plan had passed from the scene by the 1920s, to be succeeded by the more discriminating objectivity of the urban design historian Elbert Peets, the first to write about the McMillan Plan in the longer perspective; see Paul D. Spreiregen, ed., *On the Art of Designing Cities: Selected Essays of Elbert Peets* (Cambridge, MA: MIT Press, 1968). Peets was succeeded by John W. Reps, whose *Monumental Washington* (Princeton, NJ: Princeton University Press, 1967) described the McMillan Plan as the "first and greatest essay in civic design of the American twentieth century." In his standard history of city planning in the United States, Mel Scott, *American City Planning Since 1890*, 2nd ed. (Berkeley: University of California Press, 1971), found the principal achievement of the plan to be the city's central core, fatally outmoded by the automobile so as to become a "historical artifact, an elaborate set piece immune to the whims of time and chance, a sacrosanct expression of the national past and the national destiny" untouched by the realities of national history or geography. In his biography of Daniel Burnham, Thomas S. Hines, *Burnham of Chicago: Architect and Planner* (New York: Oxford University Press, 1974), recognizes the plan as "a major renewal effort" to replace an "eclectic and textured homogeneity [with a] homogeneous uniformity."

This catalog of characterizations could be considerably expanded, but it is clear that no one has yet taken full measure of the McMillan Plan. As for the City Beautiful formula, see further Charles Mulford Robinson, *Modern Civic Art, or The City Made Beautiful* (New York: G. P. Putnam's Sons, 1903). To evaluate the McMillan Plan in light of later City Beautiful schemes, see Ira L. Bach, "A Reconsideration of the 1909 Plan of Chicago," *Chicago History* 2 (Spring–Summer 1973), and "The City Beautiful and the San Francisco Fair," in Kevin Starr, *Americans and the California Dream* (New York: Oxford University Press, 1973).

In *The Birth of City Planning in the United States, 1840–1917* (Baltimore: Johns Hopkins University Press, 2003), Jon A. Peterson examines the role of the McMillan Plan in the development of planning in the United States and refers to the plan as the "foundation story of American city planning." An examination of aspects of the McMillan Plan and its influence on development in the city and metropolitan area at the turn of the twentieth century is provided in two volumes of *Washington History*: 14, no. 1 (Spring–Summer 2002), and 14, no. 2 (Fall–Winter 2002). Edited by Pamela Scott, both volumes commemorate the plan's centennial.

6. Toward Metropolis, 1902-1926

THE PLAUSIBLE PATTERN AND A QUEST FOR NEW PLANNING

The annual reports of the chief of the Army Corps of Engineers provide the essential background to the widening de facto planning responsibilities of the federal government before the corps's absorption—along with the office of the superintendent of the State, War and Navy Building—in 1925 into the independent Office of Public Buildings and Public Parks of the National Capital. The 1925 legislation is 43 Stat. 983.

URBAN PARK DEVELOPMENT: THEORY AND PRACTICE IN WASHINGTON

The best general introductions to urban park development for the early decades of the twentieth century are found in Mel Scott, *American City Planning since 1890*, 2nd ed. (Berkeley: University of California Press, 1971), and John W. Reps, *Monumental Washington* (Princeton, NJ: Princeton University Press, 1967). Information on specific projects is best obtained from primary sources, including the Minutes and *Annual Report of the Commission of Fine Arts* for the years 1910–1926; the Minutes of the National Capital Park Commission for the years 1924–1926; the *American Planning and Civic Annual* of the American Planning and Civic Association; and the annual reports of the chief of the Army Corps of Engineers.

PUBLIC ARCHITECTURE: CONSTITUENT BUILDINGS AND ORCHESTRATED URBAN FORM

The philosophy and importance of the eclectic nationalized style and of the Classical Revival in Washington can best be gleaned from manuscript sources, especially the records of federal agencies concerned with design in the city. These include Minutes and the *Annual Report of the Commission of Fine Arts* for the years 1910–1926; the Minutes of the National Capital Park Commission; annual reports of the Public Buildings Commission; records of the Office of the Supervising Architect of the Treasury; and the manuscript diaries of Edward Bennett. Issues of the *American Planning and Civic Annual* also contain substantial material. For serial articles on individual projects and architects, see the *Avery Index to Architectural Periodicals*, 15 vols., 2nd ed. (Boston: G. K. Hall, 1973).

Additional information on the architecture of the period can be found in Pamela Scott and Antoinette J. Lee, *Buildings of the District of Columbia* (New York: Oxford University Press, 1993); Sue A. Kohler, *The Commission of Fine Arts: A Brief History, 1910–1990* (Washington: Commission of Fine Arts, 1990); and Christopher A. Thomas, *The Lincoln Memorial & American Life* (Princeton, NJ: Princeton University Press, 2002).

CIVIC DESIGN: FIRST QUARTER OF THE CENTURY

The *Annual Report of the Commission of Fine Arts* for 1910–1926 emphasizes the aesthetic aspects of the official city but allows for transmittal of many McMillan Plan recommendations into the work schedules of the National Capital Park Commission and the National Capital Park and Planning Commission.

According to tradition, the "White Lot" was so named because of a whitewashed wooden fence that surrounded it. This area, roughly equivalent to the present Ellipse, is bounded by Constitution Avenue, 17th and 18th streets, and the White House grounds. One of the major problems that had confronted the Quartermaster Corps in Washington during the Civil War was the storage of supplies, particularly livestock, for the army's use. The creation of this White Lot as a holding area for cattle awaiting slaughter was a typical solution to supply problems, though the area's name persisted in common usage long after the problems and the war were over.

VARIETIES OF RESIDENTIAL DEVELOPMENT: HOMES AND HOUSES IN CITY AND SUBURB

For details on the private development of the city, see further in the Martin Luther King Jr. Memorial Library, Washington, DC, Washingtoniana Division, the vertical files s.v. Residential Sections. For the reference to Foxhall Village, for example, see the vertical files s.v. Residential Sections–Foxhall; on the electric railroad to Glen Echo, see Residential Sections–Palisades. An exhaustive survey of Massachusetts Avenue as exemplary of gracious Washington architecture is published by the Commission of Fine Arts, *Massachusetts Avenue Architecture,* 2 vols. (Washington, DC, 1973–1975). On the Larz Anderson House, see further James Orr Denby, *The Society of the Cincinnati and Its Museum* (Washington, DC, 1967); Rita Reif, *Treasure Rooms of America's Mansions, Manors and Houses* (New York: Coward-McCann, 1970); and Herbert P. Weissberger, "Notes on Anderson House," 1971 (typewritten).

Studies of the development of Washington subdivisions are provided in Christopher Michael Shaheen, "Beyond the Grand Design: City Planning in Washington beyond the Federal Core, 1919–1941" (master's thesis, George Washington University, 2000); Sharon MacDonald, "Row House Construction in DC between the World Wars" (master's thesis, George Washington University, 1995); and Diane Shaw Wasch, "Models of Beauty and Predictability: The Creation of Wesley Heights and Spring Valley," *Washington History*, vol. 1, no. 2 (Fall 1989), 58–76.

Larz Anderson III was born in Paris in 1866. After being educated at Harvard, he entered the US diplomatic service, serving first as the second secretary at the American legation in London (1891) and then as the first secretary at the American embassy in Rome (1894–1897). Anderson served in the Spanish-American War as a captain and assistant adjunct general of volunteers and then resumed his diplomatic career. He was appointed minister to Belgium in 1911 and ambassador to Japan from 1912 to 1913. He resigned from the diplomatic service before the outbreak of World War I. During the war, Anderson was very active in volunteer relief work in Washington, DC, and traveled extensively. He died in 1937 and was buried in St. Mary's Chapel at the National Cathedral in Washington.

Between 1902 and 1905, Anderson and his wife, Boston heiress Isabel Weld Perkins, built the fifty-room late Renaissance-Revival-style house at 2118 Massachusetts Avenue NW. Designed by the Boston architectural firm of Little and Browne, the house was a center for local and international society until Anderson's death. Anderson's great-grandfather had been one of the founders of the Society of the Cincinnati, and in 1939 Mrs. Anderson donated the house and most of its furnishings to the society for a national headquarters.

7. The Year of Decision, 1926
LEGITIMIZATION OF PLANNING: METROPOLITAN CITY, NATIONAL CAPITAL
For documenting national and local advancements toward creation of professional planning bodies, see the annual reports of the Washington Board of Trade, the Commission of Fine Arts, the US Chamber of Commerce, and the American Planning and Civic Association. For the John Nolen Sr. summarizing work on citizens' groups, see the report of the 1924 National Conference on City Planning, "The Importance of Citizens' Committees in Securing Public Support for a City Planning Program."

For the early work of Harlean James, see her *Land Planning in the United States for the City, State and Nation* (New York: McMillan Company, 1926). The 1923 remarks by Colonel C. O. Sherrill are quoted in the *Evening Star,* May 2, 1923. John M. Gries and James Ford edited the proceedings of the thirty-one committees that constituted the influential President's Conference on Home Building and Home Ownership; see especially the volume entitled *Planning for Residential Districts* (Washington, DC, 1931), where photographs of sections of Washington are used to illustrate the best and the worst of the national housing picture. President Herbert Hoover traced the development of his personal interest and commitment to housing and planning issues in Washington in *The Memoirs of Herbert Hoover* (New York: Garland Publishers, 1979). For the Civic Development Department's statements on planning, see US Chamber of Commerce, *The National Chamber's Civic Work* (Washington, DC). For the Washington Board of Trade's view of itself as a voluntary and unofficial organization, see *Nation's Capital Magazine* (November 1930).

LEGISLATION FOR COMPREHENSIVE PLANNING: THE ACTS OF 1924 AND 1926
The act creating the National Capital Park Commission in 1924 (43 Stat. 463) represents the first step toward a planning body, legislated two years later with the 1926 act providing for the National Capital Park and Planning Commission (44 Stat. 374). Rationale for this 1926 act is illustrated in the Minutes of the National Capital Park Commission, on file at the National Capital Planning Commission. They testify, among other things, to the low levels of funding and the shortcomings of park acquisition powers without a comprehensive planning context in which to act.

THE PUBLIC BUILDINGS ACT OF 1926: THE FEDERAL TRIANGLE PROJECT
The development of the Federal Triangle and changing justifications for the project can be studied through the *Annual Report of the Public Buildings Commission* for the years 1922–1932. The articles in the *Federal Architect* published from July 1930 through 1946 by the Association of Federal Architects under the spirited editorship of Edwin B. Morris of the Treasury Department reflect the changing tastes in civic design at the federal level. The diaries of Edward H. Bennett are housed at the Art Institute of

Chicago, Chicago, Illinois. For the addresses delivered at the April 25–26, 1929, conference at the US Chamber of Commerce, see *The Development of the United States Capitol,* 71st Cong., 1st sess., H. Doc. No. 35, 1930. For Andrew Mellon's statement on responsibility to the McMillan Plan, see Andrew W. Mellon, "A Unified Plan for Public Buildings," *American Planning and Civic Annual* (Washington, DC, 1930). For Bennett's notes on modern "blunt" architecture, see the diary entry for April 13, 1931. See there also the quoted remarks of President Hoover.

Philip Sawyer, "The Design of Public Buildings," *Architectural Forum* 55 (September 1931), outlines the difference in design between public and private architecture, with the "economy" characteristic emphasized in the Federal Triangle. Mellon's suggestions to Bennett on the "harmonious design" for the Federal Triangle are quoted in Edward H. Bennett's article, "The Architecture of the Capitol," in *The Development of the United States Capitol,* 71st Cong., 1st sess., H. Doc. No. 35, 1930; see there also Bennett's view (cited here in the text) of the plazas' unifying function in the Federal Triangle. The rationale behind the civic center element of City Beautiful design as represented by the Federal Triangle is developed in Warner Hegemann and Elbert Peets, *The American Vitruvius: An Architect's Handbook of Civic Art* (1922; reprint, New York: B. Blom, 1972). For the remark of John Russell Pope on the role of the Board of Architectural Consultants, see the miscellaneous papers accompanying the diaries of Edward H. Bennett dated September 21, 1931, Art Institute of Chicago. The annual reports and Minutes of the National Capital Park and Planning Commission covering the 1930s shed considerable light on the commission's entry into Federal Triangle planning after this planning was well under way. These documents also highlight the rising issues of traffic, parking, and design that compromised Bennett's plan for the Apex Building of the Triangle composition.

For Karl K. Hardy's remarks on the soundness of the Federal Triangle building program, see his "Economic Justification for the New Public Buildings," *American Planning and Civic Annual* (Washington, DC, 1932). George Gurney, *Sculpture and the Federal Triangle* (Washington, DC: Smithsonian Institution Press, 1985), provides an appreciation of the artworks that adorned the Federal Triangle complex, and Sally Kress Tompkins, *A Quest for Grandeur: Charles Moore and the Federal Triangle* (Washington, DC: Smithsonian Institution Press, 1993), traces the evolution of the Federal Triangle from the McMillan Commission plan to the Triangle's completion.

8. Expansive Planning Visions, 1926-1933

PLANNING IN THE NATION'S CAPITAL

The work schedules of the National Capital Park and Planning Commission are recorded in detail in the Minutes of the commission covering the years studied and are summarized for public inspection in the commission's annual reports for the years 1927–1932. These documents are on file at the National Capital Planning Commission, Washington, DC. For correspondence describing the commission members as "men of the widest experience," see Louis C. Cramton to Mr. H. M. Lord, Director of the Budget, January 29, 1929, Louis C. Cramton Papers, Library of Michigan History, University of Michigan, Ann Arbor, Michigan. For Charles Eliot's remarks on his "strong sense" of history and his job as a professional planner, see the newspaper article dated July 1931, Charles Eliot II Papers, Graduate School of Design, Harvard University, Cambridge, Massachusetts. The anecdote about Harlean James's viewing Eliot as "that kid" was recounted to the author in a personal interview with Charles Eliot II, Cambridge, Massachusetts. Statements by Eliot, U. S. Grant III, and Major Carey Brown to the House Committee on the District of Columbia are quoted in *The Work of the National Capital Park and Planning Commission,* Final Report of the House Committee on the District of Columbia, 70th Cong, 1st sess., March 10, 1928. A similar collection of statements to introduce the commission to the national planning profession were made to the National Conference on City Planning; see the report, *The Development of the National Capital and Its Environs* (Philadelphia: Wm. F. Fell Co., 1928).

THE AUTOMOBILE

For the views of J. C. Nichols, see his article "Economic Saving in City Planning" in the report of the National Conference on City Planning, *The Development of the National Capital and Its Environs* (Boston: Wm. F. Fell Co., 1928). The molding of residential development to the natural topography as articulated by Nichols is illustrated in promotional literature found in the neighborhood files, Martin Luther King Jr. Memorial Library, Washington, DC, Washingtoniana Division. For Harland Bartholomew's resume of street development, see the *Annual Report of the National Capital Park and Planning Commission,* 1928. Annual reports of this commission are on file at the National Capital Planning Commission, Washington, DC. On the special interest maps prepared by the commission, see the newspaper article dated July 1931, Charles Eliot II Papers, Graduate School of Design, Harvard University, Cambridge, Massachusetts. See this collection also for the statement on Georgetown and Boston's Beacon Hill as quoted in the section on housing in this chapter.

HOUSING

For John Ihlder's housing proposal, see his article "A Housing Program for the District of Columbia," in National Capital Park and Planning Commission, *Reports and Plans, Washington Region: Supplementary Technical Data to Accompany Annual Report* (Washington, DC, 1930).

PARK PLANNING

For the views of T. H. MacDonald on the road to Mount Vernon, see the Minutes of the National Capital Park and Planning Commission for December 1926. For the views of Milton Medary, see his article "The Aesthetic Value of City Planning in the National Capital," in the report of the National Conference on City Planning, *The Development of the National Capital and Its Environs* (Philadelphia: Wm. F. Fell Co., 1928). For Charles Eliot's report on the park system, see the Minutes of the National Capital Park and Planning Commission for December 1926; see also the 1927 annual report.

PUBLIC BUILDINGS: LOCATION, DESIGN, AND CONCENTRATION

Architectural control over new development adjacent to key federal lands and enclaves as mandated by the 1930 Shipstead-Luce Act (Public Law 71-231) is discussed in *The Shipstead-Luce Act: Rules and Regulations* (Washington, DC, 1938).

Frederick Law Olmsted Jr. shaped the Planning Commission's views on the Jefferson Memorial. See "Memorandum Report by Frederick Law Olmsted on Proposed Sites for a Memorial to Thomas Jefferson in the National Capital," included as Appendix A in the Minutes of the National Capital Park and Planning Commission for August 1933. For the views of the Commission of Fine Arts on the Jefferson Memorial, see Appendix B in the same Minutes, the "Memorandum with Reference to Proposed Sites for a Memorial to Thomas Jefferson in the National Capital," signed by Gilmore D. Clarke and William T. Partridge.

The "Key of Keys"—or "Quay of all the Quays," as the variant title and spelling go—was a large rocky projection jutting into the Potomac approximately at the foot of the Naval Observatory on 23rd Street NW. During the eighteenth century, this projection was a popular landing point for river traffic—hence the name. According to tradition, some of General Edward Braddock's troops landed here in 1755 and then marched west along the Frederick Road to Fort Cumberland. This story has never been confirmed, but the rock was often referred to as "Braddock's Rock." During the 1790s, it was decided that the rock would make excellent foundation stone. This site was the source, in fact, for much of the stone used for foundation walls in the Capitol and the White House.

Some of the rock was still extant in the early 1830s when the Chesapeake & Ohio Canal was extended to meet the Washington City Canal, and it became necessary to blast away a large piece of this rock to clear the right-of-way for the canal and its towpath.

REGIONAL PARKS AND PLANNING

Representative Cramton's reference to "artificial beauties such as monuments, boulevards, and pretentious buildings" occurs in a letter from Cramton to Mr. H. M. Lord, Director of the Budget, July 29, 1929, Louis C. Cramton Papers, Library of Michigan History, University of Michigan, Ann Arbor, Michigan. See this same collection for materials covering the prelude to the Capper-Cramton Act. These papers discuss the acute environmental issues at stake and reveal the high levels of support for the work of the National Capital Park and Planning Commission.

Documentation for planning activities in the suburban Maryland counties is found in the Maryland-National Capital Park and Planning Commission Minutes for 1927 to 1930 and in the *Twenty-Fifth Annual Report—Anniversary Edition, 1927–1952* (Silver Spring: Maryland-National Capital Park and Planning Commission, 1952), as well as in newspaper articles on file at local libraries: at the Montgomery County Library, Rockville Branch, see issues of the *Sentinel* dated December 10, 1926, January 7, 1927, February 4, 1927, May 6, 1927, and June 20, 1930; *Evening Star* (Washington), November 10, 1926; at the Maryland-National Capital Park and Planning Commission library, see *Riverdalian*, January 26, 1927, and March 2, 1927. See also Roland W. Rogers, "A Park System for the Maryland Washington Metropolitan District," *City Planning* (January 1931), and Irving C. Root, "Planning Progress in Maryland Washington Metropolitan District," *City Planning* (January 1931). Additional source materials are letters to E. Brooke Lee (Democratic political leader of Montgomery County), dated 1926–1927, Maryland-National Capital Park and Planning Commission library, Silver Spring, Maryland. The legislation creating the Maryland-National Capital Park and Planning Commission is Sec. 17, chap. 448, Acts of the General Assembly of Maryland, 1927.

For Eliot's remarks about the close relationship between the two planning commissions, see *The Work of the National Capital Park and Planning Commission*, Final Report of the House Committee on the District of Columbia, 70th Cong., 1st sess., March 10, 1928. For the reports of the Washington Region Water Supply Committee and the Washington Region Drainage and Sewerage Committee, see National Capital Park and Planning Commission, *Reports and Plans, Washington Region; Supplementary Technical Data to Accompany Annual Report* (Washington, DC, 1930). Eliot's penultimate remarks on planning needs are reported in the Minutes of the National Capital Park and Planning Commission for June 1933. Certain planning activities in the suburban Virginia counties are also reflected in this body of Minutes.

9. The New Deal in Planning, 1933-1941

THE SHIFT FROM COMPREHENSIVE PLANNING TO SHORT-TERM GOALS

On the need to reorganize the National Capital Park and Planning Commission, as well as the need for a comprehensive plan, see the American Planning and Civic Association Papers, Wisconsin State Historical Society; see also Papers of Frederic A. Delano, Harland Bartholomew, and U. S. Grant III, Architecture and City Planning Collection, Olin Library, Cornell University, Ithaca, New York. Charles Eliot's 1927 memorandum, "Union Square and the Mall," is included as Appendix A to the Minutes of the National Capital Park and Planning Commission for October 1933. See there also the statement and suggestions of Henry V. Hubbard quoted here in the text. In the same Minutes for October 1933, see also Appendix B, John Nolen Jr., "Program and Policies for Progressive Improvement of the Mall and Adjacent Areas," for the views of Nolen as quoted in the text. A fine picture of Greenbelt's history is offered in Cathy D. Knepper, *Greenbelt, Maryland: A Living Legacy of the New Deal* (Baltimore: Johns Hopkins University Press, 2001).

The controversial confrontation of architectural classicism with the modern movement is best illustrated by discussions presented in Henry Hope Reed, *The Golden City,* 2nd ed. (New York: Doubleday, 1959), and Christopher Tunnard and Henry Hope Reed, *American Skyline* (New York: New American Library, 1956).

REDUCED INFLUENCE OF THE PLANNING COMMISSION

The new federal programs that mushroomed in response to emergencies of the Depression—and overwhelmed plans previously developed by the National Capital Park and Planning Commission—are discussed in the Minutes of the commission for the years 1933–1941, the period covered by this chapter. The 1934 traffic study referred to in the text is by Charles Herrick, "General Conclusions from the Employees' Transportation Survey, 1934," included in the Minutes of the commission for January 1933. The "grab bag" statement is from Harold L. Ickes, "Warnings Against Further Encroachment upon the Parks and Playgrounds of the National Capital," included as Appendix F in the Minutes of the Park and Planning Commission for October 1941. For Frederic Delano's letter of resignation and the statement of the American Planning and Civic Association as quoted in the text, see the association's papers, Wisconsin Historical Society; see also Papers of Frederic Delano, Archi-

tecture and City Planning Collection, Olin Library, Cornell University, Ithaca, New York.

Symptomatic of the times was the 1939 exhibition, Washington: The Planned City without a Plan. Had not ten young architects organized an exhibition at the national convention of the American Institute of Architects in Washington in 1939, that convention might have been remembered only by the architects. In fact, however, a group of young architects led by Alfred Kastner and Chloethiel Woodard staged an exhibition entitled Washington: The Planned City without a Plan. Kastner and Woodard, both on the Committee on Housing and City Planning of the Washington chapter of the American Institute of Architects, wrote an accompanying essay, "Social Function of the Architect." In this essay, the authors expounded on the modern democratic city, quoting the wisdom of Lewis Mumford and Frank Lloyd Wright. In casting aside the City Beautiful ideal, they saw the McMillan Plan in Washington as well as the river drives along the Schuylkill River in Philadelphia as "typical of the escapism" of an earlier time. Philadelphia, they said, was planned with beautiful commuting strips so that the affluent could drive between work and home shielded from the "oceans of slums." They described Washington's more recent planning as "equally futile. The new federal buildings form a federal island which pulls traffic through the Washington downtown area. For both examples the formula is equally simple: be effective to sightseers, concentrate your efforts in the smallest possible area, and forget the total picture as much as you can. . . . The plan of Washington in 1939 is obsolete and inappropriate."

These harsh words were followed by the authors' suggestions for a remedied approach to planning: competitions on master plans and sectional plans should be held to dramatize the issues to the public; other professions such as medicine and sociology should have a collaborative role on planning problems; a City Planning Institute ought to be created to serve as an educational and political body "which would stimulate the average citizen to active participation in the rational development of the city"; and a city planning "museum" should be established to educate the citizenry and professionals, since such education was "necessary to develop political action for city planning."

This blistering attack on the planning agencies in Washington, particularly the National Capital Park and Planning Commission, was spread beyond the boundaries of the District as the exhibition traveled around the country. Soon after the convention closed, a special meeting of the Planning Commission was held. The president of the Washington chapter of the American Institute of Architects, Philip Schreier, disclaimed any endorsement of the exhibition and maintained that many members of the chapter objected strenuously to it. Woodard was unable to formulate precisely what her criticisms were of Washington planning but argued that her exhibition and essay were "done in the spirit of 'let's talk about it.'" The Planning Commission staff listened sympathetically, explaining that much of the commission's weakness stemmed from lack of funds, small staff, the need to cope with the immediate problems posed by the Depression and now the rumblings of another World War. (For further details, see Alfred Kastner and Chloethiel Woodard, "Social Function of the Architect," paper presented in connection with the exhibition Washington: The Planned City without a Plan, included as Appendix D in the Minutes of the National Capital Park and Planning Commission for October 1939.)

Samuel Milner, a historian at the Federal Aviation Administration, has investigated Washington's early airport history, beginning with the privately owned flying field built by Henry Berliner near the Virginia end of the 14th Street Bridge. Begun in 1927, this airport—later called Hoover Airport—accommodated scheduled service as well as private flights. The airport (as well as the amusement park next to it) was reached by streetcar from 12th Street and Independence Avenue. Hoover Airport could also be reached via Military Road. Across this highway, on the site of a former racetrack, a second privately owned commercial airport was established after 1928, largely on filled land. This hazardous situation was ultimately resolved by the consolidation of the two airfields into one, called Washington-Hoover or more properly Washington Municipal Airport. Washington Municipal Airport was Washington's only airport until the opening of National Airport at Gravelly Point in 1941. See further Constance McLaughlin Green, *Washington: Capital City, 1879–1950* (Princeton, NJ: Princeton University Press, 1963), and especially for maps, Herman R. Friis, *Geographical Reconnaissance of the Potomac River Tidewater Fringe of Virginia from Arlington Memorial Bridge to Mount Vernon* (Washington, DC: Association of American Geographers, 1968). Concerning the extensive brickyards along the Virginia shore, see William B. Clark and Benjamin L. Miller, "The Physiography amid Geology of the Coastal Plain Province of Virginia," *Virginia Geological Survey Bulletin* 4 (1912). See also Fairfax County Board of Supervisors, *Industrial and Historical Sketch of Fairfax County, Virginia* (Falls Church, VA, 1907).

The recent expansion of National Airport (now the Ronald Reagan Washington National Airport) inspired the article by James M. Goode, "Flying High: The Origins and Design of Washington National Airport," *Washington History*, vol. 1, no. 2 (Fall 1989), 4–25. This article describes Franklin Delano Roosevelt's influence on the location and design of the airport, including the introduction of the concrete facade of eight piers. This was based on Roosevelt's affection for Mount Vernon and its portico. The rest of the building, as designed by Charles M. Goodman, was a streamlined art deco structure.

THE MULTICENTERED REGIONAL CITY

For the report of John Nolen Jr. on building site shifts, in particular the Department of Agriculture's Arlington Experimental Farm, see the Minutes of the National Capital Park and Planning Commission for October 1933, Appendix B. For actions of the commission surrounding selection and planning for the Pentagon site itself, see the Minutes for March 20, 1941, July 31, 1941, September 18, 1941, and March 20, 1942. For the press release referred to in the text, see the Minutes of the Commission of Fine Arts, on file (indexed) at the commission's office in Washington, DC. For Harold Ickes's warnings about the Pentagon site, see his "Warnings Against Further Encroachment upon the Parks and Playgrounds of the National Capital," included as Appendix F in the Minutes of the National Capital Park and Planning Commission for October 1941. Other documents important for their anticipation of urban regional diffusion include the Maryland State Planning Commission report, Baltimore-Washington-Annapolis Area (Baltimore, 1937), and the National Resources Planning Board report, "Regional Factors in National Development," by John M. Gaus (Washington, DC, 1938).

10. World War II and Postwar Years, 1941-1952
WORLD WAR II GROWTH AND DEVELOPMENT

The measure of the city's wartime and postwar growth is traced in District of Columbia Department of Highways, "Twenty-four Years of Progress in Highway Development, 1924–1948," mimeographed (Washington, DC, n.d.). For the Planning Commission's recommendation on temporary federal office buildings, see the Minutes of the Special Committee to Consider Sites for Office Buildings, December 22, 1941, included as Appendix A in the Minutes of the National Capital Park and Planning Commission. For the reference to the "small village" of blacks that was relocated from the Pentagon site in Arlington over to Anacostia, see Herman R. Friis, *Geographical Reconnaissance of the Potomac River Tidewater Fringe of Virginia from Arlington Memorial Bridge to Mount Vernon* (Washington, DC: Association of American Geographers, 1968). This "small village" settlement appears to have had origins dating to the Civil War era.

A recent study of the Defense Homes Corporation's work in the Washington area is provided in Holly Knowles Chamberlain, "The Defense Homes Corporation: World War II Defense Housing for the Home Front" (master's thesis, George Washington University,

1990). For the statements of Alfred Bettman, the Cincinnati lawyer and planning expert, see the Minutes of the National Capital Park and Planning Commission for February and April 1943.

MOBILITY

Background to the development of the highway system in the District of Columbia and environs is provided in District of Columbia Department of Transportation, "Twenty-four Years of Progress in Highway Development, 1924–1948," mimeographed (Washington, DC, n.d.).

THE 1950 COMPREHENSIVE PLAN

The 1950 Comprehensive Plan for the National Capital and Its Environs is contained in five published volumes (Washington, DC, 1950): *Washington: Present and Future, A General Summary of the Comprehensive Plan for the National Capital and Its Environs,* Monograph No. 1 (April 1950); *People & Land: A portion of the comprehensive plan for the national capital and environs,* Monograph No. 2 (June 1950); *Housing & Redevelopment: A portion of the comprehensive plan for the national capital and environs,* Monograph No. 3 (June 1930); *Open Space & Community Services: A portion of the comprehensive plan for the national capital and environs,* Monograph No. 4 (June 1950); and *Moving People & Goods: A portion of the comprehensive plan for the national capital area and environs,* Monograph No. 5 (June 1950); on rapid transit, see *Moving People & Goods,* and for the "obsolete, blighted, and satisfactory" categories, see *Housing & Redevelopment.*

METROPOLITAN CITY AT MID-CENTURY

For general background on the year 1950, see the Minutes of the National Capital Park and Planning Commission so dated. See also the series of monographs published by the commission, *Washington: Present and Future* (Washington, DC, 1950).

DEVELOPMENT IN SUBURBAN VIRGINIA

For the statement of John Nolen Jr. opposing high-rise buildings, see the Minutes of the National Capital Park and Planning Commission for January 1942. On the projected development next to Arlington National Cemetery, see the Letter from Gilmore D. Clarke, chairman of the Commission of Fine Arts, to General Ulysses S. Grant III, dated May 9, 1943, included in the Minutes of the National Capital Park and Planning Commission for May 1945. As to the Planning Commission's suggestions for Springfield, see the Minutes for March 1948.

PLANNING FOR GROWTH IN THE MARYLAND COUNTIES

For wartime and postwar developments in suburban Maryland, see The Brookings Institution study, the Government of Montgomery County, *Maryland: A Survey* (Washington, DC: The Brookings Institution, 1941). See also *Looking Forward* (Silver Spring, MD, 1942), a report dated October 19, 1942, on progress made to that time by the Maryland-National Capital Park and Planning Commission, including an outline of work to be undertaken in the future by the commission and its staff. For additional background materials on Maryland development, see the Mary P. Vinton Collection in the Municipal Room at the Montgomery County Public Library, Rockville Branch, for the years 1950–1965. For the statement of M. Bond Smith quoted here in the text, see the Minutes of the National Capital Park and Planning Commission for December 1949; for Fred Tuemmler's statement, see the Minutes for September 1946.

11. Planning the City of Tomorrow, 1952-1960

NEW PLANNING VISIONS AND AUTHORITIES

Many books have been written about the planning environment of the post–World War II period. One of the most convincing and concise of these is by Michael Johns, *Moment of Grace: The American City in the 1950s* (Berkeley: University of California Press, 2003). Johns lays out the tenor of the times: the triumph of the technological know-how of the United States during World War II led to a nearly blind faith in professional planners and planning. Coupled with generous government-sponsored programs that funded massive public works projects, planning for cities and the nation's infrastructure proceeded with little input from affected residents and communities.

The National Capital Planning Act, 66 Stat. 781 (1932), reorganized the planning agency into the National Capital Planning Commission, created the National Capital Regional Planning Council, and outlined the responsibilities of each organization. For the legislative and administrative history of the Planning Commission, see *Planning Washington 1924–1976: An Era of Planning for the National Capital and Environs* (Washington, DC, 1976).

REDEVELOPMENT

A good summary of urban renewal in Washington is provided in Douglas Harmon, *The National Capital Planning Commission and the Politics of Planning in the Nation's Capital* (Washington, DC: Washington Center for Metropolitan Studies, 1968). For the 1942 Goodwillie report and plan, see Arthur Goodwillie, *The Rehabilitation of Southwest Washington as a War Housing Measure: A Memorandum to the Federal Home Loan Bank* (Washington, DC, 1942). For the views of Louis Justement, influential in the early phases of post–World War II redevelopment, see his *New Cities for Old: City Building in Terms of Space, Time and Money* (New York: McGraw-Hill Book Company, 1946). For discussion on the 1945

District of Columbia Redevelopment Act and the 1949 Housing Act (63 Stat. 420), see correspondence dated 1941–1955 in Papers of the American Planning and Civic Association (later merged into the National Urban Coalition), Social Action Archives, Wisconsin State Historical Society. Also see correspondence dated 1941–1955, Papers of Frederic Delano, Harland Bartholomew, and U. S. Grant III, Architecture and City Planning Collection, Olin Library, Cornell University, Ithaca, New York.

On the urban philosophy current in the 1930s and 1940s, see Frank Lloyd Wright, *Disappearing City* (New York: W. F. Payson, 1932), and Eliel Saarinen, *The City, Its Growth, Its Decay, Its Future* (New York: Reinhold Publishing Corporation, 1943). For Louis Justement's 1944 statements on advanced city planning, see the Minutes of the National Capital Park and Planning Commission for May 1944. On Barry Farms and Marshall Heights, see the records of the Redevelopment Land Agency, whose project files, newspaper clippings, and annual reports are in the library of the District of Columbia Department of Housing and Community Development, Washington, DC. The "Study of Barry Farms Area," Parts 1 and 2, are included in the Minutes of the National Capital Park and Planning Commission for November 1944. For the "Study of Marshall Heights Area," see the commission's Minutes for April 1945. The Greiner-DeLeuw report is appended to the commission's Minutes for December 1946 and March 1947.

For general background on post-1945 redevelopment planning, see the Minutes of the National Capital Park and Planning Commission. Microfilm graphic records are cataloged and shelved at the Planning Commission in Washington, DC. Early textual records other than the Minutes and meeting transcripts are stored at the National Archives, Washington, DC. Initial plans proposed for redevelopment of the Southwest include the Peets plan dated April 15, 1952, and the November 1952 plan prepared by Elbert Peets and the Planning Commission staff, *The Redevelopment Plan for the Southwest Project Area B* (Washington, DC, 1952). The Justement-Smith plan of May 1952 is entitled *Rebuilding Southwest Washington: A Report to the District of Columbia Redevelopment Land Agency* (Washington, DC, 1952).

The 1955–1956 study on rezoning (cited in the text) prepared for the Washington Zoning Revision Office by Harold M. Lewis, the New York consultant, produced the following planning reports: "General Background and History of Zoning in the District of Columbia" (January 1955); "Population and Employment in the District of Columbia" (March 1955); "Height and Bulk of Commercial Buildings in the District of Columbia" (September 1955); "Density of Residential Population" (December 1955); "Relation of Assessed Value to Zoning" (January 1956); "Off-Street Parking and Loading" (April 1936); "A New Zoning Plan for the District of Columbia" (November 1936); and "Land Use in the District of Columbia" (June 1936).

The Harland Bartholomew compromise report of May 1952 referred to in the text is *Redevelopment Plans for the Southwest Survey Area in the District of Columbia,* prepared under the direction of the National Capital Park and Planning Commission for the District of Columbia Redevelopment Land Agency (Washington, DC, 1952). For the Zeckendorf plan, see—in the files at the District of Columbia Department of Housing and Community Development—Webb and Knapp, Inc., "The Urban Renewal Plan for Project Area C" (March 1956). The relocation of major portions of the old Southwest's population was studied by Daniel Thursz in *Where Are They Now? A Study of the Impact of Relocation on Former Residents of Southwest Washington Who Were Served in an HWC Demonstration Project* (Washington, DC: Health and Welfare Council of the National Capital Area, 1966). The report referred to in the text is James W. Rouse and Nathaniel S. Keith, *No Slums in Ten Years: A Workable Program for Urban Renewal* (Washington, DC, 1955), prepared for the commissioners of the District of Columbia.

Background for major redevelopment areas in Washington other than the Southwest is provided in the project files and annual reports of the Redevelopment Land Agency (now the District of Columbia Department of Housing and Community Development).

TRANSPORTATION

For the Mass Transportation Survey, consultants produced several reports in the 1955–1959 period, but the overall findings were summarized in the *Transportation Plan, National Capital Region: The Mass Transportation Survey Report* (Washington, DC: National Capital Planning Commission and National Capital Regional Planning Council, 1959). The specialized consultant reports and the summary reports are on file at the National Capital Planning Commission library in Washington, DC. The work of the Joint Committee on Washington Metropolitan Problems is detailed in the staff reports to the 85th Congress and 86th Congress, 1958–1960, and the hearings conducted by the Joint Committee in 1938.

For the survey and its recommendations, see the hearings of the Joint Committee on Washington Metropolitan Problems, 85th and 86th Cong. (1958–1960). One of the published reports of the Joint Committee, *A Discussion Guide to Washington Area Metropolitan Problems* (Washington, DC, 1960), includes a transportation section with bibliography.

Development of the Metro rail system can be traced through the National Capital Transportation Agency, *Recommendations for Transportation in the National Capital Region* (Washington, DC, 1962). Note that the

National Capital Transportation Act of 1965 (79 Stat. 664) authorized the creation of a regional system, the Washington Metropolitan Area Transit Authority, and allowed for the phasing out of the original agency.

A short history of Metro from the 1950s to late 1969 is sketched by William J. Murin, *The Evolution of Metro* (Washington, DC, 1970). Murin notes that two important landmarks in the design of the system are these reports: *Transit Development Program for the National Capital Region*, 88th Cong., 1st sess., H. Rept. No. 1005, 1963, and *National Capital Transit Authority, Rapid Rail Transit for the Nation's Capital—Transit Development Program, 1965* (Washington, DC, 1965). More recent scholarly treatments of the development of the Metro system include Zachary M. Schrag, "Mapping Metro, 1955–1968: Urban, Suburban, and Metropolitan Alternatives," *Washington History* 13, no. 1 (Spring–Summer 2001), 4–23, and his comprehensive study, *The Great Society Subway: A History of the Washington Metro* (Baltimore: Johns Hopkins University Press, 2006).

Transportation studies on the Capital Beltway include *The Socio-Economic Impact of the Capital Beltway in Northern Virginia* prepared by the Bureau of Population and Economic Research, University of Virginia, Charlottesville, in cooperation with the Virginia Department of Highways and the US Department of Transportation, Bureau of Public Roads (Washington, DC, 1968), and Wilbur Smith and Associates, *Maryland Capital Beltway Impact Study: Final Report, Washington Standard Metropolitan Statistical Area and Maryland Counties* (Silver Spring, MD, 1968).

METROPOLITAN WASHINGTON: CITY, SUBURB, AND REGION

On Rosslyn, see G. Brian Kelly, "Rosslyn: Double Decker City Rises beside Potomac," *Christian Science Monitor*, 1967 (offprint).

12. The Environmentally Conscious City and Region, 1960–1975

RETHINKING THE URBAN AGENDA

For a compelling portrait of urban America in the early 1960s, see Jane Jacobs, *The Death and Life of Great American Cities* (1961; reprint, New York: Vintage Books, 1992). For a brief status report on the city in the early 1960s, see "The Capital: Washington Reborn," *Time*, November 17, 1961. For the views of Allan Temko, see "Capital's Growth Crisis Seen as Global in Scope," *Washington Post*, August 12, 1962. On the remarks of William Finley to the Washington Building Congress, see the *Washington Post*, November 16, 1958. *The Crack in the Picture Window* was the title of Washington writer John Keats's critique of suburbia (Boston: Houghton Mifflin, 1957) based largely on the experience of Montgomery County, Maryland.

The report by Douglas Harmon, "The National Capital Planning Commission and the Politics of Planning in the Nation's Capital" (Washington, DC: Washington Center for Metropolitan Studies, 1968), provides a detailed account of 1950s-style planning giving way to more environmentally conscious planning in the 1960s.

THE 1961 POLICIES PLAN FOR THE YEAR 2000

A Policies Plan for the Year 2000, published by the National Capital Planning Commission and the National Capital Regional Planning Council (Washington, DC, 1961), is the key document for this section. For background on the wedges and corridors plan for metropolitan growth, see the essays written by Hans Blumenfeld and edited by Paul D. Spreiregen in *The Modern Metropolis: Its Origins, Growth, Characteristics, and Planning* (Cambridge, MA: MIT Press, 1967). For the Council of Governments' views on metropolitan growth, see *Metropolitan Growth Policy Program* (Washington, DC, 1975). The library of the Washington Center for Metropolitan Studies contains a specialized collection of reports and other material on regional structure, growth, planning, and government. On planning activities in the Maryland suburbs, see the following documents: Allied Civic Group, Inc., *Survey of Montgomery County: Report and Recommendations of Government Operations Committee* (Silver Spring, MD, 1962); the Institute of Public Administration, *The Regional Planning Role of the Maryland-National Capital Park and Planning Commission* (New York, 1962); the annual reports of the Maryland-National Capital Park and Planning Commission for the years from 1957 on; special reports and statements of the Montgomery County Citizens Planning Association (in particular, *Background on Montgomery County Planning Problems,* February 26, 1962; *Report on Issues,* April 20, 1962; and Statement of Ramsey Wood, February 28, 1963) on file at the Montgomery County Public Library, Rockville Branch; Ladislas Segoe Associates, *Preliminary Report—Survey and Review of Organization and Activities of the M–NCPPC* (October 1956); the Mary P. Vinton Collection in the Municipal Room at the Montgomery County Public Library Rockville Branch; Madeline Baker, "Politics of Planning in Montgomery County" (master's thesis, George Washington University, 1966); and Charles Puffenbarger, "Montgomery County Planning: A Study in Politics" (master's thesis, George Washington University, 1963).

Virginia's planning activities were less coordinated with other planning agencies in the metropolitan area. See the annual reports of the Northern Virginia Regional Planning and Economic Commission, the Fairfax County Planning Commission, and the Northern Virginia Planning District Commission, most of which are available in the Virginia Collection, Fairfax County Public Library.

See also Jean Gottman, *Megalopolis: The Urbanized Northeastern Seaboard of the United States* (Cambridge, MA: MIT Press, 1961).

National Capital Planning Commission reports, in addition to published modifications and additions to the Comprehensive Plan for the National Capital, reflect the conservation-oriented approach to the city's future development and a concern with environmental quality emphasizing natural features and landmarks of the built environment; see the *Quarterly Review of Commission Proceedings* published from 1974 forward. See also *Downtown Design and Development* (Washington, DC, 1974) and *The Urban River* (Washington, DC, 1972), which proposes general policies and programs for implementing Comprehensive Plan policies. *Shoreline Acquisition and Development Policies and Programs* (Washington, DC, 1976) is a further detailing of policies and programs for implementing Comprehensive Plan policies. An argument for continuation of the traditional scale of Georgetown across its waterfront is made by the Georgetown Planning Group, *Georgetown Waterfront Area Study,* prepared for the Planning Commission and the District of Columbia Department of Transportation. This study includes three reports: *Phase I Report: Development Concept Alternatives* (Washington, DC, 1972); *Phase IIA Report: Preliminary Development Plan and Program* (1973); and *Consultants' Final Report: Recommended Development Plan and Program* (1975). See also *Downtown Progress, Action Plan for Downtown* (Washington, DC: National Capital Downtown Committee, Inc., 1962). For background on major projects in the central city, see Helen Merryman Legg, "Watergate," *Washingtonian* (October 1965), 21–23, and Sue A. Kohler, *The Commission of Fine Arts: A Brief History, 1910–1990* (Washington, DC: Commission of Fine Arts, 1990).

NEW PLANNING DIRECTIONS

Major planning reports form the primary source for this section: the "Brown Book" or *1965/1985: Proposed Physical Development Policies for Washington, D.C.,* published by the National Capital Planning Commission (Washington, DC, 1965); the "Green Book" or *The Proposed Comprehensive Plan for the National Capital,* published by the National Capital Planning Commission (Washington, DC, 1967); and the ongoing Comprehensive Plan, known as the "Red Book." Under the full title, *Comprehensive Plan for the National Capital, Adopted Pursuant to the National Capital Planning Act of 1952, as amended,* this plan was published by the National Capital Planning Commission in 1968, and elements of the plan were first adopted at that time. The document was published in binder format to facilitate the incorporation of modifications and additions to the Comprehensive Plan. For the landscape identity study referred to in the text,

see *Toward a Comprehensive Landscape Plan for Washington, D.C.,* prepared for the National Capital Planning Commission by the firm of Wallace, McHarg, Roberts, and Todd (Washington, DC, 1967). This study is often referred to as the McHarg report.

For bibliographic notes on Elizabeth Rowe, William E. Finley, Wilmer Dutton, and other members and executive directors of the National Capital Planning Commission, see *Planning Washington 1924–1976: An Era of Planning for the National Capital and Environs* (Washington, DC, 1976).

NEW DESIGN INITIATIVES

The reports documenting the evolution of Pennsylvania Avenue design proposals are the *Report to the President by the Ad Hoc Committee on Federal Office Space,* May 23, 1962; see there the much-quoted declaration that "Pennsylvania Avenue should be lively, friendly, and inviting, as well as dignified and impressive." *The Report of the President's Council on Pennsylvania Avenue* (Washington, DC, 1964) provides the fundamental and detailed statement of the plan put forward in the 1960s. Immediate steps to implement the plan are traced in the *Report of the President's Temporary Commission on Pennsylvania Avenue* (Washington, DC, 1967); see also later reports of the Pennsylvania Avenue Development Corporation. Efforts to redesign Pennsylvania Avenue were visualized in the Library of Congress exhibition entitled The Grand Design and especially in the exhibition catalog (Washington, DC: Library of Congress, 1967).

"Guiding Principles for Federal Architecture" is contained in the *Report to the President by the Ad Hoc Committee on Federal Office Space,* May 23, 1962. The monthly column "Washington Perspective" in *Progressive Architecture* for the years 1953–1958 traces planning necessities and federal architecture in the capital city. See also Frederick Gutheim, "Urban Space and Urban Design," in *Cities and Space: The Future Use of Urban Land,* edited by Lowdon Wingo Jr. (Baltimore: Johns Hopkins Press, 1963). For useful commentary on urban design in Washington, see the writings of Ada Louise Huxtable in the *New York Times* and those of Wolf von Eckardt in the *Washington Post.* Zachary M. Schrag conducted an extensive research project on the history of the Washington Metro system and wrote about it in "Mapping Metro, 1955–1968: Urban, Suburban, and Metropolitan Alternatives," *Washington History,* vol. 13, no. 1 (Spring–Summer 2001), 4–23, and *The Great Society Subway: A History of the Washington Metro* (Baltimore: Johns Hopkins University Press, 2006). For a summary of the evolution of the built environment around the White House and the development of the Lafayette Square project in the early 1960s, see Antoinette J. Lee, "The White House and the Monumental City," *White House History,* no. 11 (Summer 2002), 4–13.

GROWTH CENTERS

For the *Washington Post* article on Crystal City, see Phil Stanford, "Crystal City—A Self-Contained World," *Washington Post, Potomac Magazine,* March 15, 1970. See also Nan Netherton, *Reston: A New Town in the Old Dominion* (Norfolk: Donning Company, 1989); Tom Grubisich and Peter McCandles, *Reston: The First Twenty Years* (Reston, VA: Reston Publishing Company, Inc., 1985); and Robert Tennenbaum, ed., *Creating a New City: Columbia, Maryland* (Columbia, MD: Partners in Community Building and Perry Publishing, 1996). For an evaluation of Reston and Columbia, see Hammer, Greene, Siler Associates for the Metropolitan Washington Council of Governments, *The Economy of Metropolitan Washington* (Washington, DC, 1969).

For additional insights into the development of Cross Keys in Baltimore and Columbia in Howard County, Maryland, as well as the hiring of William E. Finley and another National Capital Planning Commission staff member, Morton Hoppenfeld, see the recent biography of James W. Rouse by Joshua Olsen, *Better Places, Better Lives: A Biography of James Rouse* (Washington, DC: Urban Land Institute, 2003).

REDEVELOPMENT PROJECTS OF THE 1960S

Background for major redevelopment areas in Washington other than the Southwest is provided in the project files and annual reports of the Redevelopment Land Agency (now the District of Columbia Department of Housing and Community Development). See there especially *Urban Renewal Plan for the Fort Lincoln Urban Renewal Area* (Washington, DC, 1972) and *A Program for Bates Street* (Washington, DC, 1969).

On the 7th Street corridor reconstruction, see the report of the Redevelopment Land Agency, *Washington Goes Forward, 1968–1976* (Washington, DC, 1976), and the report of the Metropolitan Washington Board of Trade, "The Board of Trade Riot Response Project," Report No. 1, prepared by Robert Gladstone and Associates, April 1968 (mimeographed). See also the article "City Pushes to Meet Deadline on Plan to Rebuild Riot Areas," *Washington Post,* July 23, 1968.

The recent article "The 1968 Washington Riots in History and Memory" by Dana Lanier Schaffer that appeared in *Washington History,* vol. 15, no. 2 (Fall–Winter 2003–2004), 4–33, describes the riots as lasting twelve days. Most of the official reports that address the damage caused by the riots, however, focus on April 4–8 as constituting the major period of unrest.

HOME RULE

A discussion of the political ferment of the 1960s, which led to home rule for the city during the 1970s, is presented in Howard Gillette, *Between Justice and Beauty: Race, Planning, and the Failure of Urban Policy in Washington* (Baltimore: Johns Hopkins University Press, 1995). For a history of the development of community development corporations (CDCs), see Alexander von Hoffman, *House by House, Block by Block: The Rebirth of America's Urban Neighborhoods* (New York: Oxford University Press, 2003).

13. Changing Dynamics in the Metropolitan Area, 1976-1990

THE BEST AND WORST OF TIMES

The bicentennial parade in Washington, DC, is recorded in the July 4, 1976, issues of the *Washington Post* and the *Washington Star News*. Haynes Johnson's commentary, "Upbeat Tone Marks Varied Tributes to Nation's Birthday," was part of the *Washington Post*'s coverage. A discussion of the federal interest in national capital planning was at the heart of the report, US General Accounting Office, "Mission and Functions of the National Capital Planning Commission," RCED-83-115 (Washington, DC, June 1983).

The progress in preparing the federal elements of the comprehensive plan can be gathered from the National Capital Planning Commission's quarterly reports for the 1976–1988 period and from National Capital Planning Commission, "Comprehensive Plan for the National Capital: Federal Goals for the National Capital," adopted February 4, 1982 (Washington, DC, 1982). The District's planning activities are recorded in the Government of the District of Columbia, "Comprehensive Plan for the National Capital, Planning Report" (August 1983), and "District of Columbia Comprehensive Plan, 1983" (August 18 1983).

UPGRADING DOWNTOWN

Warren J. Cox, Hugh Newell Jacobsen, Francis D. Lethbridge, and David R. Rosenthal, in *A Guide to the Architecture of Washington, D.C.*, 2nd ed. (New York: McGraw-Hill Book Company, 1974), are particularly effective in providing a portrait of the District and surrounding jurisdictions at the mid-1970s. Many of the development projects of this era are summarized in Sue A. Kohler, *The Commission of Fine Arts: A Brief History, 1910–1990* (Washington, DC, 1990). The quarterly reports of the National Capital Planning Commission from 1976 to 1988 provide summaries of major developments in both the District of Columbia and the suburban jurisdictions. The scale of development activities is captured in Bartlett Naylor, "Boomtown," *Washingtonian* 21, no. 12 (September 1986), 266, 268, 271–272.

The work of the Pennsylvania Avenue Development Corporation is covered in the report of the PADC, including "Amendments to the Pennsylvania Avenue Plan, November 1990" and "Historic Preservation Plan of the Pennsylvania Avenue Development Corporation" (Washington, DC, 1980). The report by Robinson & Associates, Inc., in association with Architrave P.C., Architects, "Pennsylvania Avenue National Historic Site, National Register of Historic Places Documentation, Final Submittal," prepared for the National Park Service, National Capital Region (February 27, 2003), covers the development of all of the major Pennsylvania Avenue projects.

Developments elsewhere in the downtown area are covered in Pamela Scott and Antoinette J. Lee, *Buildings of the District of Columbia* (New York: Oxford University Press, 1993); Claudia D. Kousoulas and George W. Kousoulas, *Contemporary Architecture in Washington, DC* (Washington, DC: Preservation Press, 1995); and Christopher Weeks, *AIA Guide to the Architecture of Washington, DC*, 3rd ed. (Baltimore: Johns Hopkins University Press, 1994).

OTHER DEVELOPMENT PROJECTS

The outline for the revitalized downtown is provided in the document "A Living Downtown for Washington, DC: Planning Concept" (Washington, DC: Government of the District of Columbia, 1981). These development projects also are covered in the quarterly reports of the National Capital Planning Commission and Sue A. Kohler, *The Commission of Fine Arts: A Brief History, 1910–1990* (Washington, DC, 1990). The Georgetown waterfront planning effort is summarized in Marie Ridder, "Georgetown Waterfront: The Last and Best Mile?" *Washingtonian* (September 1975), 84–90, and Kenneth Bredemeier, "New Waterfront Plan Opposed in Georgetown," *Washington Post*, March 5, 1980.

HISTORIC PRESERVATION IN THE DISTRICT OF COLUMBIA

There is no comprehensive history of historic preservation in the District of Columbia. Several summaries are helpful in filling in the story, however. These include "League Celebrates 20th Anniversary" in the DC Preservation League *Reporter* (Spring 1991); Suzanne Ganschinietz, "A Brief History," in DC Preservation League, 25th Anniversary Celebration Commemorative Program (May 17, 1996); and the introduction by Richard Longstreth in James M. Goode, *Capital Losses: A Cultural History of Washington's Destroyed Buildings* (Washington, DC: Smithsonian Institution Press, 2003). Richard W. Longstreth, *History on the Line: Testimony in the Cause of Preservation* (Ithaca, NY: Historic Urban Plans, Inc., for the National Council for Preservation Education and the National Park Service, 1998), provides annotated transcriptions of testimony in seven major preservation cases in the District.

NEW IMMIGRATION SHAPES THE CITY AND REGION

Francine Curro Cary, ed., *Urban Odyssey: A Multicultural History of Washington, DC* (Washington, DC: Smithsonian Institution Press, 1996), 231–249, offers an essential introduction to the histories of major cultural groups in the Washington area. Of particular importance to this period are the following chapters: Olivia Cadeval, "The Latino Community: Creating an Identity in the Nation's Capital"; Keith Q. Warner, "From 'Down the Way Where the Nights are Gay': Caribbean Immigration and the Bridging of Cultures"; Bereket H. Selassie, "Washington's New African Immigrants"; Beatrice Nied Hackett, "'We Must Become Part of the Larger American Family': Washington's Vietnamese, Cambodians, and Laotians"; and Meeja Yu and Unyong Kim, "We Came Here with Dreams: Koreans in the Nation's Capital."

SUBURBAN GROWTH AND SELF-SUFFICIENCY

The prediction of future dispersed development centers was recorded in the Metropolitan Washington Council of Governments, *Metropolitan Growth Policy Statement, The Metropolitan Growth Policy Program*, Adopted by the Board of Directors (October 1977). The explosive growth of Fairfax County receives careful attention in Ross and Nan Netherton, *Fairfax County: A Contemporary Portrait* (Virginia Beach, VA: Donning Company/Publishers, 1992). Agricultural protection programs are covered in the Maryland-National Capital Park and Planning Commission's report "Functional Master Plan for the Preservation of Agriculture and Rural Open Space in Montgomery County" (October 1980).

The evolution of the metropolitan area is captured in Peter McGrath and Howard Means, "A Special Report: How Washington Became a Real City," *Washingtonian* (October 1980), 130–160. A discussion of the Topographical Bowl and the Mall vista cone can be found in the National Capital Planning Commission *Quarterly* (Fall 1980), 1–4.

The protection of the Alexandria, Virginia, waterfront is documented in the quarterly reports of the National Capital Planning Commission and in Larry Van Dyne, "Power Rangers," *Washingtonian* (May 1996). The Arlington County projects are covered in Sherman Pratt, *Arlington County, Virginia: A Modern History* (Chelsea, MI: BookCrafters, 1997).

14. The Global Capital City, 1991-Present
A GOLDEN ERA?

Both the edge city and edgeless city phenomena are discussed in Joel Garreau, *Edge City: Life on the New Frontier* (1991; reprint, New York: Anchor Books, 1992), and Robert E. Lang, *Edgeless Cities: Exploring the Elusive Metropolis* (Washington, DC: The Brookings Institution Press, 2003). Garreau defines the "edge city" as having 5 million square feet of office space; six hundred thousand square feet of retail space; more jobs than bedrooms; and a single location for jobs, shopping, and entertainment. Finally, it is a place that was not a city thirty years ago.

EXTENDING THE LEGACY

The Legacy Plan in both its draft and final forms is available in the National Capital Planning Commission's *Extending the Legacy: Planning America's Capital for the 21st Century* (Washington, DC, 1996) and *Extending the Legacy: Planning America's Capital City for the 21st Century* (Washington, DC, 1997). Follow-up studies to the Legacy Plan include National Capital Planning Commission, *Memorials and Museums Master Plan—Draft* (December 2000) and *Memorials and Museums Master Plan* (September 2001). The Commemorative Works Act of 1986, as amended in 1991, provides the adopted guidelines for new commemorative works in the District of Columbia.

POLISHING THE CITY'S IMAGE IN THE GLOBAL COMMUNITY

The special issue of the American Planning Association's *Planning* magazine on Washington, DC (April 1992) presents a good summary of the economically perilous times for the District and the development of "edge cities" in the suburbs. The National Capital Planning Commission quarterly reports for 1989 and from 1998 through 2003 help to document the various projects over which it had jurisdiction. During the period from 1993 to 1998, the Planning Commission's in-house staff newsletter, *Plan-ly Speaking,* provides more superficial coverage of planning topics.

A July 8, 2003, memorandum from Tersh Boasberg to Antoinette J. Lee summarizes the downtown rezoning of 1990 that reinforced the retail destination, created the arts district, refurbished Chinatown, buttressed the downtown historic district, and provided for a critical mass of downtown housing. An interview with Andrew Altman on March 5, 2004, provided insight into the rebuilding of the District's Office of Planning and recent major planning projects. Also, see "National Capital Launches Invigorating Inner City Program," *Architectural Record* (July 2000).

The architectural development of the District during this period, including postmodern and neomodern buildings, is covered in the following: "The World Bank," *Progressive Architecture* (January 1991), 106–108; "Capital Gains: The Lansburgh," *Architecture* (April 1992), 74–79; "Bracing History: Connecting New Construction with Old Buildings Required Structural Integrity," *Architecture* (April 1991), 85–89; "Cultural Sensibilities," *Architecture* (July 1993), 53–65; "Memory Too Politic," *Progressive Architecture* (October 1995), 62–69; "Memorial Mania,"

Architecture (September 1997), 94–97; "Cesar Pelli's New Passenger Terminal at National Airport in Washington, D.C. Eases the Life of the World-Weary Traveler," *Architectural Record* (October 1997), 89–95; "Washington's Planning Politics," *Architecture* (November 1997), 47–51; "Despite Arguments over Site, Work Is Started on D.C. Center," *Architectural Record* (November 1998), 48; "War and Regret," *Architecture* (September 2000), 158; "D.C. Metro Chooses Canopy Design," *Architecture* (August 2001), 33; and Monte Reel, "Preservation Law Put Leash on Mall Projects," *Washington Post,* November 20, 2003.

Additional coverage is provided in Adam Macy, "Building Big in DC: Innovative Solutions to Create Vast New Washington Convention Center," *Washington, D.C. Hot Projects*, McGraw Hill Construction Regional Publication (January 2003), 74–76, and "Despite Arguments over Site, Work Is Started on D.C. Center," *Architectural Record* (November 1998), 48.

HISTORIC DISTRICTS

The achievements of the District of Columbia's historic preservation program during the 1980s and 1990s are summarized in a memorandum from Tersh Boasberg to Antoinette J. Lee dated July 8, 2003. The transformation of the Tariff Commission Building is covered in "In Washington, D.C., The Landmark Tariff Building Is Restored and Retrofitted as the New Hotel Monaco," *Architectural Record* (June 2003), 220–224.

PROTECTING THE CITY FROM TERRORISM

Protecting the national capital city from terrorism through design is described in the National Capital Planning Commission report *Designing for Security in the Nation's Capital: A Report by the Interagency Task Force of the National Capital Planning Commission* (October 2001).

EXPLODING SUBURBS

The planning work in the District and the suburban jurisdictions is addressed in the report by the Department of Metropolitan Development and Information Resources, Metropolitan Washington Council of Governments, "Local Planning Activities in Metropolitan Washington" (1992).

Important planning documents include County of Fairfax, *Policy Plan: The Countywide Policy Element of the Comprehensive Plan for Fairfax County, Virginia* (2000), and Loudoun County, Virginia, *Loudoun County General Plan* (1991, amended 2003). Montgomery County's update of the wedges and corridors plan is covered in Maryland-National Capital Park and Planning Commission, *General Plan Refinement of the Goals and Objectives for Montgomery County*, December 1993. Other planning documents include Maryland-National Capital Park and

Planning Commission, *Prince George's Approved General Plan* (October 2002); Frederick County, *Frederick County Land Preservation and Recreation Plan* (December 2000); and Howard County, *Howard County General Plan 2000* (November 2000).

The expansion of Dulles Airport is covered in "SOM's Addition to Dulles International Airport Respects Eero Saarinen's 'Modern Masterpiece,'" *Architectural Record* (March 1997), 163–167.

For information on the privatization of the federal government and its ramifications, see Stephen S. Fuller, "The Impact of Federal Procurement on the National Capital Region, Prepared for the Federal Office Space Task Force / National Capital Planning Commission" (October 2002). Fuller's report addresses the federal government's support of jobs and income growth and the tendency of federal contractors to cluster with suppliers, competitors, and subcontractors.

Articles on the Kentlands development in Montgomery County include "Plan Meets Reality," *Architecture* (December 1991), 74–77, 116. The Reston Town Center is addressed in "New Town Downtown," *Architecture* (December 1991), 56–61. Dolores Hayden, *Building Suburbia: Green Fields and Urban Growth, 1820–2000* (New York: Pantheon Books, 2003), provides a thoughtful discussion of the importance of preserving older suburbs. One of the most complete discussions of regional planning needs is provided in the chapter "Responsible Regionalism" in Howard County, Maryland, *General Plan 2000 . . . A Six Point Plan for the Future* (November 2000).

Epilogue: The National Capital City in the New Century

CENTRAL CITY AND DISTRICT

The Pentagon 9/11 memorial and the Air Force Memorial are covered in "Two New Memorials in the Capital: One Grand, the Other Minimal," *Architecture* (April 2003), 17. The Newseum is covered in "On the Boards: Polshek Partnership Architects, Newseum, Washington, DC," *Architecture* (January 2003), 36. The Frank Gehry design for the Corcoran Gallery is covered in "Gehry Throws Another Curve with Extension to Corcoran Gallery," *Architectural Record* (August 1999), 60.

The development of the District is covered in "Andrew Altman: Planning for Our Nation's Capital," *Architectural Record* (March 2002), 240; Neil Irwin, "Altman Backs Urban Vision with Substance," *Washington Post,* January 6, 2003; Neil Irwin, "Where to Build Next: As Downtown Fills In, Only Way for Construction Is Out," *Washington Post,* February 24, 2003. Additional insight into the District's resurgence is available in Debbi Wilgoren, "A New Beginning for the District's East End," *Washington Post,* March 7, 2004, and "Architect Named to

Develop Site of Former D.C. Convention Center," *Architectural Record* (January 2004). The development of the Southeast Federal Center is covered in Dana Hedgpeth, "Developer Chosen for Southeast Federal Center," *Washington Post,* January 30, 2004. For the federal elements of the comprehensive plan, see National Capital Planning Commission, *Comprehensive Plan for the National Capital: Federal Elements,* August 2004.

THE REGION

The status of growth in the region is covered in Neil Irwin, "Developer Smith Altering Course as Market Wilts," *Washington Post,* May 26, 2003, and Kenneth Bredemeier, "Gimmicks Fail to Fill Empty Offices," *Washington Post,* May 26, 2003.

The loss of green space around the National Capital Region at the end of the twentieth century is captured in Glenn Frankel and Stephen C. Fehr, "As the Economy Grows, the Trees Fall," *Washington Post,* March 23, 1997, and Stephen C. Fehr, "Montgomery's Line of Defense against Suburban Invasion," *Washington Post,* March 25, 1997. The influence of growth controls on sprawl is described in Peter Whoriskey, "Density Limits Only Add to Sprawl," *Washington Post,* March 9, 2003. A summary of growth issues in the region is presented in Larry Van Dyne, "Our Washington," *Washingtonian* (May 2003), 64–96. The Chesapeake crescent paradigm is presented in Carl Abbott, *Political Terrain: Washington, D.C. from Tidewater Town to Global Metropolis* (Chapel Hill: University of North Carolina Press, 1999).

THE CAPITAL CITY'S SPECIAL CHARACTER

The multicultural nature of the Washington, DC, metropolitan area is covered in a series of articles, "Many Paths to Here: Washington's Multicultural Mosaic," that appeared in the *Washington Post.* Articles include D'Vera Cohn and Pamela Constable, "Lives Transplanted, A Region Transformed," *Washington Post,* August 30, 1998; Pamela Constable and D'Vera Cohn, "Immigrants: More Boon than Burden," *Washington Post,* August 31, 1998; and Pamela Constable and D'Vera Cohn, "Culture Clashes Put Immigrant Women on the Front Lines," *Washington Post,* September 1, 1998.

Washington, DC, as one of the top cities for the "creative class" is addressed in Richard Florida, *The Rise of the Creative Class* (New York: Basic Books, 2002), and in D'Vera Cohn, "Leadership, Tax Issues Hamper Growth," *Washington Post,* November 10, 2003. Observations of Stephen S. Fuller and John Parsons on the character of the Washington, DC, metropolitan region were expressed at the National Capital Planning Commission, "Worthy of a Nation" Work Session, June 10, 2003.

The Historical Society of Washington, DC, formerly the Columbia Historical Society, offers detailed studies and contemporary interpretations of the city in light of new research in its flagship publication, *Washington History.* In this continuing series, fifteen individual volumes have been published since 1989; volume 15 covers the 2003 calendar year. *Washington History*'s predecessor publication, the *Records of the Historical Society of Washington, DC,* served as its functional equivalent from 1897 through 1988; fifty-one volumes contain primary source materials and scholarly articles. Unlike *Washington History,* the *Records* do not follow a consistent numbering system on the book spines, although there is internal consistency in numbering. For the clearest presentation to researchers, references to these volumes are given here as follows: vols. 1–28 are cited by volume numbers and year of publication; from vol. 29 forward, only the years covered and year of publication are shown. The Historical Society maintains a manuscript collection. References to this collection are identified by Historical Society of Washington, DC, Manuscript Collection and the year. For more about the historical society and its collections, consult www.citymuseumdc.org/library.

Classic Washington histories include Wilhelmus Bogart Bryan, *A History of the National Capital from Its Foundation through the Period of the Adoption of the Organic Act,* 2 vols. (New York: McMillan, 1914–1916), which skillfully traces the city's history to 1878 and provides a remarkable emphasis on the physical format of the city; Constance McLaughlin Green, *Washington: Village and Capital, 1800–1878,* vol. 1 (Princeton, NJ: Princeton University Press, 1962), and *Capital City, 1879–1950,* vol. 2 (Princeton, NJ: Princeton University Press, 1963), which assesses the evolving social atmosphere in juxtaposition with development of the political and cultural city; and John Clagett Proctor, ed., *Washington Past and Present: A History,* 5 vols. (New York: Lewis Historical Publishing Co., Inc., 1930). For an additional rich source of information, see the "Articles on Early Washington" written by John Clagett Proctor for the *Sunday Star* for the run of dates from January 22, 1928, to September 7, 1952. These articles are on file at the Martin Luther King Jr. Memorial Library, Washingtoniana Division, in Washington, DC. The Junior League of Washington's *An Illustrated History: The City of Washington* (New York: Knopf, 1977) provides a popular introduction to the subject. For an extensive visual documentation of Washington architecture, see the Dunlap Society publication, *The Architecture of Washington, D.C.,* 2 vols. (Essex, NY, 1976–1977). Volume 1 presents slides and microfiche on ten major buildings in Washington; volume 2 deals with the Capitol and the Federal Triangle.

Studies of the greater physical region that defined and nurtured the city include Frederick Gutheim, *The Potomac* (New York: Rhinehart, 1949). A graphic description and interpretative view of the Washington topography is explored by the National Capital Planning Commission, *Toward a Comprehensive Landscape Plan for Washington, D.C.* (Washington, DC, 1967). John W. Reps, *Tidewater Towns: City Planning in Colonial Virginia and Maryland* (Williamsburg, VA: Colonial Williamsburg Foundation, 1972), describes and compares the many human settlements that formed along the tidewater rivers and inlets. In *Monumental Washington: The Planning and Development of the Capital Center* (Princeton, NJ: Princeton University Press, 1967), Reps presents a history of the ceremonial/governmental core of the city, with particular emphasis on the L'Enfant plan and the McMillan Commission plan. See also Reps, *Washington on View: The Nation's Capital since 1790* (Chapel Hill: University of North Carolina Press, 1991), for images and descriptions of the city from its founding through 1985. Iris Miller's *Washington in Maps: 1606–2002* (New York: Rizzoli, 2002) serves as a useful complement to Reps's work. It provides a comprehensive overview of the planning of the city, explores the origins of the city plan, and assesses its role as a model in urban planning. See also Richard Longstreth, ed., *The Mall in Washington, 1791–1991* (Washington, DC: Smithsonian Institution Press, 1991). Washington in context with the growth of the planning profession nationwide can be evaluated in Mel Scott, *American City Planning since 1890* (Berkeley: University of California Press, 1971), which also offers a provocative analysis of the McMillan Commission plan as exemplary of the City Beautiful movement.

Various monographs illuminate specific eras in Washington's history. See Kenneth R. Bowling, *The Creation of Washington, D.C.: The Idea and the Location of the American Capital* (Fairfax, VA: George Mason University Press, 1991), for a discussion of the political struggle between North and South over the location of the national capital and the origin of exclusive congressional jurisdiction. Because of the key role of William Thornton, the *Papers of William Thornton, 1781–1802,* vol. 1, edited by C. M. Harris (Charlottesville: University Press of Virginia, 1995), provides insight into a range of topics in the early capital city. Stanley Harrold's *Subversives: Antislavery Community in Washington, D.C., 1828–1865* (Baton Rouge: Louisiana State University Press, 2003) chronicles "practical" abolitionism conducted in the streets, homes, and businesses of the nation's capital and moves beyond political debate to explore how free and enslaved African Americans and sympathetic whites campaigned to eradicate the peculiar institution from DC and the Chesapeake region. Alan Lessoff explores the politics behind the building of a modern capital city in the wake of the Civil War and discovers a unique "American" approach to urban, political, economic, and aesthetic issues in *The Nation and Its City: Politics, Corruption, and Progress in Washington, D.C., 1861–1902* (Baltimore: Johns Hopkins University Press, 1994). Howard Gillette Jr. limns the intersection of federal and local politics with particular emphasis on the impact of Marion Barry in *Between Justice and Beauty: Race, Planning and the Failure of Urban Policy in Washington, D.C.* (Baltimore: Johns Hopkins University Press, 1995). Carl Abbott uses a variety of political and literary sources to place Washington in a regional and international context in *Political Terrain: Washington, D.C., from Tidewater Town to Global Metropolis* (Chapel Hill: University of North Carolina Press, 1999).

An introduction to the city of Washington is also provided by several recent guidebooks: Christopher Weeks, *AIA Guide to the Architecture of Washington, D.C.*, revised edition (Baltimore: Johns Hopkins University Press, 1994); Pamela Scott and Antoinette J. Lee, *Buildings of the District of Columbia* (New York: Oxford University Press, 1993); and Sandra Fitzpatrick and Maria R. Goodwin, *The Guide to Black Washington: Places and Events of Historical and Cultural Significance in the Nation's Capital* (1990; revised edition, New York: Hipprocrene Books, 1999). For walking tours and maps of Washington, DC, and Old Town, Alexandria, see John J. Protopappas and Alvin R. McNeal, *Washington on Foot*, revised edition (Washington, DC: National Capital Area Chapter, American Planning Association and Smithsonian Institution Press, 1997). For the city as expanded over its bridges, see Donald Beckman Myer, *Bridges and the City of Washington* (Washington, DC: Commission of Fine Arts, 1974). US Works Progress Administration, Federal Writers' Project, *Washington, City and Capital* (Washington, DC, 1942), which meshes history, critique, and tours, remains a classic. For a list of earlier guidebooks and Washington directories, see Constance M. Green, Washington: *Village and Capital, 1800–1876* (Princeton, NJ: Princeton University Press, 1962).

This revised edition of *Worthy of the Nation* benefits from two decades of scholarship in the field of social history. *Washington at Home: An Illustrated History of Neighborhoods in the Nation's Capital,* edited by Kathryn Schneider Smith (North Ridge, CA: Windsor Publications, 1988), describes the development of the city in terms of its numerous communities. Catherine Allgor examines the role women played in creating a social sphere to support the relationships politics needed to work during the early national period in *Parlor Politics: In Which the Ladies of Washington Help Build a City and a Government* (Charlottesville: University of Virginia Press, 2000). Katherine Allamong Jacob continues the theme into the next century in *Capital Elites: High Society in Washington, D.C., after the Civil War* (Washington,

DC: Smithsonian Institution Press, 1995). Cindy Sondik Aron explores the simultaneous formation of the first white-collar bureaucracy in the United States in *Ladies and Gentlemen of the Civil Service: Middle-Class Workers in Victorian America* (New York: Oxford University Press, 1987).

Contributions in African American history are particularly strong. Chronologically, these include Letitia Woods Brown, *Free Negroes in the District of Columbia, 1790–1849* (New York: Oxford University Press, 1972); James Borchert, *Alley Life in Washington: Family, Community, Religion and Folklife in the City, 1850–1870* (Urbana: University of Illinois Press, 1980); Allan Johnston, *Surviving Freedom: The Black Community of Washington, D.C., 1860–1880* (New York: Garland Press, 1993); Willard Gatewood, *Aristocrats of Color: The Black Elite, 1880–1829* (Bloomington: Indiana University Press, 1990); and Elizabeth Clark-Lewis, *Living In, Living Out: African American Domestics in Washington, D.C., 1900–1940* (Washington, DC: Smithsonian Institution Press, 1994).

BIBLIOGRAPHIES

Several bibliographies offer an introduction to the study of Washington. *A Historical Bibliography of the Built Environment in the Washington, D.C., Metropolitan Area* (www.sah.org/bibs/wshbib.html), compiled by Richard Longstreth in 2001, focuses on historical studies with an emphasis on scholarly work published since 1960. The bibliography includes sources for Montgomery and Prince George's counties in Maryland and Arlington and Fairfax counties in Virginia, as well as the municipalities of Alexandria and Falls Church, Virginia. Although dated, Perry G. Fisher and Linda J. Lear, *A Selected Bibliography for Washington Studies and Descriptions of Major Local Collections* (Washington, DC: GW Washington Studies no. 8, 1981), remains useful. See also Fisher's *Materials for the Study of Washington* (Washington, DC: George Washington University, 1974) for commentary on many basic sources, including planning studies, novels, and specialized histories. An emphasis on the development of the physical city and urban planning is provided in Anne Llewellyn Meglis, *A Bibliographic Tour of Washington, D.C.* (Washington, DC: Redevelopment Land Agency, 1974). The National Capital Planning Commission, *Bibliography of Studies and Reports in the District of Columbia and the Washington Metropolitan Area* (Washington, DC: National Capital Planning Commission, 1967), lists contemporary reports covering the topics of population, economics, land use, housing, and visitors and tourism. Kathleen Collins, *Washington Photographs: Collections in the Prints and Photographs Division of the Library of Congress* (Washington, DC: Library of Congress, 1989), is an essential source for images of the capital city.

ANNUAL REPORTS

The published annual reports of the following agencies were consulted: National Capital Park and Planning Commission, Commission of Fine Arts, Army Corps of Engineers, Board of Commissioners of the District of Columbia, Maryland-National Capital Park and Planning Commission, Metropolitan Washington Council of Governments, District of Columbia Redevelopment Land Agency (now a part of the Department of Housing and Community Development of the District of Columbia), Public Buildings Commission, and Office of the Supervising Architect of the Treasury.

MANUSCRIPT COLLECTIONS

In the course of this study, the following manuscript collections were consulted:

Records of the National Capital Park and Planning Commission, National Archives, Record Group 42, Section 328.

Records of the Commission of Fine Arts, National Archives, Record Group 42, Section 66; Charles Moore's unpublished memoirs are included herein.

Papers of the American Planning and Civic Association, Social Action Archives, Division of Archives and Manuscripts, Wisconsin State Historical Society, Madison, Wisconsin.

Diaries of Edward H. Bennett, Office of Edward H. Bennett Jr., Chicago, Illinois.

Minutes of the National Capital Park Commission for the years 1924–1926, National Capital Planning Commission, Washington, DC.

Minutes of the National Capital Park and Planning Commission for the years 1926–1952, National Capital Planning Commission, Washington, DC.

Records of Jesse C. Nichols, including papers and short biographies, J. C. Nichols Company, Kansas City, Missouri.

Papers of Louis C. Cramton and Charles Moore, Library of Michigan History, University of Michigan, Ann Arbor, Michigan.

Papers relating to Frederic A. Delano and John Ihlder, Franklin Delano Roosevelt Library, Hyde Park, New York.

Papers of Frederic A. Delano, Harland Bartholomew, the American Planning and Civic Association, and Ulysses S. Grant III, Architecture and City Planning Collection, Olin Library, Cornell University, Ithaca, New York.

Papers of Henry V. Hubbard, Frederick Law Olmsted Jr., and Charles Eliot II, Graduate School of Design, Harvard University, Cambridge, Massachusetts.

Papers relating to Frederick Law Olmsted Jr., Office of Olmsted Brothers, Brookline, Massachusetts.

Papers of Oscar Stonorov and materials relating to the Corcoran Gallery of Art 1950 Sesquicentennial Exhibition.

Archives of Contemporary History, University of Wyoming, Laramie, Wyoming.

Papers of Frederick Law Olmsted Sr., Huntington Library, San Marino, California.

Papers of William W. Wurster, Office of Wurster, Bernardi and Eulmons, San Francisco, California.

Papers of Frederick Law Olmsted Sr., especially those relating to the US Capitol grounds, Library of Congress, Manuscript Division, Washington, DC.

ICONOGRAPHIC COLLECTIONS

The following public sources in Washington, DC, were consulted for illustrative material: at the Library of Congress, the Geography and Map Division, which holds many original maps dated to the eighteenth and nineteenth centuries, and the Prints and Photographs Division; the Washingtoniana Division of the Martin Luther King Jr. Memorial Library, District of Columbia Public Library System; the Historical Society of Washington, DC; the US Chamber of Commerce; the National Capital Planning Commission; the National Archives; the District of Columbia Department of Transportation; and the District of Columbia Redevelopment Land Agency (now a part of the Department of Housing and Community Development of the District of Columbia government). For additional sources, see Chalmers M. Roberts, *Washington, Past and Present* (Washington, DC: Washington Public Affairs Press, 1950).

Several private collections have also been consulted: in Washington, DC, the Bernstein and Kiplinger collections, and at George Washington University, the Wright collection; in New York, at the New York Public Library, the Stokes collection.

PERSONAL INTERVIEWS

The following individuals who played key roles in the planning of Washington graciously submitted themselves to taped interviews and thus provided a personal dimension to this book: Horace M. Albright, Sherman Oaks, California; Harland Bartholomew, St. Louis, Missouri; Charles Conrad, Washington, DC; Wilmer C. Dutton Jr., Riverdale, Maryland; Charles W. Eliot II, Cambridge, Massachusetts; William E. Finley, Miami Lakes, Florida; Colonel E. Brooke Lee, Damascus, Maryland; Mrs. James H. Rowe Jr., Washington, DC; and Paul Thiry, Seattle, Washington. Additional interviews were conducted with members of the National Capital Planning Commission staff.

INDEX

Page numbers followed by *f* indicate illustrations and photographs.

Abert, S. T., 89–90, 94, 95

ACE. *See* US Army Corps of Engineers

Adams, Henry, on city, 4

Adams Morgan, 312, 340

Ad Hoc Committee on Federal Office Space, 301, 323

Advisory Neighborhood Commissions, 384

African American Civil War Memorial, 348

agriculture, 20, 51

air raid protection, 233

Alexandria: Cameron Station, 367f; canal system and, 49; during Civil War, 66; decline of, 52–53; description of, 18–19, 41; Freedmen's Barracks in, 71f; growth and development of, 20, 368; in late 19th century, 114; National Airport and, 228; planning and, 217; Scottish character of, 21; sketch of (1844), 40f; slave dealership in, 51f; tripartite rivalry and, 37; waterfront, 344; wharf of, 66f

alley dwellings, 199, 261, 263f

Altman, Andrew, 357

American Association for the Advancement of Science Building, 362, 362f

American Institute of Architects (AIA), 122–26, 142

American Notes (Dickens), 4

American Pharmaceutical Association Building, 156

American Planning and Civic Association, 170–71

American Society of Landscape Architects, 355

American University, 108

The American Vitruvius: An Architect's Handbook of Civic Art (Hegemann and Peets), 185

America Online, 369

Anacostia, 114

Anacostia Metro station, 354f

Anacostia Park, 148, 215

Anacostia River, 33, 34, 59f, 147–48, 378–79, 381, 381f. *See also* Eastern Branch

Anacostia Waterfront Initiative Framework Plan, 357, 379, 382f

Analostan Island, 89, 215

Anderson, Larz, residence of, 162

Annandale, 340

Annapolis Freeway, 255

apartment houses, 114–15, 160f, 163f, 239–41, 357–58

Apex Building, 186, 189

aqueduct, 57–58, 92, 93

Aqueduct Bridge, 97f

Archbold, Anne, 178

architecture: Ad Hoc Committee on Federal Office Space and, 301; Beaux-Arts style, 152, 153, 156, 157, 163, 184, 211; Classical Revival style, 142, 153, 167; Collegiate Gothic style, 164; for Federal Triangle, 184; of Latrobe, 44–45; modern movement in, 226, 361; municipal architect position, 164–65; nationalized style, 152–54; neoclassicism, 26–27; neomodernism, 361–62; postmodernism, 330–31, 361. *See also specific architects*

Archives Building, 184

Arlington County, Virginia: depopulation of, 318; dispersal plan and, 249; high-rise construction in, 252, 341–42; Metro and, 368; Pentagon, 230–33, 232f; planning and, 217; subdivision in, 240f; view of Washington from, 210f

Arlington Experimental Farm, 230, 231

Arlington Memorial Bridge, 139

Arlington National Cemetery, 74, 78f, 231

Arlington Towers, 253

Armory Square, 89, 99

Army Corps of Engineers. *See* US Army Corps of Engineers (ACE)

Army War College, 148

arsenal, federal, 48–49, 58

Ashford, Snowden, 164

atomic attack, fear of, 247–50, 288

automobile: Federal Triangle and, 187–89; impact of, 165; mobility and, 158, 227–28; planning and, 145–46, 196–98; suburbs and, 258

Ayers, Louis, 183–84, 185

Babcock, Orville E., 86, 88–89, 90

Bache, Alexander Dallas, 71

Bacon, Henry, 139, 152, 153–54

balloon ascensions, 67–68, 69

Ballston Metro Station, 342, 367f

Baltimore corridor, 284

Baltimore & Ohio Railroad, 49–50

Baltimore plan, 275

Baltimore & Potomac Railroad Station, 85

Baltimore/Washington International Airport, 373

Banks, Ulysses J., 265

Banneker Recreation Center, 203

Barlow, Joel, 44

Barry, Marion S., 321, 356

Barry Farms, 75, 263–64, 265, 275

Bartholomew, Harland: Comprehensive Plan and, 245; highways and, 195; Planning Commission and, 246; southwest redevelopment and, 269; street study by, 197–98; zoning and, 169, 173

Barton, Clara, 358

Bates Street proposal, 311–12

Battery Rogers, 69

Bauer, Catherine K., 246

Beauchamp, Tanya Edwards, 107

Beaux-Arts architecture: Federal Triangle, 184; Jefferson Memorial, 211; MC and, 152, 157; Memorial Building to the Women of the Civil War, 156; National Museum, 153; Wood and, 163. *See also* École des Beaux-Arts

Belknap, William, 90

Bennett, Edward: Burnham and, 152, 168; Federal Triangle project and, 183, 184, 186, 188, 189; Hoover and, 170

Berman v. Parker, 271

Better Homes in America, 172

Bettman, Alfred, 241, 262

bicentennial celebration, 319–20

Bingham, Theodore A., 100–101, 103, 104, 121–22

Bird, Byron, 252

Black, Fischer, 242

Bladensburg Road, 79

Blumenfeld, Hans, 289–90

Board of Architectural Consultants, 183–84, 188

Board of Engineers, 95

Board of Public Works, 86, 87, 90, 91, 92

Board of Survey, 89–90

Bolling Anacostia Tract, 148, 301, 312

The Book of Washington, 175–76

Boring, William A., 126

Boschke Topographical Map, 84f

Botanic Garden, 56, 99

Boutwell, George S., 90

Bowling, Kenneth R., 35

Brady, Mathew, 71

Breuer, Marcel, 274, 301

bridges, 50, 57, 196, 301. *See also specific bridges*

Brinkley, David, on city, 6

British invasion in 1814, 42

Brookland, 113

Brown, Arthur, Jr., 183–84, 185, 188

Brown, Carey, 195

Brown, George H., 89

Brown, Glenn, 122, 123–24, 126, 138, 140

Brown, J. Carter, 350

Brown, John, 64

Brown, S. P., 112

Brown Book, 297, 298

Brownlow, Louis, 169

Broyhill, Joel, 259

Bryan, Wilhelmus Bogart, 39, 60

B Street, 87, 183

Buberl, Casper, 103

building city, first decades of, 41–52

built environment, 19th century, 116–17

Bulfinch, Charles, 42

Bureau of Alcohol, Tobacco, Firearms and Explosives Building, 379, 380f

Burleith, 160

Burnham, Daniel: Bennett and, 183; CFA and, 157; Chicago plan and, 168; MC and, 126–27, 128, 129, 132, 136, 138, 139; nationalized style and, 152

Burrville, 163

Busey, Samuel C., 77–78

Bush, Laura, vii, 286

business district, 52

business support for planning, 173–75

Cafritz and Tompkins, 305

Canadian Embassy, 325, 327

canal system, 17, 33–34, 49, 78, 82, 87. *See also* City Canal

Cannon, Joseph, 138, 140

Capital Beltway, 242–43, 255, 281f, 281–82, 282f

capital city: advocates for moving, 79–80; siting of, 10, 15–16

Capitol Building: daguerreotype of, 43f; development south of, 33–34; dome of, 57, 75; extensions to, 57;

Capitol Building (*continued*)
  grounds of, 86, 99f, 99–100, 104f; Latrobe and, 41–42;
    location of, 25; vault of, 65–66
Capitol Hill neighborhood, 52, 112, 211, 212, 338
Capitol Park, 271–73, 273f
Capper, Arthur, 213–14
Capper-Cramton Act, 214, 215, 254, 255, 258
Capper-Cramton park program, 140
Cardozo High School, 278
Carroll, Daniel, 20, 29–30, 33
Carroll, David, 15
Carrollsburg, 38
cascade and L'Enfant's design, 17, 25–26
Casey, Edward Pearce, 104, 156
Casey, Thomas Lincoln, 90, 93, 103, 104
Cassatt, Alexander J., 129
Catholic University, 108
centennial celebration, 119–20, 120, 122–23
Center Market, 78–79, 82, 182
Center Market, scene near, 182f
central city, 376–82
central core, in McMillan Plan, 132–33, 133f
Central High School, 164, 278
Centreville, 371f
Century Association, 152
CFA. *See* Commission of Fine Arts
Chamber of Commerce Building, 173–74
Charles E. Smith Company, 382
Chesapeake crescent, 383
Chesapeake & Ohio Canal, 48f, 49
Chevy Chase, 114
Chinatown, 339f, 356
churches, 107–8
Circulator, 352
city: as bucolic, 38; as cosmopolitan, 59–60; as decentral-
    ized and multicentered, 15; demilitarization of, 77–78;
    as destination, 357–58; formal, 26; as horizontal, 211,
    250–51, 376; of illusion, 25–26; indigenous, 38–40; mod-
    ern, beginning of, 97; physical, spread of, 145, 165;
    polarization of, 77
City Beautiful movement: architecture and, 152; elements
    of, 156, 167; Federal Triangle and, 185–87, 188; McMillan
    Plan and, 141, 168; in Washington, 142
City Canal, 25, 33–34, 42–43, 58
City Hall, 45f, 46
City Museum of Washington, DC, 360, 360f
civic center ideal, 185
civil defense, 247–50
Civil War, 4, 63–75
Clarendon, 340
Clark, Appleton P., Jr., 176
Classical Revival style, 142, 153, 167
Cluss, Adolph, 103, 106–7, 108–9
Cluss and Schulze, 115

Coldren, Fred, 177, 178
Columbia, 308–10, 310f, 368
Columbia Heights, 113, 113f
Columbian College, 108
Columbian Institute, 53–54, 56
Columbia Plaza, 277, 277f, 294f, 305
Commemorative Works Act, 334, 348, 354
Commerce Department Building, 157, 184, 185, 190
commercial structures, 104, 106, 331
commissioners, 28–29, 42
Commission of Fine Arts (CFA): Anacostia Park and, 148;
    analysis by, 34; Georgetown and, 252, 337; mandate of,
    139, 384; McMillan Plan and, 154, 157; Meridian Hill
    Park and, 150; Metro design and, 302–3; Moore and,
    127; Pentagon and, 232; Planning Commission and, 213;
    as planning entity, 157; Shipstead-Luce Act and, 208–9
Committee of 100, 171, 179, 230
Committee on Bridges, 176
Committee on Municipal Art, 176
Committee on Parks and Reservations, 177–78
Committee on Public and Private Buildings, 176
Committee on Public Buildings and Grounds, 83
Committee on Sewerage, 176–77
Committee on Streets and Avenues, 176
community development corporations (CDCs), 312–13
Community Reinvestment Act, 312–13
Company H, Tenth Veteran Reserve Corps, 70f
Comprehensive Plan: DC, 380–81; of 1926–1927, 179–81; of
    1950, 244f, 245–46, 255, 267; of 1983, 321–22; of 2004,
    381–82
Compromise of 1850, 52
Conrad, Charles H., 297
conservation in suburbs, 343–45
constituent city, 81, 110–11, 245–46
Constitution, Article I, section 8, 10
Constitution Avenue, 149f, 155f
Constitution Hall, 156
Control Board, 356–57
convention center, 328, 359–60, 363
convention center site, 379–80
Cooke, Henry, 72, 87
Cooke, Jay, 87
Coolidge, J. R., Jr., 126
Cooper, James S., 160
Coordinating Committee, 194, 242
Corcoran, William W., 56
Corcoran Gallery of Art, 61, 65, 90, 132, 156, 304
Cramton, Louis C., 189, 193, 213–14
Cret, Paul, 152, 156
Crystal City, 305–6, 306f, 368, 382
Cunningham, Ann Pamela, 60, 61
Curtis, George C., 132
Custis-Lee mansion, 45

Dalecarlia Reservoir and Dam, 93–94

Daughters of the American Revolution, buildings of, 156, 157f

DC Auditorium Commission, 295, 296

DC Heritage Tourism Coalition, 360

DC Law 2-144, 337–38

DC Office of Planning, 357, 380, 384

Deakins, Francis, 20

Deanwood, 163

The Death and Life of Great American Cities (Jacobs), 287

Defense Homes Corporation, 240

Delano, Frederic, 170, 179, 188, 189, 194, 229–30

Delano, William Adams, 152, 183–84, 185

DeLeuw, Cather & Company, 302

demilitarization of city, 77–78

Democracy in America (Tocqueville), 3–4

Department of Agriculture: building of, 138–39; Forest Service, 209

destination, city as, 357–58

"The Development of the United States Capital" conference, 183–85

Devrouax, Paul, 335

Dewey, Charles S., 183, 189

Dickens, Charles, *American Notes*, 4

disease, threat of, 73, 82, 94, 147

dispersal policy, 247–50

District Building, 139

Domestic Manners of the Americans (Trollope), 4, 60

Douglass, Frederick, on city, 5–6

Downing, Andrew Jackson, 55–56, 56f, 125

downtown, 322–34, 356, 358–60

Downtown Progress, 293–94

drainage, 16–17, 88–89

Drayer, Donald H., 253

dredging of rivers, 83, 89–90, 96f, 147–48

Duany, Andres, 371

Dulles, John Foster, 308

Dulles Access Road, 341

Dulles International Airport, 307f, 307–8, 373

Dunbar High School Building, 164, 338

Dupont Circle, 108f, 109–10, 115

Eames, W. S., 126

early settlement and development, 11, 32–34

East Building of National Gallery of Art, 332, 332f

East Capitol Street corridor, 211–12, 212f

Eastern Branch, 58, 60, 63, 66. *See also* Anacostia River

East-West Highway, 285f

Eckington Center, 203

École des Beaux-Arts, 124, 127, 136, 163. *See also* Beaux-Arts architecture

Economic Recovery Tax Act, 330, 338–39

Edbrooke, Willoughby J., 104

edge cities, 368

Eisenhower, Dwight, 307

11th Street, 236f, 323f

11th Street wharves, 147f

Eliot, Charles W., II: Mall and, 224; NCPPC and, 172, 194, 195, 219; parkway proposal of, 206, 208; recreation centers and, 202

Ellicott, Andrew, 29, 29f, 30f, 31, 95

Elliott, George H., 93

Elliott, Richard M., 183

embassies, 109, 151f, 162, 316, 325, 327

Embassy Apartments, 163f

entrances to city, 208, 300–301

Erickson, Arthur, 325, 327

Euclid Street, 113f

Everett, Edward, 60–61

Executive Group, 154, 156, 213, 304

Executive Order 11035, 249–50

Extending the Legacy: Planning America's Capital for the 21st Century, 348–55, 351f, 353f, 379, 386f

facade projects, 363, 363f

Fairfax County, Virginia: growth of, 340–41; planning in, 217, 292; Reston, 308–9, 309f, 311, 341; suburbs of, 307; traffic in, 368–69; Tysons Corner, 343, 368

fallout shelter, 288f

Farragut Square, 86, 89

Fauntroy, Walter, 311

Federal Aid Highway Act, 228

federal buildings, dispersal of, 247–50

federal bureaucracy: employees of, 237–38, 246–47; growth of, 104, 181; in 1990s, 347; outsourcing and, 345, 372, 383

Federal Bureau of Investigation Building, 323

"Federal City: Plans and Realities" exhibit, 320

federal district, 9–10

"federal interest," 320–21

federal procurement, 372

Federal Reserve Building, 156

Federal Triangle: buildings of, 143, 154, 157; completion of, 358; congestion and, 211; development of, 182–90, 186f, 187f

Fehr, Stephen C., 382–83

ferries, 50, 59

field forts, 69

Finley, David, 251–52, 295

Finley, William E., 284, 288, 289f, 294, 309

Finnish Embassy, 316

fire department, establishment of, 72–73

Fish, Hamilton, 87, 90

fisheries, 16, 50

Flagg, Ernest, 152, 156

Fleet, Henry, 16

flood of 1881, 94

Foggy Bottom, 66, 276f, 277, 277f, 294f, 296f

food for troops, 65–66

Ford, James, 172

Ford's Theatre, 74f, 100

foreign missions, 322, 352

forest, 209

Fort Drive Parkway, 204f, 205

Fort Dupont housing, 239f

Fort Foote, 69

Fort Lincoln, 68f, 312

Fort McNair, 272

Fort Reno, 69

forts, chain of, 68–69, 74

Fort Stevens, 69f

Fort Washington, 63

Foster, William Dewey, 226

4th Street SW, before renewal, 267f

Foxhall Village, 160–61

Frankel, Glenn, 382–83

Franklin School, 106f, 106–7

Franklin Square, 86

Franzheim, Kenneth, 239

Frederick County, Maryland, 370

free blacks, 52, 60, 71–72

Freed, James Ingo, 350, 358

Freedmen's Barracks, 71f

Freedmen's Bureau, 71–72, 74–75

Freedom Plaza, 326

Freer Gallery, 154

French, Daniel Chester, 157

freshets, 94

Friedberg, J. Paul, 326

Friendship Arch, 339f

F Street, 236f, 241f

Fuller, Stephen S., 372, 383

Gaillard, D. D., 93

Gallagher, Patricia, 364

Gallaudet College, 108

Gallinger, Jacob H., 126

Gardner, Alexander, 71

General Services Administration, 328, 358, 363, 378–79

geology of area, 16. *See also* topology of area

George Mason University, 341

Georgetown: Aqueduct Bridge, 97f; canal system and, 49; congressional visit to, 10; decline of, 52–53; description of, 18–19, 40–41; growth of, 20; harbor of, 89–90; as historic and distinctive neighborhood, 199–201, 200f; as historic district, 252; lithograph of, mid-19th century, 39f; Scottish character of, 21; ca. 1795, 19f; tripartite rivalry and, 37; urban river and, 301; waterfront, 201f, 251f, 335–37, 336f, 337f. *See also* Whitehurst Freeway

Georgetown Park, 331

Georgetown University, 108

George Washington Memorial Parkway, 98, 205, 207f, 214–15, 253, 283f

Gibson, James O., 321

Giesboro Point, 66, 74

Gilbert, Cass: as architect, 152; Executive Group plan of, 154, 174, 304; Lafayette Square proposal of, 175f; McMillan Plan and, 157; monumental groups and, 123

Glen Echo Amusement Park, 164f

global city, 355–63

Glover, Charles, 96, 178

Glover-Archbold Parkway, 178, 179f, 240

Glovers Park, 159

Goodhue, Bertram, 156

Goodman, Charles M., 228, 308

Goodwillie, Arthur, 260–61

Gordon, J. B., 218

Government Printing Office, 153, 153f

Granger, Alfred, 190

Grant, Albert, 112

Grant, Ulysses S., 88, 92

Grant, Ulysses S., III, 139, 195, 241, 246

Grant Memorial, 139

Gravelly Point, 228

Graves, Michael, 361

Great Depression, 219

Great Falls, 57–58, 93, 214

Green, Bernard R., 139

Greenbelt, 222, 222f

Green Book, 298, 300f

Greenleaf, John, 38

Greenway shopping strip, 246f

Greiner-DeLeuw report, 243

Gries, John M., 172

Gulledge, Charles, 340–41

Gund, Graham, 358

Hadfield, George, 41, 42, 45f, 46

Hains, Peter Conover, 94–95, 98, 114

Hallett, Stephen, 42

Hamilton, Alexander, 10

harbors, dredging and, 89–90. *See also* waterfront

Hardy, Karl K., 190

Harewood estate, 65

Harpers Ferry arsenal, 63–64

Harris, Albert L., 164–65

Hartman-Cox, 327, 330

Harts, W. W., 155

Hastings, Thomas, 157

Hay, John, 132

Hay-Adams House, 174f

Heaton, Arthur, 160

Hegemann, Werner, 185

height limits on buildings, 211, 252, 260, 342

Hellmuth, Obata + Kassabaum, 301, 362

Henderson, Mrs. John B., 150

Henderson Castle, 117f

Henry, Joseph, 56, 67

Herndon, 341f

Herrick, Charles, 227–28

high-rise construction, 250–51, 252, 342

highways: 1893 plan for, 198; in Foggy Bottom, 296f; growth of, 301; housing and, 199–201; legislation about, 115–16, 197, 228; in Maryland, 217, 254–55; parkland acquisition and, 151–52; Rowe and, 297

Hill, James G., 153

historic districts, 252, 356, 362–64

historic landmarks, 100

historic preservation, 318–19, 337–39, 343–45

Historic Preservation Review Board, 337

Hoban, James, 42

home rule, 254, 314–15, 321

Home Rule Act, 315

"Hookers' Division," 73, 82

Hoover, Herbert, 171–72, 182, 183, 184, 189, 195

Hoover, Kenneth M., 278

Hopkins, Mrs. Archibald, 199

horizontal city, 211, 250–51, 376

Hornblower & Marshall, 152

Hotel Monaco, 358, 363–64

housing: in downtown area, 358; fight for better, 171–72; highway plan and, 199–201; in-fill, 361f; luxury, 360–61; along Pennsylvania Avenue, 327; private developments, 227–28; public, 261, 262–63; types of, 38–40; during WWII, 235–36, 239–41. See also residential areas; specific types of housing

Housing Act (1954), 275

Housing and Urban Development Department Building, 301, 301f

Howard County, Maryland, 308–10, 310f, 370–71

Howard University, 75, 81

Hoxie, Richard L., 92

Hubbard, Henry V., 219, 224

Huxtable, Ada Louise, on city, 6

Ickes, Harold, 223, 226, 229, 232–33

Ihlder, John, 172, 174–75, 195, 199, 261–62

"I Love Washington" (McCullough), 6

image at mid-century, 285

immigration, 339–40, 373, 384

Independence Avenue, 274–75

Inner Loop Freeway System proposal, 243f

institutions, 27–28, 58, 61

Interior Department: Arlington site, 231; building of, 154, 163, 225–26

Internal Revenue Service Building, 185

International Center, 322, 352

International Finance Corporation, 361

Interstate Commerce Commission Building, 185

Interstate 270, 255

Ittner, William B., 164

Jacobs, Jane, 287

Jadwin, Edgar, 214

James, Harlean, 170, 171, 194

Jefferson, Thomas, 10, 29, 31, 38, 41

Jefferson at Penn Quarter, 358

Jefferson Memorial, 210–11, 226

Jenkins Hill, 20

Johnson, Haynes, 319

Johnson, Lady Bird, 385

Johnson, Lyndon B., 312, 315, 320, 323

Johnson, Thomas, 15

Joint Committee on Landmarks, 337

Joint Committee on Washington Metropolitan Problems, 282–83

Judiciary Square, 46, 89, 108–9

Justement, Louis, 175, 259–60, 268–69

Justice Department Building, 185, 190

Kalorama, 44, 110, 163

Kearney, James, 95

Keith, Nathaniel S., 275

Kelly, Sharon Pratt, 356

Kelsey, Albert, 156

Kennedy, Jacqueline, 385

Kennedy, John F., 291, 301, 303, 305, 323, 385

Kennedy Center, 295f, 295–96

Kentlands, 370f, 371

Key Bridge, 283, 306f, 336f

Keys Condon Florance, 331

Kidwell, John L., 96

Kimball, Fiske, 34, 210–11

King, Martin Luther, Jr., 313, 376

Kingman Lake, 148

Korean War Veterans Memorial, 349, 349f

K Street, 227f

Kutz, Charles W., 148, 169

Labor Department Building, 185

Lafayette Park, 304f, 305f

Lafayette Square: Babcock and, 89; buildings around, 154, 173–74, 174f; drainage and, 85; Gilbert and, 175f; redevelopment of, 303–5; White House and, 303f

laissez-faire growth, 287–88

landmarks, 100, 203

landscape design, 26

Landscape Identity Study, 298f, 299f

Langdon, J. G., 128

Langdon, James C., 179

Lansburgh, 357–58

Lansburgh, Mark, 262

La Rochefoucauld-Liancourt, journal of, 17–18

Latrobe, Benjamin, 41–42, 44–45
Law, Thomas, 33
LeDroit Park, 113
Lee, E. Brooke, 216
Lee, Robert E., plantation of, 72, 74
Legacy Plan. See *Extending the Legacy: Planning America's Capital for the 21st Century*
L'Enfant, Pierre Charles: analysis of plan of, 34–35; biographers of, 14; characteristics of, 15; charm of drawing by, 18; compensation and, 31; early life and career of, 14–15; influence of, 387; mandate of, 13; manuscript map of, 31; "Map of Dotted Lines," 22f, 23; MC and plan of, 140, 141; meanings of plan of, 26–28; original plan of, 3, 9, 22–26; permanency for plan of, 80–81; Plan of 1791, 24f; preservation of plan of, 251–52; recognition of, 103; resignation of, 29–30; selection of, 12–13; silhouette of, 12f; survey of (March 1791), 19–21; unified view of, 24–25, 35; Washington and, 13–14, 28
L'Enfant Plaza, 272f, 274
Le Nôtre, 26, 129, 130
Lewis, Harold M., 275–76
Library of Congress, 103–4, 104f
Lin, Maya, 332
Lincoln, Abraham, 385
Lincoln Memorial, 134–35, 137f, 139, 140, 153–54, 376
Lincoln Square, 86
living downtown concept, 328
Logan Park, 150, 151f
Long Bridge, 78, 83, 94, 196
lots, sale of, for new city, 28–29, 32
Loudoun County, Virginia, 249, 292, 369, 383
Lowe, Thaddeus, 67, 69
L Street Bridge, 195f
luxury projects, 360–61
Lydecker, G. J., 92, 93

MacDonald, Thomas H., 206
Mall: defining width of, 136; in 1863, 64f; MC and, 130, 134–38; Michler and, 85–86; in 19th century, 53–57, 54f, 56f, 80–81; in 1937, 225f; redesign of, 331–34; romantic vision of, 98–99; use of, 376; views of, 124f, 125f
Mall Development Plan, 223–24
Mall vista cone, 342
Manassas National Battlefield Park, 342, 368f, 369–70
mansions, 39
manuscript map (L'Enfant), 31
mapmaking, 71
March on Washington, 377f
Market Square, 78–79, 79f, 327
Marshall Heights, 263, 264–65, 265f, 275
Martin, Thomas S., 126
Martin F. Morris et al., appellants v. United States, 96
Martin Luther King Jr. Memorial Library, 357, 363

Maryland, 176, 215–16, 242, 253–55, 370–72. *See also specific cities and counties*
Maryland-National Capital Park and Planning Commission, 216–17, 292
Massachusetts artillerymen, 69f
Massachusetts Avenue, 86, 161f, 162–63, 321f
Mass Transportation Survey, 278–79
mathematics, 26, 27
Mather, Stephen T., 205
MC. *See* McMillan Commission
McClellan Memorial, 139
McCullough, David, "I Love Washington," 6
McFarland, H. B. F., 123
McHarg, Ian, 297–98
MCI Center (Verizon Center), 359, 359f, 363
McKim, Charles F.: architecture of, 152; MC and, 127, 128, 129, 131, 132, 138
McKim, Mead and White, 163, 210
McKinley, William, 119, 120
McKinley Center, 203
McLean Gardens, 239–41, 240f
McMillan, James, 120–21, 122, 126–28, 131, 138
McMillan Commission (MC): accomplishments of, 142–43; Anacostia flats and, 148; basis of design of, 127–28; CFA and, 154, 157; endorsement of plan of, 178; Grand Tour of, 128–29; implementation of plan of, 191; Lincoln Memorial and, 134–35, 137f; Mellon and, 184; members of, 126–27; NCPPC interpretation of, 134f; optical survey by, 128; origins of, 126; park system and central core in plan of, 132–33; plan of, in 1926, 168; reaction and response to plan of, 140–43; rendering of plan for, 135f, 136f; report of, 131–32; search for support for, 130–31; selling of plan by, 138–40; three-dimensional scale model of, 130f, 131f; urban ambience in plan of, 137–38; Washington Monument, Memorial Bridge, Jefferson Memorial, and, 209–11; work of, 129–30
McMillan Reservoir, 92–93
McNee dredge, 96f
Medary, Milton, 183, 185, 195–96, 206
Meigs, Montgomery C.: aqueduct of, 57, 92; Board of Public Works and, 86; bridge of, 85; in Civil War, 71; headquarters of, 65; public buildings of, 103; street paving and, 82–83
Mellon, Andrew W., 182–83, 184, 185, 189
Meloney, Mrs. William Brown, 172
Memorial Bridge, 209f, 209–10
Memorial Building to the Women of the Civil War, 156
Memorials and Museums Master Plan, 353–55, 354f, 376
Meridian Hill, 45, 65, 83, 85, 117f
Meridian Hill Park, 150, 151f
Metro Center concept, 290–91
metropolitan area, ix, 258
metropolitan city, mid-20th century, 246–52

Metropolitan Railroad Company, 72

Metropolitan Square project, 331

Metropolitan Washington Board of Trade, 175–78, 242

Metropolitan Washington Council of Governments, 258, 292–93

Metro rail system: canopy design, 362, 362f; completion of, 367; construction of, 302f, 318, 318f; design of, 302–3; Metro Center, 319f; planning for, 280; stops, development at, 334, 342, 354f, 367f

Michler, Nathaniel, 81, 82, 83, 85–86

Military District of Washington, 72, 74

military preparedness, 63–64

Miller Company, 161–62

Millet, Francis Davis, 157

Mills, Robert, 46–47, 53f, 54f, 54–55, 55f

mobility, 227–28, 241–42, 255, 258. *See also* transportation

Model Inner City Community Development Organization, 311, 312

modern city, beginning of, 97

modern movement in architecture, 226

Montgomery County, Maryland: DC and, 341; Park Lands and Open Spaces (map), 369f; parks in, 215, 216–17; population of, 254; preservation in, 344, 383, 385f; redevelopment in, 284; smart growth in, 370; wedges and corridors concept in, 292

monumental core, 53–57, 223f, 238f, 351f, 351–52, 377

Moore, Arthur Cotton, 336

Moore, Charles: CFA and, 157; conference on capital's development and, 183; Federal Triangle and, 189; influence of, 142, 385; on Mall, 155; MC and, 125, 126, 127, 128, 130, 131; McMillan and, 120–21; McMillan Plan and, 140; on parking, 188; selling of plan by, 138; suburbs and, 165

Moretti, Luigi, 294

Morrill, Justin, 99

Mount Pleasant, 112–13, 340

Mount Vernon, preservation of, 60–61

Mount Vernon Parkway, 205–6

Moynihan, Daniel Patrick, 385–86

M Street High School, 107

mud machines, 59

Mullett, Alfred B., 86, 87, 90–91

Mullett, Thomas A., 175

multiple-family dwellings, 114–15

municipal government by commissions, 91–92, 107

Murder Bay, 73, 73f, 82, 123, 182

Myer, Albert J., 70–71

National Academy of Sciences Building, 156

National Air and Space Museum, 301

National Airport, 228–29, 229f, 372, 372f

National Arboretum, 148

National Archives Building, 137, 185–86

National Capital Housing Authority, 261–62

National Capital Memorial Commission, 334, 349

National Capital Park and Planning Commission (NCPPC): CFA and, 213; comprehensive plan of, 179–81; decision making by, 219; establishment of, 140, 167; funding for, 222–23, 227; membership of, 193–94; New Deal and, 227–30; park system of, 203f; Potomac River Parks plan of, 148, 206; real estate interests and, 162; Regional Highway Committee, 242; regional planning and, 215; reorganization of, 258–59; Settle and, 233; suburban transit diagram, 198f; work plan of, 194–96

National Capital Park Commission, 146, 177–79

National Capital Planning Act, 259

National Capital Planning Commission (NCPC): analysis by, 34; award for, 355; Brown Book, 297, 298; comprehensive plan of (2004), 381–82; creation of, 259; exhibit of, 320; focus of, 384; GAO report on, 320–21; Green Book, 298–99, 300f; Home Rule Act and, 315; Legacy Plan of, 348–55, 379, 386f; members, viii; *Memorials and Museums Master Plan,* 354; mission, ix; *A Policies Plan for the Year 2000,* 288–96, 297–300; publication of, 320; Red Book, 299–300; Rowe and, 296–97; security plan, 364–67; *Urban River,* 301

National Capital Region, 383

National Capital Regional Planning Council, 288, 320

National Capital Transportation Act, 279–80

National Capital Transportation Agency, 279–80

National Capital Urban Design and Security Plan, 366

National Gallery of Art, 183, 226

National Gallery of Art, East Building, 332, 332f

National Garages, Inc., 188

National Historic Preservation Act, 337–38, 344, 363

National Historic Site, 325

National Housing Act, 262–63, 265

National Industrial Recovery Act, 227

National Institutes of Health, 251

National Japanese American Memorial, 348–49

National Law Enforcement Officers Memorial, 348, 348f

National Museum Arts and Industries Building, 103, 140, 153

National Museum of African American History, 376

National Museum of Natural History, 152

national organizations, headquarters of, 155–57, 250

National Park Service, 328, 331

National Permanent Building, 330, 330f

National Place, 327

National Register of Historic Places, 345

National World War II Memorial, 350f, 350–51

National Zoological Park, 97

natural landmarks, 203

natural setting, 10–11, 15–16

Navy Department, 212

Navy Yard, 48–49, 50f

NCPPC. *See* National Capital Park and Planning Commission

neighborhood life, 111–14

neighborhoods. *See* residential areas

neoclassicism, 26–27

neomodernism, 361–62

New Deal initiatives, 221–23, 227

Newlands, Francis G., 114, 136, 138

Newseum, 377

new urbanism, 371

New York Avenue Presbyterian Church, 70f

Nichols, J. C., 195, 197

Nixon, Richard M., 319

Nolen, John, Jr., 219, 224, 225, 231, 252, 253

Nolen, John, Sr., 168, 169–70

NoMa, 378, 379

Northwest Freeway proposal, 242

Northwest Rectangle, 212–13, 224–25, 226f

Norton, Eleanor Holmes, 286

Octagon, 39, 52, 115

office buildings, late 20th century, 306–7, 330–31, 378, 382

office centers during World War II, 238–39

Office of Public Buildings and Public Parks of the National Capital, 146, 195

Old Lock House, 149f

Old Post Office, 325

Olmsted, Frederick Law, Jr.: career of, 127; CFA and, 157; as designer, 99; influence of, 142; influences on, 138; landscape design and, 123, 168–69; MC and, 129, 132–33; National Mall and, 224; NCPPC and, 194, 195; recreation centers and, 202; report by, 131–32; retirement of, 219; Union Square and, 224

Olmsted, Frederick Law, Sr., 71, 86, 99–100, 201

Olmsted Brothers, 127, 150

omnibus line, 49, 82

open space, 382–83

Organic Act, 86, 91

Owen, Robert Dale, 46, 47

Owings, Nathaniel, 323

oyster shucking, 11th Street wharves, 147f

packaged-living model, 305–6

Pan American Union Building, 156

"paper towns," 21

parking lots, 188–89

parks: ACE and, 100–101, 103; active use of, 148–49; Babcock and, 89; after Civil War, 74; desire for, 85; emphasis on, 168–69; extension of, 86; land for, 96–97, 151–52, 178–79, 204–5; in Maryland, 254–55; in McMillan Plan, 132–33; neighborhood and recreation centers, 202f, 202–3; open valley treatment and, 219; Parsons and, 122; along Pennsylvania Avenue, 325–26; planning for, 201–2; proposed, 180f; regional, 213–19; urban, 147–52

Parsons, John, 383

Parsons, Philip Archibald, 202

Parsons, Samuel, Jr., 122

Parsons, W. L., 224

Partridge, William T.: as draftsman, 31, 34, 129; drawings of, 32f, 33f, 34f, 35f

Patent Office, 46–47

Patowmack Canal, 40–41

Patterson House, 163, 163f

Peabody, Robert S., 123

Peaslee, Horace, 150, 155, 175, 200

Peets, Elbert, 31–32, 34, 185, 267–68, 269

Pei, I. M., 271, 332

Pelli, Cesar, 372

Pelz, Paul J., 104, 108, 123

Penn Quarter, 327, 361

Pennsylvania Avenue: after Civil War, 81–82; commerce and, 106; Federal Triangle and, 190–91; in front of White House, 365, 366f, 367; intersection with 11th Street NW, 323f; L'Enfant and, 24–25; National Permanent Building on, 330f; north side of, 224; paving and planting, 83, 87; as principal avenue, 23; procession along, 98f; proposed municipal center for, 191f; redesign of, 378, 378f; redevelopment of, 322–23, 324f, 325–28, 326–27f, 328f

Pennsylvania Avenue Bridge, 85

Pennsylvania Avenue Development Corporation, 325–28, 358

Penn Theater project, 331

Pension Office Building, 102f, 103

Pentagon, 230–33, 232f

Perpetual Savings Building, 247f

Perry, Clarence Arthur, 203, 222

Pershing Park, 326

Peter, Robert, 20

Petersen House, 100, 110

Petworth neighborhood, 113–14, 159, 159f

Pickins, Mrs. Robert S., 249

Piedmont Plateau, 16

Piney Branch Hotel, 101f

Pittman, W. Sidney, 165

planning: battle cries for, 168–69; business support for, 173; citizens' groups working for, 169–70; in DC, 321–22, 357; home rule and, 315; Hoover and, 171–72; legitimization of, 167–68; location and design of public buildings, 208–13; New Deal and, 221, 222–23; post-WWII, 241–43, 258; zoning ordinance (1920), 169, 173. *See also* Comprehensive Plan; *Extending the Legacy: Planning America's Capital for the 21st Century;* Federal Triangle; McMillan Commission

planning authorities, 384

plantation system, 11

Plater-Zyberk, Elizabeth, 371

Platt, Charles A., 152, 154

playgrounds, 149

Poinsett, Joel R., 54–55

polarization of city, 77

police force, 72

A Policies Plan for the Year 2000, 288–96, 297–300

Pope, John Russell: as architect, 152, 183–84; Constitution
Hall, 156; Jefferson Memorial, 210, 226; National
Archives, 185–86; parking and, 188

population, 235–36, 317–18, 321, 382, 384

Portland Flats, 115

Post, George B., 126, 183

postmodernism, 330–31, 361

Post Office Building, 47, 104, 105f, 184, 185

postwar planning, 241–43

Potomac flats suit, 80

Potomac Palisades Parkways, 206, 208

Potomac Park, 96–97, 133, 148, 149–50

Potomac Quay design, 133f

Potomac River: flood (1881), 94; plans for dredging of, 83,
89–90; pollution of, 176–77, 218–19; reclamation of
river flats, 94–103, 96f; siting of city along, 10, 15–16. *See
also* Great Falls

Potomac Valley, 11–12

Powell, Charles J., 116

Presidential Building, 323, 325

President's Conference on Home Building and Home
Ownership, 172

President's House: after Civil War, 82; construction of, 42;
location of, 25, 83, 84f, 85; residential areas near, 52;
sanitary conditions of, 94. *See also* White House

Prince George's County, Maryland: Bowie subdivision,
310f; description of, 370; Greenbelt, 222, 222f; growth
of, 253–54; parks in, 217; planning in, 216

Prince William County, Virginia, 292, 342, 369–70, 383

Principal Problem Areas map, 266f

A Program for Bates Street, 311–12

Progressive era, 167–68

Progressive movement, 101

proprietors, 20–22

public buildings: ACE and, 103–4, 106–8; architecture of,
152–54; grab-bag method of development of, 229–30;
height and location of, 211; Mall development and site
of, 224–26

Public Buildings Act, 167, 182–89

Public Buildings Commission, 146, 154

Public Health Department Building, 156

Public Law 69-159, 140

Public Law 1036, Mall parkway development, 140

public works, 81–91, 107

Public Works Administration, 227

radial corridor option, 289f, 289–90, 290f

railroad, 49–50, 72, 75

rapid transit, 245

Rawlins Square, 89

real estate boom, 328, 330–31, 375–76

reconstructions of manuscript map (L'Enfant Plan),
31–32, 32f, 33f, 34f, 35f

recreation centers, 202f, 202–3

Red Book, 299–300

Red Cross Building project, 363

redevelopment, public: Barry Farms and Marshall
Heights, 263–65; demolition and, 259–60; Foggy Bottom, 276f, 277, 277f; justifications for, 260; National
Capital Housing Authority, 261–62; National Housing
Act, 262–63; in 1960s, 311–14; postwar era and, 255;
rehabilitation and, 275, 311; southwest quadrant, 259,
260–61, 265–75; zoning studies and, 275–77

Redevelopment Act, 262

Redevelopment Land Agency, 260, 262–63, 267–68, 271,
314

redevelopment of Pennsylvania Avenue, 322–23, 324f,
325–28, 326–27f, 328f

Red Lion Row development, 331

Frank D. Reeves Center, 334–35, 335f

Regional Plan for Washington and Its Environs, 1930, 218f

regional planning, 213–19, 258

Regional Thoroughfare Plan proposal, 244f

rehabilitation, 275, 311

Renwick, James, 55, 61, 90

Reps, John, 34

Reserve on National Mall, 354, 355f, 376

Residence Act (1790), 15

residential areas: automobile and, 197; distinct communities, 300f; growth of, 108–15; historic designations for,
338; legislators and, 60; neighborhood centers, 202–3;
in 19th century, 52; segregation of, 277–78; varieties of
development in, 158–65; water supply and, 58

Reston, 308–9, 309f, 311, 341, 368

Reston Town Center, 361

Reynolds, W. E., 251

Reynolds Aluminum Service Corporation, 273

rezoning: in 1990, 356; in 2005, 378

Richardson, H. H., 132, 152

Ring of Hills, 67f, 67–69

riots (1968), 313f, 313–14

Ritz Carlton, 360–61

River Park Housing Cluster, 274f

rivers, 300–301. *See also* dredging of rivers; *specific rivers*

riverside drives, 149–50, 150f. *See also* George Washington
Memorial Parkway

River Terrace, 159

Robinson, Charles Mulford, 141, 185

Rock Creek, 16, 17, 49

Rock Creek Park, 85, 150–51, 215

Rock Creek Parkway design, 132f

Rogers, Isaiah, 90

Rogers, Roland W., 215

Ronald Reagan Building and International Trade Center,
358f, 358–59

Ronald Reagan Washington National Airport, 372, 372f

Roosevelt, Franklin, 170, 228, 230

Roosevelt, Theodore, 132, 138

Root, Elihu, 131, 132

Root, Irving R., 215, 217

Rosslyn: in 1964, 283f; packaged-living model and, 305; role of, 283–84; skyline of, 306f, 343f; transportation in, 114; waterfront of, 214–15

Rouse, James W., 275, 297, 308–9

Rowe, Elizabeth, 296

row houses: examples of, 158f, 159f, 177f; postbellum period, 80; Shepherd and, 109; vernacular of, 38–39, 110–11, 159

Saarinen, Eero, 152–53, 308

Saarinen, Eliel, 152–53, 260

Saint-Gaudens, Augustus, 128, 129

Savannah Street, 133–34

Scheuer, James, 271

school buildings, 106f, 106–7, 163–65

school system, 107, 278

Scott, Thomas A., 69–70

Searles, John R., Jr., 262–63

Seaton Park, 99

security planning, 364–67, 373, 375

Seeler, Edgar, 123

Senate Park Commission, 126–28

service employment, 250

Settle, T. S., 233

7th Street corridor, 313, 314

sewer system, 87, 218–19

Shaw Street, 311

shelter for troops, 64–65

Shepherd, Alexander R., 86–88, 90, 91, 109, 385

Shepley, Henry R., 304

Sherrill, C. O., 171, 179

Shipstead-Luce Act, 208–9

Shirley Highway, 253, 254f, 284f

shoaling process, 38

shopping, regional centers, 343

Sibour, Jules H. de, 156, 163

signaling, 70–71

Silver Spring, 114

Simon, Louis E., 152, 182, 184

Simon, Robert E., 308

16th Street and Columbia Road NW, aerial view of, 169f

Skidmore, Owings & Merrill, 331, 373

slavery, 51–52

sluicing basins, 95

slum clearance, 172

Small, John H., III, 161

smart growth, 370, 371–72, 383

Smith, Chloethiel Woodard, 268–69, 308

Smith, Franklin W., 121

Smith, Howard W., 258–59

Smith, M. Bond, 253

Smith, Margaret Bayard, 38, 41

Smithmeyer, J. L., 104, 108

Smithson, James, 54

Smithsonian Institution: Castle, 55f, 136; establishment of, 54–55; influence of, 61, 80; Mills and, 53; Pleasure Grounds, 99; security measures for, 367

Somervell, Brehon B., 214

South Capitol Street, 352f, 353f, 379f

Southeast Federal Center, 378–79

southwest quadrant, 259, 260–61, 265–75, 271f

Southwest Triangle, 224–25

Southwest Urban Renewal Area, 270f

sprawl, 371–72, 383

Springfield, 253

Spring Valley, 161f, 161–62, 162f

Spy Museum, 358, 363

St. Florian, Friedrich, 350

St. John's Episcopal Church, 45

Stanford, Phil, 306

State, War and Navy Building, 90–91, 91f, 103

State Department Building, 61, 173

Stein, Clarence S., 249

Stephen, Frederick F., 201

Stevens, Roger, 271

Stewart's Castle, 108f, 109

Stoddert, Benjamin, 20

Stone, Edward Durrell, 275, 295

Stoneleigh Court Apartment Building, 163f

streetcars, 72, 75, 106, 111f, 158

street peddlers, 111

streets and avenues: Bartholomew and, 197–98; L'Enfant and, 23; in Maryland, 50, 217; McMillan Plan and, 133–34; military, 68; Nichols and, 197; paving of, 72, 88; in *A Policies Plan for the Year 2000*, 291f; regulation of, 115–16; riverside drives, 149–50, 150f. *See also specific streets*

Stuart, David, 15

suburbs: boom in, 257–58; after Civil War, 74, 75; growth of, 108–9, 340–45; in-fill housing, 361f; New Deal and, 221; Reston, Columbia, and, 308–11, 309f, 310f, 341, 368; Uniontown, 60, 114

Suitland Parkway, 248f

Sullivan, Louis Henry, 152

Sumner School, 106–7

Sumner Square project, 331

Symons, Thomas W., 93

Takoma Park, 114, 278

Tariff Commission Building, 363–64

Tarsney Act, 142

Tax Reform Act, 312–13

Tayloe, John, 39

Tech World Building, 331
telegraph, communication by, 69–70
Temko, Allan, 287–88
Tenallytown Trolley Car, 111f
ten-square mile area, 10
territorial government, 86–91
terrorism, protection from, 364f, 364–67, 365f, 373, 377–78, 378f
terrorist attacks, 375
Thomas Circle underpass, 196f
Thorn, F. M., 80
Thornton, William, 39, 41–42
Thurgood Marshall Federal Judiciary Building, 361
Tiber Creek, 16–17, 84f
Tidal Basin, 95–96, 149, 150f, 176–77
tidewater character of area, 16
tobacco trade, 11–12, 20, 40, 41
Tocqueville, Alexis de, *Democracy in America,* 3–4
Tompkins, Charles H., 273
Topographic Bowl, 342
topology of area, 67–69, 71
Totten, George Oakley, Jr., 123, 152, 175
tourism, 4–5, 6, 17–18, 60, 360
Toward a Comprehensive Landscape Plan for Washington, D.C., 297–98, 298f, 299f
town houses, 367f, 371f
towns: "paper," 21; planned, 11–12
Townsend, Richard, H., residence of, 162
transportation: Capital Beltway, 281f, 281–82; Circulator, 352; ferries, 50, 59; Mass Transportation Survey, 278–79; McLean Gardens and, 240; National Capital Transportation Act, 279–80; omnibus line, 49, 82; post-WWII plan for, 242–43; railroad, 49–50, 72, 75; trolley car, 146f, 158. *See also* automobile; Metro rail system; streetcars; streets and avenues; *specific airports*
Transportation Department Building, 378–79, 379f
Treasury Building Annex, 154
Treasury Department: building of, 43, 46, 47f; Federal Triangle project and, 182
triangle, 73–74. *See also* Federal Triangle
Trinidad neighborhood, 159f
trolley car, 146f, 158
Trollope, Frances, *Domestic Manners of the Americans,* 4, 60
Trowbridge and Livingston, 156
Truman, Harry S., 246, 304
Tuemmler, Fred, 254
Tugwell, Rexford, 222
Twining, William J., 95
Tysons Corner, 343, 368

Udall, Stewart, 325
Union Square, 139, 223, 224
Union Station: interior of, 239f; McMillan Plan and, 129, 138; rehabilitation of, 339; after restoration, 338f; in 20th century, 129f; WWI dormitories near, 156f
Uniontown, 60, 114
urban design, 14–15, 27, 31–32, 141, 147–52
urban growth, 24–25
urban living, 317
urban planning and New Deal, 221
urban redevelopment or renewal, 260, 311–14. *See also* redevelopment, public
US Army Corps of Engineers (ACE): Office of Public Buildings and Grounds, 147, 157; parks and, 100–101, 103; planning and, 146–47; public buildings and, 103–4, 106–8; public works and, 81–86, 87, 92
USA Today towers, 342
US Capitol Visitors Center, 376–77
US Chamber of Commerce, 172, 173–75
Usher, John P., 72
US Holocaust Memorial Museum, 349–50
US Navy Memorial, 327, 328f
US Route 50, 255

van der Rohe, Mies, 357
Van Ness House, 44–45, 52
Van Ness mausoleum, 45–46
Van Valkenburgh, Michael, 378
Venturi, Robert, 326
Verizon Center (MCI Center), 359, 359f, 363
Vietnam Veterans Memorial, 332–34, 333f, 349
Virginia: development in, 252–53; extension of city into, 176; federal functions in, 97–98; land use control, 372; planning in, 215, 217; stream valleys in, 292; suburban growth in, 368–70. *See also specific cities and counties*
von Ezdorf, Richard, 90, 103

Walker, C. Howard, 123
Walker, George, 21
Wallach School, 106–7
Walter, Thomas U., 46, 47, 57
Walton, William, 304, 305
War Department, 69, 212, 230. *See also* Pentagon
Waring, George E., 94
Warnecke, John Carl, 153, 304
Warner Theater project, 331
Washington, George: influence of, 385; L'Enfant and, 13–14, 28; Mount Vernon and, 11; Patowmack Canal and, 40–41; Potomac River site and, 10; President's House and, 42; proprietors and, 20–22; size of city and, 21–22; statue of, 104f
Washington, Walter, 314, 321, 337
Washington Channel, 95–96, 148
Washington Circle, 70f
Washington City, 52
Washington Harbour complex, 336–37, 337f
Washington High School, 107

Washington Metropolitan Area Transit Authority, 280, 302

Washington Monument: dedication of, 98f; design and construction of, 53, 53f; drainage system, 88–89; grounds of, 65, 65f, 135–36; MC and, 209; security measures for, 364f, 366f, 367, 378

Washington Municipal Airport, 228, 231

Washington Navy Yard Annex, 334

Washington Region Water Supply Committee, 217–18

Washington Suburban Sanitary Commission, 216

watercourses, 16–17, 58–59

waterfront: Alexandria, 344; Anacostia River, 38, 378–79, 381, 381f; Georgetown, 201f, 251f, 335–37, 336f, 337f; Potomac River, 33–34, 38; Rosslyn, 214–15; silting and, 58. *See also* Anacostia Waterfront Initiative Framework Plan

Watergate complex, 294f, 294–95, 305

water supply, 57–59, 92–94, 112, 121, 217–18

wedges and corridors theory, 289–90, 292

Weese, Harry, 271, 302, 303

Wesley Heights, 161f, 161–62

Western High School, 107

Wheat Row, 38

Wheeler, Harry A., 172, 173

White House, 135–36, 303f, 304. *See also* President's House

Whitehurst Freeway, 251f, 252, 301, 335, 336f

Wicomico-Sunderland escarpment, 15, 16, 21

Willard Hotel, 325, 327

Williams, Anthony A., 356, 357, 380

Wilson, James, 138

winter season, 79–80

Wolf Trap National Park for the Performing Arts, 341

women: on bicycles, 109f; dormitories for, 156f, 170

Women in Military Service Memorial, 348

Wood, Waddy B., 163, 165, 226

World Bank headquarters, 316

World's Columbian Exposition, 119, 120f, 126, 141

World War I temporary buildings, 155, 155f, 156f, 170, 181

World War II, 223, 235–41, 237f, 241f

Worthy of the Nation: The History of Planning for the National Capital (NCPC), 320

Wright, Frank Lloyd, 152, 184, 260

Wurster, William C., 246

Yasko, Karel, 301

Young, George Washington, mansion of, 66

Zeckendorf, William, 271f, 271–73

Zoning Commission hearing, 276f

zoning ordinance (1920), 169, 173

zoning studies, 275–77

SCALE